# Flea Market Trader

**THOUSANDS OF ITEMS
WITH
CURRENT VALUES**

*Twelfth* edition

## COLLECTOR BOOKS
*A Division of Schroeder Publishing Co., Inc.*

### Searching For A Publisher?

We are always looking for knowledgeable people considered to be experts within their fields. If you feel that there is a real need for a book on your collectible subject and have a large comprehensive collection, contact Collector Books.

**Editorial Staff**
*Editors*
Sharon and Bob Huxford
*Research and Editorial Assistants*
Michael Drollinger, Nancy Drollinger, Linda Holycross, Donna
Newnum, Loretta Woodrow

*Cover Design:* Beth Summers
*Book Design:* Joyce Cherry

COLLECTOR BOOKS
P. O. Box 3009
Paducah, Kentucky 42002-3009

Copyright ©1999 by Schroeder Publishing Company, Inc.

# INTRODUCTION

The *Flea Market Trader* is a unique price guide, geared specifically for the convenience of the flea market shopper. Several categories have been included that are not often found in general price guides, while others on antiques not usually seen at flea markets have been omitted. The new categories will serve to introduce you to collectibles that are currently coming on, the best and often the only source for which is the market place. As all of us who religiously pursue the circuits are aware, flea markets are the most exciting places in the world to shop; but unless you're well informed on current values those 'really great' buys remain on the table. Like most pursuits in life, preparation has its own rewards; and it is our intention to provide you with the basic tool of education and awareness toward that end. But please bear in mind that the prices in this guide are meant to indicate only general values. Many factors determine actual selling prices; values vary from one region to another, dealers pay various wholesale prices for their wares, and your bargaining skill is important too.

We have organized our listings into general categories for easy use; if you have trouble locating an item, refer to the index. The values we have suggested reflect prices of items in mint condition. NM stands for minimal damage, VG indicates that the items will bring 40% to 60% of its mint price, and EX should be somewhere between the two. Glassware is assumed clear unless a color is noted. Only generally accepted abbreviations have been used.

We would like to take this opportunity to thank each author, dealer, and auction house who allowed us to use their photographs.

The Editors

# Action Figures

The first line of action figures Hasbro developed in 1964 was GI Joe. It met with such huge success that Mego, Kenner, Mattel, and a host of other manufacturers soon began producing their own lines. Though GI Joe, Marx's Best of the West series, and several of Mego's figures were 12", others were 8" or 9" tall, and the most popular size in the last few years has been 3¾". Many lines came with accessory items such as vehicles, clothing, and guns. Original packaging (most now come on cards) is critical when it comes to evaluating your action figures, especially the more recent issues — they're seldom worth more than a few dollars if they've been played with. Values given for MIB or MOC can be reduced by 40% to 60% when appraising a 'loose' figure in even the best condition. For more information, you'll want to read *Collectible Action Figures* by Paris and Susan Manos, *Mego Toys* by Wallace M. Crouch, and *Schroeder's Toys, Antique to Modern,* all published by Collector Books.

See also GI Joe; Star Wars; Star Trek.

Action Jackson, accessory, Rescue Squad outfit, Mego, MIB .**10.00**
Action Jackson, figure, Action Jackson, fatigues, red hair, 8", EX ................................**20.00**
Adventures of Indiana Jones, figure, Indiana, Kenner, MOC ..................**125.00**

Aliens, accessory, Evac Fighter, Kenner, MIB .................**30.00**
Aliens, accessory, Queen Hive playset, Kenner, MIB ...**50.00**
Aliens, figure, Bishop, Gorilla, Killer Crab or Mantis, MOC, ea ....................................**10.00**
Aliens, figure, Night Cougar, Panther, Ripley or Wild Boar, MOC, ea .......................**10.00**
Batman (animated), accessory, Batmobile, Kenner, MOC .......**40.00**
Batman (animated), accessory, Joker Mobile, Kenner, MOC .....**30.00**
Batman (animated), figure, Bane or Ras A Gual, Kenner, MOC, ea ....................................**20.00**
Batman (animated), figure, Bruce Wayne, Kenner, MOC ..**20.00**
Batman (animated), figure, Killer Kroc or Clayface, Kenner, MOC, ea ........................**30.00**
Batman (animated), figure, Poison Ivy, Kenner, MOC ........**30.00**
Batman (animated), figure, Scarecrow, Kenner, MOC ..........**30.00**
Batman (movie), accessory, Batmobile, Toy Biz, 1989, 2nd series, NRFB .................**45.00**
Batman Returns, accessory, Custom Coupe, w/figure, Kenner, MIB ................................**40.00**
Batman Returns, figure, Catwoman or Robin, MOC, ea .........**15.00**
Battlestar Galactica, accessory, Colonial Scarab, Mattel, MIB ............................**60.00**
Battlestar Galactica, figure, Colonial Warrior, Mattel, 12", VG ......................**30.00**
Battlestar Galactica, figure, Commander Adama, Mattel, 3¾", VG ................................**10.00**

4

**Battlestar Galactica, figure, Cylon Raider, Mattel, MIB, $60.00.**

Battlestar Galactica, figure, Starbuck, Mattel, 3¾", MOC ...............**30.00**

Beetlejuice, accessory, Gross Out Meter, Kenner, 1990, MIB .**15.00**

Beetlejuice, accessory, Vanishing Vault, Kenner, 1990, MIB .**15.00**

Beetlejuice, figure, Showtime or Shipwreck, Kenner, 3¾", MOC, ea .........................**12.00**

Best of the West, accessory, Circle X Ranch, Marx, MIB ...**175.00**

Best of the West, accessory, Johnny West Adventure Jeep, Marx, VG ......................**40.00**

Best of the West, figure, Geronimo, Marx, complete, NMIB .**140.00**

Best of the West, figure, Jaimie West, Marx, complete, MIB .......**85.00**

Best of the West, figure, Johnny West, Marx, complete, VG+ ............**40.00**

Big Jim, accessory, Sky Commander Jet, MIB .................**50.00**

Big Jim, figure, Big Jack, complete, MIB ......................**40.00**

Big Jim, figure, Capt Flint, complete, MIB .....................**40.00**

Bonanza, figure, any, MIB, from $200 to .........................**250.00**

Bonanza, horse, American Character, EX ...........................**30.00**

Buck Rogers in the 25th Century, accessory, Command Center, MIB .............................**110.00**

Buck Rogers in the 25th Century, figure, Buck, Mego, 12", NRFB .............................**75.00**

Buck Rogers in the 25th Century, figure, Killer Kane, Mego, 3¾" ...............................**25.00**

Capt Action, accessory, Parachute Pack, Ideal, complete, EX ..**70.00**

Capt Action, figure, Action Boy, Ideal, complete, 12", EX .............**400.00**

Capt Action, figure, Batman, Ideal, complete, 12", EX ........**200.00**

Capt Planet & the Planeteers, accessory, Geo Cruiser, MIB ......**25.00**

Capt Planet & the Planeteers, figure, any, Tiger/Kenner, 3¾", MOC ...............................**15.00**

Capt Power, figure, Capt Power or Corp Pilot Chase, Mattel, MOC, ea .........................**15.00**

Capt Power, figure, Tritor, Stingray or Scout, Mattel, MOC, ea .........................**20.00**

CHiPs, figure, Jon, Mego, 8", MOC ..............................**35.00**

CHiPs, figure, Ponch, Mego, 8", MOC ..............................**25.00**

CHiPs, figure, Sarge, Mego, 8", MOC ..............................**40.00**

Chuck Norris, figure, Chuck, 2 different Ninjas or Kimo, MOC, ea ....................................**15.00**

Clash of the Titans, figure, Kraken Sea Monster, MIB ..**190.00**

DC Comics Super Heroes, figure, Aquaman, 3¾", MOC ...**25.00**

5

DC Comics Super Heroes, figure, Batman characters, 3¾", MOC, ea ........................**20.00**

DC Comics Super Heroes, figure, Green Lantern, 3¾", MOC ...**5.00**

DC Comics Super Heroes, figure, Hawkman or Two-Face, 3¾", MOC, ea ........................**25.00**

**Dukes of Hazzard, figure, Bo, Mego, 8", MOC, $35.00.**

Dukes of Hazzard, accessory, Sheriff's car, Mego, rare, NM ...........................**100.00**

Dukes of Hazzard, figure, any except Coy, Mego, 8", MOC, ea ...............................**35.00**

Dukes of Hazzard, figure, Coy, Mego, 8", MOC .............**40.00**

Dukes of Hazzard, figure, Daisy, Mego, 3¾", MOC ..........**25.00**

Dukes of Hazzard, figure, Uncle Jesse, Mego, 3¾", MOC ......................**35.00**

Emergency, accessory, fold-out playset, vinyl, VG .........**45.00**

Emergency, figure, John or Roy, 8", MOC, ea ..................**70.00**

ET, accessory, Stunt Spaceship, LJN, MOC .....................**10.00**

ET, figure, w/pop-up head, LJN, 4", MOC ........................**20.00**

Flash Gordon, figure, Flash Gordon, Mattel, MOC .........**25.00**

Flash Gordon, figure set, Flash, Dr Zarkov & Thun, Mattel, MIB .................................**40.00**

Flash Gordon, figure set, Ming, Lizard Woman & Beastman, Mattel, MIB .................**40.00**

Generation X, figure, any except Marrow or White Queen, MOC, ea ........................**15.00**

Generation X, figure, Marrow or White Queen, MOC, ea ....**20.00**

Happy Days, accessory, Fonz's Garage, Mego, MIB ......**75.00**

Happy Days, figure, any character, Mego, 8", MOC, ea .**60.00**

He-Man, accessory, Monstroid, Mattel, MIB .................**40.00**

He-Man, accessory, Point Droid & Talon Fighter, Mattel, MIB .............................**45.00**

He-Man, figure, any character, Mattel, MOC, ea ...........**15.00**

James Bond (Dr No), accessory, Dragon Tank & Yacht, Gilbert, 1965, MOC ......**40.00**

James Bond (Goldfinger), figure, Oddjob, Gilbert, 12", M (EX box) ..............................**385.00**

James Bond (Moonraker), figure, Bond, Mego, 12", MIB ..**95.00**

James Bond (Moonraker), figure, Drax or Holly, Mego, 12", NMIB, ea ....................**135.00**

Knight Rider, figure & KITT car, EX ................................**40.00**

Land of the Lost, accessory, Land Master Jeep, MIB .........**20.00**

Land of the Lost, figure, Talking Stink, Annie or Kevin, MOC, ea ....................................**15.00**

Last Action Hero, figure, any except Evil Eye Bandit, Mattel, MOC, ea ....................**5.00**

Last Action Hero, figure, Evil Eye Bandit, Mattel, MOC ....**10.00**

Legends of Batman, figure set, Egyptian Batman & Catwoman, Kenner, MOC ....................**25.00**

Legends of the Lone Ranger, figure, any, Gabriel, 3¾", MOC, ea ....................................**20.00**

Lone Ranger Rides Again, accessory, Blizzard Adventure, Gabriel, NRFB .............**35.00**

Lone Ranger Rides Again, figure, Lone Ranger, Gabriel, 9", EX ........................**20.00**

Love Boat, figures, any, Mego, 3½", MOC, ea ................**25.00**

M*A*S*H, figure, Klinger, 3¾", MOC .............................**20.00**

M*A*S*H, figure, Klinger in drag outfit, 3¾", MOC ..........**40.00**

Major Matt Mason, accessory, Space Bubble, complete, Mattel, EX ............................**35.00**

Major Matt Mason, accessory, Unitred Hauler, Mattel, EXIB .............................**75.00**

Major Matt Mason, figure, Matt Mason, Mattel, EX ....**60.00**

Man From UNCLE, accessory, Uncle Husky Car, Gilbert, MOC ..........................**220.00**

Man From UNCLE, figure, Illya Kurakin, Gilbert, 12", VG (VG box) ..............................**150.00**

Marvel Super Heroes, figure, Aqualad, Mego, complete, NM ..............................**120.00**

Marvel Super Heroes, figure, Capt America, Mego, complete, NMIB ..........................**200.00**

Marvel Super Heroes, figure, Catwoman, Mego, complete, EX ..............................**125.00**

Marvel Super Heroes, figure, Green Arrow, Mego, complete, EX ................................**95.00**

Masters of the Universe, accessory, Jet Sled, Mattel, MOC ..........................**20.00**

Masters of the Universe, figure, King Randor, Mattel, 3¾", MOC ..........................**25.00**

**Masters of the Universe, figure, Ram Man, Mattel, MOC, $35.00.**

Masters of the Universe, figure, Skeletor, Mattel, 3¾", MOC ......................**30.00**

Masters of the Universe, figure, Teela, Mattel, 3¾", MOC ..........................**40.00**

7

Mike Hazard, accessory, trench coat, Marx, NM ..............15.00

Mike Hazard, figure, complete, Marx, NM (EX box) ....150.00

Official Scout High Adventure, figure, Craig Cub Scout, Kenner, NRFB ..............................30.00

Official Scout High Adventure, figure, Steve Scout, Kenner, NRFB ..............................30.00

Official World's Greatest Super Heroes, figure, Aquaman, Mego, 8", EX .................45.00

Official World's Greatest Super Heroes, figure, Batman, Mego, 12", MIB ..............75.00

Official World's Greatest Super Heroes, figure, Hulk, Mego, 8", MIB ........................100.00

Official World's Greatest Super Heroes, figure, Joker, Mego, 8", M ..............................55.00

Official World's Greatest Super Heroes, figure, Robin, Mego, 8", M ............................125.00

Official World's Greatest Super-Gals, figure, Supergirl, Mego, 8", MOC ..........................20.00

Pee-Wee's Playhouse, figure, Miss Yvonne, Matchbox, 6", MOC ..............................30.00

Pee-Wee's Playhouse, figure, Pee-Wee, Matchbox, 6", MOC ..............................25.00

Pee-Wee's Playhouse, figure, Ricardo or Reba, Matchbox, 6", MOC, ea ..................20.00

Power Rangers, figure, girls (pink or yellow), Bandai, 1st issue, MIB ..............................20.00

Power Rangers, figure, guys (red, blue or black), 1st issue, MIB, ea ...................................15.00

Power Rangers, figure, White Ranger & Tigerzord, Bandai, set, MIB ........................50.00

Predator, figure, Lasershot, Lava or Nightstorm, Kenner, MOC, ea ....................................20.00

Predator, figure, Spiked Tail or Stalker, Kenner, MOC, ea ..........20.00

Rambo, accessory, Savage Trike Cycle, Coleco, EX ..........15.00

Rambo, figure, Rambo, Coleco, 6", MOC ..............................25.00

Rambo, figure, Sgt Havoc, Gripper or Turbo, Coleco, 6", MOC, ea ......................20.00

Real Ghostbusters, figure, any except Stay Puft MOC, ea ...................................25.00

Real Ghostbusters, figure, Stay Puft, Kenner, MOC .......30.00

Robin Hood Prince of Thieves, accessory, Battle Wagon, Kenner, MIP ........................15.00

Robin Hood Prince of Thieves, figure, Azeem, Kenner, MOC ............................15.00

Robin Hood Prince of Thieves, figure, Friar Tuck, Kenner, MOC ..............................30.00

Robin Hood Prince of Thieves, figure, Little John, Kenner, MOC ..............................15.00

Robin Hood Prince of Thieves, figure, Robin Hood, Kenner, MOC ..............................8.00

RoboCop, accessory, Skull Hog or Robocycle, Kenner, MOC, ea ....................10.00

RoboCop, figure, any except Gatlin Blast, Kenner, 3¾", MOC, ea ......................15.00

RoboCop, figure, Gatlin Blast, Kenner, 3¾", rare, MOC ......25.00

8

Robotech, figure, Lyn, Dana or Lisa, Matchbox, 12", MIB, ea ...............................30.00

Robotech, figure, Max or Roy, Matchbox, MOC, ea .......15.00

Robotech, figure, Rook, Matchbox, MOC ...............................25.00

Spawn, accessory, Spawn Alley Playset, Todd Toys, MIB .........40.00

Spawn, accessory, Spawnmobile, Todd Toys, MOC ............30.00

Spawn, figure, any from 1st or 2nd series, Todd Toys, MOC, ea ................................30.00

Spawn, figure, any from 3rd or 4th series, Todd Toys, MOC, ea ................................15.00

Super Mario Brothers, figures, any, Ertl, 3¾", MOC, ea .........10.00

Super Powers, accessory, carrying case, Kenner, EX ............15.00

Super Powers, accessory, Darkseid Destroyer, Kenner, MIB .............................45.00

Super Powers, figure, Batman, Kenner, MOC (unpunched) ........55.00

Super Powers, figure, Cyclotron, Kenner, MOC .................50.00

Super Powers, figure, Darkseid, Kenner, complete, NM ..15.00

Super Powers, figure, Flash, Kenner, MOC ......................15.00

Super Powers, figure, Orion, MOC ...............................55.00

Super Powers, figure, Penguin, Kenner, complete, NM ..25.00

Super Powers, figure, Tyr, Kenner, MOC ..............................60.00

Super Powers, figure, Wonder Woman, Kenner, MOC .30.00

Swamp Thing, figure, Capture Swamp Thing, Kenner, 2nd series, MOC ...................10.00

Swamp Thing, figure, Climbing Swamp Thing, Kenner, 2nd series, MOC ...................10.00

Teenage Mutant Ninja Turtles, figure, any, Playmates, 3¾", MOC, ea .......................20.00

Terminator 2, figure, Blaster T1000 or Damage Repair, Kenner, MOC, ea .........20.00

Terminator 2, figure, John Conner, Kenner, MOC ........25.00

Terminator 2, figure, Power Arm or Secret Weapon, MOC, ea .20.00

Terminator 2, figure, Techno Punch, Kenner, MOC ...20.00

Terminator 2, figure, Terminator, poseable, Kenner, 11", EX.................................20.00

Toy Story, figure, any, Thinkway Toys, 6", MOC, ea .........15.00

Universal Monsters, figure, Frankenstein, glow type, 3¾", MOC ...............................35.00

Universal Monsters, figure, Mummy, glow type, Remco, 3¾", MOC ......................75.00

Universal Monsters, figure, Phantom, glow type, Remco, 3¾", MOC ...............................35.00

Willow, figure, any except Ufgood, Tonka, 1988, MIP, ea .....5.00

Willow, figure, Kael or Sorsha w/Horses, Tonka, 1988, MIP, ea ....10.00

Willow, figure, Ufgood w/Baby, Tonka, 1988, rare, MIP .10.00

World Wrestling Federation, figure, Brutus Beefcake, Hasbro, MOC ...............................30.00

World Wrestling Federation, figure, Crush, Hasbro, MOC .....25.00

World Wrestling Federation, figure, Headshrinker Fatu, Hasbro, MOC ......................15.00

**Welcome Back Kotter, figure, Mr Kotter, Mattel, M (EX card), from $35.00 to $40.00.**

World Wrestling Federation, figure, Jake the Snake, Hasbro, MOC ..............................**20.00**
World Wrestling Federation, figure, Sgt Slaughter, Hasbro, MOC ..............................**30.00**

# Advertising Characters

As far back as the turn of the century, manufacturers used characters that identified with their products. They were always personable, endearing, amusing, and usually succeeded in achieving just the effect the producer had in mind, making their product line more visual, more familiar, and therefore one the customer would more often than not choose over the competition. Magazine ads, display signs, product cartons, and TV provided just the right exposure for these ad characters. Elsie the Cow became so well known that at one point during a random survey, more people recognized her photo than one of the presidents!

There are scores of advertising characters, and many have been promoted on a grand scale. Today's collectors search for the dolls, banks, cookie jars, mugs, plates, and scores of other items modeled after or bearing the likenesses of their favorites, several of which are featured below.

Condition plays a vital role in evaluating vintage advertising pieces. Our estimates are for items in at least near-mint condition, unless another condition code is present in the description. Try to be very objective when you assess wear and damage.

For more information we recommend *Zany Characters of the Ad World* by Mary Jane Lamphier; *Advertising Character Collectibles* by Warren Dotz; and *Huxford's Collectible Advertising*. All are published by Collector Books.

See also Advertising Watches; Breweriana; Bubble Bath Containers; Cereal Boxes and Premiums; Character and Promotional Drinking Glasses; Radios, Novelty; Novelty Telephones; Pin-Back Buttons.

A&W Root Beer bear, stuffed plush, 1975, 13", EX .....**35.00**

Actigall Guy doll, squeeze vinyl, 1989, 4", M ...................**40.00**

Actigall Guy memo holder, MIB ..**10.00**

Alpo dog, stuffed plush w/T-shirt, suction-cup paws, VG .....**6.00**

Apple Jack mug, w/hat lid, plastic, Kellogg's, 1967, VG+ ....**50.00**

Archie Archway display figure, composition, 1970s, 5", NM ..**60.00**

Atlas Annie doll, printed cloth, 1977, 15½", NM ...........**10.00**

Aunt Jemima Breakfast Bear, blue plush velour, dated 1984, 13" ................................**175.00**

Aunt Jemima Day spatula, metal w/plastic handle, 1940s, EX ................**125.00**

Aunt Jemima Junior Chef Pancake Set, Argo Industries, 1949, NMIB ................**185.00**

Aunt Jemima place mat, Aunt Jemima at Disneyland, dated 1955, M .........................**35.00**

Aunt Jemima syrup pitcher, plastic figure, F&F Mold, 5½", EX ...............................**70.00**

Baby Ruth doll, printed cloth, boy or girl, 1920, 16", EX, ea ...................................**20.00**

Baskin Robbins spoon figure, pink plastic w/white hands & feet, 4", M ..............................**5.00**

Bazooka Joe doll, stuffed cloth, 1973, EX .......................**20.00**

Bertoli Chef figure/toothpick holder, composition, 1970, 6", NM ...............................**30.00**

Betty Crocker doll, stuffed cloth, Kenner, 1974, 13", VG ..**20.00**

Big Boy ashtray, white w/figure on edge, 1950s, M ...........**350.00**

Big Boy bank, brown ceramic, 1965, NM ...................**500.00**

Big Boy decal, Big Boy for President, M ...........................**5.00**

Big Boy figure, PVC, 1994, 3" .**20.00**

Big Boy key chain, flat silver-tone figure, M .......................**25.00**

Big Boy kite, paper, 1960s, NM .**350.00**

Big Boy pennant, Big Boy Club, 1950s, NM ...................**50.00**

Big Boy playing cards, complete, NM ...............................**35.00**

Big Boy salad bowl, Frisch's, green, 1960s ...............**100.00**

Blue Bonnet Sue bank, NM .**35.00**

Buster Brown & Tige clicker, embossed tin, head images, EX .................................**11.00**

Buster Brown & Tige rug, head images, yellow & blue, 47" dia, VG ..............................**375.00**

**Joe Camel, necktie, $25.00. (Photo courtesy Pamela Apkarian-Russel)**

Campbell Kids bank, Kid as chef, ceramic, EX ..................46.00

Campbell Kids calendar, 1990s, ea .....................................3.00

Campbell Kids cookie jar, ceramic, Kid graphics, Westwood, 1991, MIB ......................35.00

Campbell Kids decal, Kid chef in front of barbecue, Meyercord, 1954, M ............................8.00

Campbell Kids paperweight, etched glass, 1978, M ...45.00

Campbell Kids shakers, Kids as chefs, plastic, 1950s, 4½", MIB, pr ........................100.00

Campbell Kids thimble, china, girl at stove, Franklin Mint, 1980, M ....................................15.00

Cap'n Crunch & the Fountain of Youth comic book, 1967, G ...........20.00

Cap'n Crunch bank, Treasure Chest, painted plastic, 1973, VG .....................................65.00

Cap'n Crunch hand puppet, plastic, 1960s, VG ...............15.00

Cap'n Crunch Rescue Kit, paper, 1986, MIP ......................10.00

Charlie the Tuna alarm clock, blue & white, 1969, 4" dia, M ................................65.00

Charlie the Tuna bathroom scales, painted metal, 1970s, NM .75.00

Charlie the Tuna bracelet, embossed figure on gold-tone disk, M ............................10.00

Charlie the Tuna doll, squeeze vinyl, 1974, EX .............50.00

Charlie the Tuna lamp, painted plaster figure, EX ........75.00

Charlie the Tuna pendant, Charlie on anchor, M ..........10.00

Charlie the Tuna wristwatch, stemwind, NM, from $55 to ...75.00

Cheesasaurus Rex bank, plastic figure w/treasure chest, Kraft, M ..15.00

Cheesasaurus Rex figure, NBA or skating outfit, Kraft, M, ea ..8.00

Chiquita Banana doll, inflatable, 48", NM .........................20.00

Chore Boy doll, vinyl, EX ....30.00

Chucky Cheese bank, vinyl, 7", EX ................................10.00

Coco Bear doll, plush w/cloth shirt, Coco Wheats, 1988-91, 12", EX ................................15.00

Colonel Sanders mask, plastic, 1960s, M .........................38.00

Colonel Sanders name badge, 1960s, M ......................25.00

Colonel Sanders shakers, plastic figures, pr ......................45.00

Coppertone Candi doll, Mego, 1980, 11½", MOC .........12.00

Count Chocula doll, squeeze vinyl, 1977, 8", NM ...............125.00

Count Chocula mini mug, yellow plastic, 1973, M ............30.00

Curad's Taped Crusader bank, vinyl, NM ......................75.00

Dairy Queen Girls salt & pepper shakers, ceramic, 1960s, 4", EX, pr .........................225.00

Del Monte Brawny Bear doll, stuffed, wearing denim overalls, 8", NM ..................15.00

Del Monte Country Yumkin, plush, 1980s, NM .........12.00

Diaparene Baby doll, jointed vinyl, 1980, 5", NM .................40.00

Dino the Dinosaur soap, figural, Sinclair, MIB ................10.00

Elsie the Cow, Fun Book/Cut Out Toys & Games, 1940s, 10x7", EX ................................65.00

Elsie the Cow & Her Twins coloring book, late 1950s, EX .......25.00

Elsie the Cow dexterity game, shake to get horns on ring, 1941, EX ........................65.00

Elsie the Cow doll, plush w/vinyl head, brown & yellow, 16", M ..............................135.00

Elsie the Cow lamp base, ceramic Elsie sitting w/baby Beauregard, 8" ........................215.00

Elsie the Cow letter opener, red plastic, flashing Elsie image, 16", M ...........................135.00

Elsie the Cow needle book, black & white image on red, 1940s, 5", EX ...................................55.00

Elsie the Cow night light, Elsie's head, EX ........................35.00

Elsie the Cow place mat, w/family, M .....................................8.00

Elsie the Cow thermometer, Borden's Milk & Cream, white, 27x8", EX ........................75.00

Energizer Bunny doll, plush, battery-op, 24", M ..............45.00

Energizer Bunny flashlight, squeezable vinyl, MIP ....8.00

Entenmann's Chef bank, figural, ceramic, 10", M ..............75.00

Eskimo Pie Boy doll, stuffed cloth, Chase Bag Co, 1975, 15", NM ........................20.00

Esso Drop ornament, figure w/legs & arms spread, multicolored, 4", EX .............................85.00

Esso Tiger bank, hard rubber figure, 8", NM ....................45.00

Eveready Cat bank, black plastic, 1981, NM ......................23.00

Fisk Tire Boy ashtray, ceramic, white w/image & phrase, sq, EX .................................90.00

Fisk Tire Boy bank, ceramic figure, M ........................55.00

Fisk Tire Boy display figure, composition, 32", EX ........800.00

Florida Orange Bird bank, plastic, 1980s, 5", M ..................25.00

Florida Orange Bird candle, orange-shaped base, 1980, NM ...............................15.00

Florida Orange Bird pin, bird on outline of state, NM ........5.00

Frankenberry doll, squeeze vinyl, 1977, 8", NM ..............125.00

Frankenberry pencil topper/eraser, figural, 1973, EX .....15.00

Frito Bandito pencil topper/eraser, 1960s, 1½", M ..............20.00

Fruit Stripe Gum Yipe zebra figure, bendable, EX ........25.00

Funny Face backpack, Goofy Grape, 1975, EX ...........95.00

Funny Face frisbee, different characters, white plastic, M, ea .10.00

Funny Face kite, Goofy Grape, 1970s, MIP ..................45.00

Funny Face mug, different characters, plastic, F&F Mold, ea ...............................15.00

Funny Face pitcher, Goofy Grape, 1969, M ..........................10.00

Funny Face ramp walker, 1969 .75.00

Funny Face T-shirt, all characters on front, M ....................15.00

Geoffrey jack-in-the-box, musical, Toys R Us, NM .............38.00

Geoffry bank, vinyl, Toys R Us, 1980s, NM ....................55.00

Gold Dust Twins At Work & Play drawing & painting book, EX+ ............................110.00

Green Giant dinnerware set, cup, plate, knife & fork, 1991, MIB ............................10.00

Green Giant doll, cloth, 1966, 16", M (original mailer) .......45.00

Green Giant Farm & Factory set, MIB ..............**200.00**

Green Giant footprint rug, 1970s, M ...................**55.00**

Green Giant puzzle, Planting Time..., 1000 pcs in can, 1981, NM ..................**15.00**

Hamburger Helper Helping Hand clock, plastic figure, 1980s, 6", M .......................**40.00**

Hamburger Helper Helping Hand radio, plastic hand figure, 1980s, 7", M ..................**45.00**

Harley Hog doll, stuffed, w/leather jacket, 9", M ..................**20.00**

Hawaiian Punch Punchy doll, stuffed cloth, 20", EX **50.00**

Hawaiian Punch Punchy game, 1978, EXIB ....................**30.00**

Heinz Mr Tomato alarm clock, hard plastic, talking, 1980s, 9", EX ..........................**165.00**

Heinz Picnic Ant figure, bendable, M ...................**15.00**

Honey Nut Bee doll, plush, NM .**15.00**

Hood Dairyman doll, squeeze vinyl, 1981, M ...............**65.00**

Jack Frost Sugar doll, stuffed cloth, 17", EX ................**25.00**

Jiffaroo Kangaroo kite, paper, 1950s, M .......................**35.00**

Jiffaroo Kangaroo periscope, M .**15.00**

Joe Camel apron, Max & Ray's barbecue, NM ...............**30.00**

Joe Camel license plate, NM **14.00**

Joe Camel mug, Joe w/Hard Pack & pals playing cards in bar, 7", NM .........................**20.00**

Joe Camel T-shirt, Beach Club, MIB ...............**20.00**

Kahn's Beefy Frank mustard dispenser, plastic figure, 1980s, 5½", M ..........................**25.00**

Keebler Elf baseball cap, embroidered front, NM ..............**7.00**

Keebler Elf doll, rubber, 6½", NM ...............**18.00**

Keebler Elf doll, stuffed plush, 1981, 24", EX ...............**45.00**

Keebler Elf spoon rest, painted ceramic, M .....................**12.00**

Keebler Elf wristwatch, battery-operated, MIB ..............**45.00**

Ken-L-Ration Cat wall pocket, F&F Mold, EX ..............**40.00**

Ken-L-Ration Cat/Dog salt & pepper shakers, F&F Mold, EX, pr ..................................**20.00**

Kodak Colorkins doll, stuffed cloth, 1990, 8" or 10", ea .........**20.00**

Kool-Aid Awsome Dude, stuffed cloth w/surfer shorts & sunglasses, MIP ..................**15.00**

Little Miss Sunbeam doll, stuffed cloth, Sunbeam Bread, 17", EX ................................**30.00**

**Little Sprout, planter, Benjamin Medwin, 1988, $40.00. (Photo courtesy Lil West)**

Little Sprout bank, composition figure, musical, Green Giant, 9", NM ...........................**50.00**

Little Sprout cookie jar, Benjamin Medwin, Green Giant, 1988, MIB ................................**50.00**

Little Sprout hand puppet, cloth, Green Giant, NM ..........**20.00**

Little Sprout jump rope, Green Giant, MIB ....................**20.00**

**Lotta Light cloth doll, Mazda/Westinghouse, original uncut cloth, 17", NM, $85.00.**

M&M dispensers, regular or peanut shape, 1991, lg, ea ..........**15.00**

M&M doll, stuffed plush, blue, 4½" ...............................**10.00**

M&M Happy Lights, string set, 1996, MIB ......................**20.00**

M&M Peanut doll, stuffed plush, yellow or green, 14", NM ......**18.00**

Mars Snickers Olympic Dog, stuffed, 1994, NM .........**12.00**

Mary Ann doll, North American Van Lines, MIB ............**70.00**

Meow Mix cat figure, vinyl, EX .**35.00**

Michelin Man figure, plastic, 12", NM+ ............................**100.00**

Michelin Man ramp walker, wind-up, MIB .........................**25.00**

Milton the Toaster, bank, vinyl, Kellogg's, 1970s, MIB, minimum value ..................**100.00**

Mother Nature doll, stuffed, yarn hair, Chiffon Margarine, 15", MIB ...............................**30.00**

Mr Bubble bank, plastic figure, 1970s, 7" or 9½", NM, ea .**75.00**

Mr Bubble doll, squeeze vinyl, 1990, 8", NM .................**35.00**

Mr Peanut American Presidents paint book, 32 pages, 1960s, NM ...............................**22.00**

Mr Peanut bookmark, cardboard diecut, orange, 1950s, 8x3", EX .................................**15.00**

Mr Peanut cocktail glass, plastic, blue, green or red, 1950s, EX .............................**25.00**

**Mr Peanut wood-jointed figure, 12", EX, from $150.00 to $250.00. (Photo coutesy Dunbar Gallery)**

Mr Peanut walker, wind-up, black & tan, 1984, 2¾", MIP ..**15.00**

Mr Wiggle hand puppet, red rubber, Jell-O, 1966, 6", M ........**175.00**

Mr Zip figure, wooden pop-up, US Mail, 1960s, 6½", EX ..**125.00**

Mr Zip/US Mail truck pull toy, plastic, red, white & blue, 1970s, EX ....................**125.00**

Naugie figure, vinyl, M .......**45.00**

Nestle Chocolate Man doll, stuffed cloth, Chase Bag Co, 1970, 15", NM .........................**20.00**

Nestle Quik Bunny doll, plush, 1985, 16", M .................**20.00**

Nestle Scotchie Chip doll, plush, 1984, NM ......................**12.00**

Nipper display dog figure, composition, RCA, 33", G .....**300.00**

Nipper display dog figure, felt over pot metal, RCA, 6", NM .**185.00**

Northern Tissue Girl doll, M ..**25.00**

Oreo Cookie Man figure, bendable, M ....................................**15.00**

Oscar Mayer Boy display figure, inflatable, 1960s, MIP ..**75.00**

**Pillsbury Doughboy Funfetti utensil holder, 1992, MIB, $25.00. (Photo courtesy Lil West)**

Pillsbury Doughboy bank, carboard biscuit tube w/images, 1970s, 7", NM ...............**15.00**

Pillsbury Doughboy bank, skinny figure, ceramic, 1985, M .**25.00**

Pillsbury Doughboy decals, set of 18, MIP .........................**18.00**

Pillsbury Doughboy doll, squeeze vinyl, 1970s, 6½", VG ...**12.00**

Pillsbury Doughboy mug, plastic, 1979, 4½", EX ..............**15.00**

Pizza Hut Pete bank, plastic, 1969, NM ................................**55.00**

Poll Parrot spinner, For Boys & Girls..., EX .....................**11.00**

Quick doll, stuffed cloth, Tyson Chicken, 13", VG .........**15.00**

Raid Bug banner, Raid Kills Bugs Dead, 48x24", M ...........**28.00**

Raid Bug beach bag, NM .....**15.00**

Raid Bug doll, inflatable vinyl, MIP ................................**20.00**

Raid Bug playing cards, double deck, MIP (sealed) ........**10.00**

Raid Bug telephone, plastic figure, 1980s, 9", MIB, from $100 to ......................**125.00**

Ralston Purina Chuck Wagon, squeeze vinyl, EX .........**40.00**

Rastus doll, printed cloth, assembled, Cream of Wheat, NM+ ...**150.00**

Red Goose display figure, chalkware, 12", NM+ ..........**400.00**

Red Goose give-away figure, chalkware, 4", NM+ ..............**40.00**

Red Goose rug, Half the Fun of Having Feet..., 27x59", rare, EX ...............................**325.00**

Reddy Kilowatt ashtray, glass, sq, NM ................................**10.00**

Reddy Kilowatt apron, plastic w/multicolored graphics, 1960s, M ......................**35.00**

Reddy Kilowatt coaster, cardboard, 3½", NM ............8.00

**Reddy Kilowatt figure (unusual style), 1950s, 6", $200.00. (Photo courtesy Lee Garmon)**

Reddy Kilowatt folder, clear plastic w/Reddy in corner, M ....20.00

Reddy Kilowatt napkins, set of 8, 1970, MIP ......................32.00

Reddy Kilowatt postcard, 1¢, Reddy in cowboy hat, M ..8.00

Reddy Kilowatt pot holder, MIP .30.00

Reddy Kilowatt Take It Easy Recipes for Modern Homemakers, NM ..................12.00

Revlon doll, vinyl w/outfit, 1950, 10½", M ........................25.00

Ritalin Man figure, plastic, happy or sad, 1970s, 5½", ea ..75.00

Ritalin Man figure & pen holder, plastic, 1970s, 7", EX ....35.00

Scrubbin' Bubble bank, ceramic, M ................................20.00

Scrubbin' Bubble doll, 1990s, NM ........................20.00

Shoney's Bear bank, plastic w/red shirt & blue pants, 8", M .15.00

Sleepy Bear doll, stuffed, Travel Lodge, EX ......................45.00

Sleepy Bear doll, vinyl, Travel Lodge, EX ......................65.00

Smokey the Bear plate, w/friends in center, Melmac, 1960s, 7", NM ................................25.00

Smokey the Bear postcard, Courtesy National Auto Club of CA, 1965, NM ..............11.00

Smokey the Bear spoon, plastic figural handle ..............12.50

Smokey the Bear target set, Prevents Wildfires, Gordy, MOC ..........................12.00

Snap! Crackle! & Pop! canteen, plastic, Kellogg's, 1973, NM ..........................25.00

Snap! Crackle! & Pop! key chain, Kellogg's, 1980s, EX .....10.00

Snap! Crackle! & Pop! stickers, glow-in-the-dark, Kellogg's, 1971, M ..........................10.00

Spam Bear necklace, NM ....10.00

Sparkle telephone, blue figural plastic, Crest, 1980s, 11", NM ..............................40.00

Speedy Alka-Seltzer bank, vinyl, 5½", EX ......................85.00

Sun Maid Raisin/California Raisin bank, rubber, 6½", EX+ ..............................20.00

Swiss Miss doll, stuffed cloth w/cloth dress, yarn hair, 17", EX ................................20.00

Tagamet Stomach figure, bendable, EX+ ......................15.00

Tastee Freeze doll, hard plastic, 7", NM ..........................20.00

Texaco Cheerleader doll, 11½", NMIB ..........................65.00

Tony the Tiger doll, stuffed cloth, Kellogg's, 1973, 14", EX .40.00

Tony the Tiger place mat, vinyl, Kellogg's, 1981, EX .......**10.00**

Tony the Tiger radio, plastic, battery-op, Kellogg's, 1980, 7", MIB ...............................**30.00**

Tony the Tiger's Secret Message pen, Kellogg's, 1980s, M .**3.00**

Tony the Tiger valentines, set of 30, Kellogg's, 1986, MIB ......**10.00**

Toucan Sam drinking glass, Kellogg's, 1977, VG ............**20.00**

Toucan Sam figure, bendable, Kellogg's, 4", NM .................**28.00**

Toucan Sam Funscope, Kellogg's, 1982, M ...........................**10.00**

Toucan Sam license plate, blue plastic, Kellogg's, 1973, 3x6", EX ..................................**20.00**

Trix Rabbit spoon, stainless steel, NM ..................................**5.00**

Twinkles bank, orange plastic elephant figure, 1960s, 7½", NM .............................**125.00**

Vlasic Pickles Stork doll, white fur, Trudy Toys, 1989, 22", NM ..................................**40.00**

Wizard of O's bank, cast iron, Franco American, NM ..**40.00**

Woodsy Owl bank, ceramic, Give a Hoot!... on round base, 8½", NM ..................................**60.00**

Woodsy Owl lapel button, Give a Hoot!..., 1960s, 1" dia, EX .**28.00**

# Advertising Watches

The concept of advertising timepieces goes back to the turn of the century when wall clocks featuring specific products were produced, and to some extent the idea was pursued throughout each suc-ceeding decade. But it was in the 1970s that advertising watches really came into vogue. Today these are among the newest stars on the collectibles scene. Included are mechanical/battery-operated pocket watches, mechanical/battery-operated wrist watches, digital/analog watches, dress or sport watches, company logo and character watches, event watches, corporate watches, catalog/store retail watches, and giveaway and premium watches. Condition, originality, cleanliness, scarcity, cross-collectibility, and buyer demand affect value. The newer the watch, the better its condition must be. Original mint packaging, including paperwork, can triple value. Watches featuring a popular character or event are especially desirable to collectors, while those that are produced in great numbers are generally less valuable. Copyright dates are not manufacturing dates — learn to date watches by style and features. Analogs are more collectible than digitals.

Our advisor for this category is Sharon Iranpour, editor of *The Premium Watch Watch*, a newsletter devoted to the interests of ad-logo watch collectors. See Clubs and Newsletters for information. (Note: watches described in the following listings are all wristwatches unless noted otherwise.)

1930s, Ever Ready Safety Razor Pocket Watch, VG .......**275.00**

1930s, Reddy Kilowatt 5-Sided Pocket Watch, VG .......**250.00**

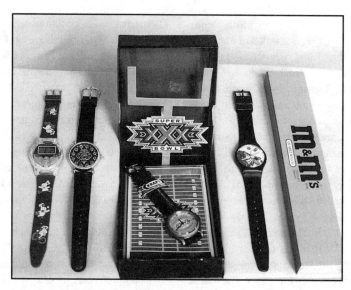

**The 1996 most collectible advertising-logo watches: Pillsbury Doughboy Talking Watch, $15.00; Oreo Cookie Watch, $50.00; Kraft Super Bowl XXX Watch in Goal Post box, $20.00; and the New Blue M&M's Watch and box cover, $20.00. (Photo courtesy Sharon Iranpour)**

1960s, Buster Brown Pocket Watch, VG ......................**75.00**

1970s, Buster Brown, red costume, VG ..................................**75.00**

1970s, Ernie the Keebler Elf, G ...**50.00**

1970s, Irish Spring, EX .......**10.00**

1970s, Punchy, mechanical, digital, red strap, VG ..........**50.00**

1971 or 1973, Charlie the Tuna, VG, either ......................**50.00**

1980s, Dukes of Hazzard, new old stock, any style, from $5 to .**10.00**

1980s, Kraft Cheese & Macaroni Club, M ..........................**10.00**

1984, Ronald McDonald House & Coca-Cola, MOC, from $3 to ..........**5.00**

1986, Charlie the Tuna 25th Anniversary, MIB .........**25.00**

1987, Max Headroom by Coca-Cola, lady's, M ..............**10.00**

1987, Max Headroom by Coca-Cola, man's, M ..............**25.00**

1990, Eggo Waffles Eggosaurus, M ....................................**15.00**

1991, Kool Aid Hologram, M .**15.00**

1993, Nightmare Before Christmas by Burger King, set of 4, MIP, ea ......................................**3.00**

1994, Campbell Kids 125th Anniversary, M .............**50.00**

1994, Snicker's Anniversary, M ...**35.00**

1995, Congo the Movie by Taco Bell, set of 3, MIB, ea .....**3.00**

1996-97, Mr Peanut Wrist Watch, yellow face, VG, ea ........50.00

1997, Fisher-Price Little People, M ....................................**50.00**

1997, Lost World of Burger King, set of 4, MIB, ea ..............**3.00**

# Akro Agate

This company operated in

Clarksburg, West Virginia, from 1914 to 1951, manufacturing marbles, novelties, and the children's dishes, for which they are best known. Though some were made in transparent colors, their most popular, easy-to-identify lines were produced in a swirling opaque type of glass similar to that which was used in the production of their marbles. Their trademark was a flying eagle clutching marbles in his claws. Refer to *The Collector's Encyclopedia of Children's Dishes* by Margaret and Kenn Whitmyer (Collector Books) for more information.

Ashtray, green & white, hexagonal, 4½" ........................**28.00**
Ashtray, oxblood & white, 3" sq .........................**18.00**
Chiquita, creamer, crystal, 1½" .........................**24.00**
Chiquita, cup, transparent cobalt, 1½" ..................................**8.00**

Chiquita, 12-pc set, opaque colors other than green, MIB ........................**150.00**
Chiquita, 22-pc set, opaque green, MIB ................................**78.00**
Concentric Rib, cup, opaque colors other than green or white, 1¼" ..................................**8.00**
Concentric Rib, set, opaque green or white, sm, 10-pc MIB ................................ **53.00**
Concentric Rib, teapot, opaque green or white, sm, 3⅜" .12.00
Concentric Ring, cereal, cobalt, lg, 3⅜" ..................................**35.00**
Concentric Ring, plate, solid opaque color, lg, 4¼" .......**7.00**
Concentric Ring, plate, transparent cobalt, sm, 3¼" .......**20.00**
Concentric Ring, teapot, blue marbleized, with lid, lg, 3¾" ......................**125.00**
Flowerpot, Banded Darts, orange & white, #301 ................**65.00**
Flowerpot, Graduated Darts, orange, #307 ..................**45.00**

**Chiquita (all in transparent cobalt): Open teapot, $12.00; Sugar bowl, $8.00; Creamer, $7.00.**

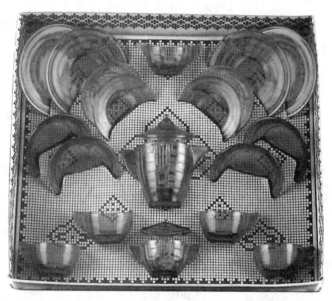

Concentric Ring, transparent cobalt, large, 21-piece boxed set, $560.00. (Photo courtesy Margaret and Kenn Whitmeyer)

Flowerpot, Ribbed Top, black, #294 ..............................**75.00**

Flowerpot, Thumbpots, marbleized, #290 .................**28.00**

Interior Panel, creamer, marbleized green & white, lg, 1⅜" ..............................**25.00**

Interior Panel, creamer, pink lustre, sm, 1¼" ..................**27.00**

Interior Panel, cup, azure blue, sm, 1¼" ..........................**30.00**

Interior Panel, plate, transparent green, lg, 4¼" ..................**6.00**

Interior Panel, teapot, transparent green, sm, 3⅜" .............**30.00**

JP (for J Pressman Co), creamer, light blue or crystal, lg, 1½" ......**32.50**

JP (for J Pressman Co), creamer, transparent green, lg, 1½" ..........................**45.00**

JP (for J Pressman Co), plate, transparent green, lg, 4¼" .......**12.00**

JP (for J Pressman Co), 21-pc set, baked-on colors, lg, MIB ........................**150.00**

Lamp, crystal, 5-pc .............**45.00**

Lamp, marbleized, 5-pc .......**95.00**

Miss America, creamer, white, 1¼" ..............................**50.00**

Miss America, cup, orange & white, 1⅝" ....................**65.00**

Miss America, plate, forest green, 4½" ..............................**45.00**

Miss America, sugar bowl, white w/decal, w/lid, 2" ..........**85.00**

Octagonal, creamer, pink or yellow opaque, closed handle, lg, 1½" ..............................**10.00**

Octagonal, saucer, green, white or dark blue, lg, 3⅜" ..........**3.00**

Octagonal, tumbler, dark green, blue or white, sm, 2" .....**12.00**

Octagonal, 17-pc set, lemonade & oxblood, lg, MIB .........**325.00**

Powder jar, Colonial lady figural, pink ...............................**80.00**

Powder jar, sawtooth, crystal .**75.00**

Raised Daisy, cup, blue, sm, 1¾" ...........................**45.00**

Raised Daisy, teapot, green, 2⅜" ...........................**25.00**

Raised Daisy, tumbler, beige, sm, 2" ....................................**35.00**

Stacked Disc, cup, opaque green or white, sm, 1¼" ...............**6.00**

Stacked Disc, plate, opaque green or white, sm, 3¼" ............**3.00**

Stacked Disc, tumbler, green or white, sm, 2" ...................**8.50**

Stacked Disc, tumbler, opaque colors other than green, sm, 2" ...................................**14.00**

Stacked Disc, 21-pc set, green or white, sm, MIB ...........**130.00**

Stacked Disc & Interior Panel, cereal, transparent green, 3⅜" ...............................**22.00**

Stacked Disc & Interior Panel, cup, solid opaque color, lg, 1⅜" ...............................**22.00**

Stacked Disc & Interior Panel, cup, transparent cobalt, lg, 1⅜" ...............................**27.50**

Stacked Disc & Interior Panel, plate, opaque colors, sm, 3¼" ...............................**8.00**

Stacked Disc & Interior Panel, teapot, opaque colors, lg, 3¾" ...............................**50.00**

Stippled Band, creamer, amber, lg, 1¼" ...............................**22.00**

Stippled Band, pitcher, green, sm, 2⅞" ...............................**15.00**

Stippled Band, tumbler, amber, sm, 1¾" ...........................**11.00**

Stippled Band, 7-pc set, green, sm, MIB ...............................**70.00**

Stippled Interior Panel, creamer, opaque yellow, lg, 1⅜" ..**35.00**

Stippled Interior Panel, cup, pumpkin, sm, 1¼" .........**20.00**

Stippled Interior Panel, plate, green, lg, 4¼" ..................**6.00**

Stippled Interior Panel, saucer, lemonade & oxblood, lg, 3⅛" ...........................**10.00**

Westite, ashtray, blue, hexagonal ...............................**28.00**

Westite, bowl, fruit; marbleized, ftd ...............................**125.00**

Westite, flowerpot, green, #301 .**40.00**

# Aluminum

From the late 1930s until early in the 1950s, kitchenwares and household items were often crafted of aluminum, usually with relief-molded fruit or flowers on a hammered background. Today many find that these diversified items make an attractive collection. Especially desirable are those examples marked with the manufacturer's backstamp or the designer's signature.

You've probably also seen the anodized (colored) aluminum pitchers, tumblers, sherbet holders, etc., that were popular in the late '50s, early '60s. Lately they're everywhere, and with a wide range between asking prices. Tumblers in good condition with very little wear seem to be about $3.00 to $4.00 each. The pitchers are fairly common and shouldn't be worth much more than $12.00 or so.

Our advisor for this category

is Everett Grist, author of *Collectible Aluminum, An Identification and Value Guide* (Collector Books). He is listed in the Directory under Tennessee.

**Buffet server, ends of draped flower-cut ribbon form feet, applied tulip on lid, Rodney Kent, from $35.00 to $45.00. (Photo courtesy Everett Grist)**

Ashtray, water lilies & pods, sq with ruffled edge, Arthur-Armour ..........................**25.00**

Basket, floral & leaf band, ruffled edge, Everlast, 6x9" ......**10.00**

Basket, hammered, serrated edge, floral handle, footed, unmarked, 4x4" ..............................**10.00**

Basket, mums, hammered, saddlebag shape, Continental, 3x7" ..............................**25.00**

Basket, mums, sq with rolled-up edges, Continental Silver, 8" ..................................**20.00**

Basket, poinsettias, fluted with serrated edge, Farber & Shlevin ..........................**5.00**

Basket, tulips, hexagon with upturned serrated edge, R Kent, 7" ..........................**30.00**

Basket, wild rose, fluted serrated edge, Continental, 6" ....**20.00**

Beverage server, concentric circles, ball finial, Kromex, 11" ............................**25.00**

Beverage set, 8 hammered tumblers in handled holder, unmarked, 13" ..............**35.00**

Beverage spoons, leaf-shaped bowls, anodized, Color Craft, set of 6 ..........................**30.00**

Bowl, bamboo, faint serrated edge, Everlast, 1x8" ..............**10.00**

Bowl, dogwood, fluted & crimped edge, Wendell August Forge, 2x7" ..............................**20.00**

Bowl, dogwood & butterflies on anodized gold, A Armour, 1x8" sq ..................................**25.00**

Bowl, ducks, scalloped serrated edge, Wendell August Forge, 10" ..................................**65.00**

Bowl, hammered, serrated, 2 3-loop coil handles, Buenilum, 2x12" ..............................**5.00**

Bowl, mums, serrated edge, beaded pedestal, unmarked, 4x9" .**20.00**

Bowl, mums in bottom, fluted edge, Continental, 1x5½" .......**20.00**

Bowl, tulips, hammered, loop handles, pedestal, R Kent, 2x10" ..............................**25.00**

Bowl, wheat design, smooth edge, Palmer-Smith, 4x14" ....**60.00**

Butter dish, bamboo, Everlast, 4x4x7" ..........................**10.00**

Cake stand, band of shields, serrated edge, Wilson Metal, 8x12" ..............................**15.00**

Candle holder, oak-leaf shape with acorn holder, Bruce Fox, 10" ..................................**35.00**

Candlesticks, hammered, scalloped & fluted bobeche, Everlast, 4x3", pr ..................**20.00**

Candlesticks, S-shaped w/tulips, Farberware, 8", pr ........**45.00**

Candy dish, pine cones, serrated, coil handle, unmarked, 6" sq ..............**5.00**

Candy dish, ship on leaf shape, curled handle, World Hand Forge, 8" ..........**15.00**

Candy dish, 2 leaves w/loop handle, serrated edge, Buenilum, 5x6" ................**10.00**

Casserole, bamboo, handles, w/lid, Everlast, 5x7" ..............**10.00**

Casserole, dogwood & butterflies, ring finial, A Armour, 4x10" ..........**50.00**

Casserole, hammered, beaded trim, double loop finial, Buenilum, 6x8" ....................**5.00**

Casserole, hammered, tulips, R Kent, 6x8" ....................**10.00**

Cigarette box, bittersweet, hinged lid, Wendell August Forge, 3x5" ................**75.00**

Cigarette box, pine cones, hinged lid, Town, 1¾x5½" ........**75.00**

Coaster, Capitol building on hammered ground, Alpha Swiss, 4½" ....................**3.00**

Coaster, cricket, smooth edge, Wendell August Forge, 3½" ....**35.00**

Coaster, Scottie dog sitting, deep smooth edge, unmarked, 3½" ..............**3.00**

Coaster set, bamboo, 4 in trivet-type footed holder, Everlast, 3½" ..............**20.00**

Coaster set, mums, 12 in basket holder, Continental, 4" dia ......**30.00**

Coffee urn, mums, glass finial, handled, Continental, 15" ..**75.00**

Collapsible cup, w/lid, souvenir, unmarked ..................**5.00**

Compote, flowers, fluted edge, double-loop pedestal, unmarked, 5x8" ..............**5.00**

Compote, hammered deep bowl with flared rim, pedestal, unmarked, 5x6" ........**10.00**

Crumb brush & tray, grapevines, Lucite brush handle, Everlast ..............**10.00**

Crumb brush & tray, 6-petal flowers on hammered ground, unmarked ..................**25.00**

Dip server, bamboo, hammered, 3 bowls on rods with wheels, Everlast, 11" ..............**35.00**

Dish, fish shape, Bruce Fox/Royal Hickman, 19x8" ..................**85.00**

Dish, lobster shape, Bruce Fox, 15x11" ..................**85.00**

Double boiler, polished, wood handle & finial, Pyrex liner, Buenilum ..............**10.00**

Fruit bowl w/knives, fruit & flowers, loop handles, pedestal, unmarked ..................**15.00**

Gravy boat, bamboo, Wendell August Forge ..............**20.00**

Gravy boat, mums, attached tray, side handle & spout, Continental, 6" ..................**25.00**

Huricane lamp, 2 sockets, twisted-loop center handle, Buenilum, 9x11" ..............**30.00**

Ice bucket, acorns, cane-shaped handles, open, Continental, 3x7" ..............**15.00**

Ice bucket, hammered, fluted edge, barbell handles, Everlast, 5x10" ..............**15.00**

Ice bucket, intaglio flowers, open, open tab handles, Everlast, 3x7" ..............**10.00**

Ice bucket, mums, mushroom & leaf finial, ribbon handles, Continental ....................**40.00**

Ice tongs, hammered, unmarked ...**4.00**

Jelly jar w/ladle, beaded lid & low pedestal plate, Nekrassoff, 5" dia ...................................**35.00**

Lazy Susan, ivy, deep well, upturned rim & leaf handles, unmarked, 13" ..............**10.00**

Lazy Susan, tulips, 2 applied flower & ribbon tabs, R Kent, 18" dia ..........................**15.00**

Letter basket, world map, silver anodized, Arthur Armour, 6x7x5" ..........................**175.00**

Match box cover, acorn & oak leaves, Wendell August Forge ...........................**35.00**

Match box cover, shotgun w/flying ducks, Wendell August Forge ...........................**75.00**

Meat server, mums, Forman Family, 14x18" ......................**20.00**

Mint dish, dogwood, glass insert, Wendell August Forge, 12" dia ...................................**45.00**

Napkin holder, dogwood, convex sides, Wendell August Forge, 5x4x3" ...........................**30.00**

Napkin holder, thistle, crimped scalloped edge, unmarked, 4x2x6" ...........................**10.00**

Nut bowl, flower & leaf, ruffled serrated rim, pedestal, Wilson, 4x7" ........................**10.00**

Pitcher, acorn & leaf, bulbous w/coiled handle, Continental, 8" ....................................**20.00**

Pitcher, bamboo, ice lip on rolled edge, Everlast, 5x8" ......**25.00**

Pitcher, tulips, ice lip, serrated, ear handle, R Kent, 9" ..**35.00**

Pitcher, wild rose, ice lip, serrated, ear handle, Continental, 8" ......**35.00**

Silent butler, bamboo, Everlast, 6" dia .................................**10.00**

Silent butler, bird on branch, fluted rim, open handle, NS Co .**15.00**

Silent butler, wheat, Kraftware, 6½" dia ..........................**10.00**

Syrup pitcher, plain, hinged lid, angled strap handle, Viko, 6" .....................................**10.00**

Tidbit, single, grapes, fluted, loop handle, Designed Aluminum, 6" dia ..............................**5.00**

Tidbit, 2-tier, ducks, rectangular, Everlast, 12" .................**25.00**

Tidbit, 2-tier, tulips, upturned serrated rims, unmarked, 10x11" ...........................**15.00**

Tidbit, 3-tier, rose, upturned fluted rims, unmarked, 11" ..**5.00**

Tray, bar; anchor, rope & sea gulls, handles, Everlast, 9x15" .............................**30.00**

Tray, bar; pine cone, raised flat rim, no handles, Everlast, 8x20" .............................**10.00**

Tray, bar; water lilies, self-handled, Arthur Armour, 8x17" ....**45.00**

Tray, beverage; vine & flower, twisted handles, Keystone Ware, 10x14" .................**10.00**

Tray, bread; mums, scalloped rim, Continental, oval, 8x11" ..**25.00**

Tray, bread; tulips, applied flower & ribbon handles, R Kent, 8x13" .............................**25.00**

Tray, cheese & cracker; floral & vine, serrated, Handwrought, 20" dia ...........................**5.00**

Tray, crane & bamboo, applied handles, Hand Forged, 9" dia .............................**30.00**

**Tray, vegetable pattern, Wendell August Forge, 9x14",**
**$85.00. (Photo courtesy Dannie Woodard)**

Tray, deer & geese, hammered, with handles, Continental, 12x16" ........................**60.00**

Tray, dogwood, center well, fluted, Admiration, 10" dia ........**5.00**

Tray, flying ducks, upturned rim, Everlast, oval, 10x12" ...................**15.00**

Tray, fox hunt scene on handles, Kensington, 14x23" .......**10.00**

Tray, fruit, hammered, center well, coil handles, Hand Forged, 17" dia ................**5.00**

Tray, fruit band, wire loop handles, fluted, Cromwell, oblong, 13x19" ...........................**5.00**

Tray, goldfish, walnut handles, beaded hammered rim, unmarked, 10x14" ........**45.00**

Tray, horse head in horseshoe, self-handled, W August Forge, 9x15" ............................**60.00**

Tray, larkspur, plain upturned rim, Wendell August Forge, 13x20" ...........................**75.00**

Tray, Pittsburgh skyline, Wendell August Forge, oval, 11x13" .....................**60.00**

Tray, relish; geese, 4 compartments, self-handled, A Armour, 5x16" ...............**75.00**

Tray, sailboat, hammered, upturned rim, open handles, Everlast, 11x18" ..........................**25.00**

Trivet, acorn, lg-scalloped serrated rim, Continental, 10" dia ..................................**10.00**

Trivet, pine cone, Everlast, oval, 8x11" ...............................**5.00**

Wastebasket, pine cone, ruffled rim, Wendell August Forge, 11" ...............................**150.00**

## Animal Dishes With Covers

Popular novelties for much of this century as well as the last, figural animal dishes were made by

26

many well-known glasshouses in milk glass, slag, colored opaque, or clear glass. Many were produced from 1930 through 1960 and beyond, and these are what you'll most often encounter. Some are reproductions of earlier styles, and though they're well worth your attention, don't overpay, thinking they're the originals. Beware! Refer to *Covered Animal Dishes* by Everett Grist (Collector Books) for more information.

Boar's head, milk glass, Atterbury, patent date May 29, 1888 ......................**1,250.00**
Bulldog, Doeskin, with WG (Westmoreland) mark, sm ...........................**30.00**
Cat on nest, purple slag iridescent, Westmoreland ...............**95.00**
Cat on wide-rib base, #18, Westmoreland, various colors, 5", from $45 to....................**75.00**
Chicken & eggs on basket nest, milk glass, glass eyes, Westmoreland ......................**95.00**
Dolphin, blue, Joe St Clair ...**175.00**
Dove & hand, milk glass, Atterbury, lid dated August 27, 1889 .............................**125.00**
Duck, pink carnival, Imperial, #146, 5" ..........................**30.00**
Duck on flange base, milk glass, LG Wright .....................**50.00**
Duck on nest, jade slag satin, Imperial, #146 ...............**65.00**
Duck on wavy base, milk glass, US Glass, 8" ......................**125.00**
Hen & chicks on base, custard, LG Wright, 5½" ..................**75.00**

Hen on basketweave base, amberina, red or vaseline, LG Wright, 7½", ...................**75.00**
Hen on basketweave base, blue slag, LG Wright, 7½" ....**95.00**
Hen on basketweave base, purple slag or caramel slag, LG Wright, 5½ .....................**55.00**
Hen on basketweave base, red slag, LG Wright, 7½", minimum value .............................**125.00**
Hen on diamond basketweave base, blue w/white head, Westmoreland ...............**65.00**
Hen on lacy base, #1, milk glass, Westmoreland, 7½" ....**125.00**
Hen on nest, milk glass, Imperial, #1950/145, 4¼" ..............**25.00**
Hen on nest, red carnival, Westmoreland, 5½" ................**85.00**
Horse on basketweave base, purple slag or caramel slag, LG Wright, 5½"....................**55.00**

Lion on lacy base, amber, Imperial (marked IG inside lid) from $75.00 to $90.00.

Lamb on picket fence base, white, Westmoreland Specialty, 5½" ...........**95.00**
Lion on lacy base, amber, Imperial, #159, from $75 to ...........**90.00**

**Rabbit on diamond nest, purple slag, $175.00. (Photo courtesy Frank J. Grizel)**

Lion on lacy base, purple slag satin, Imperial, #159 ..**185.00**

Lion on picket fence base, milk glass, Westmoreland Specialty, 5½" ..............**95.00**

Mother eagle & babies on basketweave base, chocolate, Levay, Westmoreland ...**250.00**

Owl on basketweave base, amber, LG Wright, 5½" .............**35.00**

Owl on basketweave base, custard, LG Wright, 5½" .............**65.00**

Rabbit, mule-earred; on picket base, milk glass, Westmoreland ...............................50.00

Rabbit on picket fence base, #5, purple slag, Westmoreland ..........................**95.00**

Ribbed fox on lacy Atterbury base, milk glass, dated, 6¼" ........................**175.00**

Ribbed fox on ribbed base, milk glass, dated ................**225.00**

Ribbed lion on ribbed base, milk glass, dated ................**225.00**

Rooster, standing; Crystal Mist with/red trim, Westmoreland, 8½" ...............................**95.00**

Rooster on basketweave base, purple slag, LG Wright, 5½" .......**55.00**

Rooster on lacy base, caramel slag satin, Imperial, #158 ..**160.00**

Rooster on wide-rib base, white with blue head, Westmoreland ...........................**70.00**

Rooster standing, white carnival, LE Smith ......................**75.00**

Seashell & dolphin, candy dish, blue opaque, Westmoreland, 5½" ...............................**75.00**

Swan, Block; milk glass, Challinor Taylor & Company .....**300.00**

Turkey on basketweave base, lilac mist, LG Wright, 5½" ...**55.00**

Turtle, Knobby Back, amber, LG Wright, lg ......................**95.00**

Turtle, Thousand Eye, cigarette box, black, Westmoreland .....**150.00**

Turtle on basketweave base, amber, LG Wright, 5½" .**20.00**

# Appliances

Old electric appliances are collected for nostalgic reasons as well as for their unique appearance and engineering. Especially interesting are early irons, fans, vacuum cleaners, and toasters. Examples with Art Deco styling often bring high prices at today's auctions and flea markets. But remember, condition is important. Be sure they're reasonably clean and in excellent working condition before paying listed prices.

For more information we recommend *Collector's Guide to Electric Fans* by John M. Witt, and *Collector's Guide to Toasters and Accessories* by Helen Greguire. Both are published by Collector Books.

Beater, Vidrio, paneled custard slag container, 1930s ....**60.00**

Blender, Knapp-Monarch Liquidizer, Deco style, 1940s, EX ...............................**55.00**

Coffee set, Krome Kraft, gold Bakelite handles .........**140.00**

Coffee urn, chrome & yellow Bakelite, Manning-Bowman, 14x11", VG ....................**70.00**

Corn popper, Dominion .......**75.00**

Egg boiler, El Eggo, Pacific Electric Heating Co, 1890s, NM ..**50.00**

Fan, Emerson #5460 Silver Swan, 12" blades, 3-speed, 1937-40, EX ..............................**250.00**

Fan, Emerson #6250-D Jubilee, overlapping 10" brass blades, 1939, EX ........................**30.00**

Fan, GE #FM10V1, 10" blades, 2-speed, oscillating, 1947, NM ...........................**38.00**

Fan, GE #33X164 Quiet Fan, 10" blades, 1932, EX ..........**65.00**

Fan, Westinghouse #12PA2 Power-Aire, 12" blades, 1941-49, EX ...........................**35.00**

Frappe mixer, Hamilton Beach, tan porcelain, EX+ ........**90.00**

Ice cream freezer, Hamilton Beach Iceless..., ca 1934, w/box ...........................**40.00**

**Sandwich grill, chrome with embossed top, Bakelite handles, Waage Mfg Co Chicago ILL, 1930s, 13½" long. (Photo courtesy Helen Greguire)**

Mixer, Dormeyer, chrome, 1950s ..........................**85.00**

Mixer, Hamilton Beach Model C, 1930s ............................**75.00**

Mixer, Sunbeam Mixmaster Model 9 .......................................**75.00**

Mixer, Whip-All, Air-O-Mix, cast & sheet metal, 1920s, rare ...........................**100.00**

Percolator, Hotpoint, #114517 ..**85.00**

Refrigerator, General Electric, coil top ...............................**300.00**

Toaster, Bersted #72 ............**45.00**

Toaster, Dominion, #1000, EX ......................**45.00**

Toaster, Electrahot, chrome & black enamel, 1920s, 7⅜" ..........**55.00**

Toaster, General Electric #119T48, late 1930s, 7⅝" ................**50.00**

Toaster, Hotpoint, #1Z6T33 .**95.00**

Toaster, Samson Tri Matic ..**95.00**

Toaster, Simplex, #212 ........**85.00**

Toaster, Toastwell, #791 .....**65.00**

Toaster, Universal, #E7812 ..**95.00**

Toaster stove, Westinghouse, rectangular, cabriole legs, early ...........................**65.00**

Vacuum cleaner, Airway, 1922, w/original bag .............**145.00**

Vacuum cleaner, Universal Supreme Model No E440, ca 1942 .........................**125.00**

Waffle iron, Dominion, #377 ..................**35.00**

Waffle iron, Hotpoint, #226Y53 .**45.00**

Waffle iron, Lady Hibbard on ceramic insert, Bakelite handles ....................**135.00**

Waffle iron, Westinghouse, WD-2 ...................................**65.00**

Washing machine, Maytag, double wringer, on casters, ca 1914 .........................**150.00**

# Ashtrays

Even though the general public seems to be down on smoking, ashtrays themselves are beginning to be noticed favorably by collectors, who perhaps view them as an 'endangered species'! Some of the more desirable examples are those with embossed or intaglio designs, applied decorations, added figures of animals or people, Art Deco styling, an interesting advertising message, or an easily recognizable manufacturer's mark.

For further information we recommend *Collector's Guide to Ashtrays, Identification and Values,* by our advisor, Nancy Wanvig (published by Collector Books). She is listed in the Directory under Wisconsin.

Brass, camel figural, solid, 2 rests, 5¼" long ........................**26.00**

Brass, Chinese dragons on rim, China mark (old), 5" .....**13.00**

Brass, reticulated 1" rim, Forman Bros, 5⅞" dia .................**10.00**

Brass, ship's compass & wheel form, 1930s, 6" ..............**60.00**

Brass, Zodiac symbols on rim, glass insert w/snufferette, 7⅜" dia .........................**18.00**

Bronze, sailfish at side of oval tray, some patina, 4¼x5½" ......**30.00**

Ceramic, drum major figural, lustreware, 1 rest, 3¼" ......**22.00**

Ceramic, hand w/thumb & finger raised, white, 1 rest, 4½" long ...........................**17.00**

Ceramic, Mexican sombrero, flowers & black decor, 5" ......**9.00**

Ceramic, man with trombone, majolica-type glaze, German, $275.00. (Photo courtesy Nancy Wanvig)

Ceramic, pelican figural, lustre, 4⅝" long ..........................17.00

Ceramic, pixie beside tray, multicolor & white, 7⅛" long ............................10.00

Ceramic, Serving You in Europe, white w/blue, J Haviland, 4¼" dia .....................................8.00

Chalkware, boss at desk figural, Old Bosses Never Die..., 5⅜" ..............................30.00

Chrome-like dish on pedestal, 3 rests, 4⅜" dia .................8.00

Chrome-plated fretwork frame w/matchbox holder, ruby glass insert, 4" ........................20.00

Copper plated, Indian arrowhead shape w/Indian portrait center, 5⅝" .........................15.00

Glass, amber iridescent, UAW-CIO, 1961, 4⅛" sq .........10.00

Glass, blue delphite, hat form w/cord around crown in relief, 6⅛" ................................28.00

Glass, blue opaque, 3 rests, matchbox holder & match pack holder, 4" ..............................16.00

Glass, clear paperweight type, 5-sided, white flower at bottom, 3" ....................................23.00

Glass, coal scuttle form, black, 2 rests, 2¾" ......................10.00

Glass, cobalt, boot form, 1 rest, 3¾" ...............................12.00

Glass, cobalt, cloverleaf shape, Tiffin, 4¾" .........................28.00

Glass, duck figural, clear, Duncan & Miller, 7x5" ..............40.00

Glass, elephant figural, black amethyst, Greensburg, 6" dia .....................................30.00

Glass, green, pressed pattern base, 4 rests extend inward, 5½" dia ........................10.00

Glass, green, w/3 match strikers, New Martinsville, 4½" dia .........25.00

Glass, Italian clown figural, sitting w/top hat, no hands, 2 rests, 5" ....................................95.00

Glass, Manhattan, Anchor Hocking, may have gold rim, 4" dia ................................11.00

Glass, Ovide, fired-on gray, Hazel Atlas, 3½" sq ...................7.00

Glass, Queen Mary, Forest Green, Hocking Glass, 1950s, 3½" dia ..................................6.00

Glass, vaseline, hat form w/2 rests, 1⅝" ...................................12.00

Glass, windmill scene, fired-on orange, 3 wide rests, 5¼" dia ............................25.00

Lacquered wood, metallic gold fish, copper lining, Oriental, 4½" ....................................35.00

Marble, yellow w/gray streaks, 4 rests, 4¼" sq ..................18.00

Metal, chrome-plated fretwork frame w/cobalt insert, Hong Kong, 4" dia ..................25.00

**Plastic, Lions International, 9", $10.00. (Photo courtesy Nancy Wanvig)**

Metal, 3 swans, silver-tone, 3 rests, 3½" ......................**24.00**

Nodder, lady pulling up skirt, yellow dress, orange shoes ...........**85.00**

Plastic, bowling pin shape w/black glass insert, 8⅜" long .....**9.00**

Plastic, Smokey the Bear Snuffit, snufferette in his hat, 2" .**15.00**

Pot metal w/bronze coating, squirrel sitting on log, 3⅛" ...**20.00**

Pottery, elephant w/howdah, green & tan, 4 rests, 5⅜" .........**27.00**

Pottery, toilet form, black, wall mount, 5" ......................**13.00**

Silverplate, embossed animal scenes, center matchbox, 6¼" dia ..................................**48.00**

Smoker, cat's face, smoke comes from nose, 3⅝" ..............**18.00**

Smoker, distorted face w/top hat, Wanna See Smoke..., 5¼" ..**45.00**

Smoker, Indian w/teepee, smokes comes from top, 4¼" .....**25.00**

Sterling, horseshoe shape, 2⅞" long ...............................**15.00**

**Tire Ashtrays**

Tire ashtrays were introduced in the teens as advertising items. The very early all-glass or glass-and-metal types were replaced in the early 1920s by the more familiar rubber-tired varieties. Hundereds of different ones have been produced over the years. They are still distributed (by the larger tire companies only), but no longer contain the detail or color of the pre-World War II tire ashtrays. Although the common ones bring modest prices, rare examples demand retail prices of up to several hundred dollars.

Our tire ashtray advisor is Jeff McVey; he is listed in the Directory under Idaho. You'll also find information on how to order his book, *Tire Ashtray Collector's Guide,* which we recommend for further study.

Barmstrong Miracle SD, glass insert with manufacturer's imprint .........................**25.00**

Bridgestone D-Lug 33.25.35 .**30.00**

**Goodrich Silvertone Heavy Duty Cord 36x6, clear glass insert with advertising label, $50.00. (Photo courtesy Jeff McVey)**

Dayton Thorobred Heavy Duty
Six Ply 7.50-18, green
insert ......................**100.00**
Dunlop Gold Seal 78 ...........**30.00**
Fisk Glider 6.00-16, embossed
clear insert .................**125.00**
Goodrich Powersaver Radial .**25.00**
Hood Arrow ..........................**65.00**
Miller Tires, 8 rests ............**45.00**
Mohawk Super Chief ...........**40.00**
Phillips 66 Radial Steel Belted ...**25.00**
Seiberling All-Tread ............**25.00**
Vogue Twin Tread Tyre .......**60.00**
Yoodyear Vector, clear imprinted
insert ...........................**20.00**
Zenith ...................................**40.00**

# Autographs

Autographs of famous people
from every walk of life are of
interest to students of philogra-
phy, as it is referred to by those
who enjoy this hobby. Values
hinge on many things — rarity of
the signature and content of the
signed material are major con-
siderations. Autographs of
contemporary sports figures or
entertainers often sell at $10.00
to $15.00 for small signed photos.
Beware of forgeries. If you are
unsure, ask established dealers to
help you.

Adams, Edie; signed black
& white photo, 8x10" ..**25.00**
Albert, Eddie; signed black &
white still from Madison
Avenue, 8x10" ..............**25.00**
Anderson, Loni; signed color
photo, 8x10" .................**30.00**

**Minnesota Twins, 1987 World
Champions, team-signed baseball,
from $200.00 to $250.00.**

Ball, Lucille; signed black &
white photo, playing sax,
8x10" ......................**150.00**
Berenger, Tom; in-person signed
color photo, 8x10" .........**60.00**
Bissette, Jacquelyn; signed black
& white photo, head shot,
8x10" .............................**25.00**
Cage, Nicholas; in-person signed
color photo, 8x10" .........**65.00**
Campbell, Bruce; in-person signed
color photo, 8x10" .........**50.00**
Carson, Johnny; signed black &
white photo, head shot,
8x10" ...........................**40.00**
Chen, Joan; in-person signed color
photo, 8x10" ..................**35.00**
Christiansen, Helena; in-person
signed color photo, 8x10" ..**85.00**
Costner, Kevin; signed color photo,
as Robin Hood, 8x10" ...**50.00**
Crawford, Cindy; in-person signed
color photo, 8x10" .........**50.00**
D'Errico, Donna; in-person signed
color photo, 8x10" .........**50.00**
DeNiro, Robert; signed color photo
from Deerhunter, 8x10" ..**95.00**

DeVito, Danny; in-person signed color photo, 8x10" .........**60.00**

DiCaprio, Leonardo; in-person signed color photo, 8x10" .**75.00**

Douglas, Michael; in-person signed color photo, 8x10" ...........**60.00**

Duvall, Robert; in-person signed color photo, 8x10" .........**50.00**

Elliot, Allison; in-person signed color photo, 8x10" .........**35.00**

Foster, Jody; in-person signed color photo, 8x10" .......**150.00**

Fox, Michael J; in-person signed color photo, 8x10" .........**60.00**

Frankel, Mark; in-person signed color photo, 8x10" .........**50.00**

Gershon, Gina; in-person signed color photo, 8x10" .........**40.00**

Graham, Heather; in-person signed color photo, 8x10" .................**50.00**

Grant, Hugh; in-person signed color photo, 8x10" .........**60.00**

Harris, Richard; in-person signed color photo, 8x10" .........**60.00**

Hawke, Ethan; in-person signed color photo, 8x10" .........**60.00**

Holly, Lauren; in-person signed color photo, 8x10" .........**35.00**

Hunt, Helen; in-person signed color photo, 8x10" .........**60.00**

Hurley, Elizabeth; in-person signed color photo, 8x10" ............**75.00**

Ireland, Kathy; in-person signed color photo, 8x10" .........**75.00**

Keitel, Harvey; in-person signed color photo, 8x10" .........**75.00**

Kilmer, Val; in-person signed color photo, 8x10" .................**85.00**

Lane, Nathan; in-person signed color photo, 8x10" .........**60.00**

Lee, Jason Scott; in-person signed color photo, 8x10" .........**60.00**

Liotta, Ray; in-person signed color photo, 8x10" .................**40.00**

Lollabrigida, Gina; signed black & white photo, 8x10" .......**30.00**

Lords, Traci; in-person signed color photo, 8x10" .........**60.00**

Moore, Demi; in-person signed color photo, 8x10" .......**100.00**

**Neill, Noel 'Lois Lane'; photo with Superman, matted and framed, 16x12", $55.00.**

Newman, Paul; signed black & white photo, head shot, 8x10" .........................**100.00**

Nicholson, Jack; signed black & white photo, from Two Jakes, 8x10" .............................**65.00**

Nolin, Genna Lee; in-person signed color photo, 8x10" ...........**40.00**

O'Donnell, Chris; in-person signed color photo, 8x10" .........**50.00**

Pacino, Al; in-person signed color photo, 8x10" .................**100.00**

Parker, Sarah Jessica; in-person signed color photo, 8x10" .........................**40.00**

Perez, Vincent; in-person signed color photo, 8x10" ................45.00

Pryce, Jonathan; in-person signed color photo, 8x10" .........35.00

Rea, Stephen; in-person signed color photo, 8x10" .........50.00

Refro, Brad; in-person signed color photo, 8x10" ...................40.00

Russell, Kurt; in-person signed color photo, 8x10" .........50.00

Seagel, Steven; signed black & white photo, from Under Seige, 8x10" ...................35.00

Slater, Christian; in-person signed color photo, 8x10" .........60.00

Sorbo, Kevin; in-person signed color photo, 8x10" ................60.00

Spacey, Kevin; in-person signed color photo, 8x10" .........45.00

**Springsteen, Bruce; on 45 record sleeve, $95.00.**

Stallone, Sly; in-person signed color photo, 8x10" .......100.00

Swayze, Patrick; signed color photo, sexy head shot, 8x10" ......................40.00

Tarrantino, Quentin; in-person signed color photo, 8x10" ..75.00

Travolta, John; in-person signed color photo, 8x10" .........75.00

Walken, Christopher; in-person signed color photo, 8x10" ......................60.00

Weller, Peter; in-person signed color photo, 8x10" .........40.00

Willis, Bruce; signed color photo, from Pulp Fiction, 8x10" ..........................50.00

## Automobilia

Many are fascinated with vintage automobiles, but to own one of those 'classy chassis' is a luxury not all can afford! So instead they enjoy collecting related memorabilia such as advertising, owners' manuals, horns, emblems, and hood ornaments. The decade of the 1930s produced the items that are most in demand today, but the '50s models have their own band of devoted fans as well. Usually made of porcelain on cast iron, first-year license plates in hard-to-find excellent condition may bring as much as $200.00 for the pair. (More information and values may be found in the License Plates category.)

Bank, Buick Fireball Eight, globe shape, white on red, 5", EX+ .....................110.00

Bank, Dodge, metal barrel shape, white on red, 3", EX+ ...50.00

Banner, Chevrolet Task-Force Trucks, 1956, cloth, 33x91", VG .................................70.00

Blotter, Buick, 1924, touring car in landscape, 4x9", NM .....**28.00**

Blotter, Ford Parkway Sales & Service, girl in tam, 3x6", EX ..............**50.00**

Book, Funny Stories About the Ford, Volume 1, Presto Pub, 1915, EX .........**35.00**

Brochure, Packard, Luxurious Motoring, ca 1925, 11x6", EX ..............**150.00**

Calendar, Pontiac, 1949, complete pad, 32x20", NM .........**185.00**

Car jack, Ford Model T, script lettering, EX .......................**15.00**

Catalog, Buick Valve-in-Head Motor Cars, 1915, 32 pages, EX .**110.00**

Catalog, Locomobile, 1906, different car models, 36 pages, EX ..............**150.00**

Cigarette box, Porsche 10-year award, engraved silver & wood, 3x4", EX ............**165.00**

Clock, alarm; Packard Master Salesman 1926, Seth Thomas, 5x4", VG .....................**500.00**

Clock, Oldsmobile, light-up, logo at 12, 18x15", EX+ ...**275.00**

Clock, Pontiac, plastic neon, logo with red numbers, 19" dia, VG .....................**375.00**

Compact, Dodge Brothers Coupe, sky blue & yellow, 2" dia, EX .....................**360.00**

Compass, Airglide Nomas Deluxe Auto, self-illuminating, with bracket, MIB ....................**35.00**

Display, Buick color guide, 1960, illuminated wooden cabinet, 16", VG ......................**200.00**

Display, Pontiac, 1930s, wire logo on circle on wire base, 20x47", M ................**275.00**

Display, Steelcote Rubber Enamel, cardboard easel w/samples, 30", EX ........................**775.00**

Emblem, Packard 8, cloisonne, 2x1½", EX ....................**40.00**

Fan, Chevrolet, cardboard paddle shape, girl in early touring car, EX ..........................**90.00**

Gearshift knob, glass w/brown & tan swirls, 2" dia, EX ...**50.00**

Hood ornament, GMC, chrome w/green & black inlay, 3x6½", EX+ .....................**60.00**

Key chain, Chevrolet, 50 Years, EX ................................**10.00**

Lamp shade, Chevrolet, plastic stained-glass look, 15" dia, VG ..............................**250.00**

License attachment, Ford, Let's Take It Easy, cartoon cop, 4x7", EX ........................**20.00**

Lighter, Buick, 1940s, silver-tone car shape, Occupied Japan, 5", EX ................................**220.00**

Lighter, Chevrolet School Bus, gold-tone, image on porcelain inlay, EX ......................**55.00**

Matchbooks, Dealers (1953-1967), M, ea .............................**11.00**

Necklace, 1963 Buick Riveria, sterling-silver car pendant, 1", EX ..**45.00**

Paperweight, Henry Ford Centennial, 1963, brass, oval, M ............................**55.00**

Pen, Oldsmobile, Golden Anniversary, car floats in pen top, 5", EX .....................**30.00**

Pennant, Paige-6, image of 1915 auto for $1385, red on white, 37", EX ........................**165.00**

Pin, Packard Master Service Mechanic, red, white & blue, 2x1½", VG ..................**100.00**

**Symbol, Ford, composition with blue, orange, cream, red, and gray paint, 20x17", VG, $85.00.**

Pin-back button, Pontiac Excitement, 1985, 3" dia, EX ..**5.00**

Plate, Ford, Shenango China, name on rim, building in center, 6", EX ....................**45.00**

Playing cards, Cadillac emblem, double deck in plastic box, EX ...............................**10.00**

Pocketknife, Chevrolet, blue logo on cream plastic, 3½", EX ...........................**20.00**

Postcard, 1966 Ford GT 2+2 Fastback, EX .........................**8.00**

Postcard, 1970 Chevrolet Monte Carlo, unused, M ...........**5.00**

Poster, Ford, 1939 Baseball All-Stars w/dealer names, 32x17", EX+ .............................**650.00**

Poster, 1958 Chevy Impala Convertible, driver/beach scene, 19x32", EX ..................**100.00**

Promotional vehicle, 1960 Chevy Nova, light metallic tan, EX+ ..........................**130.00**

Promotional vehicle, 1966 Pontiac GTO, silver 2-door hardtop, NM ...............................**450.00**

Promotional vehicle, 1972 Dodge Challenger, red, M ......**165.00**

Promotional vehicle, 1975 Ford Mustang, silver, MIB ......................**35.00**

Radio, Audi, AM-FM transistor, plastic w/repeated logos, 4½", EX ...................................**15.00**

Ruler, Ford, plastic, logo on front, 8-cylinder cars on back, EX .**35.00**

**Sign, 1956 Clipper, celluloid, 12x16", EX+, $80.00.**

Sign, Fordor Sedan, 1940s, cardboard, green car on yellow, 25x37", EX+ .................**75.00**

Sign, The New Willys Cars..., paper, car graphics, 25x41", VG ..**150.00**

Tape measure, Royal Packard Co, Ask the Man Who Owns Me in script, M ......................**85.00**

Thermometer, Ford Sales/Service, wood, tractor & car graphics, 14", VG ......................**175.00**

Tie tack, Cadillac crest, Certified Craftsman, 1951, gold-tone, EX .....**25.00**

Tire pressure gauge, Buick, round w/chrome frame, EX+ ...**75.00**

Token, Chevrolet, aluminum, logos on front, Father Time on back, EX ......................**45.00**

TV tray, Ford, metal w/folding stand, black w/gold graphics, 29", EX ......................**15.00**

Watch fob, Ford emblem, silvertone w/blue cloisonne, 1x2", EX+ ...............................**50.00**

Weather vane, Pontiac logo, diecut metal, 42x53", NM .......**250.00**

Yardstick/cane, Studebaker-Packard Spring Driveway, May 1957, M .................**25.00**

# Autumn Leaf

Autumn Leaf dinnerware was a product of the Hall China Company, who produced this extensive line from 1933 until 1978 for exclusive distribution by the Jewel Tea Company. The Libbey Glass Company made co-ordinating pitchers, tumblers, and stemware. Metal, cloth, plastic, and paper items were also available. Today, though very rare pieces are expensive and a challenge to acquire, new collectors may easily reassemble an attractive, usable set at a reasonable price. Hall has produced special club pieces (for the NALCC) as well as some limited editions for an Ohio company, but these are well marked and easily identified as such. Refer to *The Collector's Encyclopedia of Hall China* by Margaret and Kenn Whitmyer (Collector Books) for more information.

Our advisor for this category is Gwynne Harrison; she is listed in the Directory under California.

Baker, souffle; 4½", from $40 to ...**50.00**

Book, Autumn Leaf Story, from $40 to .............................**60.00**

Bowl, flat soup; 8½", from $16 to ...............................**20.00**

Bowl, salad; 9", from $15 to ...**20.00**

Bud vase, sm or regular decal, from $175 to ................**225.00**

Butter dish, regular, ruffled top, ¼-lb .............................**250.00**

Butter dish, regular, 1-lb, from $350 to .........................**500.00**

Cake plate, on metal stand, from $150 to .........................**200.00**

Cake safe, metal, from $25 to ..**50.00**

Candlesticks, metal, 4", pr, from $70 to ............................**100.00**

**Butter dish, regular, #1, from $350.00 to $500.00.**

**Casserole, twq-quart, from $30.00 to $45.00.**

Casserole, Heatflow clear glass, Mary Dunbar, w/lid, 2-qt, from $85 to .................**125.00**

Casserole, round, w/lid, 2-qt, from $30 to .............................**45.00**

Casserole, Royal Glasbake, milk white, round, w/lid, from $65 to ............................................**90.00**

Clock, salesman's award, from $300 to .........................**400.00**

Coffeepot, Rayed, 9-cup, from $30 to .....................................**40.00**

Cookie jar, Tootsie, Rayed, from $250 to .........................**300.00**

Creamer & sugar bowl, Rayed, 1930s style, from $60 to .**80.00**

Cup, St Denis, from $25 to .**30.00**

Dripper, coffeepot; metal, from $20 to ............................**25.00**

Dutch oven, metal & porcelain, w/lid, 5-qt, from $125 to ...........**175.00**

French baker, 2-pt, from $150 to ............................**175.00**

Goblet, gold & frost on clear, footed, Libbey, 10-oz, from $50 to .........................**65.00**

Gravy boat, from $20 to ......**30.00**

Jug, ball form, #3, from $35 to ...........................**40.00**

Marmalade, 3-pc, from $80 to ..**100.00**

Meat chopper, Griswold, from $250 to .........................**400.00**

Mug, Irish coffee ...............**125.00**

Plate, 6", from $5 to ..............**8.00**

Plate, 8", from $12 to ..........**18.00**

Plate, 9", from $8 to ............**12.00**

Platter, oval, 13½", from $20 to ...........................**28.00**

Salt & pepper shakers, Casper, regular, ruffled, pr, from $20 to ....................................**30.00**

Salt & pepper shakers, range; left & right handled, pr, from $20 to ....................................**30.00**

Saucer, St Denis, from $6 to .**8.00**

Skillet, metal & porcelain, 9½", from $100 to ...............**125.00**

Teapot, Aladdin, from $50 to .**70.00**

Teapot, Newport, 1978, from $175 to ....................................**200.00**

Tin, fruitcake; tan or white, from $7 to .............................**10.00**

Tray, coffee service; oval, 18¾", from $75 to ..................**100.00**

Tumbler, iced tea; frosted, Libbey, 5½", from $15 to ...........**20.00**

Warmer, round, from $125 to .**160.00**

# Avon

Originally founded in 1886 under the title California Perfume Company, the firm became officially known as Avon Products Inc. in 1939. Among collectors they are best known not for their cosmetics and colognes but for their imaginative packaging and figural bottles. Avon offers something for almost everyone including such cross-collectibles as Fostoria, Wedgwood, commerative plates, Ceramarte steins, and hundreds of other quality items. Also sought are product samples, awards, magazine ads, jewelry, and catalogs. Their Cape Cod glassware has been sold in vast quantities since the '70s and is becoming a common sight at flea markets and antique malls. For more information we recommend *Hastin's Avon Collector's Price Guide* by Bud Hastin.

**Calling for Men Decanter, gold paint on clear glass with black plastic ear piece, 1969, M, $12.00.**

Antiseptic Mouthwash, white cap, paper label, 1955-59, 7-oz ..................................**7.50**

Bay Rum After Shave, clear w/black cap, 1964-65, MIB ..............**12.50**

Brilliantine, green label & lid, 1936-54, 2-oz, MIB ....................**20.00**

Cotillion Treasures Set, 3-pc set w/gold caps, 1957, MIB ....**75.00**

Country Peaches Soap Jar & Soaps, blue glass jar w/soaps, 1977-79, MIB ....................................**8.50**

Daisies Won't Tell Bubble Bath, blue & white bottle, 1964, MIB ....................................**7.50**

Deluxe Manicure Set, 5 bottles & accessories, 1950-51, MIB ..............**25.00**

Electric Pre-Shave Lotion, black & white w/red cap, 1959-62, MIB ..................................**12.50**

Elusive Beauty Dust, pink plastic w/silver, 1969-74, MIB ......**4.50**

Gardenia Perfume, flowered cap, painted label, 3 drams, 1948-52, MIB ..................................**75.00**

Here's My Heart Cologne Mist, blue bottle w/gold cap, 1957-58, MIB ..................................**17.50**

Lavender Toilet Water, lavender cap, 1945-46, 4-oz, M ......**40.00**

Nearness Seashell Necklace, gold-tone chain w/pearl, 1956, M ............**24.00**

Persian Wood Mist, red w/gold cap, 1956-59, MIB ....................**8.50**

Pierre Decanter, white glass pig figural, 1984, 8-oz, MIB ........**10.00**

Regence Gift Set, sachet, mist & mirror, 1966, MIB ...........**35.00**

Short Pony Decanter, green glass, 1968-69, 4-oz, MIB ..........**10.00**

Somewhere Soap, 3 bars, 1968-69, MIB ..................................**12.50**

Spring Chimes Porcelain Bell, pink w/pink ribbons, 1991, 6", MIB ..................................**17.50**

**Somewhere Cologne, Gay Nineties girl, 1974, MIB, $12.50.**

Sunny the Sunfish Soap, on a rope, 1966, MIB ............**22.50**

Sweet Honesty Perfume Soaps, 3 bars, 1978, MIB ......................**7.50**

Sweetheart Set, To a Wild Rose dust & cologne, 1956, MIB .......**40.00**

Tribute Talc, blue & silver can with blue lid, 1963-66, M ............................**6.50**

Volkswagon Rabbit Decanter, blue glass w/silver, 1980-82, MIB ..............................**7.50**

Wishful Thoughts Figurine, blue & white porcelain, 1982-83, 5½", MIB ......................**16.00**

## Banks

After the Depression, everyone was aware that saving 'for a rainy day' would help during bad times. Children of the '40s, '50s, and '60s were given piggy banks in forms of favorite characters to reinforce the idea of saving. They were made to realize that by saving money they could buy that expensive bicycle or a toy they were particularly longing for. Today, on the flea market circuit, figural ceramic banks are popular collectibles, especially those that are character-related — advertising characters and Disney in particular. For more information on banks of this type, we recommend *Ceramic Coin Banks* by Tom and Loretta Stoddard, and *Collector's Guide to Banks* by Beverly and Jim Mangus, both published by Collector Books. See also Advertising; Specific companies.

Ice Wagon, marked Treasure Craft, 5½", from $40.00 to $45.00. (Photo courtesy Beverly and Jim Mangus)

Alvin & the Chipmunks, vinyl, figure w/harmonica, Alvin, 1984, 9", EX ...........................**15.00**

Baba Louie, plastic, figure w/removable hat, EX ....**10.00**

Bart Simpson, plastic, any color variation, Street Kids, MIB ...........................**12.00**

Batman, ceramic nodder, unmarked, 5", scarce, NM ................**450.00**

Batman, painted ceramic, Japan, 1966, 7", from $125 to .**130.00**

Bear, pottery, white with gold, Pearl China...22 K Gold USA, 7" .........................**80.00**

Betty Boop, Bank & Trust, Vandor, 1981 ....................**150.00**

Betty Boop, bust w/hand to cheek, Vandor, 1994 ................**18.00**

Bionic Woman in running suit, on rocks, Animals Plus, 1970s, NM .................................**40.00**

Black baby in washtub, green glossy, US (?), 1930s, 4", from $175 to ......................**200.00**

Black boy w/accordion on melon, painted bisque, Germany (?), 1920s, 4" .....................**265.00**

**Banks Teddy Bear, American Bisque, from $40.00 to $50.00. (Photo courtesy Beverly and Jim Mangus)**

Black girl w/watermelon, painted ceramic nodder, unmarked Japan, 7" ......................**65.00**

Boy w/bow tie, marked Duncan Ceramic Productions, Inc 1970, 6" ..........................**25.00**

Bugs Bunny w/bag of carrots, pottery, Warner Bros...1981, 5½" ..............................**55.00**

Bugs Bunny w/carrot by tree trunk, multicolor painted metal, 6", EX ...........**135.00**

Bull's head, pottery, realistic paint, ca 1920, US, 3¼", from $175 to........................ **200.00**

Bulldog head, Rockingham (?), ca 1920s, English (?), 3" ..**175.00**

Cable car, pottery, multicolor paint, US, San Francisco, 1940s, 4½" .....................**85.00**

Charlie McCarthy standing, no monocle, composition & tin, 10", EX ......................**250.00**

Charlie McCarthy stands by trunk, pot metal, no trap, 7¾", VG ...............................**110.00**

Conch shell, porcelain, tan lustreware, European (?), 1930s, 4" ..............................**375.00**

Daffy Duck leaning on tree trunk, painted metal, 6", EX .**135.00**

Davy Crocket, bronze ..........**68.00**

Donald Duck, tin litho, Disney, Marx, 1950s, 4", NMIB .**550.00**

Donald Duck atop green van, ceramic, Disney, MIB ...**25.00**

Drum, porcelain, blue & white, Germany, ca 1925, from $175 to .................................**225.00**

Elephant in tutu, pottery, painted details, ca 1940, US, from $75 to .....................................**90.00**

Ernie in Train, painted ceramic, Applause, Jim Henson..., 4", from $30 to ....................**35.00**

Felix the Cat, nodding head atop soccer ball, cast metal, 5½" .**850.00**

Fred Flintstone, gumball bank, plastic head figure, 1968, 8", EX ...................................**50.00**

Fred Flintstone, Homecraft, 1973, NM ...................................**25.00**

Fred Flintstone, plastic figure, 1973, EX ........................**30.00**

Fred Flintstone, vinyl, holding bowling ball, 1977, 11", EX .....**35.00**

Garfield, ceramic, bowling ..**65.00**

Garfield, ceramic, in chair, Enesco, from $110 to ...............**125.00**

Garfield, ceramic, on skis, Enesco ........................**70.00**

Garfield, ceramic, the graduate, Enesco, 1978, 5½" .........**55.00**

General Lee (Dukes of Hazzard car), red plastic, 14" long, EX ..............................**15.00**

Grimace, paper label: Grimace 1985 McDonald's...Thailand, 8½" ...............................**50.00**

Heathcliffe, plastic figure, EX .**10.00**

Hershey Kiss, ceramic, unmarked, 4¼" ...............................**24.00**

Horse (stylized), porcelain with painted details, Occupied Japan, 3¼" ...............................**85.00**

Humpty Dumpty, hand-painted ceramic, Corl...USA 1995, 6¾" ...............................**85.00**

Incredible Hulk's head, vinyl, M ...............................**20.00**

Lump of coal, pottery, black, unmarked, 7¼" ...........**20.00**

Mac Saver (Scotsman), painted ceramic, Heilig Meyers..., Japan, 6¾" ...............**25.00**

Mickey Mouse, Ucago, 1960s, 5", MIB ...............................**55.00**

Mickey Mouse, vinyl, Animals Plus, 1977, 12", NM ......**25.00**

Mickey Mouse & Minnie, glass, round w/molded faces on sides, M ...............................**10.00**

Mickey Mouse standing beside trunk, composition, Crown, crazing, 6" ...............**75.00**

Monkey swatting fly, pottery, brown w/multicolor details, 4½" ...............................**115.00**

Neal the Frog, pottery, glossy green, Sears Roebuck...1977 Japan, 5" ...............**45.00**

Nipper, ceramic, paper label; Nipper GE Comp Made in Korea, 5¾" ...............................**27.50**

Panda bear walking, pottery, black & white, 2½", from $35 to ...............................**50.00**

Pebbles Flintstone & Dino, blue vinyl, 13", EX ...............**45.00**

Pig sitting, ceramic, roses on white, 1948 Chick Pottery, 6¾" ...............................**75.00**

Pinocchio on whale, ceramic, musical, Schmid ...............**60.00**

Pinocchio standing by stump, composition, Crown, 5", EXIB ..**200.00**

Pluto, composition figural, Disney, MIB ...............................**65.00**

Poodle w/padlock at neck, ceramic, shiny black, unmarked Japan, 6½" ...............................**50.00**

Popeye Daily Dime, metal box w/canted corners, KFS, 1956, 2⅝", EX ...............**450.00**

Porky Pig, AJ Renzi, 1964, 15½", EX ...............................**45.00**

Porky Pig bust, painted bisque, Marked Japan, 5", EX .........................**50.00**

Puppy, pottery, gold trim, LePere Pottery, 5", from $40 to .**45.00**

Rabbit, long-eared; ceramic, white w/pink details, US, ca 1930, 2⅞" ...............................**115.00**

Rabbit, pottery, brown, pink & white, NAPCO Japan, 7" ..........**30.00**

Robin, ceramic, paper label: National Periodical...1966 Japan, 6½" ...............**125.00**

Rocky & Bullwinkle's Mr Sherman, Pat Ward, 1960, ceramic, 6", NM ...............**550.00**

Romper Room, Do-Bee sitting on flower base, plastic w/clear wings, 5" ...............**55.00**

Scarecrow (Wizard of Oz), hand painted, Arnart Imports, 1960s, 7", NMIB .........**100.00**

Scooby Doo, vinyl w/felt vest, NM ...............................**25.00**

Snoopy, silverplate, Leonard #9669, MIB ...............**30.00**

Snow White & 7 Dwarfs, Dopey, Crown, composition, EX .................200.00
Snow White & 7 Dwarfs Dime Register, metal box, 2½" sq, EX+ ...........................150.00
Speedy Gonzalez on wedge of cheese, ceramic figural, M .........................35.00
Spider-Man bust, plastic, Renzi, 1979, 15", EX, from $15 to ..........20.00
Spinach can w/Popeye & Olive portraits, ceramic, unmarked, 5" .....................................14.00
Superman Dime Register, DC Comics, metal box, 2½", EX/NM, $200 to ..........275.00
Tasmanian Devil, ceramic, w/Looney Tunes tag, 1990, 5½", EX ...........................45.00
Taz – Do Not Feed, pottery, Applause, Warner Bros...1988 Taiwan, 6" ......................50.00
Thumper, ceramic, pink, Schmid Musical ...........................65.00
Thumper on block, pottery, paper label: Sigma Thumper, 6¼" ..............................35.00
Top Cat on trash can, plastic figural, 1962, 10", NM ..........45.00
Toucan (stylized), painted pottery, Czechoslovakia, ca 1930, 3⅞" ...................185.00
Uncle Scrooge, Brechner, M ........................125.00
Winnie the Pooh, ceramic figural, Disney, Enesco, 5" ........45.00
Wise Pig, pottery, multicolor details, US, ca 1935, 6⅛" .............85.00
Woody Woodpecker, ceramic, multicolor, NM ....................18.00
Yogi Bear, plastic, 14", EX ......................35.00

# Barware

Gleaming with sophistication and style, vintage cocktail shakers are skyrocketing in value as the hot new collectible of the '90s. Young trend-setters are using this swank and practical objet d'art to serve their pre-dinner drinks. Form and function never had a better mix. The latest acquisition from America's classic Art Deco past is occasion enough for a party and a round of martinis.

In the 1920s it was prohibition that brought the cocktail hour and cocktail parties into the home. Today the high cost of dining out along with a more informed social awareness about alcohol consumption brings at-home cocktail parties back into fashion. Released across the country from after a half century of imprisonment in attics and china closets, these glass and chrome shaker sets have been recalled to life — recalled to hear the clank of ice cubes and to again become the symbol of elegance.

Our advisor for this category is Stephen Visakay, author of *Vintage Bar Ware* (Collector Books). Mr. Visakay, is listed in the directory under New Jersey.

Cocktail cup, chrome plated w/glass insert, Farber Bros, 4¼" ....10.00
Cocktail cup, Manhattan, chrome-plated copper, Revere, 4¼x2½" ........................125.00
Cocktail cup, silverplated with wood, Hammacher Schlemmer, 5¾" .................................20.00

Cocktail shaker, end-of-day glass, 1930s, 7", from $75 to ...**85.00**

Cocktail stem, chrome base w/amber Cambridge glass insert, 3½" ....................**20.00**

Cocktail stem, ruby glass w/chrome base, SW Farber, 5x3¼", from $7 .............**12.00**

Cup, chrome plated, footed, 3¼x3" dia, from $20 to .............**30.00**

Highball glass, decal of female on clear, 1941, 4¾x2⅝" .....**12.00**

Ice bowl & tongs, chrome plated, Russell Wright, Chase #28002, 7" dia ...............**35.00**

Ice bucket, chrome w/yellow Bakelite, Keystone, 10½x6¼" dia ...............................**75.00**

Ice bucket, clear glass, silverplate holder, 1920s-30s, 7¼" .**45.00**

Pitcher, martini; nickel plated, cork-based stopper, Keystoneware .....................**45.00**

Set, Spun Crystal, Imperial Glass, 11" shaker+6 3x3" tumblers ....................**175.00**

Shaker, aluminum, Emson Products...Conn, ca 1947, 12½", from $55 to ....................**65.00**

Shaker, amber glass w/chrome top, Cambridge, 1927, 12", from $55 to ....................**65.00**

Shaker, chrome plated, rocket ship base, jade Catalin mounts, 13"................................**400.00**

Shaker, cobalt blue dumbbell shape, 13x4" dia, from $250 to ...............................**325.00**

Shaker, cobalt glass w/recipes, silverplated top, 1930s, 10½" ..**120.00**

Shaker, Cone, silverplated w/red bands at base, Napier, 9x3¾" ..........................**95.00**

Mixer, cobalt with fired-on recipes, 12" overall, from $90.00 to $110.00.

Shaker, cranberry-flashed heavy pressed glass w/silverplated top, 11" ........................**145.00**

Shaker, etched rooster on green glass, silverplated top, 1926, 10½" ...............................**70.00**

Shaker, frosted glass with sterling trim, 1930s-40s, from $38 to ......................**48.00**

Shaker, lady's high-heeled slipper, chrome & ruby glass, 15½" ...........................**375.00**

Shaker, Manhattan, chrome plate over brass, Revere, 12¾" ..........**425.00**

Shaker, nickel plated, hammered & plain, Expressware NY, 17½" ............................**150.00**

Shaker, nickel plated with engraved painted rooster, Meriden,1927, 56-oz ....**135.00**

Shaker, pewter, handmade by Max Rieg for Mary Ryan, 1935, 13½" ..................**165.00**

Shaker, silver overlay roosters on ruby glass, chrome top, 1930s, 12" ..............**275.00**

Shaker, silverplate & clear glass, hourglass shape, 1930s, 13x5" dia ..................**65.00**

Shaker, silverplated with grape leaves, unstamped, late 1920s, 12½" ..................**85.00**

Shaker, Steward, chrome plated, walnut trim, unmarked, ca 1934 ..............**70.00**

Shot jigger, graduated, silverplated, Napier, 4", from $20 to ...**30.00**

Traveling bar, nickel-plated shaker form, Germany, ca 1928, 9-pc ..................**95.00**

Tray, canape; chromium over brass, N Bel Geddes, Revere, 6¾x4⅝" ..........................**10.00**

Tray, Doric, chrome plated with white or blue, Chase, 12" dia, $20 to ..............**40.00**

Tray, red & black cocktail glasses enameled on metal, 1940-50s, 13x18" ..........................**20.00**

Tray, reverse painted w/gold & silver geometric, wooden frame, 17½" ..............................**75.00**

Tray, silverplate & plastic, 14" dia, from $35 to ..................**45.00**

## Bauer

The Bauer Company moved from Kentucky to California in 1909, producing crocks, gardenware, and vases until after the Depression when they introduced their first line of dinnerware. From 1932 until the early 1960s, they successfully marketed several lines of solid-color wares that are today very collectible. Some of their most popular lines are Ring, Plain Ware, and Monterey Modern. Refer to *The Collector's Encyclopedia of Bauer Pottery* by Jack Chipman (Collector Books) for more information.

Bowl, #9 nappy, Ring, from $65 to ..................**95.00**

Bowl, batter; Ring, 2-qt, from $85 to ..................**125.00**

Bowl, divided vegetable; Ring, oval, from $150 to ......**225.00**

Bowl, fruit; Monterey, footed, 9", from $45 to ..................**65.00**

Bowl, Indian, by Tracy Irwin, speckled pink, lg ..........**95.00**

Bowl, Matt Carlton, orange-red, 5½x6" sq ......................**75.00**

Bowl, mixing; Gloss Pastel, green, #12 ..................**35.00**

Bowl, Monterey Moderne, brown, 13" ..................**75.00**

Bowl, salad; Ring, 12", from $100 to ..................**150.00**

Bowl, souffle/ice; Ring, from $200 to ..................**300.00**

Candle holder, Monterey, from $45 to ..................**65.00**

Candle holder, Ring, 2½", from $45 to ..........................**65.00**

Chop plate, Monterey Moderne, chartreuse ....................**40.00**

Coffee server, Ring, wooden handle, from $65 to ............**95.00**

Creamer, Ring, from $20 to ..**30.00**

Cup, El Chico, burgundy, minimum value ..................**45.00**

Cup, Monterey, from $17.50 to ...**25.00**
Cup & saucer, La Linda, matt colors ...................................**24.00**
Figurine, Cal-Art, duck, matt white, 2¼x4¼" ..............**35.00**
Figurine, Cal-Art, duck, orange-red (rare color), minimum value ............................**100.00**
Mug, Kitchenware, 8-oz .......**18.00**
Mug, Ring, barrel shape, from $100 to .........................**150.00**
Pitcher, Al Fresco, ice lip, raffia-wrapped handle, Dubonet, 2-qt ....................................**75.00**
Pitcher, Gloss Pastel, ivory, 1-qt ..............................**35.00**
Pitcher, Ring, ball shape, 2-qt, from $250 to ................**375.00**
Pitcher, Ring, 3-qt, from $125 to .............................**175.00**
Plate, Brusche Al Fresco, 11½" ....**12.00**
Plate, Contempo, 8" ...............**8.00**
Plate, Mission Moderne, chartreuse & brown, 6" ........**12.50**
Plate, Monterey Moderne, olive green, 6½" .......................**8.00**
Plate, Ring, 10½", from $65 to .**95.00**
Plater, Ring, 6", from $10 to .**15.00**
Ramekin, Monterey Moderne ..**12.00**

**Refrigerator jar, Ring, from $40.00 to $60.00; Wooden frame, from $30.00 to $45.00. (Photo courtesy Jack Chipman)**

Relish plate, Ring, from $85 to .**125.00**
Rose bowl, Hi-Fire, yellow, 6" ..**50.00**
Sherbet, Ring, from $75 to ..**100.00**

Soup plate, Ring, 7½", from $75 to ...............................**100.00**
Sugar shaker, Ring, from $200 to ..............................**300.00**
Swan dish, Cal-Art by Ray Murray, white matt, 4x13" .........**125.00**
Teapot, Monterey Moderne, yellow, 6-cup ......................**65.00**
Vase, Cal-Art, matt pink, flared rim, sm low handles, footed, 10" ..................................**85.00**
Vase, Hi-Fire, olive green, attributed to Jim Johnson, cylindrical, 9" ...........................**100.00**
Vase, Hi-Fire, turquoise, shouldered, #213, 7" ..............**85.00**
Vase, Matt Carlton, Chinese Yellow, ruffled rim, 3" .................**75.00**

# Beanie Babies

What's behind the current new Beanie Babies collecting phenomenon? Two things, obviously: 1, they're loads of fun, and 2, they're appreciating faster than just about any commodity you could invest in. Where will it end? No one knows, but for the time being, these beanbag toys are definitely 'where it's at.' They came out in 1993, and estimates of how many have been made hover around the one billion mark. We'll list current values on some of the retired Beanie Babies, but if you plan to collect them, you'll really need a book to learn about tags, differences in various issues, retirements and, of course, values. Our values are for retired

Beanie Babies in mint condition. By press time, there will undoubtedly be more retirements, so our listing is very likely incomplete.

**Ally the Alligator, #4032, retired, $65.00. (From the collection of Robin Hicks)**

Baldy the Eagle #4074 ........**25.00**

Bessie the Cow, brown, #4009 ..**70.00**

Blizzard the Tiger, white, #4163 ......................**25.00**

Bones the Dog, brown, #4001 .**25.00**

Bongo the Monkey, brown, #4067, from $65 to ....................**80.00**

Bronty the Brontosaurus, blue, #4085 ..........................**900.00**

Brownie the Bear, #4010, with hang tag, minimum value ................**3,000.00**

Bubbles the Fish, yellow & black, #4078 ..........................**185.00**

Bucky the Beaver, #4016 ....**40.00**

Caw the Crow, #4071, from $500 to ................................**600.00**

Chilly the Polar Bear, #4012, minimum value ..............**1,600.00**

Chops the Lamb, white w/black face, #4019 ..................**200.00**

Coral the Fish, tie-dyed, #4079 ...........................**125.00**

Cubbie the Bear, brown, #4010 ...**35.00**

Digger the Crab, orange, #4027, minimum value ..........**700.00**

Doodles the Rooster, tie-dyed, #4171 .............................**60.00**

Ears the Rabbit, brown, #4018 ..**25.00**

Echo the Dolphin, #4180 .....**25.00**

Flash the Dolphin, #4021 ..**100.00**

Flip the Cat, white, #4012 ..**35.00**

Floppity the Bunny, lilac, #4118 ........................**25.00**

Flutter the Butterfly, tie-dyed, #4043, minimum value .....................**850.00**

Garcia the Teddy, tie-dyed, #4051, from $100 to ................**200.00**

Goldie the Goldfish, #4023 ..**35.00**

Gracie the Swan, #4126, from $15 to .....................................**25.00**

Grunt the Razorback Pig, #4092 .....................**175.00**

Happy the Hippopotamus, gray, 1st issue, #4061, minimum value ...........................**400.00**

Happy the Hippopotamus, lavender, 2nd issue, #4061 ..........................**25.00**

Hippity the Rabbit, light green, #4119 ............................**25.00**

Hoot the Owl, #4073 ............**40.00**

Hoppity the Rabbit, pink, #4117 .......................**25.00**

Humphrey the Camel, #4060, minimum value .................**850.00**

Inch the Worm, #4044 .........**25.00**

Inky the Octopus, tan, 1st issue, #4028, minimum value .....................**400.00**

Jolly the Walrus, #4082 ......**25.00**

Kiwi the Toucan, #4070, minimum value ............................**125.00**

Lefty the Donkey, w/American flag, #4057, minimum value .......................**200.00**

Legs the Frog, #4020 ...........**35.00**

Lizzy the Lizard, #4033, minimum value ...........................**425.00**

Lucky the Ladybug, w/11 spots, #4040, from $15 to ........**25.00**

Lucky the Ladybug, w/21 spots, #4040 ...........................**400.00**

Magic the Dragon, #4088, from $30 to ..............................**40.00**

Manny the Manatee, #4081 .**125.00**

**Maple, sold only in Canada, current but hard to find, from $180.00 to $275.00; Libearty, #4057, retired, from $200.00 to $300.00; Brittania, sold only in England, current but hard to find, from $410.00 to $550.00. (Photo courtesy Amy Hopper)**

Mystic the Unicorn, 1st issue, #4007 ...........................**500.00**

Nip the Cat, gold, 1st or 2nd issue, #4003, minimum value .**700.00**

Nip the Cat, gold w/white paws, 3rd issue, #4003, from $25 to ................................**30.00**

Patti the Platypus, hot pink, #4025, from $20 to ........**25.00**

Patti the Platypus, maroon, #4025, minimum value .......**1,000.00**

Peking the Panda Bear, #4013, minimum value .......**1,500.00**

Pinchers the Lobster, #4026, from $15 to ...........................**25.00**

Quackers the Duck, no wings, #4024, minimum value ...........**1,000.00**

Quackers the Duck, w/wings, #4024, from $15 to ........**25.00**

Radar the Bat, #4091, minimum value ...........................**100.00**

Rex the Tyrannosaurus, tie-dyed, #4086, minimum value ......................**600.00**

Righty the Elephant, w/American flag, #4086, minimum value .......................**200.00**

Rover the Dog, red, #4101 ...**25.00**

Scottie the Terrier, #4102, from $15 to ...........................**25.00**

Seamore the Seal, white, #4029 .....................**125.00**

Slither the Snake, #4031, minimum value .................**750.00**

Sly the Fox, all brown, 1st issue, #4115 ...........................**165.00**

Sparky the Dalmatian, #4100 .**85.00**

Speedy the Turtle, #4030, from $25 to ..............................**30.00**

Splash the Whale, #4022 ...**100.00**

Spooky the Ghost, #4090, minimum value ...................**40.00**

Spot the Dog, black spot on back, 2nd issue, #4000 ...........**50.00**

Spot the Dog, no spot on back, 1st issue, #4000 .............**1,600.00**

Squealer the Pig, #4005 ......**30.00**

Steg the Stegosaurus, tie-dyed, #4087, minimum value .**600.00**

Sting the Stingray, tie-dyed, #4077, minimum value ............**140.00**

Stripes the Tiger, #4065 ....**450.00**

Stripes the Tiger, #4065, 2nd issue, from $15 to .........**25.00**

Tabasco the Bull, red, #4002, minimum value ...............**225.00**

Tank the Armadillo, #4031, minimum value .................**150.00**

Teddy Bear, brown, #4050, new face, from $65 to ...........**70.00**

Teddy Bear, brown, #4050, old face ...........................**2,300.00**

Teddy Bear, cranberry, #4052, old face ............................**1,800.00**

Teddy Bear, cranberry, #4052, new face ...................**2,000.00**

Teddy Bear, jade, #4057, new face ............................**2,000.00**

Teddy Bear, jade, #4057, old face ........................**1,800.00**

Teddy Bear, magenta, #4056, new face ...........................**2,000.00**

Teddy Bear, magenta, #4056, old face ...........................**1,800.00**

Teddy Bear, teal, #4051, new face ..............................**2,000.00**

Teddy Bear, teal, #4051, old face ........................**1,800.00**

Teddy Bear, violet, #4055, new face ...........................**2,000.00**

Teddy Bear, violet, #4055, old face ...........................**1,800.00**

Trap the Mouse, #4042, minimum value .........................**1,000.00**

Tusk the Walrus, #4076, minimum value ..................**125.00**

Twigs the Giraffe, #4068 .....**25.00**

Velvet the Panther, #4064 ..**35.00**

Waddle the Penguin, #4075 ..**25.00**

Waves the Whale, #4084, from $10 to .....................................**25.00**

Web the Spider, #4041, minimum value .........................**1,000.00**

Weenie the Dachshund, #4013 .**30.00**

Ziggy the Zebra, #4063 ........**25.00**

Zip the Cat, all black, #4004, minimum value ..............**1,500.00**

Zip the Cat, black w/white paws, #4004 ............................**35.00**

Zip the Cat, black w/white tummy, #4004, minimum value .**450.00**

# The Beatles

Beatles memorabilia is becoming increasingly popular with those who grew up in the '60s. Almost any item that could be produced with their pictures or logos was manufactured and sold by the thousands in department stores. Some have such a high collector value that they have been reproduced, beware!

Our advisor for this category is Bojo (Bob Gottuso), who is listed in the Directory under Pennsylvania. Refer to *The Beatles: A Reference and Value Guide* by Michael Stern, Barbara Crawford, and Hollis Lamon (Collector Books) for more information.

Beach hat, blue & white w/faces & signatures, NM ...........**125.00**

Beach towel, Cannon, wearing old-fashioned swimsuits, VG .**200.00**

Book, Apple to the Core, softcover, 1972, NM ......................**10.00**

Book, Beatles Quiz Book, United Kingdom, softcover, 1964, VG ..............................**10.00**

Booklet, concert souvenir, black & white photos, 1965, VG .**45.00**

Brooch, United Kingdom, plastic guitar w/group photo, 3½", EX ................................**75.00**

Bulletin, Special International Album, April 1977, 16 pages, EX ................................**45.00**

Charms, plastic records w/faces & labels, set of 4, EX ........**25.00**

Coin holder, black rubber squeeze purse, white images & names, EX ................................**55.00**

**Candy cigarettes, Primrose Confectionary, EX/M, $175.00. (Photo courtesy Stern, Crawford, and Lamon)**

Cup, United Kingdom, ceramic w/fired-on decal, EX ...**130.00**
Diary, vinyl w/black & white photos inside, 1965, EX ......**45.00**
Dolls, Applause, Sgt Pepper costumes, 1988, 22", set of 4, M .........................**385.00**
Figures, lead, snow scene pose from the movie Help!, set of 4, EX ................................**95.00**
Game, Flip Your Wig, complete, NMIB ...........................**190.00**
Game, Hullabaloo, 1965, VG .**75.00**
Guitar, Four Pop by Mastro, red & pink w/faces & names, 21", EX ..............................**400.00**
Guitar strings, Hofner, NMIP .**80.00**
Hairbrush, Genco, blue, w/autographed picture card, MIP .**70.00**
Handkerchief, United Kingdom, With Love From Me To You, 8½" sq, EX .....................**80.00**
Headband, Dame, portraits & autographs in black on blue, 1964, EX .......................**85.00**

Key chain, Yellow Submarine by Pride Creations, plastic, EX ...........**60.00**
Lobby card, Help!, 11x14", VG .**60.00**
Magazine, Beatles at Carnegie Hall, United Kingdom, 1964, VG ..................................**40.00**
Matchbook cover, Holland, group photo, EX .......................**25.00**
Necklace, mop-haired figures w/guitars on chain, EX .**60.00**

**Necklace, 'yeh yeh yeh,' Randall, EX/M, $175.00. (Photo courtesy Stern, Crawford, and Lamon)**

Nesting dolls, Russian, Sgt Pepper suits, hand-painted wood, EX .................................**50.00**
Nylons, Ballito, textured mesh, MIP .............................**130.00**

Pencil case, Ramat/London, yellow vinyl, 8x3½", EX .........**200.00**

Pennant, felt, I Love the Beatles & hearts, white on red, 29", VG ..............................**125.00**

Pillow, group photo on red or blue background, EX ...........**160.00**

Pressbook, Let It Be, 6 pages, EX .............................**100.00**

Pressbook, Magical Mystery Tour, 4 pages, rare, EX ..........**70.00**

Purse, Canadian, John Lennon on silky material, gold clasp, 1970s, EX ......................**35.00**

Record carrier, PYX, blue vinyl w/group photo insert, 7x7", NM ..............................**200.00**

Scrapbook, Whitman, color photos on front & back, unused, EX ..............................**75.00**

Stationery, Yellow Submarine, 4 sheets w/matching envelopes, 1968, EX .......................**20.00**

Sticker, from gumball machine, gold & black w/faces & names, EX ...................................**25.00**

Wig, Lowell, MIP ..............**125.00**

# Beatrix Potter

If you enjoyed *The Tale of Peter Rabbit* as a child, you'll love these whimsical little figurines reminiscent of the characters illustrated in Beatrix Potter's books. Beswick issued ten of them in 1947 including Peter Rabbit himself, Benjamin Bunny, Squirrel Nutkin, Jemima Puddleduck, Timmy Tiptoes, Tom Kitten, Mrs. Tittlemouse, Mrs. Tiggywinkle, Little Pig Robinson, and Samuel Whiskers. Characters from other stories were eventually added to the line, some with variations that evolved over time. Colors indicate issue dates as do the different backstamps that were used. There have been several stamps since the first figures were issued. There are three basic styles: Beswick brown, Beswick gold, and Royal Albert — with many variations on each of these.

Our advisor for this category is Nicki Budin; she can be found in the Directory under Ohio.

Aunt Petitoes, BP-6B ...........**65.00**
Cecily Parsley, BP-3B ..........**80.00**
Chippy Hackee, BP-B3 ........**35.00**
Cousin Ribby, BP-6B ...........**55.00**
Goody Tiptoes, BP-3B ..........**45.00**
Hunca Munca, BP-3C ..........**75.00**
Jemima Puddleduck/Nest, BP-3B ..............................**65.00**
Johnny Townmouse, BP-3B .**55.00**
Little Pig Robinson, BP-3B .**45.00**
Mr Drake Puddleduck, BP-3B ...**60.00**
Mrs Flopsy Bunny, BP-3B ..**65.00**
Mrs Tiggy Winkle, BP-3B ...**55.00**
Mrs Tittlemouse, BP-6B ......**50.00**

**Old Woman in Shoe, BP-3B, $45.00.**

Poorly Peter Rabbit, BP-6B ..**45.00**
Ribby & Patty Pan, BP-6B ..**45.00**
Samuel Whiskers, BP-3B ....**45.00**
Tabitha Twitchit, BP-6B .....**45.00**
Timmy Wille, BP-B3 ............**60.00**
Tom Kitten, BP-4B ..............**85.00**

# Birthday Angels

Here's a collection that's a lot of fun, inexpensive, and takes relatively little space to display. They're not at all hard to find, but there are several series, so completing 12-month sets of them all can provide a bit of a challenge. Generally speaking, angels are priced by the following factors: 1) company — look for Lefton, Napco, Norcrest, and Enesco marks or labels (unmarked or unknown sets are of less value); 2) application of flowers, bows, gold trim, etc., (the more detail, the more valuable); 3 ( use of rhinestones, which will also increase price; 4) age; and 5) quality of the workmanship involved, detail, and accuracy of painting.

#1600 Pal Angel, month series of both boy & girl, 4", ea, from $12 to ............................**15.00**
Kelvin, C-230, holding flower of the month, 4½", ea, from $15 to ....................................**20.00**
Kelvin, C-250, holding flower of the month, 4½", ea, from $15 to ....................................**20.00**
Lefton, #1323, angel of the month, bisque, ea, from $18 to .**22.00**
Lefton, #2600, birthstone on skirt, 3¼", ea, from $25 to ......**30.00**

Relco, 4¼", from $15.00 to $18.00; 6", from $18.00 to $22.00. (Photo courtesy Denise and James Atkinson)

Lefton, #3332, bisque, w/basket of flowers, 4", ea, from $18 to .........**22.00**
Lefton, #489, holding basket of flowers, 4", ea, from $25 to ....**30.00**
Lefton, #6224, flower/birthstone on skirt, 4½", ea, from $18 to ...............................**20.00**
Lefton, #985, flower of the month, 5", ea, from $25 to .........**30.00**
Napco, A1360-1372, angel of the month, ea, from $20 to .....**25.00**
Napco, A1917-1929, boy angel of the month, ea, from $20 to ............................**25.00**
Napco, A4307, angel of the month, sm, ea, from $22 to .......**25.00**
Napco, C1361-1373, angel of the month, ea, from $20 to ..**25.00**
Napco, C1921-1933, boy angel of the month, ea, from $20 to .....**25.00**
Napco, S1361-1372, angel of the month, ea, from $22 to .**25.00**
Napco, S401-413, angel of the month, ea, from $20 to ...........................**25.00**
Norcrest, F-120, angel of the month, 4½", ea, from $18 to ..........**22.00**
Norcrest, F-340, angel of the month, 5", ea, from $20 to ...........**25.00**
Norcrest, F-535, angel of the month, 4½", ea, from $20 to .........**25.00**
SR, angel of the month, w/birthstone & 'trait' of month, ea, from $20 to ...................**25.00**

TMJ, angel of the month, w/flower, ea, from $20 to .............**25.00**

# Black Americana

This is a wide and varied field of collector interest. Advertising, toys, banks, sheet music, kitchenware items, movie items, and even the fine arts are areas that offer Black Americana buffs many opportunities to add to their collections. Caution! Because some pieces have become so valuable, reproductions abound. Watch for lots of new ceramic items, less detailed in both the modeling and the painting.

Our advisor for this category is Judy Posner, who is listed in the Directory under Pennsylvania. Refer to these books for more information: *Black Collectibles Sold in America* by P.J. Gibbs, and *Black Dolls Book II, An Identification and Value Guide, 1820 – 1991*, by Myla Perkins. (Both are published by Collector Books.)

Book, All About Little Black Sambo, Cupples & Leon, 1917, 48 pages, EX ....................**200.00**

Book, Little Black Sambo, by Helen Bannerman, hardcover, 1943, M ........................**235.00**

Book, Little Brown Koko, 1st edition, hardcover, 1940, 96 pages, EX .....................**95.00**

Book, Pickanninny Twins, by Lucy Fitch Perkins, 1931, 149 pages, EX ...........**165.00**

**Notepad holder, hard plastic, ca 1940s, replaced pencil, EX, $75.00.**

Book, Songs of Stephen Foster, Sweetheart Soap premium, 1940, EX .......................**40.00**

Book, Uncle Tom's Cabin, by Harriet Beecher Stowe, hardcover, 1897, EX .................**95.00**

Bottle, Luzianne Mammy Instant Coffee, tin lid, 1953, 4½", M .....................**125.00**

Card game, Game of Dixieland, Fireside Game Co, 1897, EX in worn box .................**255.00**

Clicker, Minstrel Sam, litho tin, 1920s, 1¾", EX .............**95.00**

Coloring book, Little Brown Koko, illustrated by Dorothy Wadstaff, 1941, EX ...........**125.00**

Cookbook, Aunt Jemima's Magical Recipes, 1954, 26 pages, EX .............................**65.00**

Decanter, boy atop elephant, ceramic, 1949, 7", w/4 plastic cups ............................**90.00**

Doll, golliwog, hand-knit yarn w/felt features, 1930s, 17", EX ..............150.00

Doll, golliwog, stuffed cloth w/plush hair, 12", EX ...65.00

Doll, pickaninny, inflatable plastic, flasher eyes, 1950s, 10", EX ...............................50.00

Doll kit, Sambo, Bucilla Needlework, 1950s, EX ......................100.00

Figure, child sleeping, terra cotta, 1930s, 3½", EX ..............75.00

Figure, girl on potty, cast metal w/painted details, 4", EX ..250.00

Figure, jockey on horse, cast metal w/painted details, 1930s, 3", EX ...............................50.00

Figure, man w/watermelon slice, cast metal, Manoil, 1930s, 3", EX ..............................165.00

Game, Golli-Pop Target, Chad Valley, heavy cardboard, NMIB ..........................550.00

Game, Zoo Hoo, Lubbers & Bells, 1924, NM (EX box ).....165.00

Pennant, Alabama - The Cotton State, cotton picker image, 11½", M ........................50.00

Place mat, Story of Aunt Jemima, Pancake Days, 1950s, 11x14", M .....................................35.00

Pull toy, Little Jasper, Wood Commodities, 1944, 10", NMIB .........................300.00

Puppet Theater, Little Black Sambo Playette, cardboard, 1942, MIB ..................225.00

Record & book set, Little Black Sambo's Jungle Band, Paul Wing, EX ....................110.00

Salt & pepper shakers, Mammy & Chef bust figures, ceramic, 1930s, pr ......................195.00

Pincushion, velvet and cotton, 4½", $65.00.

Salt & pepper shakers, man w/watermelon slice, porcelain, 1930s, 3", pr ...............295.00

Spoon rest, chef atop frying pan, glazed pottery, 1930s, 6", EX ...............................95.00

Tambourine, Amo's Singing Minstrels, tin, unmarked, 1910-20, 6", EX ....................900.00

Towel, Mammy at clothesline, printed cloth, 1930s, EX ..........70.00

Wall caddy, Mammy w/ruffle collar, diecut utensils hold hooks, 9½" ................................95.00

Whisk broom, Mammy figure, red bristles form skirt, 1930s, 4¼", EX ........................80.00

## Black Cats

This line of fancy felines was marketed mainly by the Shafford (importing) Company, although black cat lovers accept similarly modeled, shiny glazed kitties of other importing firms into their collections as well. Some of the more plentiful items maybe purchased for $15.00 to $35.00, while the Shafford six-piece spice set in a wooden rack usually sells for as much as $145.00. These values and the ones that follow are for items with mint paint, a very important consideration in determining a fair market price. Shafford items are often minus their white whiskers and eyebrows, and this type of loss should be reflected in your evaluation. An item with poor paint may be worth even less than half of given estimates. Note: Unless 'Shafford' is included in the descriptions, values are for cats that were imported by other companies.

Ashtray, head shape w/open mouth, Shafford, 3" ......**18.00**

Bank, seated, coin slot in top of head, Shafford .............**125.00**

Cigarette lighter, Shafford, 5½" .........................**175.00**

Cookie jar, lg head, Shafford .**85.00**

Cruet, slender, gold collar & tie, tail handle .....................**12.00**

Decanter, upright, holds bottle w/cork stopper, Shafford .**50.00**

Decanter set, upright, yellow eyes, w/6 plain wines .............**35.00**

Desk caddy, spring body holds letters, pen forms tail, 6½" .**8.00**

Egg cup, cat face on bowl, pedestal foot, Shafford .................**30.00**

Ice bucket, cylindrical w/embossed cat face, 2 sizes, ea .......**75.00**

Mug, Shafford, 3½" .............**50.00**

Demitasse pot, Shafford, 7½", $95.00.

Paperweight, cat's head on chrome base, yellow eyes, rare ..**75.00**

Planter, cat & kitten in hat, Shafford-like paint ...............**30.00**

Planter, upright, Napco label, Shafford-like paint, 6" ..**20.00**

Salt & pepper shakers, crouching cat w/shaker at ea end, Shafford, 10" .........................**85.00**

Salt & pepper shakers, seated, blue eyes, Enesco label, 5¾" ...........................**15.00**

Spice set, 6 sq shakers in wooden frame, Shafford .............**145.00**

Stacking tea set, mama pot w/kitty creamer & sugar bowl, yellow eyes ................................**65.00**

Teapot, bulbous body w/head lid, green eyes, Shafford, 4½" .**30.00**

Teapot, bulbous body w/head lid, green eyes, Shafford, 7" .**75.00**

Teapot, panther-like appearance, gold eyes, sm .................**20.00**

Thermometer, standing w/paw on round dial, yellow eyes .**30.00**

Toothpick holder, cat on vase atop
book, Occupied Japan ...**12.00**
Tray, flat face, wicker handle,
Shafford, rare, lg ........**125.00**
Utensil rack, flat-backed cat w/3
slots for utensils ..........**90.00**

# Blade Banks

In 1903 the safety razor was
invented, making it easier for men
to shave at home. But the old, used
razor blades were troublesome,
because for the next 22 years,
nobody knew what to do with
them. In 1925 the first patent was
filed for a razor blade bank, a container designed to hold old blades
until it became full, in which event
it was to be thrown away. Most
razor blade banks are 3" or 4" tall,
similar to a coin bank with a slot in
the top but no outlet in the bottom
to remove the old blades. These
banks were produced from 1925 to
1950. Some were issued by men's
toiletry companies and were often
filled with shaving soap or cream.
Many were made of tin and printed
with an advertising message. An
assortment of blade banks made
from a variety of materials —
ceramic, wood, plastic, or metal —
could also be purchased at five-
and-dime stores.

For information on blade
banks as well as many other types
of interesting figural items from
the same era, we recommend *Collectibles for the Kitchen, Bath &
Beyond* (featuring napkin dolls,
egg timers, string holders, children's whistle cups, baby feeder
dishes, pie birds, and laundry
sprinkler bottles) by Ellen Bercovi-
ci, Bobbie Zucker Bryson, and
Deborah Gillham. (Available
through Antique Trader Books).

Barber, wood w/Gay Blade bottom,
Woodcroft, 1950, 6", from $65
to .................................**75.00**
Barber, wood w/key & metal hold-
ers for razor & brush, 9", from
$85 to .............................**95.00**

**Barber bust, handlebar mustache,
in coat and tie, from $55.00 to
$65.00. (Photo courtesy Deborah
Gillham)**

Barber chair, lg, from $100 to ..**125.00**
Barber chair, sm, from $100 to .**125.00**
Barber head, different colors on
collar, Cleminson, from $30
to .................................**40.00**
Barber holding pole, Occupied
Japan, 4", from $50 to ..**60.00**
Barber pole, red & white, w/ or
w/out attachments, from $20
to .................................**25.00**

Barber pole w/barber head & derby hat, white, from $35 to ..............................**40.00**

Barber pole w/face, red & white, from $30 to ...................**35.00**

Barber standing in blue coat & stroking chin, from $75 to .**80.00**

Barber w/buggy eyes, full-figure, Gleason look-alike, from $65 to .....................................**75.00**

Barbershop quartet, 4 singing barber heads, from $95 to .**125.00**

Box w/policeman, metal, marked Used Blades, from $75 to ..........**100.00**

Dandy Dans, plastic w/brush holders, from $30 to .............**40.00**

Frog, green, marked For Used Blades, from $65 to .......**75.00**

Half barber pole, hangs on wall, may be personalized, from $50 to .....................................**60.00**

Half shaving cup, hangs on wall, marked Gay Blades, from $65 to .....................................**75.00**

**Shaving brush, American Bisque (?), from $50.00 to $60.00. (Photo courtesy Deborah Gillham)**

Half shaving cup, hangs on wall, marked Gay Old Blade, from $65 to .........................**75.00**

Listerine donkey, from $20 to .**30.00**

Listerine elephant, from $25 to ...**35.00**

Listerine frog, from $15 to ..**20.00**

Looie, right- or left-hand version, from $85 to ..................**100.00**

Man shaving, mushroom shape, Cleminson, from $25 to .**30.00**

Razor Bum, from $95 ........**125.00**

Safe, green, marked Razor, from $45 to .............................**55.00**

Tony the barber, Ceramic Arts Studio, from $85 to .......**95.00**

# Blue Ridge

Some of the most attractive American dinnerware made in the twentieth century is Blue Ridge, produced by Southern Potteries of Erwin, Tennessee, from the late 1930s until 1956. More than four hundred patterns were hand painted on eight basic shapes. Elaborate or appealing designs sell for 25% more than the prices we suggest for simple, plain patterns. The Quimper-like peasant-decorated line is one of the most treasured and should be priced at double the amounts recommended for the higher-end patterns. Refer to *Blue Ridge Dinnerware, Revised Third Edition,* by Betty and Bill Newbound (Collector Books) for more information.

Ashtray, simple or solid pattern, individual, from $8 to ...........................**10.00**

Bonbon, elaborate/appealing pattern, divided, center handle, from $75 to.................. **90.00**

Bowl, cereal/soup; simple or solid pattern, 6", from $4 to ....**6.00**

Bowl, divided vegetable; simple or solid pattern, oval, 9", $15 to ......................**20.00**

Bowl, fruit; simple or solid pattern, 5¼", from $2 to ......**4.00**

Bowl, salad; elaborate/appealing pattern, 10½", from $45 to .....**50.00**

Butter pat/coaster, elaborate/appealing pattern, from $25 to ..**30.00**

Cake lifter, elaborate/appealing pattern, from $20 to .....**25.00**

Candy box, china, artist signed, 6" dia, from $90 to ...........**100.00**

Creamer, simple or solid pattern, regular, from $3 to ..........**6.00**

Cup & saucer, simple or solid pattern, regular, from $5 to .**7.00**

Egg cup, double, elaborate/appealing pattern, from $20 to .**30.00**

Gravy boat, elaborate/appealing pattern, from $15 to .....**22.00**

Jug, batter; elaborate/appealing pattern, w/lid, from $55 to .....**75.00**

Pie baker, elaborate/appealing pattern, from $25 to .....**30.00**

Pitcher, Betsy, elaborate/appealing pattern, from $75 to .......**90.00**

Pitcher, Spiral, china, artist signed, rare, sm, from $70 to ..............................**85.00**

Plate, cake; elaborate/appealing pattern, 10½", from $25 to .....**30.00**

Plate, cake; simple or solid pattern, 10½", from $18 to ...........**20.00**

Plate, child's, elaborate/appealing pattern, from $25 to .....**30.00**

Plate, elaborate/appealing pattern, 10½", from $25 to ..........**30.00**

**Salt and pepper shakers, Mardi Gras, $40.00 for the pair.**

Plate, elaborate/appealing pattern, 8", from $8 to .......**10.00**

Plate, simple or solid pattern, 10", from $8 to ......................**10.00**

Platter, Turkey with Acorns or Thanksgiving, from $190 to ...........................**200.00**

Salad fork, elaborate/appealing pattern, from $25 to .....**30.00**

Shakers, Apple, pr, from $10 to .**12.00**

Shakers, Chickens, pr, from $80 to ...................................**90.00**

Sugar bowl, demitasse; elaborate/appealing pattern, from $25 to ............................**30.00**

Teapot, Charm House, elaborate/appealing pattern, from $100 to .................................**150.00**

**Teapot, Lorraine, $135.00.**

Teapot, Piecrust, elaborate/
appealing pattern, from $75
to ..................................**90.00**
Teapot, Woodcrest, elaborate/appeal-
ing pattern, from $95 to ....**125.00**
Tidbit, 3-tier, elaborate/appealing
pattern, from $20 to .....**30.00**
Tidbit, 3-tier, simple or plain pattern, from $17 to ...........**20.00**
Tray, waffle set; elaborate/appeal-
ing pattern, from $50 to .**55.00**
Tumbler, juice; elaborate/ appealing pattern, glass, from $9
to ...................................**12.00**
Vase, Boot, elaborate/appealing pattern, 8", from $75 to ..............**85.00**
Wall sconce, elaborate/appealing
pattern, from $60 to .....**65.00**

## Blue Willow

Inspired by the lovely blue
and white Chinese exports, the
Willow pattern has been made by
many English, American, and
Japanese firms from 1950 until
the present. Many variations of
the pattern have been noted —
mauve, black, green, and multicolor Willow ware can be found in
limited amounts. The design has
been applied to tinware, linens,
glassware, and paper goods, all of
which are treasured by today's
collectors. Refer to *Blue Willow* by
Mary Frank Gaston (Collector
Books) for more information. See
also Children's Dishes; Royal
China.

Ashtray, unmarked Japan, 7½"
sq ..................................**50.00**
Bowl, child's, Japan, 3½" ....**10.00**

Bowl, salad; unmarked Japan,
3½x10", w/matching fork &
spoon ...........................**140.00**
Bowl, soup; Japan, 6½" .........**4.00**
Bowl, soup/cereal; Shenango
China ............................**20.00**
Bowl, vegetable; pictorial border,
Royal Sometuke ............**75.00**
Bowl, vegetable; Shenango China,
8" ...................................**30.00**
Bowl, vegetable; w/lid, Japan,
child's, 3¼x4¼" .............**40.00**
Bowl, vegetable; w/lid, WR Mid-
winter Ltd, 10" ..............**75.00**

**Butter dish, Japan, from $60.00 to
$75.00. (Photo courtesy Mary
Frank Gaston)**

Butter warmer, unmarked
Japan .........................**85.00**
Candelabra, brass & ceramic, 3-light,
Shenango China, 11" .......**245.00**
Chop plate, Buffalo, 11¾" .**150.00**
Coffeepot, cylindrical, Japan,
7" ...........................**115.00**
Compote, footed, Shenango China,
3x6" ..............................**60.00**
Creamer, scalloped rim, England,
2" ...................................**45.00**
Creamer & sugar bowl, gold
trim, with lid, unmarked
Japan, 3½" .................**60.00**
Creamer & sugar bowl, oval,
Japan ...........................**40.00**

Cup, England ...................12.00
Cup & saucer, Buffalo .........30.00
Cup & saucer, Johnson Bros .12.50
Cup & saucer, USA, stacking .6.00
Egg cup, double; unmarked Japan, 3¾" .................................20.00
Egg cup, single, gold trim, unmarked Japan ...........35.00
Flatware, 4-pc place setting, plastic & stainless steel, Japan ...........................50.00
Lamp, electric, oil-lamp style, Made in Japan, 7¼" ....................55.00
Mug, farmer's; Japan, 4" .....40.00
Mug, Japan ..........................15.00
Napkin ring, unmarked, 1½" .80.00
Pie server, Moriyama Made in Japan 10" .....................40.00
Plate, grill; Occupied Japan, 10½" .............................30.00
Plate, Made in Japan, 8¾" ..14.00
Plate, Shenango China, 9" ..35.00
Plate, variant center pattern w/pictorial border, unmarked, 6" ....................................12.00
Platter, unmarked, 14x11½" .45.00
Salt & pepper shakers, barrel form, Japan, pr .............20.00
Salt box, wooden lid, unmarked Japan, 5x5" .................135.00
Snack Hound, 5 sections, Japan ........................70.00
Snack set, Japan, cup & 9" plate w/cup ring ....................35.00
Spoon rest, double style, unmarked Japan, 9" long ...............50.00
Teacup, porcelain, pictorial border pattern, Noritake mark, 3" ...................................45.00
Teapot, musical, unmarked Japan ..........................140.00
Toothpick holder, Buffalo China ...................235.00

Tumbler, glass ....................18.00
Wall pocket, teapot form w/traditional pattern & floral border, Japan ...........................50.00

## Bobbin' Head Dolls

Bobbin' head dolls made of papier-mache were produced in Japan during the 1960s until about 1972. They are about 7" tall, hand painted in bright colors, then varnished. The most colledtible represent sports teams and their mascots. They've been made in countless variations. Base color indicates when the doll was made. During 1961 and '62, white bases were used; today these are very scarce. Green bases are from 1962 to '66, and gold bases were used from 1967 until 1972. We recommand *The Bobbin' Head Collector and Price Guide* by our advisor Tim Hunter, who listed in the Directory under Nevada. Another scource that deals primarily with nodders but includes bobbin' heads as well is *Figural Nodders* by Hilma R. Irtz (Collector Books).

See also Clubs and Newsletters.

### Baseball

Atlanta Braves, team mascot, gold base, 1967-72, NM .....................135.00
Baltimore Orioles, team mascot, white base, 1961-62, rare, NM ...........................350.00
Cincinnati Reds, Black player, green base, 1962-66, NM ..................1,500.00

Cleveland Indians, team mascot, white base, 1961-62, rare, NM ..............................**485.00**

Los Angeles Dodgers, Black player, green base, 1962-66, NM ............................**800.00**

Mickey Mantle, sq or round white base, 1961-62, NM, ea ..............................**600.00**

New York Mets, blue base, 1960-61, NM .........................**200.00**

New York Yankees, white base, 1961-62, NM ..............**225.00**

Roger Maris, white base, 1961-62, NM ..............................**485.00**

St Louis Cardinals, team mascot, white base, 1961–62, minimum value ......**400.00**

Willie Mays, white base, 1961-62, NM ..............................**300.00**

Chicago Bears, gold base, 1967, NM ...............................**100.00**

Dallas Cowboys, round base, 1965, NM ...............................**200.00**

Detroit Tigers, team mascot, green base, 1962-66, minimum value ...........................**180.00**

Green Bay Packers, gold base, 1967, NM .....................**150.00**

Houston Oilers, gold base, 1966-67, NM ...........................**55.00**

Kansas City Chiefs, gold base, 1968, NM, from $50 to .**75.00**

Los Angeles Rams, gold base, 1966-68, NM .................**75.00**

Minnesota Vikings, gold base, from $100 to ...............**150.00**

Philadelphia Eagles, 1960 Champions on green base, 1961-62, NM ...............................**135.00**

## Basketball

Baltimore Bullets, Little Dribblers, NM ...................**200.00**

Harlem Globetrotters, 1962, NM ..........................**350.00**

Los Angeles Lakers, 1962, NM ......................**225.00**

Seattle Sonics, yellow uniform, 1967, NM ....................**225.00**

## Football

Atlanta Falcons, gold base, 1967, NM ................................**75.00**

Baltimore Colts, realistic face, gold base, 1966-68, NM .......**250.00**

Boston Patriots, Type VI, lg shoulder pads, from $300 to ..........................**400.00**

Chicago Bears, Black player, gold base, 1965, NM ...........**350.00**

**Purdue Boilermakers, toes up, smaller shoulder pads, early 1960s, minimum value, $75.00. (Photo courtesy Tim Hunter)**

Washington Redskins, Merger series, gold base, NM .**200.00**

## Hockey

Baltimore Clippers ............**200.00**

Boston, 1962 ......................450.00
Boston Braves ...................475.00
Chicago, 1962, mini .............65.00
Detroit, Canada, high skate ..425.00
Los Angeles, 1967, gold base .425.00
New York, 1962, sq ...........175.00
Portland Buckaroos ...........400.00
San Diego Gulls .................375.00
St Louis, 1967, gold base (gold uni-
    form add 20%) .............450.00
Toronto, 1962, mini .............35.00

## Nonsports

Beetle Bailey, NM ..............125.00
Ben Casey, from 1960s TV show,
    NM, from $100 to .......125.00
Bugs Bunny, NM, from $100 to .175.00
Charlie Brown, sq black base,
    NM ...............................95.00
Colonel Sanders, Kentucky
    Fried Chicken, 2 different,
    NM, ea ......................100.00
Danny Kaye & girl kissing, NM,
    pr .................................150.00

**Donald Duck, copyright WDP, Irwin Toys, 5", from $90.00 to $100.00. (Photo courtesy Hilma R. Irtz)**

Dobie Gillis, NM, from $250 to .300.00
Donny Osmond, white jumpsuit
    w/microphone, NM, from $100
    to .................................150.00
Dumbo, round red base, NM .100.00
Eisenhower, blue coat, NM, from
    $100 to ........................125.00
Flapper girl kicks legs in bathtub
    ashtray, Japan, 5½" .....70.00
Foghorn Leghorn, NM, from $100
    to .................................175.00
Goofy, Disneyland, arms at side,
    white base, NM ............75.00
Little Audrey, NM, from $100
    to .............................150.00
Lt Fuzz (Beetle Bailey), NM .125.00
Lucky Leo Lion, MIB ...........25.00
Mickey Mouse, Walt Disney World,
    blue shirt & red pants,
    NM ...............................75.00
Mr Peanut, w/cane, moves at waist,
    NM, from $150 to .........200.00
New York World's Fair, globe,
    1964, NM ......................75.00
Oodles the Duck (Bozo the Clown),
    NM ..............................150.00
Pappy (Dogpatch USA), NM ..75.00
Phantom of the Opera, sq brown
    base, NM .....................500.00
Porky Pig, NM, from $100 to .175.00
Rabbit, life-like, Japan, 1960s,
    MIB ...............................55.00
Smokey Bear, holding shovel, sq
    or round base, ea from $125
    to .................................200.00
Snoopy, sq black base, Lego,
    NM ............................95.00
Space Boy, black spacesuit & hel-
    met, NM ......................75.00
Three Little Pigs, blue overalls &
    yellow cap, round red base,
    NM, ea ........................100.00
Tweety Bird, NM, from $100 to .175.00

Winnie the Pooh, 1970s, no base, sm, NM ...........................**40.00**
Woodstock, no base, 1970s, NM .**45.00**
Yosemite Sam, NM, from $100 to ..............................**175.00**
Zero (Beetle Bailey), NM ...**125.00**

# Bookends

Bookends have only recently come into their own as a separate category of collectibles. They are so diversified in styling, it's easy to find those that appeal to you, no matter what your personal tastes and preferences. Metal examples seem to be most popular, especially those with the mark of their manufacturer, and can still be had at reasonable prices. Glass and ceramic bookends by noted makers, however, may be more costly — for example, those made by Roseville or Cambridge, which have a cross-over collector appeal.

Our advisor for this category is Louis Kuritzky, author of *Collector's Guide to Bookends* (Collector Books); he is listed in the Directory under Florida. See also Clubs and Newsletters.

Angelfish, painted gray metal on polished stone base, ca 1930, 6", pr ...........................**120.00**
Baby shoes on books, painted gray metal, Pat 1940, 5½", pr .**75.00**
Bedouin, man on camel, painted cast iron, Hubley, ca 1925, 5¾", pr ...........................**125.00**
Cape Cod fisherman, cast iron, Connecticut Foundry, 1928, 5½", pr ...........................**65.00**
Cowboy & bronco, cast iron, Connecticut Foundry, #923, 1930, 6", pr ...........................**125.00**
Dutch boy & girl, gold on gray metal, Frankart, 1934, 5½", pr ..................................**150.00**
Elephant at tree, painted cast iron, Judd Co, ca 1925, 4½", pr ..................................**150.00**
End of Trail, rider on horse, painted metal, Ronson, 1930s, 6", pr ..................................**110.00**
German shepherd, cast iron, unmarked, ca 1928, 4¾", pr ...........................**45.00**

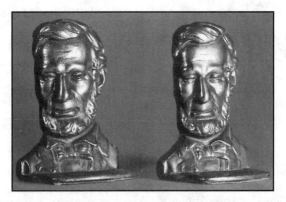

**Abraham Lincoln, Verona, 1928, 6½", $65.00. (Photo courtesy Louis Kuritzky)**

**Rearing Horse, LE Smith, 5", $150.00. (Photo courtesy Louis Kuritzky)**

Gleaners, gathering scene relief, painted metal, K&O, 1925, 4¼", pr ........................**125.00**

Hound, hunter on point, gray metal, Ronson, ca 1930, 5¾", pr ................................**150.00**

Igloo, Eskimo at door, painted aluminum, Glenmore Distilleries, 5", pr ...........................**295.00**

Indiana Pigeon, white opalescent, Indiana Glass, 1940s, 5½", pr ........................**70.00**

Library monk, figure in red w/books, painted metal, Ronson, 1920, pr ................**125.00**

Lincoln seated in relief, bronze, Solid Bronze, 1930s, 3¾", pr ................................**90.00**

Lindy, bust of Charles Lindbergh, cast iron, Verona, 1928, 6", pr ..............................**110.00**

Madrigal, Oriental musician relief, bronze-painted metal, PB, 1925, pr .................**75.00**

Maple leaf, painted gray metal, PM Craftsman, ca 1965, pr ..**40.00**

Menora & IOBB in relief, cast iron, ca 1935, 5", pr ......**75.00**

Nude on book, cast iron, Litco (not always marked), ca 1929, 8", pr ................................**160.00**

Nude woman kneeling, gray metal, 1933, 5" ...........**140.00**

Nymph on dolphin, green paint on gray metal, ca 1929, 5¾", pr ...............................**175.00**

Odd Fellows, eye & hands, Vergne Artware #119, pr ........**125.00**

Penguin family, 3 figures on rocky base, gray metal, 1925, 5", pr .........................**225.00**

Roar of the Tiger, gray metal, Ronson, ca 1925, 7½", pr ..............**175.00**

Sajous' Cyclopedia, cast iron, ca 1925, 6½", pr .................**75.00**

Scarf Dance, nude dancing figure, CI, ca 1930, 6½", pr ....**195.00**

Scottie, cast iron, Hubley, ca 1925, 5", pr ............................**50.00**

Sitting Bull, bust of chief in headdress, brass, ca 1924, 6¾", pr .....................**275.00**

Washington bust, cast iron, ca 1920, pr ........................**75.00**

Ye Olde Inn, scene in relief, Syroco Wood, ca 1940, 6¼", pr .**45.00**

# Bottle Openers

Figural bottle openers are models of animals, people, and various inanimate objects designed for the sole purpose of removing a bottle cap. To qualify as an example, the cap lifter must be part of the figure itself. Among the major producers of openers of this type were Wilton Products, John Wright Inc., L & L Favors, and Gadzik Sales. These and advertising openers are very collectible.

Our advisor for this category is Charlie Reynolds; he is listed in the Directory under Virginia. The FBOC (Figural Bottle Opener Collectors) are listed under Clubs and Newsletters.

Alligator, cast iron, F-136, VG .**70.00**

Auto jack, chrome, F-211, NM, from $35 to ....................**45.00**

Bear, cast iron, repainted, F-426, EX ................................**150.00**

Bulldog's head, cast iron, Wilton, wall mount, F-425, NM ..........................**110.00**

Clown, brass, F-417, EX ......**55.00**

Cowboy & signpost, cast iron, J Wright, F-14, EX ........**125.00**

Dachshund, brass, F-83 .......**80.00**

Elephant, plated aluminum, F-49 ................................**38.00**

False teeth, painted cast iron, F-420, EX original ............**80.00**

Flamingo, cast iron, hollow, Wilton Pdts, F-120 **100.00**

Hockey skate, pot metal ......**50.00**

Lamppost drunk, bronze, F-2A, NM ................................**25.00**

Lobster, white metal, F-169, EX ............................**45.00**

Karate Man, cast iron, F-250, $95.00. (Photo courtesy Charlie Reynolds)

Monkey, cast iron, Wright, F-89, EX ................................**135.00**

Parrot, long blue tail, painted cast iron, J Wright, F-108, 5¼" ..............................**50.00**

Pelican, cast iron, bright multicolor paint, F-129 ..............**65.00**

Pretzel, aluminum, F-230, EX paint ..............................**42.50**

Salted pretzel, F-230 ...........**40.00**

Sea gull, cast iron, bright 3-color paint, F-123 ...................**60.00**

Squirrel, nickeled cast iron, Norlin Enterprises, F-91d, 1¾x3" ..........................**50.00**

Streetwalker, aluminum, original paint, F-5, 4½", NM ....**160.00**

4-eyed lady, painted cast iron, J Wright, F-407, EX ......**100.00**

# Bottles

Bottles have been used as containers for commercial products since the late 1800s. Specimens from as early as 1845 may still be occasionally found today (watch for a rough pontil to indicate this early production date). Some of the most collectible are bitters bottles, used for 'medicine' that was mostly alcohol, a ploy to avoid paying the stiff tax levied on liquor sales. Spirit flasks from the 1800s were blown in the mold and were often designed to convey a historic, political, or symbolic message. Even bottles from the 1900s are collectible, especially beer or pop bottles and commercial containers from defunct bottlers. Refer to *Bottle Pricing Guide, Third Revised Edition,* by Hugh Cleveland (Collector Books) for more information.

## Dairy Bottles

The storage and distribution of fluid milk in glass bottles became commonplace around the turn of the century. They were replaced by paper and plastic containers in the mid-1950s. Perhaps 5% of all US dairies are still using some glass, and glass bottles are still widely used in Mexico and some Canadian provinces.

Milk-packaging and distribution plants hauled trailer loads of glass bottles to dumping grounds during the conversion to the throwaway cartons now in general use. Because of this practice, milk bottles and jars are scarce today. Most collectors search for bottles from hometown dairies; some have completed a fifty-state collection in the three popular sizes.

Bottles from 1900 to 1920 had the name of the dairy, town, and state embossed in the glass. Nearly all of the bottles produced after this period had the copy painted and then pyro-glazed onto the surface of the bottle. This enabled the dairyman to use colors and pictures of his dairy farm or cows on the bottles. Collectors have been very fortunate that there have been no serious attempts at this point to reproduce a particularly rare bottle!

Ben-Dor Farms Dairy, farm scene, orange pyro, sq, 1-qt ............................**6.00**
Blue Ribbon Dairies...NJ, red pyro (worn), sq, 1-qt ................**4.00**
Bonnie Brook Green Spot..., green pyro, orange peel 2 sides, sq, 1-qt ................................**10.00**
Brookfield Dairy.../Premium, low baby-face top, ½-pt ....................**35.00**
Dairymen's Co-Op Assn embossed, round, 1-qt ......................**6.00**
Desmarais embossed, round, 1-qt ............................**9.00**
Elliot F Walker Dighton Rock Farm... embossed, round, 1-pt, haze ................................**15.00**
Farmer's Dairy Inc New Bedford MA embossed, round, 1-qt .....**10.00**
Farmer's Dairy Inc...Mass embossed, round, ½-pt .**10.00**
Francis S Cummings...West Somerville embossed, round, 1-qt ................................**8.00**
Highland Farm Lenox Mass embossed, round, ½-pt .................**6.00**

Hobart Farms Jersey Cream, cow's head, tin top, ½-pt ........................**75.00**

Hood Dairy Experts & spider web design embossed, round, ½-pt ..............................**7.00**

Hope Street Dairy... Mulberry St embossed, round, 1-pt ..........................**12.00**

HP Hood & Sons Dairy Experts...1939 embossed, round, ½-pt ......................**6.00**

HP Hood & Sons Dairy Experts...1941 embossed, round, 1-qt ......................**7.50**

It's Hoods, orange pyro, sq, ½-pt ..............................**8.00**

JA DeMarchi Reading w/lg JAD monogram embossed, round, 1-qt ..................................**10.00**

JB Heywood Fall River Mass Pasteurized...embossed, round, 1-qt .....................................**12.00**

Laudholm Farms, Wells ME w/lg monogram embossed, round, 1-qt ...................................**9.00**

Martin & Oliveira Fall River, cow's head embossed, round, 1-pt ................................**18.00**

Speedwell Farms, cow's head, tin top, ½-pt ........................**70.00**

Tripp's Dairy...Mass w/T monogram embossed, round, 1-pt ...........................**15.00**

Universal Store Bottle...5¢ embossed, round, 1-qt .....**6.00**

WC Viall E Providence w/lg WCV monogram embossed, round, 1-qt ..................................**12.00**

WD Whittemore Bellevue Dairies embossed, round, 1-qt .....**6.00**

Whitings Milk...Over a Century, red pyro, round, ½-pt ...**10.00**

Whittaker East Fairhaven embossed, round, ½-pt .**12.00**

**I Want Rainier's Milk, screaming baby in red pyro, cream top, from $20.00 to $25.00.**

## Soda Bottles With Applied Color Labels

This is an area of bottle collecting that has recently shown strong and sustained growth. Market prices have been climbing steadily.

Our advisor for this category is Thomas Marsh, author of *The Official Guide to Collecting Applied Color Label Soda Bottles, Volumes I and II*. Mr. Marsh is listed in the Directory under Ohio.

A&W Root Beer, clear, 10-oz .**10.00**

Apollo, clear, 1-qt ................**15.00**

Badger State, clear, 7-oz .....**15.00**

Birdsboro, clear, 1-qt ..........**20.00**

Brookdale, green, 8-oz .........**10.00**

Click, green, 7-oz .................**25.00**
Crown Club, clear, 7-oz .......**15.00**
Dr Swett's, clear, 12-oz ........**10.00**
Fawn, clear, 1-qt .................**20.00**
Frontenac, clear, 1-qt .........**15.00**
Gill's, clear, 10-oz ................**20.00**
Golden Valley, clear, 12-oz ..**15.00**
Grapeteen, clear, 6-oz .........**50.00**
Holiday, green, 1-qt .............**15.00**
Isaly's Mountain Air, clear, 12-oz ................................**20.00**
Lemon Blossoms, green, 10-oz ..**10.00**
Little Tom, clear, 6-oz .........**15.00**
LLL Triple, green, 7-oz ........**15.00**
Mrs Lombardi's, clear, 12-oz .**75.00**
Orangette Lemonette, clear, 10-oz ................................**15.00**
Phoenix, clear, 1-qt .............**15.00**
Pittsford, green, 7-oz ...........**10.00**
Quicky, green, 7-oz ..............**10.00**
Robersons, clear, 10-oz ........**10.00**
Skipper, green, 1-qt .............**15.00**
Smack, clear, 12-oz ..............**40.00**
Sun Flower Beverages, clear, 10-oz ................................**20.00**
Verners, clear, 12-oz ............**10.00**
Walsh's, green, 7-oz .............**10.00**
Wondor, clear, 7-oz ..............**10.00**

Amber glass, circa 1950s – 60s, any shown, $125.00. (Photo courtesy Thomas Marsh)

## Miscellaneous

Atwood's Vegetable Dyspeptic Bitters, aqua, sq, lt haze ......**65.00**

**Augauer Bitters, bright yellow-green, NM labels, 8", $80.00; Dr. Bell's Blood Purifying Bitters, yellow-amber, 9½", $75.00.**

Ayers Hair Vigor, peacock blue, original stopper, 7", NM .......................**75.00**
Baby Brand Trade Mark Castoria... on 2 sides, sun-colored amethyst ..........................**5.00**
Barry's Tricopherous, aqua, smooth base ..................**15.00**
Benjamin's Wonder Oil, rare .**35.00**
Blankenheym & Nolet, embossed key, green, case gin ......**22.00**
Brant's Pulminary Balsam, aqua, smooth base, 6¼" ..........**15.00**
Brystol Myers Co New York w/monogram, amber, dug .............**20.00**
Carl Schultz, aqua, 10-pin soda .**75.00**
CH Daniels Brewery Manistee, Mich, amber, blob top, 1-qt ........**45.00**
Chamberlain's Immediate Relief... Elkhart IN, aqua, dug .............................**90.00**

Curtis & Perkins Wild Cherry Bitters, aqua, open pontil, EX ...............115.00

Dabrooks' Perfumes, Detroit, clear, smooth base, 3½" ...........10.00

Davis Vegetable Pain Killer, haze ..............................3.00

Dr G Barber's Instantaneous Relief From Pain, aqua .........175.00

Dr Harter's Iron Tonic, amber, smooth bottom ..............15.00

Dr Hoofland's German Bitters, aqua ..............................25.00

Dr Hul Cee's Blood Building Tonic Louisville KY, aqua, open pontil .............................40.00

Dr J Hostetter's Stomach Bitters, honey amber ................55.00

Dr JW Bull's Cough Syrup, AC Meyer...Baltimore USA, dug ..............................8.00

Dr Kennedy's Medical Discovery, aqua, smooth base, 9" ............................13.00

Dr King's New Discovery for Consumption, aqua, smooth base, 8½" ................................12.00

Dr Langley's Root & Herb Bitters...Boston, aqua ........70.00

Dr Lawrences' Wild Cherry Bitters, amber, sample size .......350.00

Dr S Pitcher's Castoria, aqua, bubbles, hinged mold ..........10.00

Dr Thacher's Worm Syrup, aqua, smooth base, 4¼" ..........10.00

EG Lyons Jamaica Ginger, SF, applied top ....................14.00

Eye w/rays (picture) ROL Co, cobalt blue, cylinder, water bottle ..............................59.00

F Brown's Ess of Jamaica Ginger, aqua, smooth base, 5½" ............................7.00

FA Sherwin Pharmacist Ashland OR, amethyst, 4¼" ..........8.00

Farmer's Horse Medicine, SF Cal, aqua, tooled top, 8¼" ....65.00

Fellows Syrup of Hypo-phosphites ............................8.00

Four Roses, Paul Jones, Louisville KY, amber, minor stain, dug, 11" .............25.00

Frankfort Safe Cure, emerald, blob top, full, 1-pt .......500.00

Gargling Oil Lockport NY, medium emerald green, smooth base, 5¾" .......................60.00

Garner & Auch Consohocken PA, aqua, Hutchinson .........10.00

Gwinn Bottling Works Register Gwinn MI, light amethyst, w/stopper .....................150.00

HHH Horse Medicine, light green aqua, lg .........................25.00

Hirsch's Malt Whiskey Reliable Stimulant, amber, cylinder ...........40.00

Indian Vegetable Cough Syrup & Blood Purifier, SG Goff, aqua, 7⅝" ..............................35.00

JJW Peters on base, trademark (dog) on front, amber, bubbles ..............................40.00

JL Laufer's Pure Horseradish, Buffalo NY, aqua, smooth base ..............................13.00

John Bull's Extract of Sarsaparilla, Louisville KY, aqua ......................150.00

JP Brady's Family Bitters, dark amber ..........................220.00

Lashes Kidney & Liver Bitters Best Cathartic, honey amber to amber, NM ................35.00

Lydia E Pinkham's Vegetable Compound, bubbles, neck stress ..........................12.00

Lyon's Katheron for the Hair, aqua, open pontil, minor stain ............................**35.00**

Mexican Mustang Liniment, aquamarine, open pontil, rolled lip, 4¼" ................................**70.00**

Parker's Celebrated Stomach Bitters, amber, crooked neck ............................**70.00**

Pepper sauce, aqua, concave panel, smooth base, crude rolled lip ........................**15.00**

Peptenzyme, Reed & Carnrick, NJ, cobalt, oval, smooth base, 2½" ................................**25.00**

Pof DeGrath's Electric Oil, Phila, clear, 2¾" ....................**55.00**

Pomeroy Bottling Works, Manistee, amber, rough lip, 1-pt ....**75.00**

R Riddle Philada, green, squat .**20.00**

Registered Pottstown PA, amber, squat ..............................**27.00**

Rev T Hills Vegetable Remedy, aqua, NM ....................**175.00**

Sanford's Radical Cure, Weeks & Potter Boston, cobalt ....**70.00**

Sarasina Stomach Bitters, medium amber ......................**155.00**

Schenck's Pulmonic Syrup Philada, aqua ........................**12.00**

Scott's Emulsion Cod Liver Oil w/Lime & Soda, flask, aqua, EX embossing ...............**15.00**

Stoddard Double Eagle, golden olive-amber, bubbles, 1-pt .....................**150.00**

Underberg Bitters, amber, lady's leg ..................................**35.00**

Union Clasped Hands, E Wormser, flask, blue, blob lip, aqua, 1-qt ....................**140.00**

Union Clasped Hands, flask, deep aqua, 1-pt ...................**70.00**

Utility, yellow-olive citron, 12-sided cylinder, 7¾" .......**39.00**

Warner's Safe Kidney & Liver Cure Rochester NY, amber, left-handed ....................**79.00**

Warner's Safe Tonic, amber, slug plate, 1-pt ...................**300.00**

Warner's Sample Safe Cure, London, honey yellow .......**500.00**

Wolf & Hornkohl Manistee, Hutchinson, NM ...........**45.00**

Wright & Taylor, Louisville KY (whiskey), dark amber, 1-pt ............................**75.00**

# Boyd Crystal Art Glass

Since it was established in 1978, this small glasshouse located in Cambridge, Ohio, has bought molds from other companies as they went out of business, and they have designed many of their own as well. They may produce several limited runs of a particular shape in a number of the lovely colors of glass they themselves formulate, none of which are ever reissued. Of course, all of the glass is handmade, and each piece is marked with their 'B-in-diamond' logo. Most of the pieces we've listed are those you're more apt to find at flea markets, but some of the rarer items may be worth a great deal more.

Our advisor for this category is Joyce Pringle who is listed in the Directory under Texas.

Airplane, Carnival Red ........**20.00**

Airplane, Heather Gray ......**15.00**

**Tramp or Baby Shoe, Bermuda Slag (ca 1985), and Deep Purple, $15.00 each.**

| | |
|---|---|
| Angel, Vaseline | 28.00 |
| Artie Penguin, Classic Black | 8.25 |
| Bear, Chocolate | 8.00 |
| Bow Slipper, Caramel | 6.00 |
| Boyd Special, 6-pc Train, Cobalt | 85.00 |
| Bunny Salt, Banana Cream | 8.00 |
| Bunny Salt, Gold Delight | 20.00 |
| Chick Salt, Crystal Carnival | 8.50 |
| Chick Salt, Oxford Gray | 22.00 |
| Chick Salt, Pocono Blue | 21.00 |
| Colonial Doll, Caramel | 12.00 |
| Debbie the Duck, Furr Green | 6.00 |
| Duckling, Kumquat | 5.00 |
| Elephant Head Toothpick, Willow Blue | 14.00 |
| Fuzzy the Teddy Bear, Plum | 15.00 |
| Hand Dish, Pippin Green | 9.50 |
| JB Scotty, Sunburst | 17.50 |
| Jeremy Frog, Nile Green | 9.50 |
| Lamb Salt, Windsor Blue | 8.50 |
| Louise Doll, Ice Blue | 36.50 |
| Louise Doll, Purple Slag | 12.00 |
| Lucky the Unicorn, Bermuda | 8.00 |
| Miss Cotton the Kitten, Mulberry Carnival | 8.00 |
| Owl, Lime | 12.00 |
| Parlour Pup, Bermuda | 10.00 |
| Pooch, Buttercup Slag | 24.00 |
| Pooch, Patriot White | 8.00 |
| Swan, Green Slag, Cambridge mold, 5" | 55.00 |
| Teddy the Tugboat, Mint Green | 12.50 |
| Willie the Mouse, Buckeye | 7.00 |
| Woodchuck, Classic Black | 12.00 |
| Zak the Elephant, Crown Tuscan | 15.00 |
| Zak the Elephant, Flame | 50.00 |

# Breweriana

Beer can collectors and antique advertising buffs as well enjoy looking for beer-related memorabilia such as tap knobs, beer trays, coasters, signs, and the like. While the smaller items of a more recent vintage are quite affordable, signs and trays from defunct breweries often bring three-digit prices. Condition is important in evaluating early advertising items of any type.

Our advisor for this category is Dan Andrews; he is listed in the Directory under California.

| | |
|---|---|
| Ashtray, Ballantine metal, 2 rests, 3-circle logo, 3½" dia, M | 15.00 |
| Bar caddy, Piel Bros Bert & Harry figures, 8½x8x3½", EX | 90.00 |
| Bottle, Claussen-Sweeny Brewing Co, Seattle WA, green blob top, 12" | 8.00 |
| Bottle opener, Schlitz Beer, wood & metal bottle shape, preprohibiton | 12.00 |
| Bottle topper, Knickerbocker Beer, trademark boy w/tray, 11x5", VG+ | 20.00 |

Calendar, Pabst Old Tankard Ale, 1936, tavern scene, 19x15", VG+ ............135.00

Clock, Dawson's Beer, pictures king, metal frame, glass front, EX ...................65.00

Clock, Lone Star Beer, plastic light-up bottle shape, NM .....165.00

Coaster, Ruppert Beer & Ale, cardboard, hands w/beer mugs, 4½", NM .........................6.00

Corkscrew, Anheuser-Busch, metal bottle shape, 23", EX .....40.00

Decal, Trommer's Beer, glass & horseshoe, 1952, 9x5", EX .5.00

Display, Coors, diecut easel, Elvira & black bat, 1992, 71", NM ..35.00

Display figure, Blatz man w/mug on tray, 1960s, 16", EX ...........................65.00

Display figure, Pabst Blue Ribbon bartender, painted pot metal, NM ...............................60.00

Drinking glass, Atlantic Premium Beer, pilsner, painted label, 5½" ...............................12.00

Foam scraper, Crown Premium Lager, plastic, 1950s, EX .25.00

Foam scraper, Rheingold, celluloid, M ...........................26.00

Label, Birk's Beer, lion logo, 1933-50, 1-qt, VG ...................16.00

Match safe, Bowler Bros, celluloid over metal, orange leaf design, G .....................................35.00

Menu cover, Hull's Beer & Ale, with insert, 1950s, 8x11", unused ...........................4.00

Mirror, Weidemann Fine Beer, reverse-painted glass, 1981, 14x20" .............................5.00

Mug, Busch Bavarian Beer, metal can shape, 1970, EX .....10.00

Mug, Miller High Life, red-painted label on clear glass, EX .............................12.00

Plate, Budweiser, Winter Day, 24k-gold trim, 1989, 8½" dia, M ...................................75.00

Playing cards, Ballantine Beer, 3-ring logo, 1960s, complete, MIB ..............................23.00

Pocket mirror, Anthracite Brewing Co, bust image of girl, VG ...................................65.00

Pocketknife, Bergner & Engle Brewing, 3-blade, VG ...60.00

Postcard, Uncle Vistar's Saloon, Tacoma WA, interior view, EX ...............................12.00

Poster, Acme Beer, colorful western scene, 1950s, 19x25", EX .................50.00

Pretzel holder, Anheuser-Busch, eagle logo, 1940s, EX .........................90.00

Stein, Budweiser, ceramic, 8½", $30.00.

Sign, Budweiser, red neon w/plastic base, 11x18", EX ......**60.00**

Sign, Miller High Life, neon, script logo, EX ...............**250.00**

Sign, Pabst, tin, train porter & conductor in window, EX ..**125.00**

Sign, Schaefer Beer, plastic light-up w/metal back, 1960s, 16" dia, EX ..........................**70.00**

Sign, Schmidt's, plastic light-up, 1980, 13x20", NM ..........**5.00**

Stein, Falstaff, w/lid, 1971, 10½", M .................................**125.00**

Tap handle, Walter's Premium Draft Beer, 1960s, EX ..**32.00**

Thermometer, Bud Lite/Spuds McKenzie, 12" dia, EX ..**12.00**

Thermometer, Old Export Beer, bottle graphic, 15x6", VG .....**40.00**

Tip tray, Adam Scheidt Brewing Co/Standard Beer, 4½" dia, VG+ ............................**130.00**

Tip tray, Hamm's Beer, cartoon bear, 1981, NM .............**10.00**

Tip tray, Indianapolis Brewing Co, 5" dia, EX ......................**45.00**

Tray, Pabst Blue Ribbon Beer, blue embossed plastic, 13" dia, NM ..................................**8.00**

Tray, Schlitz, Real Gusto, yellow & white, 13" dia, EX .........**25.00**

Tray, Trenton Old Stock Beer, 12" dia, EX ..........................**50.00**

Tumbler, Bartholomy Rochester logo, enamel on crystal, 4", EX ...............................**25.00**

# Breyer Horses

Breyer collecting has grown in popularity throughout the past several years. Though horses dominate the market, cattle and other farm animals, dogs, cats, and wildlife have also been produced, all with exacting details and lifelike coloration. They've been made since the early 1950s in both glossy and matt finishes. (Earlier models were glossy, but from 1968 until the 1990s when both glossy and semigloss colors were revived for special runs, matt colors were preferred.) Breyer also manufactures dolls, tack, and accessories such as barns for their animals.

Our advisor for this category is Carol Karbowiak Gilbert, the author of several articles for *The Model Horse Gazette* on model collecting, values, and care; she is listed in the Directory under Michigan. For more information we recommend *Schroeder's Collectible Toys, Antique to Modern* (Collector Books), and *Breyer Animal Collector's Guide* by Felicia Browell.

Appaloosa Performance Horse, gray blanket, 1984, NM ......................**95.00**

Arabian Foal, matt alabaster, 1973-82, NM ................**30.00**

Arabian Stallion, matt sorrel, 1980-93, NM ................**15.00**

Belgian, glossy dapple gray or black, 1964-67, NM, ea ...........**650.00**

Black Beauty, 1979-88, NM .**30.00**

Bucking Bronco, matt gray, 1961-67, NM .......................**150.00**

Cantering Welsh Pony, matt bay w/yellow ribbons, 1971-73, NM ..............................**100.00**

Clydesdale Stallion, glossy dapple gray w/gold bobs, 1961-65, NM ...............**150.00**

Clydesdale Stallion, woodgrain, 1960-65, NM .............**250.00**

Family Arabian Foal, glossy palomino, 1961-66, NM **15.00**

Family Arabian Mare, woodgrain, 1963-67, NM .............**100.00**

Five-Gaiter Commander, woodgrain w/blue & white ribbons, 1963-65, NM .............**200.00**

Hanoverian, matt bay, 1980-84, NM ...............**55.00**

Justin Morgan, matt bay, 1990-92, NM ...............**35.00**

Lipizzan Stallion, matt alabaster, 1975-80, NM .............**40.00**

Lying Foal, matt red roan, 1969-73, NM ...............**75.00**

Mustang, glossy alabaster, semi-rearing, 1961-66, NM .**200.00**

Mustang Foal, matt chestnut, 1976-90, G6 ...............**15.00**

Pony of the Americas, chestnut leopard appaloosa, 1976-80, NM ...............**50.00**

Proud Arabian Foal, glossy alabaster, 1956-60, NM .**40.00**

Quarter Horse Gelding, woodgrain, 1963-65, NM ....**225.00**

Quarter Horse Stallion, matt palomino, 1974-93, NM ...............**15.00**

Racehorse, woodgrain, 1958-66, NM ...............**250.00**

Ruffian, matt bay, 1977-90, NM ...............**35.00**

Running Foal, matt alabaster, 1963-71, NM ...............**45.00**

Running Stallion, matt alabaster, 1968-71, NM ...............**125.00**

Stock Horse Mare, matt sorrel, 1983-86, NM ...............**35.00**

Stock Horse Stallion, appaloosa, 1981-86, NM ...............**40.00**

Western Horse, glossy black, 1959-62, NM .............**150.00**

Western Pony, glossy palomino, 1956-67, NM ...............**40.00**

**Traditional Scale: Running Mare and Running Foal, glossy dapple gray, 1963 – 73, $75.00; $45.00.**

# Bubble Bath Containers

Figural bubble bath containers were popular in the 1960s and have become highly collectible today. The Colgate-Palmolive Company produced the widest variety, called Soakies. Purex's Bubble Club characters were also popular. Most Soaky bottles came with detachable heads made of brittle plastic which cracked easily. Purex bottles were made of a softer plastic but lost their paint easier. Condition affects price considerably.

The interest collectors displayed in the old bottles prompted many to notice foreign-made products. Some of the same characters have been licensed by companies in Canada, Italy, the UK, Germany, and Japan, and the bottles they've designed have excellent detail. They're usually a little larger than domestic bottles and though fairly recent are often reminiscent of those made in the US during the 1960s.

For more information we recommend *Collector's Guide to Bubble Bath Containers* and *Schroeder's Collectible Toys, Antique to Modern*. Both are published by Collector Books. The following prices are for containers in excellent to near-mint condition, unless noted otherwise.

Alvin (Chipmunks), Soaky, red sweater w/white A, w/puppet ..............................**75.00**
Atom Ant, Purex, orange w/red accents ...........................**50.00**
Baba Louie, Purex, brown w/blue scarf & green hat ..........**35.00**
Barney Rubble, Purex, brown & yellow, 1960s .................**30.00**
Big Bad Wolf, Tubby Time, gray & red w/cap head, 1960s ......................**40.00**
Brutus (Popeye), red shorts with red & white striped shirt ........................**40.00**
Cinderella, Soaky, movable arms, 1960s ...........................**35.00**
Cookie Monster, Minnetonka, holding sailboat ..............**8.00**
Deputy Dawg, Colgate-Palmolive, 1960s ..........................**30.00**

Droop-A-Long Coyote, Purex, pink w/blue & orange accents, green hat .......................**40.00**
Elmer Fudd, Soaky, in hunting outfit .............................**30.00**
Flipper, Kid Care, riding a wave ..**8.00**
Fozzie Bear, Calgon, Treasure Island outfit .................**10.00**

**Frankenstein, Colgate-Palmolive, NM, $100.00.**

Goofy, Colgate-Palmolive, red, white & black w/cap head, 1960s ............................**25.00**
Huckleberry Hound, bank, Knickerbocker, red & black, w/contents ....................**65.00**
Irwin Troll, Lander, 1970s, w/contents ..............................**25.00**
King Louie, Colgate-Palmolive, slipover only, 1960s ......**25.00**
Lucy (Peanuts), Avon, red dress, 1970, MIB ......................**25.00**
Magilla Gorilla, Purex, movable or non-movable arms, 1960s, ea ................................**60.00**

Mighty Mouse, Soaky .........25.00
Miss Piggy, Calgon, Treasure Island outfit ..............10.00
Mouseketeer Girl, Colgate-Palmolive, red outfit, 1960s .............30.00

**Mr. Magoo, 10", NM, $50.00.**

Oscar the Grouch, Minnetonka, holding trash can lid .......................10.00
Panda Bear, Tubby Time, cap head, 1960s ..................30.00
Pebbles Flintstone, Purex, 1960s .........................40.00
Popeye, Soaky, white suit w/blue accents, 1960s, MIB ......55.00
Punkin' Puss, Purex, orange body w/blue clothes ..............40.00
Ricochet Rabbit, Purex, movable or non-movable arms, 1960s, ea ....................50.00
Santa Claus, Colgate-Palmolive, NMIB .........................30.00
Schroeder (Peanuts), Avon, 1970, MIB ...........................35.00

Simon (Chipmunks), Soaky, green sweater with white S, with/puppet .................75.00
Snoopy, Avon, Flying Ace outfit, 1969, MIB .....................30.00
Snow White, Soaky, movable arms ...........................35.00
Spider-Man, Colgate-Palmolive, NMIB ...........................55.00
Superman, Soaky, blue with red outfit ...........................50.00
Tasmanian Devil, Kid Care, standing in inner tube .............8.00
Tidy Toy Race Car, red or blue w/movable wheels, ea .50.00

**Top Cat, Colgate-Palmolive, 1960s, NM, $45.00.**

Tweety Bird, Soaky, standing on cage ..............................30.00
Wendy the Witch, Soaky, NM .30.00
Yakky Doodle Duck, Roclar (Purex), w/contents .......25.00
Yogi Bear, bank, Purex, 1961 .40.00

# Cake Toppers

The first cake toppers appeared on wedding cakes in the 1880s and were made almost entirely of sugar. The early 1900s saw toppers carved from wood and affixed to ornate plaster pedestal bases and backgrounds. A few single-mold toppers were even made from poured lead. From the 1920s to the 1950s bisque, porcelain, and chalkware figures reigned supreme. The faces and features on many of these were very realistic and lifelike. The beautiful Art Deco era was also in evidence.

Celluloid kewpie types made a brief appearance from the late 1930s to the 1940s. These were quite fragile because the celluloid they were made of could be easily dented and cracked. The true Rose O'Neill kewpie look-alike also appeared for awhile during this period. During and after World War II and into the Korean Conflict of the 1950s, groom figures in military dress appeared. Only a limited amount was ever produced; they are quite rare. From the 1950s into the 1970s, plastics were used almost exclusively. Toppers took on a vacant, assembly-line appearance with no specific attention to detail or fashion.

In the 1970s, bisque returned and plastic disappeared. Toppers were again more lifelike. For the most part, they remain that way today. Wedding cakes now often display elegant and elaborate toppers such as those made by Royal Doulton and Lladro.

Toppers should not be confused with the bride and groom doll sets of the same earlier periods. While some smaller dolls could and did serve as toppers, they were usually too unbalanced to stay upright on a cake. The true topper consisted of a small bride and groom anchored to (or part of) a round flat base which made it extremely stable for resting on a soft, frosted cake surface. Cake toppers never did double-duty as play items.

Our advisor for this category is Jeannie Greenfield, who is listed in the Directory under Pennsylvania.

Art Deco-style heads, crepe-paper, 1920s ............................**75.00**
Basalt carved figures, 1940s, single-pc ...........................**20.00**

**Sailor and bride, chalkware, 4½", $35.00. (Photo courtesy Jeannie Greenfield)**

Kewpies, bisque w/molded plaster base .................................**95.00**
Kewpies, celluloid w/crepe-paper outfits, bride wears headband, 3" .........................**25.00**
Kissing couple, bisque, newer .**20.00**
Marine dress uniform on groom, bisque, 4½" ....................**35.00**
Sailor uniform on groom, all plaster, 4½" ..........................**35.00**
World War II military couple, plaster w/paper base ....**30.00**
1920s couple, all bisque, bride in dropped-waist gown, 4" .**30.00**

# California Potteries

In recent years, pottery designed by many of the artists who worked in their own small studios in California during the 1940s through the 1960s has become highly sought after, and prices on the secondary market have soared. As more research is completed and collectors are introduced to the work of previously unknown artists, the field continues to expand. Items made by Kay Finch, Brayton, Howard Pierce, and Sascha Brastoff often bring high prices (especially the Finch pieces) and have been considered very collectible for several years. Now such names as Matthew Adams, Marc Bellaire, and deLee are attracting their share of attention as well.

It's a fascinating field, one covered very well in Jack Chipman's *Collector's Encyclopedia of California Pottery, Second Edition.* Specific companies/designers are featured in these books: *Collector's Encyclopedia of Howard Pierce Porcelain* by Darlene Hurst Dommel; *Collectible Kay Finch* by Martinez, Frick, and Frick; *Collector's Encyclopedia of Sascha Brastoff* by Steve Conte, A. Dewayne Bethany, and Bill Seay; and *Collector's Guide to Don Winton Designs* by Mike Ellis. All are published by Collector Books. See also Bauer; Fransiscan; Metlox.

### Adams, Matthew

Bowl, seal, oval, 9" ...............**60.00**
Cup & saucer, sled on blue .**25.00**
Pitcher, Eskimo, 13" ...........**90.00**
Platter, house, 12" ..............**50.00**
Tumbler, cabin ....................**24.00**

### Bellaire, Marc

Ashtray, Bird Isle, black birds on cream, 8" ......................**85.00**
Bowl, Mardi Gras, free-form, lg .**125.00**
Box, Mardi Gras, 10" dia ...**200.00**

**Ashtray, Mardi Gras, $165.00. (Photo courtesy Pat and Kris Secor)**

Platter, Friendly Island, 10" .**135.00**
Vase, Mardi Gras, hourglass
shape, 8" ....................**125.00**
Vase, Polynesian Woman, 9" .**125.00**

## Brayton Laguna

Ashtray, hand painted, marked, 7"
sq ...................................**30.00**
Box, French peasants, round .**50.00**
Cookie jar, Calico Dog .......**595.00**
Figurine, Dopey, Disney ....**325.00**
Figurine, horse, abstract, black,
9½" ...............................**250.00**
Figurine, horses, Pa & Ma, pr ..**225.00**
Figurine, matador & bull, multi-
color & woodtone ........**250.00**
Figurine, quails, B-40/B-41, pr .**225.00**
Figurine, ringmaster, 8" ......**85.00**
Figurine, toucan, 9" ...........**150.00**
Figurine, zebra, sm ............**100.00**
Flower holder, peasant lady, 8" ..**85.00**
Flower holder, Sally ............**50.00**
Planter, rabbit, sm ...............**75.00**
Teapot, Provincial, brown, tulip
stand ............................**125.00**
Toothbrush holder, Gingham
Dog ............................**125.00**

## Cleminson Pottery

Ashtray, stylized fruit, footed,
7" ...............................**32.00**
Butter dish, Distlefink ........**25.00**
Cookie jar, Potbellied Stove .**200.00**
Creamer, rooster .................**20.00**
Cup & saucer, Gramma's ....**35.00**
Drip jar, Cherry, w/lid .........**40.00**
Hairpin holder, soldier ........**30.00**
Pitcher, Distlefink, 9½" .......**35.00**
Plaque, grapes, 6½x6½" ......**35.00**
Ring holder, bulldog ............**25.00**
Shakers, Katrina, pr ...........**40.00**

Bank, jalopy, 3¾", $40.00. (Photo
courtesy Beverly and Jim Mangus)

Spoon rest, fruit ...................**27.00**
Sprinkler, Chinese boy ........**40.00**
String holder, heart form ....**45.00**
Tray, Distlefink, 12" ............**30.00**
Wall pocket, frying pan .......**45.00**

## DeForest of California

Condiment jar, Cheezy ........**30.00**
Dip set, Dippy Pig, Dippy at cen-
ter, 11" tray ...................**85.00**
Hors de'oeuvre, Pig, unmarked ..**15.00**
Pitcher, Perky, 2-qt .............**70.00**
Plate, salad; Bar-B-Cutie, 6" .**20.00**
Platter, Hammy, Go Ahead Make
a Pig of Yourself ...........**65.00**
Rolling pin, Don't Dally in This
Galley, from $75 to .......**85.00**
Shakers, Bar-B-Cutie, unmarked,
pr ...................................**35.00**
Shakers, Cocky & Henny chickens,
unmarked, pr ...............**50.00**
Spoon rest, Spooners, couple's
heads, from $75 to ........**95.00**
Tea set, stacking teapot, creamer,
sugar bowl w/lid, 4-pc ...**70.00**
Tureen, Bar-B-Cutie, w/ladle .**200.00**

## deLee

Ashtray, skunk match holder in
tail, 5" dia, from $45 to .**60.00**

Candle holder, Twinkle or Star, ea, from $25 to ..............**35.00**

Figurine, Danny, tipping bowler hat, incised deLee Art 1947, 9" .................**50.00**

Figurine, June, girl seated w/open book, 4", from $65 to .....**85.00**

Figurine, Mickey, kitten playing w/ball, 4", from $45 to ..**60.00**

Head vase, Bobby Pin Up, lady w/locket, 3½", from $60 to ...........**90.00**

## Finch, Kay

Ashtray, German shepherd, #5331, 5¾" sq, from $65 to .......**85.00**

Canister, Santa's face on white cylinder, 10½" .............**275.00**

Figurine, angel, #114A, #114B or #114c, from $75 to ......**100.00**

Figurine, camel, #464, 5", minimum value ..................**450.00**

Figurine, colt, #4806, 11", from $250 to .........................**350.00**

Figurine, donkey, long-eared, #4768, 4" .....................**120.00**

**Cat, Ambrosia, 10½", minimum value, $700.00. (Photo courtesy Pat and Kris Secor)**

Figurine, elephant, Mumbo, #4804, 4" .......................**250.00**

Figurine, fish, #5008, 7" ..**150.00**

Figurine, Jezebel, #179, 6x9", from $300 to .........................**325.00**

Figurine, lamb, kneeling, #136, 2¼" ................................**65.00**

Figurine, minkey, Socko, #4841, 4¼" ...............................**235.00**

Figurine, owl, Tootsie, #189, 3¾" ...............................**65.00**

Figurine, pig, Winkie, #185, or Sassy, #144, 4", ea ...**150.00**

Figurine, Scandie boy & girl, #126/127, 5¼", pr, from $125 to ..................................**150.00**

Mug, Missouri Mule, solid green, 4½" ...............................**100.00**

## Florence Ceramics

Note: The amount of applied decoration — lace, flowers, etc. — has a great deal of influence on values. Our ranges reflect this factor.

Ann, any color other than yellow, 6", from $55 to ...........**190.00**

Beth, beige or green, 7½", from $100 to .........................**150.00**

David, pink or green, 7½", from $100 to .........................**275.00**

Eugenia, moss green, 9", from $250 to .........................**400.00**

Karla (Ballerina), various colors, 9¾", from $200 to .....**450.00**

Love Letter, yellow, 10", from $450 to ..................................**900.00**

Matilda, green w/violet trim, 8½", from $100 to ...............**250.00**

Prince Charming & Cinderella, white w/gold trim, 11¾", from $900 to .....................**1,300.00**

Sally, rose or white w/gold trim, 6¾", from $35 to ...........**50.00**

Suzette (flower holder), peasant girl, 7" ...........................**65.00**

Virginia, rose on green, 8½x7", from $400 to ................**600.00**

Wendy (flower holder), ivory with pink trim, 6½", from $50 to .........................**75.00**

## Freeman-McFarlan

Ashtray, turquoise ..............**15.00**

Figurine, bald eagle, 13" ...**185.00**

Figurine, Mickey, pomeranian dog .............................**185.00**

Figurine, snow owl, 5" .........**45.00**

## Gilner

Figurine, Bali dancer, lg .....**60.00**

Figurine, pixie sits on plants & mushrooms ....................**30.00**

Pin dish, pixie inside, turquoise, 6" ...................................**23.00**

Planter, pixie sits on log ......**25.00**

## Kindell, Dorothy

Ashtray, Beachcombers .......**75.00**

Lamp bases, Siamese dancers, pr ............................**375.00**

Mug, nude handle, from $28 to .**35.00**

Shakers, nude handles, pr ..**75.00**

## Schoop, Hedi

Bowl, Oriental style w/dragons .**65.00**

Darner Doll, pink & green stripes .......................**250.00**

Figurine, Dutch girl, 10½" ..**85.00**

Figurine, rooster, lg ..........**175.00**

Lamp, peasant lady figural .**225.00**

Hula girl, 11¾", $165.00. (Photo courtesy Pat and Kris Secor)

Vase, duck form ..................**75.00**

## Simmons, Robert

Figurine, Chirpee, bird on branch, 6½" ...............................**12.50**

Figurine, collie ....................**45.00**

Figurine, Dear Me, deer ......**45.00**

Figurine, Nutsy or Frisky squirrel, ea ...................................**12.00**

Figurine, Skidoo, giraffe, #2021, 7" ..................................**25.00**

## Twin Winton

Ashtray, Bambi ..................**100.00**

Bank, kitten .........................**50.00**

Candy jar, turtle, rabbit finial .**85.00**

Canister, House (tea) ...........**50.00**

Ice bucket, Men of the Mountains, Clem w/jug sitting on barrel .........................**200.00**

Lamp, monkey figural .......**175.00**

Mug, Men of the Mountains, w/hillbilly handle .........**30.00**

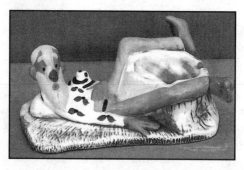

**Twin Winton, Ashtray, Hillybilly Line, Men of the Mountains, Clem, 3½" tall, $50.00. (Photo courtesy Michael Ellis)**

Napkin holder, cow ............**85.00**
Planter, bear beside stump .**50.00**
Punch cup, Men of the Mountains, w/hillbilly handle ..........**15.00**
Salt & pepper shakers, churn, pr ..............................**40.00**
Salt & pepper shakers, foo dog, pr ...............................**125.00**
Salt & pepper shakers, pirate fox, pr ..................................**45.00**
Spoon rest, cow ...................**40.00**
Stein, Ladies of the Mountains, w/lady handle ...............**70.00**

## Weil Ware

Coffee server, Malay Blossom .**30.00**
Dealer's plaque ....................**75.00**
Dish, dogwood, divided, square, 10½" ............................**15.00**
Figure vase, standing child, 8" .**35.00**
Pitcher, Malay Blossom .......**30.00**
Plate, dinner; Bamboo .........**12.00**

## Will-George

Figurine, cardinal on branch, 10" ............................**75.00**
Figurine, flamingo, head up, 12" ..........................**135.00**

Figurine, monk, terra-cotta face w/brown robe, 4" ..........**50.00**
Pitcher, chicken figural, multicolor, 7" ...........................**125.00**
Wine, chicken figural, multicolor, 5" ...................................**55.00**

## Yona

Figurine, mother & daughter, 9½" & 7½", pr ....................**175.00**
Planter, embossed man & woman, 2 handles, footed, 6x8" .**35.00**
Sugar bowl, clown ...............**20.00**
Wall pocket, clown & pig, tub forms pocket, dated 1957, 7" ...............................**65.00**

# Cameras

Whether buying a camera for personal use, adding to a collection, or for resale, use caution. Complex usable late-model cameras are difficult to check out at sales, and you should be familiar with the camera model or have confidence in the seller's claims before purchasing one for your personal use. If you are just beginning a camera collection, there are a multitude of different types and models and special features to select from in building your collection; you should have on hand some of the available guide books listing various models and types. Camera collecting can be a very enjoyable hobby and can be done within your particular funding ability.

Buying for resale can be a very profitable experience if you are careful in your selection and have made arrangements with buyers who have made their requirements known to you. Generally, buying low-cost, mass-produced cameras is not advisable; you may have a difficult time finding a buyer for such cameras. Of these low-cost types, only those that are mint or new in the original box have any appreciable appeal to collectors. Very old cameras are not necessarily valuable — it all depends on availabilty. The major criterion is quality; prices offered for mint-condition cameras may be double or triple those of average-wear items. You can expect to find that foreign-made cameras are preferred by most buyers because of the general perception that their lenses and shutters are superior. The German- and Japanese-made cameras dominate the 'classic' camera market. Polaroid cameras and movie cameras have yet to gain a significant collector's market.

The cameras listed here represent only a very small cross section of thousands of cameras available. A (+) at the end of the line indicates cameras that are generally considered the most popular user-type cameras, not including later model AutoFocus cameras or point-and-shoot cameras. Values are given for cameras with average wear and in good working order; they represent average retail prices with limited guarantees. It is very important to note that purchase prices at flea markets, garage sales, or estate sales would have to be far less for them to be profitable for a resaler because of the significant expense of servicing the camera, testing it, and guaranteeing it to a user or collector.

Our advisor, Gene Cataldo (of Gene's Cameras), is listed in the Directory under Alabama.

Agfa, Isolette .........................**25.00**
Agfa, Karat 3.5, 1940 ..........**35.00**
Aires, 35III, 1958 .................**40.00**
Ansco, Memar, 1956-59 .......**25.00**
Ansco, Speedex, Standard, 1950 .**15.00**
Argus A2F, 1939-41 .............**20.00**
Argus C4, 50/2.8 lens w/flash .**25.00**
Baldi, by Balda-Werk, Germany, 1930s ............................**35.00**
Bolsey, B2 ............................**25.00**
Braun Paxette I, 1952 .........**40.00**
Canon A-1 ..........................**190.00**
Canon AE-1 ........................**110.00**
Canon AE-1P .....................**140.00**
Canon F-1 ...........................**225.00**
Canon IIB, 1949-52 ...........**250.00**
Canon III, 1951-53 .............**225.00**
Canon S-11, 1947-49 .........**375.00**
Canon 7, 1961-64 ...............**300.00**
Ciroflex, TLR, 1940s ...........**40.00**

Contax II or III, 1936-42, from $300 to ........................**450.00**

Contessa 35, 1950-55 ........**150.00**

Detrola Model D, Detroit Corp, 1938-40 ........................**30.00**

Eastman Folding Brownie Six-20 ..............................**15.00**

Eastman Premo, many models available, any ...............**35.00**

Edinex, by Wirgin ...............**40.00**

Exakta VX, 1951 ................**80.00**

Fujica AX-3 ........................**100.00**

Fujica ST-701 ......................**70.00**

Hit Camera, sm novelty, Japan, various names, any .......**12.00**

**Kodak Retina Model IIIc, 35mm, Germany, 1954 – 57, $150.00. (Photo courtesy Gene's Cameras)**

Kodak Autoreflex TC, various models, from $60 to .....**90.00**

Kodak Baby Brownie, Bakelite .**12.00**

Kodak Bantam, Art Deco design, 1935-38 ......................**350.00**

Kodak Box Brownie 2A ........**7.00**

Kodak Box Hawkeye No 2A ..**8.00**

Kodak Hawkeye, plastic ......**10.00**

Kodak No 1 Folding Pocket .**30.00**

Kodak No 3A Folding Pocket .**40.00**

Kodak Retina I ...................**50.00**

Kodak Retina II .................**65.00**

Kodak Retina IIa ................**90.00**

Kodak Retinette, various models, from $30 to ...................**45.00**

Kodak Signat 35 .................**30.00**

Kodak 35, with range finder, 1940-51 ........................**30.00**

Konica III, 1956-59 .............**80.00**

Mamiya-Sekor 500TL, 1966 .**35.00**

Mamiyaflex 1, TLR, 1951 ..**140.00**

Mercury, Model II, 1945 .....**40.00**

Minolta HiMatic Series, various models, from $15 to ........................**20.00**

Minolta SR-7 .....................**50.00**

Minolta SRT 101 ...............**75.00**

Minolta SRT 202 ...............**90.00**

Minolta XD-11, 1977 ........**175.00**

Minolta XG-1 .....................**60.00**

Minolta X700 ....................**145.00**

Minolta-16, miniature, various models ...........................**25.00**

Minox B (Spy Camera) ......**125.00**

Miranda Automex II, 1963 ..**70.00**

Nikkormat FTN ................**125.00**

Nikon EM ...........................**75.00**

Nikon FG ...........................**135.00**

Nikon FM ...........................**195.00**

Olympus CM-2 ..................**150.00**

Olympus OM-1 ..................**120.00**

Olympus OM-10 .................**75.00**

Olympus Pen EE, compact half frame ...........................**35.00**

Olympus 35IV, 1949-53 .......**50.00**

Pax-M3, 1957 ....................**50.00**

Pentax Spotmatic, many models, from $50 to .................**125.00**

Pentex K-1000 ..................**110.00**

Pentex ME .........................**100.00**

Petri FT, FT1000 or FT-EE, ea ..**70.00**

Petri 7, 1961 .....................**20.00**

Polaroid, most models, from $5 to .................................**10.00**

Polaroid, SX-70, from $30 to .**50.00**

Praktica FX, 1952-57 ..........**50.00**

Praktica Super TL, 1968-74 .**60.00**

Realistic Stereo, 3.5 lens ...**120.00**

Regula, King, various models, fixed lens ........................**40.00**
Ricoh Diacord L, TLR, built-in meter, 1958 ..................**80.00**
Ricoh KR-30 .......................**115.00**
Rolleicord II, 1936-50 .........**90.00**

**Rolleiflex 2.8E2, circa 1960, from $400.00 to $600.00. (Photo courtesy Gene's Cameras)**

Rolleiflex Automat, 1937 ...**125.00**
Samoca 35, 1950s .................**35.00**
Seroco 4x5, Folding Plate, Sears, 1902, from $90 to ........**125.00**
Topcon Super D, 1963-74 ..**135.00**
Topcon Uni ...........................**50.00**
Tower 50 (Sears), w/Cassar lens ..**18.00**
Univex, Universal Camera Co, 1935-39 ..........................**25.00**
Voigtlander Bessa, various folding models, 1931-49 ............**40.00**
Voigtlander Bessa, w/range finder, 1936 .............................**140.00**
Voigtlander Vito II, 1950 ....**50.00**
Yashica A, TLR ...................**45.00**
Yashica Electro 35, 1966 .....**30.00**
Yashica FX-1, 1975 ..............**50.00**
Yashica FX-70 ......................**75.00**
Zeiss Baldur Box Tengor, Frontar lens, ca 1935, from $35 to .**50.00**
Zeiss-Ikon Box Tengor 43/2, 1934-38 ..................................**40.00**

Zenit E, Russian .................**35.00**
Zorki 4, Russian ..................**70.00**

# Candlewick

Candlewick was one of the all-time bestselling lines of The Imperial Glass Company of Bellaire, Ohio. It was produced from 1936 until the company closed in 1982. More than 741 items were made over the years; and though many are still easy to find today, some (such as the desk calendar, the chip and dip set, and the dresser set) are a challenge to collect. Candlewick is easily identified by its beaded stems, handles, and rims characteristic of the tufted needlework of our pioneer women for which it was named. For a complete listing of the Candlewick line, we recommend *Elegant Glassware of the Depression Era* by Gene Florence (Collector Books).

Ashtray, eagle, #1776/1, 6½" .**55.00**
Ashtray, sq, #400/651, 3¼" .........**40.00**
Bell, #400/108, 5" .................**80.00**
Bowl, belled, #400/63B, 10½" .**60.00**
Bowl, fruit; #400/3F, 6" .......**12.00**
Bowl, jelly; w/lid, #400/59, 5½" .**65.00**
Bowl, salad; #400/75B, 10½" .**45.00**
Candle holder, urn, holders on circle center bead, #400/129R, 6", ea .................................**200.00**
Cigarette box, w/lid, #400/134 ..**45.00**
Compote, low, plain stem, #400/66B, 5½" ..............**25.00**
Creamer, bridge; #400/122, individual ...........................**14.00**
Egg cup, lg bead foot, #400/19 .**47.50**

**Cake stand, high foot, 11", $80.00.**

Icer, seafood or fruit cocktail; #400/53/3, 3-pc ..............95.00
Marmalade set, liner saucer, jar, lid & spoon, #400/89, 4-pc ...48.00
Oil, beaded base, #400/164, 4-oz ..50.00
Pitcher, low foot, #400/19, 16-oz .300.00
Plate, birthday cake (holes for 72 candles), #400/160, 14" .425.00
Plate, salad; #400/3D, 7" .......8.00
Plate, w/indent, #400/50, 8" 13.00
Plate, 2 handles, crimped, #400/52C, 6¾" ..............32.00
Salt dip, #400/61, 2" .............11.00
Saucer, after dinner; #400/77AD ..10.00
Stem, cordial; #400/190, 1-oz ........................85.00
Stem, wine; #3400, 4-oz .......25.00
Tray, condiment; #400/148, 5¼x9¼" ..........................65.00
Tumbler, footed, #3400, 12-oz .17.00
Vase, beaded foot, flared rim, #400/21, 8½" ..............225.00

## Candy Containers

If you're old enough to be the parents of a baby boomer, you'll remember the glass candy containers we used to buy at the 5-&-10¢ store filled with tiny, multicolored candies. Dogs, guns, lanterns, cars, ships, rabbits, horns, busses, trains, and lamps were common. But as each new design hit the store counters, we'd scurry to buy it up, and add the container to the rows and rows we already had at home. Today's collectors have a little more serious approach to their shopping — some of the rarer examples can carry four-figure price tags. For instance, Felix on the Pedestal with original black paint intact carries a value of $4,000.00! A Flossie Fisher Bed realized an auction price of over $5,000.00! But there are many that can still be bought for under $100.00, so don't let those extremely high prices discourage you.

For more information, we recommend *The Collector's Guide to Candy Containers* by Doug Dezso and Leon and Rose Poirier (Collector Books). References to plate numbers in the descriptions that follow correspond with this book. Our values are given for candy containers that are undamaged, in good original paint, and complete (with all parts and closure). See also Clubs and Newsletters.

Airplane (Boyd), plate #77, from $25 to ..........................30.00
Baby Chick, plate #7, from $100 to ...........................125.00
Barney Google on pedestal, plate #189, from $250 to ...350.00
Circus dog w/hat, plate, #21, from $20 to ..........................40.00
Dog by barrel, plate #19, from $225 to ......................250.00

Fish, plate #44, from $200 to .**250.00**
Gun, grooved barrel, plate #392, from $25 to ................**35.00**
Jack-o'-lantern, slant eyes, plate #265, from $175 to .................**225.00**
Pumpkin witch, plate #272, from $550 to .....................**650.00**

**Rabbit With Laid Back Ears, plate 70, LE Smith, early 1900s, 4¼", from $100.00 to $125.00.**

Rabbit eating carrot, plate #55, from $60 to ..................**80.00**
Rabbit on dome, plate #65, from $450 to ........................**525.00**
Rabbit w/basket on arm, plate #64, from $100 to ...............**150.00**
Rocking horse w/rider, plate #47, from $175 to ...............**225.00**
Rolling pin, plate #310, from $250 to ...............................**300.00**
Santa in chimney, plate #281, from $125 to ...............**200.00**
Scotty dog, plate #35, from $20 to ...............................**35.00**

Turkey gobbler, plate #75, from $175 to .......................**225.00**
Victory Lines bus, plate #156, from $45 to ...........................**75.00**

# Cape Cod by Avon

Now that Avon has discontinued their Cape Cod line, don't be surprised to see prices on the upward swing. They'd been making this dark ruby red glassware since the '70s, and there seems to be a good supply of it around today. In addition to the place settings (there are plates in three sizes, soup and dessert bowls, a cup and saucer, tumblers in two sizes, three different goblets, a mug, and a wine glass), there are many lovely accessory items as well. Among them you'll find a cake plate, a pitcher, a platter, a hurricane-type candle lamp, a butter dish, napkin rings, and a pie plate server. Note: mint-in-box items are worth about 20% more than the same piece with no box.

Our advisors for this cateogry, Debbie and Randy Coe, are listed in the Directory under Oregon.

Bell, hostess; marked 1979, 6½" ..........................**22.50**
Bell, hostess; unmarked, 1979-80, 6½" .....................**17.50**
Bowl, dessert; 1978-90, 5" ...**14.50**
Bowl, rimmed soup; 1991, 7½" ....**18.00**
Bowl, vegetable; 100th Anniversary, Centennial Edition..., 8¾" ..............................**34.50**
Bowl, vegetable; unmarked, 1986-90, 8¾" ......................**24.50**

Butter dish, 1983 – 84, ¼-lb, 7" long, $22.50. (Add 20% for original box.)

Box, heart form, w/lid, 1989-90, 4" wide ..............................**18.00**

Cake knife, plastic handle, Regent Sheffield, 1981-84 ..........**9.50**

Candle holder, hurricane type w/clear chimney, 1985, 13" ...........**35.00**

Candlestick, 1975-80, 8¾", ea .**12.50**

Candlestick, 1983-84, 2½", ea ..**9.75**

Christmas ornament, 6-sided, marked Christmas 1990, 3¼" ..............................**10.00**

Creamer, footed, 1981-84, 4" .**12.50**

Cup & saucer, 15th Anniversary, marked 1975-90 on cup, 7-oz ............................**24.50**

Cup & saucer, 1990-93, 7-oz .**19.50**

Decanter, w/stopper, 1977-80, 16-oz ....................................**20.00**

Goblet, champagne; footed, 1991, 8-oz, 5¼" ........................**9.50**

Goblet, claret; footed, 1992, 5-oz, 5¼" ..............................**8.50**

Goblet, water; footed, 1976-90, 9-oz ......................................**9.50**

Goblet, wine; footed, 1977-80, 3-oz ................................**5.00**

Gravy boat w/attached liner, 1988 only ..............................**28.50**

Mug, pedestal foot, 1982-84, 6-oz, 5" ....................................**12.50**

Napkin ring, 1989-90, 1¾" dia .**9.50**

Pie plate, server, 1992-93, 10¾" dia ..................................**19.50**

Pitcher, water; footed, 1984-85, 60-oz ............................**50.00**

Plate, dessert; 1980-90, 7½" ....................**9.50**

Plate, dinner; 1982 – 1990, 10", $19.50. (Add 20% for original box.)

Platter, oval, 1986, 13" ........**35.00**

Salt & pepper shakers, marked 1978, ea ..........................**8.50**

Sugar bowl, footed, 1980-83,
3½" ..............................**12.50**
Tidbit tray, 2-tier (7" & 10" dia),
1987, 9¾" ......................**49.50**
Tumbler, straight sided, footed,
1988, 8-oz, 3¾" ...............**8.50**
Tumbler, straight sided, 1990, 12-
oz, 5½" ............................**9.50**
Vase, footed, 1985, 8" .........**20.00**

Reading Girl, 1910-25, 12x8½" .**85.00**
Sailor Girl, by Jenkins, 1934,
13½" ..............................**70.00**
Shirley Temple, ca 1935-45,
10" .........................**165.00**
Snow White, 1937-50, 14" ...**85.00**
Three Little Pigs, ashtray, ca
1935-45, 6½x5¼" ..........**40.00**
Windmill, 1935-40, 10¾" .....**25.00**

# Carnival Chalkware

Chalkware statues of Kew-
pies, glamour girls, assorted dogs,
horses, etc., were given to winners
of carnival games from about 1910
until the 1950s. Today's collectors
especially value those representing well-known personalities such
as Disney characters and comic
book heroes. Refer to *The Carnival
Chalk Prize* by Tom Morris for
more information. Mr. Morris is in
the Directory under Oregon.

Apache Babe, 1936-45, 15" ..**75.00**
Buddy Lee, ca 1920-30, 13½" .**95.00**
Elephant, standing & dancing, ca
1930-40, 10" .................**45.00**
Girl w/Banjo, 1940s, 13¼" ...**85.00**
Hula Girl, ca 1940-50, 17" .**175.00**
I Love Me Girl, 1915-30, 11¼" .**85.00**
Lighthouse, 1935-40, 12¼" ..**45.00**
Majorette, 1949, 12" ...........**50.00**
Mexican Girl, marked Jenkins, ca
1925, 14½" ...................**195.00**
Ming Toy, marked Jenkins, ca
1924, 13" ......................**195.00**
Miss America, ca 1940-50, 15¾" ..**85.00**
Owl, sm prize, flat back, ca 1935-
50, up to 5½" .................**10.00**
Piano Baby, 1910-25, 10½" .**120.00**

**Bashful Nude Bather, no mark, ca
1930s, $55.00. (Photo courtesy Tom
Morris)**

# Cat Collectibles

Cat lovers are often quite fer-
vent in their attachment to their
pets, and for many their passion
extends into the collecting field.
There is no shortage of items to
entice them to buy, be they figural pieces, advertising signs, postcards, textiles, books, candy containers, or what have you. Mar-
bena Fyke has written two amusing and informative books called
*Collectible Cats, Identification*

and *Value Guide, Volume I* and *Volume II*. If you're a cat lover yourself, you're sure to enjoy them.

Our advisor for this category is Mariyn Dipboye; she is listed in the Directory under Michigan. See the Clubs and Newsletters section for ordering information concerning her newsletter *Cat Talk*. See also Black Cats; Character Collectibes.

Cookie jar, blue-gray cat with pink trim, painted ceramic, 10", $40.00. (Photo courtesy Cat Collector)

Book, A Dog & His Cat, Kurt Unkelbach, Prentice-Hall, 1969, w/jacket ...............**20.00**

Bottle, Cleopatra's Cat, w/bath oil beads, Elizabeth Arden, 1982, 7" ...................................**60.00**

Box of catnip leaves, VO Toys, 29¢ original price, 1-oz, 4½x5", NM, $15.00. (Photo courtesy Cat Collector)

Christmas pin, gold cat w/silver stocking ...........................**8.00**

Clock, plastic Garfield face, digital with alarm, M, 7" ......................**55.00**

Cookie jar, black & gray fat cat w/pink trim & rosebud, ceramic, 10" ..................**40.00**

Cookie jar, black & white cat w/fish, King Fong Pottery, 10¾" ..............................**35.00**

Cuff links, black arch-backed cats, silver details .................**25.00**

Figurine, Cat Nap, pewter, Little Gallery/Hallmark, 1981, 2¾" ..............................**50.00**

Figurine, Figaro, ceramic, Hagen-Renaker/Walt Disney, 1955-60, 2½" ..........................**75.00**

Figurine, resin composition, Whiskers, Martha Carey, 1985, 3¾" ......................**32.50**

Figurine, Tender Loving Care, pewter, Little Gallery/Hallmark, 1½" ..................................**50.00**

Lamp, ceramic tiger figural, ca 1950-60, 14½", shade not original ................................**35.00**

Pin, Scottish clan crest badge, pewter w/lion & SANSPEUR, 1¾" ...............................**20.00**

Plate, Mother's Day 1971, mother/daughter w/cats, Royal Copenhagen, 6" ............**28.00**

Plate, tabby face on cream, gold border, Mt Clemens, Hallmark, 1935, 6" ...............**25.00**

Stringholder, black & cream cat face w/string ball, chalkware, 6¾" ..............................**65.00**

Towel, day of week w/cat doing chores, cross-stitch, 1940s, set of 7 ................................**75.00**

## Cattail Dinnerware

Cattail was a dinnerware pattern popular during the late 1920s until sometime in the 1940s. So popular, in fact, that ovenware, glassware, tinware, and even a kitchen table was made to coordinate with it. The dinnerware was made primarily by Universal potteries of Cambridge, Ohio, though a catalog from Hall China Co. circa 1927 shows a three-piece coffee service, and there may have been other pieces made by Hall as well. Cattail was sold for years by Sears Roebuck and Company, and some items bear a mark with their name.

The pattern is unmistakable — a cluster of red cattails (usually six but sometimes only one or two) with black stems on creamy white. Shapes certainly vary; Universal used a minimum of three of their standard mold designs — Camwood, Old Holland, Laurella — and there were possibly others. Some Cattails say 'Wheelock' on the bottom. Wheelock was a department store in Peoria, Illinois.

If you are trying to decorate a '40s vintage kitchen, no other design could afford you more to work with. To see many of the pieces that are available and to learn more about the line, read *The Collector's Encyclopedia of American Dinnerware* by Jo Cunningham (Collector Books).

Our advisors for Cattail Dinnerware are Ken and Barbara Brooks, who are listed in the Directory under North Carolina.

Batter jug, w/metal lid, from $80 to ...................................**100.00**

Bowl, mixing; 9", from $28 to .**30.00**

Bowl, Old Holland shape, marked Wheelock, 6" ....................**7.00**

Butter dish, w/lid, 1-lb ........**50.00**

Cake cover & tray, tinware .**35.00**

Canister set, tinware, 4-pc, from $45 to .............................**60.00**

**Casserole, lid doubles as pie plate, $45.00. (Photo courtesy Ken and Barbara Brooks)**

Casserole, w/lid ....................**30.00**

Coffeepot, 3-pc ......................**70.00**

Cookie jar, from $85 to ......**100.00**

Cracker jar, barrel shape, from $75 to .............................**85.00**

Creamer, Laurell shape, from $20 to ...................................**25.00**

Custard cup ............................**8.00**

Gravy boat, w/liner, from $35 to ...............................**45.00**

Jug, refrigerator; w/handle .35.00
Jug, side handle, cork stopper .35.00
Kitchen scales, tinware .......40.00
Match holder, tinware .........35.00
Pie plate ...............................30.00
Pie server, hole in hanger for hanging, marked Universal Potteries ........................25.00
Pitcher, glass, w/ice lip, from $100 to ...................................125.00
Pitcher, utility or milk .........30.00
Pitcher, w/ice lip, from $75 to .80.00
Plate, dinner; Laurell shape, from $15 to ............................20.00
Plate, dinner; 3-compartment ..30.00
Plate, salad or dessert ...........6.50
Plate, serving; early, marked Universal...OvenProof...Ohio, from $35 to ....................40.00
Platter, oval ..........................30.00
Salad set (fork, spoon & bowl), from $50 to ....................60.00
Salt & pepper shakers, different styles, ea pr, from $15 to .............................20.00
Saucer, Old Holland shape, marked Wheelock ...........6.00
Shaker set (salt/pepper/flour/sugar), glass, on red metal tray, $40 to ....................45.00
Stack set, 3-pc w/lids, from $35 to ..................................40.00
Sugar bowl, 2-handled, w/lid, from $20 to ............................25.00
Tablecloth ............................90.00
Teapot, w/lid, from $40 to ...50.00
Tumbler, iced tea; glass, from $35 to ...................................40.00
Tumbler, marked Universal Potteries, scarce, from $65 to .............70.00
Tumbler, water; glass ..........35.00
Waste can, step-on style, tinware ...........................35.00

# Ceramic Arts Studio

Whether you're a collector of American pottery or not, chances are you'll like the distinctive styling of the figurines, salt and pepper shakers, and other novelty items made by the Ceramic Arts Studio of Madison, Wisconsin, from about 1938 until approximately 1952. They're not especially hard to find — a trip to any good flea market will usually produce at least one good buy from among their vast array of products. They're easily spotted, once you've seen a few examples; but if you're not sure, check for the trademark — most are marked.

The CAS Collector's Association is listed under Clubs and Newsletters in the back of this book. They not only publish a quarterly newsletter but a comprehensive value guide as well.

**Bell, Lillibell, 6½", from $85.00 to $90.00.**

Bank, Mr Blankety Blank, 4½" .90.00
Figurine, Al, hunter, 6¼" ....90.00
Figurine, Bedtime Girl, 4¾" .75.00
Figurine, Bright Eyes, cat, 3" .38.00
Figurine, Dinky, girl skunk ..25.00
Figurine, Drummer Girl ......75.00

**Figurines, Gay '90s couple, 6¾", 6½", $130.00 for the pair.**

Figurine, Hansel & Gretel, pr .100.00
Figurine, Little Bo Peep, 5½" ..28.00
Figurine, Lucindy & Col Jackson, pr ..................................100.00
Figurine, mouse & cheese, snuggle type, pr .........................25.00
Figurine, Mr Skunk, 3" long .50.00
Figurine, panda w/hat, 2½" .145.00
Figurine, sea horse & coral, snuggle type, 3½", 3", pr ......70.00
Figurine, Violet Ballerina, 3" ..125.00
Figurine, Wee Dutch boy & girl, 3", pr ..............................32.00
Head vase, African man, 8" .160.00
Metal accessory, birdcage w/perch for Birds, 14" .................65.00
Metal accessory, sofa, for Maurice & Michele, 10x3¾" ........65.00
Pitcher, Pine Tree ...............50.00

Planter, Bamboo ..................22.00
Plaque, Comedy, 5" ..............75.00
Plaque, Greg & Grace, pr ..135.00
Plaque, Harlequin & Columbine, black & white w/green, pr ..........135.00
Salt & pepper shakers, boy in chair, snuggle type, 2¼", pr .......75.00
Salt & pepper shakers, Calico Cat & Gingham Dog, pr ....125.00
Salt & pepper shakers, Dem & Rep, 4½", pr ................200.00
Salt & pepper shakers, elf & mushroom, pr ................65.00
Salt & pepper shakers, mouse in cheese, snuggle type, 2½", pr ...............................38.00
Salt & pepper shakers, ox & covered wagon, 3", pr .......125.00
Salt & pepper shakers, spaniel mom & pup, 2¼", 2¾", pr .........80.00
Salt & pepper shakers, Wee Chinese boy & girl, sm, pr .............45.00
Shelf sitter, boy w/dog, 4¼" .65.00
Shelf sitter, farm girl ...........45.00
Shelf sitter, Jack & Jill, 4¾", 5", pr ...................................80.00
Shelf sitter, Pete parrot, maroon ......................65.00
Teapot, swan form, open, mini .50.00
Vase, bud; Lu Tang by bamboo, 7" ...................................45.00
Vase, rose motif, round, 2¼" ..30.00

# Cereal Boxes and Premiums

When buying real estate, they say 'location, location, location.' When cereal box collecting its 'character, character, character.' Look for Batman, Quisp, Superman, or Ninja Turtles — the so-called 'Grain Gods' emblazoned across the box. Dull adult and health cereals such as Special K or Shredded Wheat, unless they have an exciting offer, aren't worth picking up (too boring). Stick to the cavity-blasting presweets aimed at kids, like The Jetsons, Froot Loops, or Trix. You can hunt down the moldy FrostyOs and Quake from childhood in old stores and pantries or collect the new stuff at your supermarket. Your local cereal aisle — the grain ghetto — is chock full of future bluechips, so squeeze the moment! The big question is: once you've gotten your flaky treasures home, how do you save the box? If you live where pests (bugs or mice) aren't a problem, display or store the box unopened. Otherwise, eat its contents, then pull out the bottom flaps and flatten the package along the fold lines. If you don't want to flatten the box, empty it by gently pulling out the bottom flaps and removing the bag. Be sure to save the prize inside, called an inpack, if it has one; they're potentially valuable too. Prices are for cereal boxes that are full or folded flat, in mint condition.

Our advisor for this category is Scott Bruce (Mr. Cereal Box); he is listed in the Directory under Massachusetts. For further information we recommend *Cerealizing America, The Unsweetened Story of American Breakfast Cereal,* by Scott Bruce and Bill Crawford; and *Cereal Box Bonanza* and *Cereal Boxes & Prizes: 1960s,* both by Mr.

Bruce. See Clubs and Newsletters for information on *Flake, The Breakfast Nostalgia Magazine.*

**Boxes**

All Stars, walking finger puppets (Wizard of Oz), 1960 ...**150.00**
Alpha Bits, baseball cards, 1963 ........................**175.00**
Cap'n Crunch, comic books, 1963 ........................**250.00**
Cheerios, King Leonardo mask, 1961 ............................**100.00**

Kellogg's Cocoa Krispies, Snagglepuss on front, $225.00. (Photo courtesy Scott Bruce)

Cocoa Puffs, train station (Cocoa Puff kids), 1961 ...........**250.00**
Corn Flakes, Huck Hound stampets printing set, 1961 ...**125.00**
Count Off, astronaut book, 1962 ........................**200.00**
Crispy Critters, football cards, 1962 ............................**350.00**

Frosted Flakes, Tony Tiger stuffed toys, 1963 ....................**200.00**

FrostyO's, Indian bead set (Frosty bear), 1962 ..................**200.00**

Grape Nut Flakes, modern jetliner models, 1960 ...............**125.00**

Jets, tooter-tune toys, 1960 .**150.00**

Krinkles, Plymouth (So-Hi), 1960 ..........................**125.00**

Life, Shari Lewis finger puppets, 1962 ............................**125.00**

Maypo, Marky Maypo shirt offer, 1961 ............................**200.00**

OK's, pin-me-ups (Yogi Bear), 1962 ............................**300.00**

Raisin Bran, Bugs Bunny postcards, 1961 ...................**100.00**

Rice Krispies, Yogi & Huck stuffed toys, 1960 ....................**200.00**

Spoon Size Shreaded Wheat, totem-pole head, 1961 ..**65.00**

Sugar Crisp, baseball trading cards, 1961, from $250 to ........**350.00**

Sugar Pops, Mark Wilson's trick (Sugar Pops Pete), 1961 .........................**125.00**

Sugar Smacks, color-by-numbers (Smaxey Seal), 1960 ...**125.00**

Sugar Stars, supersonic jet model, 1962 ............................**500.00**

Top 3, introductory (3 sheep), 1960 ..........................**125.00**

Trix, Nestle's Quik (rabbit puppet), 1961 ...................**200.00**

Twinkles, grab-bag flaps, 1963 .**175.00**

Wheaties, classic comics, 1960 .**150.00**

## Premiums

Bullwinkle electronic quiz game, 1962 ...............................**75.00**

Car, 1960 Impala model, 1960 ....................**175.00**

Car, 1963 Ford hardtop, 1963 ..**125.00**

Cocoa Puff kids crazy train, 1959-61 ..................................**100.00**

Dennis the Menace mug & bowl, 1962 ..............................**50.00**

Frontier hero medals, 1960, ea ..........................**10.00**

Handy & Dandy bears mug & bowl, 1960 .....................**75.00**

Howdy Doody rings, 1960 ...**25.00**

Huck Hound stampets printing set, 1961 ........................**45.00**

Linus the Lion stuffed toy, 1963 .........................**95.00**

Tony the Tiger stuffed toy, 1963 .........................**75.00**

Toucan Sam stuffed toy, 1964 ...**45.00**

Trix the Rabbit breakfast set, 1964 ............................**125.00**

Twinkle the Elephant sponge, 1960-61 ..........................**50.00**

USS Nautilus model, 1961 ..**75.00**

Window banner, I Want My Maypo!, 1961 ...............**400.00**

**Yogi Bear bank, Kellogg's, 1965, 9½", from $25.00 to $35.00. (Photo courtesy Scott Bruce)**

Woody Woodpecker door knocker, 1964 .......................**100.00**

Yogi Bear game cloth, 1962 ..**65.00**

## Character and Promotional Glassware

Once routinely given away by fast-food restaurants and soft-drink companies, these glasses have become very collectible; and though they're being snapped up by avid collectors everywhere, you'll still find there are bargains to be had. The more expensive are those with Disney or Walter Lantz cartoon characters, super-heroes, sports greats, or personalities from Star Trek or the old movies. For more information refer to *Collectible Drinking Glasses* by Mark E. Chase and Michael J. Kelley (Collector Books), and *The Collector's Guide to Cartoon and Promotional Drinking Glasses* by John Hervey (L-W Book Sales). See Club and Newsletters for information on Collector Glass News.

Al Capp, Brockway, 1975, footed, 16-oz, 5 different, ea from $30 to .......................**50.00**

Animal Crackers, Chicago Tribune, 1978, any except Louis, ea from $7 to ..............**10.00**

Animal Crackers, Chicago Tribune, 1978, Louis, scarce, from $25 to ..................**50.00**

Apollo Series, Marathon Oil, 4 different, ea from $2 to .......**4.00**

Archies, Welch's, 1971, 6 different, ea .................................**3.00**

Archies, Welch's, 1973, 6 different, ea .................................**3.00**

Avoid the Noid, Domino's Pizza, 1988, 4 different, ea ........**7.00**

Battlestar Galactica, Universal Studios, 1979, 4 different, ea .............................**10.00**

BC Ice Age, Arby's, 1981, 6 different, ea from $3 to ...........**5.00**

Cleveland Browns, Wendy's/Dr Pepper, 1981, 4 different, ea from $5 to .......................**8.00**

Currier & Ives, Arby's, 1978, numbered, 4 different, ea from $3 to .....................................**5.00**

Dallas Cowboys, Dr Pepper, 6 different, ea from $7 to .......................**15.00**

Dinosaurs, Welch's, 1989, 4 different, ea ...........................**2.00**

Donald Duck, Donald Duck Cola, 1960s-70s, from $15 to .**20.00**

Elsie the Cow, Borden, 1960s, yellow daisy image, from $10 to .................................**12.00**

ET, Pepsi/MCA Home Video, 1988, 6 different, ea from $15 to .................................**25.00**

ET, Pizza Hut, 1982, 4 different, ea from $2 to ..................**4.00**

Flintstone Kids, Pizza Hut, 1986, 4 different, ea from $2 to ....**4.00**

Friendly Monsters, Burger Chef, 1977, 6 different, ea from $20 to ..................................**35.00**

Goonies, Godfather's Pizza/ Warner Bros, 1985, 4 different, ea $4 to ...............................**8.00**

Great Muppet Caper, McDonald's, 1981, 4 different, ea ........**2.00**

Happy Days, Dr Pepper, 1977, Fonzie or Richie, ea from $8 to .................................**12.00**

**Archies, Welch's Jellies & Preserves, set of six, $3.00 each. (Photo courtesy Paris and Susan Manos)**

Hot Dog Castle, Collector Series, 1977, 3 different, ea from $6 to ......................................**8.00**

Howdy Doody, Welch's/Kagran, 1950s, 6 different, ea from $15 to ....................................**20.00**

Indiana Jones & the Temple of Doom, 7-Up, 1984, 4 different, ea $8 to ..........................**15.00**

Jungle Book, Disney/Canada, 1966, 6 different, ea from $30 to ....................................**60.00**

Jungle Book, Disney/Pepsi, 1970s, Bagheera or Shere Kahn, ea from $60 to ....................**90.00**

Jungle Book, Disney/Pepsi, 1970s, Mowgli, from $40 to .....**50.00**

Jungle Book, Disney/Pepsi, 1970s, Rama, from $50 to ........**60.00**

Keebler, Soft Batch Cookies, 1984, 4 different, ea from $7 to ...**10.00**

King Kong, Coca-Cola/Dino De Laurentis Corp, 1976, from $5 to ......................................**8.00**

Mark Twain Country Series, Burger King, 1985, 4 different, ea ...........................**10.00**

Masters of the Universe, Mattel, 1983, 4 different, ea from $5 to ....................................**10.00**

McDonaldland Action Series, McDonald's, 1977, 6 different, ea ....................................**5.00**

McVote, McDonald's, 1986, 3 different, ea ........................**10.00**

Mickey's Christmas Carol, Coca-Cola, 1982, 3 different, ea ...............................**10.00**

Mister Magoo, Polomer Jelly, several variations, ea from $25 to ....................................**35.00**

NFL, Mobil Oil, rocks, flat, 4 different, ea from $2 to ....**4.00**

NFL, Mobil Oil, rocks, footed, 5 different, ea from $3 to .**5.00**

Night Before Christmas, Pepsi, 1982-83, 4 different, ea from $4 to ...............................**6.00**

Norman Rockwell Summer Scenes, Arby's, 1987, 4 different, ea from $3 to ...........**5.00**

Philadelphia Eagles, McDonald's, 1980, 5 different, ea from $4 to ....................................**6.00**

Pillsbury Doughboy, 1991, premium, w/musical instruments, from $6 to ......................12.00

Pinocchio, Dairy Promo/Libbey, 1938-40, 12 different, ea from $15 to ..........................25.00

Pocahontas, Burger King, 1995, 4 different, MIB, ea ...........3.00

Popeye Pals, Popeye's Fried Chicken, 1979, 4 different, ea from $10 to ..........................20.00

Presidents & Patriots, Burger Chef, 1975, 6 different, ea from $7 to ......................10.00

Rescuers, Pepsi/Brockway, 1977, 4 different, ea from $8 to .15.00

Ringling Bros Circus Clowns, Pepsi/Federal, 1976, 8 different, ea ......................12.00

Roy Rogers Restaurant, 1883-1983 logo, from $8 to ............12.00

Sleeping Beauty, American, 1950s, 6 different, ea from $15 to ..........................20.00

Smurf's, Hardee's, 1982, 8 different, ea from $1 to ...........3.00

Snoopy for President, Dolly Madison Bakery, 4 different, ea from $4 to ......................6.00

Snoopy Sport Series, Dolly Madison Bakery, 4 different, ea from $4 to ......................6.00

Snow White & the Seven Dwarfs, Bosco, 1938, ea from $25 to ..........................45.00

Star Trek, Dr Pepper, 1976, 4 different, ea from $20 to ...25.00

Star Trek, Dr Pepper, 1978, 4 different, ea from $30 to ..........................40.00

Star Trek: The Motion Picture, Coca-Cola, 1980, 3 different, ea from $10 to ..............15.00

Sunday Funnies, 1976, any except Broom Hilda, ea from $8 to ..........................15.00

Sunday Funnies, 1976, Broom Hilda, from $100 to ....150.00

Super Heroes, Marvel/Federal, 1978, 5 different, ea from $100 to ..........................200.00

Super Heroes, Marvel/7-Eleven, 1977, 5 different, ea from $20 to ..........................25.00

Twelve Days of Christmas, Pepsi, 1976, ea from $1 to .........3.00

Universal Monsters, 1980, footed, 6 different, ea from $75 to .125.00

Universal Monsters, 1980, tapered, 4 different, ea from $35 to ..........................50.00

Urchins, Coca-Cola, 1976-78, 6 different, ea from $3 to ......5.00

**Wolfman, Universal Monsters, from $35.00 to $50.00.**

Warner Bros, Welch's, 1974, sayings around top, 8 different, ea from $2 to ..................4.00

99

Warner Bros, Welch's, 1976, names around bottom, 8 different, ea from $5 to ......**7.00**

Winnie the Pooh, Sears/WDP, 1970s, 4 different, ea from $7 to ..................**10.00**

Wizard of Oz, Swift's, 1950s-60s, Glinda, fluted bottom, from $15 to ..................**25.00**

Wizard of Oz, Swift's, 1950s-60s, Wicked Witch, fluted bottom, from $35 to ..................**50.00**

Ziggy, 7-Up Collector Series, 4 different, ea from $4 to ......**7.00**

## Character Clocks and Watches

The first character timepieces were designed in the 1930s, when Ingersoll made not only a clock, but a wristwatch and a pocket watch as well, all featuring that popular Disney character, Mickey Mouse. Since then, hundreds of comic and sports figures have graced the faces of as many watches. Of course, these were designed for kids, so few of the older models exist today in a state good enough to interest collectors. Rust, fading, scratches, or other signs of wear sharply devaluate a clock or a watch, while original packaging can add a great deal — in some cases, as much as the watch itself.

If you're going to collect them, you'll need to study *Comic Character Clocks and Watches* by Howard S. Brenner (Books Americana) for more information.

Batman & Robin, talking alarm clock, 3-D image, Janex, 1974, EX ..................**50.00**

Betty Boop, pendulum, painted wood figure w/center dial, Poppo, EX ..................**500.00**

Bozo the Clown, alarm clock, Larry Harmon/French, 1960s, rare, EX ..................**150.00**

**Bugs Bunny Talking Alarm Clock, Janex, 1974, 'Eh, Wake Up Doc,' MIB, $75.00.**

Bugs Bunny, travel alarm, glow-in-the-dark hands, Seth Thomas, 1970, M ..........**65.00**

Cinderella, alarm clock, leaving slipper on steps, Bradley, MIB ..................**125.00**

Fred Flintstone, ceramic figure w/dial in center, Sheffield, 1960s, EX ..................**185.00**

Max Headroom, wall clock, NMIB ..................**65.00**

Mickey Mouse, alarm clock, analog movement, Phinney-Walker, 1960s, EX ..................**75.00**

Mickey Mouse, wall clock, metal alarm clock shape, Hamilton, 1970s, EX ..................**75.00**

Mighty Mouse, alarm clock, Mighty mouse points time, 1960s, NM ..................**85.00**

Pinocchio, alarm clock, Jiminy Cricket on his head, Bayard, 1939, NM .....................**250.00**

Pluto, wall clock, plastic figure, hands shaped as dog bones, 8", NMIB .....................**450.00**

**Raggedy Ann and Andy Talking Alarm Clock, Equity, NM, from $25.00 to $35.00.**

Roy Rogers, alarm clock, Roy on Trigger, Ingraham, 1940, NM (VG box) .....................**385.00**

Tweety Bird, talking alarm clock, Janex, 1978, EX ............**75.00**

Woody Woodpecker, alarm clock, image at Cafe tree, Westclox, 6", EX .........................**175.00**

## Watches

Archie, head revolves as it ticks, red band, Rouan, 1960s, NM .**100.00**

Batman, Batwing hands, black plastic wings enclose face, Marcel, 1960, EX ..........................**200.00**

Bozo the Clown, Bozo on face, red band, Bradley, 1960s, EX ...........................**75.00**

Cinderella, pink band, w/plastic Cinderella figure, Timex, 1958, NMIB .................**150.00**

Dick Tracy, beige band, New Haven/New Syndicate, 1948, EX (EX box) ................**300.00**

Dukes of Hazzard, stainless steel band, LCD Quartz, 1981, NRFB ............................**40.00**

Flintstones, image of Fred & Pebbles, red band, Bradley, 1960s, NM .....................**65.00**

Mickey Mouse, rectangular face, red band, Ingersoll, 1947, NMIB ..........................**350.00**

Nightmare Before Christmas, digital, Timex, MIP ....................**45.00**

Porky Pig, Porky tipping hat, blue band, Sheffield, 1960s, NMIB .........................**150.00**

Roy Rogers, rectangular face, brown band, Ingraham, 1951, NMIB ..........................**400.00**

Rudolph, rectangular chrome case, red band, USA, EX ......................**75.00**

**Snoopy, Hero-Time Watch, with patch, Determined, MIB, $100.00.**

Space Mouse, black & white image, red band, Webster, 1960s, MIB ....................**65.00**
Tom Corbett, lightning bolt hands, metal band, Ingraham, 1951, NM ..............................**165.00**

# Character Collectibles

One of the most active areas of collecting today is the field of character collectibles. Flea markets usually yield some of the more common items — toys, books, lunch boxes, children's dishes, and sheet music are for the most part quite readily found. Trade papers are also an excellent source. Often you will find even the rare and hard-to-find listed for sale. Disney characters, television personalities, and comic book heroes are among the most sought after.

For more information, refer to *Schroeder's Collectible Toys, Antique to Modern*; *Cartoon Toys & Collectibles* by David Longest; *Collector's Guide to TV Toys & Memorabilia, 2nd Edition,* by Greg Davis and Bill Morgan; *G-Men and FBI Toys and Collectibles* by Harry and Jody Whitworth; and *Cartoon Friends of the Baby Boom Era* by Bill Bruegman (see the Directory under Ohio). With the exception of the Brugeman book, all are published by Collector Books.

See also Advertising; Advertising Watches; Banks; Books; Bubble Bath Containers; Cereal Boxes and Premiums; Character and Promotional Glassware; Character Clocks and Watches; Cookie Jars; Fast Foods; Games; Lunch Boxes; Novelty Telephones; Pencil Sharpeners; Puzzles; Radios, Novelty; Star Trek; Star Wars; View-Master Reels and Packets; Western Heroes.

## Batman

Batman was created in 1939 by Bob Kane. He's been imortalized in comic books, TV and movie cartoons, and finally on the silver screen. A plethora of related merchandise has been marketed over the years. Items from the late '60s are often marked National Periodical Publications.

Batarang, Ideal, 1966, black plastic, came w/utility belt, 8", NM ..............................**100.00**
Batmobile pedal car, 1966, plastic, 34", EX ........................**575.00**

**Batman charm bracelet, National Periodical Publications, 1966, MOC, $125.00. (Photo courtesy June Moon)**

Cartoon-a-Rama Animation Art Set, 1977, MIB (sealed) ..**50.00**
Colorforms, 1966, few pcs missing, NMIB ............................**40.00**
Flicker ring, plastic, NM .....**20.00**
Hat/mask, 1966, felt hat w/dropdown mask, Pow! patch on front, NM ......................**25.00**

Helmet & cape, plastic & vinyl, Ideal, 1966, NM (EX box) .........**200.00**

Mask, Batman Returns, Penguin, Morris, 1992, latex, EX .**50.00**

Magic slate, Watkins-Strathmore, 1966, VG .......................**50.00**

Magic slate, Batman Returns, Golden, 1992, MIP (sealed) .........**4.00**

Official Bat Chute, NPPI, 1966, MOC .............................**40.00**

Thingmaker mold, Mattel, 1965, for rings or rubber stamps, EX ...............................**35.00**

## Betty Boop

Betty Boop was developed by the Fleischer Studios in 1930. All in all, there were about one hundred black and white cartoons produced during that decade. Very few of these early cels remain today. Many of the cartoons were copied and colored in the '60s, and these cels may still be found. Hoards of related items were marketed in the '30s, and many others were produced over the next forty years. During the '80s, still others graced the retail market. One of the leading companies in this resurgence of popularity was Vandor; they came out with dozens of different ceramic items. Another innovative company is Bright Ideas of San Francisco; they feature items ranging from playing cards to Christmas tree light sets. King Features still owns the copyright, and all items should carry the appropriate labeling.

Ashtray, Betty sitting at piano, Vandor #0618, from $75 to .............**80.00**

Bookends, jukebox, 1981 ...**165.00**

Napkin holder with salt and pepper shakers, Vandor, from $50.00 to $65.00. (Photo courtesy Helene Guarnaccia)

Box, bust, Vandor, 1985 ......**60.00**

Box, T-Bird, 1986 ................**85.00**

Clock, Betty's Kitchen, Vandor, 1995 .............................**50.00**

Creamer & sugar bowl, Tropico, w/lid .............................**75.00**

Dish, Betty sitting on cresent moon face, Vandor #0676, 1989, from $30 to .........**35.00**

Doll, compo & wood, original decal, 12", EX .......................**685.00**

Doll, Play by Play Toys, 1992, stuffed cloth w/vinyl head, 14", EX .........................**15.00**

Doll, stuffed cloth w/mask face, redressed, rare, EX .....**100.00**

Fan, Japan, prewar, image of Betty w/movable eyes, 12", NM ...............................**400.00**

Figure, Japan, prewar, bisque, playing drum, 3½", EX ........**125.00**

Figure, Jaymar, 1930s, jointed wood, 4¼", M ..............**100.00**

Figure, marked Made in USA, cardboard, metal joints, wood base, 9", EX .................**450.00**

Figure, NJ Croce, 1988, bendable, 8", MOC .........................**15.00**

Frame ................................**45.00**

Mask, Bimbo, celluloid, 6x6",
NM ............................**175.00**
Mask, head, 1981 .................**65.00**
Mug, bust, 1981 ...................**35.00**
Music box, piano or jukebox, ea .**125.00**
Stringholder, Vandor ...........**65.00**
Teapot, 1 arm is handle, 2nd is
spout, Vandor, 1995, mini-
mum value .....................**35.00**
Transfers, Japan, 1935, set of 12,
NMOC ...........................**25.00**
Utensil holder, Vandor, 1995, sm,
from $15 to ....................**25.00**

## California Raisins

In the fall of 1986, the California Raisins made their first com-
mercials for television. In 1987 the
PVC figurines were introduced.
Initially there were four: a singer,
two conga dancers, and a saxophone player. At this time, Hardee's issued similar but smaller figures. Later that year Blue Surfboard (horizontal), and three Ben-
dees (which are about 5½" tall
with flat pancake-style bodies)
were issued for retail sale.

In 1988 twenty-one Raisins
were made for sale in retail stores
and in some cases used for promo-
tional efforts in grocery stores:
Blue Surfboard (vertical), Red
Guitar, Lady Dancer, Blue/Green
Sunglasses, Guy Winking, Candy
Cane, Santa Raisin, Bass Player,
Drummer, Tambourine Lady
(there were two styles), Lady
Valentine, Male Valentine, Boy
Singer, Girl Singer, Hip Guitar
Player, Sax Player with Beret, and
four Graduates. The Graduates

are identical in design to the original four characters released in
1987 but stand on yellow pedestals
and are attired in blue graduation
caps and yellow tassels. Bass Player and Drummer were initially distributed in grocery stores along
with an application to join the California Raisin Fan Club located in
Fresno, California. Later that year
Hardee's issued six more: Blue
Guitar, Trumpet Player, Roller
Skater, Skateboard, Boom Box,
and Yellow Surfboard. As was true
with the 1987 line, the Hardee's
characters were generally smaller
than those produced for retail
sales.

Eight more made their debut in
1989: Male in Beach Chair, Green
Trunks with Surfboard, Hula Skirt,
Girl Sitting on Sand, Piano Player,
'AC,' Mom, and Michael Raisin. Dur-
ing that year the Raisins starred in
two movies: *Meet the Raisins* and *The
California Raisins — Sold Out*, and
were joined in figurine production by
five movie characters (their fruit and
vegetable friends): Rudy Bagaman,
Lick Broccoli, Banana White,
Leonard Limabean, and Cecil
Thyme.

The latest release of Raisins
came in 1991 when Hardee's issued
four more: Anita Break, Alotta Stile,
Buster, and Benny. All Raisins
issued for retail sales and promotions
in 1987 and 1988, including Hardee's
issues for those years, are dated with
the year of production (usually on the
bottom of one foot). Of those Raisins
released for retail sale in 1989, only
the Beach Scene characters are

dated, and they are actually dated 1988. Hardee's Raisins, issued in 1991, are also undated.

In the last two years, California Raisins have become extremely popular collectible items and are quickly sold at flea markets and toy shows. On Friday, November 22, 1991, the California Raisins were enshrined in the Smithsonian Institution to the tune of *I Heard It Through the Grapevine*. We recommend *Schroeder's Collectible Toys, Antique to Modern*, for further information about the many miscellaneous items relating to California Raisins that are available. Listings are for loose items in mint condition unless noted otherwise.

Applause, Captain Toonz, w/boom box, Hardee's 2nd Promotion, 1988 ...............................**3.00**

**Applause, Michael Raisin, Special Edition, 1989, M, $20.00.**

Applause, Rollin' Rollo, Hardee's 2nd Promotion, 1988, sm ...............................**3.00**

Applause, SB Stuntz, Hardee's 2nd Promotion, 1988, sm .........**3.00**

Applause, Trumpy Trunote, Hardee's 2nd Promotion, 1988, sm .........................**3.00**

Applause, Waves Weaver I, Hardee's 2nd Promotion, 1988, sm .........................**4.00**

Applause, Waves Weaver II, Hardee's 2nd Promotion, 1988, sm ....**6.00**

Applause-Claymation, Banana White, Meet the Raisins 1st Edition, 1989 ................**20.00**

Applause-Claymation, Lick Broccoli, Meet the Raisins 1st Edition, 1989 ......................**20.00**

Applause-Claymation, Rudy Bagaman, Meet the Raisins 1st Edition, 1989 ................**20.00**

CALRAB, Blue Surfboard, connected to foot, Unknown Promotion, 1988 ................**35.00**

CALRAB, Blue Surfboard, not connected to foot, Unknown Promotion, 1987 ................**50.00**

CALRAB, Christmas Issue, w/red hat, 1988, ........................**9.00**

CALRAB, Guitar, red guitar, 1st Commercial Issue, 1988 .............................**8.00**

CALRAB, Hands, left hand up, right down, Post Raisin Bran Issue, 1987 ......................**4.00**

CALRAB, Microphone, Post Raisin Bran Issue, 1987 .............**6.00**

CALRAB, Saxophone, gold sax, no hat, 1st Key Chains, 1987 .**5.00**

CALRAB, Saxophone, inside of sax painted red, Post Raisin Bran Issue ...............................**4.00**

CALRAB, Sunglasses, index finger touching face, 1st Key Chains ........................**5.00**

CALRAB, Sunglasses, Post Raisin Bran Issue ......................**4.00**

CALRAB, Sunglasses II, eyes not visible, 1st Commercial Issue ..............................**6.00**

CALRAB, Sunglasses II, eyes visible, 1st Commercial Issue .......**25.00**

CALRAB, Winky, hitchhiking, 1st Commercial Issue ...........**6.00**

CALRAB-Applause, Alotta Stile, Hardee's 4th Promotion, MIP ..............................**12.00**

CALRAB-Applause, Bass Player, 2nd Commercial Issue ....**8.00**

CALRAB-Applause, Boy in Beach Chair, Beach Theme Edition .......................**15.00**

**CALRAB-Applause, Boy With Surfboard, Beach Theme Edition, purple board, brown base, 1988, $10.00.**

CALRAB-Applause, Cecil Tyme (carrot), Meet the Raisins 2nd Promotion ....................**175.00**

CALRAB-Applause, Drummer, 2nd Commercial Issue ....**8.00**

CALRAB-Applause, Hands, graduate w/thumbs at head, Graduate Key Chains ..........**85.00**

CALRAB-Applause, Hip Band Guitarist (Hendrix), 3rd Commercial Issue ................**25.00**

CALRAB-Applause, Lenny Lima Bean, Meet the Raisins 2nd Promotion ....................**150.00**

CALRAB-Applause, Microphone (female), 2nd Key Chains ....................**45.00**

**CALRAB-Applause, 'Mom' Lulu Arborman, Meet the Raisins, Second Promotion, yellow hair, pink apron, 1989, $150.00.**

CALRAB-Applause, Mom, Meet the Raisins 2nd Promotion .**150.00**

CALRAB-Applause, Saxophone, 3rd Commercial Issue ..**15.00**

CALRAB-Applause, Singer (female), 2nd Commercial Issue .....**16.00**

CALRAB-Applause, Valentine, Special Lover's Edition ...**8.00**

Backpack, maroon & yellow w/3 figures, 1987, EX ..........**35.00**

Ballpoint pen, set of 3 w/figures on top, M ..........................**65.00**

Baseball cap, 1988, EX ..........**5.00**

Belly bag, blue or yellow nylon fabric w/Conga Line, 1988, EX ................................**25.00**

Book, Birthday Boo Boo, 1988, EX ................................**12.00**

Bulletin board, Singer & Conga Line, Rose Art, 1988, MIP ..............**35.00**

Clock, wall-type wristwatch, red or blue, 1987, EX, ea ........**85.00**

Coloring book, Sports Crazy, 1988, EX ..................................**5.00**

Doll, vinyl w/suction cups, 1987, sm version, EX .............**10.00**

Figural, Imperial Toy, 1987, inflatable vinyl, 42", MIB ........**55.00**

Game, California Raisins board game, Decipher Inc, 1987, MIB ..............................**25.00**

Halloween costume, complete with gloves, M, from $25 to ...........................**45.00**

Lapel pin, girl, base player or microphone, PVC, 1988, MOC, ea ...................................**15.00**

Official Fan Club Watch set, MIP ..............................**50.00**

Picture album, 1988, EX .....**25.00**

Puffy Stick-On, 1987, EX ....**10.00**

Puppet, female w/yellow shoes, Bendy/Sutton Happenings, 1988, MIB ......................**30.00**

Puzzle, American Publishing, 1988, 500-pc, MIB .........**20.00**

Radio, AM/FM, figure with posable arms & legs, 1988, MIB ..........................**75.00**

Record, I Heard It Through the Grapevine, 45rpm, 1987, EX (EX sleeve) ...................**20.00**

Record, Meet the Raisins, 33⅓ rpm, EX (EX cover) ......**20.00**

Refrigerator magnets, Hands, Orange Sunglasses, Microphone, 1988, ea .............**75.00**

School kit, w/promotion ideas, activities, recipes, etc, 1998, M ...............................**30.00**

Shoulder bag, blue & orange w/dancing Raisins, 1988, MOC ..............................**25.00**

Sleeping bag, purple, 1988, EX ............................**40.00**

Slippers, fuzzy, child's, 1988, M ................................**55.00**

Sticker book, unused, M ......**25.00**

Tambourine, Raisins on stage, 1987, EX ........................**15.00**

Tote bag, yellow w/Conga Line, 1987, EX ........................**20.00**

Umbrella, lady Raisins on beach, 1988, EX ........................**45.00**

Video, Meet the Raisins, 1988, MIP ..............................**25.00**

Watercolor-Paint-by-Numbers, Rose Art, complete, 1988, EX ..............................**30.00**

Windup toy, figure w/yellow or green shoes & bracelet, 1988, MOC, ea ........................**25.00**

Wristwatch, lady Raisin w/yellow tambourine, 1988, M ....**75.00**

## Dick Tracy

The most famous master detective of them all, Dick Tracy stood for law and order. Whether up against Boris Arson or the Spider Gang, he somehow always came out on top, teaching his young followers in no uncertain terms that 'Crime Does Not Pay.' Many companies parlayed his persona through hundreds of items for retail sales; and radio premiums such as badges, buttons, secret code books, and rings were free just for 'sending in.' In 1990 with the release of the movie, a new round of potential collectibles appeared.

Camera, Seymour, 1950s, 127mm, scarce, NMIB .............. **100.00**

Cartoon kit, Colorforms, 1962, complete, EX (EX box) ..**75.00**

Figure, Bonnie Braids, Charmore, 1951, plastic, 1¼", NMOC .**50.00**

Figure, Dick Tracy, Rubb'r Niks, complete, NMOC .......... **45.00**

Figure, Dick Tracy, 1930s, painted lead, EX .......................... **30.00**

Film, Trick or Treat, 1960s, 8mm, EX (EX box) ................... **50.00**

Fingerprint Lab, Parliament Toys, 1953, complete, EX (EX box) ............................. **135.00**

Greeting cards, Norcross, 1960s, many styles, neon backgrounds, NM, ea ........... **20.00**

ID Composit Kit, Playmates, 1990, MIB ................................ **15.00**

Magnifying glass, Larami, 1979, MOC ............................. **20.00**

Mask, Einson-Freeman, 1933, paper, rare, EX ........... **100.00**

Mini Color Televiewer, Larami, 1972, NMIP ................... **25.00**

**Sub-Machine Water Gun, plastic, 1950s, MIB, $225.00. (Photo courtesy Dunbar Gallery)**

Transistor Radio Receiver, American Doll & Toy, 1961, MIB .............................. **100.00**

TV Watch, Ja-Ru, NMOC ....**20.00**

Valentine, 1940s, Say..., You May Detect It..., NM (original envelope) ....................... **50.00**

Wallet, 1973, black vinyl, w/6 Crimestopper textbook cards, NM ................................ **20.00**

Wrist radios, Remco, MIB .**100.00**

## Disney

The movies of Walt Disney have been a part of every child's growing-up years and the characters they feature as familiar as family. Though it's the items from the '30s and '40s that generally bring the high prices, even memorabilia from more recent movies is collectible. There are many books available for further study: *Character Toys and Collectibles, First and Second Series,* and *Antique & Collectible Toys, 1870 – 1950,* by David Longest; *Stern's Guide to Disney Collectibles* by Michael Stern (there are three in the series); and *The Collector's Encyclopedia of Disneyana* by Michael Stern and David Longest.

Aladdin, doll, Genie or Prince Ali, Applause, 10", M, ea .....**15.00**

Alice in Wonderland, figure, Tweedle Dum, Shaw, 1940s, ceramic, EX .......................... **300.00**

Aristocats, doll, Duchess, 1970, stuffed plush, 15", NM .**50.00**

Bambi, fork & spoon set, Walt Disney Stainless, 5", EX, pr ............................. **50.00**

Bambi, pencil sharpener, Plastic Novelties, Bakelite, 1¾", EX .............................. **65.00**

Beauty & the Beast, doll, Beast or Lumiere, Applause, 12", M, ea ...............**15.00**

Cinderella, apron, cloth w/colorful image, NM ...............**25.00**

Cinderella, purse, 1970s, green slipper w/zipper closure, 5", MIP ...............**20.00**

Disney, kaleidoscope, WDP, 1950s, litho cardboard, 9", EX ...............**75.00**

Disney, Scramble 4 Faces, Halsam Products, 1950s, MIP ...**50.00**

Disney, top, 1930s, litho tin, 9" dia, VG ...............**65.00**

Disneyland, Character Play World, fold-away, unused, MIB ...............**125.00**

Disneyland, xylophone, Original Concert Grand, w/music stand, NMIB ...............**135.00**

Donald Duck, camera, Herbert George/WDP, 3x5", MIB .**75.00**

Donald Duck, figure, Enesco, 1970s, ceramic, 4", M ...**15.00**

Donald Duck, figure, 1930s, chalkware, EX ...............**125.00**

Donald Duck, jack-in-the-box, early, celluloid, EX+ ...**850.00**

Donald Duck, magic slate, Whitman, 1970s NM ...............**25.00**

Donald Duck, soap, Cussons, 1939, 5", M (M red lift-top box) ......**150.00**

Donald Duck, watering can, Ohio Art, litho tin, EX .........**200.00**

Dumbo, figure, American Pottery, 1940s, no label, 5", NM .**100.00**

Fantasia, figure, Centaurette, Vernon Kilns #17, 1940 .......**635.00**

Fantasia, figure, unicorn, Vernon Kilns #14, 1940 ...........**365.00**

Ferdinand the Bull, figure, Seiberling, rubber, 6", VG ...........**75.00**

Goofy, doll, Merry Thoughts, England, stuffed cloth, 12", EX ...............**75.00**

Horace Horsecollar, figure, Fun-E-Flex, wood w/rope tail, rare, EX ...............**1,000.00**

Jungle Book, figure, Baloo, Japan, 1966, velvet & felt, 6", NM .**50.00**

Lady & the Tramp, Colorforms Cartoon Kit, 1962, complete, NMIB ...............**50.00**

Ludwig Von Drake, Erase-a-Board, 1960s, MIB (sealed) .......**65.00**

Mickey Mouse, ball, Eagle, 1950s, rubber, EX (EX box) .....**45.00**

Mickey Mouse, Bubble Buster, Kilgore, 1930s, 7", NM ......**275.00**

Mickey Mouse, Colorforms, 1970s, complete, EX (EX box) ..**20.00**

Mickey Mouse, doll, Dean's Rag Book Co, original tag, 5", EX ...............**700.00**

Mickey Mouse, doll, Posie, 1950s, EX (EX box) ...............**50.00**

Mickey Mouse, doll, Sun Rubber, 1950s, 10", VG .............**65.00**

Mickey Mouse, figure, American, 1931-32, jointed wood, rare, 5" ...............**750.00**

Mickey Mouse, figure, 1970s, bisque, Mickey on sled, 4", M ......**20.00**

Mickey Mouse, Kodak Theatre, MIP ...............**35.00**

Mickey Mouse, music box, Schmid, Mickey as cowboy, 6", M .**85.00**

Mickey Mouse, pencil box, Dixon, figural, rare, G ............**400.00**

Mickey Mouse, Pin the Tail on Mickey Mouse, Hallmark,WDP, MIP ...............**25.00**

Mickey Mouse, purse, American, 1930s, mesh w/chain handle, NM ...............**550.00**

Mickey Mouse and Donald Duck pencil case, 1930s, EX, $65.00. (Photo courtesy Dunbar Gallery)

Mickey Mouse, Shooting Gallery, Classic Toy, 1970s, MOC .**55.00**

Mickey Mouse, soap, Cussons, 1939, 4½", M (M red lift-top box) ..............................**125.00**

Mickey Mouse, stamp pad, WDE, 1930s, tin w/ink pad, 2x3", EX ................................**50.00**

Mickey Mouse, tool chest, 1930s, litho metal, EX ............**275.00**

Mickey Mouse, washing machine, Ohio Art, litho tin, EX .**400.00**

Mickey Mouse & Donald Duck, fire truck, red rubber, 6½", EX ..............................**100.00**

Mickey Mouse & Minnie, masks, WDE, 1933, paper, 9", VG ..............**75.00**

Mickey Mouse & Minnie, tambourine, Noble Cooley/WDE, EX ..............................**250.00**

Mickey Mouse Club, Build-Up Blocks, Eldon, 1950s, M (NM box) ..............................**45.00**

Mickey Mouse Club, Mouseketeer Ears, Kohner, MIP .......**75.00**

Mickey Mouse Club, wallet, features Donald Duck, NMIB ........**75.00**

Minnie Mouse, doll, Sun Rubber, 1950s, 10", VG ..............**65.00**

Minnie Mouse, figure, Japan, 1930s, bisque, in nightshirt, 4", EX .........................**225.00**

Minnie Mouse, figure, 1970s, bisque, w/golf clubs, 4", M .............**20.00**

Nightmare Before Christmas, doll, Jack, Applause, MIB ..**225.00**

Nightmare Before Christmas, doll, Sally, Applause, MIB ....................**350.00**

Nightmare Before Christmas, figure, Sally, Hasbro, 1993, MOC ..........................**100.00**

Pinocchio, clicker, Jiminy Cricket, yellow plastic head figure, EX ................................**20.00**

Pinocchio, doll, Figaro, jointed composition, 7", EX .....**465.00**

Pinocchio, doll, Jiminy Cricket, Ideal, 1940, 8½", EX, from $300 to ......................**500.00**

Pinocchio, figure, Geppetto, Multi-Products, 1940s, bisque, 2¼", EX ................................**100.00**

Pinocchio, figure, Honest John, 1930s, bisque, 3", EX ....**40.00**

Pinocchio, figure, Pinocchio, Occupied Japan, ceramic, 5", NM ................................**55.00**

Pinocchio, roly poly, celluloid, 5", EX ...............175.00
Pinocchio, tea set, ceramic trimmed in red, 8-pcs, EX ..........250.00
Pinocchio, wallet, Jiminy Cricket, leather, EX ...................30.00
Pluto, pencil sharpener, Bakelite, 1½" dia, EX ..................35.00
Pocahontas, figure set, Applause, PVC, set of 7, 3", EX .....15.00
Rocketeer, Gee Bee plane, Spectra Star, MIB ......................45.00
Silly Symphony, Christmas tree light set, Noma, complete, rare, EXIB .................250.00
Sleeping Beauty, Magic Bubble Wand, 1950s, MIP ........40.00
Sleeping Beauty, sewing set, Transogram, 1959, unused, scarce, EX ...............65.00
Snow White & the Seven Dwarfs, doll, Grumpy, Knickerbocker, 8", EX ..........................250.00
Snow White & the Seven Dwarfs, doll, Snow White, Ideal, 1937, 16", NM ......................400.00
Snow White & the Seven Dwarfs, figure, Dopey, 1930s, bisque, 3", EX ...........................50.00
Snow White & the Seven Dwarfs, kitchen set, Wolverine, 1970s-80s, EX ........................110.00
Three Little Pigs, figure set, Fun-E-Flex, wood, EX ........400.00
Three Little Pigs, tea set, Ohio Art/WDE, 1935, green litho tin, NM ......................225.00
Toy Story, Colorforms, 1993, MIB ...........................15.00
Toy Story, Mr Potato Head, Hasbro, MIB .......................20.00
Who Framed Roger Rabbit, Dip Flip, LJN, 1987, MIB ...25.00

Who Framed Roger Rabbit, figure, Jessica, LJN, bendable, 6", MOC ...........................30.00

**Winnie the Pooh bookends, painted ceramic, Enesco, 1960s, M, pair, $425.00.**

Winnie the Pooh, doll, Piglet, Sears, 1964-68, stuffed cloth, 7", NM ........................100.00
Winnie the Pooh, doll, Pooh, Knickerbocker, 1963, blue shirt, 13", EX ...............75.00
Winnie the Pooh, squeeze toy, Roo or Tigger, NM, ea .........30.00
101 Dalmatians, Colorforms, 1961, complete w/booklet, NM (EX box) ..............................40.00
101 Dalmatians, squeeze toy, EX ............................30.00

**Flintstones**

Anyone alive today knows that Fred, Wilma, Barney, Betty, Pebbles, and Bamm-Bamm lived in Bedrock, had a dinosaur for a pet, and preferred bowling over any other sport. This invention of Hanna-Barbera, who introduced them all in 1959, met with immediate, sustained success. To date literally thousands of items featuring the Flintstone crew have been sold such as games, playing cards, pin-back buttons, cookie jars, puzzles, toys, dolls, T-shirts, etc., so today's collectors can build a large and varied collection of Flintstones memorabilia with ease.

**Flintstones, Pebbles and Bamm-Bamm in cradle, Ideal, plastic, 14½" long, EX, $125.00.**

Baby Pebbles Cave House, Ideal, 1964, M .....................175.00
Bookends, Fred & Wilma, Vandor, 1989, paper label, pr, from $65 to .....................................75.00
Bubble pipe, Bamm-Bamm, 1960s, 8", EX ............................20.00
Building Boulders, Kenner, MIB, from $75 to ................100.00
Cockamamies, 1961, complete, NMIB ............................30.00
Coin purse, Barney, 1975, NM ...25.00
Doll, Barney, Knickerbocker, 1960s, plush & vinyl, 12", EX ...............................75.00
Doll, Fred, Knickerbocker, 1960s, plush & vinyl, 12, NM ..85.00
Doll, Pebbles, Mighty Star Ltd, 1982, cloth & vinyl, 12", MIB ...............................60.00
Figure, Flintstone Kids, any, Coleco, MOC, ea ...................15.00
Gumball machine, Fred head figure, Hasbro, plastic, 1968, 8", EX ...............................50.00

Mug, Betty Rubble face, Vandor, 1990, from $15 to ...........20.00
Pencil-by-Number Set, Transogram, 1960s, complete, EX (EX box)...........................130.00
Play Fun Set, Whitman, 1965, complete, EX (EX box) ..65.00
Shakers, Pebbles & Bamm-Bamm, Vandor, pr, from $40 to .50.00
Squeeze toy, any character, Lanco, 1960s, NMIP, ea ........135.00

## Garfield

America's favorite grumpy cat, Garfield has his own band of devotees who are able to find a good variety of merchandise modeled after his likeness. Garfield was created in 1976 by Jim Davis. He underwent many changes by the time he debuted in newspapers in 1978. By 1980 his first book was released, followed quickly in 1981 by a line of collectibles by Dakin and Enesco. The stuffed plush animals and ceramic figures were a huge success. There have been thousands of items made since, with many that are hard to find being produced in Germany, the Netherlands, England, and other European countries. Banks, displays, PVCs, and figurines are the most desirable items of import from these countries.

Bib, Garfield in sleigh, MOC .2.00
Book, Scary Tales, Grosset Dunlap ......................................4.00
Bookends, w/Odie, ceramic, Enesco, pr, from $100 to ...........125.00

**Garfield wall-mount toothbrush holder, United Features, copyright 1978, plastic, from $25.00 to $30.00.**

Cookie tin, Garfield tangled in lights ..................................6.00
Doll, as Santa Claus, plush, original tag, M ....................16.00
Doll, Mattel, 1983, talker, 10", EX ................................60.00
Doll, Spaghetti Attack, Dakin, stuffed plush ................15.00
Figure, as Santa, vinyl, 6" ...25.00
Figure, as tennis player, ceramic, 4" ...................................20.00
Figure, as witch, vinyl, 6" ...25.00
Figure, Enesco, as Uncle Sam, I Want You on base, 3" ...20.00
Figure, in workout suit, ceramic, 4½" ..................................20.00
Figure, on roller skates, ceramic, 2", EX ............................10.00
Figure, To Dad From a Chip Off the Old Block, ceramic, EX ..12.00
Growth chart, 3 sheets, MIB .16.00
Jack-in-the-box, Pop Goes the Odie, MIB .....................30.00
Music box, Baby's First Christmas, train circles Garfield ....20.00
Necklace, Avon, MIB ..........10.00
Night light, Garfield on cloud, MOC ............................15.00

Night light, head figural, MOC ......................15.00
Ornament, on a star, Hallmark, 1991, MIB .....................20.00
Play money, MIP .................3.00
Slide-tile puzzle, MIP ............5.00

## Howdy Doody

The Howdy Doody show was introduced in 1951, and the puppet host and his cast of friends, Buffalo Bob, Flub-a-Dub, Clarabelle, Mr. Bluster, and the Princess became pals to their rapt TV audiences. Merchants filled their shelves with an enormous variety of licensed merchandise. Even into the '70s and '80s, Howdy Doody continued to be marketed, though on a much smaller scale. For further reading see *Howdy Doody, Collector's Reference and Trivia Guide,* by Jack Koch (Collector Books).

Bee-Nee Kit, 1950s, NMIB ..65.00
Bookends, Vandor #0579, from $70 to ..................................80.00
Booklet, Howdy Doody's Big Prize Doodle List, 1954-55, 4 pages, EX ................................40.00
Boxing gloves, Parvey, 1950s, tan w/black image of Howdy, 6", NMIB ..........................325.00
Bubble pipes, Lido, complete w/2 pipes, cup & bubbles, NM (NM box) ....................175.00
Catcher's mitt, 1950s, brown vinyl w/silver image of Howdy, VG .................100.00
Clock-a-Doodle, 1950s, litho tin wind-up, NMIB ........1,600.00

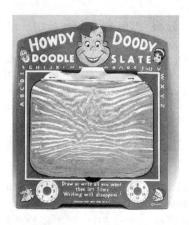

**Howdy Doody Doodle Slate, 1950s, from $35.00 to $45.00. (Photo courtesy Dunbar Gallery)**

Doctor kit, Ja-Ru, 1987, MOC .**15.00**

Figure set, Tee-Vee Toys, 1950s, set of 5 different characters, EX .................................**150.00**

Flip-A-Ring, Flub-A-Dub, Flip-A-Ring Inc, 1950s, MIP ....**45.00**

Handkerchief, 1950s, colorful image of Howdy spinning lasso, 8x8", EX .............**25.00**

Magnet, Vandor, from $4 to ..**6.00**

Paint set, Milton Bradley, complete, NM (NM box) ....**200.00**

Pen, Leadworks, 1988, posable plastic figure, 6", M ........**5.00**

Pencil case, 1950s, red vinyl w/lg image of Howdy on front, 4x8", EX .........................**65.00**

Pencil topper, Leadworks, 1988, vinyl, head figure, 1½", M .**5.00**

Phono Doodle, 1950s, sq record player w/colorful images, EX .........................**250.00**

Picture frame, Howdy sitting in right-hand corner, Vandor, from $25 to ...................**30.00**

Ranch House tool box, Kagran, 1950s, metal, EX .........**200.00**

Sparkler, Ja-Ru, 1987, MOC. **10.00**

Squeak toy, 13", NM ...........**85.00**

Uke, Emenee, plastic, 17", NM (EX box) ....................**165.00**

## Peanuts

First introduced in 1950, the *Peanuts* comic strip has become the world's most widely read cartoon. It appears daily in about 2,200 newspapers. From that funny cartoon about kids (that readers of every age could easily relate to) has sprung an entertainment arsenal featuring movies, books, Broadway shows, toys, theme parks, etc. And surely as the day follows the night, there comes a bountiful harvest of *Peanuts* collectibles. If you want to collect, you should know that authenticity is important. To be authentic, the United Features Syndicate logo and copyright date must appear somewhere on the item. In most cases the copyright date simply indicates the date that the character and his pose as depicted on the item first appeared in the comic strip.

Colorforms, Peanuts Preschool, VG (VG box) ..................**25.00**

Doll, Charlie Brown, 1950s, vinyl, 9", VG ...........................**75.00**

Doll, Lucy, Ideal, rag-type, red dress, 14", VG ...............**20.00**

Doll, Snoopy, World Wonder, 1986, talker, MIB .................**100.00**

Doll, Snoopy as chef, rag-type, 6", VG .................................**10.00**

Doll, Snoopy w/rattle, plush, 9", MIP .................................**10.00**

**Charlie Brown figure, push down head and body pivots, EX, $135.00.**

Figure, Linus w/blanket, 3", M ..**8.00**
Figure, Lucy in hula skirt, 1989, 3", M ..............................**6.00**
See & Say, Snoopy Says, Mattel, VG ..............................**50.00**
Snoopy Sign-Mobile Coloring set, Avalon, 1977, MIB ........**70.00**

## Smurfs

A creation of Pierro 'Peyo' Culliford, the little blue Smurfs that we have all come to love have found their way to the collectibles market of today. There is a large number of items currently available at reasonable prices, though some, such as metal lunch boxes, cereal premiums and boxes, and promotional items and displays, are beginning to attract special interest. Because the Smurfs' 'birthplace' was in Belgium, many items are European in nature.

Banner, Happy Smurfday, MIP .**20.00**
Chalkboard, Smurfette, EX .**25.00**
Coin purse, To Paint a Rainbow Life, cloth, EX ..............**10.00**
Colorforms, complete, EX (EX box) ..............................**35.00**
Figure, Papa Smurf, ceramic, VG ..............................**30.00**
Figure, Smurf Village, ceramic, VG ..............................**30.00**
Figurine, PVC, several different, from $2 to ......................**4.00**
Fun Club Packet, w/newsletters & stickers, EX ..................**45.00**
Paint-by-Numbers, #263, EXIB .**30.00**
Record player, 1982, EX .....**20.00**
Sand bucket & shovel, plastic, EX ..............................**10.00**
Serving tray, VG ..................**15.00**
Sewing cards, MIB (sealed) .**25.00**
Shrinky Dinks, MIB ...........**20.00**
Smurf Amaze-ing Action Maze, EX ..............................**20.00**
Smurfettes Amaze-ing Action Maze, EX ......................**20.00**
Wrap-'em-Egg set, MIB .......**10.00**

## Warner Brothers

Bugs Bunny and Porky Pig were among the original Warner Brothers characters, first appearing in cartoon form in 1938. The studio closed in 1963, but they and several other characters (some of which we've featured below) remained popular with kids and collectors alike, since the cartoons have been in syndication for TV ever since.

Bugs Bunny, Chatterchum, Mattel, 1976, 7", VG ...........**30.00**

**Bugs Bunny Cartoon-O-Graph Sketch Board, 1950s, NMIB, $50.00.**

Bugs Bunny, doll, stuffed felt w/mask face, 24", EX ..**175.00**

Bugs Bunny, doll, 1950s, dressed as Davy Crockett, EX .**325.00**

Bugs Bunny, figure, 1988, bendable, 8", EX ..................**20.00**

Bugs Bunny, magic slate, Golden, 1987, MIP (sealed) ..........**5.00**

Bugs Bunny, ring toss, Larami, 1981, MOC ....................**15.00**

Bugs Bunny, Silly Putty, Ja-Ru, 1980, MOC ......................**5.00**

Bugs Bunny, sleeping bag, 1977, features Bugs & friends, VG ................**15.00**

Bugs Bunny's Uncle Bugs, vinyl, Great America, 1978, EX ..................**25.00**

Daffy Duck, doll, Mighty Star, 1971, stuffed plush, 19", NM ...........................**25.00**

Porky Pig, figure, Sun Rubber, 1950s, 6", EX (EX box) .**100.00**

Porky Pig, figure, 1930s, chalkware, 7", EX ..................**75.00**

Porky Pig, gumball machine, Banko Matic, 1970s, plastic, 9½", EXIB ....................**25.00**

Porky Pig, jack-in-the-box, Mattel, M, from $100 to ..........**150.00**

Road Runner, doll, Mighty Star, 1971, stuffed w/wire frame, 17", EX ..........................**35.00**

Road Runner, Magic Cartoon Board, 1971, unused, M .**25.00**

Skediddler, Mattel, 1966, MIB .**85.00**

Sylvester, roly poly, EX .......**25.00**

Tasmanian Devil, doll, Mighty Star, 1970s, stuffed cloth, EX .............................**40.00**

Tasmanian Devil, doll, 1980, stuffed plush, 13" ..........**15.00**

Tasmanian Devil, figure, vinyl, 6", NM ...............................**25.00**

Tasmanian Devil, magic slate, Golden, 1992, M (sealed) .**5.00**

Tweety Bird, doll, Chatterchum, Mattel, 1976, MIB ........**45.00**

**Miscellaneous Cartoon and TV Show Characters**

Remember those great shows like 'Charlie's Angels' (it had beautiful girls with character *and* morals), 'Happy Days' (whose reruns are just as funny today as they were back 'when'), 'Six Million Dollar Man,' 'Gilligan's Island,' and so many others? If you do, you may be among the many collectors that today for reasons of nostalgia search out character-related memorabilia that reminds them of a more innocent era of TV entertainment. Greg Davis and Bill Morgan have written a comprehensive book called *Collector's Guide to TV Toys and Memorabilia* (now in its second edition). It contains chapter after chapter of photographs and values along with information concerning the shows and their casts. (Available from Collector Books.)

Alvin & the Chipmunks, doll, Alvin, Ideal, talker, plush, 18" ..............................**55.00**

Alvin & the Chipmunks, squeeze toy, Alvin, Holland, 1964, rubber, EX ..........................**60.00**

Alvin & the Chipmunks, Treat Mobile, Ideal, 1984, MIB .**40.00**

Andy Panda, doll, stuffed cloth w/red overalls, w/tag, NM, from $250 to ...............**450.00**

Archies, Jughead Jr Shaving Kit, 1986, MOC ...................**15.00**

Archies, stencil set, 1983, MOC .**15.00**

Archies, sticker, Everything's Archie, 1968, 5" dia, EX .**35.00**

Baby Huey, figure, Alvimar, 1960s, inflatable vinyl w/bells, 9", EX .............................**25.00**

Banana Splits, flute set, Larami, 1973, plastic, set of 3, MOC .........**55.00**

Banana Splits, pillow, Fleegle, Kellogg's, 1960s 10", minor fading, EX .....................**50.00**

Beetle Bailey, doll, Presents, cloth w/vinyl head, original tags, M .........................**40.00**

Beetle Bailey, puffy stickers, Ja-Ru, 1983, MIP (sealed) ...............**20.00**

Bozo the Clown, Circus Train or Wagon, Multiple Toys, 1970, MIB, ea .........................**20.00**

Bozo the Clown, doll, Mattel, 1963, talker, 18", VG ..............**45.00**

Bozo the Clown, sticker board, 1983, MIB .....................**15.00**

Bozo the Clown, Stitch-A-Story, Hasbro, 1967, MOC (sealed) ...................**50.00**

Brady Bunch, banjo or guitar, Larami, 1973, EX, ea ....**30.00**

Brady Bunch, brain twisters, Larami, 1973, EX .........**25.00**

Brady Bunch, dominos, Larami, 1973, EX .......................**25.00**

Brady Bunch, sticker fun book, Whitman, 1973, EX ......**50.00**

Casper the Ghost, chalkboard, 12x18", MIP (sealed) ....**40.00**

Casper the Ghost, figure, Sutton, 1972, vinyl, 7", NM .......**25.00**

Charlie's Angels, adventure van, Hasbro, for 8½" dolls, 1978, EX .................................**50.00**

Charlie's Angels, board game, Milton Bradley, 1978, EX ...........**15.00**

**Charlie's Angels Cosmetic Beauty Kit, H.G. Toys, 1977, MIB, from $50.00 to $75.00. (Photo courtesy Greg Davis and Bill Morgan)**

CHiPs, Free-Wheeling Motorcycle, for 8" dolls, Mego, 1980, EX .................................**25.00**

CHiPs, notebook, Ponch, Stuart Hall, 1979, EX ...............**10.00**

Dennis the Menace, Creepy Bugs, Larami, 1988, MOC ......**15.00**

Dennis the Menace, doll, Joey, Presents, 1980s, cloth, EX .......**25.00**

Doctor Dolittle, Cartoon Kit, Colorforms, 1967, NMIB, from $25 to ..........................**35.00**

Doctor Dolittle, Mystery Chamber Magic Set, Remco, 1939, NMIB ............................30.00

Doctor Dolittle, Ride-Em Rocker, Pushmi-Pullyu, AJ Renzi, 1974, NM ......................50.00

Doctor Dolittle, wrist flashlight, Bantamlite, NM ............30.00

Dr Seuss, doll, Horton the Elephant, Coleco, 1983, stuffed plush, EX ......................35.00

Dr Seuss, doll, Yertle the Turtle, Coleco, 1983, stuffed plush, EX ................................35.00

Droopy Dog, squeeze toy, Alan Jay, 1960s, rubber, 4", EX .....35.00

**Felix the Cat Button Sew-On Cards, 1959, M, $95.00.**

Felix the Cat, doll, 1982, stuffed plush, 14", NM ..............25.00

Felix the Cat, figure, Germany bisque, 1½", NM .........350.00

Felix the Cat, squeak toy, Germany, paper litho w/wood & paper, 6", EX ..............400.00

Flipper, doll, Knickerbocker, plush, NM ....................25.00

Gilligan's Island, Floating Island Playset, Playskool, 1977, EX ....................80.00

Gilligan's Island, writing tablet, Gilligan & Skipper, 1960s, EX ...............................20.00

Gremlins, figure, Gizmo, LJN, 1984, bendable, MOC ...35.00

Gumby & Pokey, figure, Pokey, Jesco, 1980s, bendable, 12", MOC ..............................15.00

Gumby & Pokey, paint set, rare, NM ..............................200.00

Happy Days, belt, Fonz & the Gang, Paramount, 1981, EX ..........................10.00

Happy Days, board game, Parker Brothers, 1976, EX .......15.00

Happy Days, Colorforms, Fonz, 1976, EX ........................20.00

Happy Days, pinball machine, Coleco, electric, 1976, 36x20", EX ................................80.00

Happy Days, record player, Fonz in lid, Vanity Fair, 1976, EX ....................35.00

I Dream of Jeannie, doll, Jeannie, Remco, 1977, 6", EX .....60.00

I Dream of Jeannie, halloween costume, Jeannie, Ben Cooper, 1974, EX ......................25.00

I Dream of Jeannie, magic slate, Rand McNally, 1975, EX ..........................30.00

Jetsons, doll, Elroy, plush w/plastic hat, 14", NM ...........15.00

Jetsons, film, 1960s, 8mm, NMIB ......................15.00

Krazy Kat, doll, stuffed felt, orange neck ribbon, 18", VG ........................500.00

Laverne & Shirley, purse, Harmony, 1977, EX ..........................15.00

Laverne & Shirley, secretary set, Harmony, 1977, EX ......**15.00**

Linus the Lion-Hearted, doll, Mattel, 1965, talker, 21", VG .............................**85.00**

Little House on the Prairie, Colorforms, 1978, EX ............**35.00**

Little Lulu, doll, 1940s, stuffed cloth w/cowgirl outfit, 16", NM .............................**500.00**

Little Rascals, pencil sharpener, Spanky, 1930s, Bakelite, 1⅛", NM ...............................**60.00**

Mork & Mindy, Colorforms, 1979, EX ...................................**15.00**

Mork & Mindy, 4-wheel drive Jeep, Mattel, for 8" dolls, 1979, EX ........................**45.00**

Mr Magoo, doll, Ideal, 1961, stuffed cloth & vinyl, 16", EX ...............................**75.00**

Munsters, figure, Grandpa, Applause, 1991, MIP ....**40.00**

Partridge Family, guitar, David Cassidy, Carnival Toys, 1970s, EX ...................**100.00**

Pee-Wee's Playhouse, Colorforms, 1988, MIB (sealed) ........**20.00**

Pink Panther, doll, plush, 6", M ..**10.00**

Popeye, figure, KFS, jointed wood, 6", EX+ ........................**125.00**

Popeye, figure, plaster, 7", EX ....................**165.00**

Popeye, Flip-Show, 1961, EX (EX box) ...............................**40.00**

Popeye, Paint-a-graf, Milton Bradley, 1935, complete, EX (EX box) ......................**350.00**

Punky Brewster, doll, Galoob, 1984, 18", NRFB ..........**40.00**

Rainbow Brite, figures, PVC, set of 5 .....................................**25.00**

Rat Fink, decal, 1990, NM ....**5.00**

Scooby Doo, doll, stuffed plush, 16", EX .........................**40.00**

Sesame Street, doll, Ernie, stuffed cloth, 18", EX ..............**20.00**

Sesame Street, figure, Kermit the Frog, Bend 'Ems, MOC .....................**10.00**

Simpsons, doll, Bart, Dandee, soft vinyl, 10", MIB .............**10.00**

Simpsons, figure, Lisa, Jasco, bendable, 3½", MOC .......**6.00**

Simpsons, Fun Dough Model Maker, MIB ..................**20.00**

Spider-Man, Colorforms Adventure Set, 1974, unused, MIB ...............................**15.00**

Starsky & Hutch, radio-controlled car, Galoob, 1977, EX .............................**45.00**

**Six Million Dollar Man Bionic Transport and Repair Station, Kenner, 1975, MIB, from $25.00 to $35.00. (Photo courtesy Greg Davis and Bill Morgan)**

Superman, belt buckle, Pioneer, 1940s, bronze w/image, rectangular, EX ...............**450.00**

Superman, Cartoonist Stamp Set, 1966, complete, MOC ...**75.00**

Superman, doll, Applause, 1988, 18", NM .........................**25.00**

Superman, kite, Hi-Flyer, 1984, MIP ...............................**30.00**

Superman, Sparkle Paints, 1966, w/5 pictures to paint, NMIB .........................**65.00**

Teddy Ruxpin, doll, Baby Teddy Ruxpin, 1986, VG .........**70.00**

Terrytoons, Monkey Stix, Ideal, 1960, M (NM sealed container) ...................................**70.00**

Tom & Jerry, figure, painted plaster, 5", EX .....................**85.00**

Tom & Jerry, guitar, Mattel, 1965, musical windup, EX .....**40.00**

Winky Dink, outfit, 1950s, yellow, red & white felt, scarce, EX ....**85.00**

Wizard of Oz, figure, Cowardly Lion, Multiple, 1960s, rubber, 6", EX .............................**55.00**

Wizard of Oz, figure, Tin Woodsman, Multiple, 1960s, rubber, 6", EX .............................**55.00**

Wizard of Oz, flasher ring, Cowardly Lion or Tin Woodsman, M, ea .............................**100.00**

Wizard of Oz, Magic Kit, Fun Inc, 1960s, complete w/10 tricks, NMIB ............................**50.00**

Wonder Woman, figure, Ideal, 1966, painted plastic, 4", EX .............................**45.00**

Woody Woodpecker, harmonica, early, plastic figure, 6", EX ...........**30.00**

Woody Woodpecker, jack-in-the-box, Mattel, M, from $100 to ...................**150.00**

Woody Woodpecker, ring, 1970s, cloisonne, M .................**15.00**

**Yogi Bear, Huckleberry Hound, and Quick Draw McGraw TV tray, EX, $30.00. (Photo courtesy June Moon)**

Yogi Bear, doll, Applause, 1970s-80s, stuffed plush, 9", NM ............................**20.00**

Yogi Bear, mug, 1961, painted plastic, NM ....................**20.00**

## Cherished Teddies

First appearing on dealers' shelves in the spring of 1992, Cherished Teddies found instant collector appeal. They were designed by artist Priscilla Hillman and produced in the Orient for the Enesco company. Besides the figurines, the line includes waterballs, frames, plaques, and bells. For more information we recommend *Secondary Market Price Guide for the Cherished Teddies Collection* by Rosie Wells, who is also the founder of the collector organization called *Just the Bear Facts Bear Club*. Ms. Wells is listed in the Directory under

Illinois; see also Clubs and Newsletters.

#903337, Jointed Bear Christmas, musical (Jingle Bells), 1993 ..............................**70.00**

#906530, Angel Bear, bell, Christmas 1992 ..............**65.00**

#951226, Sister w/Blue Hat, ornament, Christmas 1992 ......................**20.00**

L/R 910678, Charity, I Found a Friend in Ewe, Easter 1993 ...........**75.00**

L/R 910708, Heidi & David, Special Friends, Easter 1993 .....**75.00**

L/R 950440, Katie, A Friend Always Knows..., 1992 ....**65.00**

L/R 950459, Anna, Hooray for You, 1992 ..............................**65.00**

L/R 950491, Zachary, Yesterday's Memories Are..., 1992 ........................**50.00**

L/R 950572, Mandy, I Love You Just the Way..., 1992 ....**95.00**

L/R 95072, Charlie, Spirit of Friendship..., Christmas 1992 ..............................**45.00**

L/R 950726, Sammy, Little Lambs..., Nativity, 1992 .**55.00**

3/R 624888, Father, ...Bearer of Strength, Our Cherished Family, 1994 ................**22.00**

3/R 910732, Amy, Hearts Quilled w/Love, 1993 valentine ............................**27.50**

3/R 911348, Age 1, Beary Special One, Through the Years, 1993 ............................**25.00**

3/R 911356, Baby, Cradled with Love, Through the Years, 1993 ........................**25.00**

3/R 911747, Freda & Tina, Our Friendship Is..., 1993 ....**75.00**

3/R 912816, Brenda, How I Love Being Friends, Thanksgiving 1993 ...............................**30.00**

3/R 913855, Bear in Scarf, stocking holder, Christmas 1993 ..........................**30.00**

3/R 916307, Kelly, You're My One & Only, valentine, 1994 .**50.00**

3/R 916404, Bessie, Some Bunny Loves You, Easter 1994 ...........................**70.00**

3/R 916447, Kathleen, Luck Found Me..., St Patrick's 1994 .**35.00**

3/R 950564, Beth & Blossom, Friends Are Never..., w/butterfly, 1992 .................**125.00**

4/R 103659, Cupid Baby Boy on Pillow, valentine, 1995 .**25.00**

4/R 617296, Ebearnezer Scrooge, Bah Humbug!, Dickens Village, 1994 ......................**32.00**

4/R 61764, Willie, Bears of a Feather..., Thanksgiving 1994 ..............................**25.00**

4/R 61780, Brenna, Pumpkin Patch Pals, Halloween 1994 ....**28.00**

4/R 626066, Betty, Bubblin' Over w/Love, 1994 .................**37.50**

4/R 651095, Cow, nativity pull toy, That's What Friends..., 1994 ............................**28.00**

4/R 903620, Alice, Cozy Warm Wishes..., Christmas 1993, 9" ..............................**115.00**

4/R 912786, Gary, True Friendships Are Scarce, Halloween 1993 ............................**25.00**

## Children's Books

Books were popular gifts for children in the latter 1800s; many were beautifully illustrated, some by notable artists such as Frances Brundage and Maxfield Parrish. From this century tales of Tarzan by Burroughs are very collectible, as are those familiar childhood series books — for example, The Bobbsey Twins and Nancy Drew. For more information we recommend *Collector's Guide to Children's Books, Volumes I and II,* by Diane McClure Jones and Rosemary Jones (Collector Books).

## Big Little Books

Probably everyone who is now forty to sixty years of age owned a few Big Little Books as a child. Today these thick hand-sized adventures bring prices from $10.00 to $75.00 and upwards. The first was published in 1933 by Whitman Publishing Company. Dick Tracy was the featured character. Kids of the early '50s preferred the format of the comic book, and the Big Little Books were gradually phased out. Stories about super heroes and Disney characters bring the highest prices, especially those with an early copyright. For more information see *Big Little Books, a Collector's Reference and Value Guide,* by Larry Jacobs (Collector Books).

Bambi's Children, Whitman #1497, 1943, VG ............**45.00**
Billy the Kid, Whitman #773, 1935, EX .......................**35.00**
Blondie & Baby Dumpling, Whitman #1415, 1937, NM ..............**50.00**

Captain Midnight & the Secret Squadron, Whitman #1488, 1941, NM .....................**100.00**
Dan Dunn on the Trail of Wu Fang, Whitman #1454, 1938, EX ...............................**35.00**
Dick Tracy & the Tiger Lily Gang, Whitman #1460, 1949, VG ...............................**35.00**
Flash Gordon & the Monsters of Mongo, Whitman #1166, 1935, EX ...............................**100.00**
Gunsmoke, Whitman #1647, 1958, EX ................................**20.00**
Jimmy Allen in the Air Mail Robbery, Whitman #1143, 1936, EX ...................................**35.00**
Junior G-Men, Whitman #1442, 1937, EX .......................**40.00**
Li'l Abner in New York, Whitman #1198, 1936, EX ......................**60.00**

**Lone Ranger and the Red Renegades, Better Little Book, VG, $32.50.**

Mandrake the Magician, Whitman #1167, 1935, VG ............**30.00**

Mickey Mouse & Pluto the Racer, Whitman #1128, 1936, EX .................... **75.00**

Popeye Ghost Ship to Treasure Island, Whitman #2008, 1967, VG ................................ **10.00**

Red Ryder in Circus Luck, Whitman #1466, 1947, EX ....................... **35.00**

Smitty & Herman Lost Among the Indians, Whitman #1404, 1941, EX ....................... **35.00**

Tom Mix & His Circus on the Barbary Coast, Whitman #1482, 1940, EX ...................... **45.00**

## Dick and Jane

Dick and Jane readers were very common first-grade textbooks from the 1930s until the mid-1970s. Not only were they used in public schools in the United States, they were also used on military bases worldwide and in Roman Catholic and Seventh Day Adventists' schools. Even today they're used by the Mennonite and Amish. These books have been published in the US, Canada, the Philippine Islands, Australia, and New Zealand.

Before We Read, softcover, school stamp, 1962, EX .......... **75.00**

Fun Wherever We Are, softcover, 1962, VG ....................... **70.00**

Fun With Dick & Jane, hardcover, 1946, NM .................... **350.00**

Fun With Our Family, softcover, 1962, VG ....................... **70.00**

Good Times With Our Friends, softcover, 1954, G ......... **50.00**

Friends and Neighbors, second grade reader, 1946 – 1947, from $85.00 to $100.00.

Guess Who, softcover, 1951, VG .......................... **70.00**

Happy Days With Our Friends, Scott Forsman, 1954, VG .......... **60.00**

New Fun With Dick & Jane, hardcover, 1951, VG ............. **45.00**

New We Work & Play, 2nd of 3 pre-primers, softcover, 1956, VG ................................ **65.00**

Our Big Book, teacher's edition, easel size, M ............... **275.00**

Sally, Dick & Jane, softcover, 1962, VG ....................... **70.00**

We Read More Pictures, softcover, 1963, EX ...................... **75.00**

We Read Pictures, Scott Foresman, softcover, 1951, VG .............. **50.00**

We Talk, Spell & Write, softcover, 1951, VG ..................... **75.00**

## Little Golden Books

Little Golden Books (a registered trademark of Western Publishing Company Inc.), introduced in October of 1942, were an overnight success. First published with a blue paper spine, the later spines were of gold foil. Parents and grandparents born in the '40s, '50s, and '60s are now trying to find the titles they had as children. From 1942 to the early 1970s, the books were numbered from 1 to 600, while books published later had no numerical order. Depending on where you find the book, prices can vary from 25¢ to $30.00 plus. The most expensive are those with dust jackets from the early '40s or books with paper dolls and activities. The three primary series of books are Regular (1 – 600), Disney (1 – 140), and Activity (1 – 52).

Television's influence became apparent in the '50s with stories like the Lone Ranger, Howdy Doody, Hopalong Cassidy, Gene Autry, and Rootie Kazootie. The '60s brought us Yogi Bear, Huckleberry Hound, Magilla Gorilla, and Quick Draw McGraw, to name a few. A TV Western title from the '50s is worth around $12.00 to $18.00. A Disney from 1942 to the early '60s will go for $15.00 to $25.00 (a few even higher; reprinted titles would be lower). Cartoon titles from the '60s would range from $6.00 to $12.00. Books with the blue spine or gold paper spine (not foil) can bring from $8.00 to $15.00. If you are lucky enough to own a book with a dust jacket, the jacket alone is worth $20.00 and up. Paper doll books are worth around $30.00 to $36.00. These prices are meant only to give an idea of value and are for 1st editions in mint condition. Condition is very important when purchasing a book. You normally don't want to purchase a book with large tears, crayon or ink marks, or missing pages.

As with any collectible book, a 1st edition is always going to bring the higher price. To determine what edition you have on the 25¢ and 29¢ cover price books, look on the title page or the last page of the book. If it is not on the title page, there will be a code of 1/(a letter of the alphabet) on the bottom right corner of the last page. A is for 1st edition, Z would refer to the twenty-sixth printing.

There isn't an easy way of determining the condition of a book. What is 'good' to one might be 'fair' to another. A played-with book in average condition is generally worth only half as much as one in mint, like-new condition. To find out more about Little Golden Books, we recommend *Collecting Little Golden Books* (published by Books Americana) by Steve Santi.

A Day at the Beach, #110, A edition, EX .........................**25.00**
Animal Counting Book, #584, A edition, EX ....................**10.00**
Bible Stories of Boys & Girls, #174, A edition, EX .......**10.00**
Big Brown Bear, #89, A edition, EX ..............................**18.00**
Bugs Bunny & the Indians, #120, B edition, EX .................**12.00**

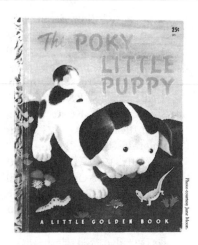

**The Poky Little Puppy, 1941, A (first) edition, NM, $24.00. (Photo courtesy June Moon)**

Christmas Story, #158, E edition, EX ...................................10.00
Donald Duck Private Eye, #D94, A edition, VG ....................20.00
Frosty the Snowman, #142, B edition, EX ...........................6.00
Hansel & Gretel, #17, H edition, VG ...................................10.00
Huckleberry Hound Builds a House, #376, B edition, EX .............8.00
Jolly Barnyard, #200-44, A edition, EX ...........................5.00
Let's Go Shopping, #208-58, C edition, EX ...........................3.00
Mister Ed, #483, A edition, EX .18.00
My Own Grandpa, #208-56, A edition, EX ...........................5.00
Oscar's New Neighbor, #109-67, A edition, EX ......................5.00
Peter & the Wolf, #D5, I edition, EX ...................................8.00
Pinocchio & the Whale, #D101, A edition, VG ...................20.00
Rocky & His Friends, #408, A edition, EX .........................22.00

Rumpelstiltskin, #498, B edition, EX ...................................8.00
Seven Sneezes, #51, B edition, VG ...................................12.00
Surprise for Sally, #84, A edition, VG ...................................22.00
Three Little Pigs, #D10, K edition, VG ...................................10.00
Twelve Days of Christmas, #526, A edition, EX ...................12.00
Wild Animal Babies, #309-58, A edition, EX ......................6.00

## Series

Everyone remembers a special series of books they grew up with: The Hardy Boys, Nancy Drew Mysteries, Tarzan — there were countless others. And though these are becoming very collectible today, there were many editions of each, and most are very easy to find. As a result, common titles are sometimes worth very little. Generally the last few in any series will be the most difficult to locate, since fewer were printed than the earlier stories which were likely to have been reprinted many times. As is true of any type of book, first editions or the earliest printing will have more collector value. For further reading see *Collector's Guide to Children's Books, 1850 to 1950,* by Diane McClure Jones and Rosemary Jones (Collector Books).

Beverly Gray's Reporter, Clair Blank AL Burt, 1934, w/dust jacket, VG......................75.00

Beverly Gray's Surprise, Clair Blank, McLoughlin, #00024 1955, G+ .........................**20.00**

Bobbsey Twins on Airplane Trip, LL Hope, Grosset Dunlap, 1933, w/jacket, VG.........**35.00**

**Cherry Ames Flight Nurse, Grosset Dunlap, #25 in series, pictorial boards, 1945, from $7.00 to $12.00.**

Cherry Ames Army Nurse, Helen Wells, Grosset Dunlap, w/jacket, VG.....................**6.00**

Hardy Boys: Detective Handbook, FW Dixon, Grosset Dunlap, 1959, VG.........................**10.00**

Hardy Boys: Secret of Pirates' Hill, FW Dixon, 1st edition, 1956, w/jacket, VG...................**45.00**

Hardy Boys: Secret of the Caves, Dixon, Grosset Dunlap, 1929, EX+.................................**22.50**

Lone Ranger, Fran Striker, Grosset Dunlap, 1938, w/dust jacket, VG.............................**15.00**

Lone Ranger, Outlaw Stronghold, Fran Striker, Grosset Dunlap, 1939, w/jacket, EX........**22.00**

Nancy Drew, Double Jinx Mystery, #50 Grosset Dunlap, 1973, w/jacket, EX..........**5.00**

Secret in Old Attic, Keene, 1st edition, 1944, w/jacket VG .**55.00**

Oz, Emerald City of, Baum, Rand McNally, 1939, G...........**10.00**

Oz, Woodsman of Oz — Original Story, Baum, Reilly Lee, cloth cover, VG.......................**20.00**

Penny Parker: Danger at the Drawbridge, red cloth cover, w/jacket VG...................**30.00**

Tom Swift, Race to the Moon, hardcover, decorated boards, VG................................**20.00**

Tom Swift & his Motorboat (#2), 1910, 2 dust jackets, VG ...........................**35.00**

**Whitman Tell-A-Tale Books**

Though the Whitman Company produced a wide variey of children's books, the ones most popular with today's collectors (besides the Big Little Books which are dealt with earlier in this category) are the Tell-A-Tales. They were published in a variety of series, several of which centered around radio, TV, and comic strips. For more information, photos, and current values, we recommend *Whitman Juvenile Books, Reference & Value Guide*, by David and Virginia Brown (Collector Books).

Bedknobs & Broomsticks, #2541, 1971, EX .......................**5.00**

Billy Bunnyscoot the Lost Bunny, #888, 1948, VG ...............**6.00**
Corky's Hiccups, #2428, 1968, EX ................................**5.00**
Disneyland, 1964, 28 pgs, NM .**25.00**
Donald Duck & the New Birdhouse, #2520, 1956, VG/EX .........**8.00**
Donald Duck in Frontierland, #2445, 1957, VG ..............**8.00**

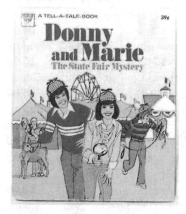

**Donnie and Marie, The State Fair Mystery, 1977, from $3.00 to $5.00. (Photo courtesy Greg Davis and Bill Morgan)**

Flying Sunbeam, #849, 1950, EX ..............................**10.00**
Ho-Hum, #2525, 1957, EX .....**5.00**
Johnny Appleseed, #808, 1949, EX ..............................**20.00**
Little Red Hen, #2431, 1953, EX .**5.00**
Mother Goose on the Farm, #2415-4, 1975, EX .....................**5.00**
Pink Panther Rides Again, #2403-1, 1976, EX .....................**6.00**
Road Runner & the Birdwatchers, #2518, 1968, VG/EX .......**5.00**
Roy Rogers' Surprise for Donnie, #943, 1954, EX ..............**20.00**
Snow White & 7 Dwarfs, #2533, 1957, VG/EX ...................**5.00**

Three Bears, #2592, 1968, EX .**5.00**
Tweety & Sylvester at the Farm, #2642, 1978, EX .............**4.00**
Yogi Bear Takes a Vacation, #2406, 1965, EX ...........**10.00**
101 Dalmatians, #2622, 1960, VG/EX .............................**5.00**

**Wonder Books**

Though the first were a little larger, the Wonder Books printed since 1948 have all measured 6½" x 8". They've been distributed by Random House, Grosset Dunlap, and Wonder Books Inc. They're becoming very collectible, especially those based on favorite TV and cartoon characters. Steve Santi's book *Collecting Little Golden Books* includes a section on Wonder Books as well.

A Horse for Johnny, #754, 1952, EX ...............................**5.00**
Cozy Little Farm, #749, 1946, EX ...............................**8.00**
Crusader Rabbit, 1958, EX .**20.00**
Famous Fairy Tales, #505, 1949, VG/EX ...........................**10.00**
Fred Flintstone, The Fix-It Man, #917, 1976, VG/EX .........**8.00**
Gandy Goose, #695, 1957, EX ......................**10.00**
Heidi, #532, 1950, VG/EX ...**10.00**
Hoppy the Curious Kangaroo, #579, 1952, EX .............**10.00**
Kewtee Bear's Christmas, #867, 1956, EX .........................**8.00**
Little Peter Cottontail, #641, Thornton W Burgess, 1956, VG/EX .............................**7.00**

127

Mother Goose, #501, in bonnet on cover, 1946, VG/EX .........**5.00**

Once There Was a House, #842, 1965, EX .........................**8.00**

Picture Story of Davy Crockett, #2525, 1955, EX ..............**5.00**

Pinocchio, #615, 1954, VG/EX .**6.00**

Raggedy Ann's Merriest Christmas, 1952, EX ...............**12.00**

Romper Room Book of Happy Animals, #587R, 1957, VG/EX ...........................**8.00**

Soupy Sales & the Talking Turtle, #960, 1965, EX ..............**10.00**

Three Little Pigs/Red Riding Hood, #609, 2-in-1 book, 1975, VG/EX ...........................**14.00**

Tuggy the Tugboat, #696, 1958, EX ....................................**8.00**

Wonder Book of Christmas, #575, 1951, EX .........................**8.00**

**Miscellaneous**

Adventures of Robin Hood & His Merry Men, Elf/Rand McNally, 1955, EX ...................**10.00**

Aladdin & the Wonderful Lamp, McLoughlin Bros, 1940, EX .**20.00**

Andy Panda's Rescue, Whitman, 1969, softcover, NM ........**8.00**

Batman Vs the Joker, Signet, 1966, 1st edition, softcover, NM ...............................**25.00**

Bobby Bear's Busy Day, Saalfield, 1952, hardcover, EX .....**15.00**

Dennis the Menace, Holt, 1953, hardcover, rare, EX ......**30.00**

Dr Seuss, Scrambled Eggs, Random House, 1953, hardcover, EX ....................................**8.00**

Hansel & Gretel, Samuel Lowe, 1944, softcover, EX .......**10.00**

Land of Peek-A-Boo, Treasure Books, 1955, EX ............**20.00**

Little Red Riding Hood, Jr Elf/ Rand McNally, 1933, EX .**20.00**

Mickey Mouse's Summer Vacation, Whitman, 1949, softcover, NM ...........................**18.00**

Mother Goose Rhymes, Whitman, 1934, softcover, NM ......**10.00**

One, Two, Cock-A-Doodle Doo, Jr Elf/Rand McNally, 1944, EX ...............................**10.00**

Peter Pan, Grosset & Dunlap, 1942, hardcover, EX .....**15.00**

Puppy Dog Tales, Random House, 1964, EX .......................**10.00**

Raggedy Ann & the Laughing Brook, Perks, 1946, softcover, EX ................................**35.00**

Superboy & the Legions of Super Heroes, Tempo, 1977, softcover, EX ...........................**20.00**

Superman, Lowther-Random House, 1942, hardcover, EX ......**125.00**

Three Bears Visit Goldilocks, Elf/ Rand McNally, 1950, EX ..**15.00**

# Children's Dishes

In the late 1900s glass companies introduced sets of small-scaled pressed glass dinnerware, many in the same pattern as their regular lines, others designed specifically for the little folks. Many were of clear glass, but milk glass, opalescent glass, and colors were also used. Not to be outdone, English ceramic firms as well as American potteries made both tea sets and fully accessorized dinnerware sets decorated with decals of nursery

**Edwin M, Knowles China Co., Circus theme: Plate, 6½", from $5.00 to $7.00; Cup and saucer, from $10.00 to $12.00; Teapot, $35.00. (Photo courtesy Margaret and Kenn Whitmyer)**

rhymes, animals, or characters from children's stories. Though popularly collected for some time, your favorite flea market may still yield some very nice examples of both types. Refer to *The Collector's Encyclopedia of Children's Dishes* by Margaret and Kenn Whitmyer (Collector Books) for more information.

## China and Pottery

Bowl, soup; Dimity, green on cream, England, 4¼" ....**10.00**

Creamer, Blue Banded, Dimmock, 2¾" ................................**25.00**

Creamer, Butterfly, Japan, 2¼" ..**7.50**

Creamer, Three Little Pigs on tan lustre, Japan ................**15.00**

Creamer & sugar bowl, Blue Willow, w/lid, 2", 2¾" .........**40.00**

Cup & saucer, Pagoda, on white, Japan ..............................**3.00**

Cup & saucer, Punch & Judy, 1⅞", 4¼" ................................**42.50**

Feeding set, Raggedy Ann & Andy, Crooksville, 1941, 3-pc .**60.00**

Plate, Embossed Leaf, burgundy, Made in Japan, 5½" ........**5.00**

Plate, Flow Blue Dogwood, Minton, 4" ....................**22.00**

Plate, grill; children playing on cream, ca 1930, 7¼" ......**12.00**

Plate, Hansel & Gretel, pink lustre, Germany, 5" ..........**24.00**

Plate, House That Jack Built, Germany, 5¼" ......................**8.00**

Plate, 2 girls playing game, black transfer, Dawson, 6½", EX .............................**70.00**

Sugar bowl, dog on ball, blue lustre rim, Japan, with lid, 2⅝" .**14.00**

Tea cup, Alice, Hammersley, 1930s ..........................**25.00**

Tea set, floral on tan lustre, Japan, 2-place ..............**30.00**

Tea set, Merry Christmas, pink lustre & gold, 12-pc ....................**385.00**

Tea set, Pink Rose, decal on white, unmarked, 6-place ......**185.00**

Teapot, Dutch figures, Japan .**8.50**

Teapot, Silhouette, Japan, w/lid, 4⅛" ................................**30.00**

Teapot, tan lustre, Occupied Japan ...............................12.00

Warming dish, Hansel & Gretel, Holland, 1930s ..............65.00

### Glass

Butter dish, Beaded Swirl, crystal, w/lid ................................55.00

Butter dish, Buzz Star (Whirligig), crystal, w/lid...................35.00

Butter dish, Colonial, crystal, Cambridge, w/lid............25.00

Cake stand, Fine Cut Star & Fan, crystal ............................35.00

Cake stand, Louisiana, crystal ..45.00

Cake stand, Ribbon Candy, green footed .............................75.00

Creamer, Arrowhead in Ovals, crystal ............................25.00

Creamer, Bead & Scroll, crystal ..70.00

Creamer, Lamb, crystal .......85.00

Cup & saucer, Loops & Ropes, crystal ............................30.00

Mug, Dewdrop, blue, 3¼" ....72.00

Mug, Eastlake, amber .........22.00

Mug, Hobnail, crystal .........50.00

Mug, Prism Panel, crystal, Sandwich ..............................15.00

**Mug, Butterfly, 2x2" or 2½x2¼", crystal, from $40.00 to $45.00.**

Mug, Squirrel, crystal .........**25.00**

Pitcher, Galloway, crystal ...**32.00**

Pitcher, Pattee Cross, crystal .**90.00**

Pitcher, water; Portland, crystal w/gold trim .....................**28.00**

Punch bowl, Wheat Sheaf, crystal ................................**35.00**

Punch cup, Oval Star, crystal .**9.00**

Punch cup, Wild Rose, milk glass ............................**15.00**

Spooner, Beaded Swirl, crystal .**40.00**

Spooner, Menagerie, fish, amber .....................**145.00**

Spooner, Rex (Fancy Cut), crystal ................................**35.00**

Sugar bowl, Arrowhead-In-Ovals, crystal ............................**35.00**

Sugar bowl, Beaded Swirl Variant, crystal ............................**40.00**

Sugar bowl, Wild Rose, milk glass, open .............................**100.00**

Tumbler, Nursery Rhyme, crystal ................................**25.00**

## Christmas

No other holiday season is celebrated to such an extravagant extent as Christmas, and vintage decorations provide a warmth and charm that none from today can match. Ornaments from before 1870 were imported from Dresden, Germany — usually made of cardboard and sparkled with tinsel trim. Later, blown glass ornaments were made there in literally thousands of shapes such as fruits and vegetables, clowns, Santas, angels, and animals. Kugles, heavy glass balls (though you'll sometimes find fruit and vegetable

**Bells, Criterion Bell & Specialty, tin decorations for miniature trees, rung by electrical Santa, MIB, $65.00. (Photo courtesy Kenn and Margaret Whitmyer)**

forms as well) were made from about 1820 to late in the century in sizes up to 14". Early Santa figures are treasured, especially those in robes other than red. Figural bulbs from the '20s and '30s are popular, those that are character related in particular. Refer to *Christmas Collectibles* by Margaret and Kenn Whitmyer and *Christmas Ornaments, Lights & Decorations, Volumes I, II and III*, by George Johnson (all by Collector Books) for more information.

Bubble light, celluloid Santa in cardboard disc, Japan, 2¼" ....**20.00**

Bubble light, generic type, 4¼" to 5½", from $2 to ...............**8.00**

Bubble light, Noma, clear base, ca 1988 ...................**1.50**

Bubble light, Noma Biscuit, common form, 1946-60, EX .........................**5.00**

Bulb, apple, milk glass, oval shape, Japan, 2½" .........**12.50**

Bulb, banana w/face, milk glass, Japan, 1950s, 2¾", from $20 to ....................................**30.00**

Bulb, bell, milk glass, Christmas Greetings, Japan, 1950, mini ............................**12.50**

Bulb, bird in birdhouse, milk glass, 1935-50, 1½", from $15 to ....................................**20.00**

Bulb, cat begging, lg eyes, milk glass, Japan, 1930s, 2½" .**25.00**

Bulb, cottage in hillside, milk glass, Japan, 1950s, 2¼" ..........**55.00**

Bulb, Joey clown head, milk glass, Japan, 1935-50, 2", from $25 to ....................................**30.00**

Bulb, Mickey Mouse, milk glass, Disney, Diamond Brite, from $14 to .............................**18.00**

Bulb, puppy on ball, milk glass, Japan, 2¼", from $25 to .**35.00**

Bulb, rooster playing golf, milk glass, Japan, 2¾", from $20 to ....................................**25.00**

Bulb, 3-faced Santa, milk glass, Japan, 2¼", from $20 to .**30.00**

Bulb cover, Santa, early plastic, 3¼" ....................................**25.00**

Candy container, lady's high-heeled boot, satin over cardboard, 5½" ....................**50.00**

Candy container, Santa, papier-mache & fur, wire neck, Germany, 9" ........................**35.00**

Candy container, snowman, papier-mache w/glass eyes, Germany, 5" ................**38.00**

Figure, reindeer, celluloid w/glitter, hollow, 5" ................**25.00**

Figure, reindeer, plaster over wood & compo, Germany, 2½" ..............................**25.00**

Figure, sheep, wooly w/wooden legs, 3¼" ........................**75.00**

**Figurines, angels, red and white glossy glazes, 'real' hair, Norcrest, Made in Japan label, from $8.00 to $12.00 each; Angel music box, red and white glossy glazes, Norcrest, Made in Japan label, from $18.00 to $22.50. (Photo courtesy Carole Bess White)**

Kugel, grapes w/embossed leaves, various colors, Indian repro, 4" ......................................**8.00**

Lantern, Santa head, milk glass, double-faced, battery, Amico, 6" ....................................**40.00**

Nodder, Santa, composition, Japan ............................**50.00**

**Ornaments, teapot and coffeepot sold as part of a series, Montgomery Ward, 1950s, $25.00 each. (Photo courtesy Margaret and Kenn Whitmyer)**

Ornament, angel w/harp on cloud, scrap, 6", from $10 to ...**15.00**

Ornament, beaded object or figure, flat, 2" to 6", from $2 to ..**8.00**

Ornament, beads & tubes, flat, Japan or Czech ...............**8.00**

Ornament, bell (common), free blown, 4", from $3 to ......**7.00**

Ornament, bird, mold blown, spun glass wings, Germany, 3½" ..............................**40.00**

Ornament, bird, spun cotton, varying sizes, from $15 to ...**25.00**

Ornament, birdhouse w/doves, mold blown, 3", from $20 to .....**30.00**

Ornament, cat, free blown, tubular w/annealed legs, Germany, 3" ........................**45.00**

Ornament, elf head, mold blown, Germany, 1970s, 3", from $15 to ...................................**18.00**

Ornament, football, mold blown, hanger in top, 1980s, 3¼" ...............**55.00**

Ornament, Joey clown head, mold blown, Germany, 1950s, 3½" ...................**75.00**

Ornament, man in the moon (frowning), mold blown, 2¾" ...........................**85.00**

Ornament, pear, spun cutton, varying sizes, from $15 to .....**50.00**

Ornament, rosette, spun glass w/scrap angel on 1 side, 6" dia ...............................**55.00**

Ornament, Teddy bear, mold blown, East Germany, 1970s, 2", from $70 to ..............**90.00**

Ornament, trumpet flower, mold blown, indented center, 2¾" ...................**40.00**

Ornament, windmill on disc, mold blown, 2¼", from $30 to .**40.00**

Santa, celluloid, red & white, Irwin, 8¼" ....................**75.00**

**Santa, ceramic figure, ca 1960s, 7", $30.00.**

Santa, plastic, red & white w/green, lights up, lg, EX ..............**75.00**

Tree, bubble light; green or white, US, 24", from $100 to .**125.00**

Tree, cellophane, green, ca 1935, from $20 to ...................**35.00**

Tree, crepe paper, ca 1940, from $30 to ............................**40.00**

Tree, feather; green w/red berries, sq red base, 1930s, 37" ............................**300.00**

Tree, Visca, green & white, ca 1950, 42" to 60", from $30 to ............................**45.00**

Tree stand, cast iron, green paint, gold star ea leg (4), 3" opening ......................**55.00**

Tree topper, angel in cloud wreath, plastic, American, 1958, 8" ..........................**6.00**

## Cigarette Lighters

Pocket lighters were invented sometime after 1908 and were at their peak from about 1925 to the 1930s. Dunhill, Zippo, Colibri, Ronson, Dupont, and Evans are some of the major manufacturers. An early Dunhill Unique model if found in its original box would be valued at hundreds of dollars. Quality metal and metal-plated lighters were made from the '50s to about 1960. Around that time disposable lighters never needing a flint were introduced, causing a decline in sales of figurals, novelties, and high-quality lighters.

What makes a lighter collectible? — novelty of design, type of mechanism (flint and fuel, flint and gas, battery, etc.), and manufacturer (and whether or not the company is still in business). For further information, we recommend *Collector's*

Guide to Cigarette Lighters, Books I and II, by James Flanagan (Collector Books).

Advertising, Alpine Cigarettes, Japan, 1960s, 2x1⅜", from $10 to ..............................15.00

**Advertising, Sherwin-Williams, chromium, Lansing, ca 1975, 1¾" x 2", from $10.00 to 20.00. (Photo courtesy James Flanagan)**

Advertising, Tribune Vermouth, bottle figural, 1950s, 5¼", from $15 to ...................20.00

ATC, Super de Lux, brushed satin chromium, 1950s, 2¼", MIB, from $10 to ...................20.00

Bently, chromium, butane, mid-1950s, 1½x2⅛", from $10 to ...........20.00

Continental, chromium w/red leather band, 1950s, 1¼x1¼", from $10 to ...................20.00

Dunhill, gold-plated metal, ca 1934, 2½x⅞", from $175 to ....225.00

Elgin, American Lite-O-Matic .20.00

Evans, Spitfire, US army insignia on black enamel, ca 1940s ....30.00

Figural, Book of Smoking, Corona ..............................20.00

Figural, camel, table model, Japan, 1960s, 3½x4", from $20 to ..............................30.00

Figural, cowboy boot w/spur, Evans ..............................15.00

Figural, derringer, brass-plated metal, Made in Japan, 1970s, 8" ....................................20.00

Figural, donkey, brass, Japan, mid-1950s, 2x2½", from $15 to ........................................20.00

Figural, gun, Henry 42 caliber derringer, Swank ..............20.00

Figural, ice cream cone, plastic, ca 1960s, 3½" ....................15.00

Figural, motorcycle, front wheel turns, chromium, butane, 1980s, 6" ........................40.00

Figural, potbellied stove, black paint on brass, ca 1955, 5½" ............................30.00

Figural, rose, table model, chromium, 1960s, 2¼x1¾", from $20 to ....................................30.00

Figural, table-top, brass, ca early 1930s, 4x1¼" dia, from $40 to ..................................60.00

Figural, television, table model, Swank, 1960s, 2¾x3⅞", from $25 to ............................40.00

Gibson, Windproof, ostrich leather w/engravable shield, 1950s .10.00

Hyalyn, ceramic w/brown & orange on cream, table size ........................15.00

Marvel Pocket Lighter, w/Ray-O-Lite Fluid, MIB ............35.00

May Fair, brass & Bakelite w/lift arm, 1930s, 2x1⅝", from $50 to ..................................70.00

Myflam/England, embossed florals on chromium, 1½x1⅜", $40 to ..........................60.00

Occupied Japan, chromium, lift arm, ca 1948, 1x⅞", from $20 to ..................................40.00

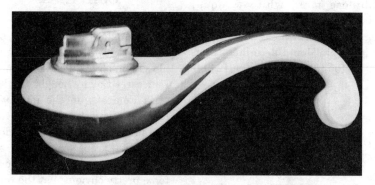

**Ronson, gold on white china, 2½" x 8", $15.00.**

Parker, Flaminaire, polished chromium, ca 1951, 2¾", MIB, $25 to ............................**40.00**

Partlow Kase Lighter, polished chrome, MIB ................**20.00**

Perfecto, plain chromium, ca 1930, 2½x1½", from $40 to ............................**50.00**

Ronson, Banker, 14k gold, engine-turned, 1950s ..............**150.00**

Ronson, Diana model, silver-plated table model, ca 1950, 2¼" ............................**20.00**

Ronson, Mastercase, chromium, case & lighter combo, 1933, 4½" ............................**35.00**

Ronson, Princess, enameled florals on black, 1950s ............**45.00**

Waterford crystal, butane, ca 1975, 3x3½" dia ............**60.00**

Weston, Ball of Flint, pen form w/ball top ......................**40.00**

Weston, Mighty Midget, 3" ..**35.00**

Zippo, Civil War, Cherokee rifleman, 1991 .....................**25.00**

Zippo, Landing on the Moon, 1969, from $25 to ..................**30.00**

Zippo, 60th Anniversary Zippo Co, 1932-92 ......................**25.00**

# Clothes Sprinkler Bottles

From the time we first had irons, clothes were sprinkled with water before ironing for the best results. During the 1930s until the 1950s when the steam iron became a home staple, some of us merely took sprinkler tops and stuck them into bottles to accomplish this task. The more imaginative enjoyed the bottles made in figural shapes and bought the ones they particularly liked. The most popular, of course, were the Chinese men marked Sprinkle Plenty. Some bottles were made by American Bisque, Cleminson of California, and other famous figural pottery makers. Many were made in Japan for the export market.

Cat, marble eyes, American Bisque, from $195 to .**250.00**

Chinese man, holding iron, from $125 to ........................**150.00**

Chinese man, Sprinkle Plenty, yellow & green, Cardinal China, $20 to ............................**30.00**

Chinese man, white & aqua, Cleminson, from $30 to ..........................**40.00**

Clothespin, hand decorated, from $100 to ........................**125.00**

**Dearie Is Weary, ceramic, Enesco, $200.00 minimum value. (Photo courtesy Ellen Bercovici)**

Dutch boy, green & white, from $150 to ........................**175.00**

Elephant, trunk forms handle, American Bisque, minimum value ...........................**300.00**

Iron, blue flowers, from $75 to **.95.00**

Iron, lady ironing, from $60 to **.70.00**

Iron, souvenir of Florida, pink flamingo, from $150 to **.200.00**

Mary Maid, all colors, plastic, Reliance, from $15 to ....**35.00**

Peasant woman, w/laundry poem on label .......................**250.00**

Rooster, green, tan & red detailing over white, from $100 to ...........................**125.00**

# Coin Glass

Coin glass was originally produced in crystal, ruby, blue, emerald green, olive green, and amber. Lancaster Colony bought the Fostoria Company in the mid-1980s and is currently producing this line in crystal, green, blue, amber, and red. Except for the red and crystal, the colors are 'off' enough to be pretty obvious, but the red is so close it's impossible to determine old from new. Here is some (probably not all) of the items currently in production: bowl, 8" diameter; bowl, 9" oval; candlesticks, 4½"; candy jar with lid, 6¼"; cigarette box with lid, 5¾" x 4½"; creamer and sugar bowl; footed comport; decanter, 10¼"; jelly; nappy with handle, 5¼"; footed salver, 6½"; footed urn with lid, 12¾"; and wedding bowl, 8¼". Know your dealer!

Emerald green is the most desired by collectors. You may also find some crystal pieces with gold decorated coins. These will be valued at about double the price of plain crystal if the gold is not worn. Worn or faded gold seems to have little value. Numbers included in our descriptions were company-assigned stock numbers that collectors use as a means to distinguish variations in stems and shapes. For futher information we recommend *Collectible Glassware from the 40s, 50s & 60s*, by Gene Florence (Collector Books).

Bowl, #1372/199, blue, footed, 8½" ..............................**90.00**

Bowl, ruby, oval, 9", $50.00.

Candy box, #1372/354, green, w/lid, 4⅛" ......................**75.00**

Cigarette holder, #1372/372, crystal, w/ashtray lid ..........**45.00**

Cigarette urn, #1372/381, olive, footed, 3⅜" ......................**20.00**

Condiment tray, #1372/738, blue, 9⅝" ................................**75.00**

Creamer, #1372/680, ruby ...**16.00**

Decanter, #1372/400, blue, 1-pt, w/stopper, 10¼" ..........**195.00**

Lamp, coach; #1372/320, amber, oil, 13½" ......................**135.00**

Lamp, patio; #1372/466, blue, electric, 16⅝" ....................**275.00**

Nappy, #1372/499, crystal, w/handles, 5⅜" ......................**15.00**

Candy dish, green, 6", 75.00.

Pitcher, #1372/453, amber, 32-oz, 6⅜" ................................**55.00**

Plate, #1372/550, olive, 8" ...**20.00**

Punch cup, #1372/615, crystal ........................**32.00**

Salver, #1372/630, green, footed, 6½" ..............................**250.00**

Shaker, #1372/652, ruby, with chrome top, 3¼", pr ......**45.00**

Stem, goblet; #1372/2, ruby, 10½-oz ....................................**95.00**

Sugar bowl, #1372/673, olive, with lid ................................**35.00**

Tumbler, iced tea; #1372/58, crystal, 14-oz, 5¼" ..............**35.00**

Tumbler, juice/old fashioned; #1372/81, crystal, 9-oz, 3⅝" ........................**30.00**

Vase, bud; #1372/799, ruby, 8" ..**45.00**

## Coloring Books

This is a branch of toy collecting that has become so popular that it now stands on its own merit. Throughout the '50s and even into the 1970s, coloring and activity books were produced by the thousands. Whitman, Saalfield, and Watkins-Strathmore were some of the largest publishers. The most popular were those that pictured well-known TV, movie, and comic book characters, and these are the ones that are bringing top dollar today. The better the character, the higher the price, but condition is important as well. Compared to a coloring book that was never used, one that's only partially colored is worth from 50% to 70% less.

Agent Zero, Whitman, 1966, unused, NM ..................**25.00**

Andy Panda, Whitman, 1944, few pages colored, EX ..........**25.00**

Batman, Whitman, 1967, unused, NM ................................**30.00**

Beverly Hillbillies, Whitman, 1964, several pages colored, EX ................................**25.00**

**The Beverly Hillbillies, Whitman #1137, 1963, EX, from $20.00 to $25.00. (Photo courtesy Greg Davis and Bill Morgan)**

Captain America, Whitman, 1966, few pages colored, EX ...**25.00**

Choo Choo Charlie, Whitman, 1970, rare, few pages colored, EX ................................**50.00**

Davy Crockett, Whitman, 1950s, few pages colored, VG ..........................**25.00**

Dick Tracy, Saalfield, 1946, unused, EX ....................**45.00**

Donald Duck, Watkins-Strathmore, 1963, unused, EX ............**25.00**

Elizabeth Taylor, Whitman, 1952, few pages colored, EX ...**35.00**

F-Troop, Saalfield, 1960, few pages colored, EX ..........**28.00**

Felix the Cat, Whitman, 1957, unused, M ......................**50.00**

Gentle Ben, Whitman, 1968, unused, EX ....................**20.00**

Gilligan's Island, Whitman, 1965, several pages colored, NM ............................**55.00**

Hey There It's Yogi Bear, Whitman, 1964, few pages colored, EX ................................**30.00**

Huck & Magilla Join the Circus, Modern, 1977, unused, NM .........**25.00**

Johnny Tremain, Whitman, 1957, few pages colored, EX ...**25.00**

Krazy Cat, Lowe, 1963, unused, M ................................**25.00**

Land of the Giants, Whitman, 1969, unused, NM ........**45.00**

Laurel & Hardy, Whitman, 1968, unused, NM ..................**25.00**

Little Lulu, Whitman, 1944, several pages colored, EX .....**40.00**

**Huckleberry Hound, Western Printing, 1962, EX, $12.00. (Photo courtesy June Moon)**

Mary Poppins, Whitman, 1964, few pages colored, EX ...**25.00**

My Three Sons, Whitman, 1967, unused, NM ..................**45.00**

Partridge Family, Saalfield, 1970, several pages colored, VG ............................**25.00**

Porky Pig, Saalfield, 1938, several pages colored, NM ........**70.00**

Raggedy Ann, Whitman, 1968, few pages colored, NM ........**30.00**

Ripcord, Saalfield, 1963, unused, NM ...............................**30.00**

Roy Rogers & Dale Evans, Whitman, 1958, several pages colored, VG .......................**25.00**

Six Million Dollar Man, Whitman, 1977, unused, EX ..........**10.00**

Smokey Bear, Whitman, 1958, few pages colored, EX ..........**15.00**

Steve Canyon, Saalfield, 1952, few pages colored, EX ..........**30.00**

Stingray, Whitman, 1966, few pages colored, EX ..........**30.00**

Super Circus, Whitman, 1953, unused, NM ...................**30.00**

Tammy's Vacation, Watkins-Strathmore, 1960, unused, M ....**20.00**

Tarzan, Whitman, 1966, unused, EX ...............................**20.00**

Tweety Bird, Whitman, 1955, few pages colored, EX ..........**20.00**

Wacky Races, Whitman, 1971, unused, NM ...................**35.00**

Wagon Train, Whitman, 1959, several pages colored, EX ..**25.00**

Walt Disney Around the World, Whitman, 1957, few pages colored, VG .......................**10.00**

Waltons, Whitman, 1975, unused, EX ...............................**15.00**

101 Dalmatians, Whitman, 1960, few pages colored, VG ..**20.00**

# Comic Books

Factors that make a comic book valuable are condition, content, and rarity, not necessarily age. In fact, comics printed between 1950 and the late 1970s are most in demand by collectors who prefer those they had as children to the earlier comics. Issues where the hero is first introduced are treasured. While some may go for hundreds, even thousands of dollars, many are worth very little; so if you plan to collect, you'll need a good comic book price guide such as Overstreet's to assess your holdings. Condition is extremely important. Compared to a book in excellent condition, a mint issue might be worth six to eight times as much, while one in only good condition should be priced at less than half the price of the excellent example. For more information see *Schroeder's Collectible Toys, Antique to Modern* (Collector Books).

Adventures of Bob Hope, Dell #30, VG ...............................**25.00**

Apache Trail, Dell #3, 1958, NM ............................**15.00**

Batman & Robin Battle Mutiny in the Big House, DC Comics #46, 1948, EX .............**145.00**

Beany & Cecil, Dell #2, 1962, rare, EX ...............................**25.00**

Best of Donald Duck & Scrooge, Dell #2, 1967, EX .........**40.00**

Buck Jones, Dell Four-Color #652, 1955, EX .......................**10.00**

Bullwinkle & Rocky, Gold Key #9, 1973, EX .......................**12.00**

Challengers of the Unknown, Dell #28, EX .......................**40.00**

Christmas & Archie, Archie Comics #1, 1974, EX ...**10.00**

Christmas in Bedrock, Gold Key #31, 1965, EX ...............**20.00**

Conan the Barbarian, Marvel Treasury #4, 1975, oversized, NM ...................................**8.00**

Dark Shadows, Gold Key #5, 1970, NM ...................................**50.00**

David & Goliath, Dell Four-Color #1205, 1961, VG ..........**20.00**

Dennis the Menace, Standard #13, 1955, EX ........................**25.00**

Dick Tracy, Dell #4, NM ..**100.00**

Donald Duck in Disneyland, Dell #1, NM ..........................**125.00**

Dr Who & the Daleks, Dell #1, 1966, VG ........................**15.00**

Felix the Cat, Dell #2, 1948, VG ............................**25.00**

**Flying Nun, Dell, #1 – #4, 1967, from $10.00 to $20.00 each. (Photo courtesy Greg Davis and Bill Morgan)**

Flipper, Gold Key #2, 1966, EX ............................**35.00**

Gentle Ben, Dell #4, 1968, VG ..**6.00**

George of the Jungle, Dell Giant #1, EX ............................**40.00**

Gidget, Dell #1, 1966, VG ....**25.00**

**Green Lantern, DC Comics #7, 1960, NM, from $175.00 to $200.00.**

Howdy Doody, Dell #1, 1952, EX ............................**25.00**

Hunchback of Notre Dame, Dell #854, 1957, EX ..............**40.00**

Josie & the Pussycats, Archie #18, 1966, EX ........................**10.00**

Lone Ranger, Dell #70, 1954, EX ...............................**20.00**

Marge's Little Lulu, Dell #42, 1951, VG ......................**20.00**

Mod Squad, Dell #5, 1970, NM ......................**10.00**

Mutt & Jeff, DC Comics #39, 1948, EX ...................................**12.00**

Nick Fury Agent of Shield, Marvel Comics, EX ...................**15.00**

Oswald the Rabbit, Dell Four-Color #102, 1946, VG ........................**25.00**

Popeye, Dell #48, 1959, EX .**12.00**

Raggedy Ann & Andy, Dell Giant #2, 1965, EX ...................**8.00**

Red Ryder, Dell #69, 1949, EX ........................**20.00**

Restless Gun, Dell #1045, EX ..**55.00**

Richie Rich, Dell #23, VG ....**15.00**

Rifleman, Gold Key #16, 1963, VG ...............15.00
Rudolph the Red-Nosed Reindeer, DC Comics, 1952, EX ...........25.00
Ruff & Reddy, Dell #7, EX ..35.00
Secret Agent, Gold Key #1, 1966, EX ...............30.00
Silly Symphonies, Dell #7, NM .100.00
Space Mouse, Dell Four-Color #132, 1960, VG .............15.00
Superman's Pal Jimmy Olsen, Dell #23, VG ..................15.00
Tarzan's Jungle Annual, Dell Giant #4, 1955, EX .......25.00
Terry & the Pirates, Dell #101, 1945, EX .......................80.00
Texas Kid, Dell #9, VG ........15.00
That Darn Cat, Gold Key, 1965, EX ................20.00
Three Stooges, Dell #1170, 1961, VG .................30.00
Tom Corbett Space Cadet, Dell #9, EX ...................50.00
Tom Mix, Fawcett #10, 1948, VG .............40.00
Voyage to the Bottom of the Sea, Gold Key #1, 1964, EX .20.00
Woody Woodpecker, Dell Four-Color #374, 1952, NM ...25.00
Zorro, Dell #13, 1961, EX ....35.00
101 Dalmatians, Dell Four-Color #1183, 1961, EX .............25.00

## Compacts

Prior to World War I, the use of cosmetics was frowned upon. It was not until after the war when women became liberated and entered the work force that their use became acceptable. A compact became a necessity as a portable container for cosmetics and usually contained a puff and mirror. They were made in many different styles, shapes, and motifs and from every type of natural and man-made material. The fine jewelry houses made compacts in all of the precious metals — some studded with precious stones. The most sought-after compacts today are those made of plastic, Art Deco styles, figurals, and any that incorporate gadgets. Compacts that are combined with other accessories are also very desirable.

Our advisor for this category is Roselyn Gerson; she is listed in the Directory under New York. For further information we recommend these books: *Collector's Encyclopedia of Compacts, Carryalls & Face Powder Boxes, Volumes I and II*, by Laura M. Muller; and *Vintage Ladies' Compacts* by Ms. Gerson. All are published by Collector Books. See also Clubs and Newsletters.

Ebonite w/white metal & faceted rhinestones, 2¾" dia, from $50 to .................................60.00
Gold-tone, Art Moderne sunray & monogram, vanity, 2" dia, from $45 to ...................60.00
Gold-tone, ballet duo by C Golding, Stratton, 3¼" dia, from $75 to .........................90.00
Gold-tone, butterfly logo, Lucretia Vanderbilt, 2" dia, from $50 to .................................65.00
Gold-tone, domed w/embossed petals, Majestic, 2" dia, from $30 to .........................45.00

**Black and white dice motif on gold-tone, $125.00. (Photo courtesy Roselyn Gerson)**

Gold-tone w/embossed nude, Deere script logo, 2⅜" dia .......60.00

Gold-tone w/enameled lady w/fan, Colgate & Co, 2½" dia ...........................85.00

Gold-tone w/faux tortoise-shell enamel, Paris France, 3½x2¾" ......................120.00

Gold-tone w/maroon enamel & repousse floral, snuff box form, Elmo, 3" ...............75.00

Gold-tone w/painted roses, Kigu of London, 2½" sq, from $25 to ................................40.00

Gold-tone w/silver-tone overlay, engraved circles, Belle Fifth Ave, 4" .........................85.00

Green marbled vinyl over white metal, shutter button, Zell, 3¼x2" ........................75.00

Gunmetal with Deco lid inset, octagon, vanity, Seventeen, 1⅞" .........................100.00

Ivorene, lady in full skirt on lid, pressed powder vanity, triangular ......................75.00

Leather horseshoe with gilt dots, Rothena, 3¾x3⅝", from $45 to .............................60.00

Lucite, cerice w/pierced quatrefoil lid ornament, 4½x4¼" ..135.00

Mother-of-pearl cross-banded lid, gold-tone base, 2¾x2⅜" .75.00

Plastic, aqua flapjack w/mermaid, coin-purse closures, Revlon, 4" dia ................................80.00

Plastic, ivory dome w/Atlantic City NJ transfer, flapjack, 5" dia ...............................265.00

Plastic, Schiaparelli on shocking pink, 2¾" dia, from $35 to ..........50.00

Plastic domed case, coin-purse closure, Victoria Vogue, 2⅜" dia .......................20.00

Spun aluminum, embossed Deco flowers, Hampden, 3" dia, from $50 to ...................65.00

Spun aluminum, Fleurs d'Amour, Cupid logo, Roger & Gallet, 3¼" dia .........................................85.00

Sterling w/blue Lucite lid w/dove relief, unmarked, 2⅞" sq .....................135.00

White metal, Spanish fan dancer on brown enamel, glove vanity, 2½" ..........................60.00

White metal, wood-encased w/burned initials, glove vanity, 2½" ..........................45.00

White metal book w/black & gold floral, vanity, 3x2⅛", from $75 to .................................90.00

White metal w/champleve enamel Art Moderne comet on lid, 2" dia .................................75.00

Wood & plastic flapjack w/painted flamingo, Zell, 4" dia, from $45 to ...........................60.00

**Related Items and Accessories**

Creme perfume, flower basket form w/porcelain lid, Max Factor, 1½" .......................50.00

Lipstick, black Bakelite w/rhine-
stones & gold beads, 2¼", from
$40 to .................................60.00
Lipstick, Cracker Jack, black &
gold stripes, Helena
Rubenstein, 2¾"............60.00
Lipstick, Evening in Paris, red,
white & blue plastic, 2" ..30.00
Lipstick, gold-tone w/Lucite
base, Tangee, 2", from $15
to .................................25.00
Lipstick, rabbit fur covering,
Lucien Lelong, 2¼", from $45
to .................................65.00
Mirror, gold-tone w/red & blue
enamel hearts, 1¾" sq .20.00
Mirror, polished gold-tone w/red &
black card symbols, Carolee,
2¼" .................................25.00
Mirror/matchbook combination,
filigree with stones, Zell,
2x1¾" .........................20.00
Pearlized plastic w/gold-tone &
rhinestones, 2⅝" sq ......45.00
Solid perfume, blue enamel purse
w/twist closure, Viviane
Woodward ...................60.00
Solid perfume, brushed gold-tone
shell, Givenchy, 1⅞", from $20
to .................................25.00
Solid perfume, pink frost cat on
silver-tone pillow, Estee
Lauder, 2" ...................60.00
Solid perfume pendant, brushed gold-
tone heart w/rhinestone, 1" ..35.00
Solid perfume pendant, silver-tone
kidney shape, Estee Lauder,
2" .................................35.00

## Cookbooks

Advertising cookbooks, those by
well-known personalities, and figural
diecuts are among the more readily
available examples on today's market.
    Our advisor for this catego-
ry is Colonel Bob Allen, author
of *A Guide to Cookbook Collecting.* Other suggested reading:
*The Price Guide to Cookbook
and Recipe Leaflets* by Linda
Dickinson. (Both are published
by Collector Books.)

### Advertising

American Beauty Recipes Using
Macaroni Products, 1930s, 16
pages ...........................15.00
Aunt Jemima's Magical Recipes,
Quaker Oats Co, 1962, 26
pages ...........................10.00
Baker's Cocoanut Cut-Up Cakes,
General Foods, 1956, 28
pages ..............................8.00
Beech-Nut Book of Menus &
Recipes, Ida Bailey Allen,
1923, 32 pages ............20.00
Betty Crocker's Bisquick Party
Book, softcover, 1957, 24
pages ..............................6.00
Blue Ball Book, 1933, 56
pages ...........................15.00
Bond Bread Cook Book, Gener-
al Baking Co, softcover,
1933 .........................14.00
Borden's Eagle Brand 70 Magic
Recipes, softcover, 1952, 26
pages ..............................8.00
Bouquets for the Cook,
Gulden's, 1950s, 6-page
pamphlet ...................6.00
C&H Cane Sugar Presents 'Dri-
vert' Fondant Icings, 1957, 28
pages ..............................6.00

Calumet Baking Powder, ca 1918, 32 pages, EX, $16.00.

Calumet Cook Book, 1922, 80 pages ..............................**14.00**

Carnation Cook Book, Mary Blake, 1942 ...............................**10.00**

Chiquita Banana Presents 18 Recipes From Her Minute Movies, 1951 ...................**8.00**

Chocolate Cookery, Baker's GF Corp, 1929, 36 pages .**14.00**

Chiquita Banana's Recipe Book, 1960, $6.00. (Photo courtesy Colonel Bob Allen)

Cox's New Simple Recipes — What To Do w/Gelatin, 1930s, 31 pages ...............................**12.00**

Cream Top Book of Tested Recipes, Cream Top Bottle Corp, 1935 .....................**15.00**

Creative Cooking Made Easy — Golden Fluffo, spiral bound, 1956 ................................**8.00**

Del Monte Tomato Sauce Recipes, CA Packing Corp, 1930, 24 pages ..............................**14.00**

Downright Delicious Sun-Maid Raisin Recipes, HJ Heinz, 1949, 32 pages ..............**10.00**

Everyday Recipes, Wesson Oil People, 1950, 29 pages .**14.00**

Fascinating Foods w/Swift'ning, 1940s ...........................**10.00**

Fleischmann Treasury of Yeast Baking, 1962, 51 pages ..**6.00**

General Foods Cook Book, hardcover, 1932, 1934, 370 pages .........................**20.00**

Good Things To Eat — My Favorite Breads, Arm & Hammer, 1939, 15 pages .........................**12.00**

Heinz Recipe Book, HJ Heinz Co, spiral bound, 1939 ........**25.00**

Here's How by Stouffers, Stouffer Foods Corp, 1962 ............**8.00**

Hershey Recipe Book, Caroline B King, 1930, 80 pages ....**14.00**

Jelke Good Luck Oleomargarine Quick Breads, 1933 ......**14.00**

Kooking with Inspiration, Kitchen Bouquet, 1962, 48 pages ........................**6.00**

Kraft Cheese & Ways To Serve It, 1921, 32 pages ..............**20.00**

Let's Bake the Robin Hood 'No-Sift' Way, Rita Martin, 1976, 15 pages .........................**4.00**

Let's Eat Outdoors, American Dairy Association, 1950s, 28 pages ...............6.00

Margaret Mitchell's Cooking, Aluminum Cooking Utensil Co, 1932 ...............30.00

Maxwell House Coffee Cookbook, Ellen Sattoustall, hardcover, 1964 ...............15.00

Minute Gelatin Cook Book, 1926, 16 pages ...............16.00

Mr Peanut's Guide to Entertaining, Planters Peanuts... Kitchen, 1960s ...............8.00

Nescafe — 4 New Coffee-Flavored Desserts, Nestle Co, 1949, 14 pages ...............10.00

New Cake Secrets, F Barton, Swans Down Flour, Igleheart Brothers, 1931 ...............15.00

New Sealtest Book of Recipes & Menus, 1940s, 96 pages .8.00

Rawleigh's Good Health Guide Almanac & Cook Book, 1956, 32 pages ...............6.00

Recipes To Stretch Your Sugar Ration, Arm & Hammer, 1942, 8 pages ...............6.00

Rumford Book of Home Managemant, H Wing, gray cover, 1920s, 64 pages ...............14.00

Spry 20th Anniversary Cookbook of Old & New Favorites, 1955, 25 pages ...............8.00

Staley's Approved Recipes, 1928, 30 pages ...............14.00

Sunsweet Recipes, 1950, 46 pages ...............8.00

Tempting Dishes the Easy Way..., Pet Milk, 1930s, 16 pages ...............14.00

Time Tested Royal Recipes, Standard Brands, 1950s, 31 pages ...............8.00

Vermont Maid Pancake Cookbook, 1968 reprint, 10 pages, 8½x11" ...............5.00

100 Recipes Using Campfire Marshmallows & Creme, 1920s ...............14.00

75 Delicious Desserts, Nabisco, Mary Ellen Baker, 1957, 28 pages ...............8.00

## Appliances

Coldspot Operating Suggestions & Recipes, Sears Roebuck, 1930s ...............15.00

Cook Book & Instructions, Standard Electric Stove Co, 1930, 32 pages ...............20.00

Cooking w/Cold, Kelvinator, softcover, 1933 ...............15.00

French Fried Delicacies, Wear-Ever French Fryer, 1926, 16-page foldout .......20.00

Frigidaire Recipe Book, Miss Verna L Miller, Frigidaire Corp, 1933 ...............15.00

Frigidaire Recipes, hardcover, copyright Union 1910, 1928, 77 pages ......35.00

Gem Chopper Cook Book, Sargent & Co, 1902 ...............25.00

How To Use Your General Electric Refrigerator, 1940s, 24 pages ...............8.00

Kenmore Cook Book — US Regional Cook Book, 1939, 1940, 1947 ...............20.00

Magic Chef Cooking, Shank, American Stove Co, 1924, 1934, 1935 ...............15.00

Majestic Recipes, Dorothy A Louden, 1931, 40 pages ...............15.00

Monarch Cook Book, hardcover, Malleable Iron Range Co, 1905 ..............................**45.00**

Robertshaw Oven Heat Control Cooking Suggestions, 1920s ........................**17.50**

Sunbeam Mixmaster, 1957, 42 pages ..............................**6.00**

**Westinghouse Refrigerators, 1948, $12.50. (Photo courtesy Colonel Bob Allen)**

## Jell-O

The Jell-O® Story: Peter Cooper dabbled with and patented a product which was 'set' with gelatin, a product that had been known in France since 1682. His patent for an orange-flavored gelatin was granted in 1845 and was marketed from the 1890s through the early 1900s. Suffice it to say, it never did 'jell' with the American public.

In 1897 Pearl B. Wait, a carpenter in Le Roy, New York, was formulating a cough remedy and laxative tea in his home. He experimented with gelatin and came up with a fruit-flavored dessert. His wife coined the name Jell-O®, and production began with four flavors: lemon, orange, raspberry, and strawberry.

Jell-O® is 'America's Most Famous Dessert.' In the infancy of advertising campaigns, this was the campaign slogan of a simple gelatin dessert that would one day become known around the world. The success story is the result of advertising and merchandising methods, new and different, having never before been employed. Well-groomed, well-trained, and well-versed salesmen went out in 'spanking' rigs drawn by beautiful horses into the roads, byroads, fairs, country gatherings, church socials, and parties to advertise their product. Pictures, posters, and billboards covered the American landscape, and full-page ads in magazines carried Jell-O® with her delicious flavored product into American homes.

A Jell-O Year — America's Most Famous Desert, 1924, 16 pages ..............................**20.00**

Charm of Jell-O, lady w/tray & Jell-O mold, 1926 ..........**15.00**

Dessert Magic (Jell-O), 6th printing, 1944, 26 pages .......**15.00**

For Economy Use Jell-O, 1920, 14 pages ..............................**16.00**

Gayer Mealtimes w/New Jell-O, 1934 ..............................**14.00**

Greater Jell-O Recipe Book, 1931, 47 pages ........................**14.00**

**Jell-O Rhymes, geese on cover, Lucille Patterson Marsh, 6½x4¼", EX, $15.00.**

Joys of Jell-O — Story of Jell-O & Why It Grew, 5th edition, 95 pages ...............................**6.00**

Quick & Easy Jell-O Wonder Dishes, 1930, 23 pages .........**14.00**

What Mrs Dewey Did w/the New Jell-O, 1933, 23 pages ..**14.00**

## Pillsbury

Ann Pillsbury's Baking Book, 1st Grand National, hardcover, 1950 ..............................**50.00**

Bake Off Cookie Favorites, 1969, 64 pages ..........................**3.00**

Baking Is Fun, Ann Pillsbury, 1946 ................................**10.00**

Fabulous Pies From Pillsbury, Ann Pillsbury, 1961, 24 pages ............................**6.00**

Pillsbury's Butter Cookie Booklet, 1961, leaflet, 22 pages, EX ..................................**4.00**

Pillsbury's Cook Book, Pillsbury's Laboratory, 1929, 46 pages .........**14.00**

Pillsbury's Recipes You'll Use Over & Over Again, leaflet .....**10.00**

Recipes From Pillsbury Bake Off 1949, package insert, 1953 ...........................**3.50**

Self-Frosted Yellow Cake, 1967, 1968 ................................**3.00**

Short-Cut Breads, Pillsbury's Best, 1960 ......................**6.00**

Story of Flour, Pillsbury Flour Mills, hard cover, 1922, 28 pages ..............................**25.00**

100 Prize-Winning Recipes, 2nd Grand National, 1951, from $15 to ............................**20.00**

1950 Grand National Recipe & Baking Contest, 100 Prize Winning Recipes ..........**65.00**

1950s Grand National Recipe & Baking Contest, #s 3 through 10, ea ............................**10.00**

1960s Grand National Recipe & Baking Contest, #s 11 through 20, ea ..............................**8.00**

1970s Grand National Recipe & Baking Contest, #s 21 through 30, ea ..............................**5.00**

## Miscellaneous

Adjustable Diet Cook Book, Suzy Chaplin, 1967, hardcover, 346-pages ......................**10.00**

American Girl Cook Book, hardcover, 1966 ....................**20.00**

Amy Vanderbilt's Complete Cook Book, hardcover, 1961, 811 pages ............................**20.00**

Better Homes & Gardens Vegetable Cookbook, hardcover, 1965, 160 ......................**10.00**

Better Meals for Less Money, Green, hardcover, 1931 .**25.00**

Christmas Cookie Book, Virginia Pasley, Little, Brown & Co, 1949 ............................**25.00**

Diners Club Cook Book — Great Recipes, Myra Waldo, hardcover, 1959 ...................**20.00**

Family Circle Dessert & Fruit Cook Book, 1st edition, hardcover, 1954 ...................**20.00**

**The First Ladies Cook Book, 1969, EX, $15.00. (Photo courtesy Colonel Bob Allen)**

Going Wild in the Kitchen, G Parke, David McKay Co, hardcover, 1965 ............**15.00**

Hot Dog Cookbook, Wm Kauffman (autographed), hardcover, 1966 ..............................**10.00**

Ida Bailey Allen's Modern Cook Book, hardcover, 1924, 1008 pages ............................**40.00**

James Beard Cook Book w/Isabel E Calvert, 1959, 1961, 456 pages ............................**20.00**

Ladies' Home Journal Cook Book, 1st edition, Truax, Doubleday, 1960 ............................**15.00**

New Book of Cookery, Fannie M Farmer, 1st edition, 1912, 440 pages ............................**60.00**

Newlywed's Handbook, Rogers Publishing, 1st edition, 1937, 104 pages ......................**20.00**

Palmer House Cook Book, Ernst E Amiet, hardcover, 1935 .**35.00**

**Peanuts Cook Book, 1969, EX, $8.00. (Photo courtesy Colonel Bob Allen)**

Peter Hunt's Cape Cod Cookbook, Peter Hunt, 1957, 1962, 181 pages ............................**15.00**

Pressure Cooking, Ida Bailey Allen, 1947, 403 pages .**25.00**

Recipes of All Nations, Countess Morphy, hardcover, 1945 .**25.00**

Salads, Sandwiches & Specialty Dishes, Emory Hawcock, hardcover, 1932 ............**35.00**

Sea Food Cookery, Wallace, Blue Ribbon Books, 1949 ......**25.00**

## Cookie Cutters and Shapers

Cookie cutters have come into their own in recent years as wor-

San Diego Zoo elephant and lion cutters, painted white plastic, Monogram Products, Inc., M on card, $8.00 each. (Photo courtesy Rosemary Henry)

thy kitchen collectibles. Prices on many have risen astronomically, but a practiced eye can still sort out a good bargain. Advertising cutters and product premiums, especially in plastic, can still be found without too much effort. Aluminum cutters with painted wooden handles are usually worth several dollars each if in good condition. Red and green are the usual handle colors, but other colors are more highly prized by many. Hallmark plastic cookie cutters, espcially those with painted backs, are always worth considering, if in good condition.

Be wary of modern tin cutters being sold for antique. Many present-day tinsmiths chemically antique their cutters, especially those done in a primitive style. These are often sold by others as 'very old.' Look closely, because most tinsmiths today sign and date these cutters.

To learn more, check *The Cookie Shaper's Bible* by Phillis Wetherill and Rosemary Henry. Ms. Henry also publishes *Cookies*, a newsletter for collectors. She is listed in the Directory under Virginia. See also Clubs and Newsletters.

Bunny head, blue soft plastic w/eyelet, Hallmark, 1980, 4" .....**5.50**
Chicken, aluminum, strap handle, 3½" .....................................**5.00**
Chickory Chick, yellow, blue or pink hard plastic, Hallmark, 1978, ea ..........................**7.50**
Christmas tree, aluminum, strap handle, 4" ........................**5.00**
Christmas tree, green soft plastic, Hallmark, 1983, 2½" .........................**2.50**
Circus animals, Hultzer, 1960s, MIP ...................................**5.00**
Duck, yellow soft plastic, Hallmark, 1983, 4" .................**3.00**
Enesco, Vending Machine, from $50 to ...........................**60.00**

Formay rabbit, machine-formed metal w/self handle, ca 1930, 6", G .................................**10.00**

Ghost, white hard plastic, Hallmark, 1979, MIP, from $8 to ..............................**10.00**

Gingerbread Boy, blue or red, Betty Crocker Gingerbread Mix ....................................**3.50**

Halloween cat, dark orange hard plastic w/eyelet, 1976 .....**5.00**

Heart, tin, strap handle, marked Kreamer, 3¼" ..................**7.50**

Holly Hobbie, plastic, American Greetings, set of 7 .........**20.00**

KO Biscuit & Cookie, spring-action handle, VG ...........**8.00**

Lamb, aluminum, 4" ..............**5.00**

Lamb, white soft plastic w/eyelet, Hallmark, 1980, 4" .........**4.00**

Mickey or Minnie Mouse, plastic, Loma, 1950s, ea ...........**10.00**

Mr Peanut, blue, Planters Peanuts, set of 2 ...........**40.00**

Mr Peanut, red, Planters Peanuts, set of 2 ...........................**25.00**

Pilgrim boy, hard plastic w/eyelet, Hallmark, 1976, 2¾" .............................**8.00**

Precious Moments, Christmas, pink plastic, Enesco, 1991, set of 6, MIP .......................**18.00**

Santa in sleigh, red hard plastic, painted details, Hallmark, 1979, 3" ..........................**12.00**

Shaper, black cat face, black soft plastic, Hallmark, 1995 ..**3.00**

Shaper, Christmas bell, red, Hallmark, 1985 ......................**3.00**

Shaper, graduation cap, royal blue, Hallmark, 1997 ....**10.00**

Shaper, heart w/arrow, hard plastic, Hallmark, 1986 .........**3.00**

Shaper, hippopotamus, lavender, Hallmark, 1988 ..............**5.00**

Shaper, lips, red, Hallmark, 1985 ............................**4.00**

Turkey, brown soft plastic, Hallmark, 1984 ......................**3.00**

# Cookie Jars

McCoy, Metlox, Twin Winton, Robinson Ransbottom, and American Bisque were among the largest producers of cookie jars in the country. Many firms made them to a lesser extent. Today cookie jars are one of the most popular of modern collectibles. Figural jars are the most common (and the most valuable), made in an endless variety of subjects. Early jars from the 1920s and '30s were often decorated in 'cold paint' over the glaze. This type of color is easily removed — take care that you use very gentle cleaning methods. A damp cloth and a light touch is the safest approach.

For further information we recommend *Collector's Encyclopedia of Metlox Potteries* by Carl Gibbs, *Collector's Guide to Don Winton Designs* by Mike Ellis, *Collector's Encyclopedia of McCoy Pottery* by Sharon and Bob Huxford, *Collector's Encyclopedia of Cookie Jars* by Joyce and Fred Roerig (there are three in the series), and *An Illustrated Value Guide to Cookie Jars* by Ermagene Westfall (all published by Collector Books). Values are for jars in mint condition unless otherwise noted. Beware of

modern reproductions!
See also Club and Newsletters.

Abingdon, Money Bag, #588 ................................**70.00**

Abingdon, Old Lady, plain, #471, 1942 ............................**210.00**

Abingdon, Pineapple, #664 ..**95.00**

Abingdon, Three Bears, #696 ..**90.00**

Abingdon, Windmill, #678 .**185.00**

American Bisque, Cookieville Bus Co ....................................**350.00**

American Bisque, Farmer Pig .**145.00**

American Bisque, French Chef .**125.00**

American Bisque, Gift Box .**150.00**

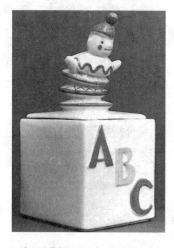

**American Bisque, Jack-in-the-Box, #611, $275.00.**

Applause, Sylvester Head w/Tweety, from $75 to ..**90.00**

Applause, Tasmanian Devil, from $65 to ............................**80.00**

Brush, Cinderella Pumpkin, #W32 ............................**250.00**

Brush, Clown, yellow pants .**250.00**

Brush, Cookie House, #W31 .**125.00**

Brush, Dog & Basket ........**300.00**

Brush, Gas Lamp, #K1 ........**75.00**

Brush, Hen on Basket, unmarked ..................**125.00**

Brush, Night Owl ..............**125.00**

Brush, Old Clock, #W10 ....**165.00**

Brush, Panda, #W21 ..........**125.00**

Brush, Peter Pan, sm ........**550.00**

Brush, Squirrel on Log, #W26 ..**100.00**

Brush, Stylized Owl ..........**350.00**

Brush, Teddy Bear, feet apart ..................**250.00**

Brush, Teddy Bear, feet together ....................**200.00**

Brush, Treasure Chest, #W28 ..**150.00**

California Originals, Bear, #2648 ..........................**75.00**

California Originals, Monkey w/Bananas ..................**160.00**

**California Originals, Ernie, from $50.00 to $65.00.**

California Originals, Strawberry Jar ..................................**25.00**

California Originals, Taxi Cab, from $85 to ..................**125.00**

Clay Art, Chicken Racer, from $50 to ..................................**65.00**

Clay Art, Humpty Dumpty, from $100 to ..........................**135.00**

Cleminson, Carrot Head ...**165.00**

Cleminson, Gingerbread House **200.00**

Dayton Hudson, Pinocchio ..**60.00**

DeForest, Buddha, from $100 to ............................**145.00**

Dept 56, Cowboy in Silhouette, red & yellow, 10½" ............**110.00**

Dept 56, McNutts Chicken Coop, McNutts Dept 56 Japan c 1988 ..............................**175.00**

Dept 56, McNutts Egg, McNutts c 1988 Dept 56 Japan, from $65 to ....................................**70.00**

Dept 56, Mirage Cactus, Mirage c, from $35 to ....................**45.00**

Dept 56, Peasant Woman, Peasant People c 1980, from $100 to ........**150.00**

Dept 56, Short-Order Toaster, Short-Order Made in Japan... ......................**55.00**

Dept 56, Ugly Stepsisters, Tea Time Ugly Stepsisters 1989 ..........................**65.00**

Dept 56, Vegetable Cottage, #1001, from $50 to ........**60.00**

Dept 56, Vegetable House, c Dept 56 1990, from $60 to .....**75.00**

Dept 56, Witch, unmarked, from $50 to ............................**70.00**

Doranne of California, Dinosaur, from $200 to ................**250.00**

Doranne of California, Ketchup Bottle, from $55 to ........**70.00**

Enesco, Gingerbread House, from $30 to ............................**40.00**

Enesco, Jack & the Beanstalk, from $40 to ....................**50.00**

Enesco, Woodland Commune, from $125 to ................**145.00**

Fitz & Floyd, Ballooning Bunnies ............................**85.00**

Fitz & Floyd, Berry Patch Lamb, from $50 to ....................**65.00**

Fitz & Floyd, Bunny Bonnet .**110.00**

Fitz & Floyd, Cat Holding Fish .**65.00**

Fitz & Floyd, Cinderella Fairy Godmother ..................**100.00**

Fitz & Floyd, Hat Box Bunnies .**160.00**

Fitz & Floyd, Jungle Elephant .**250.00**

Fitz & Floyd, Queen of Hearts ..**175.00**

Fitz & Floyd, Santa in Chair .**125.00**

Fitz & Floyd, Wanda the Witch .**190.00**

Ganz Co, Little Cheezer, from $100 to ........................**125.00**

Gilner, Rooster, from $60 to .**70.00**

**Gonder, Sheriff, from $600.00 to $700.00.**

Grant Howard, School Bus, from $50 to ............................**75.00**

Hallmark, Maxine ............**125.00**

Hearth & Home, Stagecoach, from $60 to ............................**75.00**

Hirsch, Covered Wagon, from $65 to ....................................**85.00**

Home Collection, Goldilocks & the Three Bears, from $40 to ................................**55.00**

House of Webster, Coffee Grinder, from $30 to ....................**35.00**

JC Miller, Grandfather Washington, from $100 to ...................**135.00**
Lotus, Witch .........................**50.00**
Maddux, Calory Hippy ......**300.00**
Maddux, Scottie .................**75.00**
Maddux, Strawberry ...........**35.00**
Maurice of California, Train .**65.00**
McCoy, Apple on Basketweave ..**70.00**
McCoy, Asparagus ...............**50.00**
McCoy, Basket of Eggs ........**60.00**
McCoy, Blue Willow Pitcher .**50.00**
McCoy, Burlap Sack, from $25 to ...............................**35.00**
McCoy, Chipmunk .............**150.00**
McCoy, Clown Bust .............**85.00**
McCoy, Cookie Boy ............**225.00**
McCoy, Covered Wagon .....**150.00**
McCoy, Eagle on Basket ......**35.00**
McCoy, Elephant ...............**200.00**
McCoy, Engine, black ........**175.00**
McCoy, Snow Bear .............**100.00**
McCoy, Woodsy Owl .........**300.00**
Metlox, Chef Pierre Mouse, from $100 to ......................**125.00**
Metlox, Grapefruit, from $175 to .............................**200.00**
Metlox, Loveland, from $65 to ..**75.00**
Metlox, Noah's Ark, bisque, from $125 to ......................**150.00**
Metlox, Scottie Dog, white, from $175 to ......................**200.00**
Metlox, Slenderella Pig .....**150.00**
Metlox, Teddy Bear, brown, from $45 to ............................**50.00**
Napco, Miss Cutie Pie, from $225 to ...............................**275.00**
Newcor, Cookie Monster .....**45.00**
Norcrest, Chipmunk ............**65.00**
Omnibus, European Santa ..**50.00**
Omnibus, Pirate, from $50 to .**75.00**
Otagiri, Penguin, from $150 to .**175.00**
Pacific Stoneware, Dog, from $45 to ...............................**55.00**

Pamona, Alien Pig, from $35 to ...........................**50.00**
Papal, Cathy, from $75 to .**100.00**
Pottery Guild, Dutch Girl, from $65 to ............................**85.00**
Red Wing, Chef Pierre, brown .................**200.00**
Red Wing, Friar Tuck, green, marked ......................**300.00**
Red Wing, Pineapple, yellow ..**200.00**
Red Wing, Queen of Tarts, marked ......................**550.00**
Regal China, Churn Boy ...**275.00**
Regal China, Davy Crockett ..**550.00**
Regal China, French Chef .**375.00**
Regal China, Old McDonald's Barn ...........................**275.00**
Rick Wisecarver, Cookstove Mammy, from $150 to .**200.00**
Rick Wisecarver, Hill Folk .**225.00**
Robinson Ransbottom, Cow Jumped Over Moon ....**275.00**
Robinson Ransbottom, Wise Owl (Hootie), gold trim ......**175.00**
Rose Collection, Watermelon Girl ..........................**175.00**
Schmid, Pumbaa, musical .**150.00**
Schmid, 101 Dalmatians, from $100 to ......................**135.00**
Shawnee, Dutch Girl, green, marked Great Northern 1026, minimum value ..........**250.00**
Shawnee, Jug, Pennsylvania Dutch design, marked USA, minimum value ......**150.00**
Shawnee, Smiley Pig, blue bib, marked USA, minimum value .........................**150.00**
Shawnee, Snowflake, bean pot, yellow, marked USA, minimum value ...................**50.00**
Sierra Vista, Clown Bust, from $55 to .........................**75.00**

**Sierra Vista, Elephant, from $125.00 to $150.00.**

Sierra Vista, Tugboat ........**165.00**
Sigma, Miss Piggy on Couch .**85.00**
Sigma, Santa w/Toy Sack ....**75.00**
Starnes, Gangster Car, from $150 to ..............................**175.00**
Storyteller Art, Cowboy Boot, from $60 to ...........................**80.00**
Terrace Ceramics, Fluffy Cat ..**25.00**
Terrace Ceramics, Muggsy Dog .......................**120.00**
Treasure Craft, Dopey .........**55.00**
Treasure Craft, Fozzie Bear .**45.00**
Treasure Craft, Gardener Bunny .......................**55.00**
Treasure Craft, Noah's Ark, from $50 to ............................**75.00**
Treasure Craft, Sweetheart Cat, from $50 to ...................**75.00**

**Twin Winton, Raggedy Ann, Collector Series USA, from $125.00 to $150.00.**

Twin Winton, Barrel of Cookies (mouse finial) ...............**75.00**
Twin Winton, Barrel of Cookies (no mouse finial) ...........**75.00**
Twin Winton, Cookie Barn, wood stain w/painted detail or gray, ea ...................................**80.00**
Twin Winton, Gunfighter Rabbit ...........................**200.00**
Twin Winton, Sheriff Bear, Collector Series, fully painted ...................**200.00**
Twin Winton, Squirrel with Acorns, wood stain with painted details ...........**75.00**
Twin Winton, Teddy Bear, wood stain with painted detail .**85.00**
Vallona Starr, Squirrel on Stump, #86 ................................**75.00**
Vandor, Baseball ..................**50.00**
Vandor, Betty Boop Kitchen .**40.00**
Vandor, Happy Trails ..........**70.00**
Vandor, Radio, from $80 to ..**100.00**
Vandor, Socks, from $50 to .**65.00**
Warner Brothers, Olympic Torch .......................**135.00**
Warner Brothers, Space Jam w/Michael Jordan & Bugs Bunny ..........................**150.00**
Weiss, Bear, many variations, from $30 to ...................**60.00**
Weiss, Mother Goose, from $150 to ...............................**175.00**
Wolfe Studio, Purdue Pete .**150.00**

# Cracker Jack

The name Cracker Jack was first used in 1896. The trademark as well as the slogan 'The more you eat, the more you want,' were registered at that time. Prizes first appeared in

Cracker Jack boxes in 1912. Prior to then, prizes or gifts could be ordered through catalogs. In 1910 coupons that could be redeemed for many gifts were inserted in the boxes.

The Cracker Jack boy and his dog Bingo came on the scene in 1916 and have remained one of the world's most well-known trademarks. Prizes themselves came in a variety of materials, from paper and tin to pot metal and plastic. The beauty of Cracker Jack prizes is that they depict what was happening in the world at the time they were made. All items listed are marked Cracker Jack.

To learn more about the subject, you'll want to read *Cracker Jack Toys, The Complete Unofficial Guide for Collectors,* and *Cracker Jack Advertising Collectibles,* both by our advisor, Larry White; he is listed in the Directory under Massachusetts.

Airplane cards from the 1940s, ea .................................**20.00**
Alphabet charms, plastic, various colors, ea .........................**2.50**
Bank, tin, w/Cracker Jack & airplane .............................**70.00**
Baseball card, Topps or Donruss, mini, ea ...........................**1.00**
Building, plastic snap-together .**7.50**
Delivery truck, tin litho, black, red & white .........................**45.00**
Games or toys to assemble, plastic, mini, MIP, ea ..................**8.00**
Kerchoo, plastic .....................**7.50**
Magnifying glass, clear plastic .**50**
Mini-book, Sailor Jack's Wisecracks ..............................**7.50**
Mustache, black paper ........**10.00**

Palm puzzle, face, Gee Cracker Jack Is Good on back ....**80.00**
Pipe, dog's face, ceramic, pink ..**4.00**
Postcard, Cracker Jack Bears .**40.00**
Riddle card ..........................**20.00**
Standup, comic character, tin litho, 1940s ...................**55.00**
Standup, plastic, various figures, marked NOSCO ..............**4.50**
Steel ball puzzle, assortment of games 1970s, ea, from $5.00 to ................................**$20.00**
Stud, Uncle Sam, pot metal .**45.00**

**Top, tin, 1933, 1½" diameter, NM, $60.00.**

Traffic signs, yellow, marked CJ Co .....................................**5.00**
Trophy, snap-together, silver or gold ...............................**5.00**

## Crackle Glass

Most of the crackle glass you see on the market today was made from about 1930 until the '70s. At the height of its popularity, almost five hundred glasshouses produced it; today it is still being made by Blenko, and a few pieces are coming in from Taiwan and China. It's hard to date, since many pieces were made for years. Some colors, such as red, amberina, cobalt, and cranberry, were more expensive to produce; so today, these are scarce and therefore more expensive. Smoke gray was made for only a short time, and you can expect to pay a premium for that color as well. For more information we recommend *Crackle Glass, Books I and II,* by Stan and Arlene Weitman (Collector Books).

Apple, orange, Hamon, late 1940-70s, 4", from $75 to .....................**100.00**

Basket, amberina, ruffled top, clear handle, Kanawha, 6", from $60 to ....................**85.00**

Basket, topaz, ovoid, ring foot, clear handle, Pilgrim, 4¾", from $60 to ....................**75.00**

Candle holders, clear w/aquamarine rosettes, flared foot, pr, from $100 to ................**125.00**

Candy dish/ashtray, topaz, wide rim w/indent, footed, Bischoff, 3x6" ................................**75.00**

Compote, clear w/aquamarine rosettes, flared rim, Blenko, 4x12" ............................**125.00**

Creamer, emerald green, dropover handle, Pilgrim, 3", from $25 to .............................**40.00**

Creamer & sugar bowl, blue, drop-over handle, Boniat, 2¾", pr ........................**85.00**

Cruet, blue, cylindrical, teardrop stopper, Pilgrim, 6¾", from $50 to ........**75.00**

Cruet, sea green, matching ball stopper, Pilgrim, 6", from $45 to ..................................**75.00**

**Cruet, blue with clear drop-over handle, Rainbow, 1940s – 1960s, 6½", from $50.00 to $75.00. (Photo courtesy Stan and Arlene Weitman)**

Decanter, blue, stick neck, oval drop stopper, Blenko, 14¾" ....**175.00**

Decanter, clear, pinched body, stick neck, blue stopper, Blenko, 11" ..................**125.00**

Decanter, topaz, crocodile figural, 1960s, 17", from $125 to ...........................**150.00**

Decanter, topaz, stick neck, lg ball stopper, Rainbow, 8½", from $80 to ................**100.00**

Jug, blue, clear drop-over handle, Pilgrim, 4", from $35 to ............................**40.00**

Pear, rose crystal, Blenko, 5", from $75 to .........................**100.00**

Perfume bottle, blue teardrop w/flower-shaped stopper, 4½", from $50 to ....................**65.00**

Pitcher, amberina, cylindrical, clear handle, Pilgrim, 3½" ........................**50.00**

Pitcher, blue, mug style, drop-over handle, 3", from $35 to ............................**40.00**

Pitcher, golden amber, drop-over handle, Pilgrim, 4", from $30 to ....................................**35.00**

Salt & pepper shakers, amethyst, metal lids, 3¼", pr, from $55 to ....................................**80.00**

Tumbler, topaz, unknown maker, 6¾", from $40 to ..........**55.00**

Vase, amberina, cylindrical, 13", from $110 to ................**125.00**

Vase, blue, flared cylinder w/crimped rim, Bischoff, 10½", from $105 to .....**130.00**

Vase, clear, bulbous w/can neck, green handles, Blenko, 7", from $80 to ..................**95.00**

Vase, clear w/green snake, bulbous w/can neck, Blenko, 9½", from $100 to ..........................**125.00**

Vase, cobalt satin, ball form w/can neck, 6", from $85 to ...**110.00**

Vase, green, cylinder w/stick neck, Made in Spain label, 11½" .**100.00**

Vase, lemon-lime, bulbous with pinched sides, Pilgrim, 5", from $40 to ....................**45.00**

Vase, olive green, bulbous, rope twist on neck, Pilgrim, 6¾" ........**75.00**

Vase, rose crystal, waisted cylinder, Blenko, 11", from $110 to ............................**135.00**

Vase, sea green, clear angle handles, Blenko, 7½", from $55 to ....................................**80.00**

Vase, tangerine, cylindrical with stick neck, footed, Blenko, 17" ............................**175.00**

Vase, vaseline, shouldered, stick neck, unknown maker, 6", from $50 to ....................**75.00**

# Credit Cards

Credit items predate the 20th century and have been made from various types of materials. Celluloid tokens and paper cards were among the earliest, followed by paper and metal plates with holders, metal tokens, and, finally, plastic cards. They have been issued by merchants, oil companies, the travel and entertainment industries, and banks to name the most common sources. Credit card collecting is one of the fastest growing hobbies today. By their very nature, credit cards and charge tokens were usually deliberately destroyed, making older credit items fiercely sought after. Our advisor, Walt Thompson, is listed in the Directory under Washington.

Air Travel Card Co, America, 1950s ...............................**6.00**

American Express, plastic, 1963 ...........................**58.00**

American Express, 1971 ......**11.50**

Bank Royale, Visa, Canadian .**6.50**

Boggs & Buhl, metal charge coin .............................**8.00**

BonWhit Teller Credit Card, plastic ......................................**3.85**

Carter Oil Co, paper, 1950 ..**88.50**

Chevron USA, national .........**2.00**

Esso Standard Co, 1959, M .**50.00**

Florida Bank & Trust Co, 1950s ..**20.00**

Gimbels Co, metal charge coin .**4.00**

Hilton Hotel, plastic, 1960s ...**8.75**

Hotel Clinton, 1921, paper, G ..**15.50**

Hotel Emery, paper ..............**9.50**

Norwalk/Hancock Oil Co, 1950s .**135.00**

Pennsylvania Refining Co, 1934 .**137.50**
People's Bank .........................**2.50**
Playboy Presidential Key, plastic ..................................**8.00**
Rogers Co, charge coin ........**21.00**
Seaside Oil Co, 1960s ........**255.00**
Signal Gas, national, 1962 .**180.00**

**Signal Oil Co., plastic, 1960s, $123.00. (Photo courtesy Walt Thompson)**

Sinclair Motoring, 1969 .......**26.00**
Sinclair Refining Co, 1947 ..**41.00**
Sun Oil Co, paper charge card ..**20.00**
Utah Oil, metal charge coin .**28.00**
Walt Schroeder Hotels, metal charge coin ....................**18.00**
Western Union, 1950s .........**11.50**

## Cuff Links

What is this new attraction to cuff links as a collectible? To the surprise of many, cuff links are not really new to the hobby scene; they have been collectible for years. In fact, one of the main reasons for the formation of the National Cuff Link Society in 1991 was to provide a networking mechanism for collectors. The Society's quarterly publication, *The Link*, unites collectors throughout the world and provides ideas and research. Veteran collectors describe the hobby as ideal. They point out that cuff links are very available, affordable, easy to display, and do not require a lot of room to store. They also boast that it is the only collectible that can be worn on one's shirt sleeve.

Collectors also enjoy the virtually infinite number of cuff link designs available and the opportunities to specialize. Some of the most popular subjects for specialization are sports, fraternal emblems, advertising logos, animals, cars, and ships. Other enthusiasts limit their collections to the types of materials used in the manufacturing process. Examples of this category include wood, leather, plastic, fur, silver, and gold. Some collectors concentrate on the back of the cuff link — they specialize in various fastening devices that have evolved over the years.

Cuff link collecting is educational. They have always mirrored the economy, lifestyle, and history of their time. For example, the Victorian period's accent on color, glitter, and enamel was clearly reflected in the design of its cuff links. Likewise, the post-World War II era's preference for ostenatious fashion gave birth to the bright and over-sized cuff links of that day. Cuff links also reveal a lot about the state-of-the art of design and workmanship at the time of their manufacture.

Our advisor for this category is

Greek profile, ca 1910, from $110.00 to $125.00. (Photo courtesy National Cuff Link Society)

Gene Klompus, president of the National Cuff Link Society; he is listed in the Directory under Illinois. See also Clubs and Newsletters.

Abacus (working), gold-plated sterling, toggle closure, Hong Kong ...........................**150.00**

Atlantic Companies logo, silver, swivel closure, ca 1950, ¾" dia ..............................**140.00**

Aztec masks, sterling, toggle closure, ca 1950, ½" ..........**95.00**

Buckle, brown leather, American Toggle closure, 1950, ¾x⅞" ........**30.00**

Car (generic), blue enameled metal, ca 1920, ½x1¼", EX .......**175.00**

Clowns, tempered base metal, chain closure, ca 1930,¾" dia, EX ..................................**45.00**

Comedy/Tragedy, silver-tone, American Toggle closure, 1965, ½x½" ....................**40.00**

Devil's head, sterling, ca 1940, ¾" dia ..............................**95.00**

Elephants, sterling, EX detail, toggle closure, ca 1955, 1x1½" ...........................**60.00**

Horse heads, black gunmetal, ball-shape closure, ca 1915, 1" .**55.00**

Indian head pennies w/relief removed, toggle closure, ca 1955 ...............................**45.00**

Initial F on oval, sterling, ca 1960, 1x½" ..............................**65.00**

Lovebirds, multicolor enameled porcelain w/gold leaf, disc closure, VG ........................**95.00**

Microphone, sterling, Fenwick & Sailor, ca 1950, 1" .........**45.00**

Minotaur w/bow & arrow, gold-tone metal, toggle closure, 1950, ⅞" ........................**40.00**

Mother-of-pearl, silver-tone surround, toggle back, 1950s, 1¼" dia ..................................**30.00**

Peace sign, silver-tone base metal, ca 1960, ¾" dia ..............**50.00**

Pistols, sterling w/mother-of-pearl handles, ca 1955, ¾" .......................**110.00**

Presidential seal, Richard Nixon 37th President, pewter, 1968, ⅞" ..................................**175.00**

Separable/snappers, black celluloid w/stone center, 1923, ½x½", VG .....................**50.00**

Star of David, red enameled base metal, Made in Palestine, ca 1945 ...........................**175.00**

Venus DeMilo cameo on wood base, gold-tone surround, ca 1950, 1⅛" ......................**60.00**

1972 Olympics logo, silver-tone base metal, toggle back, ¾" dia ..............................**125.00**

# Czechoslovakian Glass

Items marked Czechoslovakia are popular modern collectibles. Pottery, glassware, jewelry, etc., were produced there in abundance. Refer to *Czechoslovakian Glass and Collectibles* by Dale and Diane Barta and Helen M. Rose (Collector Books) for more information. See also Clubs and Newsletters.

Atomizer, blue crystal, cut ridge design on base, gold-tone sprayer ..........................**75.00**

Basket, red & yellow swirled (cased), crystal thorn handle, 6¼" ..............................**75.00**

Beverage barrel, clear frosted overshot w/4 metal bands, 8½" ..............................**70.00**

Bottle, scent; amethyst, 6-sided, etched decor, matching stopper, 5" ..........................**70.00**

Bottle, scent; clear, ribbed, rectangular, w/stopper, 5¼" ...**50.00**

Bottle, scent; crystal w/cut diamond design, 4-sided drop stopper, 6" ..................**180.00**

Bottle, scent; purple lustre, bulbous, flower stopper, 4½" .......**140.00**

Bottle, topaz sq w/Witch Hazel on front, 4½" .....................**95.00**

Bowl, red cased w/gold flecks, 3", pr, from $80 to ..............**85.00**

Bowl, white cased, fluted crystal rim, 3", from $40 to ......**50.00**

Candlesticks, mottled autumn colors, satin glass, 4¼", pr .**65.00**

Candy basket, blue mottle w/yellow ruffled rim, jet handle, 8" ............................**250.00**

Candy basket, red w/black-edged petal rim, crystal handle, 6½" ............................**200.00**

Champagne glass, cranberry w/crystal stem, 6", from $40 to ...............................**45.00**

Compote, orange cased, applied jet feet, 5¾", from $80 to ...**90.00**

Creamer, yellow & white mottle cased, cobalt trim & handle, 6" ...............................**80.00**

Decanter, crystal waffle weave, sq sides, no top, 6½" .........**20.00**

Decanter, green w/wheel-cut vintage, 8½", from $85 to ..**90.00**

Flower holder, cream cased, red overlay, 5", from $50 to .**60.00**

Lamp, table; dark blue lustre, replaced shade, 13¼" ..**175.00**

Perfume, clear w/cut design base, cut panel on stopper, 5½" ......**85.00**

Pitcher, amber w/green overlay, cobalt handle w/threading, 10¼" ............................**180.00**

Pitcher, orange cased w/cobalt thread at rim, white handle, 6" ...............................**75.00**

Powder dish, clear w/bubble design, ball handle, 3¾" ..............**40.00**

Salt & pepper shakers, crystal w/black base, 1¾", pr, from $35 to ............................**40.00**

Salt & pepper shakers, cut crystal, 2", pr, from $20 to .........**25.00**

Tumbler, hunt scene enameled on bubbly green, 5¾" .........**65.00**

**Vase/pitcher, cased yellow and light blue spatter with cobalt rim and handle, 6", from $80.00 to $85.00. (Photo courtesy Dale and Diane Barta and Helen M. Rose)**

Vase, black amethyst, flared rim, 6", from $30 to .............**35.00**
Vase, green cased, applied pink serpentine & leaves, slim, 8" ................................**80.00**
Vase, jack-in-the-pulpit; multicolor variegated cased, 9½" ....**85.00**
Vase, mottled reds & yellows cased, clear feet, slim, 13¼" ......**65.00**
Vase, multicolor spatter w/aventurine, 4½" ....................**45.00**
Vase, red & white mottle on inverted cylinder, 5⅞" ..**50.00**
Vase, red cased, black rim & bottom, painted bird on branch, 6¼" ................................**60.00**
Vase, white cased w/applied crystal fluted rim, 5¼" ........**80.00**
Vase, white w/embossed decor, applied crystal pleated rim, 5½" ................................**85.00**

Vase, yellow cased w/black serpentine decor, stick neck, 9" .**50.00**

# Dakin

From about 1968 through the late 1970s, the R. Dakin Company produced a line of hollow vinyl advertising and comic characters licensed by such companies as Warner Brothers, Hanna-Barbera, and the Disney corporation as well as others. Some figures had molded-on clothing; others had felt clothes and accessory items. Inspiration for characters came from TV cartoon shows, comic strips, or special advertising promotions. Dakins were offered in different types of packaging. Those in colorful 'Cartoon Theatre' boxes command higher prices than those that came in clear plastic bags. Plush figures were also produced, but the vinyl examples we've listed below are the most collectible. Assume all to be complete with clothes, accessories, and original tags unless otherwise noted. For further information and more listings we recommend *Schroeder's Collectible Toys, Antique to Modern* (Collector Books).

Baby Puss, Hanna-Barbera, 1971, EX+ .............................**100.00**
Benji, 1978, cloth, VG .........**30.00**
Bob's Big Boy, missing hamburger otherwise VG ...............**80.00**
Bugs Bunny, Warner Bros, 1971, MIP ...............................**30.00**
Christian Bros Brandy, St Bernard, 1982, cloth, VG ..............**30.00**

**Pinocchio, molded shoes, red and yellow clothes, blue tie, 1960s, 8", EX, $20.00.**

**Yosemite Sam, red beard, blue hat, molded shoes, 1968, 7½", EX, $20.00.**

Cool Cat, Warner Bros, w/beret, 1970, EX+ ......................**40.00**

Daffy Duck, Warner Bros, 1968, EX ..................................**30.00**

Dewey Duck, Disney, straight or bent legs, EX .................**40.00**

Dream Pets, Bull Dog, cloth, EX .............................**15.00**

Dream Pets, Midnight Mouse, cloth, EX ........................**15.00**

Droopy Dog, 1971, 8½", EX .**25.00**

Dumbo, Disney, 1960s, cloth collar, MIB ..........................**25.00**

Elmer Fudd, Warner Bros, 1978, MIP (Fun Farm bag) ....**35.00**

Glamour Kitty, 1977, EX ..**150.00**

Goofy Gram, Bull, I'm Mad About You, EX .........................**25.00**

Goofy Gram, Kangaroo, World's Greatest Mom!, EX .......**25.00**

Hoppy Hopperoo, Hanna-Barbera, 1971, EX+ ....................**100.00**

Lion in Cage, bank, 1971, EX .**25.00**

Merlin the Magic Mouse, Warner Bros, 1970, EX+ ............**25.00**

Mighty Mouse, Terrytoons, 1978, EX ...............................**100.00**

Monkey on a Barrel, bank, 1971, EX ..................................**25.00**

Opus, 1982, cloth, w/tag, 12", EX ...................................**15.00**

Pepe Le Peu, Warner Bros, 1971, EX ..................................**55.00**

Popeye, King Features, 1974, cloth clothes, MIP .................**50.00**

Porky Pig, Warner Bros, 1968, EX ..................................**30.00**

Quasar Robot, bank, 1975, NM .**150.00**

Ren & Stimpy, water squirters, Nickelodeon, 1993, EX .................**10.00**

Road Runner, Warner Bros, 1976, MIB ..............................**45.00**

Sambo's Tiger, 1974, MIP ...**60.00**

Scooby Doo, Hanna-Barbera, 1980, EX ..................................**75.00**

Smokey Bear, 1976, MIB (TV Cartoon Theatre box) .........30.00
Snagglepuss, 1971, EX ......100.00
Sylvester, Warner Bros, 1968, EX ............................20.00
Tiger in Cage, 1971, EX ......25.00
Wile E Coyote, bank, 1971, EX ........................230.00
Woodsey Owl, 1974, missing clothes, EX ...................30.00
Yogi Bear, Hanna-Barbera, 1970, EX ..............................60.00

# Decanters

The James Beam Distilling Company produced its first ceramic whiskey decanter in 1953 and remained the only major producer of these decanters throughout the decade. By the late 1960s, other companies such as Ezra Brooks, Lionstone, and Cyrus Noble were also becoming involved in their production. Today these fancy liquor containers are attracting many collectors.

Our advisors for decanters are Judy and Art Turner of Homestead Collectibles, who are listed in the Directory under Pennsylvania.

Aesthetic Specialties (ASI), 1910 Oldsmobile, Black .........70.00
Beam, Casino Series, HC Covered Wagon .....................10.00
Beam, Casino Series, HC Man in Barrel #2 ...................150.00
Beam, Casino Series, Reno, Prima Donna ..........................10.00
Beam, Centennial Series, Civil War, North ................15.00

Beam, Centennial Series, Hawaii 200th .....................15.00
Beam, Club Series, Beaver Valley ..............................10.00
Beam, Club Series, Fox, Gold .25.00
Beam, Club Series, Fox, White Coat ..........................20.00
Beam, Club Series, Twin Bridges .....................25.00
Beam, Convention Series, #13 St Louis, Stein ................49.00
Beam, Convention Series, #20 Florida .........................45.00
Beam, Convention Series, #22 Showgirl, Blond or Brunette, ea ...................................40.00
Beam, Convention Series, #24 Cowboy on Horse .........75.00
Beam, Convention Series, #3 Detroit, 1973 ................10.00
Beam, Customer Series, Harry Hoffman ........................10.00
Beam, Customer Series, Ponderosa Ranch ...............15.00
Beam, Customer Series, Sheraton Inn ..........................10.00
Beam, Executive Series, Carolier Bull, 1984 .....................20.00
Beam, Executive Series, Tavern Scene, 1959 .................35.00
Beam, Executive Series, 1975 Reflection ....................15.00
Beam, Foreign Series, Australia, Sydney Opera ...............25.00
Beam, Foreign Series, Boystown ...........................10.00
Beam, Foreign Series, Queensland ...........................22.00
Beam, Opera Series, Falstaff, w/base .........................125.00
Beam, Organization Series, Ducks Unlimited #12, Redhead, 1986 .........................50.00

**Jim Beam, Clint Eastwood Invitational Celebrity Tennis Tournament, 1973, ⅕-quart, 14½", $25.00.**

Beam, Organization Series, Ducks Unlimited #5, Canvasback Drake, 1989 ...................**45.00**

Beam, Organization Series, Legion Music .................**10.00**

Beam, Organization Series, Telephone #4, 1919 Dial ......**45.00**

Beam, People Series, Campaigner Donkey, 1960 ...**20.00**

Beam, People Series, Emmet Kelley ................................**35.00**

Beam, People Series, Hannah Dustin ...........................**30.00**

Beam, People Series, Mr Goodwrench ..........................**70.00**

Beam, Political Series, Clown Donkey, 1968 ......................**20.00**

Beam, Regal China Series, Cable Car, 1968 ......................**10.00**

Beam, Regal China Series, Globe, Antique .........................**10.00**

Beam, Regal China Series, Jukebox ................................**60.00**

Beam, Sports Series, Bing Crosby 29th, 1970 .....................**10.00**

Beam, State Series, Delaware .**10.00**

Beam, State Series, Pennsylvania ................**15.00**

Beam, Trophy Series, Doe ...**15.00**

Beam, Trophy Series, Dog, St Bernard .......................**30.00**

Beam, Wheel Series, Ambulance ..........................**70.00**

Beam, Wheel Series, Dump Truck ..........................**50.00**

Beam, Wheel Series, Train, Casey Jones, Box Car ..............**30.00**

Beam, Wheel Series, Volkswagon, Red ...............................**75.00**

Beam, Wheel Series, 1914 Stutz, Gray ..............................**50.00**

Beam, Wheel Series, 1930 Ford Paddy Wagon ..............**150.00**

Beam, Wheel Series, 1957 Chevy Corvette, Green ........**175.00**

**Ezra Brooks, Gold Panner, 1969, $8.00.**

Beam, Wheel Series, 1974 Mercedes, Blue ....................50.00

Ezra Brooks, Automobiles & Transportation Series, Ontario Racer #10 ........25.00

Ezra Brooks, Automobiles & Transportation Series, 1978 Corvette, Pace Car ........50.00

Famous Firsts, Automobiles & Transportation Series, Duesenberg ....................95.00

Famous Firsts, Locomotive, Dewitt Clinton .............35.00

Famous Firsts, Spirit of St Louis, lg ................................150.00

Hoffman, College Series, Helmet, Georgia ..........................40.00

Hoffman, College Series, Mascot, LSU, Running or Passing .40.00

Kontinental, Editor .............35.00

Kontinental, Lumberjack ....25.00

Lionstone, Basketball Players ..60.00

Lionstone, Buffalo Hunter ..20.00

Lionstone, Chinese Laundryman ..............................20.00

Lionstone, Firefighter w/Child #2 ...............................50.00

Lionstone, Judge Roy Bean .22.00

Lionstone, Tribal Chief ........20.00

McCormick, Bicentennial Series, Betsy Ross ....................28.00

McCormick, Henry Ford, mini .25.00

McCormick, Jimmy Durante .50.00

McCormick, JR Ewing .........40.00

McCormick, Muhammad Ali .200.00

Old Commonwealth, Boot, Western ....................................25.00

Old Commonwealth, Golden Retriever ......................50.00

Old Fitzgerald, Irish Charm, 1977 ............................22.00

Old Fitzgerald, Sons of Ireland, 1969 ............................15.00

Pacesetter, Ahrens Fox, Red & White ............................125.00

Pacesetter, American La France ..65.00

Ski Country, Bull Rider .......75.00

Ski Country, Flycatcher ....130.00

Ski Country, Indian, Great Spirit, mini ..............................25.00

Ski Country, Salmon, Landlocked ..........................50.00

Wade, Garman Beamers Club, 1995 ............................40.00

Wade, Scottie 'Nennie' ........50.00

Wade, 200th Anniversary Barrel, Blue ..............................45.00

Wild Turkey, #1, In Flight ..90.00

Wild Turkey, #2, w/Bobcat ..95.00

Wild Turkey, #4, w/Eagle ....90.00

Wild Turkey, #11, w/Falcon .90.00

Wild Turkey, Lore Series, #1 .25.00

Wild Turkey, Lore Series, #4 .35.00

Wild Turkey, Standing Turkey, 1971, mini ....................10.00

Wild Turkey, Turkey Taking Off, 1977 ............................15.00

# Department 56 Inc.

This is an importing and distributing firm located in Eden Prairie, Minnesota. Their merchandise is well done and appealing; some of their more collectible items are listed here. For more information refer to *Collector's Encyclopedia of Cookie Jars Vol. I, II, and III,* by Fred and Joyce Roerig (Collector Books).

Cowboy (in silhouette), salt & pepper shakers, pr, from $25 to ................................30.00

Dickens, Denton Mill..........30.00

Mirage: Cookie jar, from $35.00 to $45.00; Salt and pepper shakers, from $15.00 to $18.00 for the pair; Teapot, from $30.00 to $35.00. (Photo courtesy Joyce Roerig)

Dickens, King's Road Printer....**25.00**

Dickens, Knottinghill.............**32.00**

Dickens, Old Michaelchurch ....**20.00**

Dickens, Puddlewick Spectacle..**20.00**

Le Chef Cuisine, salt & pepper shakers, chef's head, pr, from $25 to..............................**30.00**

McNutts, Chicken, creamer .**35.00**

McNutts, teapot from $40 to........................**50.00**

McNutts, Corn, butter dish, from $35 to ............................**45.00**

McNutts, Egg, salt & pepper shakers, pr, from $15.00 to ........................ **20.00**

North Pole Village, Doll & Santa Bear Works ....................**55.00**

North Pole Village, Reindeer Barn.............................**24.00**

Snow Village, Coca-Cola Bottling Plant...............................**40.00**

Snow Village, Good Shepard Chapel/School.................**40.00**

Snow Village, Gothic Farm ..**28.00**

Snow Village, Library...........**32.00**

Snow Village, Queen Anne...**30.00**

Snow Village, Reindeer Bus Depot ..........................**25.00**

Snow Village, Used Car Lot .**27.00**

Snowbabies Dancing to a Snowbabies Tune, #6808 ...........**18.00**

Snowbabies, I'll Put Up a Tree, #6800 ............**15.00**

Snowbabies, Look What I Can Do, #6819 ....................**10.00**

Snowbabies, Playing Games #7947..............................**20.00**

Snowbabies, Special Delivery, # 7918..............**9.00**

Someone's in the Kitchen (Mammy), butter dish, from $70 to ............................**90.00**

Someone's in the Kitchen (Mammy), napkin holder, from $30 to ...................**40.00**

Someone's in the Kitchen (Mammy), planter/utensil holder, from $35 to ....**45.00**

Someone's in the Kitchen (Mammy), platter, lg, from $75 to ...........................................**95.00**

Someone's in the Kitchen (Mammy), teapot, from $100 to .....................................**125.00**

## Depression Glass

Depression glass, named for the era when it sold through dime stores or was given away as premiums, can be found in such varied colors as amber, green, pink, blue, red, yellow, white, and crystal. Mass-produced by many different companies in hundreds of patterns, Depression glass is one of the most sought-after collectibles in the United States today. For more information, refer to *The Pocket Guide to Depression Glass, 11th Edition; Collector's Encyclopedia of Depression Glass, 13th Edition;* and *Collectible Glassware of the 40s, 50s & 60s, 4th Edition;* all are by Gene Florence (Collector Books). See also Fire-King; Forest Green; Royal Ruby; Clubs and Newsletters.

Adam, ashtray, green, 4½" ..**25.00**
Adam, bowl, pink, 7¾" ........**28.00**
Adam, cake plate, pink, footed, 10" ..............................**28.00**
Adam, platter, green, 11¾" .**35.00**
American Pioneer, bowl, console; pink, 10¾" ...................**55.00**
American Pioneer, creamer, green, 3½" .................................**22.00**
American Pioneer, ice bucket, green, 6" .......................**60.00**
American Pioneer, plate, pink, 8" ...............................**10.00**
American Sweetheart, bowl, flat soup; Monax, 9½" .........**85.00**
American Sweetheart, plate, salad; pink ...................**11.00**
American Sweetheart, platter, Monax, oval, 13" ..........**67.50**
American Sweetheart, tumbler, pink, 10-oz, 4¾" .........**115.00**
Anniversary, cup, pink .........**8.00**
Anniversary, relish dish, crystal, 8" .....................................**5.00**
Anniversary, vase, pink, 6½" ..**30.00**

Aunt Polly, bowl, berry; blue, 4⅜" ...............................**18.00**
Aunt Polly, bowl, berry; blue, 8" ................................**45.00**
Aunt Polly, butter dish, green, w/lid ..............................**235.00**
Aunt Polly, sugar bowl, green .**25.00**
Aurora, cup, cobalt ..............**15.00**
Aurora, plate, cobalt, 6½" ....**12.00**
Aurora, tumbler, cobalt, 4¾" .**25.00**
Avocado, bowl, relish; pink or green, footed .................**25.00**
Avocado, saucer, green ........**24.00**
Avocado, sherbet, pink ........**55.00**
Beaded Block, bowl, opalescent, flared, 7¼" ....................**38.00**
Beaded Block, creamer, opalescent ...............................**35.00**
Beaded Block, vase, green, 6" .**25.00**
Beaded Edge, plate, dinner; decorated, 10½" ...................**35.00**
Beaded Edge, relish, plain, 3-part ...............................**22.50**
Block Optic, candlesticks, green, 1¾", pr .......................**110.00**
Block Optic, goblet, cocktail; pink, 4" ................................**40.00**
Block Optic, plate, luncheon, pink or green, 8" ......................**5.00**
Block Optic, plate, sherbet; pink or green, 6" .......................**2.00**
Block Optic, tumbler, green, footed, 9-oz .........................**18.00**
Bowknot, bowl, cereal; green, 5½" .................................**25.00**
Bowknot, plate, salad; green, 7" ..**13.00**
Bowknot, tumbler, green, 10-oz ...............................**25.00**
Cameo, bowl, cream soup; green, 4¾" ...............................**135.00**
Cameo, compote, mayonnaise; green, 4" ......................**32.00**
Cameo, cookie jar, green, w/lid .**55.00**

Cameo, cup, yellow, 2 styles ..**7.50**
Cameo, plate, sandwich; green, 10" ................................**14.00**
Cameo, sherbet, yellow, 5" ..**45.00**
Cherry Blossom, bowl, cereal; green, 5¾" ....................**48.00**
Cherry Blossom, coaster, pink .**15.00**
Cherry Blossom, creamer, pink .**22.00**

**Cherry Blossom, pitcher, green or pink, 8", $58.00.**

Cherry Blossom, plate, dinner; pink or green, 9" ..........**25.00**
Cherry Blossom, saucer, pink or green ................................**5.00**
Cherryberry, bowl, salad; pink or green, deep, 6½" ..........**25.00**
Cherryberry, pickle dish, pink or green ..............................**20.00**
Cherryberry, sherbet, pink or green ...............................**10.00**
Chinex Classic, bowl, cereal; decorated, 5¾" ........................**9.00**
Chinex Classic, butter dish, decorated, w/lid ....................**80.00**
Chinex Classic, plate, sandwich or cake; ivory, 11½" .............**7.50**
Circle, bowl, pink or green, 9½" ..........................**22.00**
Circle, pitcher, pink or green, 80-oz ...................................**30.00**

Circle, plate, luncheon; pink or green, 8¼" ......................**4.00**
Cloverleaf, bowl, cereal; green, 5" ................................**32.00**
Cloverleaf, plate, luncheon; yellow, 8" ..........................**14.00**
Cloverleaf, sugar bowl, green, footed, 3½" ..........................**10.00**
Colonial, cup, pink or green .**12.00**
Colonial, goblet, water; green, 8½-oz, 5¾" ....................**30.00**
Colonial, plate, dinner; pink, 10" ................................**55.00**
Colonial Block, bowl, pink or green, 7" ......................**20.00**
Colonial Block, candy dish, pink or green, w/lid, 8½" ..........**40.00**
Colonial Block, pitcher, pink or green ..............................**45.00**
Colonial Fluted, bowl, berry; green, 4" ......................**8.00**
Colonial Fluted, plate, luncheon; green, 8" ......................**5.00**
Columbia, bowl, cereal; crystal, 5" ................................**18.00**
Columbia, cup, pink .............**25.00**
Columbia, saucer, pink ........**10.00**
Coronation, bowl, nappy; red, 6½" ................................**12.00**
Coronation, plate, luncheon; pink, 8½" ................................**5.00**
Cube, bowl, dessert; green, 4½" ...**7.00**
Cube, cup, pink ......................**7.50**
Cube, sugar bowl, green, 3" ...**8.00**
Diamond Quilted, bowl, cream soup; blue, 4¾" .............**20.00**
Diamond Quilted, compote, green, w/lid, 11½" ....................**95.00**
Diamond Quilted, plate, salad; blue, 7" ............................**9.00**
Diamond Quilted, tumbler, water; green, 9-oz ......................**9.00**
Diana, bowl, cereal; amber, 5" ..**12.00**

Diana, coaster, pink, 3½" ......7.00
Diana, tumbler, amber, 9-oz, 4" ...27.50
Dogwood, bowl, cereal; pink, 5½" ........................33.00
Dogwood, plate, luncheon; green, 8" ........................8.00
Dogwood, sugar bowl, pink, thin, 2½" ........................18.00
Doric, bowl, cereal; green, 5½" .75.00
Doric, coaster, pink or green, 3" ...18.00
Doric, plate, dinner; pink, 9" ...16.00
Doric, relish tray, green, 4x8" .18.00
Doric, sugar bowl, pink ......12.00
Doric & Pansy, creamer, pink ...35.00
Doric & Pansy, plate, salad; ultramarine, 6" ...................38.00
Doric & Pansy, saucer, ultramarine ........................8.00
English Hobnail, bowl, cream soup; pink or green ......25.00
English Hobnail, candlesticks, pink or green, 3½", pr ..40.00
English Hobnail, egg cup, pink or green ........................36.00
English Hobnail, marmalade, pink or green, w/lid ..............40.00
English Hobnail, plate, pie; pink or green, 7¼" .................9.00
English Hobnail, tumbler, iced tea; pink or green, 12-oz, 5" ........................30.00
Floral, bowl, salad; pink, 7½" .22.00
Floral, cup, green .................14.00
Floral, plate, dinner; pink, 9" ..18.00
Floral, sugar bowl, green ....12.00
Floral & Diamond Band, bowl, nappy; pink or green, handled, 5¾" ...................12.00
Floral & Diamond Band, plate, luncheon; pink or green, 8" ........................45.00
Floral & Diamond Band, tumbler, water; pink, 4" .............40.00

Florentine No 1, bowl, berry; yellow, 5" ...................15.00
Florentine No 1, pitcher, green, footed, 36-oz, 6½" .........40.00
Florentine No 1, plate, dinner; yellow, 10" ........................25.00
Florentine No 1, plate, salad; yellow, 8½" ........................12.00
Florentine No 1, saucer, green ..3.00
Florentine No 2, bowl, cream soup; green, 4¾" ...................14.00
Florentine No 2, custard, green .....60.00
Florentine No 2, plate, dinner; green or yellow, 10" ......15.00
Florentine No 2, sherbet, green, footed ...................10.00
Flower Garden w/Butterflies, bowl, console; pink or green, footed, 10" ...................85.00
Flower Garden w/Butterflies, candlesticks, pink or green, 8", pr ...................145.00
Flower Garden w/Butterflies, powder jar, pink or green, flat ........80.00
Fortune, bowl, dessert; pink, 4½" ........................9.00
Fortune, candy dish, pink, flat, w/lid ...................25.00
Fortune, cup ........................7.00
Fruits, bowl, cereal; pink, 5" ..23.00
Fruits, cup, green .................8.00
Fruits, saucer, green .............5.00
Georgian, bowl, cereal; green, 5¾" ........................24.00
Georgian, butter dish, green, w/lid ...................75.00
Georgian, sherbet, green .....12.00
Hex Optic, bowl, berry; pink or green, ruffled, 4¼" .........6.00
Hex Optic, plate, sherbet; pink or green, 6" ...................2.50
Hobnail, decanter, crystal, w/stopper, 32-oz .................30.00

Hobnail, saucer, crystal .........**2.00**

Hobnail, tumbler, juice; crystal, 5-oz ................................**4.00**

Homespun, ashtray/coaster, pink ...........................**6.50**

Homespun, bowl, cereal; pink, 5" ............................**28.00**

Homespun, plate, dinner; pink, 9¼" ................................**17.00**

Homespun, tumbler, water; pink, 9-oz, 4" ...........................**20.00**

Indiana Custard, butter dish, ivory, w/lid ...................**60.00**

Indiana Custard, platter, ivory, oval, 11½" ......................**30.00**

Indiana Custard, sugar bowl, ivory ...........................**12.00**

Iris, bowl, salad; crystal, 9½" .**12.50**

Iris, creamer, crystal or iridescent, footed ............................**12.00**

Iris, goblet, wine; iridescent, 4" .**30.00**

Iris, sugar bowl, crystal or iridescent ................................**11.00**

**Iris, crystal: Footed tumbler, 6", $18.00; Wine, 4½", $17.00; Pitcher, 9½", $38.00.**

Jubilee, creamer, pink .........**35.00**

Jubilee, cup, yellow ..............**12.00**

Jubilee, plate, luncheon; pink, 8¾" ..............................**27.50**

Jubilee, sherbet, yellow, 8-oz, 3" ..............................**70.00**

Laced Edge, bowl, blue or green, 5" ....................................**37.50**

Laced Edge, mayonnaise, blue or green, 3-pc ...................**135.00**

Laced Edge, plate, bread & butter; blue or green, 6½" .........**18.00**

Laced Edge, tidbit, blue or green, 8" & 10" plates ............**100.00**

Lake Como, bowl, cereal; 6" ...**25.00**

Lake Como, salt & pepper shakers, pr .....................................**42.50**

Laurel, bowl, cereal; ivory, 6" ..**9.00**

Laurel, creamer, ivory or green, tall ................................**12.00**

Laurel, salt & pepper shakers, green, pr ......................**65.00**

Laurel, sugar bowl, ivory, tall ...**12.00**

Lincoln Inn, ashtray, blue or red ............................**17.50**

Lincoln Inn, comport, cobalt .**15.00**

Lincoln Inn, nut dish, blue or red, footed ............................**20.00**

Lincoln Inn, saucer, amethyst ...**3.50**

Lorain, bowl, cereal; green, 6" ........................**45.00**

Lorain, cup, yellow ..............**15.00**

Lorain, relish, green, 4-part, 8" ...**20.00**

Lorain, tumbler, yellow, footed, 9-oz, 4¾" ...........................**33.00**

Madrid, bowl, salad; amber, 8" ..**14.00**

Madrid, butter dish, green, w/lid ...........................**90.00**

Madrid, jam dish, amber, 7" ....................................**25.00**

Madrid, salt & pepper shakers, green, flat, 3½", pr ........**65.00**

Manhattan, ashtray, crystal, round, 4" ........................**11.00**

Manhattan, coaster, crystal, 3½" ............................**15.00**

Manhattan, compote, pink, 5¾" .**35.00**

Manhattan, sherbet, crystal ..**9.00**

Manhattan, vase, crystal, 8" .**18.00**

Mayfair (Federal), bowl, sauce; amber, 5" ........................9.00

Mayfair (Federal), creamer, green, footed ............................16.00

Mayfair (Federal), sugar bowl, green, footed ................16.00

Mayfair/Open Rose, bowl, vegetable; pink, 7" ..............28.00

Mayfair/Open Rose, cake plate, pink, footed ...................33.00

Mayfair/Open Rose, pitcher, blue, 37-oz, 6" ......................150.00

Mayfair/Open Rose, plate, grill; pink, 9½" ......................40.00

Mayfair/Open Rose, salt & pepper shakers, pink, flat, pr ..........................65.00

**Mayfair, pitcher, 80-oz, 8½": Green or yellow, from $750.00 to $800.00; Pink, $115.00; Blue, $210.00. (Photo courtesy Gene Florence)**

Miss America, bowl, berry; pink, 6¼" .................................25.00

Miss America, celery dish, crystal, oblong, 10½" ..................15.00

Miss America, plate, dinner; pink, 10½" ..............................30.00

Miss America, platter, crystal, oval, 12" ........................14.00

Moderntone, bowl, cereal; amethyst or cobalt, 6½" ..................75.00

Moderntone, cup, amethyst or cobalt ............................11.00

Moderntone, plate, luncheon; cobalt, 7¾" ....................12.50

Moderntone, saucer, amethyst ...4.00

Moondrops, ashtray, red or blue ...32.00

Moondrops, bowl, vegetable; pink, oval, 9¾" ......................25.00

Moondrops, candy dish, red or blue, ruffled, 8" ............40.00

Moondrops, decanter, green, 8½" ............................45.00

Moondrops, pitcher, amber, 22-oz, 7" ...................................90.00

Moondrops, plate, dinner; red or blue, 9½" ......................25.00

New Century, bowl, casserole; green, w/lid, 9" ..............65.00

New Century, plate, breakfast; green, 7" ..........................9.00

New Century, plate, grill; green, 10" ....................................15.00

New Century, tumbler, green, 12-oz, 5¼" ......................30.00

No 610 Pyramid, bowl, pickle; pink, 9½" ......................35.00

No 610 Pyramid, sugar bowl, yellow ..............................40.00

No 610 Pyramid, tumbler, pink, footed, 11-oz ..................55.00

No 612 Horseshoe, bowl, cereal; green or yellow, 6½" .....30.00

No 612 Horseshoe, plate, salad; green or yellow, 8½" .....12.00

No 612 Horseshoe, plate, sandwich; green or yellow, 11¼" ......................23.00

No 616 Vernon, creamer, green or yellow, footed ..............25.00

No 616 Vernon, cup, green or yellow ..............................18.00

**No 610 'Pyramid', creamer and sugar bowl, pink, $30.00 each.**

No 616 Vernon, sugar bowl, green or yellow, footed ............**25.00**

No 618 Pineapple & Floral, bowl, crystal, 4¾" ..................**25.00**

No 618 Pineapple & Floral, plate, dinner; crystal, 9½" ......**17.50**

No 618 Pineapple & Floral, saucer, crystal or amber .............**4.00**

No 622 Pretzel, bowl, fruit cup; crystal, 4½" ....................**5.00**

No 622 Pretzel, cup, crystal ..**6.00**

No 622 Pretzel, plate, crystal, tab handles, 6" ......................**3.00**

Normandie, bowl, vegetable; amber, 10" ....................**20.00**

Normandie, plate, grill; pink, 11" ..............................**20.00**

Normandie, sugar bowl, amber ..**8.00**

Old Cafe, candy dish, red, low, 8" ...............................**16.00**

Old Cafe, olive dish, pink, oblong, 6" .......................................**7.00**

Old Cafe, plate, dinner; pink, 10" ...............................**55.00**

Old Colony, bowl, cereal; pink, 6½" ...............................**25.00**

Old Colony, cookie jar, pink, w/ lid ...............................**75.00**

Old Colony, plate, dinner; pink, 10½" ..............................**33.00**

Parrot, bowl, berry; green, 5" .**25.00**

Parrot, jam dish, amber, 7" .**35.00**

Parrot, sugar bowl, green ....**35.00**

Patrician, bowl, cereal; amber, 6" ...............................**25.00**

Patrician, pitcher, green, 75-oz, 8" ..............................**125.00**

Patrician, plate, luncheon; green, 9" ...............................**11.00**

Patrician, salt & pepper shakers, amber, pr ......................**55.00**

Patrick, candlesticks, yellow or pink, pr ......................**150.00**

Patrick, saucer, yellow ........**10.00**

Patrick, sherbet, pink, 4¾" .**60.00**

Petalware, bowl, cream soup; pink or monax, 4½" .............**12.00**

Petalware, plate, dinner; pink, 9" ...............................**14.00**

Petalware, saucer, monax .....**1.50**

Primo, bowl, yellow or green, 4½" .............................**18.00**

Primo, plate, yellow or green, 7½" .............................**10.00**

Primo, tumbler, yellow or green, 9-oz, 5¾" .........................**22.00**

Princess, bowl, salad; pink or green, octagonal, 9" ......................**40.00**

Princess, butter dish, pink or green, w/lid ...............**100.00**

Princess, relish, pink, divided, 7½" ...............................**30.00**

Queen Mary, bowl, berry; crystal, 5" ..........................................**7.00**

Queen Mary, candy dish, pink, w/lid ...............................**40.00**

Queen Mary, cup, crystal ......**5.00**

Queen Mary, plate, dinner; crystal, 9¾" ...........................**18.00**

Queen Mary, saucer, pink .....**2.00**

Radiance, bowl, amber, 2-part, 7" ...............................**18.00**

Radiance, bowl, celery; red or blue, 10" .....................................**30.00**

Radiance, comport, amber, 5" ...**18.00**

Radiance, plate, luncheon; red or blue, 8" ...........................**16.00**

Radiance, tumbler, amber, 9-oz ...**20.00**

Raindrops, bowl, cereal; green, 6" ................................**9.00**

Raindrops, plate, luncheon; green, 8" ......................................**6.00**

Raindrops, sugar bowl, green .**7.50**

Ribbon, bowl, berry; green, 4" .**28.00**

Ribbon, plate, luncheon; black, 8" ...............................**14.00**

Ribbon, salt & pepper shakers, green, pr ........................**32.00**

Ring, bowl, berry; crystal, 5" .**3.50**

Ring, ice bucket, green or crystal w/decoration ................**35.00**

Ring, sandwich server, crystal, w/center handle .............**17.50**

Rose Cameo, bowl, cereal; green, 5" ...............................**18.00**

Rose Cameo, sherbet, green ..**12.00**

Rosemary, bowl, cream soup; amber ...............................**17.00**

Rosemary, cup, green ...........**9.50**

Rosemary, plate, dinner; amber ...**9.00**

Rosemary, saucer, green .......**5.00**

Roulette, pitcher, pink or green, 64-oz, 8" ........................**35.00**

Roulette, sherbet, green ........**5.50**

Roulette, tumbler, iced tea; pink, 12-oz, 5" ........................**28.00**

Round Robin, cup, green or iridescent, footed ....................**5.00**

Round Robin, plate, luncheon; green or iridescent, 8" ....**4.00**

Round Robin, sherbet, green .**5.00**

Roxana, bowl, berry; yellow, 5" .**11.00**

Roxana, plate, yellow, 6" .......**7.50**

Royal Lace, bowl, berry; pink, 5" ...............................**30.00**

Royal Lace, cup, blue ...........**35.00**

Royal Lace, plate, dinner; pink, 10" .....................................**30.00**

Royal Lace, saucer, blue ......**12.50**

Royal Ruby, ashtray, 4½" square ..........................**5.00**

Royal Ruby, creamer, footed .**9.00**

Royal Ruby, sugar bowl, footed ..**8.00**

Royal Ruby, tumbler, water; 9-oz .**6.50**

S Pattern, bowl, cereal; crystal, 5½" ..................................**5.00**

S Pattern, pitcher, crystal, 80-oz ........................**52.50**

S Pattern, plate, grill; amber .**9.00**

S Pattern, sherbet, amber, low-footed ...............................**7.50**

Sandwich (Hocking), bowl, cereal; crystal, 6¾" ..................**35.00**

Sandwich (Hocking), custard cup, green ...............................**1.50**

Sandwich (Hocking), punch bowl, crystal, 9¾" ..................**20.00**

Sandwich (Indiana), bowl, berry; crystal, 4¼" ....................**3.50**

Sandwich (Indiana), candlesticks, crystal, 7", pr ................**27.50**

Sandwich (Indiana), plate, dinner;
pink, 10½" .....................18.00
Sandwich (Indiana), sherbet, crystal .....................................6.00
Sharon, bowl, cream soup; amber,
5" ....................................28.00
Sharon, cake plate, pink, footed,
11½" ...............................43.00
Sharon, tumbler, pink, thin, 12-oz,
5½" ..................................50.00

**Sharon, salt and pepper shakers,
pair: pink, $50.00; amber, $40.00.**

Sierra, bowl, vegetable; pink, oval,
9½" ..................................50.00
Sierra, plate, dinner; green, 9" ...25.00
Sierra, tray, pink, handled ..18.00
Spiral, bowl, mixing; green, 7" ..9.00
Spiral, ice or butter tub, green .30.00
Spiral, saucer, green ...............1.50
Strawberry, bowl, berry; pink or
green, 4" ........................12.00
Strawberry, pickle dish, green ..20.00
Sunburst, bowl, crystal, 11" .25.00
Sunburst, cup, crystal ...........8.00
Sunburst, plate, crystal, 5½" ..4.00
Sunburst, saucer, crystal ......3.00
Sunflower, ashtray, pink, center
design only, 5" ................9.00
Sunflower, cake plate, pink or
green, footed, 10" ..........15.00
Sunflower, sugar bowl, green ..22.00

Swirl, bowl, cereal; ultramarine,
5¼" .................................18.00
Swirl, candy dish, pink, open,
footed ..............................14.00
Swirl, tumbler, ultramarine, 9-oz,
4" ....................................35.00
Tea Room, bowl, banana split;
pink, 7½" ........................90.00
Tea Room, creamer, pink or green,
4" ....................................26.00
Tea Room, relish, green, divided .25.00
Tea Room, sugar bowl, pink, 4" .18.00
Thistle, cup, pink, thin ........20.00
Thistle, saucer, pink or green ..10.00
Tulip, bowl, amber or crystal,
6" ....................................15.00
Tulip, plate, amethyst, blue or
green, 6" .......................10.00
Tulip, tumbler, juice; amber or
crystal ............................20.00
Twisted Optic, bowl, cereal; pink
or green, 5" ......................7.00
Twisted Optic, cup, pink or
green ................................5.00
Twisted Optic, saucer, pink or
green ................................2.00
Twisted Optic, tumbler, pink or
green, 12-oz, 5¼" ..............9.00
US Swirl, bowl, pink or green,
oval, 8¼" ........................45.00
US Swirl, plate, salad; green, 8" ...6.00
US Swirl, vase, pink, 6½" ...25.00
Victory, bonbon, blue, 7" .....20.00
Victory, creamer, pink .........15.00
Victory, goblet, pink, 7-oz, 5" ..20.00
Victory, plate, salad; blue, 7" ..20.00
Vitrock, bowl, berry; white, 4" .4.50
Vitrock, cup, white .................3.50
Vitrock, plate, dinner; white,
10" ....................................9.00
Waterford, bowl, berry; crystal,
4¾" ..................................6.50
Waterford, cup, pink ...........15.00

Waterford, saucer, pink .........**6.00**
Waterford, tumbler, crystal, 10-oz,
5" .....................................**13.00**
Windsor, ashtray, crystal, 5¾" .**13.50**
Windsor, bowl, cream soup; pink,
5" ....................................**22.00**
Windsor, platter, crystal, 11½" ..**8.00**
Windsor, tumbler, crystal, 9-oz,
4" ...................................**7.00**

# Dollhouse Furnishings

Collecting antique dollhouses
and building new ones is a popular hobby with many today, and
all who collect houses delight in
furnishing them right down to the
vase on the table and the scarf on
the piano! Flea markets are a good
source of dollhouse furnishings,
especially those from the 1940s
through the '60s made by
Strombecker, Tootsietoy, Renwal,
or the Petite Princess line by
Ideal.

For an expanded listing see

*Schroeders Collectible Toys,
Antique to Modern.*

Armoire, Mattel Littles .........**8.00**
Baby bath, pink w/duck or bunny
decal, Renwal, #122, ea .**15.00**
Bathtub, ivory w/blue, Ideal .**10.00**
Bed, bright yellow, Superior, ¾"
scale ................................**5.00**
Bed, green-painted cast iron, Kil-
gore ...............................**60.00**
Bed, w/headboard, Wolverine .**12.00**
Bedroom set, dark ivory, hard
plastic, 8-pc, Marx, ¾"
scale ........................**40.00**
Boudoir chaise lounge, blue, Ideal
Petite Princess ..............**25.00**
Buffet, brown, opening drawer,
Renwal .............................**8.00**
Chair, dining room; brown or
ivory, Tootsietoy, ea ........**7.00**
Chair, kitchen; white, Donna
Lee ...............................**5.00**
Chair, living room; red, hard plas-
tic, Marx, ½" scale .........**3.00**
China closet, brown, stenciled,
Renwal, #K52 ...............**15.00**

**Bed, Ideal Petite Princess, pink, MIB, $30.00.**

**Kitchen set, Renwal, complete in box, $150.00; Mother, #43, $25.00; Stool, #12, $12.00; Table radio #16, $15.00. (Photo courtesy Judith Mosholder)**

Clock, mantel; ivory or red, Renwal, #14, ea .................10.00

Cradle, pink, spread insert, Renwal, #119 ......................30.00

Doll, baby; w/diaper, Ideal ..10.00

Doll, father; blue suit, metal rivets, Renwal, #44 ............30.00

Doll, mother; pink, plastic rivets, Renwal, #43 .................25.00

Dresser, tan, w/mirror, hard plastic, Marx, ½" scale .........3.00

Dresser, w/mirror, Wolverine .10.00

Highboy, ivory w/blue, Ideal .18.00

Hutch, brown, soft plastic, Marx, ¾" scale ..........................3.00

Kitchen counter, white w/blue base, Plasco .....................6.00

Lamp, floor; yellow w/ivory shade, Renwal, #70 .................20.00

Night stand, ivory w/blue, Ideal .8.00

Night stand, yellow, hard plastic, Marx, ½" scale ..............15.00

Piano, baby grand; walnut, Strombecker, ¾" scale ..20.00

Piano & bench, Marx Little Hostess, MIB ......................35.00

Playground slide, blue w/red, Renwal, #20 ........................22.00

Radio, floor; walnut w/etched detail, Strombecker, ¾" scale ...........................12.00

Refrigerator, white, hard plastic, Marx, ½" scale ................3.00

Refrigerator, white, Superior, ¾" scale ...............................5.00

Rocker, stained wood, Grand Rapids, 1½" scale .........18.00

Rocking horse, pink, Best ....12.00

Sink, bathroom; blue w/yellow, Ideal ...............................10.00

Sink, bathroom; blue-painted cast iron, Kilgore .................50.00

Sink, kitchen; Ideal ............15.00

Sofa, light green fabric, Sonia Messer .........................80.00

Sofa, red w/brown base, Renwal, #78 ................................15.00

Stove, ivory, Endeavor ..........5.00

Stroller, pink w/blue or white wheels, Acme/Thomas, ea .6.00

Table, cocktail; brown, Renwal, #72 ................................10.00

Table, dining; dark marbleized maroon, Ideal ...............**20.00**
Table, dressing; white w/pink, Blue Box ........................**4.00**
Telephone, yellow w/red, Renwal, #28 ...............................**22.00**
Telephone set, Fantasy; Ideal Petite Princess, #4432-1 ...........**22.00**
Vacuum cleaner, Renwal .....**25.00**
Vanity, tan w/heart-shaped mirror, Blue Box ...................**3.00**
Washing machine, white, Superior, ¾" scale ....................**5.00**

# Dolls

Doll collecting is no doubt one of the most popular fields today. Antique as well as modern dolls are treasured, and limited edition or artists' dolls often bring prices in excess of several hundred dollars. Investment potential is considered excellent in all areas. Dolls have been made from many materials — early to middle 19th-century dolls were carved of wood, poured in wax, and molded in bisque or china. Primitive cloth dolls were sewn at home for the enjoyment of little girls when fancier dolls were unavailable. In this century from 1925 to about 1945, composition was used. Made of a mixture of sawdust, clay, fiber, and a binding agent, it was tough and durable. Modern dolls are usually made of vinyl or molded plastic.

Learn to check your intended purchases for damage which could jeopardize your investment. In the listings, values are for dolls in excellent condition unless another condition is noted in the line. They are priced 'mint in box' only when so indicated. Played-with, soiled dolls are worth from 50% to 75% less, depending on condition. Authority Pat Smith has written many wonderful books on the subject: *Patricia Smith's Doll Values, Antique to Modern; Modern Collector's Dolls* (eight in the series); *Vogue Ginny Dolls, Through the Years With Ginny;* and *Madame Alexander Collector's Dolls.* Patsy Moyer's books, *Modern Collector's Dolls, Volumes 1, 2, and 3,* and *Doll Values, Third Edition,* are also highly recommended. (All are published by Collector Books.) See also Action Figures; Advertising Characters; Character Collectibles; Holly Hobbie and Friends; Strawberry Shortcake; Trolls; Clubs and Newsletters.

## American Character

In business by 1918, this company made both composition and plastic dolls, all of excellent quality. Many collectors count them among the most desirable American dolls ever made. The company closed in 1968, and all of their molds were sold to other companies. The hard plastic dolls of the 1950s are much in demand today. See also Betsy McCall.

Eloise, cloth w/yarn hair, crooked smile, 1950s, original clothes, 15", M ...........................**250.00**
Mary/Magic Makeup, 1965-66, pale face, no lashes, bent knees, M ......................**45.00**

Pixie, or Granny, Whimette/Little People, 1963, 7½", M, ea ................................30.00
Pre-Teen Tressy, M .............75.00
Ricky Jr, vinyl baby boy, 1955-56, original clothes, 13", M..50.00
Sally Says, 1965, plastic & vinyl talker, 19", M ................70.00
Talking Marie, 1963, record player in body, battery operated, 18", M ................................90.00
Tiny Tears, hard plastic & vinyl, 1955-62, 8", M...............50.00
Tressy, in Miss America character outfit, NM ......................50.00
Tressy w/Magic Makeup Face, M ...............................20.00

## Annalee

Annalee Davis Thorndike made her first commercially sold dolls in the late 1950s. They're characterized by their painted felt faces and the meticulous workmanship involved in their manufacture. Most are made entirely of felt, though Santas and rabbits may have flannel bodies. All are constructed around a wire framework that allows them to be positioned in imaginative poses. Depending on rarity, appeal, and condition, some of the older dolls have increased in value more than ten times their original price. Dolls from the 1950s carried a long white red-embroidered tag with no date. The same tag was in use from 1959 until 1964, but there was a copyright date in the upper right-hand corner. In 1970 a transition period began. The company changed its tag to a white satiny tag with a date preceded by a copyright symbol in the upper right-hand corner. In 1975 they made another change to a long white cotton strip with a copyright date. In 1982 the white tag was folded over, making it shorter. Many people mistake the copyright date as the date the doll was made — not so! It wasn't until 1986 that they finally began to date the tags with the year of manufacture, making it much easier for collectors to identify their dolls. Besides the red-lettered white Annalee tags, numerous others were used in the 1990s, but all reflect the year the doll was actually made.

Our advisor for this category is Jane Holt; she is listed in the Directory under New Hampshire. For more information, refer to *Teddy Bears, Annalee's, and Steiff Animals,* by Margaret Fox Mandel (Collector Books).

Bat, 1991, 12" ......................50.00
Boating Mouse, 1985, 7" ......40.00
Bunny on Sled, 1987, 7" ......45.00
Caroller Girl, on stand, 1987, 3" ............................25.00
Country Girl Bunny, 1981, 18" ..75.00
Cupid in Hot Air Balloon, 1987, 3" ................................75.00
Devil Kid, 1994, 12" .............55.00
Ghost, 1994, 7" ....................35.00
Hobo Cat, 1986, 18" .............75.00
Jogger Boy, 1984, 7" ...........35.00
Jogger Mouse, 1979, 7" ........30.00
Mouse w/Presents, 1986, 7" ..25.00
Pilot Duck, 1984, 5" .............40.00
Pixie Piccolo Player, 1995, 5" ...45.00

**Annalee, Santa on ski-bob with sack, 1971, 7", $150.00.**
**(Photo courtesy Jane Holt)**

Santa in Rocking Chair, 1986,
  18" ...........................**75.00**
Santa w/Red Nose Reindeer, 1979,
  7" ....................................**40.00**
St Nicholas w/Plaque, 1988, 10" .**60.00**
Witch, 1987, 3" ....................**75.00**

## Arranbee

Made during the 1930s
through the '50s, these composition or plastic dolls will be marked
either 'Arranbee,' 'R&B' (until
1961), or 'Made in USA - 210.'

Littlest Angel, 1956+, hard plastic
  walker, 10", NM .........**185.00**
My Angel, 1957-59, walker, 30",
  M ...............................**150.00**
My Angel, 1961, hard plastic &
  vinyl, 17", M .................**45.00**
Nancy Lee, 1950-59, hard plastic,
  14", G ...........................**125.00**
Nanette Walker, 1957-59, 17",
  NM ............................**425.00**

## Barbie and Friends

Barbie has undergone some
minor makeovers since 1959 — the
first one had just white irises but
no eye color. Today those early
Barbie dolls are almost impossible
to find, but if you can find one in
mint condition, she's worth about
$5,500.00 – $2,000.00 more if the
original box is with her. There are
several reference books available
for further study: *The World of
Barbie Dolls* and *The Wonder of
Barbie, 1976 to 1986,* by Paris, and
Susan Manos; *The Collector's Encyclopedia of Barbie Dolls and Collectibles* by Sibyl De Wein and Joan
Ashabraner; *Barbie Fashions, Vol I
and Vol II,* by Sarah Sink Eames;
*Barbie Exclusives, Book I and Book
II,* by Margo Rana; *The Story of Barbie* by Kitturah B. Westenhouser;
*Barbie Doll Exclusives and More* by
J. Michael Augustyniak; and *The*

*Barbie Doll Years* by Patrick and Myrazona Olds. All these books are published by Collector Books.

Values given for mint-in-the-box dolls will be from three to as much as seven times higher than the same doll in very good, played-with condition.

Allan, 1963, painted red hair, straight legs, NRFB ...**165.00**
Barbie, #3, 1960, brunette hair, original swimsuit, NM ........**950.00**
Barbie, #5, 1961, red hair, MIB .**900.00**
Barbie, Benefit Ball, 1992, Classique Collection, NRFB ...........**150.00**
Barbie, Bubble-Cut, 1961, brunette hair, NM ......**200.00**
Barbie, Circus Star, FAO Schwarz, 1994 department store special, NRFB .....................**95.00**
Barbie, Eskimo, 1981, Dolls of the World series, NRFB ......**75.00**
Barbie, Gold & Lace, 1989, Target, NRFB .............................**35.00**
Barbie, Holiday, 1988, original dress, EX .....................**325.00**
Barbie, Holiday, 1990, original dress, VG ......................**85.00**
Barbie, Kissing, 1979, original outfit, M ........................**20.00**
Barbie, Malibu, 1971, original blue swimsuit, VG ................**20.00**
Barbie, Nigerian, 1989, Dolls of the World series, NRFB .......**65.00**
Barbie, Pink & Pretty, 1982, original outfit, M ..................**15.00**
Barbie, Pretty in Purple, 1992, K-Mart, NRFB .................**25.00**
Barbie, Solo in the Spotlight, porcelain, 1989, NRFB .........**200.00**
Barbie, Superstar, 1976, original outfit, M ......................**25.00**

Barbie, Twist 'N Turn, 1966, brunette hair, redressed, G .............................**45.00**
Curtis, Free Moving, 1975, MIB .**50.00**
Francie, Malibu, 1970, original swimsuit, VG ...............**45.00**

**Magic Earrings Ken, real clip-on earrings, 12", $100.00. (Photo courtesy June Moon)**

Ken, Busy, 1972, painted brown hair, original outfit & accessories, VG .....................**65.00**
Ken, Malibu, 1971, original swimsuit, VG ........................**20.00**
Ken, Spanish Talking, 1970, MIB ...........................**200.00**
Midge, Earring Magic, 1993, MIB ...........................**25.00**
PJ, Gold Medal Gymnast, 1975, MIB ..............................**85.00**

Skipper, Growing Up, 1975, original outfit, VG ................**35.00**

Skipper, 1963, brunette hair, straight legs, MIB .......**300.00**

Skooter, 1965, blond hair, bendable legs, original outfit, NM ...........................**100.00**

Tutti, 1966, blond or brunette hair, MIB ......................**175.00**

## Betsy McCall

Tiny 8" Betsy McCall was manufactured by the American Character Doll Company from 1957 until 1963. She was made from fine quality hard plastic with a bisque-like finish and had hand-painted features. Betsy came with four hair colors — tosca, blond, red, and brown. She has blue sleep eyes, molded lashes, a winsome smile, and a fully jointed body with bendable knees. On her back is an identification circle which reads ©McCall Corp. The basic doll could be purchased for $2.25 and wore a sheer chemise, white taffeta panties, nylon socks, and Maryjane-style shoes.

There were two different materials used for tiny Betsy's hair. The first was soft mohair sewn onto mesh. Later the rubber scullcap was rooted with saran which was more suitable for washing and combing.

Betsy McCall had an extensive wardrobe with nearly one hundred outfits, each of which could be purchased separately. They were made from wonderful fabrics such as velvet, felt, taffeta, and even real mink fur. Each ensemble came with the appropriate footware and was priced under $3.00. Since none of Betsy's clothing is tagged, it is often difficult to identify other than by its square snap closures (although these were used by other companies as well).

**Betsy McCall starter kit with rare side-part doll, $175.00. (Photo courtesy Leslie Robinson; from the collection of Marci Van Ausdall)**

Betsy McCall is a highly collectible doll today but is still fairly easy to find at doll shows. The prices remain reasonable for this beautiful clothes horse and her many accessories, some of which we've included below.

Our advisor for this category is Marcy Van Ausdall; she is listed in the Directory under California. For further information we recommend her book, *Betsy McCall, A Collector's Guide*. See also Clubs and Newsletters.

Clothes, #8204 Birthday Party outfit, for 8" doll, MOC .....................**95.00**
Clothes, Prom Time formal, pink, for 8" doll ........................**65.00**
Doll, American Character, 14", M ...............................**225.00**
Doll, w/tissue & original pamphlet, 8", MIB .............**225.00**
Little Golden Book, #559, EX & complete ........................**25.00**
Magazine sheet, McCalls's, uncut paper doll, 1970s, from $3 to ....................**4.00**
Paper doll book, Whitman's #1969 ............................**20.00**
Rothschild Betsy McCall Goes to a Tea Party, #800B, NRFB .**45.00**
Shoes, Maryjane, black or white, pr, EX ............................**20.00**

## Cameo

Best known for their Kewpie dolls, this company also made some wood-jointed character dolls with composition heads during the 1920s and '30s. Although most of the Kewpie molds had been sold to another company by then, the few they retained were used during the 1970s to produce a line of limited edition dolls. Kewpies marked 'S71' were actually made by Strombecker.

Miss Peep, ball-jointed shoulders & hips, 1970s-80s, 17", M ..**45.00**
Miss Peep, Black, vinyl, 1950s, 18", M ...........................**65.00**
Miss Peep, Newborn, 1962, vinyl & rigid plastic, 18", M ......**40.00**
Miss Peep, vinyl, 1960s, 15", M .**40.00**
Pinkie, 1950s, 10-11", M, ea .**150.00**
Scootles, vinyl, 1964, 14", M, minimum value .................**185.00**

## Celebrities

Dolls that represent movie or TV personalities, fictional characters, or famous sports figures are very popular collectibles and can usually be found for well under $100.00. Mego, Horsman, Ideal, and Mattel are among the largest producers. Condition is vital. To price a doll in mint condition but without the box, deduct about 65% from the value of one mint-in-the-box. Dolls in only good or poorer condition drop at a very rapid pace.

Our advisor for this category is Henri Yunes; he is listed in the Directory under New Jersey. For an expanded listing, see *Schroeder's Collectible Toys, Antique to Modern*.

Andy Gibb, Ideal, 1979, w/disco dancing stand, 7½", NRFB .........**50.00**

**Brooke Shields, Prom Party, LJN, 1983, third issue, 11½", rare, MIB, $200.00.**

Boy George, LJN, 1984, scarce, 11½", MIB ..................**125.00**

Cher, Mego, 1977, 2nd issue, Growing Hair, 12¼", NRFB .............**80.00**

Diana Ross, Mego, 1977, white & silver dress, 12", NRFB ....**125.00**

Dolly Parton, Eegee, 1987, 2nd issue, cowgirl outfit, 11½", MIB ..............................**45.00**

Groucho Marx, Effanbee, 1983, 17", MIB ......................**90.00**

Kate Jackson (Sabrina of Charlie's Angels), Hasbro, 1977, 8½", MOC ............................**40.00**

Marie Osmond, Mattel, 1976, 11", MIB ..............................**50.00**

Michael Jackson, LJN, 1984, any of 4 outfits, 11", NRFB, ea ..**60.00**

New Kids on the Block, 1990, 1st issue, Hangin' Loose, 12", MIB, ea ..........................**35.00**

Redd Fox, Shindana, 1977, talker, stuffed doll, MIB ..........**45.00**

Robin Williams (Mork), Mattel, 1979, 9", MIB ...............**45.00**

Shirley Temple, Ideal, 1972, Stand Up & Cheer outfit, 16", MIB ...........................**160.00**

Vivian Leigh (Scarlett), World Dolls, 1980, 1st edition, 12", NRFB ...........................**65.00**

## Chatty Cathy

Made by Mattel, this is one of the most successful lines of dolls ever made. She was introduced in the 1960s as either a blond or a brunette. By pulling a string on her back, Chatty Cathy could speak eleven phrases. During the next five years, Mattel added to the line with Chatty Baby, Tiny Chatty Baby, Tiny Chatty Brother, Charmin' Chatty, and Singing' Chatty. The dolls were taken off the market only to be brought out again in 1969. But the new dolls were smaller and had restyled faces, and they were not as well received.

Our advisors for this category are Kathy and Don Lewis, authors of *Chatty Cathy Dolls, An Identification and Value Guide;* they are listed in the Directory under California.

Black Chatty Baby, M .......**325.00**

Black Tiny Chatty Baby, M .**300.00**

Chatty Baby, open speaker, brunette w/blue eyes, M .**90.00**

Chatty Cathy, later issue, open speaker, brunette w/blue eyes, M ................................**150.00**

Doll, mid-year or transitional, brunette w/brown eyes, M ......**135.00**

**Porcelain, 1980, MIB, $700.00.**
**(Photo courtesy Kathy and Don**
**Lewis)**

Doll, Patent Pending, cloth over speaker, blond w/blue eyes, M ...**150.00**

Doll, Singin' Chatty, blond, M .**100.00**

Doll, soft face, blond, brunette or auburn pigtails, M ......**200.00**

Doll, Tiny Chatty Baby, brunette w/brown eyes, M .........**125.00**

Doll, Tiny Chatty Baby, brunette w/blue eyes, M ..............**90.00**

## Deluxe, Deluxe Topper

Dolls by the Deluxe Reading Corporation may be marked either Deluxe Topper, Topper Corp., Topper Toys, Deluxe Toy Creations, or Deluxe Premium Corp. They're most famous for their teen fashion doll, Dawn. She was produced from the late 1960s to 1970, so her wardrobe is right in step with today's retro styles. Expect to pay from $10.00 to $15.00 for any of her outfits, mint in the box.

Betty Bride/Sweet Rosemary, 1957, 1-pc vinyl, 30", M ..........**90.00**

Dancing Angie, NRFB ........**30.00**

Dancing Dawn, NRFB .........**30.00**

Dancing Jessica, NRFB ......**30.00**

Dawn Head to Toe, pink & silver dress, NRFB .................**90.00**

Dawn Majorette, NRFB .......**75.00**

Gary, NRFB .......................**30.00**

Kevin, EX ..........................**15.00**

Little Miss Fussy, battery operated, 18", M ....................**35.00**

Longlocks, NRFB ................**30.00**

Maureen, Dawn Model Agency, red & gold dress, MIB ..**75.00**

Ron, NRFB ........................**30.00**

Suzy Homemaker, 1964, hard plastic & vinyl, jointed knees, 21", M ...........................**45.00**

Tom Boy, Go Go, 1965, 6", M .**45.00**

## Eegee

The Goldberger company made these dolls, Eegee (E.G.) being the initials of the company's founder. Dolls marked 'Made in China' were made in 1986.

Andy, 1963, vinyl, teenager, molded/painted hair, painted eyes, 12", M ...........................**35.00**

Annette, 1963, vinyl, teenager, rooted hair, painted eyes, 11½", M ......................**55.00**

Baby Luv, 1973, dark hair version, all original, 15", VG ......................**25.00**

Ballerina, 1964, vinyl & hard plastic, 31", M ...................**100.00**

My Fair Lady, 1958, vinyl, fashion type, swivel waist, jointed, 20", M ..........................**75.00**

Tandy Talks, 1961, vinyl & hard plastic, pull-string talker, 20", M ......................50.00

**Effanbee**

This company has been in business since 1910, continually producing high quality dolls, some of all composition, some composition and cloth, and a few in plastic and vinyl. In excellent condition, some of the older dolls often bring $300.00 and up.

Baby Lisa, 1980, vinyl, 11", M ................................150.00
Baby Lisa Grows Up, 1983, vinyl, toddler, M in trunk with wardrobe ....................150.00
Fluffy, Girl Scout, 1954+, vinyl, M ....................................75.00
Honey, 1949-55, hard plastic, sleep eyes, hard plastic, 14", M ................................500.00
Mickey, 1956-72, vinyl, jointed, molded hat, painted eyes, 10", M ..................................75.00

Polka Dotty, 1954, vinyl head w/molded braids, cloth body, 21", M ..........................165.00
Pun'kin, 1966-83, vinyl, jointed toddler, sleep eyes, 11", M ..30.00
Suzie Sunshine, 1961-79, vinyl, jointed, sleep eyes, freckles, 18", M ..........................50.00

**Fisher-Price**

Since the mid-1970s, this well-known American toy company has been making a variety of dolls. Many have vinyl heads, rooted hair, and cloth bodies. Most are marked and dated.

Audrey, #203, 1974-78, vinyl & cloth, removable jeans ..25.00
Baby Ann, #204, 1974-78, vinyl & cloth, removable nightgown & diaper ...........................25.00
Black Elizabeth, 1974-79, vinyl & cloth, removable skirt, MIB ..........55.00
Honey, #208, 1978, yellow & white print, MIB ....................45.00

**Effanbee, Patsyette Babies, composition, caracul wigs, sleep eyes, 9", each, $265.00.**

Jenny, #0201, 1974-78, vinyl &
cloth, removable skirt ...**25.00**
Jenny, #0201, 1974-78, vinyl &
cloth, removable skirt,
MIB ...........................**50.00**
Joey, #206, 1975, vinyl & cloth,
w/jacket, lace & tie sneak-
ers ..............................**25.00**
Natalie, #0202, 1974-78, vinyl &
cloth, removable skirt & bon-
net, MIB ........................**50.00**

## Gerber Babies

The first Gerber Baby dolls
were manufactured of cloth by an
unknown maker in 1936. Since
that time six different companies
have attempted to capture the
charm of the charcoal drawing
done by Dorothy Hop Smith of her
friend's baby, Ann Turner (Cook).

Gerber began to issue premium items in the 1930s but discontinued them during World War II
(1941 – 1945); they began again in
1946. In the '70s Gerber began to
expand their interest beyond food
items into merchandising their
related baby care line and insur-
ance. Then in the '80s Gerber initi-
ated a sales program of promotional items that were available to
those who were in any way connected with the company. The '90s
saw emphasis shift toward mass
merchandising, and the company
disclosed a line of toys designed to
grow with the child. However, the
sale of high quality food items for
infants and toddlers remains their
first priority.

Besides premiums and sale
items, Gerber made many 'freebie' souvenirs available through its company
tours, the Tourist Center, and special
events which they sponsored.

Our advisor for this category is
Joan Stryker Grubaugh, the author of
an excellent new book, *Gerber Baby
Dolls and Advertising Collectibles*. She
is listed in the Directory under Ohio.

Amsco, 1972-73, vinyl, plastic
pants & bib-type shirt, 14",
EX ................................**35.00**
Arrow Rubber & Plastic Corp,
1965-67, footed clown paja-
mas, 14", VG ................**45.00**
Atlanta Novelty, 1978, 50th
Anniversary, vinyl/cloth, 17",
NRFB ...........................**95.00**
Atlanta Novelty, 1979, zipper
snowsuit, 17", NRFB ....**95.00**
Atlanta Novelty, 1979-85, Pajama
Baby, 17", MIB ..........**100.00**
Atlanta Novelty, 1981, porcelain
cloth, christening gown, 14",
NRFB ..........................**350.00**
Atlanta Novelty, 1985, foam filled,
w/tub & accessories, 12",
EX ................................**45.00**
Atlantic Novelty, 1981-84, rag
doll, 11½", NM ..............**20.00**
Lucky Ltd, 1989, Birthday Party
Twins, 6", NRFB ...........**40.00**
Sun Rubber, 1955-58, red polka-
dot dress, 12", VG .........**65.00**
Sun Rubber, 1955-58, 2-pc paja-
mas, 12", VG ................**65.00**
Toy Biz, 1994, Potty Time Baby,
vinyl, 15", NRFB ..........**25.00**
Bib, rubber, 1936, EX .........**75.00**
Picture, signed by Ann Turner
Cook in 1978, EX ..........**20.00**
Ruler, plastic, 1950s, 6" .........**5.00**

Spoon, Oneida Stainless, 1972-96,
5½" ...................................**8.00**
Tumbler, plastic, 1971, EX ....**3.00**

## Hasbro

Some of these dolls sold
extremely well on the retail level
during the 1980s — you probably
remember the 'Real Baby' dolls.
They came in two versions, one
awake, the other asleep. They
were so realistic that even grown-
up girls had them on their
Christmas lists! See also Jem and
GI Joe.

Aimee, 1972, jointed vinyl, amber
sleep eyes, 11½", M ......**85.00**
Dolly Darling, 1965, 4½", M ..**10.00**
Goldilocks, 1967, 3", M ........**50.00**
Prince Charming, 1967, 3",
VG ...................................**15.00**
Real Baby, vinyl & cloth, open/closed
mouth, 1984-86, 19", M ...**40.00**
That Kid, 1967, 21" M .........**95.00**
World of Love Doll, 1971, white,
9", M .............................**18.00**

## Horsman

During the 1930s, this company
produced composition dolls of the
highest quality. Today many of their
dolls are vinyl. Hard plastic dolls
marked '170' are also Horsmans.

Angelove, 1974, plastic & vinyl, made
for Hallmark, 12", M .........**25.00**
Baby First Tooth, 1966, vinyl & cloth, 1
tooth, rooted hair, 16", M .....**40.00**
Ballerina, 1957, vinyl, 1-pc body,
18", M ..............................**50.00**

Betty Jane, vinyl & hard plastic,
19", M ............................**60.00**
Bye-Lo Baby, 1972 reissue, vinyl
& cloth, organdy bonnet dress,
14", M ............................**55.00**
Christopher Robin, vinyl, 11",
M ..............................**35.00**
Cindy Kay, 1950s+, vinyl child
w/long legs, 15", M ........**80.00**
Crawling Baby, 1967, vinyl, rooted
hair, 14", M ...................**25.00**
Doll, Beauty Box, Horsman, 13",
MIB ............................**75.00**
Jackie, 1961, vinyl, high-heeled
feet, 25", M ..................**125.00**
Police Woman, 1976, vinyl & plas-
tic, jointed, 9", M .........**35.00**

## Ideal

For more than eighty years,
this company produced quality
dolls that were easily affordable by
the average American family.
Their 'Shirley Temple' and 'Toni'
dolls were highly successful.
They're also the company who
made 'Miss Revlon,' 'Betsy Wetsy,'
and 'Tiny Tears.' For more information see *Collector's Guide to
Ideal Dolls* by Judith Izen. See
also Shirley Temple; Tammy.

Baby Flatsy, EX ...................**10.00**
Baby Mine, 10½", MIB ........**75.00**
Chew Suzy Chew, Black, 1980,
15", NRFB ....................**30.00**
Cory Flatsy, print mini-dress,
NRFB ............................**60.00**
Crissy Baby, 1989, rooted hair,
16", MIB ......................**35.00**
Magic Hair Crissy, 1977, w/5 hair-
pieces, MIB .................**100.00**

Ideal, Toni, 14", MIB, $450.00. (Photo
courtesy McMaster Doll Auctions)

Moovin' Groovin' Crissy, 1977,
MIB ..............................**55.00**
Nancy Flatsy, nurse w/baby car-
riage, EX ......................**15.00**
Patty Playpal, 1960s, re-dressed,
36", EX ......................**225.00**
Talking Patty Playpal, 1986, 27",
MIB ..........................**225.00**
Tippy Tumbles, 1970s, NMIB .**30.00**
Twirly Bead Crissy, 1971, 19",
MIB ..............................**45.00**

## Jem

The glamorous life of Jem
mesmerized little girls who
watched her Saturday morning
cartoons, and she was a natural as
a fashion doll. In 1985 Hasbro
introduced the Jem line of 12"
dolls representing her, the rock
stars from Jem's musical group,
the Holograms, and other members of the cast, including Rio, the
only boy, who was Jem's road
manager and Jerrica's boyfriend.
Production was discontinued in
1987. Each doll was posable, jointed at the waist, heads, and wrists,
so that they could be positioned at
will with their musical instruments and other accessory items.
Their clothing, their makeup, and
their hairdos were wonderfully
exotic, and their faces were beautifully molded. Our values are given
for mint-in-box dolls. All loose
dolls are valued at about $8.00
each.

Aja, blue hair, MIB ...**40.00**
Ashley, curly blond hair, w/stand,
11", MIB ......................**25.00**
Banee, waist-length straight
black hair, w/stand, 11",
MIB ..........................**25.00**
Clash, straight purple hair, com-
plete, MIB ....................**40.00**

**Jem/Jerrica #2, flashing earrings and blond hair, MIB, $50.00. (Photo courtesy Lee Garmon)**

Danse, pink & blond hair, invents dance routines, MIB .....**40.00**
Jem/Jerrica, Glitter & Gold, complete, MIB ....................**50.00**
Jetta, black hair w/silver streaks, complete, MIB ..............**40.00**
Kimber, red hair, complete w/cassette, instrument & poster, MIB ..............................**40.00**
Krissie, dark skin w/brown curly hair, 11", MIB ..............**25.00**
Pizzaz (Misfits), chartreuse hair, complete, MIB ..............**40.00**
Raya, pink hair, MIB ..........**40.00**
Rio, Glitter & Gold, MIB .....**50.00**
Roxy, blond hair, complete, MIB ..............................**40.00**
Shana (of Holograms Band), purple hair, complete, M, from $30 to ..........................**40.00**
Stormer, curly blue hair, complete, MIB ..............................**40.00**

Video (band member who makes tapes), complete, MIB, from $30 to ..............**40.00**

## Kenner

This company's dolls range from the 12" jointed teenage glamour dolls to the tiny 3" 'Mini-Kins' with the snap-on changeable clothing and synthetic 'hair' ponytails. (Value for the latter: doll only, $8.00; doll with one outfit, $15.00; complete set, $70.00.)

Baby Bundles, 16", M .........**20.00**
Crumpet, 1970, vinyl & plastic, 8", M ....................................**30.00**
Darcy Cover Girl, 1978, blond, 12½", M ......................**30.00**
Dusty, 12", M ....................**18.00**
Gabbigale, 1972, white, 18", M ....................................**35.00**
Garden Gal, 1972, hand shaped to hold watering can, 6½", M ....................................**10.00**
Jenny Jones & baby, 1973, vinyl, 9", 2½", pr ....................**25.00**
Steve Scout, 1974, black, 9", M ....................................**25.00**
Sweet Cookie, 1972, 18", M .**30.00**

**Liddle Kiddles**

Produced by Mattel between 1966 and 1971, Liddle Kiddle dolls and accessories were designed to suggest the typical 'little kid' in the typical neighborhood. These dolls can be found in sizes ranging from ¾" to 4", all with posable bodies and rooted hair that can be restyled. Later, two more series were

**Liddle Middle Muffit and spider, #3545, complete, M, $75.00. (Photo courtesy Cindy Sabulis)**

designed that represented storybook and nursery rhyme characters. The animal kingdom was represented by the Animiddles and Zoolery Jewelry Kiddles. There was even a set of extraterrestrials. And lastly, in 1979 Sweet Treets dolls were marketed.

Items mint on card or mint in box are worth about 25% more than one in mint condition but with none of the original packaging. Based on mint value, deduct 50% for dolls that are dressed but lack accessories. For further information we recommend *Liddle Kiddles* by Paris Langford, and *Schroeder's Collectible Toys, Antique to Modern*, both published by Collector Books.

Our advisor is Cindy Sabulis; she is listed in the Directory under Connecticut.

Apple Blossom Kologne, #3707, missing cap ..................**15.00**

Baby Din-Din, #3820, complete, M ...**60.00**
Calamity Jiddle, #3506, complete, M ....................................**65.00**
Dainty Deer, #3637, complete, M ..............................**40.00**
Florence Niddle, #3507, complete, M ....................................**65.00**
Flower Pin Kiddle, #3741, complete, M..........................**20.00**
Goofy Skediddler, #3627, MIP .**70.00**
Henrietta Horseless Carriage, #3641, doll only, M ........**15.00**
Laverne Locket, #3678, gold frame, M.......................**35.00**
Lolli-Grape, #3656, doll only .**15.00**
Lou Locket, #3535, doll only .**25.00**
Nappytime Baby, #3818, complete, M ....................................**75.00**
Peter Paniddle, #3547, doll only, M....................................**30.00**
Shirley Strawberry, #3727, complete, M .........................**40.00**
Suki Skediddle, #3767, complete, M ....................................**25.00**

Vanilly Lilly, #2819, MIP ....**25.00**

## Madame Alexander

Founded in 1923, Beatrice Alexander began her company by producing an Alice in Wonderland doll which was all cloth with an oil-painted face. By the 1950s there were over six hundred employees making dolls of various materials. The company is still producing lovely dolls today. For further information, we recommend *Madame Alexander Collector's Doll Price Guide* by Linda Crowsey.

Alice in Wonderland, Maggie & Margaret, hard plastic, 1951-52, 14" ...................**575.00**
Baby Lynn, cloth & vinyl, 1973-76, 20" ...............................**135.00**
Carrot Kate, Ribbons & Bows Series, Mary Ann, #25506, 1995, 14" ....................**150.00**
Dolly Dryper, vinyl, 1952 only, 17-pc layette, 11" ........**325.00**
Flapper, Portrette, Cissette, 1988-91, 10" ...........................**75.00**
Gretel, hard plastic, straight legs, marked Alex, 1973-75, 8" ............................**75.00**
Heather, cloth & vinyl, 1990 only, 18" ..............................**100.00**
Janie, toddler, 1964-66 only, #1156, 12" ....................**350.00**
Leslie (Black Polly) vinyl, as bride, 1966-71, 17" ....................**350.00**
Maggie Teenager, hard plastic, 1951-53, 15-18", from $475 to ..............................**600.00**

Norway, hard plastic, bent knees, Wendy Ann, 1968-72, 8" .....................**100.00**
Pinocchio, Storyland Series, Wendy Ann, 1992-93, 8" ........................**65.00**
Red Riding Hood, hard plastic, bent knees, 1965-72, 8" ........................**125.00**
Sardinia, Wendy, 1989-91 only, 8" ................................**60.00**

**Scarlett O'Hara, composition, Wendy Ann, 1939 – 1946, 18", VG/EX with original tagged clothes, $425.00 (at auction).**

Southern Belle, hard plastic, Wendy Ann, 1954, 8", minimum value ...**900.00**
Tinkerbell, hard plastic, Cissette, 1969 only, 11", minimum value ...........................**475.00**
Violette, Cissette, 1987-88, 10" ........................**65.00**
Wendy Angel, hard plastic, Wendy Ann, 1954, 8", minimum value ..**850.00**

Yolanda, Brenda Starr, 1965 only, 12" ..................395.00

**Mattel**

Though most famous, of course, for Barbie and her friends, the Mattel company also made celebrity dolls, a lot of action figures (the Major Matt Mason line and She-Ra, Princess of Power, for example), and in more recent years, 'Baby Tenderlove' and 'P.J. Sparkles.' See also Barbie; Liddle Kiddles.

Baby Beans, 1971-75, vinyl & terry cloth, 12", M ...18.00
Baby Brother Tenderlove, 1969, 16", MIB ......................35.00
Baby First Step, 1964, 20", VG in original box ..................85.00
Baby Love Light, battery operated, 16", M ....................18.00
Baby Skates, 1982, 15", MIB .35.00
Baby Small Talk, 1968-69, pull-string talker, white, 10¾" ......................25.00
Baby Teenie Talk, 1965, 17", M ..............................22.00
Baby That Away, 1974, all original, 16", VG ..................25.00
Cheerful Tearful, 1966-67, vinyl, blond hair, wets & cries, 13", M ....................................25.00
Dancerella, 1978, 17", NRFB .15.00
Dancerina, 1968, original outfit, 24", VG ..........................45.00
Downy Dilly, Upsy Downsy #3832, NRFB ..........................150.00
Drowsey, 1965-75, vinyl & cloth, pull-string talker, 15½", M ..................18.00

Guardian Goddess, 1979, 11½", M ..............................165.00
Magic Baby Tenderlove, 1978, w/accessories, 14", MIB ....30.00
Shogun Warrior, plastic, battery operated, 23½", VG ......65.00
Shoppin' Cheryl, 1970, original outfit, 15", VG ..............20.00
Southern Belle, Star Spangled, 1973, M ........................45.00
Talking Baby First Step, MIB ...150.00
Talking Timey Tell, MIB ...100.00
Teachy Keen, 1966-70, Sears, vinyl & cloth, talker, 16", M ..............................32.00
Tearful Tenderlove, 1971, all original, 16", VG ..................25.00
Tickle Pickle, Upsy Downsy #3825, w/accessories & board ......................65.00
Tiny Baby Tenderlove, 1971, all original, 11½", VG ........25.00
Tippee Toes, 1967, 16", MIB .100.00

**Nancy Ann Storybook**

These dolls were first made in California during the 1940s. Some were bisque, while others were made of hard plastic. Both wigs and rooted hair were used, and they ranged in sizes from 5" up to 10" or 12". An extensive line of clothing was available, and there were wall cases and standing shelves to display them on. These dolls have been reintroduced in recent years.

Audrey Ann, toddler, marked, 6", VG ..............................250.00
Baby, 1953, hard plastic, black sleep eyes, 3½-4½", MIB ..........75.00

Baby Sue, vinyl, M .............**75.00**
Hit Parade Series, bisque or plastic, M, ea ....................**125.00**
Lori Ann, vinyl, 17½", M ...**165.00**
Miss Nancy Ann, vinyl, rooted hair, high-heeled feet, 10½", M ...................................**125.00**
Muffie, 1953-56, hard plastic, wig, non-walker, 8", M ......................**190.00**
Nancy Ann Style Show, hard plastic, sleep eyes, undressed, 17", VG ...............................**300.00**
Sports Series, bisque, VG, ea .**200.00**

## Raggedy Ann and Andy

Designed by Johnny Gruelle in 1915, Raggedy Ann was named by combining two James Whitcomb Riley poem titles, *The Raggedy Man* and *Orphan Annie*. The early cloth dolls he made were dated and had painted-on features. Though these dolls are practically nonexistent, they're easily identified by the mark, 'Patented Sept. 7, 1915.' P.F. Volland made these dolls from 1920 to 1934; theirs were very similar in appearance to the originals. The Mollye Doll Outfitters were the first to print the now-familiar red heart on her chest, and they added a black outline around her nose. These dolls carry the handwritten inscription 'Raggedy Ann and Andy Doll/Manufactured by Mollye Doll Outfitters.' Georgene Averill made them ca 1938 to 1950, sewing their label into the seam of the dolls. Knickerbocker dolls (1963 to 1982) also carry a compa-

ny label. The Applause Toy Company made these dolls for two years in the early 1980s, and they were finally taken over by Hasbro, the current producer, in 1983.

Besides the dolls, scores of other Raggedy Ann and Andy items have been marketed, including books, radios, games, clocks, bedspreads, and clothing, and we've included a few such listings here. In the last couple of years, collector interest has really taken off, and just about any antique mall you visit today will have an eye-catching display. For more information see *The World of Raggedy Ann Collectibles* by Kim Avery.

Applause, puppet dolls, 1987, 15½", ea, from $40 to ........................**45.00**
Applause, Sleepytime, 17", ea, from $30 to ...................**35.00**
Applause, 36", ea, from $65 to ..**70.00**
Bobbs-Merrill, Japan, 1972, bean bag doll, 7½", ea, from $18 to ..**20.00**
Bobbs-Merrill, Nasco Doll Inc, 1973, plastic, ea, from $35 to ..............................**40.00**
Georgene Novelties, 1946-53, yarn hair, flowered dress, 15", from $80 to ..........................**90.00**
Georgene Novelties, 1946-63, yarn hair, 19", ea, from $95 to .**125.00**
Georgene Novelties, 1950s-63, yarn hair, 15", ea, from $75 to ..**85.00**
Knickerbocker, Christmas, 1981, 12", ea, from $45 to .......**55.00**
Knickerbocker, early to mid 1970s, 15", ea, from $20 to .......**30.00**
Knickerbocker, Hong Kong, musical, 15", M, ea, from $45 to ....**55.00**

**Raggedy Andy, Knickerbocker, early to mid 1970s, 15", NM, $30.00. (Photo courtesy June Moon)**

Knickerbocker, Hong Kong, 15", ea, from $35 to ..............**40.00**

Knickerbocker, Hong Kong, 5 eyelashes (not 4), 45", ea, from $195 to ..............**215.00**

Knickerbocker, made in Taiwan, 6", ea, from $10 to .........**12.00**

Knickerbocker, Taiwan, bean bag type, 9", ea, from $10 to .**15.00**

Knickerbocker, Taiwan, Bedtime, plastic eyes, 15", ea, from $20 to ....................................**25.00**

Knickerbocker, Taiwan, Teach & Dress, 1970s, 20", M, ea, from $45 to ............................**50.00**

Knickerbocker, 7", pr, MIB, from $25 to ............................**30.00**

Playskool, Christmas, 1990, 12", ea, from $35 to ..............**40.00**

Playskool, Heart-to Heart, 1992, battery operated, 17", from $35 to ............................**45.00**

Playskool, 1989, 8½", ea, from $10 to ....................................**14.00**

Reliable Toy Co Ltd of Canada, yarn hair, 19", ea, from $175 to ...................................**195.00**

Raggedy Ann & Andy bulletin board, 1970s, 23", VG ....................**15.00**

Raggedy Ann & Andy Color-forms Dress-Up kit, Ann, 1967, M ...................**25.00**

Raggedy Ann & Andy figurine, bisque, 1988, 4", M ..........**15.00**

Raggedy Ann & Andy jewelry box, 1972, 9", VG ..................**15.00**

Raggedy Ann & Andy manicure set, Ann & Andy, Larami, 1979, MOC (sealed) ....................**10.00**

Raggedy Ann & Andy quilt, baby's, NM ................................**15.00**

Raggedy Ann & Andy TV chair, 1970s, inflatable, NMIB .**35.00**

## Remco

The plastic and vinyl dolls made by Remco during the 1960s and '70s are gaining popularity with collectors today. Many have mechanical features that were activated either by a button on their back or batteries. The Littlechap Family of dolls (1964), Dr. John, his wife Lisa, and their two children, Judy and Libby, came with clothing and fashion accessories of the highest quality. Children found the family less interesting than the more glamorous fashion dolls on the market at that time, and as a result, production was limited. These dolls in excellent condition are valued at about $20.00 each, while their outfits range from about $30.00 (loose and complete) to a minimum of $50.00 (MIB).

Addams Family, 1960-74, 5½",
  MIB, ea member ..........**20.00**
Baby Crawlalong, 1967, 20",
  VG ............................**5.00**
Baby Jumpsy, 1970, 15", MIB .**75.00**
Baby Laugh A Lot, 1970, vinyl &
  plush, battery operated, 16",
  M ................................**20.00**
Heidi, 1967, vinyl, push-button
  (waves), 5½", MIB ..........**9.00**
Jumpsy, 1970, vinyl & hard plas-
  tic, 14", M .....................**20.00**
Lisa, Littlechaps, NRFB ......**60.00**
Mimi, 1973, vinyl & hard plastic,
  Black, 19", MIB ............**60.00**
Sweet April, 1971, Black, 5½",
  MIB ..............................**15.00**
Tumbling Tomboy, 1969, vinyl &
  hard plastic, blond braids, 17",
  MIB ..............................**20.00**

## Shirley Temple

The public's fascination with Shirley was more than enough reason for toy companies to literally deluge the market with merchandise of all types decorated with her likeness. Dolls were a big part of that market, and the earlier composition dolls in excellent condition are often priced at a minimum of $600.00 on today's market. Many were made by the Ideal Company, who in the 1950s also issued a line made of vinyl.

Porcelain, 1987+, Danbury Mint,
  16", MIB .....................**90.00**

Vinyl, 1957, Ideal, hazel sleep eyes, open-closed mouth with six upper teeth, rooted hair, original clothes, 15", M, $265.00.

Vinyl, 1957, sleep eyes, 2-pc
  slip & undies, ST/12, 12",
  VG ........................**110.00**
Vinyl, 1958-61, marked ST//17 or
  ST//19, 15-19", M, from $350
  to ................................**485.00**
Vinyl, 1972, Montgomery
  Wards reissue, 17", M in
  plain box ................**225.00**
Vinyl, 1973, red dot Stand Up &
  Cheer outfit, 16", MIB ..**165.00**
Vinyl, 1982-83, 8-12", MIB, ea,
  from $30 to ..................**35.00**
Vinyl, 1984, Doll Dreams & Love,
  36", MIB .....................**300.00**

## Tammy

In 1962 the Ideal Novelty & Toy Company introduced their teenage Tammy doll. Slightly pudgy and not quite as sophisti-

195

**Misty dolls: Straight legs (two on left) and Pos'n Misty (two on right), EX, each from $20.00 to $30.00. (Photo courtesy Cindy Sabulis)**

cated as some of the teen fashion dolls on the market at the time, Tammy's innocent charm captivated consumers. Her extensive wardrobe and numerous accessories added to her popularity with children. Tammy had everything including a car, a house, and a catamaran. In addition, a large number of companies obtained licenses to issue products using the 'Tammy' name. Everything from paper dolls to nurses' kits were made with Tammy's image on them. Tammy's success was not confined to the United States. She was also successful in Canada and in several European countries. Doll values listed here are for mint-in-box examples. (Loose dolls are generally about half mint-in-box value as they are relatively common.) Other values are for mint-condition items without their original packaging. (Such items with their original packag-

ing or in less-than-mint condition would then vary up or down accordingly.)

Our advisor for this category is Cindy Sabulis; she has co-authored a book with Susan Weglewski entitled *Collector's Guide to Tammy, The Ideal Teen* (Collector Books), which we highly recommend. Cindy is listed in the Directory under Connecticut.

Black Grown Up Tammy, MIB, minimum value ..........250.00
Bud, MIB ...........................300.00
Car, minimum value ...........75.00
Dodi, MIB .........................75.00
Glamour Misty the Miss Clairol Doll, MIB .....................125.00
Grown Up Tammy, MIB ......75.00
Misty, straight legs, MIB ..100.00
Pepper, MIB ........................55.00
Pos'n Dodi, MIB .................150.00
Pos'n Tammy, MIB .............95.00
Tammy's Ideal House, minimum value ....................110.00

Ted, MIB ...............................**65.00**

## Terri Lee

There were two sizes of this chubby charmer — the larger 16" to 18", and the Tiny Terri Lee, measuring 10". She was made during the 1950s and came from the factory with a daisy tied to her wrist and dressed in a variety of costumes. Some of these dolls were 'talkers' that had an attachment at the base of the neck for a 'phone jack' to connect with a record player. Others were 'walkers,' and besides Terri Lee, the company made a variety of babies and toddlers by other names.

**Tiny Terri Lee, 10", with trunk and six outfits, $425.00. (Photo courtesy McMasters Doll Auctions)**

Benji, 1947-48, painted plastic, black lamb's wool wig, 16", VG ...............................**150.00**

Composition, 1946-47, 16", MIB ........................**375.00**
Jerry Lee, hard plastic, caracul wig, 16", M .................**500.00**
Patty Jo or Bonnie Lou, Black, 16", M, ea ...........................**600.00**
Talking, 16", VG ...............**135.00**

## Uneeda

Uneeda dolls generally date from the 1950s through the '70s; they were made of vinyl and plastic, and some had cloth bodies. They made some mechanical talkers, nursing dolls, and a walker who turned her head with each step she took. Most are marked and dated. See also Tiny Teens.

Dollikin, 1960s, muliple joints, 20", VG ..........................**13.00**
Fairy Princess, 1961, 32", M ..**110.00**

**Baby Dollikins, 1960, plastic and vinyl, jointed, 21", M, $45.00. (Photo courtesy Pat Smith)**

Freckles, 1960s, 32", M .....**100.00**
Jennifer, 1973, rooted hair, teenage body, 18", M ....**25.00**
Pollyanna, 1960, 11", M ......**35.00**
Pollyanna, 1960, 35", M ....**150.00**
Seranade, 1962, vinyl & hard plastic, phonograph & records, 21", M ............................**55.00**
Tiny Teen, 1957-59, vinyl, 6-pc body, 10½", M .............**135.00**

### Vogue

This is the company that made the 'Ginny' doll famous. She was first made in composition during the late 1940s, and if you could find her in mint condition, she'd bring about $450.00 on today's market. (Played with and in relatively sad condition, she's still worth about $90.00.) Ginny dolls from the 1950s were made of rigid vinyl. The last Ginny came out in 1969. Tonka bought the rights in 1973, but the dolls they produced sold poorly. After a series of other owners, Dakin purchased the rights in 1986 and began producing a vinyl doll that resembled the 1950-style Ginny very closely. For more information, we recommend *Collector's Guide to Vogue Dolls* by Judith Izen and Carol Stover (Collector Books).

Baby Dear One, 1962, toddler version, 2 teeth, 25", M ..**160.00**
Brikette, 1959, swivel waist, green flirty eyes, 22", M ............................**65.00**
Ginnette, 1955+, vinyl baby, 8", M ..............................**200.00**

Ginny, 1955-56, hard plastic, 7-pc body, walker, 8", VG ...**55.00**
Ginny, 1965, vinyl, straight legs, nonwalker, 8", M ..........**40.00**
Ginny Crib Crowd, 1950, Easter Bunny, 8", VG .............**350.00**
Love Me Linda, 1965-68, 15",M ..**23.00**
Wee Imp, 1960, hard plastic, red wig, freckles, 8", M ...**375.00**

# Doorstops

Doorstops, once called door porters, were popular from the Civil War period until after 1930. They were used to prop the doors open during the hot summer months so that the cooler air could circulate. Though some were made of brass, wood, and chalk, cast iron was by far the most preferred material, usually molded in amusing figurals — dogs, flower baskets, frogs, etc. Hubley was one of the largest producers. Refer to *Doorstops, Identification and Values,* by Jeanne Bertoia (Collector Books) for more information. Beware of reproductions! Assume all the examples in the listing that follows to be made of cast iron and with original paint; ranges reflect condition from VG to NM. See also Clubs and Newsletters

Beagle, realistic paint, on haunches, unmarked, 8x6½", from $175 to ........................**250.00**
Bulldog, porcelainized, full-figure, 5¾x8½", from $75 to .........................**125.00**

**Dutch girl, worn multicolor paint, $230.00; Garden Rabbit, EX white paint with pink details, $330.00.**

Cat, on haunches, black paint, full-figure, 11x7", from $125 to ...............175.00

Cocker Spaniel, Hubley, full-figure, 6¾x11", from $225 to ...........................275.00

Colonial Dame, pink & blue dress, Hubley, 8x4½", from $200 to ......................250.00

Deco Girl, blue dress held wide, #1251, cJo, 9x7½", from $300 to ..................................375.00

Doll on Base, pink tiered skirt, full-figure, 5½x5", from $75 to ...............................100.00

Donald Duck, Walt Disney...1971, 8⅜x5¼", from $200 to ..250.00

Duck Head, brass, 11½x9", from $100 to .........................150.00

El Capitan, marching soldier on base, 7¾x5¼", from $175 to .....225.00

Frog, full-figure, 6x3½", from $75 to ...............................125.00

Frog, Hubley, 1½x7½", from $100 to ...............................175.00

Giraffe, wedge base, S-110, 13½x5¼", from $250 to .275.00

Gnome, red pointed hat, full beard, full-figure, 11x5", from $225 to ......................275.00

Horse on Base, dog underfoot, unmarked, 7¼x8½", from $150 to ......................175.00

House, AM Greenblatt Copyright 1927 #114, 7½x6⅛", from $250 to ......................325.00

Japanese Spaniel, begging, cJo, #1267, 9x4½", from $275 to .........350.00

Little Red Riding Hood, National, #94, 7¼x5⅜", from $350 to .......425.00

Major Domo, Black man in uniform, #129, 8⅜x5⅛", from $175 to ......................225.00

Oxen & Wagon, c 64, 6¼x10¼", from $150 to ...............175.00

Peacock by Urn, Hubley, #208, 7½x4¼", from $175 to ..........................250.00

Pirate w/Chest, sword & red cape, unmarked, 9¾x6", from $200 to......................275.00

Poppies & Cornflowers, Hubley, #265, 7¼x6½", from $100 to ...................150.00

Poppy Basket, CH Co E110, 10½x9½", from $250 to ..**325.00**

Small Mammy, dressed in red & white, Hubley, 8½x4½", from $150 to .........................**225.00**

Swan, National Foundry, full-figure, 5¾x4½", from $175 to ...........................**250.00**

Tiger Lilies, Hubley, #472, 10½x6", from $150 to .**225.00**

Welsh Corgi, Bradley & Hubbard, 8¼x5⅞", from $175 to ..........................**250.00**

Windmill, National Foundry, 10 Cape Cod, 6¼x6⅞", from $100 to .................................**150.00**

## Early American Presscut

This line was made by Anchor Hocking from about 1960 through the mid-'70s. Few homes were without at least a piece or two. It was standard dime-store fare, inexpensive and accessible. Today it's almost as common at flea markets as it was then on the retail level, and collectors are starting to show an interest in reassembling it into table services. For more information, refer to Gene Florence's book called *Collectible Glassware of the 40s, 50s, and 60s, 4th Edition* (Collector Books).

Ashtray, #700/690, 4" ...........**3.00**

Bowl, console; #797, 9" ........**10.00**

Bowl, plain or ruffled rim, #726, 4¼" ....................................**2.50**

Bowl, salad; #788, 10¾" ......**10.00**

Bowl, 3-toed, #769, 6¾" .........**4.50**

Butter dish, #705, ¼-lb ..........**6.00**

Cake plate, footed, #706, 13½" .....................**17.50**

Candlestick, double; #784, 7x5⅝" .......................**15.00**

Candy dish, w/lid, #774, 5¼" .**10.00**

Chip & dip set, #700/733, 10¾" bowl, 5½" brass-finished holder ..........................**17.50**

Coaster, #700/702 ................**2.00**

Cruet, w/stopper, #711, 7¾" ..**6.00**

Cup, custard; 4¼" .................**2.50**

Lazy Susan, #700/713, 9-pc .**20.00**

Pitcher, #744, 18-oz .............**8.00**

**Divided relish, 10", $7.00.**

Pitcher, #791, 60-oz ............**12.50**

Plate, serving; #790, 13½" ...**10.00**

Plate, 4⅜" ................................**3.00**

Relish, oval, #778, 8½" ..........**5.00**

Server (syrup), #707, 12-oz ....**6.00**

Shakers, #700/699, pr ............**4.00**

Sugar bowl, w/lid, #753 .........**4.00**

Tray, deviled egg/relish; #750, 11¾" ..............................**25.00**

Tumbler, flared rim, 3½" .......**3.50**

Tumbler, flared rim, 4⅜" .......**6.00**

Tumbler, iced tea; #732, 15-oz, 6" ....................................**5.00**

Tumbler, old-fashioned; 7-oz, 3" .**6.00**

Vase, #741, 8½" ....................**10.00**

Vase, #742, 10" .....................**12.50**

# Egg Timers

The origin of the figural egg timer appears to be Germany, circa 1920s or 1930s, with Japan following their lead in the 1940s. Some American companies may have begun producing figural timers at about the same time, but evidence is scarce in terms of pottery marks or company logos.

Figural timers can be found in a wide range of storybook characters (Oliver Twist), animals (pigs, ducks, rabbits), career and vocational uniformed people (chef, London Bobby, housemaid), or people in native costume.

All types of timers were a fairly uniform height of 3" to 4". If a figural timer no longer has its sand tube, it can be recognized by the hole which usually goes through the back of the figure or the stub of a hand. Most timers were made of ceramic (china or bisque), but a few are of cast iron and carved wood. They can be detailed or quite plain. Listings below are for timers with their sand tubes completely intact.

Our advisor for this category is Jeannie Greenfield; she is listed in the Directory under Pennsylvania.

Bellhop, green, ceramic, Japan, 4½" ..................................**60.00**

Black mammy & chef, bisque, matching pr .................**200.00**

Black watch guard, plastic, England ..............................**40.00**

Boy on skis, bisque, Germany .**45.00**

Cat w/ribbon at neck, ceramic, marked Germany .........**85.00**

Clown on phone, standing, yellow suit, ceramic, Japan, 3¾" .**50.00**

Geisha, ceramic, Germany, 4½" ..**65.00**

Girl w/flower bouquet, plaster ..**20.00**

Housemaid w/towel, standing, earthenware, Japan, 4" .**69.00**

Leprechaun, all brass, Ireland ...**35.00**

Little Red Riding Hood w/wolf at her feet .........................**50.00**

**Dutch boy, Germany, $65.00. (Photo courtesy Jeannie Greenfield)**

Newspaper boy, ceramic, Japan, 3¾" ................................**50.00**
Rooster, plaster, England ....**35.00**
Sultan, Japan, 3½" ..............**75.00**
Veggie man or woman, bisque, Japan, 4½" ...................**60.00**

# Elvis Presley

The King of Rock 'n Roll, the greatest entertainer of all time (and not many would disagree with that), Elvis remains just as popular today as he was in the height of his career. Over the past few years, values for Elvis collectibles have skyrocketed. The early items marked 'Elvis Presley Enterprises' bearing a 1956 or 1957 date are the most valuable. Paper goods such as magazines, menus from Las Vagas hotels, ticket stubs, etc., make up a large part of any Elvis collection and are much less expensive. His 45s were sold in abundance, so unless you find an original Sun label (one recently sold at auction for $2,800.00), a colored vinyl or a promotional cut, or EPs in wonderful condition, don't pay much! The picture sleeves are usually worth much more than the record itself! Albums are very collectible, and even though you see some stiff prices on them at antique malls, there's not many you can't buy for well under $25.00 at any Elvis convention.

Remember, the early mark is 'Elvis Presley Enterprises'; the 'Boxcar' mark was used from 1974 to 1977, and the 'Boxcar/Factors'

mark from then until 1981. In 1982, the trademark reverted back to Graceland.

Our advisor is Rosalind Cranor, author of *Elvis Collectibles* and *Best of Elvis Collectibles* (Overmountain Press); see the Directory under Virginia for ordering information.

Ankle bracelet, dog-tag type, Elvis Presley Enterprises, 1950s ..........................**45.00**
Belt buckle, pewter, 1935-77 .**20.00**
Book, Are You Lonesome Tonight, Lucy DeBarbin & Dary Matera, 1987, M ..................**10.00**
Bracelet, full-color head shot, Elvis Presley Enterprises, 1977, EX ......................**25.00**
Charm bracelet, Loving You, Elvis Presley Enterprises, 1956 ...........................**40.00**

**Doll, white jumpsuit and guitar, Graceland, 1984, MIB, $75.00.**

Concert pin, back converts to easel, 6" .........................**24.00**

Decanter, no music box, Elvis Bust, McCormick, 1978 ...........**75.00**

Decanter, plays Blue Hawaii, Aloha Elvis Mini, McCormick, 1982 ..............................**175.00**

Decanter, plays Can't Help Falling in Love, McCormick, 1981 ....**55.00**

Decanter, plays GI Blues, Sgt Elvis, McCormick, 1983 ..........**295.00**

Decanter, plays Hound Dog, McCormick, 1986 ........**695.00**

Decanter, plays How Great Thou Art, Elvis Silver, 1980 .**175.00**

Decanter, plays Love Me Tender, McCormick, 1977 ........**125.00**

Decanter, plays Loving You, Elvis '55, McCormick, 1979 ......................**125.00**

Decanter, plays My Way, Elvis Gold, McCormick, 1979 ...........**175.00**

Decanter, plays White Christmas, Season's Greetings, McCormick, 1986 ....................................**195.00**

Doll, issued in 3 different outfits, Hasbro, 1993, 12", MIB .........................**40.00**

Doll, issued in 6 different outfits, Eugene, 1984, 12", MIB .**65.00**

Earrings, Loving You, 1956, MOC ............................**45.00**

Flip book, Jailhouse Rock, 1957 ..**135.00**

Menu, Las Vegas, diecut record shape, 1973 ...................**48.00**

Paint-by-Number set, Peerless Playthings, 1956, rare, EX (EX box) ....................**3,000.00**

Pennant, Elvis Summer Festival Sahara..., felt, NM ........**75.00**

Pennant, King of Rock 'n Roll..., blue & white on red, 1970s, 31", EX ..........................**40.00**

Photo, Elvis in uniform, black & white, RCA, 8x10" ........**75.00**

Photo album, 2nd tour book, 1956, from $350 to ................**400.00**

Plate, The King Remembered, by Cassidy J Alexander, 1984, M ...............................**100.00**

Playing cards, 1972 Las Vegas souvenir deck, M ...........**20.00**

Postcard, Christmas, full color, 1957, 5x7" ......................**20.00**

Postcard, Las Vegas Hilton, 1970 ...........................**35.00**

Poster, Jailhouse Rock, half sheet ...........................**28.00**

Pressbook, Speedway, M .....**25.00**

Record case, pink-tan with black & white, ca 1956, 7⅝" .....**575.00**

Ring, brass w/full-color photo under clear bubble, 1956, EX ............................**200.00**

Scrapbook, Solid Gold Memories, Ballantine, 1977, EX ....**30.00**

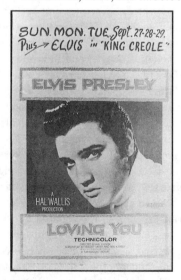

**Window card, Loving You, 14x22", minimum value $200.00. (Photo courtesy Rosalind Cranor)**

Sheet music, Burning Love, caricature portrait ..................**75.00**
Sheet music, Heartbreak Hotel .**35.00**
Sideburns sticker from gumball
machine, 1950s, EX ......**55.00**
Ukette, turn side knob for
music, Selcol, 14", EX (VG
rare box) ................**1,200.00**
Yearbook, 1960, original, from $90
to ................................**100.00**

# Enesco

Enesco is an importing company based in Elk Grove, Illinois.
They're distributors of ceramic
novelties made for them in Japan.
There are several lines styled
around a particular character or
group, and with the emphasis collectors currently place on figurals,
they're finding these especially
fascinating. During the 1960s,
they sold a line of novelties originally called 'Mother-in-the-
Kitchen.' Today's collectors refer to
them as 'Kitchen Prayer Ladies.'
Ranging from large items such as
canisters and cookie jars to toothpick holders and small picture
frames, the line was fairly extensive. Some of the pieces are very
hard to find, and those with blue
dresses are much scarcer than
those in pink. Where we've given
ranges, pink is represented by the
lower end, blue by the high side. If
you find a white piece with blue
trim, add another 10% to 20% to
the high end.

Another Enesco line destined to
become very collectible is called
'Kitchen Independence.' It features
George Washington with the Decla-
ration of Independence scroll held at
his side and Betsy Ross wearing a
blue dress and holding a large flag.

Both lines are pictured in *The
Collector's Encyclopedia of Cookie
Jars, Volumes 1, 2, and 3*, by Joyce
and Fred Roerig. See also Cookie
Jars.

Our advisor for this category is
April Tvorak, who is listed in the
Directory under Pennsylvania.

**Bank, Dear God Kids, from $40.00
to $50.00. (Photo courtesy Joyce
Roerig)**

Air freshener, Kitchen Prayer
Lady, from $125 to .....**145.00**
Bank, Human Bean series, This
Is a Retired..., 1981, from $15
to ................................**20.00**
Bank, Human Bean series, w/gold
club ................................**40.00**
Bank, Kitchen Prayer Lady, from
$145 to ........................**175.00**
Bell, Kitchen Prayer Lady, from
$75 to ............................**90.00**

Candle holders, Kitchen Prayer Lady, pr, from $95 to ............................**110.00**

Candy container, Dear God Kids (girl), 1983 ....................**75.00**

Canister, Kitchen Prayer Lady, pink, ea, from $200 to .**250.00**

Console set, swans, turquoise & black, 7" swan & 2 candlesticks ..............................**25.00**

Cookie jar, Human Bean, from $140 to ........................**150.00**

Cookie jar, Kitchen Independence, Betsy Ross, sm, from $200 to ...............**250.00**

Cookie jar, Kitchen Prayer Lady, blue ..............................**495.00**

Cookie jar, Kitchen Prayer Lady, pink ...............................**350.00**

Cookie jar, Snappy the Snail ..**175.00**

Creamer & sugar bowl, Snappy the Snail, wearing bow tie ....**35.00**

**Kitchen Prayer Lady spoon holder, from $45.00 to $50.00.**

Crumb tray & brush, Kitchen Prayer Lady, from $150 to ........**175.00**

Cup & saucer, Dutch boy & girl .**45.00**

Egg timer, Kitchen Prayer Lady, from $135 to ................**145.00**

Figurine, cat or dog w/sad eyes, 6", ea, from $6 to ..................**8.00**

Figurine, Human Bean Graduate, Teachers Are Classy, from $12 to ....................................**15.00**

Figurine, Human Bean series, Moms are Special, 1981, from $7 to ..............................**10.00**

Figurine, Jungle Book's Kaa, w/label, sm ......................**8.00**

Jar, instant coffee; Kitchen Prayer Lady, spoon-holder loop on side ..............................**95.00**

Mug, Kitchen Prayer Lady, from $100 to ..........................**125.00**

Napkin holder, Dear God Kids (girl) ..............................**25.00**

Napkin holder, Kitchen Independence, George Washington, from $18 to ......................**22.00**

Napkin holder, pink, from $25 to ..............................**30.00**

Night light, Big Bird w/book, 1993 ............................**40.00**

Picture frame, Kitchen Prayer Lady, from $100 to .....**125.00**

Planter, Kitchen Prayer Lady, from $65 to ...................**75.00**

Plaque, Kitchen Prayer Lady, full-figure, from $55 to ..........................**65.00**

Plaque, Paddington Bear, 1990, MIB ..............................**20.00**

Recipe holder, Kitchen Independence, George Washington w/scroll clip ...................**75.00**

Ring holder, Kitchen Prayer Lady, from $40 to ...................**50.00**

Salt & pepper shakers, Golden Girls, rhinestone trim, pr ..........................**16.00**

Salt & pepper shakers, Kitchen Prayer Ladies, pr, from $12 to ..................................**20.00**

Salt & pepper shakers, Snappy the Snail, w/bow tie, pr .......................... **22.00**

Scissors holder, Kitchen Prayer Lady, wall mount, from $135 to ...................................**145.00**

Snow dome, Paddington Bear, Christmas, 1992, MIB ..**15.00**

Soap dish, Kitchen Prayer Lady, from $35 to ....................**45.00**

Spoon holder, Betsy Ross, Spoon Storage on skirt, 5¾", from $22 to .............................**28.00**

Spoon rest, Granny, dressed in blue, glasses sliding off nose, 6¾" .................................**28.00**

Spoon rest, Snappy the Snail .**12.00**

Sprinkler bottle, Kitchen Prayer Lady, blue, from $300 to ...........................**400.00**

Sprinkler bottle, Kitchen Prayer Lady, pink ...................**200.00**

String holder, Kitchen Prayer Lady, from $135 to .......................**145.00**

Tea set, Kitchen Prayer Lady, pot, sugar bowl & creamer, from $175 to ........................**275.00**

Tea set, Snappy the Snail, with creamer & sugar bowl ................**125.00**

Teabag holder, Snappy the Snail ...........................**6.00**

Toothpick holder, Dutch boy & girl, E-6803 ..................**30.00**

Vase, bud; Kitchen Prayer Lady, from $95 to ..................**110.00**

# Ertl Banks

The Ertl company was founded in the mid-'40s by Fred Ertl, Sr., and until the early 1980s, they produced mainly farm tractors. In 1981 they made their first bank, the 1913 Model T Parcel Post Mail Service #9647; since then they've produced thousands of models with the logos of countless companies. The size of each run is dictated by the client and can vary from a few hundred up to several thousand. Some clients will later add a serial number to the vehicle; this is not done by Ertl. Other numbers that appear on the base of each bank are a four-number dating code (the first three indicate the day of the year up to 365, and the fourth number is the last digit of the year, '5' for 1995, for instance). The stock number is shown only on the box, never on the bank, so be sure to keep them in their original boxes. Our values are for banks that are mint and in their original boxes. For more information, see *Schroeder's Collectible Toys, Antique to Modern* (Collector Books). See also Clubs and Newsletters.

Aberfoyle Antique Market, 1938 Chevy, #4868 ................**35.00**

Alka Seltzer, 1918 Ford, #9155 ...**95.00**

Atlanta Falcons, 1913 Ford, #1248 ..........................**35.00**

Barq's Rootbeer, 1932 Ford, #9072 .........................**45.00**

**Kroger 1925 Delivery Truck, MIB, $25.00.**

Ben Franklin, 1918 Ford, #1319 ........................35.00

Breyer's Ice Cream, 1905 Ford, #9028 ...........................65.00

Campbell's Soup, 1957 Chevy Stake Truck, #F603 ..................30.00

Chicago Cubs, 1926 Mack Truck, #7545 ...........................40.00

Coca-Cola, 1925 Kenworth, #B398 ...........................25.00

Dairy Queen, 1950 Chevy, #9178 ......................135.00

Diamond Rio, 1940 Ford, #67503 ......................25.00

Dutch Girl Ice Cream, 1931 Hawkeye, #9049 ...................30.00

Eastview Pharmacy, 1913 Ford, #9896 ...........................25.00

Farm Bureau Co-op, 1918 Ford, #9220 ...........................25.00

Ford Motor Co, 1912 Ford, #9348 ..........................40.00

Global Van Lines, 1913 Ford, #1655 ...........................45.00

Granny Goose Chips, 1913 Ford, #9979 ...........................50.00

Harley-Davidson of Baltimore, 1931 International, JLE, #5033 ...........................95.00

Hershey Cocoa, 1905 Ford, #9665 ...........................55.00

Houston Rockets, 1956 Ford Pickup, #B882 ....................20.00

IGA 60th Anniversary, 1932 Ford, #9350 ...........................45.00

Iowa Hawkeyes, 1951 GMC, #B782 ...........................25.00

JC Penney, 1918 Ford, #1328 ..40.00

John Deere, 1931 Hawkeye, #5687 ...........................25.00

Kraft Foods, 1905 Ford, #B203 .45.00

Lennox, 1905 Ford, #9323 .35.00

Lone Star Beer, 1926 Mack Truck, #9168 ...........................55.00

Marathon Oil, 1929 International Tanker, JLE, #4044 ......30.00

Marsh Supermarket, 1912 Ford, #B015 ...........................25.00

Massey-Harris, 1913 Ford, #1092 ...........................25.00

Merit Oil Co, 1926 Mack Tanker, #9980 ...........................75.00

Mobil Oil, 1931 Hawkeye, #9742 ...........................60.00

New York Farm Show, 1931 International, JLE, #5040 ...................35.00

Old Milwaukee Beer, 1918 Ford, #9173 ...........................35.00

**True Value 1930 Diamond 'T' Tanker, #11 in series, $20.00.**

Orchard Supply, 1932 Ford, #B081 ...........................40.00

Pennzoil, 1918 Ford, #7676 .30.00

Pepsi-Cola, 1950 Chevy, #9635 ......................45.00

Philgas, 1938 Chevy, #B039 .125.00

Pittsburgh Steelers, 1957 Chevy, #F634 ............................25.00

Prairie Farms Milk, 1923 Chevy, #3958 ............................20.00

Purina Mills Inc, 1913 Ford, #9103 ...........................35.00

Quaker Oats, 1931 Hawkeye, #F569 ............................45.00

Quakertown National Bank, 1905 Ford, #9979 ...................65.00

Radio Flyer, 1931 Hawkeye, #3549 ............................55.00

RCA, 1926 Mack Truck, #9275 ....................45.00

Red Crown Gasoline, 1931 Hawkeye, 1st issue, #7654 ................50.00

Ringling Bros Circus, 1913 Ford, #9027 ..........................145.00

Safeguard Soap, 1950 Chevy, #7508 ............................35.00

Sears, 1913 Ford, #2129 ......45.00

Shell Oil Co, 1939 Dodge Airflow, #4866 ...........................35.00

Smokey Bear, 1913 Ford, #9124 .....................85.00

Sunbeam Bread, 1932 Ford, #1330 ...........................25.00

Tastykake, 1917 Ford, #F846 .35.00

Texaco, Stearman Plane, #F121 .......................30.00

Toy Town Museum, 1931 Hawkeye, #F779 ....................40.00

Trustworthy Hardware, 1918 Ford, #9744 ...................50.00

United Airlines, 1913 Ford, #9233 ...........................40.00

University of Notre Dame, 1938 Chevy, #B714 ...............35.00

US Mail, 1918 Ford, #9843 .45.00

Valley Forge, 1926 Mack Truck, #9616 ...........................95.00

Vintage Chevrolet Club, 1938 Chevy, #B629 ...............35.00

Watkins Inc, 1913 Ford, #F435 .45.00

Wheelers, 1913 Ford, #1358 .35.00

Winn Dixie, 1918 Ford, #9116 .25.00

Wonder Bread, 1913 Ford, #9161 .....................48.00

# Fast-Food Collectibles

Everyone is familiar with the kiddie meals offered by fast-food restaurants, but who knew that the toys tucked inside would become so collectible! Played-with items are plentiful at garage sales for nearly nothing, but it's best if they're still in the packages they originally came in. The ones to concentrate on are Barbie dolls, the old familiar Disney characters, and those that tie in with the big blockbuster kids' movies. Collectors look for the boxes the meals came in, too, and even the display signs that the restaurants promote each series with are valuable. The toys don't have to be old to be collectible.

Our values are for toys that are still in the original packaging. A loose example is worth about 35% to 50% less than one still sealed.

Our advisors for McDonald's® are Joyce and Terry Losonsky, authors of *Illustrated Collector's Guide to McDonald's® Happy Meal® Boxes, Premiums and Promotions, McDonald's® Happy Meal® Toys in the USA; McDonald's® Happy Meal® Toys Around the World;* and *Illustrated Collector's Guide to McDonald's® McCAPS®*. Terry and Joyce are listed in the directory under Maryland. Another recently published reference is *McDonald's Collectibles* by Gary Henriques and Audre DuVall (Collector Books). Our advisors for restaurants other than McDonald's are Bill and Pat Poe (see Florida). See also Character and Promotional Drinking Glasses. For information concerning a McDonald's club and newsletter see Clubs and Newsletters.

Arby's, Babar's World Tour Pull-Back Racers, 1992, ea ...........................**3.00**
Arby's, Looney Tunes Characters, 1987, oval base, ea .........**5.00**
Arby's, Mr Men, 4 different, ea .**5.00**
Arby's, Snow Domes, 1995, Yogi or Snagglepus, ea ...............**5.00**
Burger King, Bonkers, 1993, 6 different, ea ........................**3.00**
Burger King, Capitol Critters, 1992, 4 different, ea ........**2.00**
Burger King, Glow-in-the-Dark Troll Patrol, 1993, 4 different, ea ...................................**2.00**

**Burger King, Goof Troop bowlers series, MIP, each, $3.00.**

Burger King, Lion King Finger Puppets, 1995, 6 different, ea ...................................**3.00**
Burger King, Mini Sports Games, 1993, 4 different, ea ........**3.00**

Burger King, Oliver & Co, 1996, 5 different, ea ...............3.00

Burger King, Spacebase Racers, 1989, 4 different, ea ......3.00

Burger King, Super Powers Aquaman Tub Toy, 1987 .........6.00

Burger King, Toy Story, Woody, 1995 .................8.00

Burger King, Toy Story Action-Wing Buzz, 1995 ............6.00

Dairy Queen, Alvin & the Chipmunks Music Makers, 1994, 4 different, ea ....................5.00

Dairy Queen, Bobby's World, 1994, 4 different, ea .................5.00

Dairy Queen, Rock-A-Doodle, 1991, 6 different, ea ........7.00

Dairy Queen, Tom & Jerry, 1993, 4 different, ea .................6.00

Denny's, Adventure Seekers Activity Packet, 1993, ea ..........2.00

Denny's, Flintstones Fun Squirters, 1991, 5 different, ea .........4.00

Denny's, Flintstones, Pebbles & Bamm-Bamm, 1989, plush, pr .................12.00

Denny's, Jetson's Space Cards, 1992, 6 different, ea ........4.00

Dominos Pizza, Donnie Domino, 1989, 4" ...................6.00

Dominos Pizza, Noid Bookmark, 1989 ...................10.00

Hardee's, Balto, 1995, 6 different, ea ...................3.00

Hardee's, Beach Bunnies, 1989, 4 different, ea ...................2.00

Hardee's, Homeward Bound II, 1996, 5 different, ea ........3.00

Hardee's, Swan Princess, 1994, 5 different, ea ...................4.00

Jack-in-the-Box, Bendable Buddies, 1975, 4 different, ea ...................10.00

Jack-in-the-Box, Bendable Buddies, 1991, 5 different, ea .........3.00

Jack-in-the-Box, Finger Puppets, 1994, 5 different, ea .....10.00

Long John Silver's, Fish Car, 1989, 3 different, ea ........3.00

Long John Silver's, Map Activities, 1991, 3 different, ea ........4.00

Long John Silver's, Sea Watchers, 1991, 3 different, ea ........5.00

Long John Silver's, Water Blasters, 1990, 4 different, ea ........4.00

McDonald's, Airport, 1986, Ronald McDonald seaplane .......5.00

McDonald's, Animaniacs, 1995, any except under age 3, ea .....5.00

McDonald's, Animaniacs, 1995, under age 3, ea .............5.00

McDonald's, Bambi, 1988, 4 different, ea ...................5.00

McDonald's, Barbie/Hot Wheels, 1991, Hot Wheels, ea ......4.00

McDonald's, Barbie/Mini Streex, 1991, Barbie, any except under 3, ea ...................3.00

McDonald's, Batman (Animated), 1993, any except under age 3, ea ...................3.00

McDonald's, Crayola Stencils, 1987, under age 3, Ronald .........6.00

McDonald's, Flintstone Kids, 1988, any except under age 3, ea ...................8.00

McDonald's, Gravedale High, 1991, Regional, 5 different, ea ...................5.00

McDonald's, Hook, 1997, 4 different, ea ...................3.00

McDonald's, Jungle Book, 1989, 4 different, MIP .............15.00

McDonald's, Looney Tunes Quack-Up Cars, 1993, 4 different, ea ...................2.00

**McDonald's, boxes, Happy Meal McNugget Buddies, 1988, set of four, from $15.00 to $20.00.**

McDonald's, Marvel Super Heroes, 1996, any except under age 3, ea .....................................**3.00**
McDonald's, Marvel Super Heroes, 1996, under age 3 ...........**4.00**
McDonald's, McDonaldland Dough, 1990, ea ..............**5.00**
McDonald's, Oliver & Co, 1988, 4 different, M, ea ...............**2.00**
McDonald's, Peanuts, 1990, any except under age 3, ea ..........................**3.00**
McDonald's, Potato Heads, 1992, 8 different, ea .....................**4.00**
McDonald's, Power Rangers, 1995, any except under age 3, ea ..**3.00**
McDonald's, Power Rangers, 1995, under age 3 .....................**4.00**
McDonald's, Space Rescue, 1995, any except under age 3, ea ........**3.00**
McDonald's, Spider-Man, 1995, under age 3 .....................**4.00**
McDonald's, Super Mario Bros, 1990, any except under age 3, ea .....................................**3.00**
McDonald's, Tale Spin, 1990, any except under age 3, ea ....**3.00**

McDonald's, VR Troopers, 1996, any except under age 3, ea .......**3.00**
McDonald's, Water Games, 1992, ea .....................................**4.00**
McDonald's, Winter Worlds, 1983, ornament, Ronald McDonald, M .....................................**3.00**
McDonald's, Zoo Face, 1988, 4 different, ea .........................**4.00**

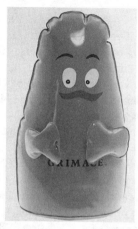

**McDonald's, Grimace inflatable figure, 1978, 8", $25.00.**

Pizza Hut, Air Garfield, 1993, kite .................................**6.00**
Pizza Hut, Air Garfield, 1993, parachute .........................**8.00**
Pizza Hut, Brain Thaws, 4 different, 1995, ea ....................**4.00**
Pizza Hut, Land Before Time, 1988, hand puppet, Sharptooth .................................**8.00**
Pizza Hut, Squirt Toons, 1995, 5 different, ea .....................**5.00**
Pizza Hut, Universal Monsters, 1991, hologram cards, 3 different, ea .............................**5.00**
Sonic, Airtoads, 6 different, ea ..**4.00**
Sonic, Bone-A-Fide Friends, 1994, 4 different, ea .................**3.00**

**Wendy's, Alien Mix-up Characters, 1990, $3.00 each.**

Sonic, Creepy Strawlers, 1995, 4 different, ea .....................**5.00**

Sonic, Totem Pal Squirters, 1995, 4 different, ea ..................**5.00**

Sonic, Very Fast Food, 1996, 4 different, ea ..........................**4.00**

Subway, Battle Balls, 1995-96, 4 different, ea .....................**3.00**

Subway, Bump in the Night, 1995, 4 different, ea ..................**5.00**

Subway, Hurricanes, 1994, 4 different, ea ..........................**4.00**

Subway, Tom & Jerry, 1995, 4 different, ea ..........................**3.00**

Taco Bell, Congo, 1995, watches, 3 different, ea .....................**5.00**

Taco Bell, Mask, 1995, It's Party Time switchplate or Milo w/mask, ea .......................**4.00**

Taco Bell, Pebble & the Penguin, 1995, 3 different, ea ........**5.00**

Target Markets, Targeteers, 1992, 5 different, ea ..................**5.00**

Target Markets, Targeteers, 1994, 5 different, rooted hair, ea ....**4.00**

Wendy's, Animalinks, 1995, 6 different, ea ..........................**2.00**

Wendy's, Cybercycles, 1994, 4 different, ea ..........................**3.00**

Wendy's, Dino Games, 1993, 3 different, ea ..........................**3.00**

Wendy's, Felix the Cat, 1990, under age 3, rub-on set ..**4.00**

Wendy's, Glo-Ahead, 1993, any except under age 3, ea ....**2.00**

Wendy's, Glo-Ahead, 1993, under age 3, finger puppet ........**3.00**

Wendy's, Jetson's Space Vehicles, 1989, 6 different, ea ........**5.00**

Wendy's, Wacky Windups, 1991, 5 different, ea .....................**4.00**

Wendy's, Yogi Bear & Friends, 1990, 6 different, ea ........**3.00**

White Castle, Camp White Castle, 1990, fork & spoon, ea ...............................**4.00**

White Castle, Fat Albert & the Cosby Kids, 1990, 4 different, ea .....................................**10.00**

White Castle, Holiday Huggables, 1990, 3 different, ea ........**6.00**

White Castle, Super Balls, 1994, 3 different, ea ....................**5.00**

# Fenton

The Fenton glass company, organized in 1906 in Martin's Ferry, Ohio, is noted for their fine art glass. Over one hundred thirty patterns of carnival glass were made in their earlier years but even their new glass is considered collectible. Only since 1970 have some of the pieces carried a molded-in logo; before then paper labels were used. For information on early Fenton, we recommend *Fenton Art Glass, 1907 to 1939*, by Margaret and Kenn Whitmyer; two of their later lines, Hobnail and Silver Crest, are shown in Gene Florence's book called *Collectible Glassware of the 40s, 50s, and 60s*. All are published by Collector Books. See also Clubs and Newsletters.

Ashtray, Thumbprint, black, #4469 ............................**15.00**
Banana bowl, Silver Crest, low foot, #5824 ....................**50.00**
Basket, Cherry Chain, plum opalescent, lg ................**60.00**

**Basket, French opalescent (iridized), Dusty Rose handle and crest, $95.00.**

Basket, Daisy & Button, amethyst, #QVC16916 .**45.00**
Basket, Emerald Crest, #7237, 7" ..............................**97.50**
Basket, Hobnail, blue opalescent, 3½" dia .........................**42.00**

Basket, Hobnail, milk glass, double crimped, #3735, 5½x5½" ....................**25.00**
Basket, Hobnail, topaz opalescent, 4½" ................................**95.00**
Basket, Peach Crest, crystal handle, 7" ............................**80.00**
Basket, Poppy, Lime Sherbet, deep, #9138, 7" ..............**75.00**
Basket, Silver Crest, yellow roses hand-painted on milk glass ...........**45.00**
Basket, strawberry, ruby w/white birds & flowers, Louise Piper, #9537 ............................**50.00**
Bell, Beauty, Blue Royale, #9665KK ........................**15.00**
Bell, Hobnail, milk glass, #3667, 6" ..................................**25.00**
Bell, Light House, #7667 .....**85.00**
Bell, milk glass w/pink roses, #8267 ............................**20.00**
Bell, Nativity, Antique White, #9463 ............................**30.00**
Bell, Syndenhan, cobalt carnival, #9063NK ......................**20.00**
Bonbon, Silver Crest, 5½" ...**12.00**
Boot, Daisy & Button, amethyst, #1990CN ........................**25.00**
Bowl, Aqua Crest, 10" .........**45.00**
Bowl, cereal; Hobnail, milk glass, #3719, 2x5" ....................**75.00**
Bowl, Gold Crest, crimped, 7½" ....**30.00**
Bowl, Hobnail, milk glass, double crimped, #3624, 10½" ...**30.00**
Bowl, Peach Crest, double crimped, 4x10¼" ...........**38.00**
Bowl, Pekin Blue, oval w/straight sides, #1663 ..................**75.00**
Bowl, Silver Crest, #7338, 8½" ...**50.00**
Bowl, soup; Emerald Crest, #680, 5½" ..................................**37.50**
Cake salver, Silver Crest, hand-painted violets ..............**70.00**

Cake stand, Emerald Crest, #7213 ............................**85.00**

Candle epergne, Hobnail, milk glass, #3746, 2-pc ..........**65.00**

Candle holder, Rose Crest, #1523, 5" ...................................**25.00**

Candlesticks, Hobnail, French opalescent, low, pr ........**40.00**

Candle holders, Hobnail, milk glass, footed, #3673, 2¾x4¼", pr ...................................**40.00**

Candle holder, Hobnail, turquoise, crimped top, #3947, pr .**40.00**

Candle holders, Silver Crest, cornucopia, #951, pr ..........**60.00**

Candy box, Hobnail, milk glass, w/lid, #3886, 6¾" ..........**35.00**

Chip & dip set, Silver Crest, #7303 ............................**75.00**

Comport, custard w/hand-painted daisies, #7429 ................**35.00**

Comport, Emerald Crest, 7" .**45.00**

Comport, Hobnail, milk glass, double crimped, #3920, 5½" .**86.00**

Compote, Gold Crest, footed, 6½x8" ..............................**30.00**

Cornucopia candlesticks, Ming Pink, #950, pr ...............**70.00**

Creamer, Emerald Crest, clear reeded handles, #7231 ..**42.50**

Creamer & sugar bowl, Hobnail, blue opalescent, individual, 3½" ....**28.00**

Cruet, Hobnail, cranberry opalescent, w/stopper, 4⅞" .....**60.00**

Cup & saucer, Silver Crest, #7209 ............................**30.00**

Figurine, bear, teal marigold carnival, sitting, #51510I ..**20.00**

Figurine, bunny, white carnival, #5162 ............................**20.00**

Figurine, duck, milk glass w/hand-painted berries & flowers, swimming ......................**35.00**

Figurine, fawn, milk glass w/hand-painted poinsettias, #5160 .**22.50**

Figurine, lion, ruby carnival, #5141RN ........................**50.00**

Figurine, Mallard duck, iridized mother-of-pearl, #5147PT ...........**15.00**

Figurine, rooster, Special Milk Glass w/hand-painted decor, 8½" ..................................**95.00**

Figurine, Snail, teal, #5134OC .**70.00**

Figurine, swan, Bairly Blue Satin, #5161BA ........................**40.00**

Goblet, wine; Hobnail, milk glass, #3843, 4-oz, 4½" ............**14.00**

Jam set, Hobnail, French opalescent, w/lid, 3-pc .............**95.00**

Jug, Rose Crest, #192, 5" ....**20.00**

Lamp, fairy; custard, owl, #5108 ........................**24.00**

Lamp, fairy; Fine Cut & Block, milk glass ......................**30.00**

Lamp, gone-w/the-wind; Roses, Honey Amber ..............**175.00**

Lamp, hurricane; Hobnail, milk glass, scalloped top, #3998, 8" ...................................**65.00**

Lamp, student; Hobnail, milk glass ...............................**20.00**

Mayonnaise, Aqua Crest, 3-pc .**45.00**

Mustard, Hobnail, blue opalescent, w/lid ......................**30.00**

Napkin ring, Hobnail, milk glass, #3904, 2" ........................**35.00**

Pitcher, Beaded Melon, Peach Crest, #7166PC .............**85.00**

Pitcher, Hobnail, milk glass, no ice lip, 54-oz, 8" ..................**65.00**

Pitcher, Sandwich, red carnival, 5" ...................................**20.00**

Planter, Hexagon, amethyst carnival, #8226CN ................**65.00**

Plate, Anniversary, white satin .......................**15.00**

Plate, Mother's Day 1972, blue satin ...............................12.00
Plate, Silver Crest, 12" ........40.00
Plate, Statue of Liberty, #7618LO ...................110.00
Plate, torte; Silver Crest, 15" .45.00
Punch cup, Hobnail, milk glass, #3847, 2¼x2¾" .............15.00
Relish, divided; Silver Crest, #7234 ...........................40.00
Rose bowl, Hobnail, cranberry opalescent, 4" ..............90.00
Rose bowl, Waffle, green opalescent, 4½" ......................35.00
Rose bowl, Water lily, Lime Sherbet, #8429 .....................22.00
Salt & pepper shakers, Hobnail, milk glass, flat, #3806, 3", pr ...............................20.00
Sherbet, Emerald Crest, footed, #7226 ...........................22.50
Sherbet, Silver Crest ...........20.00
Sherbet, Velva Rose stretch, 75th Anniversary ...................18.00
Slipper, custard w/hand-painted pink flowers, #9591PY .29.00
Sugar bowl, Silver Crest, ruffled rim ...............................45.00

**Tidbit tray, Silver Crest, two-tier, $55.00.**
Toothpick holder, Hobnail, milk glass, #3795, 3" .............12.00

Tumbler, Hobnail, French opal, flat, 4¼" ........................18.00
Tumbler, iced tea; Hobnail, milk glass, footed, #3842, 5¾" ..........................38.50
Tumbler, water; Hobnail, milk glass, footed, lg .............12.50
Vase, bud; Florentine Green stretch, #251, 12" .........30.00
Vase, Emerald Crest, bulbous base, #186, 8" ..............62.00
Vase, fan; Daisy & Button, milk glass, 8" ......................30.00
Vase, fish figural, milk glass w/black tail & eyes, 7" .425.00
Vase, Hanky, milk glass w/hand-painted green holly .......24.00
Vase, Hobnail, blue opalescent, #389, 5½" .....................32.00
Vase, Hobnail, blue opalescent, fan form, 6¼" ................42.00
Vase, Hobnail, green opalescent, green rim, mini .............30.00
Vase, Hobnail, milk glass, double crimped, #3856, 6" .......20.00
Vase, Melon, blue satin, #7451, 6" ................................12.00
Vase, Melon, Lime Sherbet, #7451 ...........................10.00
Vase, Snow Crest, amber, #3005, 7½" ................................45.00
Vase, Swirl, Lime Sherbet, #9155, 8" ....................................35.00
Vase, Wild Rose, & bow knot, coral, #2855CL, 5", .......45.00

## Fiesta

Since it was discontinued by Homer Laughlin in 1973, Fiesta has become one of the most popular collectibles on the market. Values have continued to climb until some of the more hard-to-find items now sell for several hundred dollars each. In 1986 HLC reintroduced a line of new Fiesta that buyers should be aware of. To date these colors have been used: cobalt (darker than the original), rose (a strong pink), black, white, apricot (very pale), yellow (a light creamy tone), turquoise, (country) blue, seamist (a light mint green), lilac, persimmon, perwinkle, sapphire blue (very close to the original cobalt), and chartreuse. When old molds were used, the mark will be the same, if it is a molded-in mark such as on pitchers, sugar bowls, etc. The ink stamp differs from the old — now all the letters are upper case.

'Original colors' in the listings indicates values for three of the original six colors — light green, turquoise, and yellow. The listing that follows is incomplete due to space restrictions; refer to *The Collector's Encyclopedia of Fiesta, Eighth Edition,* by Sharon and Bob Huxford (Collector Books) for more information. See aslo Clubs and Newsletters.

Ashtray, original colors .......**47.00**
Bowl, cream soup; '50s colors .**72.00**
Bowl, dessert; '50s colors, 6" ..**52.00**
Bowl, dessert; original colors, 6" ...........................**38.00**
Bowl, fruit; '50s colors, 4¾" .**40.00**
Bowl, fruit; original colors, 5½" ..**28.00**
Bowl, nappy; medium green, 8½" ..........................**140.00**
Bowl, nappy; original colors, 9½" ...........................**52.00**

Candle holders, bulb; original colors, pr ...........................**95.00**
Carafe, original colors .......**250.00**
Casserole, '50s colors .........**300.00**
Coffeepot, '50s colors .........**350.00**
Creamer, '50s colors .............**40.00**
Creamer, stick handle, original colors ...........................**45.00**
Cup, demitasse; original colors .**65.00**
Egg cup, original colors .......**58.00**
Mixing bowl, #1, original colors ..**170.00**
Mixing bowl, #4, original colors ..**130.00**
Mug, Tom & Jerry; original colors ...............................**60.00**
Pitcher, disk juice; red .......**450.00**
Pitcher, disk water; original colors ...............................**125.00**
Pitcher, jug, '50s colors, 2-pt .**150.00**
Plate, '50s colors, 6" ..............**9.00**
Plate, '50s colors, 7" .............**13.00**
Plate, calendar; 1954 or 1955, 10", ea ...................................**45.00**
Plate, chop; red, cobalt or ivory, 13" ...................................**55.00**
Plate, compartment; original colors, 10½" ........................**40.00**
Plate, compartment; red, cobalt or ivory, 12" ........................**60.00**
Plate, deep; original colors ..**40.00**
Plate, medium green, 6" ......**20.00**
Plate, original colors, 6" ........**5.00**
Plate, red, cobalt or ivory, 7" .**10.00**
Platter, original colors .........**35.00**
Relish tray base, original colors ..**65.00**
Relish tray side insert, original colors ...........................**40.00**
Salt & pepper shakers, original colors, pr .......................**22.00**
Sauce boat, '50s colors .........**78.00**
Saucer, demitasse; '50s colors .**95.00**
Saucer, red, cobalt or ivory ...**5.00**
Sugar bowl, w/lid, red, cobalt or ivory, 3¼x3½" ..............**55.00**

Syrup, original colors ........**325.00**
Teacup, red cobalt or ivory ..**35.00**
Teapot, medium; '50s colors .**325.00**
Tray, figure-8; cobalt ..........**90.00**
Tumbler, juice; rose ............**65.00**

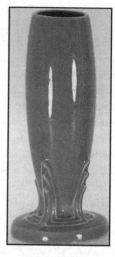

**Vase, bud; turquoise, red, cobalt, or ivory, $100.00 other original colors, $80.00.**

Vase, red, cobalt or ivory, 8" .**700.00**

# Fire-King

From the 1930s to the '60s, Anchor Hocking produced a line called Fire-King; various patterns and colors were used in its manufacture. Collectors are just beginning to reassemble sets, so pieces are relatively low, except for some of the jade-ite pieces that are especially popular. For more information we recommend *Anchor Hocking Fire-King and More* and *Pocket Guide to Depres-sion Glass 11th Edition*, both by Gene Florence (Collector Books). See also Forest Green, Kitchen Collectibles, Royal Ruby.

Alice, cup & saucer, jade-ite ..**7.00**
Alice, plate, jade-ite, 9½" .....**25.00**
Anniversary Rose, bowl, dessert; white w/decals, 4⅝" ........**8.00**
Anniversary Rose, creamer, white w/decals .........................**10.00**
Anniversary Rose, platter, white w/decals, 9x12" .............**20.00**
Blue Mosaic, bowl, vegetable; white w/decals, 8¼" ......**15.00**
Blue Mosaic, plate, salad; white w/decals, 7⅜" .................**6.00**
Bubble, plate, grill; sapphire blue, 9⅜" .............................**22.50**
Bubble, tumbler, iced tea; crystal iridescent, 12-oz, 4½" ...**12.00**
Charm, bowl, dessert; jade-ite or ivory, 4¾" ......................**10.00**
Charm, plate, dinner; jade-ite or ivory, 9¼" ......................**35.00**
Fish Scale, bowl, dessert; ivory, shallow, 5½" .................**10.00**
Fish Scale, plate, salad; ivory w/red, 7⅜" .....................**15.00**
Fleurette, creamer, white w/decals ..**5.00**
Fleurette, plate, bread & butter; white w/decals, 6¼" ......**12.00**
Forget Me Not, casserole, white with decals, 1-qt, with lid .................**24.00**
Forget Me Not, mug, white w/decals, 8-oz ...............**15.00**
Game Birds, bowl, vegetable; white w/decals, 8¼" ......**25.00**
Game Birds, plate, bread & butter; white w/decals, 6¼" ......**15.00**
Harvest, plate, dinner; white w/decals, 10" .................**6.00**

Homestead, creamer, white w/decals ............................**5.00**

**Honeysuckle, Dessert, $2.25; Plate, 9", $6.00; Bread and butter plate, rare, 6", $15.00. (Photo courtesy Gene Florence)**

Homestead, plate, dinner; white w/decals, 10" ...................**15.00**

Honeysuckle, plate, salad; white w/decals, 7⅜" ....................**5.00**

Honeysuckle, tumbler, water; white w/decals, 9-oz ......**10.00**

Jane Ray, bowl, oatmeal; jade-ite, 5⅞" ..................................**14.00**

Jane Ray, plate, dinner; ivory, 9⅛" .....................................**22.50**

Jane Ray, platter, jade-ite, 9x12" ..........................**20.00**

Laurel, bowl, vegetable; ivory or white, 8¼" ......................**35.00**

Laurel, creamer, peach lustre, footed ...............................**4.00**

Meadow Green, bowl, mixing; white w/decals, 2½-qt ...**10.00**

Meadow Green, plate, dinner; white w/decals, 10" .........**4.00**

Milk White, bowl, berry; 4½" ......................**5.00**

Philbe, bowl, cereal; pink or green, 5½" ................................**45.00**

Philbe, plate, luncheon; crystal, 8" ...................................**20.00**

Philbe, platter, blue, closed handles, 12" ......................**175.00**

Philbe, tumbler, pink or green, footed, 10-oz, 5¼" ..........**80.00**

Primrose, bowl, vegetable; white w/decal, 8¼" ..................**14.00**

Primrose, cake pan, white w/decal, 8" sq ...............................**12.00**

Restaurant Ware, bowl, cereal; jade-ite, flanged rim, 8-oz ........**16.00**

Restaurant Ware, bowl, fruit; crystal/white, 4¾" ..................**6.00**

Restaurant Ware, cup, jade-ite, tapered, 7-oz ..................**20.00**

Restaurant Ware, plate, dinner; crystal/white, 9" ............**10.00**

Restaurant Ware, platter, jade-ite, oval, 9½" ........................**30.00**

Royal Lustre & White, bowl, vegetable; white, 8½" .........**12.00**

Royal Lustre & White, cup, lustre ....**8.00**

Sheaves of Wheat, plate, dinner; jade-ite, 9" ....................**45.00**

Shell, creamer, jade-ite, footed .**12.00**

Shell, saucer, demitasse; mother-of-pearl, 4¾" .................**15.00**

Soreno, bowl, Honey Gold, 4-qt, 11⅜" ..................................**8.00**

Soreno, bowl, soup/salad; crystal, 5⅞" ..................................**4.50**

Soreno, pitcher, water; aquamarine, 64-oz .....................**18.00**

Swirl, bowl, vegetable; ivory/white, 8¼" ..................................**20.00**

Swirl, creamer, pink, flat ......**8.50**

Swirl, cup, jade-ite, 8-oz ......**20.00**

Three Bands, bowl, vegetable; burgundy, 8¼" ....................**35.00**

Three Bands, bowl, vegetable; ivory, 8¼" ......................**25.00**

Three Bands, saucer, jade-ite, 5¾" ..................................**15.00**

Turquoise Blue, bowl, berry; 4½" .**7.00**

Turquoise Blue, bowl, soup/salad; 6⅝" ..................................**20.00**

Turquoise Blue, plate, 6⅛" ..**18.00**
Vienna Lace, bowl, vegetable; white w/decals, 8¼" ......**15.00**
Vienna Lace, platter, white w/decals, 9x12" .............**12.00**
Wheat, bowl, soup plate; 6⅝" .**8.00**
Wheat, casserole, knob cover, 1-qt ...................................**10.00**
Wheat, plate, dinner; 10" ......**5.00**
1700 Line, bowl, cereal; jade-ite, 5⅞" ................................**25.00**
1700 Line, cup, coffee; ivory, 8-oz ..............................**10.00**
1700 Line, plate, dinner; ivory, 9⅛" ...................................**5.00**

# Fishbowl Ornaments

Mermaids, divers, and all sorts of castles have been devised to add interest to fishbowls and aquariums, and today they're starting to attract the interest of collectors. Many were made in Japan and imported decades ago to be sold in 5-&-10¢ stores along with the millions of other figural novelties that flooded the market after the war. The condition of the glaze is very important; for more information we recommend *Collector's Guide to Made in Japan Ceramics* by Carole Bess White (Collector Books). Unless noted otherwise, the examples in the listing that follows were produced in Japan.

Arches, green & red matt, Germany, 4¼x4½" .............**24.00**
Castle & tower, multicolor, details blurred, 4½x4½" ...........**22.00**
Castle & tower, multicolor, details sharp, 3½x3¼" .............**22.00**
Colonnade w/palm tree, multicolor, 3¾x4" ......................**20.00**
Coral reef, curved, yellow & green, 8x2" ...............................**20.00**
Fish (2) on waves, white & cobalt, 3½x3" .............................**22.00**
Houses w/water wheel & bridge, multicolor, 4½x4½" .......**26.00**

**Bathing beauty on coral, multicolor, 4",
from $20.00 to $30.00. (Photo courtesy of
Carole Bess White)**

Lighthouse, multicolor, detailed, 2x2½" ............................**16.00**

Lighthouse, multicolor, detailed, 6½x4" .............................**26.00**

Medieval gate, multicolor w/lustre, detailed, 3½x3¾" ..........**26.00**

Pagoda, triple roof, multicolor, 5½x3¼" ...........................**20.00**

Pagodas, joined by bridge, multicolor, wreath mark, 3¼x3¼" ......**22.50**

Pagodas, joined by bridge, multicolor, 6½x2½" ................**24.00**

Sign, No Fishing on tree trunk, multicolor, 2½x4" ..........**12.00**

Torii, double roof, multicolor, 2¼x3¾" ...........................**20.00**

Torii, triple roof, multicolor w/lustre, 4½x3½" ...................**22.00**

# Fisher-Price

Since about 1930 the Fisher-Price Company has produced distinctive wooden toys covered with brightly colored lithographed paper. Plastic parts were first added in 1949. The most valuable Fisher-Price toys are those modeled after well-known Disney characters and having the Disney logo. A little edge wear and some paint dulling are normal to these well-loved toys and to be expected; pricing information reflects items that are in very good played-with condition. Mint-in-box examples are extremely scarce.

Our advisor for this category is Brad Cassity. For further information we recommend *A Pictorical Guide to the More Popular Toys, Fisher-Price Toys, 1931 – 1990,* by Gary Combs and Brad Cassity; *Fisher-Price, A Historical Rarity Value Guide,* by John J. Murray and Bruce R. Fox (Books Americana); and *Schroeder's Collectible Toys, Antique to Modern* (Collector Books). See also Clubs and Newsletters.

Bouncing Buggy, #122, 1974-79, 6 wheels ............................**10.00**

Bouncy Racer, #8, 1960 .......**40.00**

Cackling Hen, #120, 1958, white .........................**40.00**

Dr Doodle, #132, 1957 .........**85.00**

Fisher-Price Zoo, #916, 1984-87, w/6 figures & accessories ........................**20.00**

Frisky Frog, #154, 1971-83 .**20.00**

Golden Gulch Express, #191, 1961 ...........................**100.00**

Happy Hoppers, #121, 1969-76 ...........................**25.00**

Hot Rod Roadster, #982, 1983-84 ..............................**65.00**

Jiffy Dump Truck, #156, 1971-73 ..............................**20.00**

Jolly Jumper, #793, 1963 ....**50.00**

Katy Kackler, #140, 1954 ....**70.00**

Magnetic Chug-Chug, 1964-69 ..**40.00**

Mother Goose, #164, 1964-66 ..**40.00**

Music Box Clock Radio, #107, 1971, plays Hickory Dickory Dock ...............................**5.00**

Music Box TV, #114, 1967 ...**10.00**

Play Family House, #952, 1987-88, complete ........................**20.00**

Play Family Western Town, #934, 1982-84, w/4 figures & accessories ............................**75.00**

Playland Express, #192, 1962 .**100.00**

Pony Chime, #127, 1962, pink plastic wheel ...............**40.00**

**Snoopy Sniffer, 1971, MIB, $50.00. (Photo courtesy Doug Dezso)**

Pull-A-Long Lacing Shoe, #146, 1970-75, w/6 figures .....**45.00**

Roly Poly Sailboats, #162, 1968-69 ................................**10.00**

Squeaky the Clown, #777, 1958 .....................**250.00**

Talking Donald Duck, #765, 1955 ..........................**125.00**

This Little Pig, #910, 1963 ..**40.00**

Three Men in a Tub, #142, 1970-73 ................................**20.00**

Tiny Ding-Dong, #767, 1940 ...**400.00**

Tip-Toe Turtle, #0773, 1962, vinyl tail ................................**20.00**

Tuggy Tooter, #139, 1967-73 .**30.00**

TV Radio, #154, 1964-67 .....**25.00**

# Fishing Collectibles

Very much in evidence at flea markets these days, old fishing gear is becoming popular with collectors. Because the hobby is newly established, there are some very good buys to be found. Early 20th-century plugs were almost entirely carved from wood, sprayed with several layers of enamel, and finished off with glass eyes. Molded plastics were of a later origin. Some of the more collectible manufacturers are James Heddon, Shakespeare, Rhodes, and Pflueger. Rods, reels, old advertising calendars, and company catalogs are also worth your attention, in fact, any type of vintage sporting goods is now collectible. For more information we recommend *Fishing Lure Collectibles* by Dudley Murphy and Rick Edmisten (Collector Books).

Our advisor for this category is Dave Hoover; he is listed in the Directory under Indiana.

### Lures

Arbogast, Jitterbug, green scale w/black plastic lip, EX+ ...**35.00**

Biff, Musky Spiral Spinner, MIB .............................**225.00**

Brown, Fisheretto, leader & spinner, orange head w/red neck, EX ................................**40.00**

Clark, Water Scout, tack eyes, black w/white ribs, EX+ ..........**30.00**

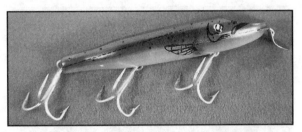

Creek Chub, trout-colored #700-P Pikie, from $25.00 to $30.00. (Photo courtesy Harold Smith)

Creek Chub, Baby Pike #901, glass eyes, MIB ......................**45.00**

Creek Chub, Beetle, Midget, deep lip, gold head w/black wings, EX+ ..............................**275.00**

Creek Chub, Crawdad #300, albino w/red blush on chin, EX .**75.00**

Creek Chub, Darter #2000, brown frog, EX ..........................**85.00**

Creek Chub, Ding Bat, perch, glass eyes, old lip, brown tails, VG+ ................................**35.00**

Creek Chub, Giant Jointed Pike #802, glass eyes, white w/red head, MIB ......................**90.00**

Fishcake, Baby #7, frog, MIB ..**15.00**

Heddon, Crazy Crawler, yellow plastic crackleback, MIB ........**20.00**

Heddon, Deep-O-Diver, goldfish, glass eyes, EX ...............**85.00**

Heddon, Dowagiac Minnow #100, fat-body style, 1917, 2½", EX ......................**85.00**

Heddon, Flap Tail, 2-pc, glass eyes, white w/red head, EX ....**75.00**

Heddon, Fly Rod, Baby Bass Bug Spook #974 RW, MIB .....................**40.00**

Jamison, Twin Spinner Bucktail, 1932, EX ......................**20.00**

Keeling, Baby Tom #210, aluminum & red hat, M (NM box) ..............................**95.00**

Miller, Min-Nix Spoon, silver finish, very old, MOC .....**25.00**

Millsite, Wig Wag, 1946, 3", EX ...........................**15.00**

Pflueger, Baby Scoop #9300, 3", EX ...................................**35.00**

Pflueger, Globe, yellow w/gold spots, tail cup, EXIB .....**55.00**

Pflueger, Mustang, perch scale, painted eyes, carver gills, VG+ ..............................**20.00**

Pflueger, Swimming Mouse, MIB ...........................**25.00**

Pflueger, Three Hook Never Fail, painted eyes, white, red, black, VG+ .....................**55.00**

Shakespeare, Floating Minnow, yellow & green w/6 tiger stripes, VG+ ..................**95.00**

Shakespeare, Plopper, frog spots, glass eyes, VG+ .............**85.00**

South Bend, Bass-Oreno, glass eyes, white, red, black, VG ...............**95.00**

South Bend, Be Bop #902 YP, yellow perch, MIB .............**25.00**

South Bend, Dive-Oreno #952P, perch scales, MIB .........**35.00**

South Bend, Fin-Dingo, yellow w/black spots, MIB .......**40.00**

South Bend, Minnow #999, glass eyes, tail cap, weighted nose, 1929, EX ........................**55.00**

Creels: Split willow with rattan hinges and metal fish-head latch, VG, $85.00; Whole reed with decorative weaving, peg-and-loop latch on lid (peg missing), EX, $140.00.

## Reels

ABU 1750, missing label, EX .**55.00**
Airex, Bache Brown Mastereel Model #3, half bail, VG ........................**20.00**
Alcedo #2, spinning, stamped PO 27, EX ...........................**75.00**
Ambassadeur 2050, EX+ .....**95.00**
Ambassadeur 5000 #027200, red, grooved rims, MIB ......**150.00**
Bushkill Trout Reel, McVicar & Sons, Tuxedo NY Pat Pend, EX ...............................**195.00**
Dam Quick 550, spinning, right-handed model, EX ........**65.00**
Garcia Mitchell 314, EX ......**20.00**
Garcia Mitchell 440, automatic bail & bail lock, NM .....**50.00**
Pflueger Supreme, cub handle, EX+ ...............................**25.00**
Roddy Roddymatic 560, star drag, free spool, NM ...............**25.00**
Shakespeare President 1970, sandwich plates, stainless steel, VG+ .....................**30.00**
South Bend 400, Model D, anti-backlash, jeweled, EX ...**20.00**
Winchester 4291, single handle, counterweight, 80-yd, NM ......**145.00**

## Miscellaneous

Catalog, Abercrombie & Fitch, 1968, The Big Little Book of Fishing, EX ...................**35.00**
Catalog, South Bend, 1931, boy on pier w/big bass, EX+ .....**85.00**
Catalog, Weber, 1938, EX+ .**95.00**
Decoy, AJ Downey, whitefish, 14", EX+ .............................**225.00**
Decoy, Carl Christenson, brown trout, glass eyes, 11", EX+ ..........**75.00**
Decoy, Dennis Wolf, golden sucker, glass eyes, 10", EX+ .....**125.00**
Magazines, Field & Stream, 1930s-40s, EX, ea .........**10.00**
Plaque, Heddon, wood, black crappie, VG .........................**40.00**
Plaque, Heddon, wood, large-mouth bass, G+ ............**30.00**
Trap, Oneida-Victor, sm size, VG ..............................**10.00**

## Flashlights

The flashlight was invented in 1898 and has been produced by the Eveready Company for these past ninety-six years. Eveready dominated the flashlight market for most of this period, but more than one hundred twenty-five other U.S. flashlight companies have come and gone, providing competition along the way. Add to that number over thirty-five known foreign flashlight manufacturers, and you end up with over one thousand different models of flashlights to collect. They come in a wide variety of styles, shapes, and sizes. The flashlight field includes tubular, lanterns, figural, novelty, and litho. At present, over forty-five different categories of flashlights have been identified as collectible. For further information we recommend consulting the *Flashlight Collectors of America*, see Clubs and Newsletters.

Our advisor for this category is Bill Utley; he is listed in the Directory under California.

Blue Cub Scout, 2C-cell, Made by BMG, NM ......................**24.00**
Bond, Vest Pocket, green marbled, EX ................................**22.00**

Bright Star Penlite, NM ........**8.00**
Burgess Sub Lithograph, NM ..**22.00**
Burgess Vest Pocket, maroon, NM ................................**15.00**
Chase, Vest Pocket, 2AA-cell, NM ............................**18.00**
Coke bottle, plastic, NM ......**12.00**
Collins Wind-up, no battery, EX+ ..........................**125.00**
Durolite, MIB ......................**20.00**
Elephant Political Lapel Pins, NM ................................**10.00**
Eveready, #1904 Midget, w/red glass switch, NM ..........**35.00**
Eveready, #2251, MIB ........**25.00**
Eveready, #2602, 2C-cell, Old Rose or Baby Blue, 1929, VG ............................**22.00**
Eveready, #3651 Liberty Daylo Lantern, blued or nickel finish, NM ..........................**20.00**
Eveready, #6961, Dec 17 1912, EX+ ..................................**8.00**
Eveready, Captain, 2C-cell, 1962, NM ................................**12.00**
Eveready, Glovecatch, flashlight pin, M ..........................**10.00**
Eveready, Glovecatch, 3D-cell, 1906, EX ......................**65.00**

**Eveready British hand lanterns, EX+, $65.00 each. (Photo courtesy Bill Utley)**

Eveready, Hand Lantern, black, 1908, NM ........................**75.00**

Eveready, Horseshoe Clock light, 1902, VG ......................**100.00**

Eveready, Lily Candle, wood base, 1900, EX ......................**110.00**

Eveready, Masterlite, tubular, 3D-cell, 1935, EX+ ..............**38.00**

Eveready, Masterlite table model, 1935, EX ........................**40.00**

Eveready, Pistol Light, nickel, 1914, VG ........................**45.00**

Eveready, Round Auto Bulb-Holder, NM+ ........................**18.00**

Eveready, tan leather cover, 1954, NM ................................**25.00**

Eveready, Vest Pocket, engraved sterling, 1907, NM ......**150.00**

Flasher Is Your Friend, red plastic dog w/tail switch, NM ...........................**28.00**

Franco, Pistol Light, black steel, 1913, VG ........................**40.00**

Franco, Vest Pocket, 2AA-cell, EX ................................**26.00**

Homart, w/compass, EX ......**16.00**

Lone Ranger, lithograph, NM .**135.00**

Masterlite, 2C-cell, red plastic lens ring, later model, 1954, NM ................................**22.00**

Pluto Lantern, lithograph, NM ...**225.00**

Popeye Lantern, lithograph, NM ...........................**225.00**

Ray-O-Vac, Miner, 2B-cell, NM ...........................**22.00**

Ray-O-Vac, Penlite, VG .......**10.00**

RCA, 2D-cell, M ..................**35.00**

Space Cadet, lithograph, VG .**48.00**

Sterling, engraved vest pocket, 1907, NM ....................**140.00**

Sterling Candle, 2C-cell, EX ..**150.00**

Tiffany, sterling w/chain, 1966, NM ................................**55.00**

Zoom-Lite Lithograph Flashlight, NM ................................**32.00**

# Flower Frogs

Nearly every pottery company and glasshouse in America produced their share of figural flower 'frogs,' and many were imported from Japan as well. They were probably most popular from about 1910 through the 1940s, coinciding not only with the heyday of American glass and ceramics, but with the gracious, much less hectic style of living the times allowed. Way before a silk flower or styrofoam block was ever dreamed of, there were fresh cut flowers on many a dining room sideboard or table, arranged in shallow console bowls with matching frogs such as we've described in the following listings. For further information see *Collector's Guide to Made in Japan Ceramics, Identification and Values*, by Carole Bess White (Collector Books). See also specific pottery and glass companies.

Bird, lustre trim, Japan, marked Niagara Falls Canada, 6" .......**15.00**

Bird, multicolor on brown rocky base, Made in Japan, 6x3" dia ................................**15.00**

Bird, pelican-like, yellow with orange & black wings, log base, Japan ..................**15.00**

Bird, red, black & white, blue stump, lustre trim, Japan, 5¼" ................................**28.00**

**Bird flower bowl with separate flower frogs, blue and tan lustre with multicolor birds, Japan, 10" wide, from $40.00 to $65.00. (Photo courtesy Carole Bess White)**

Bird, yellow & blue lustre, oval base, Made in Japan, 2½" ..........**8.00**

Crane pr on perch, w/lotus bowl, white semi-matt, Camark, 11" ...............................**50.00**

Flower bud, multicolor on blue base, lustre trim, Japan, 2½" .............................**22.00**

Oriental lady on base, lime green, 1940s, 13x3½" dia .........**15.00**

Penguin pr, multicolor w/pearl & blue lustre, Made in Japan, 4¾" ...............................**25.00**

Rosebud, pink with yellow & blue, tan lustre base, Japan, 2½" ..............**22.00**

Scarf dancer, teal, 7½", w/attached 6" scalloped bowl, Yankoware ...................**20.00**

Water lily, multicolor with green leaves, on base, 2½x3½x2¼" .............**15.00**

## Forest Green

Not a pattern but a color and one that's been at the forefront of home fashions for several years, Forest Green glassware is easy to find, not at all expensive, and comes in a wide variety of shapes and designs — all factors that contribute to its collectibility. It was made by Anchor Hocking (who patented the name) from 1950 until 1967 and widely distributed as premiums. For an expanded listing and more information, see *Collectible Glassware of the 40s, 50s, and 60s,* by Gene Florence (Collector Books).

Ashtray, 5¾" sq ......................**9.00**

Bowl, batter; w/spout ...........**25.00**

Bowl, berry; Bubble, 8⅜" .....**14.00**

Vase, 9", $8.00; Vase, 6½", $5.00; Pitcher, $30.00; Bowl, oval vegetable, 8½", $21.00; Bowl, 6", $8.50. (Photo courtesy Gene Florence)

Bowl, cereal; Bubble, 5¼" ....**12.00**
Bowl, deep, 5¼" .......................**8.50**
Bowl, fruit; Bubble, 4½" ........**7.00**
Candlesticks, Bubble, pr .....**37.50**
Creamer, Bubble ..................**12.00**
Cup, Bubble ..........................**17.00**
Pitcher, 22-oz ......................**22.50**
Plate, bread & butter; Bubble, 6¾" ...............................**15.00**
Plate, dinner; Bubble, 9⅜" ..**25.00**
Punch bowl ...........................**22.50**
Punch bowl stand ................**22.50**
Punch cup, round ...................**2.25**
Saucer, 5⅜" ...........................**1.50**
Stem, cocktail; Bubble or plain, 3½" ..................................**10.00**
Stem, cocktail; Bubble or plain, 4½-oz .............................**12.50**
Stem, goblet; Bubble or plain, 9½-oz .............................**13.00**
Stem, juice; Bubble or plain, 4-oz .**10.00**
Stem, juice; Bubble or plain, 5½-oz .............................**12.50**
Stem, sherbet; Bubble or plain, 6-oz .................................**9.00**
Sugar bowl, Bubble .............**12.00**

Tumbler, iced tea; tall, 15-oz .**12.00**
Tumbler, tall, 9½-oz .............**6.50**
Tumbler, 11-oz ......................**7.00**
Tumbler, 14-oz, 5" .................**7.50**
Tumbler, 7-oz ........................**4.00**
Vase, ivy ball, 4" ...................**4.00**

## Franciscan

When most people think of the Franciscan name, their Apple or Desert Rose patterns come to mind immediately, and without a doubt these are the most collectible of the hundreds of lines produced by Gladding McBean. Located in Los Angeles, they produced quality dinnerware under the trade name Franciscan from the mid-1930s until 1984, when they were bought out by a company from England. Many marks were used; most included the Franciscan name. An 'F' in a square with 'Made in USA' below it dates from 1938, and a double-line script F was used later. Some of this dinnerware is still being produced in England, so be sure to look for the USA mark.

Apple, bowl, fruit .................**12.00**
Apple, bowl, straight sides, lg .**65.00**
Apple, candle holders, pr ...**137.00**
Apple, creamer, individual ..**45.00**
Apple, mug, 7-oz .................**35.00**
Apple, plate, 9½" .................**22.00**
Coronado, creamer, from $12 to .**15.00**
Coronado, cup & saucer, jumbo, from $28 to ....................**35.00**
Coronado, gravy boat, attached plate, from $28 to .........**40.00**
Coronado, teapot, from $65 to .**95.00**

**Desert Rose, Grill plate, $125.00.**

Desert Rose, bowl, cereal; 6" ...**12.00**
Desert Rose, bowl, soup; footed .**32.00**
Desert Rose, butter dish ......**45.00**
Desert Rose, plate, 10½" .....**18.00**
Desert Rose, salt shaker & pepper mill, pr .........................**295.00**
Desert Rose, syrup pitcher ..**75.00**
El Patio, bowl, vegetable; oval, 10½", from $22 to .........**30.00**

El Patio, cup, from $8 to .....**10.00**
El Patio, cup & saucer, demitasse; from $28 to ....................**45.00**
El Patio, relish, handled, from $50 to ...................................**65.00**
Forget-Me-Not, bowl, vegetable; 9" ...................................**65.00**
Ivy, plate, 10½" ...................**30.00**
Ivy, teapot ..........................**175.00**
Meadow Rose, butter dish ...**65.00**
Meadow Rose, sherbet .........**25.00**
Poppy, butter dish .............**175.00**
Poppy, cup & saucer ............**35.00**

**Starburst, Divided vegetable bowl, $25.00; Salt and pepper shakers, $50.00 for the pair.**

Starburst, bowl, fruit .............**7.00**
Starburst, creamer, from $10 to ..............................**15.00**
Starburst, plate, 6½", from $5 to ................................**6.00**
Starburst, sugar bowl, w/lid ...**20.00**

# Frankoma

Since 1933 the Frankoma Pottery Company has been producing dinnerware, novelty items, vases, etc. In 1965 they became the first American company to produce a line of collector plates. The body of the ware prior to 1954 was a honey tan that collectors refer to as 'Ada clay.' A brick red clay (called 'Sapulpa') was used from then on, and this and the colors of the glazes help determine the period of production.

Our advisor for this category is Susan Cox; she is listed in the Directory under California. For more information refer to *Frankoma and Other Oklahoma Potteries* by Phyllis and Tom Bess (Schiffer), and *Frankoma Pottery, Value Guide and More*, by Susan N. Cox.

Bookends, Setter, Osage Brown, pr ................................**150.00**
Bowl, Royal Blue, oval, Ada clay, #205 ..............................**40.00**
Canteen, Thunderbird, Prairie Green, leather thong, 6¼" .............**30.00**
Catalog, 1950 .......................**30.00**
Christmas card, 1952 ..........**85.00**

Christmas card, 1953-56, ea .**75.00**
Christmas card, 1958-60, ea .**65.00**
Christmas card, 1967-68, ea .**50.00**
Christmas card, 1972 ..........**35.00**
Christmas plate, 1965 .......**310.00**
Christmas plate, 1977-82, ea .**35.00**
Flower holder, boot, star on sides, Ada clay, #507, 3½" ......**20.00**
Jug, Prairie Green, w/stopper, 3-cup .................................**75.00**
Mug, Democrat Donkey, Carter/Mondale, 1977 ...**45.00**
Mug, Republican Elephant, Nixon/Agnew, 1969 .......**75.00**
Mug, Uncle Sam, 1976 ........**15.00**
Pipe rest ............................**140.00**
Pitcher, eagle, Dusty Rose ..**25.00**
Pitcher, honey; #831, 16-oz .**25.00**
Plate, Bob White Quail, 1972 .................**100.00**
Plate, David, Teenager of the Bible, 1974 ....................**45.00**
Plate, Helen Keller .............**45.00**
Sculpture, cat reclining, black gloss, 4½x9" .................**25.00**

**Bookends, Charger, green on red clay, $165.00 for the pair.**

**Sugar bowl, Mayan-Aztec, with lid, 4", from $12.00 to $15.00; Matching teapot, 4¼", $18.00 to $22.00.**

Sculpture, Fan Dancer, green, red clay, #113, 8½x13½" ...**250.00**

Sculpture, Gardener Girl, blue ...**95.00**

Sculpture, Rearing Clydesdale, flat back, reissue .........**175.00**

Sculpture, swan, Peacock Blue, mini ..............................**50.00**

Sculpture, Trojan Horse, mini .**65.00**

Teapot, Wagon Wheel, Prairie Green, 2-cup ..................**40.00**

Trivet, Governor & Mrs David Boren, 1975 ....................**20.00**

Trivet, Prairie Green, Cattle Brands, red clay ............**10.00**

Vase, collector; V-13, black & Terra Cotta, 1981, 13" ..**65.00**

Vase, collector; V-2, turquoise, 1970, 12" ........................**70.00**

Vase, collector; V-5, Flame Red, 1973, 13" ........................**85.00**

Vase, collector; V-8, red & white, red stopper, 13" ..............**75.00**

Vase, goose, Ada clay, #60-B .**30.00**

Vase, mottled, #74 ...............**25.00**

Vase, Ring, Desert Gold, #500, mini ..............................**35.00**

Vase, Wagon Wheel, blue, Ada clay ..............................**30.00**

Wall mask, Tragedy & Comedy, white, #118T&C, pr ......**65.00**

Wall pocket, acorn, green, Ada clay ..............................**30.00**

# Fruit Jars

Some of the earliest glass jars used for food preservation were blown, and corks were used for seals. During the 19th century, hundreds of manufacturers designed over 4,000 styles of fruit jars. Lids were held in place either by a wax seal, wire bail, or the later screw-on band. Jars were usually made in aqua or clear, though other colors were also used. Amber jars are popular with collectors, milk glass jars are rare, and cobalt and black glass jars often bring $3,000.00 and up if they can be found! Condition, age, scarcity, and unusual features are also to be considered when evaluating old fruit jars.

Amazon Swift Seal (in circle), blue, 1-pt ..............................**22.00**

Atlas (clover) Good Luck, clear, qt ...................................**4.00**

Atlas E-Z Seal in Circle, light blue, qt ..................................**27.00**

Atlas Mason's Patent Nov 30th 1858, aqua, ½-gal ............**9.00**

Ball Improved, dropped A, aqua, qt ......................................**4.00**

Ball Improved Mason's Patent 1858, aqua, qt ................**4.00**

Ball Mason, aqua, blue, qt ....**2.00**

Ball Mason's Patent 1858, aqua, pt ..................................**12.00**

Ball Perfect Mason, undropped A, 8 ribs, blue, qt .................**6.00**

Ball Sure Seal, blue, full round dimples, qt .....................**20.00**

Bernardin (script) Underlined Mason, clear, pt ............**10.00**

Brockway Clear Vu Mason, clear, correct glass insert, pt ....**1.00**

Clark's Peerless, aqua, qt ......**5.00**

**Compton & Batchelder Cleveland O, bluish-aqua, wax sealer, tin lid, quart, EX, $210.00.**

Crown Cordial & Extract & Co New York, clear, ½-gal .**12.00**

Crown Crown (ring crown), aqua, qt ....................................**17.00**

Crown Mason, clear, qt ..........**2.00**

Double Safety, older narrow mouth, clear, qt ...............**2.00**

Drey Square Mason (in carpenter's sq), clear, qt .....................**6.00**

Foster Sealfast, clear, pt .......**3.00**

Genuine (Mason script in flag), aqua, qt .........................**12.00**

Hazel Atlas E-Z Seal, aqua, pt .**15.00**

HW Pettit Westville NJ, aqua, qt ...................................**8.00**

Improved Jewel Made in Canada, clear, qt ...........................**5.00**

Jos Middleby Jr Inc (vertically), correct lid, clear, ½-gal .**10.00**

Leotric (sm mouth), green, qt .**15.00**

Lockport Mason Improved, clear, qt ...................................**10.00**

Marion Jar Mason's Patent Nov 30th 1858, aqua, qt .......**15.00**

Mason's II Patent Nov 30th 1858, aqua, qt .........................**33.00**

Mason's Improved, aqua, qt ..**3.00**

Mason's KBGCo Patent Nov 30th 1858, aqua, qt ...............**25.00**

Mason's Patent, clear, qt .......**3.00**

Mason's Patent Nov 30th 1858, HGW on reverse, aqua, qt .........**20.00**

Mason's 14 (underlined) Patent Nov 30th 1858, aqua, ½-gal ...**18.00**

Mason Star, clear, qt .............**1.00**

Mountain Mason, clear, round, qt ...................................**22.00**

Perfect Seal (in circle), clear glass lid, pt ..............................**6.00**

Presto Supreme Mason clear, qt ...................................**1.00**

Safe Seal Patd July 14 1908, blue, qt .....................................**5.00**

Security Seal FG Co (in triangles), clear, qt ............................**6.00**

Swayzee's Improved Mason, Imperial, aqua, qt .................**15.00**

The Gem (1 line), Patd Nov 26 1867 on base, aqua, qt .............**12.00**

Tight Seal Pat'd July 14th 1908, blue, qt .............................**2.00**

TM Lightning, aqua, qt .........**2.00**

Trademark Banner Registered (in banner), clear, qt ..........**10.00**

True's Imperial Brand DW True Portland ME, clear, pt ....**9.00**

Victory (in shield on lid), clear, qt ....................................**5.00**

Victory Reg'd 1925 (on lid), twin side clamps, clear, qt ......**6.00**

Wears Jar (in circle), clear, qt .**9.00**

Wellman Pantry Jr (on 2 upper panels), clear, pt, w/zinc lid ...**25.00**

Whitney Mason 6 Pat'd 1858, apple green, qt ..............**25.00**

Widemouth Telephone Jar, aqua, pt ....................................**8.00**

# Gambling Collectibles

Prices for antique gambling chips and equipment have continued to escalate as evidenced by high prices realized at recent auctions. Interest should spread and increase along with the rise of legal gambling in the U.S.

When evaluating these items, add a premium for: (1) equipment rigged for cheating; (2) items bearing the name of an old-time gambling saloon or manufacturer, particularly of the American West (e.g., Will & Finck, San Francisco; Mason, Denver; Mason, San Fran-

cisco), as signed and named pieces are worth at least 50% more than unsigned ones; (3) items typically found in American gambling halls of the middle and late 19th century (parlor game items of whist, bezique, cribbage, bridge, pinochle, etc., are not as valuable as those of faro, poker, craps, roulette, etc.); and (4) gambling supply catalogs which are dated and have many large, colorful pages and good graphics.

The most valuable chips, in descending order, are ivory poker chips (elaborately scrimshawed in more than a simple concentric design), mother-of-pearl chips and markers (engraved, at least ⅛" thick and preferably colored), casino chips (preferably from Nevada, the best from Las Vegas), illegal club chips, and clay composition poker chips.

Little or no value or collector interest is found in the following gambling items: (1) made after 1945, except for casino chips, gambling supply catalogs, and some early but post-1945 casino souvenirs; (2) plain (no design) paper, wood, and composition chips, regardless of age; chips with interlocking rims; hot-stamped casino-quality chips that can not be identified (e.g., unknown monogram); and virtually all plastic (except Catalin), paper, and wood chips, unless there is some advertising connection; (3) homemade items (e.g., carnival wheels of fortune); (4) casino-type toys and combination game sets (e.g., plastic and brown Bakelite roulette wheels); and (5) narrow, bridge-sized (2¼" wide) playing card decks. (Generally, only poker decks that are 2½" wide are collectible.) Finally, beware of the heavy, bulkier gambling antiques (e.g., professional crap tables) as storage and shipping problems limit the resale market.

Not listed here but of interest to many gambling collectors are a myriad of objects with gambling/playing card motifs: paintings and lithographs, ceramics, jewelry and charms, postcards, match safes, cigarette lighters, casino artifacts (ashtrays, swizzle sticks, etc.), souvenir spoons, tobacco tins, cigar box labels, song sheets, board games, etc. Values given here are for items in fine condition.

Our advisor for this category is Robert Eisenstadt, who is listed in the Directory under New York. For further detailed information, refer to *Gambling Collectibles, A Sure Winner*, by Leonard Schneir.

Backgammon, Catalin set (30 pcs, modest size, about 1½"), from $30 to .............................**60.00**
Book, Fools of Fortune by John Philip Quinn, 1890, EX .**160.00**
Book, Foster's Practical Poker by RF Foster, 1905, EX ...**105.00**
Book, Gambler's Tricks w/Cards Exposed & Explained, JH Green, 1858, EX ..........**500.00**
Book, Official Rules of Card Games, Hoyle, US Playing Card Co, annual ............**10.00**

Book, Sucker's Success...Gambling in America, H Asbury, 1938, EX ..................................**60.00**
Book, The Gamblers, from Time-Life Old West series .....**22.00**
Book, Thompson Street Poker Club, From Life, White & Allen, 1888, EX ...........**150.00**
Book, Webster's Poker Book, HT Webster, 1925, EX ........**75.00**
Book, 40 Years Gambler on Mississippi, GH Devol, 1887, 1st edition, EX ..................**250.00**
Card press, mahogany with petit-point design, ca 1880 ....................**415.00**
Card press, plain wooden box w/loose boards & threaded wooden dowel ..............**100.00**
Card shuffler/dealer, automatic, 1940s, 5x5x5", common, ..**20.00**
Catalog, Blue Book, KC Card Co, 50+ pages, 1930s-60s, any, from $20 to ....................**63.00**
Cheating device, card trimmer, brass & steel, attached blade ........................**650.00**
Cheating device, corner rounder, brass & steel, unmarked ...........**600.00**
Cheating device, Jacob's ladder type, sleeve card hold-out w/straps ...................**3,000.00**
Chip, bone, plain, solid color, set of 100 ................................**75.00**
Chip, bone w/design or color border, 1mm thick, set of 100 ........................**150.00**
Chip, casino; Castaways...Las Vegas, $25, green w/black & yellow, 1963 .................**75.00**
Chip, casino; current or recent $1 to $5 chips, face value plus $2 to .....................................**3.00**

**Chip rack, marbleized Catalin ice-block type, 3x4x7", with 200 Catalin chips, $250.00. (Photo courtesy Robert Eisenstadt)**

Chip, Catalin or marbleized Bakelite, red, yellow & green, set of 100 ................................**60.00**

Chip, clay, embossed, inlaid or engraved, ea, from $1 to ...**7.00**

Chip, clay or metal, w/casino name, minimum value ...**3.00**

Chip, clay w/molded design, set of 100, minimum value .....**25.00**

Chip, clay w/painted engraving, set of 100, minimum value ..**45.00**

Chip, clay w/white plastic inlay, set of 100, minimum value ........................**45.00**

Chip, dealer; clay w/goat head in relief, ea ..........................**85.00**

Chip, plastic, wood or rubber, no design, set of 100 ............**5.00**

Chip, scrimshawed ivory, marked '25,' minimum value .....**50.00**

Chip, scrimshawed ivory, marked '5,' minimum value .......**35.00**

Chip, scrimshawed ivory w/concentric circle design ......**10.00**

Chip, scrimshawed ivory w/quatro or floral design, ea ........**28.00**

Chip rack, Count Rite, brown Bakelite, w/original plastic chips ..............................**100.00**

Chip rack, marbleized Bakelite, ice-block type, 3x4x7", no chips ...........................**110.00**

Chip rack, Turnit Mfg...Los Angeles Calif, 300-chip capacity, empty ...........................**125.00**

Chip rack, wood chest w/lid & pull-out rack, no chips, minimum value ..............................**70.00**

Chip rack, wood Lazy Susan (carousel) type, cover, no chips ..............................**25.00**

Counter, mother-of-pearl, etched elliptical, Canton, 1½", 1mm thick ................................**4.00**

Counter, mother-of-pearl, relief carving, 2½", 3mm thick ............................**40.00**

Dice, ivory, ⅝", pr ..............**100.00**

Dice, poker; Catalin, 2", set of 5 ............................**500.00**

Dice, poker; celluloid, card symbols on sides, set of 5, ⅝" ......**10.00**

Dice cage, felt-lined cardboard, thin wire & metal .........**40.00**

Dice cage, hide drums, heavy chrome, 9x14" .............**300.00**

Dice cup, ivory, minimum .**100.00**

Dice cup, leather .................**15.00**

Faro dealing box, metal, open top, spring for cards, minimum value ............................**400.00**

Keno goose, polished walnut bowl between posts, 13x24" ...................**750.00**

Lighter, Scripto Vu, transparent tank w/dice, original packaging ...............................**50.00**

Mah-Jong set, Catalin or bone, not extraordinary, from $70 to .................................**100.00**

Match safe, sterling w/engraved playing card etc, 1900s, from $100 to .........................**300.00**

Needlepoint card table cover w/gambling & card images, minimum value ...........**100.00**

Playing cards, faro; poker size w/sq edges, set of 52, minimum value ....................**80.00**

Roulette pocketwatch, spinner hand, red & black numbers, 1900s, minimum .........**150.00**

Roulette regulation table, w/wheel & 32" bowl, walnut, paw feet, Mason .......................**5,000.00**

Roulette wheel, 10" wood bowl w/wheel & simple design .**150.00**

Roulette wheel, 24" wood bowl w/elaborate inlays & veneer, chrome trim ................**600.00**

Roulette wheel, 32" wood bowl w/elaborate inlays & veneer ...**1,750.00**

Spinner, On Me, Bakelite, Art Deco, w/layout, MIB ...**125.00**

# Games

The ideal collectible game is one that combines playability (i.e., good strategy, interaction, surprise, etc.) with interesting graphics and unique components. Especially desirable are the very old games from the 19th and early 20th centuries as well as those relating to early or popular TV shows and movies. As always, value depends on rarity and condition of the box and playing pieces. For a greatly expanded list and more information, see *Schroeder's Collectible Toys, Antique to Modern* (Collector Books).

Amazing Spiderman, Milton Bradley, 1967, EX (EX box) ...........**125.00**

**Bewitched, Game Gems, 1965, M in (EX box), $55.00.**

Bang Box, Ideal, 1969, NMIB .**25.00**

Barney Miller, Parker Bros, 1977, VG (VG box) ..................**20.00**

Batman & Robin Pinball Game, Marx, 1966, EX ...........**175.00**

Battlestar Galactica, Parker Bros, 1978, NM (EX box) .......**20.00**

Beatlemania Trivia, 1984, EX (EX box) ...............................**20.00**

Bermuda Triangle, Milton Bradley, 1976, NMIB ...**35.00**

Big Sneeze, Ideal, 1968, NM (NM box) ...............................**30.00**

Black Beauty, Transogram, 1958, NM (EX box) .................**25.00**

Black Hole Space Alert, Whitman, 1979, MIB ......................**35.00**

Bop the Beetle, Ideal, 1962, MIB ...**45.00**

Bug-A-Boo, Whitman, 1968, EX (EX box) ..........................**25.00**

Captain Caveman, Milton Bradley, 1980, EX (EX box) .........**10.00**

Casper the Ghost, card game, 1950s-60s, NM (NM box) ............**15.00**

Charlie's Angels, Milton Bradley, 1977, NM (EX box) .......**25.00**

Chopper Strike, Milton Bradley, 1975, VG (VG box) ........**38.00**

Chutes Away!, Gabriel, 1978, EX (EX box) ..........................**65.00**

Clue, Parker Bros, 1963, EX (EX box) ...............................**25.00**

Combat, Ideal, 1963, NM (EX box) ...............................**65.00**

Countdown, ES Lowe, 1967, VG (VG box) ........................**50.00**

Crazy Clock, Ideal, 1964, NM (EX box) ...............................**75.00**

Daniel Boone, card game, Ed-U, 1965, NMIB ..................**15.00**

Davy Crockett Adventures, Gabriel, 1955, NM (EX box) ........................**95.00**

Dino the Dinosaur, Transogram, 1961, MIB ..................**100.00**

Don't Spill the Beans, Schaper, 1967, MIB (sealed) ........**25.00**

Dream House, Milton Bradley, 1968, rare, EX (EX box) ..............**60.00**

Dungeons & Dragons, Mattel, 1980, NMIB ..................**45.00**

Electra Woman, Ideal, 1977, EX (EX box) ..........................**25.00**

Fall Guy, Milton Bradley, 1982, EX (EX box) ..................**20.00**

Flintstones, card game, Ed-U, 1961, EX (EX box) ........**10.00**

Flipper Flips, Mattel, 1965, EX (EX box) ..........................**55.00**

Foto-Electric Football, Cadaco, 1965, VG (VG box) ........**25.00**

Fu Manchu's Hidden Hoard, 1967, EX (EX box) ..................**65.00**

G-Men Clue Games, Whitman, EX (EX box) ..........................**85.00**

Garrison's Gorillas, Ideal, 1967, NM (EX box) ..............**135.00**

General Hospital, Cardinal Industries, 1982, VG (VG box) ...............................**50.00**

Gidget Fortune Telling Game, Milton Bradley, 1965, NMIB ..........................**50.00**

Godfather, Family Games Inc, 1971, VG (VG box) ........**30.00**

Goldfinger, Milton Bradley, 1966, NMIB ...........................**65.00**

Great Grape Ape, Milton Bradley, 1975, EX (VG box) ........**15.00**

Green Ghost, Transogram, 1965, NMIB ...........................**90.00**

Hair Bear Bunch, Milton Bradley, 1971, NM (EX box) ......**25.00**

Hoppity Hooper, Milton Bradley, 1964, EX (EX box) ........**45.00**

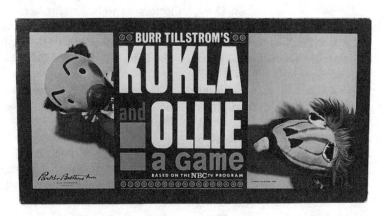

**Kukla and Ollie board game, Parker Brothers, 1962, MIB, $35.00.**
(Photo courtesy June Moon)

Hulla Baloo, Electric Teen Game, Remco, 1965, rare, NM (EX box) ..............................**150.00**

I've Got a Secret, Lowell, 1956, NM (EX box) .................**50.00**

Ipcress File, Milton Bradley, 1966, EX (EX box) ...................**25.00**

Jackson Five, Shindana, 1972, rare, NM (NM box) .**90.00**

Jeanne Dixon's Game of Destiny, 1969, MIB (sealed) ........**40.00**

Justice League of America/Flash, Hasbro, 1967, scarce, MIB (sealed) .......................**350.00**

Ka-Bala, Transogram, 1967, NM (EX box) ........................**95.00**

Kojak, Milton Bradley, 1975, VG (VG box) .......................**25.00**

Krull, Parker Bros, 1983, EX (EX box) ..............................**20.00**

Lie Detector, Mattel, 1960, EX (EX box) ..............................**35.00**

Lone Ranger, Parker Bros, 1938, VG (VG box) ..................**95.00**

Looney Tunes, Milton Bradley, 1968, VG (VG box) ..**30.00**

Lost in Space, Milton Bradley, 1965, EX (EX box) .......**95.00**

Lucky Stars, Ideal, 1960s, EX (EX box) ...............................**25.00**

Lucy Show, Transogram, 1962, MIB .............................**300.00**

Magilla Gorilla, Ideal, 1964, NMIB ..........................**150.00**

Marathon, Sports Games, 1978, VG (VG box) ..................**20.00**

Men in Space, Milton Bradley, 1960, VG (VG box) ........**95.00**

Miami Vice, Pepper Lane, 1984, EX (EX box) ..................**25.00**

Milton the Monster, Milton Bradley, 1966, NMIB ...**35.00**

Mostly Ghostly, Cadaco, 1975, EX (EX box) ........................**20.00**

New Kids on the Block, Milton Bradley, 1990, VG (VG box) ...............**20.00**

Newlywed Game, Hasbro, 1969, NMIB ............................**20.00**

Outer Limits, Milton Bradley, 1964, EX (EX box) ......**275.00**

Perils of Pauline, Marx, 1964, NM (EX box) .......................**115.00**

Peter Pan, Parker Bros, 1969, EX (EX box) ........................**45.00**

Pop Yer Top!, Milton Bradley, 1968, EX (EX box) ........**30.00**

Rat Patrol Desert Combat, Transogram, 1966, NM (EX box) .......................**125.00**

Rose-Petal Place, Parker Bros, 1984, NM (EX box) .......**25.00**

Talk to Cecil, Mattel, MIB (sealed) .....................**160.00**

Talking Football, Mattel, 1971, EX (EX box) .......................**100.00**

Tammy, Ideal, 1965, 2nd issue, NM (NM box) ...............**50.00**

Tic Tac Dough, Transogram, 1957, VG (VG box) ..................**15.00**

Trump, Milton Bradley, 1989, EX (EX box) ........................**15.00**

Underdog to the Rescue, Whitman, 1970s, EX (EX box) ........**40.00**

Yacht Race, Parker Bros, 1961, VG (VG box) .......................**85.00**

77 Sunset Strip, Lowell, 1960, NM (EX box) ........................**70.00**

# Gas Station Collectibles

From the invention of the automobile came the need for gas service stations, who sought to attract customers through a wide variety of advertising methods. Gas and oil companies issued thermometers, signs, calendars, clocks, banks, and scores of other items emblazoned with their logos and catchy slogans. Though a rather specialized area, gas station collectibles encompass a wide variety of items that appeal to automobilia and advertising collectors as well. For further information we recommend *Huxford's Collectible Advertising* by Sharon and Bob Huxford, and *Value Guide to Gas Station Memorabilia* by B.J. Summers and Wayne Priddy. Both are published by Collector Books.

Atlas, Chevron Travel Club, USA-Canada, unused ...........**10.00**

Bank, Atlas Battery, metal, EX .**22.00**

Banner, Kendall Oil, red silk w/gold fringe, EX ..........**35.00**

Blotter, Texaco Motor Oil, shows early auto, driver & garage man, EX ........................**10.00**

Calendar, Esso, 1953, w/various scenes, 29½x16", EX ......................**30.00**

Calendar, Texaco, 1941, incomplete, 19x9½", EX .........**20.00**

Can, Macmillan Grease, M & Ring Free, red & white, 1-lb, EX ................................**15.00**

Car-care guide & lube chart, Chevron, 1970, EX ........**15.00**

Cigarette box, Firestone Supreme Batteries, composition, VG .**5.00**

Clock, Firestone, tractor tire shape, EX ......................**75.00**

Cup, Shell, folding plastic, NM ..**10.00**

Dip-stick clip, Sinclair Oil, oil-can shape, EX ......................**10.00**

Display rack, Goodyear Tires, tin, 1950s-60s, 25", NM .......**80.00**

Display rack, Mohawk Tires, painted tin, arrowhead logo, 13x9", EX ......................**60.00**

Display rack, Prestone Anti-Freeze, metal, 4-legged, 20x21x16", VG .............**60.00**

Fan, Cities Service/Maron Oil Co, cardboard paddle shape, Biblical, G ..............................**15.00**

First-aid kit, Shell Oil Co, brown steel cabinet, M ..............**75.00**

Gas-mileage finder, Texaco, VG+ ............................**20.00**

Gasoline pump nozzle, brass, 15", NMIB ............................**30.00**

Globe, Aetna Oil, 3-pc, all glass, red & white, 13½", EX .......**450.00**

Globe, Atlantic Gasoline, red, white, blue, glass case, 16½", VG+ ............................**150.00**

Globe, Cities Service Oils, clover logo, 1928, 15" dia, EX .**250.00**

Grease pail, Panther Oil & Grease, red, black & silver, 10-lb, VG ......................**40.00**

Hat, attendant's, Standard Oil, summer-style mesh, 1960s, EX ...............................**175.00**

Mask, Texaco Fire Chief, diecut cardboard image of Ed Winn, 12x15", EX .....................**50.00**

Matchbook cover, Union 76, EX .**4.00**

Mug, Esso, tiger logo on milk glass, Anchor Hocking, 1970s, 3½", VG ...........................**8.00**

Oil bottle, Enarco, metal cone-shape spout, 1-qt, NM .**130.00**

Oil can, Gargoyle Mobiloil A, cream & red, sq, 1-gal, 10x5x5", EX .................**130.00**

Oil can, Gulfpride, orange & blue, sq, 5-gal, VG .................**55.00**

Oil can, Quaker Maid, waxed cardboard, 1-qt, VG .............**35.00**

**Oil rack, Brookins, embossed bottles with metal rack, 15½x18½", EX-, $120.00.**

**Maps, Tydol, paper, minor soiling, $20.00 for the pair.**

Map holder, Texaco Touring Service, metal, red shield, w/maps, EX ..................**80.00**

Paperweight mirror, Phillips 66 Silver Anniversary, 3½" dia, NM ...............................**120.00**

Pencil clip, Standard Oil, EX .**8.00**

Pump sign, Atlantic White Flash, metal, white & black on red, 17x13", M ....................**125.00**

Radio, Sinclair Dino Supreme Gasoline, resembles modern pump, 4", EX .................**40.00**

Restroom key tags, Texaco, Men/Ladies, paddle shape, 5½", M, pr ...................**135.00**

Salt & pepper shakers, Conoco Super, plastic pump form, EX, pr ...................................**40.00**

Scrapper, Sweney Motor Oil, name on wooden handle, 3½x2¼", EX ...................................**20.00**

Sign, Jenny Aero, porcelain, red, white & blue, 12x9", NM ..........................**160.00**

Thermometer, Prestone Anti-Freeze, porcelain, 1940s, 36x9", EX .....................**100.00**

Tie pin, brass-colored Goodyear figural blimp, EX ..........**15.00**

## Gaudy Italian

Here's a new category of collectible pottery you may want to start picking up while it's still very reasonable. Marked only 'Italy' it has a rather primitive style that has all the charm of the Italian countryside. It was manufactured from about 1950 until the 1970s, handmade and hand painted, and though flowers seem to be most in evidence, you'll find items decorated with fruit and animals as well. Some of the designs are very reminiscent of Blue Ridge and, in fact, may have been copies.

Basket, lg, 10" to 8", from $20 to ...............................**22.00**

Basket, med, 6" to 8", from $10 to ................................**15.00**

Basket, sm, 4", from $6 to .....**8.00**

Bowl, vegetable; w/lid ..........**15.00**

Bowl, vegetable; 9" ...............**10.00**

Bowl, 10½" dia .....................**15.00**

Box, cigarette; sq ................**15.00**

Box, ring; sm .........................**5.00**

Figurine, from 14" to 16", up to .........................**125.00**

Lamp, bedroom; sm, from $20 to .............................**35.00**

Lamp, living room; lg, minimum value ..............................**65.00**

Plate, dinner ..........................**8.00**

**Plate, floral with yellow basketweave, 10½" square, $15.00.**

## Gay Fad

Here's another new area of collecting that's just now taking off. The company started out on a very small scale in the late 1930s, but before long, business was booming! Their first products were hand-decorated kitchenwares, but it's their frosted tumblers, trays, pitchers, and decanters that are being sought out today. In addition to souvenir items and lines with a holiday theme, they made glassware to coordinate with Royal China's popular dinnerware, Currier and Ives. They're also known for their 'bentware' — quirky cocktail glasses with stems that were actually bent. Look for an interlocking 'G' and 'F' or the name 'Gay Fad,' the latter mark indicating pieces from the late 1950s to the early '60s.

Our advisor for this category is Donna S. McGrady; she is listed in the Directory under Ohio.

Ashtray, Trout Flies, clear ....**5.00**
Bent tray, Stylized Cats, clear, signed Gay Fad, 11½" dia .............**14.00**
Beverage set, magnolia, clear, 86-oz pitcher & 6 13-oz tumblers, 7-pc .....................**45.00**
Canister set, Red Rose, red lids, white interior, 3-pc .......**55.00**
Casserole, tulips (rosemaling) on lid, clear, 2-qt, w/black wire rack ...............................**20.00**
Cocktail shaker, full-figure ballerina, frosted, 28-oz, 9" .....**35.00**
Cruet set, Oil & Vinegar, Cherry, clear ...............................**15.00**
Goblet, Bow Pete, Hoffman Beer, 16-oz ..............................**12.00**
Ice tub, Gay 90s, frosted ......**16.00**
Juice set, Tommy Tomato, frosted, 36-oz pitcher & 6 4-oz tumblers, 7-pc.......................**45.00**
Mug, Notre Dame, frosted, 16-oz ...............................**15.00**
Pitcher, Currier & Ives, blue & white, frosted, 86-oz .....**50.00**
Pitcher, tulips (rosemaling), white inside, 32-oz .................**28.00**

Punch set, turquoise veiling, bowl & 8 cups in metal frame .....**65.00**
Salad set, Fruits, frosted, lg bowl, 2 cruets, salt & pepper shakers .................................**50.00**
Stem, bent cocktail; Souvenir of My Bender, frosted, 3-oz ......**11.00**

**Tumbler, Gay Nineties series, one of eight, 12-oz, from $6.00 to $8.00.**

Tumbler, Christmas Greetings From Gay Fad, frosted, 4-oz ..............................**12.00**
Tumbler, Hors D'oeuvres, clear, 14-oz ...............................**8.00**
Tumbler, Pegasus, gold & pink on black, 12-oz .....................**8.00**
Tumbler, Zombie, Giraffe, frosted, marked GF, 14-oz .........**15.00**
Tumblers, Ohio Presidents, frosted, 12-oz, set of 8 .........**60.00**
Tumblers, Sports Cars, white interior, 12-oz, set of 8 ........**45.00**
Vase, Red Poppy, clear, footed, 10" ...............................**22.00**

Wine set, Grapes, decanter & 4 2½-oz stemmed wines, clear, 5-pc ...............................**35.00**

# GI Joe

Toys are the big news of the '90s, as far as collectibles go, and GI Joe dolls vie for a spot near the top of many a collector's want list.

Introduced by Hasbro in 1964, 12" GI Joe dolls were offered in four basic packages: Action Soldier, Action Sailor, Action Marine, and Action Pilot. A Black figure was included in the line, and there were representatives of many nations as well. Talking dolls followed a few years later, and scores of accessory items such as vehicles, guns, uniforms, etc., were made to go with them all. Even though the line was discontinued in 1976, it was evident the market was still there, and kids were clamoring for more. So in 1982, Hasbro brought out the 'little' 3¾" GI Joe dolls, each with his own descriptive name. Sales were unprecedented. The small figures are easy to find, but most of them are 'loose' and played with. Collectors prefer old store stock still in the original packaging; such examples are worth from two to four times more than those without the package.

For more information we recommend *Collectible Male Action Figures, Second Edition,* by Paris and Susan Manos; *Schroeder's Collectible Toys, Antique to Modern*;

and *Dolls in Uniform* by Joseph Bourgeois. All of these books are published by Collector Books.

**12" Figures and Accessories**

Action Pack Turbo Copter, MIB (sealed) ..........................**50.00**
Action Pilot, 30th Anniversary, NRFB ..........................**140.00**
Action Soldier, original outfit, boots & hat, EX ..........**100.00**
Adventure Team Fire Suit, silver, EX ..................................**25.00**
Adventure Team Raft, yellow, EX ................................**12.00**
Adventure Team Sea Adventurer, original outfit, EX .......**155.00**
Air Cadet Hat, EX ..............**25.00**
Annapolis Cadet Jacket, G ..**25.00**
Big Trapper, VG ..................**75.00**
Bivouac Sleeping Bag, #7515, MOC ..............................**55.00**
Command Post Poncho, #7519, MOC ..............................**55.00**

**Duke, Hall of Fame, Real American Hero series, 1991, MIB, $70.00.**

Crash Crew, complete, EX .**180.00**

Deep Sea Diver, complete, MIB ........................**885.00**

Deep Sea Diver Helmet, EX .**25.00**

Fighter Pilot, complete, NM .**550.00**

German Field Pack, EX .......**25.00**

Life Ring, MOC ...................**45.00**

Medic Flag, EX ....................**32.00**

Military Policeman, complete, EX .............................**200.00**

Motorcycle & Sidecar, complete, MIB ..............................**425.00**

Parachute, white cloth w/strings, EX ..................................**25.00**

**Radio Command Unit, combination AM radio and microphone, with Morse code button, NM, $100.00. (Photo courtesy Cotswold Collectibles)**

Rifle, black, w/scope, EX .....**15.00**

Sailor Cap, EX .....................**15.00**

Scramble Pilot, complete, EX .**300.00**

Scuba Tank, NM ..................**25.00**

Ski Patrol, complete, EX ...**250.00**

Space Coveralls, white, EX .**30.00**

Team Vehicle, yellow ATV, VG (G box) ...............................**85.00**

West Point Cadet Jacket, EX .**30.00**

## 3¾" Figures and Accessories

Ace, 1983, MIP ....................**25.00**

Ammo Dump Unit, 1985, EX (EX package) ........................**20.00**

Astro Viper, 1988, MIP .......**12.00**

Attack Vehicle Vamp w/Clutch, 1982, EX ......................**40.00**

Big Boa, 1987, MIP .............**25.00**

Bomb Disposal Unit, 1985, MIP .........................**20.00**

Clutch, 1988, MOC .............**18.00**

Cobra Pom-Pom Gun, 1983, EX ...**15.00**

Cover Girl, 1983, MIP .........**45.00**

Crystal Ball, 1986, MOC .....**15.00**

D-Day, 1995, MOC ................**7.00**

Deep Six w/Finback, 1992, MOC ..**15.00**

Dictator, 1989, w/instructions, EX ...............................**10.00**

Duke, 1985, MOC ..............**100.00**

Flame Thrower, 1983, EX .....**5.00**

Flint, 1985, MOC ................**55.00**

**Hawk, 1987, missing helmet, NM, $10.00.**

Gnawgahyde, 1989, MOC ....**20.00**

Hardball, 1988, MOC ..........**18.00**

Jinx, 1987, w/accessories, EX .**9.00**

Machine Gun, 1983, EX ........**5.00**

Mainframe, 1986, MOC .......**32.00**

Maverick, 1988, MOC ..........**27.00**

Mercer, 1987, w/accessories, EX ...............................**8.00**
Motor Viper, 1986, MOC .....**22.00**
Mountain Howitzer, 1984, w/accessories, EX ............**8.00**
Ninja Force Zartan, 1993, MOC .**12.00**
Pogo, 1987, complete, EX ......**8.00**
Raptor, 1987, MOC ..............**20.00**
Ripper, 1985, MOC ..............**36.00**
Sci-Fi, 1991, MOC ................**15.00**
Slaughter's Marauders Footloose, MOC ...............................**18.00**
Steeler, 1983, MOC ..............**35.00**
Sub-Zero, 1990, MOC ..........**15.00**
Tele-Viper, 1989, MOC ........**15.00**
Topside, 1990, MOC ............**15.00**
Tunnel Rat, 1987, MOC ......**25.00**
Wild Bill, 1992, MOC ..........**10.00**

# Glass Animals and Birds

Nearly every glasshouse of note has at some point over the years produced these beautiful models, some of which double for vases, bookends, and flower frogs. Many were made during the 1930s through the '50s and '60s, and these are the most collectible. But you'll also be seeing brand new examples, and you need to study to know the difference. A good reference to help you sort them all out is *Glass Animals of the Depression Era* by Lee Garmon and Dick Spencer (Collector Books). See also Boyd; Fenton.

Angelfish, bookend, amber (crystal or frosted), Imperial ...**100.00**
Angelfish, crystal, Heisey ..**140.00**

Bird, candle holder, crystal, Fostoria, 1½" ..........................**20.00**
Bird, medium dark blue, Viking, 9½" ..................................**35.00**
Bridge hound, amber, Cambridge ..................**45.00**
Bunny, cotton-ball dispenser, blue frosted, ears back, Paden City ..................**125.00**
Bunny, crystal, head up, New Martinsville ..................**60.00**
Butterfly, Green Mist, Westmoreland, 2½" ......................**25.00**
Cardinal, Green Mist, Westmoreland ........................**20.00**
Cat, black, glossy, Tiffin, lg .**250.00**
Chick, milk glass, head up, Imperial ....................................**10.00**
Cock, Fighting; blue, LE Smith, 9" ..................................**45.00**
Colt, crystal, Fostoria ..........**50.00**
Colt, Horizon Blue, kicking, Imperial ................................**35.00**
Cygnet (baby swan), crystal, Heisey, 2½" ................**210.00**
Dolphin, candle holder, pink, hexagonal foot, 9½" ......**75.00**
Duck, ashtray, red, Duncan & Miller, 7" ......................**90.00**
Duck, orange, round, footed, Viking, 5" ......................**35.00**
Elephant, bookend, ebony, Fostoria, 6½" ...............**125.00**
Elephant, crystal, Heisey, sm .**225.00**
Fish, candlestick, Sunshine Yellow, Imperial, 5" ..........**50.00**
Goose, crystal, Paden City ..**60.00**
Goose, crystal, wings half, Heisey ......................**100.00**
Horse, bookend, ruby, rearing, LE Smith ............................**45.00**
Horse, crystal, rearing, Fostoria, #2564 ..............................**48.00**

Irish setter, ashtray, crystal, Heisey .............................**30.00**

Lady's leg, bookends, custard, Mosser, pr ....................**175.00**

Mallard, caramel slag, wings up, Imperial .........................**40.00**

Mopey dog, crystal, Federal, 3½" ............................**10.00**

Nautilus shell, bookend, crystal frost, New Martinsville, 6" .........**35.00**

**Rooster, vase, crystal, Heisey, 6¼x6", $95.00.**

Piglet, crystal, sitting; Heisey .**100.00**

Polar bear on ice, crystal, Paden City, 4½" ........................**65.00**

Pouter pigeon, bookend, crystal, Indiana, 5½" ...................**40.00**

Pouter pigeon, bookend, milk glass, Cambridge, 5½" ..**95.00**

Robin, crystal, Westmoreland, 5⅛" ................................**20.00**

Rooster, Epic; red, Viking, 9½" (reproduced) ..................**60.00**

Rooster, pink, fighting, Imperial .............................**175.00**

Rooster head, stopper, crystal, Heisey, 4½" ...................**45.00**

Seal w/ball, candle holder, crystal, New Martinsville, 4½" .**70.00**

Sparrow, crystal, Heisey ...**120.00**

Squirrel on curved log, crystal, Paden City, 5½" ............**65.00**

Swan, candle holders, ruby, New Martinsville, pr .............**70.00**

Swan, crystal, solid, Duncan & Miller, 5" .......................**30.00**

Swan, ebony, Cambridge, 3" .**65.00**

Swan, milk glass, Cambridge, 6½" .............................**125.00**

Terrier, Parlour Pup, amethyst carnival, Imperial, 3½" .**45.00**

Thrush, blue frost, LE Smith .**20.00**

Tropical fish, ashtray, pink opalescent, Duncan & Miller, 3½" .............................**50.00**

Whale, crystal, Fostoria ......**25.00**

Wood duckling, Sunshine Yellow satin, floating, Imperial .**20.00**

Wren, light blue, Westmoreland, 2½" .................................**22.50**

# Glass Knives

Glass fruit and cake knives, which are generally between 7½" and 9¼" long, were made in the United States from about 1920 to 1950. Distribution was at its greatest in the late 1930s and early 1940s. Glass butter knives, which are about 5" to 6½", were made in Czechoslovakia. Colors of the fruit and cake knives generally follow Depression glass dinnerware: crystal, light blue, light green, pink, and more rarely amber, forest green, and white (opal). The range of butter knife colors is even broader, including

**Plain handle, green, 9", $30.00.**

bicolors with crystal. Glass knives are frequently found with hand-painted decorations. Many were engraved with a name and occasionally with a greeting. Original boxes are frequently found along with a paper insert extolling the virtues of the knife and describing its care. As long as the original knife shape is maintained and the tip is not damaged, glass knives with nicked or reground blades are acceptable to collectors.

Our advisor for this category is Michele A. Rosewitz; she is listed in the Directory under California.

Aer-Flo (Grid), forest green, 7½" .........................**250.00**
Aer-Flo (Grid), pink, 7½" .....**75.00**
BK CO/ESP 12-14-20, crystal, hand-painted handle, 9" ...........**25.00**
Block, crystal, MIB .............**20.00**
Block, pink, Atlantic City engraving, 8¼" ........................**30.00**
Butter, green or crystal, 6¼", ea .**25.00**
Cryst-O-Lite (3 flowers), crystal, 8½" ................................**10.00**
Dagger, crystal, 9¼", from $75 to .............................**85.00**
Dur-X, 3-leaf, blue, 8½" & 9", ea ...........................**35.00**
Dur-X, 3-leaf, green, 8½" & 9", ea ...........................**35.00**

Dur-X, 5-leaf, blue, 9" .........**40.00**
Dur-X, 5-leaf, green, 9" ........**40.00**
Plain handle, light pink, 9" ..**35.00**
Rosespray, crystal ................**25.00**
Steel-Ite, crystal, 8½" ..........**35.00**
Steel-Ite, pink or green, 8½", ea .**65.00**
Stonex, amber, 8½" ............**200.00**
Stonex, crystal, 8½" .............**35.00**
Stonex, green, 8½" ..............**75.00**
Thumbguard, crystal, hand-painted handle, 9" .................**25.00**
Vitex (Star & Diamond), blue or pink, 8½" & 9", ea .........**30.00**
Vitex (Star & Diamond), crystal, 8½" & 9", ea ..................**15.00**

# Golden Foliage

If you can remember when this glassware came packed in boxes of laundry soap, you're telling your age. Along with 'white' margarine, Golden Foliage was a product of the 1950s. It was made by the Libbey Glass Company, and the line was rather limited; as far as we know, we've listed the entire assortment here. The glassware features a satin band with various leaves and gold trim. (It also came in silver.)

Our advisors for this category are Debbie and Randy Coe; they are listed in the Directory under Oregon.

Drink set, includes 6 jiggers & brass-finished caddy .....**35.00**
Drink set, includes 8 tumblers (9-oz), ice tub & brass-finished caddy ...........................**50.00**
Goblet, cordial; 1-oz ...............**8.50**
Goblet, sherbet; 6½-oz ...........**3.50**
Goblet, water; 9-oz .................**6.50**

**Tumbler, 10-oz, $6.50; Water goblet, 9-oz, $6.50.**

Ice tub ...................................**14.50**
Pitcher, 5¼", w/metal frame .**12.50**
Tumbler, beverage; 12½-oz ...**8.50**
Tumbler, jigger; 2-oz ..............**7.00**
Tumbler, juice; 6-oz ...............**5.00**
Tumbler, old fashioned; 9-oz ..**4.50**
Tumbler, water; 10-oz ...........**6.50**

# Graniteware

Graniteware is actually a base metal with a coating of enamel. It was first made in the 1870s, but graniteware of sorts was made well into the 1950s. In fact, some of what you'll find today is brand new. But new pieces are much lighter in weight than the old ones. Look for seamed construction, metal handles, and graniteware lids on such things as tea- and coffeepots. All these are indicators of age. Colors are another, and swirled pieces — cobalt blue and white, green and white, brown and white, and red and white — are generally older, harder to find, and therefore more expensive. For a comprehensive look at this popular collectible, we recommend *The Collector's Encyclopedia of Graniteware, Colors, Shapes and Value, Books I and II*, by Helen Greguire (Collector Books).

Baking pan, lg blue & white swirl, white interior, oblong, EX .**115.00**
Batter jug, med gray mottle, Extra Agate Nickel..., NM ....**375.00**
Bowl, mixing; lg black & cream swirl, black trim, M ....**225.00**
Bread box, white w/light blue veins, round, EX .........**395.00**
Bucket, lg black & white swirl, tin lid, wood bail, lg, M ....**575.00**
Cake pan, light green, white & black mottle, triple coated, oblong, EX ...................**350.00**
Coffee boiler, lg cobalt & white swirl, M .......................**325.00**
Coffee flask, solid blue, cork-lined screw top, seamed, NM .**285.00**
Coffeepot, fine red & white mottle, pewter trim, Manning-Bowman, NM .....................**275.00**
Colander, shaded violet, footed, EX ...............................**225.00**
Cream can, lg blue & white swirl, black trim, seamless, EX ............................**525.00**

Cup & saucer, white w/cobalt trim, child size, EX ...............**50.00**

Dipper, gray mottle, hollow handle applied w/lip-type bracket, NM ...............................**40.00**

Double boiler, lg blue & white swirl, Lava Ware, EX ......................**395.00**

Dust pan, dark blue, applied black handle, seamless, NM .........................**225.00**

Funnel, red & white 'snow on the mountain,' red trim, EX .**275.00**

Grater, solid gray, revolving, EX ...........................**145.00**

Kettle, Berlin-style, cobalt & white 'chicken wire,' Elite, w/lid, NM ...................**180.00**

Ladle, oyster; med gray mottle, perforated, EX ...............**75.00**

Ladle, soup; lg cobalt & gray mottle, white interior, EX .........................**95.00**

Measure, lg blue & white 'chicken wire,' Paragon, NM .........................**210.00**

Milk can, Boston-style, white w/dark blue trim, EX ..**125.00**

Milk can, lg blue & white mottle, black trim, flat ears, NM ...........**395.00**

Muffin pan, lg light blue & white swirl, 8-cup, EX ..........**295.00**

Mug, lg cobalt & white swirl, NM ...........................**125.00**

Mug, lg green & white swirl w/black trim, Emerald Ware, lg, G .............................**150.00**

Pie plate, lg cobalt & gray mottle, gray interior, NM .........**75.00**

Pie plate, lg cobalt & white swirl w/black trim, M ..........**125.00**

Pitcher, milk; light green & white relish, blue trim, EX ...**160.00**

Pitcher, water; lg green & white swirl w/blue trim, Chrysolite, EX ................................**595.00**

Plate, dessert; lg aqua & white swirl w/cobalt trim, EX ..........**125.00**

Plate, luncheon; lg yellow & white swirl w/black trim, M .............................**35.00**

Roaster, lg blue & white swirl w/black trim, flat top, 3-pc, NM ...............................**375.00**

Salt box, red w/black trim, NM .**145.00**

Skimmer, cobalt w/white interior, perforated, handled, EX .**135.00**

Skimmer, med black & white mottle, perforated, handled, EX ................................**85.00**

Spoon, lg blue & white swirl, white interior, NM ...............**125.00**

Strainer, lg blue & white swirl, white interior, hollow handle, EX ................................**310.00**

Sugar shaker, white w/green trim, seamless body, cork plug, M ......................**225.00**

Tea steeper, shaded violet w/black handle, tin lid, Thistle Ware, M ..................................**225.00**

Teakettle, lg blue & white swirl w/black trim, bail handle, EX .............................**395.00**

Teakettle, lg yellow & white swirl w/black trim, M ..........**195.00**

Teapot, calla lilies on white, pewter trim, M ............**295.00**

Teapot, cobalt, straight tubular handle, NM .................**240.00**

Trivet, windmill scene, dark blue on white, round, handled, EX .............................**125.00**

Wash basin, lg blue & white swirl, Blue Diamond Ware, lg, NM .......................**195.00**

# Griswold

Cast-iron cooking ware was used extensively in the 19th century, and even today lots of folks think no other type of cookware can measure up. But whether they buy it to use or are strictly collectors, Griswold is the name they hold in highest regard. During the latter part of the 19th century, the Griswold company began to manufacture the finest cast-iron kitchenware items available at that time. Soon after they became established, they introduced a line of lightweight, cast-aluminum ware that revolutionized the industry. The company enjoyed many prosperous years until its closing in the late 1950s. You'll recognize most items by the marks, which generally will include the Griswold name; for instance, 'Seldon Griswold' and 'Griswold Mfg. Co.' But don't overlook the 'Erie' mark, which the company used as well.

Our advisor for this category is Grant Windsor; he is listed in the Directory under Virginia. See also Clubs and Newsletters.

Aebleskiver pan, #32 ...........**35.00**
Cake mold, lamb form, #866 .**100.00**
Cornstick pan, #273 .............**35.00**
Dutch oven, #8, hinged lid ..**80.00**
Gem pan, #8, Erie USA .....**250.00**
Griddle, #9, Erie/slant logo, oval ...........................**175.00**
Meatloaf pan, #977, 2¾x10⅛x5½" .............**450.00**
Muffin pan, #21 .................**150.00**

Skillet, #12, block letters, smoke ring ..............................**100.00**
Skillet, #14, block logo .......**200.00**
Skillet, #6, slant logo, EPU .**40.00**
Skillet, #9, Victor .................**45.00**
Skillet lid, #3, high dome, smooth top ................................**275.00**
Skillet lid, #8, high dome, writing ...............................**50.00**

**Skillet, #80/1103, marked Double Skillet Top, Erie PA USA, with Griswold trademark, $100.00.**

Waffle iron, #11, sq, high base .**150.00**
Waffle iron, #11, sq, low base..**200.00**

# Gurley Candles

Santas, choir boys, turkeys, and angels are among the figural candles made by this company from the 1940s until as late as the 1960s, possibly even longer. They range in size from 2½" to nearly 9", and they're marked 'Gurley' on the bottom. Because they were so appealing, people were reluctant to burn them and instead stored them away and used them again and again. You can still find them today, especially at the flea market level. Tavern candles (they're marked as well) were made by a company owned by Gurley; they're also collectible.

Our advisors for this category are Debbie and Randy Coe; they are listed in the Directory under Oregon.

Birthday/wedding, bride or groom, 4½", ea ...............................**9.50**
Birthday/wedding, Western boy or girl, 3", ea .........................**8.50**
Christmas, Black man caroler, red clothes, 3" .........................**6.00**
Christmas, candelabra, green w/red candle, 5" ...............**7.50**
Christmas, deer, 3", stands before 5" candle ..........................**6.50**
Christmas, grotto w/star, angel & baby, blue, 4½" ................**7.50**
Christmas, lamppost, yellow cap & garland, 5½" ....................**3.50**
Christmas, man caroler, red clothes, 7" .........................**8.50**
Christmas, Rudolf w/red nose, 3" ...................................**2.50**
Christmas, Santa sitting on present on sled, 3" ................**8.50**
Christmas, snowman w/red hat running, 3" ......................**8.50**
Christmas, snowman w/red pipe & green hat, 5" ....................**5.00**
Easter, birdhouse, pink w/yellow bird, 3" .............................**7.50**
Easter, egg w/bunny inside, pink, 3" .......................................**8.50**
Easter, lily, white w/blue lip & green candle, 3" ..............**4.00**
Easter, rabbit w/carrot, winking, pink, 3¼" .........................**3.50**

Halloween, ghost, white, 4½" .**5.00**
Halloween, owl on stump, black & orange, 3½" .....................**2.50**
Halloween, pumpkin w/black cat, 2½" ...................................**7.00**
Halloween, skeleton, 8½" ....**18.00**
Halloween, witch, black, 8" .**15.00**
Halloween, witch w/black cape, 3½" ...................................**7.50**
Thanksgiving, Indian male, red clothes, 5" ........................**9.50**
Thanksgiving, sailing ship, gold, 7½" ...................................**6.50**

# Hall

Most famous for their extensive lines of teapots and colorful dinnerware, the Hall China Company still operates in East Liverpool, Ohio, where they were established in 1903. Refer to *The Collector's Encyclopedia of Hall China* by Margaret and Kenn Whitmyer (Collector Books) for more information. See also Clubs and Newsletters. For listings of Hall's most popular dinnerware line, see Autumn Leaf.

Acacia, casserole, Medallion .**35.00**
Arizona, salt & pepper shakers, Tomorrow's Classic, pr .**18.00**
Beauty, bowl, salad; 9½" .....**27.00**
Beauty, teapot, Rutherford ..**225.00**
Blue Blossom, custard, Thick Rim ...................................**18.00**
Blue Bouquet, ball jug, #3 ...................................**100.00**
Blue Bouquet, casserole, Radiance, lg ..........................**35.00**
Blue Willow, casserole, 5" ...**45.00**

Bouquet, butter dish, Tomorrow's Classic ...........................**95.00**

Buckingham, bowl, vegetable; 8¾" sq ....................................**18.00**

Buckingham, vase, Tomorrow's Classic ...........................**35.00**

Cameo Rose, bowl, cream soup; E-style, 5" ...........................**85.00**

Caprice, candlestick, Tomorrow's Classic, 8" .......................**30.00**

Caprice, egg cup, Tomorrow's Classic ...........................**25.00**

Carrot/Golden Carrot, bowl, batter; Five Band ...............**65.00**

Casual Living, bean pot, Ziesel ..**60.00**

Casual Living, casserole, Zeisel, individual ......................**18.00**

Century Fern, ashtray ...........**6.00**

Century Fern, casserole .....**30.00**

Christmas Tree & Holly, mug, Irish Coffee; 3-oz ...........**22.00**

Classic Spring, bowl, fruit; Tomorrow's Classic, footed, lg .....................................**32.00**

Classic Spring, gravy boat, Tomorrow's Classic ..................**25.00**

Clover/Golden Clover, casserole, round, 10" ......................**55.00**

Crocus, cake safe, metal ......**35.00**

Crocus, leftover, rectangular, D-style ...............................**55.00**

Dripolator coffeepot, Bricks & Ivy ..............................**30.00**

Dripolator coffeepot, Wicker .**40.00**

Eggshell, bean pot, New England; Dot, #3 ...........................**95.00**

Fantasy, butter dish, Tomorrow's Classic ...........................**75.00**

Fantasy, leftover, loop handle .**110.00**

Five Band, syrup, colors other than red or cobalt .........**50.00**

Floral Lattice, canister, Radiance ...................**125.00**

Floral Lattice, onion soup, individual ...................................**35.00**

Frost Flowers, creamer, Tomorrow's Classic .........**9.00**

Frost Flowers, gravy boat, Tomorrow's Classic ..................**25.00**

Game Bird, cup & saucer, E-style .............................**18.00**

Gold Label, baker, French ...**14.00**

Gold Label, jug, Rayed ........**14.00**

Heather Rose, coffeepot, Terrace .**40.00**

Heather Rose, gravy boat & underplate, E-style .................**20.00**

Holiday, bowl, fruit; Tomorrow's Classic, 5¾" .....................**5.50**

Holiday, creamer, Tomorrow's Classic ...........................**9.00**

Homewood, sugar bowl, Art Deco ...........................**30.00**

Lyric/Mulberry, butter dish, Tomorrow's Classic .......**80.00**

Meadow Flower, bowl, Thick Rim, 6" ....................................**18.00**

Meadow Flower, salt & pepper shakers, handled, pr .....**44.00**

Medallion, creamer, ivory ......**4.00**

Medallion, teapot, Lettuce, 64-oz .**90.00**

**Orange Poppy, pretzel jar, 7", from $85.00 to $95.00.**

Morning Glory, casserole, Thick Rim ................................**32.00**

Morning Glory, custard, straight-sided, 3½" ......................**13.00**

Mums, bowl, round, 9¼" ......**27.00**

Mums, coffeepot, Terrace ....**70.00**

No 488, baker, French .........**29.00**

Orange Poppy, bowl, cereal; 6" ..**16.00**

Orange Poppy, creamer, Great American .......................**18.00**

Pastel Morning Glory, bowl, Radiance, 9" ..........................**22.00**

Pert, bean pot, Cadet, tab handles ................................**32.00**

Pert, custard, Chinese Red, straight-sided ..................**9.00**

Pine Cone, bowl, Tomorrow's Classic, 9" ............................**27.00**

Pine Cone, onion soup, w/lid, Tomorrow's Classic .......**30.00**

Primrose, cake plate ............**15.00**

Radiance, casserole, ivory ...**12.00**

Radiance, teapot, red or cobalt, 6-cup ..............................**225.00**

Red Kitchenware, bowl, salad; 9" ..............................**22.00**

Red Kitchenware, pretzel jar ....**95.00**

Red Poppy, bowl, Radiance, 9" ....**18.00**

Refrigerator ware, jug, Donut, red or cobalt, lg ....................**70.00**

Ribbed, custard, russet or red, 7-oz ..................................**10.00**

Ribbed, ramekin, russet or red, scalloped, 4-oz .................**6.50**

Rose Parade, bean pot, tab handles ...............................**75.00**

Rose Parade, creamer, Pert .**16.00**

Rose White, bowl, Medallion, 7¼" ...**18.00**

Rx, casserole ........................**25.00**

Rx, gravy boat & underplate .**20.00**

Sears' Fairfax, bowl, flat soup; 8" ..**9.00**

Sears' Fairfax, plate, 10" .......**7.00**

Sears' Monticello, bowl, vegetable; w/lid ...............................**32.00**

Sears' Monticello, gravy boat & underplate ......................**18.00**

Sears' Mount Vernon, bowl, cereal; E-style, 6¼" ....................**8.00**

Sears' Richmond/Brown-Eyed Susan, pickle dish, 9" .....**5.00**

Serenade, baker, French; fluted ...**14.00**

Serenade, bowl, fruit; 5½" .....**5.50**

Shaggy Tulip, canister, Radiance ................................**140.00**

Shaggy Tulip, pretzel jar ...**145.00**

Silhouette, bowl, flared, 7¾" ..**35.00**

**Wild Poppy, dripolator, from $150.00 to $175.00.**

Silhouette, jug, Medallion, #4 .**30.00**

Springtime, pie baker ..........**20.00**

Stonewall, bowl, Radiance, 7½" .**20.00**

Stonewall, leftover, rectangular ...**60.00**

Sundial, coffeepot, red or cobalt, individual ......................**50.00**

Sundial, syrup, red or cobalt, individual ..............................**65.00**

Teapot, Airflow, cobalt w/gold, 8-cup ..................................**95.00**

Teapot, Airflow, red, 6-cup .**145.00**

Teapot, Albany, turquoise w/gold, 6-cup ..............................**45.00**

Teapot, Baltimore, Gold Label, 6-cup ..................................**50.00**

Teapot, Cleveland, emerald green, 6-cup ..............................**65.00**

Teapot, Globe, colors other than red, 6-cup ......................**85.00**

Teapot, Star, Delphinium w/gold, 6-cup ..............................**75.00**

Teapot, Starlight, Lemon Yellow, 6-cup ..............................**75.00**

Teapot, Windshield, turquoise w/gold, 6-cup .................**55.00**

Tulip, bowl, Radiance, 7½" ..**14.00**

Tulip, canister set, metal, 4-pc .**50.00**

Westinghouse, creamer, Hanging Vine ...............................**11.00**

Westinghouse, sugar bowl, Hanging Vine, w/lid ...............**15.00**

Wild Poppy, baker, oval ......**55.00**

Wildfire, bowl, oval ..............**22.00**

Wildfire, bowl, Thick Rim, 8½" ..**25.00**

Yellow Rose, plate, 9" ...........**9.00**

# Hallmark

Since 1973 the Hallmark Company has made Christmas ornaments, some of which are today worth many times their original price. Our suggested values reflect the worth of those in mint condition and in their original boxes. Refer to *The Ornament Collector's Price Guide, Hallmark's Ornaments and Merry Miniatures*, by Rosie Wells.

Our advisors for this category are the proprietors of *The Baggage Car*, which is listed in the Directory under Iowa as well as Clubs and Newsletters.

Angel Music, QX 343-9, 1979 .**22.00**

Angelic Messengers, QLX 711-3, 1987 ...............................**65.00**

Arctic Dome, QLX 711-7, 1991 ..**50.00**

Baby's Second Christmas, QX 413-3, 1986 ..........................**30.00**

Baroque Angel, QX 456-6, 1982 ......................**150.00**

Batman, QZ 585-3, 1994 .....**28.00**

Beauty of Friendship, QX 303-4, 1980 ..............................**50.00**

Bell Wreath, QX 420-9, 1983 .**35.00**

Calico Kitty, QX 403-5, 1981 ..................**22.00**

Cherry Jubilee, QX 453-2, 1989 ......................**25.00**

Chickadee, QX 451-4, 1984 .**40.00**

Country Angel, QX 504-6, 1990 ....................**150.00**

Doc Holiday, QX 467-7, 1987 .**38.00**

Dollhouse Dreams, QLX 737-2, 1993 ..............................**50.00**

Drummer Boy, QX 161-1, 1975 .**240.00**

First Christmas Together, QX 218-3, 1978 ..........................**45.00**

For Your New Home, QX 263-5, 1977 ..............................**40.00**

Friendly Fiddler, QX 434-2, 1981 ..........................**80.00**

Garfield, QX 537-4, 1992 .....**20.00**

Godchild, QX 201-7, 1983 ....**18.00**

Gone Fishing, QX 479-4, 1988 .**22.00**

Good Friends, QX 265-2, 1985 .**25.00**

Grandfather, QX 207-6, 1982 ..**18.00**

Happy the Snowman, QX 216-1, 1976 ..............................**50.00**

Heathcliff, QX 436-3, 1986 ..**25.00**

Joyful Trio, QX 437-2, 1989 .**18.00**

Kermit the Frog, QX 424-2, 1981 ..........................**110.00**

Kringle Trolley, QLX 741-3, 1994 ..........................**30.00**

Little Red Schoolhouse, QLX 711-2, 1985 ..........................**95.00**

Magical Unicorn, QX 429-3, 1986 ..........................**90.00**

Mom-To-Be, QX 491-6, 1990 ..**35.00**

New Home, QX 376-7, 1987 .**30.00**

Night Before Christmas, QX 530-7, 1991 ..........................**25.00**

Peanuts, QX 216-1, 1980 .....**30.00**

Peek-A-Boo Tree, QX 524-5, 1993 ...........................**25.00**

Peppermint Clown, QX 450-5, 1989 .............................**30.00**

**Puppy Love, QX 448-4, 1992, second in series, 2⅝", MIB, $35.00.**

Raccoon Tunes, QX 405-5, 1981 ......................**22.00**

Secret Pal, QX 542-4, 1992 .**15.00**

Sister to Sister, QX 588-5, 1993 ........................**50.00**

Swinging Angel Bell, QX 492-5, 1985 ..............................**38.00**

Sylvester & Tweety, QX 501-7, 1995 ..............................**20.00**

Ten Years Together, QX 401-3, 1986 ..............................**25.00**

Three Kittens in a Mitten, QX 431-1, 1984 ...........................**45.00**

Very Strawbeary, QX 409-1, 1988 ...........................**18.00**

Village Express, QLX 707-2, 1987 ..........................**120.00**

Winnie the Pooh & Tigger, QX 574-6, 1994 ...................**35.00**

# Halloween

Halloween items are fast becoming the most popular holiday-related collectibles on the market today. Although originally linked to pagan rituals and superstitions, Halloween has long since evolved into a fun-filled event; and the masks, noisemakers, and jack-o'-lanterns of earlier years are great fun to look for. Within the last ten years, the ranks of Halloween collectors have grown from only a few to thousands, with many overcompensating for lost time! Prices have risen rapidly and are only now leveling off and reaching a more reasonable level. As people become aware of their values, more items are appearing on the market for sale, and warehouse finds turn up more frequently.

Our advisor for this category is Pamela E. Apkarian-Russell, the Halloween Queen; she is listed in the Directory under New Hampshire. See Clubs and Newsletters for information concerning *The Trick or Treat Trader*.

Apron, crepe paper w/witch ... **30.00**

Baby dish, 3-part w/Bakelite handles, Halloween decor, 1930s, 8", NM .........................**280.00**

Batman, Ben Cooper, 1969, complete, NMIB .................**95.00**

Book, Dennison's Bogie Book, 1924, EX ......................**95.00**

Book, Georgie's Halloween, by Robert Bright, 1958, 30 pages, EX ...................................**25.00**

Book, Party, Dennison, 1928 ..**110.00**

Box, Sperry's Witch, chocolate covered marshmallows ......**50.00**

Candy container, Johnston's Shadowland Candies, tin barrel, 5", EX ................................**130.00**

Candy container, lemon-headed girl, German ................**135.00**

Catalog, Rainbo FavorWorks, Chicago, 1963 ................**65.00**

Chestnut warmer, heavy brass with witch, made in England .....**185.00**

Costume, Alf, Collegeville, MIB ..........................**20.00**

Costume, Archie, Ben Cooper, 1969, complete, NMIB ..**55.00**

Costume, Barbie, Ben Cooper, MIB ..............................**50.00**

Costume, Rocketeer, Ben Cooper, MIB ..............................**95.00**

Costume, Winky Dink, Halco, 1950s, complete, rare, NM ..........**95.00**

Crate, wood w/paper label, Halloween/Thompson Seedless, 14x18", EX ..................**100.00**

Cup, theatre; Nightmare Before Christmas, plastic .........**45.00**

**Cat pull toy, plastic, Rosen, $85.00; Clown pull toy, plastic, Rosen, USA, $85.00. (Photo courtesy Pamela Apkarian-Russel)**

Diecut, black cat atop jack-o'-lantern, 1930s, 10x12", EX ......................**175.00**

Diecut, devil, German, 1920, 5½x2½", NM ...............**100.00**

Diecut, devil w/wings, German, 1920s, 15x21", rare, EX .**100.00**

Diecut, goblin w/crepe-paper wings, USA, 1930s, 12", VG+ ...........................**85.00**

Diecut, jack-o'-lantern, Beistle, 1930s, 9", EX ................**60.00**

Diecut, witch face, German, 1920s, 13", NM .......................**100.00**

Dress, orange crepe paper w/black witch's hat .....................**35.00**

Eyeglasses, plastic, witches & jack-o'-lanterns, 1950s, NM ..........................**30.00**

Fan, black cat, 2-sided, German, 1920s, 13", EX .............**100.00**

Fan, witch, double-sided, German, 1920s, 13", EX ...............**95.00**

Figure, owl, pulp, American, 1940s, 6½", NM .........**150.00**

Figure, scarecrow, celluloid, EX ...........................**95.00**

Game, Jack-o'-Lantern Fortune, Beistle, 1920s, EX .........**40.00**

Game, Zingo Halloween Fortune & Stunt Game, Beistle, 1935, NM ................................**45.00**

Hat, yellow felt cone shape w/black cat & star, 15", EX ........**20.00**

Horn, cardboard, witch & black cat design, 1921, EX ..........**20.00**

Horn, tin, cats & witches, short, EX .................................**15.00**

Jack-o'-lantern, plastic, battery-operated, Miller, 1950s, 6", NMIB ............................**75.00**

Jack-o'-lantern, pulp, smiling face, w/insert, American, 1940s, 7", NM ...............................**150.00**

Lamp, plastic witch figure, orange & black, 1960s, 11", EX .................................**75.00**

Lamp shade, 6-panel cone shape w/upsidedown owls, 1930s, 8", EX .................................**75.00**

Lantern, black cat, full body, German, 6¼", NM .............**400.00**

Lantern, cat's head, pulp, American, 1940s-50s, 8", NM .........**375.00**

Light bulb, orange w/jack-o'-lantern face, GE 25-watt, 6¼", NM .................................**20.00**

Light set, plastic 2-sided jack-o'-lanterns & witches, Noma, 1930s, VG ....................**135.00**

Lollipop holder, devil, litho face, crepe costume, 1930s, 6", EX .............................**40.00**

Magazine, Dennison's Party Magazine, October/November, 1928, NM ....................**110.00**

Mask, skull face, papier-mache, Germany, 1920s, 8x7", EX ..**75.00**

Mug, jack-o'-lantern, Fitz & Floyd .............................**50.00**

Noisemaker, tin, double cymbal, 4 scenes on both sides, 1930s, 8", EX ..........................**250.00**

Noisemaker, tin panknocker, rectangular w/handle, 1950s, 8½", NM ........................**65.00**

Noisemaker, witch, wooden, German, 1930s, 11x6", EX .............**190.00**

Parade stick, cat face, pulp, American, 1940s, 21", EX ...................**375.00**

Poster, Unicef, 4 children ..**125.00**

Tambourine, tin, devil on yellow, Kirchof, 1950s, 6½" dia, NM ............................**115.00**

Tarot deck, Edward Gorey ..**55.00**

Teapot, witch over bat, china, English .................................**85.00**

Toasting fork, heavy brass, witch figural handle ...............**50.00**

Yard decoration, haunted house, Union Pacific, flashing lights ...........................**20.00**

# Harker

One of the oldest potteries in the East Liverpool, Ohio, area, the Harker company produced many lines of dinnerware from the late 1920s until it closed around 1970. Refer to *A Collector's Guide to Harker Pottery* by Neva W. Colbert (Collector Books) for more information.

Amy, bean pot, metal rack ..**65.00**

Amy, lifter ............................**22.00**

Amy, pie plate ......................**26.00**

Amy, teapot ..........................**37.00**

Apple & Pear, platter, 13" ...**12.50**

Cactus, cake plate ...............**24.00**

Calico Ribbon, cake plate, flat ..**15.00**

Calico Tulip, pie plate .........**20.00**

Calico Tulip, spooner ...........**28.00**

Cameo Rose, cup & saucer ....**6.00**

Cameoware, plate, 6" .............**3.00**

Cherry Blossom, plate, dinner ..**6.00**

Coronet, platter ...................**20.00**

Dainty Flower, rolling pin ...**70.00**

Deco Dahlia, custard cup ....**15.00**

Deco Dahlia, pie plate, 10" ..**30.00**

Duchess, creamer ..................**8.00**

Elk, ewer .............................**65.00**

Godey Print, bowl, fruit ........**3.00**

Godey Print, creamer ...........**8.00**

Godey Print, platter, 11¾" ..**15.00**

Heritance, bowl, divided vegetable .............................**4.00**

Ivy Vine, spoon ....................**28.00**

Melrose, lifter ......................**10.00**

Modern Tulip, cookie jar .....**48.00**

Modern Tulip, pie plate .......**24.00**

Oriental Poppy, platter, Melrose, 15" ...................................**18.50**

Petit Point I, casserole, stacking, w/lid ...............................**44.00**

Petit Point II, pie plate ........**28.00**

Pheasants, platter, signed ...**30.00**

Red Apple, casserole, w/lid, 9" .**40.00**

Red Apple, plate, 10" ...........**15.00**

**Ruffled Tulip, self-handled tray, 11¾", $25.00.**

Shadow Rose, platter ...........**13.00**

Springtime, platter ..............**20.00**

White Rose, lifter .................**12.50**

Wood Song, plate, 7" .............**8.00**

# Hartland

Hartland Plastics Inc. of Hartland, Wisconsin, produced a line of Western and Historic Horsemen and Standing Gunfighter figures during the 1950s, which are now very collectible. Using a material called virgin acetate, they molded such well-known characters as Annie Oakley, Bret Maverick, Matt Dillon, and many others, which they painted with highest attention to detail. In addition to these, they made a line of sports greats as well as religious statues. See Clubs and Newsletters for ordering information regarding the book *Hartland Horses and Riders* by Gail Fitch. Our advisor for sports figures is James Watson; he is listed in the Directory under New York.

## Sports

Babe Ruth, NM/M, from $175 to ...........................**200.00**

Dick Groat, EX, from $800 to ...................**1,000.00**

Don Drysdale, EX, from $275 to ...........................**300.00**

Don Drysdale, NM/M, from $325 to ...............................**400.00**

Duke Snider, EX, from $300 to ......................**325.00**

Duke Snider, NM/M, from $500 to ...............................**600.00**

Eddie Mathews, NM/M, from $125 to ...............................**150.00**

Ernie Banks, EX, from $200 to ...............................**225.00**

Ernie Banks, NM/M, from $250 to ...............................**350.00**

Harmon Killebrew, NM/M, from $400 to ........................**500.00**

Henry Aaron, EX, from $150 to ..........................**175.00**

Henry Aaron, NM/M, from $200 to ...............................**250.00**

Little Leaguer, 6", EX, from $100 to ...............................**125.00**

Little Leaguer, 6", NM/M, from $200 to ........................**250.00**

Louie Aparacio, EX, from $200 to ...........................**225.00**

Louie Aparacio, NM/M, from $250 to ...............................**350.00**

**Dick Grout, Pirates, NM/M, from $1,200.00 to $1,500.00; Rocky Colavito, Tigers, NM/M, from $600.00 to $700.00. (Photo courtesy James Watson)**

Mickey Mantle, NM/M, from $250 to ...................................**350.00**

Minor Leaguer, 4", EX, from $50 to ........................**75.00**

Minor Leaguer, 4", NM/M, from $100 to ........................**125.00**

Nellie Fox, NM/M, from $200 to ..**250.00**

Roger Maris, EX, from $300 to .**350.00**

Roger Maris, NM/M, from $350 to ...............................**400.00**

Stan Musial, EX, from $150 to ..**175.00**

Stan Musial, NM/M, from $200 to ...............................**250.00**

Ted Williams, NM/M, from $225 to ...............................**300.00**

Warren Spahn, NM/M, from $150 to ...................................**175.00**

Willie Mays, EX, from $150 to ...**200.00**

Willie Mays, NM/M, from $225 to ...............................**250.00**

Yogi Berra, w/mask, EX, from $150 to ........................**175.00**

Yogi Berra, w/mask, NM/M, from $175 to ........................**250.00**

Yogi Berra, w/out mask, NM/M, from $150 to ...............**175.00**

## Standing Gunfighters

Bat Masterson, NMIB .......**500.00**
Chris Colt, NM ..................**150.00**

**Brett Maverick, NM, $150.00. (Photo courtesy Ellen and Jerry Harnish)**

Clay Holiser, NM ...............**225.00**
Johnny McKay, NM ...........**800.00**
Paladin, NM .......................**400.00**
Wyatt Erp, NM .................**200.00**

## Western and Historic Horsemen

Alkine Ike, NM ..................**150.00**
Brave Eagle, NMIB ...........**300.00**
Buffalo Bill, NM .................**300.00**
Cactus Pete, NM ................**150.00**
Cheyenne, w/tag, NM ........**190.00**
Cochise, NM ........................**150.00**
Dale Evans, green, NM .....**125.00**
Davy Crockett, NM ............**550.00**
General Robert E Lee, NMIB ...**175.00**
Gil Favor, prancing, NM .....**80.00**
Hoby Gillman, NM ............**225.00**
Jim Hardy, NMIB ..............**275.00**
Josh Randle, NM ...............**650.00**
Lone Ranger, NM ..............**150.00**
Matt Dillon, w/tag, NMIB .**275.00**
Rifleman, NMIB .................**350.00**
Seth Adams, NM ................**275.00**
Sgt Lance O'Rourke, NMIB ..**250.00**
Tom Jeffords, NM ..............**175.00**
Tonto, NM ...........................**150.00**
Warpaint Thunderbird, w/shield,
    NMIB ...........................**350.00**

# Head Vases

Many of them Japanese imports, head vases were made primarily for the florist trade. They were styled as children, teenagers, clowns, and famous people. There are heads of religious figures, Blacks, Orientals, and even some animals. One of the most common types are ladies wearing pearl earrings and necklaces. Refer to *Head*

*Vases, Identification and Value Guide,* by Kathleen Cole (Collector Books) for more information.

African lady w/gold earings, yellow turban, necklace, Japan, 6½" ...............................**47.50**
Baby boy in draped blue blanket w/kitten, unmarked, 6" ..**50.00**
Baby boy in knit cap, lg black eyes, brown hair, unmarked, 5" ...................................**30.00**
Baby girl in pink ruffled bonnet w/lg bowl, unmarked, 5½" .......**45.00**
Baby w/blond hair, lg black painted eyes, unmarked, 5¼" .....**25.00**
Boy in fireman's hat, holding nozzel, Inarco label, 5" .**75.00**
Clown, red nose, green polka-dot bow tie, Napcoware, #1988, 4¾" ...............................**45.00**
Girl, long dark hair w/yellow ribbon, flower pin, Enesco label, 4½" ................................**45.00**

**Lady with pearl necklace and leaf pin, earrings missing, 7¼", $85.00.**

Girl, ponytail w/pink bow, hand w/ring up, Inarco, #E-1061, 4½" .................................**40.00**

Girl facing right, white ponytail, flowers over ear, Vcagco, 5¼" .............................**42.50**

Girl holding telephone, Inarco, #E3548, 5½" .................**65.00**

Girl holding umbrella, flowers in hair, bow at neck, unmarked, 4½" ..................................**75.00**

Girl saying prayers, blond hair, brown robe, Inarco, #E1579, 6" ......................................**45.00**

Girl w/blond flip hairdo, pearl necklace, Parma label, #A172, 5½" ..................................**65.00**

Girl w/hat & fan, blond hair, winking, unmarked, 6" .........**75.00**

Girl w/long blond hair, blue headband, Inarco, #E1967, 5½" .............................**65.00**

Girl w/long braid & knit cap, Hummel look, Relpo, #K1018B, 8" .**200.00**

Girl w/2 blond ponytails, pearl earrings, Rubens label, #4135, 5½" ..................................**75.00**

Glowing Gertie, smiling red-headed lady, Napco, 4" .........**30.00**

Indian chief, full headdress, unmarked, 8" ................**57.50**

Lady, blond curls peek from turban, rose on bodice, unmarked, 6½" .............**85.00**

Lady, blond w/flower in hair & along neckline, Napco label, #93A, 5" ........................**50.00**

Lady, frosted hair, pearl earrings/necklace, Napcoware, #C7293, 6" ......................**40.00**

Lady, white hair, hat w/bow, pearl necklace/earrings, Atlas label, 6" ......................................**50.00**

**Lady with hand to face, dark green hat and bodice, pearl necklace, 5", $45.00.**

Lady in pink, blond curls, flat hat, pearl earrings, Vcagco, 5¼" ...............................**45.00**

Lady w/black ribbon in hair, thick lashes, unmarked, #50/425, 8" .................**175.00**

Lady w/blond hair swept to side, pin on bodice, Velco, #10759, 5½" ..................................**65.00**

Lady w/hand to forehead, gold & white, pearl jewelry, unmarked, 5" .................**5.00**

Lady w/poinsettia on hat, Christmas, Inarco, #E195, 1961, 4½" ..................................**65.00**

Man, green hat & jacket, bow tie, black mustache, unmarked, 4½" ..................................**30.00**

Mary Lou, girl in bonnet w/bow at side, Relpo, 1956, 6" ...................**50.00**

Uncle Sam, allover light green, stars along hat band, unmarked, 6½" .............**30.00**

## Holly Hobbie and Friends

About 1970 a young homemaker and mother, Holly Hobbie, approached the American Greeting Company with some charming country-styled drawings of children. Since that time over four hundred items have been made with almost all being marked HH, H. Hobbie, or Holly Hobbie.

Our advisor for this category is Helen McCale; she is listed in the Directory under Missouri.

Bank, silverplated figural, Oneida, name at base, 1979, 6", from $25 to ...................**35.00**

Cookie cutters, plastic, assorted colors, 1976, set of 7, MIB, from $75 to ..................**100.00**

Cookie jar, glass, white w/blue lid, It's Cookie Time, '80, from $65 to ..................**75.00**

Doll, Country Fun Holly Hobbie, 1989, 16", NRFB ...........**20.00**

Doll, Grandma Holly, Knickerbocker, cloth, 24", MIB .**25.00**

Doll, Holly, Heather, Amy or Carrie, Knickerbocker, 16", MIB, ea ...................................**20.00**

Doll, Holly, Heather, Amy or Carrie, Knickerbocker, 27", MIB, ea ...................................**6.00**

Doll, Holly, Heather, Amy or Carrie, Knickerbocker, 33", MIB, ea ...................................**40.00**

Doll, Holly, Heather, Amy or Carrie, Knickerbocker, 9", MIB, ea ...................................**30.00**

Doll, Holly Hobbie Bicentennial, Knickerbocker, 12", MIB .**25.00**

Doll, Holly Hobbie Day 'N Night, Knickerbocker, 14", MIB ..........................**15.00**

Doll, Little Girl Holly, Knickerbocker, 1980, 15", MIB .**25.00**

Doll, Robby, Knickerbocker, 1981, 16", MIB ......................**25.00**

**Joy iron, plastics, Durham, MIB, from 20.00 to 30.00. (Photo courtesy Helen McCale)**

Doll, 25th Anniversary, cloth, Meritus, 1993, 14", MIB, from $25 to ..............................**35.00**

Doll, 25th Anniversary, cloth, Meritus, 1994, 26", MIB, from $45 to ..............................**55.00**

Dolls, Robby, Knickerbocker, 9", MIB ................................**15.00**

Figurine, Country Morning, porcelain, limited edition, 6", w/base ...........................**225.00**

Figurine, porcelain, musical base, 6", made in 6 styles, ea, from $35 to ............................**45.00**

Figurine, porcelain, 6 different made, 1973, 8", ea, from $100 to ...................................**115.00**

Jewelry box, cardboard/plastic, w/dancing figure, musical, 1982, 8", M .....................**35.00**

Jug, porcelain, May Your Days Be Happy, 6¼", from $25 to ............................**35.00**

Lamp, porcelain, complete, 1977, 7½", from $35 to ...........**45.00**

Plate, painted ceramic, 1971, 6 different made, 10", ea, from $50 to ....................................**75.00**

Plate, sterling, Franklin Mint limited edition, 1972, 10", MIB, from $600 to ................**750.00**

Store plaque, porcelain, Holly & kitten, 1973, 4¾", from $50 to ..................................**60.00**

Teapot, porcelain, 1973, 9½", from $60 to .............................**75.00**

Toy iron, plastic, Durham, 5", MIB, from $20 to ..........**30.00**

Trinket box for Mother's Day, limited edition, 1980, 4¼", from $30 to ..................**40.00**

Vase, Petite pattern, porcelain, 1980, 6" .........................**25.00**

# Holt Howard

Ceramic novelty items marked Holt Howard are hot! From the late 1950s, collectors search for the pixie kitchenware items such as cruets, condiments, etc., all with flat, disk-like pixie heads for stoppers. In the '60s the company designed and distributed a line of roosters — egg cups, napkin holders, salt and pepper shakers, etc. Items with a Christmas theme featuring Santa or angels, for instance, were sold from the '50s through the '70s, and you'll also find a line of white cats, collectors call Kozy Kittens. Most pieces are not only marked but dated as well.

Our advisors for this category are Pat and Ann Duncan, who are listed in the Directory under Missouri.

Christmas, airwick, holly girl figural ...............................**40.00**

Christmas, ashtray, Santa, med ..**25.00**

Christmas, candle holders, Santa w/climbing mouse, pr ...**35.00**

Christmas, candy container, pop-up Santa, 4¼" ..............**50.00**

Christmas, dish, tree form, 9⅞" ...........................**15.00**

Christmas, mug, tree w/Santa handle ...........................**10.00**

Christmas, planter, candy cane .**20.00**

Christmas, planter, mother deer & fawn, white w/gold, from $22 to ....................................**35.00**

Christmas, salt & pepper shakers, tree w/Santa, pr ...........**25.00**

Kozy Kitten, bud vase, cat in plaid cap & neckerchief, from $65 to ...........................**75.00**

Kozy Kitten, butter dish, cats peeking out on side, ¼-lb, rare ............................**150.00**

Kozy Kitten, cottage cheese keeper, cat knob on lid .......**100.00**

Kozy Kitten, creamer & sugar bowl, stackable ...........**195.00**

Kozy Kitten, letter holder, cat w/coiled wire back .........**75.00**

Kozy Kitten, salt & pepper shakers, cats' heads, pr .......**30.00**

Kozy Kitten, salt & pepper shakers, tall cats, pr .............**40.00**

Kozy Kitten, spice set, stacking .**175.00**

Kozy Kitten, string holder, head only ................................**95.00**

Pixie Ware, candlesticks, pr .**55.00**

Pixie Ware, cherries jar, flat head finial, w/cherry pick or spoon .........................**150.00**

Pixie Ware, chile sauce, rare, minimum value .................**300.00**

**Mustard jar, pixie head finial, from $65.00 to $75.00. (Photo courtesy Pat and Ann Duncan)**

Pixie Ware, creamer ............**55.00**

Pixie Ware, decanter, flat head stopper w/300 Proof & rose, minimum .....................**200.00**

Pixie Ware, French dressing bottle, minimum value ....**200.00**

Pixie Ware, hors d'oeuvre, head on body, tall hairdo, saucer base ............................**200.00**

Pixie Ware, ketchup jar, orange tomato-like head finial .**75.00**

Pixie Ware, mayonnaise jar, winking head finial, minimum value ............................**250.00**

Pixie Ware, olive jar, winking green head finial ...........**95.00**

Pixie Ware, salt & pepper shakers, Salty & Peppy, pr .........**65.00**

Pixie Ware, spice set, stacking .**150.00**

Ponytail Girl, candle holder, figure-8 platform, from $50 to .**60.00**

Ponytail Girl, lipstick holder, from $60 to .............................**75.00**

Ponytail Girl, salt & pepper shakers, pr ...........................**45.00**

Ponytail Girl, tray, girl between 2 joined flower cups .........**65.00**

Rooster, coffeepot, electric .**100.00**

Rooster, cookie jar, embossed rooster .........................**200.00**

Rooster, cup & saucer ..........**25.00**

Rooster, dish, figural rooster w/open-body receptacle .**30.00**

Rooster, jam & jelly jar, embossed rooster ..........................**75.00**

Rooster, mug, embossed rooster, 3 sizes, ea .........................**20.00**

Rooster, napkin holder ........**40.00**

Rooster, plate, embossed rooster, 8½" ................................**25.00**

Rooster, platter, embossed rooster, oval ................................**35.00**

Rooster, tray, facing left ......**25.00**

Water pitcher, Rooster, tail handle, $60.00; Chocolate pot, Rooster, $95.00. (Photo courtesy Pat and Ann Duncan)

Tomato, salt & pepper shakers, pr ................................**15.00**
Tomato, snack set, tomato cup on lettuce-leaf plate, 1962 .**25.00**
Tomato, soup tureen, lg, from $85 to ................................**100.00**

# Homer Laughlin

The Homer Laughlin China Company has produced millions of pieces of dinnerware, toiletry items, art china, children's dishes, and hotel ware since its inception in 1874. On most pieces the backstamp includes company name, date, and plant where the piece was produced, and most often the shape name is included. Refer to *The Collector's Encyclopedia of Homer Laughlin China* by Joanne Jasper; *Homer Laughlin China Company, A Giant Among Dishes,* by Jo Cunningham; and *The Col-*

*lector's Encyclopedia of Fiesta* by Sharon and Bob Huxford.

Our advisor for this category is Darlene Nossaman; she is listed in the Directory under Texas. See Clubs and Newsletters for information concerning *The Laughlin Eagle*, a newsletter for collectors of Homer Laughlin dinnerware. See also Fiesta; Harlequin; Riviera.

### Genessee: early 1900s (Pink Rose, Rose Spray, Gold Stamp and Band, Parisian Rose)

Bowl, fruit; 5" .........................**5.00**
Bowl, vegetable; oval, 9" ......**15.00**
Casserole, w/lid, 9" ..............**45.00**
Creamer ...............................**10.00**
Cup & saucer, AD ................**16.00**
Jug, 1½-pt ..........................**35.00**
Pickle dish ..........................**22.00**
Plate, 10" ............................**10.00**
Plate, 7" ...............................**7.50**
Platter, 13" ..........................**18.00**
Sauce boat ...........................**16.00**
Saucer ...................................**3.00**
Sugar bowl, w/lid ................**15.00**
Teacup ..................................**6.00**

### Kraft Blue and Kraft Pink Shape, 1930s

Bowl, cereal; 6" ......................**8.00**
Bowl, cream soup; 5" ...........**10.00**
Bowl, fruit; 5½" .....................**6.00**
Bowl, vegetable; 8¾" dia .....**12.00**
Creamer ..................................**8.00**
Creamer, novelty ................**12.00**
Egg cup, double ...................**12.00**
Plate, 10" ............................**10.00**
Plate, 6" ................................**5.00**
Plate, 9" ................................**8.00**

**Kraft Blue and Kraft Pink Shape, Plate, 9", $8.00; Creamer, $8.00; Sugar bowl, with lid, $10.00; Teapot, $25.00. (Photo courtesy Darlene Nossaman)**

| | |
|---|---|
| Platter, 10" | **12.00** |
| Saucer | **3.00** |
| Sugar bowl, w/lid | **10.00** |
| Teacup | **7.00** |
| Teapot | **25.00** |

| | |
|---|---|
| Casserole, w/lid | **45.00** |
| Creamer | **14.00** |
| Plate, 10" | **10.00** |
| Plate, 7" | **6.00** |

## Newell: 1927 design (Yellow Glow, Puritan, Song of Spring, Southern Pride, Poppy)

| | |
|---|---|
| Bowl, fruit; 5" | **4.00** |
| Bowl, vegetable; 9" | **12.00** |
| Casserole, w/lid | **35.00** |
| Creamer | **10.00** |
| Jug, 1½-pt | **35.00** |
| Plate, 10" | **10.00** |
| Plate, 7" | **6.00** |
| Platter, 12" | **16.00** |
| Sauce boat | **15.00** |
| Saucer | **3.00** |
| Sugar bowl, w/lid | **15.00** |
| Teacup | **7.00** |

## Virginia Rose, 1930 (Pink Wild Rose, Rose and Daisy, Patrician, Nosegay; Add 20% for JJ59 and VR128)

| | |
|---|---|
| Bowl, fruit; 5" | **5.00** |
| Bowl, vegetable; 9" | **18.00** |
| Cake plate | **25.00** |

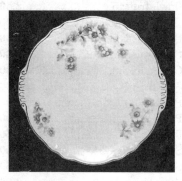

**Tray, decal JJ59, hard to find, 8", from $28.00 to $35.00.**

| | |
|---|---|
| Platter, 13" | **24.00** |
| Rimmed soup | **9.50** |
| Sauce boat | **18.00** |
| Saucer | **5.00** |
| Sugar bowl, w/lid | **16.00** |
| Teacup | **8.00** |

## Wells, 1930 (Flight of the Swallows, Cosmos, Flowers of the Dell, Gold Stripe, Hollyhock)

| | |
|---|---|
| Bowl, fruit; 5" | **4.50** |

Bowl, vegetable; oval, 9" ......**18.00**
Casserole, w/lid ....................**48.00**
Creamer ...............................**12.00**
Muffin cover .........................**45.00**
Plate, 10" .............................**10.50**
Plate, 7" .................................**6.00**
Platter, 11" ...........................**18.00**
Sauce boat ...........................**18.00**
Saucer ...................................**3.00**
Sugar bowl, w/lid .................**16.00**
Teacup ...................................**7.00**

## Yellowstone 1927 (in Moss Rose, Poppy Pastel, Golden Rose, Buttercup, Floral Spray)

Bowl, fruit; 5" ..........................**2.50**
Bowl, vegetable; 9" ..............**10.00**
Butter dish ...........................**32.00**
Casserole, w/lid ....................**30.00**
Creamer .................................**6.00**
Jug, 2½-pt ............................**28.00**
Plate, 10" ...............................**7.00**
Plate, 6" .................................**4.00**
Platter, 13" ...........................**17.50**
Sauce boat ...........................**10.00**
Saucer ...................................**2.50**
Sugar bowl, w/lid .................**10.00**
Teacup ...................................**5.00**

# Horton Ceramics

Horton Ceramics, owned by Horace and Geri Horton, began operations in Eastland, Texas, in 1947. Mrs. Geri Horton was a multi-talented artist and designed all the ceramics, while Mr. Horton ran the business end. The company produced vases, planters, figurines, ashtrays, western dinnerware, and kitchen accessories. These items were sold to florist, variety, department, grocery, and gift shops all over the United States. Each item is usually marked with a mold number and 'horton ceramics' in lower case letters. The company was sold in 1961.

Our advisor for this category is Darlene Nossaman; she is listed in the Directory under Texas.

Ashtray, fish decor, #BS120, blues & greens .........................**9.00**
Ashtray, fish head, #108, brown .........................**8.50**
Ashtray, free-form, #1811, black w/smoky gray swirls .......**8.00**
Planter, contemporary, #AT5, pink, lime or white, 6x6" .........**14.00**
Planter, contemporary, #246, fluted, pink, 6x3" .................**8.00**
Planter, contemporary, #807, gold, pink or black, 4x7" ........**14.00**
Planter, free-form, #D12, brown wood finish, 12x5" .........**11.00**
Planter, free-form, #514, 2-tone green, 14" L ...................**10.00**
Planter, free-form, Art Deco, #707, black, green & mushroom, 7x5" ...............................**12.00**
Planter, free-form, Mood, #912, 2-tone green & black, 11x5" .........**10.00**
Planter, free-form, Skirt, #H-3, 2-tone green & yellow, 4" L ........................**12.00**
Planter, free-form leaf, #805, black & lime green, 7x13" ......**10.00**
Planter, jack-in-the-box .......**20.00**
Planter, novelty, Dutch shoe, #WBN, 10" L .................**10.00**
Planter, novelty, football, #F10, brown, 11x10" ...............**10.00**

**Horton, Western jug, rearing horse on white, one-quart, $18.00; Planter, yellow, #809, $5.00. (Photo courtesy Darlene Nossaman)**

Planter, novelty, hobby horse, #H, various colors, 6" ..........**10.00**

Planter, novelty, kissing boy & girl angels, #460, 6x5" .........**10.00**

Planter, novelty, lamb, #407, pink or blue, 4x6" ....................**8.50**

Planter, novelty, nursery block, #B1, pink or blue, 5x5" ...**6.50**

Planter, window ledge, free-form, #1418, 2-tone pink, 15x5" .**15.00**

Vase, #BV19, coral, blue, black, pink or green, 9x2" .......**25.00**

Vase, #E-6, white, pink, black or green, 6x6" ....................**14.00**

Vase, #211, fan form, blue, white or ivory, 11" ..................**35.00**

# Hull

Established in Zanesville, Ohio, in 1905, Hull manufactured stoneware, florist ware, art pottery, and tile until about 1935, when they began to produce the lines of pastel matt-glazed artware which are today very collectible.

The pottery was destroyed by flood and fire in 1950. The factory was rebuilt and equipped with the most modern machinery which they soon discovered was not geared to duplicate the matt glazes. As a result, new lines — Parchment and Pine, and Ebb Tide, for example — were introduced in a glossy finish. During the '40s and into the '50s, their kitchenware and novelty lines were very successful. Refer to *Roberts' Ultimate Encyclopedia of Hull Pottery* and *The Companion Guide*, both by Brenda Roberts (Walsworth Publishing), for more information. Brenda also has authored a third book, *The Collector's Encyclopedia of Hull Pottery,* which is published by Collector Books.

Blossom Flite, candle holder, T-11, 3" ....................................**60.00**

Blossom Flite, teapot, rope handle, T-14, 8¼" ....................**145.00**

Bow-Knot, console bowl, B-16, 13½" .............................**395.00**

**Bow-Knot, whisk broom wall pocket, B-27, 8", $260.00.**

Butterfly, ashtray, matt, B-3, 7" ..**45.00**

Butterfly, serving tray, white & turquoise matt w/gold, B-23, 11½" .............................**115.00**

Calla Lily, ewer, blue & pink, #506, 10" ......................**425.00**

Camellia, cornucopia, #101, 8½" ..........................**175.00**

Camellia, vase, pink to blue, low handles, #130, 4¾" .......**80.00**

Capri, urn, lion's head in relief, #50, 9" ............................**60.00**

Classic, ewer, flower on creamy white, #6, 6" ..................**35.00**

Continental, candle holder/planter, green, unmarked, 4" ......**30.00**

Dogwood, basket, #501, 7½" .**375.00**

Early Art, vase, pink & blue stripes on turquoise, stoneware, 5½" ..............**70.00**

Ebb Tide, basket, E-5, 6¼" .**140.00**

Ebb Tide, creamer, shell form, E-15, 4" ............................**85.00**

Fiesta, flowerpot, black, ruffled rim, #40, 4¼" .................**30.00**

Fiesta, flowerpot, rose in relief, pedestal foot, #43, 6" ....**60.00**

Floral, bowl, mixing; yellow sunflower decor, #40, 5" .....**25.00**

Iris, bud vase, #410, 7½" ...**195.00**

Iris, vase, cream, flared, double handles, #403, 4¾" .......**95.00**

Magnolia, matt; candle holder, low handles, #27, 4" ............**50.00**

Mardi Gras, vase, yellow glossy cylinder w/embossed ribs, unmarked, 6" ................**25.00**

Mirror Almond, creamer .....**12.00**

Mirror Almond, French casserole, w/lid, sm ........................**15.00**

Mirror Almond, stein ............**7.00**

Mirror Brown, canister set, round, 4-pc .............................**375.00**

Mirror Brown, casserole, duck lid, 2-qt ..................................**75.00**

Mirror Brown, gravy boat, w/undertray ..................**42.00**

Mirror Brown, mug, 9-oz .......**5.00**

Mirror Brown, pitcher, w/ice lip, #514, 2-qt .....................**25.00**

Mirror Brown, plate, dinner ..**8.00**

Mirror Brown, salt & pepper shakers, table size, pr ..........**20.00**

Mirror Brown, spoon rest, oval, 6½" .................................**30.00**

Mirror Brown, vinegar cruet .**30.00**

Novelty, giraffe planter, #115, 8" ................................**45.00**

Novelty, kitten w/spool, #89, 6" .**25.00**

Novelty, piggy bank, Mirror Brown, #196, 6" ............**65.00**

Novelty, ribbon wall pocket, #71, 6" ..................................**40.00**

Novelty, telephone planter, #50, 9" ..................................**65.00**

Orchid, vase, #308, 4½" .....**100.00**

Parchment & Pine, teapot, S-15, 8" ..............................**125.00**

Poppy, vase, #607, 6½" ......**150.00**

Rosella, lamp base, L-3, 11" .**425.00**

Rosella, vase, heart form, R-8, 6½" .............................**140.00**

Serenade, ashtray, S-23, 12x10½" ....................**130.00**

Sun Glow, casserole, w/lid, #51, 7½" ................................**80.00**

Sun Glow, basket, yellow, #84, 6½" ...............................**90.00**

Tokay, cornucopia, #10, 11" ..**75.00**

Tokay, sugar bowl, pink to green, branch finial, #18 ..........**75.00**

Tulip, ewer, #109, 8" ..........**295.00**

Tuscany, urn, white w/green foliage, low handles, footed, #5, 5½" ...........................**35.00**

Water Lily, jardiniere, L-24, 8½" ........................**340.00**

Wildflower, candle holder, pink to blue, oval form, unmarked, 2½" ...............................**45.00**

**Wildflower, vase, center handles, W-6, 7½", $80.00.**

Woodland, matt; ewer, W-6, 6½" ..........................**155.00**

Woodland, vase, blue to green gloss, twig handles, W-8, 7½" ..........................**145.00**

Yellowware, cup, custard; brown banded, #114, 3" ..........**18.00**

# Indiana Carnival Glass

Though this glass looks old, it really isn't. It's very reminiscent of old Northwood carnival glass with its grape clusters and detailed leaves and vines, but this line was actually introduced in 1972! Made by the Indiana Glass Company, Harvest (the pattern name assigned by the company) was produced in blue, lime green, and marigold. Although they made a few other carnival patterns in addition to this one, none are as collectible or as easy to recognize.

This glassware is a little difficult to evaluate as there seems to be a wide range of 'asking' prices simply because some dealers are unsure of its age and therefore its value. If you like it, now is the time to buy it!

Harvest values given below are based on items in blue. Adjust them downward a price point or two for lime green and even a little more so for marigold. For further information we recommend *Garage Sale and Flea Market Annual* (Collector Books).

**Candlesticks, Harvest, comport shape, 4x4½",
$35.00 for the pair.**

Butter dish, Harvest, ¼-lb, 8" .**25.00**
Candlesticks, Harvest, comport
shape, 4x4½", pr ...........**35.00**
Candy box, Harvest, w/lace edge,
w/lid, 6½" .......................**30.00**
Canister/candy jar, Harvest, 7" ..**30.00**
Canister/cookie jar, Harvest, 9" ..**45.00**
Canister/snack jar, Harvest, 8" ..**35.00**
Center bowl, paneled sides, 4-foot-
ed, 4½x8½x12" .............**35.00**
Creamer & sugar bowl on tray,
Harvest ..........................**30.00**
Garland bowl (comport), paneled,
7½x8½" dia ...................**35.00**
Goblet, Harvest, 9-oz, set of 4,
from $25 to ....................**30.00**
Pitcher, Harvest, 10½" ........**50.00**
Plate, Bicentennial; American
Eagle, from $12 to ........**15.00**
Plate, hostess; Canterbury, allover
diamond facets, crimped rim,
10" ..................................**35.00**
Punch set, Princess, 26-pc ...**95.00**
Tidbit, embossed diamond points, shal-
low w/flared sides, 6½" .........**18.00**
Wedding bowl (sm comport),
Thumbprint, footed, 5x5" .**25.00**

# Indy 500 Memorabilia

Every Memorial Day since

1911 — if the weather cooperates
— race car drivers from all over
the world converge on the 500
mile track in Indianapolis, Indiana, for the running of the Indy
500. Since the first race, pro-
grams, tickets, yearbooks, magazines, and many other types of
memorabilia have been issued,
and today race fans prize them
highly. They also look for autographs and photos of the drivers,
pit badges, books, decanters,
model race cars, and souvenir
plates and tumblers.

Our advisor for this category
is Eric Jungnickel, he is listed in
the Directory under Illinois.

Ashtray, dark glass w/race scene,
car & IMS logo, 3½" dia .**10.00**
Book, Marlboro Salute to 75th
Anniversary of Indy 500,
1986, hardcover ...........**25.00**
Decal, IMS/USAC logo, dated
1960 .............................**12.00**
Decal, water dip style, shows IMS
Main Gate & period car,
1960s ...........................**15.00**
Decanter, Al Unser's Johnny
Lightning race car, blue
w/gold, #2 .....................**75.00**

Decanter, Mario Andretti, red #9 car, Old Mr Boston .......**50.00**

Flag, black & white checks with yellow and blue racer, Indianapolis 500, fringed, 1960s ......................**25.00**

**Flag, checkered cloth with racing car in oval, on wooden stick, 17¼x17½", EX, $85.00.**

Game, Champion Spark Plug Auto Race, premium, 1934, M ...............................**75.00**

Glass, IMS logo, 1953 .........**25.00**

Model, '64 Mustang Indy Pace Car, Monogram, 1995, complete .............................**10.00**

Mug, 1983 Indy 500 w/Shell logo, Libbey, 8" ......................**15.00**

Pamphlet, Why I Became a...Driver, by Wilbur Shaw, Firestone, 1940 ...................**10.00**

Pin-back button, Detroit Diesel Quality Club, red & blue on gold, 1944 .....................**15.00**

Pit badge, 1950, bronze ....**150.00**

Pit badge, 1956, silver, IMS Main Gate .............................**90.00**

Pit badge, 1978, bronze, STP ...**50.00**

Postcard, color photo w/Eddie Sachs in #2 Autolite Special ..........................**15.00**

Program, 1925, scored ......**350.00**

Program, 1940, M .............**100.00**

Program, 1951, EX...............**50.00**

Program, 1970-80, any, EX .**15.00**

Seat cushion, Indy 500 Speedway, black & white checks w/1970s car ................................**25.00**

Ticket, 1963, shows 1962 winner Roger Ward & car, unused ...........**15.00**

Ticket, 1973, shows 1972 winner Rick Mears .....................**10.00**

Ticket, 31st International Sweepstakes, VG ..........**40.00**

Tie bar & cuff links, Parnelli Jones in helmet, gold-filled, 3-pc ....**35.00**

Tumbler, 1972, short ..........**10.00**

Yearbook, Indy Car World Series, 1981, 144 pages ............**10.00**

Yearbook, 1961, Floyd Clymer, Foyt's 1st win ...............**50.00**

# Japan Ceramics

Though Japanese ceramics marked Nippon, Noritake, and Occupied Japan have long been collected, some of the newest fun-type collectibles on today's market are the figural ashtrays, pincushions, wall pockets, toothbrush holders, etc., that are marked 'Made in Japan' or simply 'Japan.' In her books called *Collector's Guide to Made in Japan Ceramics* (there are three in the series), Carole Bess White explains the pitfalls you will encounter when you try to determine production dates. Collectors refer to anything produced before WWII as 'old' and anything made after 1952 as 'new.' You'll find all you need to know to be a wise shopper in this book.

Our advisor for this category is Carole Bess White; she is listed in the Directory under Oregon. (Please enclose an SASE if you contact her.)

See also Black Cats; Blue Willow; Cat Collectibles; Egg Timers; Enesco; Fishbowl Ornaments; Flower Frogs; Geisha Girl; Head Vases; Holt Howard; Lefton; Moss Rose; Nippon; Noritake; Occupied Japan; Rooster and Roses; Sewing Collectibles; Toothbrush Holders; Wall Pockets.

Bell, bellhop bust, luster trim, 4" ...............................**45.00**
Butter dish, rectangular w/hobnails, flower finial on lid, 6½" .............................**32.00**
Calendar, dog w/hat before sq holder, luster trim, 2½" ........**35.00**
Candlesticks, flattened ball shape, green & white, 4¾", pr .**38.00**
Candy dish, Art Deco florals, w/lid, luster trim, 7½" ............**75.00**
Celery set, oval w/cherries, pierced handles, matt, 11½", 7-pc .**55.00**
Chocolate pot, house by lake, matt, 8½" .................................**38.00**
Clothes brush, dog w/upright ears, black & white, 3¾" .......**40.00**
Condiment set, castle towers w/black cat knob on mustard, 3¾" ...............................**135.00**
Condiment set, 2 orange tomatoes w/green leaf tray, 3-pc ..**35.00**
Creamer & open sugar bowl, cone shape, Art Deco, luster trim, 7½" .................................**55.00**

Creamer & sugar bowl w/lid+tray, blown-out pods, luster, 7½" wide ...............................**55.00**
Demitasse set, Art Deco florals, service for 6, 7¼" pot ..**135.00**
Egg cup, girl bunny w/flower-shaped cup, luster & matt glazes, 3" .......................**25.00**
Figurine, bunny standing on Easter egg, matt, 4¼" ..........**18.00**
Figurine, calico dog, seated w/red bow, 4½" ......................**18.00**
Figurine, clown, standing, ruffled collar, 4¾" .....................**18.00**
Figurine, girl holds skirt out, back arched, arm over head, 7½" ...**55.00**
Flask, spotted dog, brown bottle w/All's Well That Ends Well, 4¼" ...............................**85.00**
Flower basket, fluted sides, footed, angle handle, luster trim, 7" .................................**57.00**
Hair receiver, pink roses w/cobalt trim & handles, 2¼" .....**60.00**
Humidor, green crackle w/multicolor flowers, 5½" ..........**65.00**
Ice cream set, 6 sq plates +11" oblong tray, luster trim, 7-pc ...............................**45.00**

**Ice box set, blue shamrocks on green, 6½" wide, from $40.00 to $70.00. (Photo courtesy Carole Bess White)**

Incense burner, Asian man w/moustache, seated on chair, 4" ....................................**23.00**

Incense burner, bisque man w/feet extended, faces on feet, 3½" ...............................**30.00**

Incense burner, Tokanabe bowl & lid, black w/red & gold, 2½" ...............................**18.00**

Lamp, Buddah on elephant figural, multicolor lustres, 7" base+shade ....................**75.00**

Lemon plate, flower shape w/embossed orange at center, 6¾" ...............................**25.00**

**Liquor set, bellhop figural, multicolor glazes, 11", $150.00 to $200.00 for the set. (Photo courtesy Carole Bess White)**

Mayonnaise set, lotus bowl, matt & glossy glazes, 6¾" dia, 3-pc ...............................**35.00**

Napkin ring, elephant, graduated balls as trunk & tail, 3" .**28.00**

Pitcher, man in chair holds book, dog as handle, 6" ..........**45.00**

Powder box, lady holds skirt wide, luster trim, 5½" ............**85.00**

Relish, divided w/3 round bowls, cup handle, matt, 2½" ..**38.00**

Salt & pepper shaker flowers on basket tray, luster trim, 3½" ............................**28.00**

Swagger stick, wood w/2" ceramic baseball finial, lustres ..**65.00**

Syrup pitcher, geometric Art Deco design, w/lid & underplate, 6¼" ...............................**48.00**

Teapot, Bonzo seated, arm spout & tail handle, 7" ............**350.00**

Teapot, Pekingese figural, matt, 6¾" ...............................**150.00**

Toast rack, 6 angular arches, handle forms open diamond, matt, 8" ....................................**42.00**

Vase, blown-out poppies on cream crackle, 5½" ...................**48.00**

Vase, houses on tan luster, onion shape, 7¼" .....................**38.00**

Vase, 2 black cats, fox hunter decal, bottle shape, 4¾" ...........**20.00**

Wall plaque, Valentino-like molded face, 4¼" ..................35.00

# Jewelry

Anyone interested in buying gems will soon find out that antique gems are the best values. Not only are prices from one-third to one-half less than on comparable new jewelry, but the older pieces display a degree of craftsmanship and styling not often seen in modern jewelry. Costume jewelry from all periods is popular, especially Art Nouveau and Art Deco examples. Signed pieces are particularly good, such as those by Miriam Haskell, Eisenberg, Trifari, Hollycraft, and Weiss, among others.

There are some excellent reference books available if you'd like more information. Lillian Baker has written several: *Art Nouveau and Art Deco Jewelry; Twentieth Century Fashionable Plastic Jewelry; 50 Years of Collectible Fashion Jewelry;* and *100 Years of Collectible Jewelry.* Books by other authors include *Costume Jewelry* by Fred Rezazadeh; *Collector's Encyclopedia of Hairwork Jewelry* by C. Jeanenne Bell, G.G.; *Collectible Costume Jewelry* by Cherri Simonds; *Christmas Pins* by Jill Gallina; and *Collecting Antique Stickpins* by Jack and 'Pet' Kerins. All are published by Collector Books.

Bar pin, 10k yellow gold arrow w/arrowhead, 7 seed pearls, 2" .....................................**45.00**

Belt buckle, Art Nouveau, cut steel butterfly, ca 1905 ..........**45.00**

Bracelet, Bakelite, 4-color flattened beads on stretch band, 1930s ...........................**135.00**

Bracelet, bangle; 14k yellow gold, hinged ..........................**175.00**

Bracelet, bangle; Bakelite, apple juice w/yellow rhinestones ........**45.00**

Bracelet, bangle; Bakelite, carved golden yellow, from $65 to ......**130.00**

Bracelet, bangle; 14k yellow gold, engraved, hexagonal ...**375.00**

Bracelet, Eisenberg, rhodium w/rhinestones, wide, 1950 .............**150.00**

Bracelet, Emmons, black opaque stones in silver metal lacy chain ..............................**30.00**

Bracelet, France, sm brass sea horses on red Bakelite, brass links .............................**150.00**

Bracelet, gold-tone chain w/lg jonquil sq & oval rhinestones .......**18.00**

Bracelet, Kramer, clear rhinestones, single strand, from $35 to .............................**50.00**

Bracelet, Sarah Coventry, enamel grape leaves & metal links, from $20 to ....................**32.00**

Bracelet, Sarah Coventry, gold-tone wheat shocks design, 1950s .............................**10.00**

Bracelet, Trifari, silver-tone metal work & faux pearls, from $35 to .....................................**50.00**

Bracelet, 14k gold, white gold filigree, 6" .......................**225.00**

Bracelet, 14k yellow gold w/engraving, ½" wide, hinged, 20 grams ......................**195.00**

Bracelet, 14k yellow gold w/9 sm diamonds, 1960s .........**200.00**

Brooch, Alice Caviness, green & blue pronged stones, 2¼" .......................**85.00**

Brooch, Beau, sterling flowers & leaves on branch, from $20 to ..................................**35.00**

Brooch, Ciner, gold-plated owl on branch, green stone eyes, from $80 to .............................**95.00**

Brooch, Cini, sterling Libra ..**45.00**

Brooch, Danecraft, sterling repousse leaf form, 1940s ................**55.00**

Brooch, Eisenberg Ice, 2½", w/matching earrings ...**110.00**

Brooch, Gorham, silver dragonfly, 2½x2½" ........................**175.00**

Brooch, Hattie Carnegie, giraffe running, rhinestones on gold-tone ..................................**75.00**

Brooch, Hobe, 3-colored gemstones in gold-tone filigree, 1948, 2¾" ....................**300.00**

Brooch, Lea Stein Paris, celluloid vintage car w/long hood .**85.00**

Brooch, Marvel Boucher, gold-plated ballerina w/etched tutu, from $145 to .......**175.00**

Brooch, Miriam Haskell, peacock, blue & green stones on gold-tone ..............................**175.00**

Brooch, Monet, white & gold-metal flower shape, from $25 to ..**30.00**

Brooch, Regency, butterfly, blue-green iridescent pronged stones, 2" .......................**85.00**

Brooch, Trifari, brushed silvertone Art Moderne spiral, 2" ..............................**18.00**

Brooch, Trifari, butterfly w/colored stones, sm, from $45 to .**55.00**

Brooch, Trifari, opaque glass petals & beads form flower, from $40 to ....................**60.00**

Brooch, Weiss, apple form, black metal w/red rhinestones .**75.00**

Brooch, Weiss, faceted rhinstones in various shapes, lg, from $80 to ..................................**120.00**

Brooch & earrings, BSK, gold-plated leaves, from $40 to ...**60.00**

Brooch & earrings, Sarah Coventry, aurora borealis stones, from $25 to ....................**30.00**

Brooch & earrings, Weiss, red stones form strawberries, from $80 to ..................**110.00**

Brooch/pendant, cameo, gold-filled rope twist bezel, 1⅝x1⅛" ....................**150.00**

Chain, Sarah Coventry, rhodium twist, ca 1960 ................**10.00**

Charm, 18k yellow gold gondola, pink stone & quartz ......**85.00**

Charm, 18k yellow gold reticulated fish, green stone eyes ....**85.00**

Clip, Bakelite, deeply carved, rectangular, 2x1" ..............**28.00**

Critter pin, Coro, bird w/enamel & rhinestones on gold-tone, 2"/1", pr ..........................**14.00**

Critter pin, Trifari, silver-plated elephant w/rhinestones & crystals ..........................**95.00**

**Earrings, plastic loops with metal mounts, signed Joseff, 1950s, $135.00 for the pair.**

Earrings, Bijoux Cascio, draped rope in brushed gold-tone, 1¼" ................................**15.00**

Earrings, Coro, rhinestone leaf shape, screw backs, from $20 to ...................................**30.00**

Earrings, Czechoslovakia, filigree drops w/topaz rhinestones, 1" .....................**15.00**

**Necklace, rhinestones and three gold-tone filigree flowers on chain, unmarked, $110.00.**

Earrings, Czechoslovakia, red rhinestone clusters, screw backs, from $20 to ........**30.00**

Earrings, Eisenberg, rhinestone & rhodium drops, 1950s ...**85.00**

Earrings, Eisenberg, typical lacy pattern, clip backs, from $50 to ....................................**85.00**

Earrings, George Jensen, sterling doves ............................**130.00**

Earrings, Kalo, flower form, screw backs ............................**150.00**

Earrings, Kramer, clear rhinestone crescent shapes, from $30 to ............................**40.00**

Earrings, Kramer, pearl & rhinestone beads, clips ..........**10.00**

Earrings, Lerue, floral design w/pastel enamel & rhinestones, 2" ......................**18.00**

Earrings, Marvella, gold-tone leaf shape w/faux pearls, from $15 to ....................................**20.00**

Earrings, Robert, green beads & rhinestones, from $50 to .........................**75.00**

Earrings, Weiss, green baguette stones, from $35 to .......**50.00**

Earrings, Weiss, rhinestones w/faux turquoise drops, clips, 1950s ............................**65.00**

Earrings, Weiss, 3 lg rhinestones w/sm rhinestone accents, clips, 1" ........................**14.00**

Earrings, 14k yellow gold, ea w/1.50ct oval amethyst .**90.00**

Earrings, 14k yellow gold oak leaves, 1940s ..............**250.00**

Earrings, 14k yellow gold w/1.50ct citrine ............................**75.00**

Fur clip, Bakelite, grasshopper, apple-juice body w/rhinestones ..........................**250.00**

Locket, yellow gold filled, Egyptian princess & snake relief, 1¼" ................................**50.00**

Necklace, Arts & Crafts, clear stone w/3 sm drops, silver chain ...........................**250.00**

Necklace, BSK, gold-tone floral design w/pink rhinestones, from $30 to ....................**45.00**

Necklace, Coro, gold-tone chains w/gold-tone spatter-look beads ...............................**12.00**

Necklace, Coro, gold-tone metal w/aqua rhinestone dangle, from $125 to ................**140.00**

Necklace, cultured pearls, 1-strand, 62 6-6.5mm, silver clasp, 15" .....................**165.00**

Necklace, cultured pearls, 1-strand, 96 3-7.5 mm, 18" ...........**250.00**

Necklace, Emmons, rhodium cross w/faux turquoise & cultured pearls ............................**55.00**

Necklace, frosted amethyst 8mm beads, hand knotted, 34" **.60.00**

Necklace, jet, 51 6mm Whitby faceted beads w/50 spacers, 24" .................................**25.00**

Necklace, Jewelart, choker, roses & leaves, 1930s .............**60.00**

Necklace, Miriam Haskell, amber beads, 6-strand ...........**175.00**

Necklace, Miriam Haskell, pearls, 2-strand w/rondells .....**225.00**

Necklace, Monet, gold-plated chain, from $15 to .........**20.00**

Necklace, multicolored rhinestone floral design, from $45 to **.65.00**

Necklace, Trifari, faux turquoise beads, 2-strand, from $40 to ................**65.00**

Necklace, West Germany, faceted black glass beads, 3-strand, from $20 to ....................**35.00**

Necklace, 18k yellow gold, hollow beads on 16" chain ......**265.00**

Necklace & earrings, West Germany, blue Bohemian glass beads, from $50 to ........**75.00**

Necklace & earrings, West Germany, gold-tone filigree w/pearls, from $45 to ....**70.00**

Pendant, gutta percha w/black cameo ...........................**55.00**

Pendant, Kramer, blue & white pronged rhinestones .....**40.00**

Pendant, 14k gold with lg amethyst flower, Victorian ....................**125.00**

Pin, carved wooden Scotty w/glass eyes ...............................**35.00**

Pin, Cini, dogwood, sterling, lg ..**180.00**

Pin, Emmons, bobcat's gold-tone face w/green eyes, 1954 ..........................**75.00**

Pin, Emmons, Lambkin, oxidized brass & enamel lamb, 1960 ...........................**35.00**

Pin, Kramer, green stones, stacked, 1½x2" ..............**95.00**

Pin, scarf; Trifari, gold-tone feather design, 1960 ..............**25.00**

Pin, Trifari, poodle w/mother-of-pearl body ......................**25.00**

Pin, Trifari, sterling crown, lg .**185.00**

Pin, white gold w/6 7mm pearls & 30 seed pearls in circle .**120.00**

Ring, Eisenberg, sapphire blue rhinestones on silver-tone .......**115.00**

Ring, Emmons, aurora borealis rhinestones set in gold-tone, 1970 ...............................**30.00**

Ring, Hattie Carnegie, Lucite ram's head w/rhinestones & faux coral ...................**175.00**

Ring, man's, heavy gold, engraved initials ...........................**65.00**

Ring, Miriam Haskell, seed pearl cluster, adjustable ......**145.00**

Ring, platinum, .70ct diamond w/4 side diamonds ..............**750.00**
Ring, white gold filigree w/2 emerald-cut aquamarines, 1920s ...........................**250.00**
Ring, 10k white gold w/onyx & sm diamond .........................**50.00**
Ring, 10k yellow gold filigree w/sm ruby .............................**145.00**
Ring, 14k white gold filigree w/lg amethyst .........................**75.00**
Ring, 14k yellow gold w/.60ct round solitaire diamond .........**330.00**
Ring, 14k yellow gold w/garnet cluster ............................**70.00**
Ring, 14k yellow gold w/7.5mm cultured pearl ...............**60.00**

# Johnson Brothers

Dinnerware marked Johnson Brothers, Staffordshire, has lately become the target of some aggressive collector activity, and for good reason. They made many lovely patterns, some scenic and some florals. Most are decorated with multicolor transfer designs, though you'll see blue or red transferware as well. Some, such as Friendly Village (one of their most popular lines), are still being produced, but the lines are much less extensive now, so the secondary market is being tapped to replace broken items that are no longer available anywhere else.

For more information refer to *Johnson Brothers Dinnerware* by Mary J. Finegan. (See the Directory under North Carolina.)

Coaching Scenes, bowl, cereal; 6", from $7 to ......................**10.00**
Coaching Scenes, bowl, fruit; 5", from $5.50 to ...................**6.50**
Coaching Scenes, creamer, from $28 to .............................**32.00**
Coaching Scenes, cup & saucer, from $10 to ....................**15.00**
Coaching Scenes, plate, dinner; 10", from $12 to ...........**16.00**
Coaching Scenes, platter, 12", from $40 to ....................**55.00**
English Chippendale, bowl, cereal; 6", from $7 to ................**10.00**
English Chippendale, bowl, vegetable; 8½", from $22 to .**28.00**
English Chippendale, cup & saucer, from $12 to .......**15.00**
English Chippendale, plate, dinner; 10", from $10 to .....**15.00**
English Chippendale, sugar bowl, w/lid .............................**45.00**
English Chippendale, teapot, from $75 to .............................**85.00**
Friendly Village, bowl, cereal; 6" ...............................**9.00**
Friendly Village, bowl, vegetable; oval, from $25 to ..........**30.00**
Friendly Village, bowl, vegetable; round, from $25 to .........................**30.00**
Friendly Village, butter dish, from $45 to .............................**50.00**
Friendly Village, coffeepot, from $70 to .............................**80.00**
Friendly Village, cup & saucer, from $12 to ....................**15.00**
Friendly Village, gravy boat, from $30 to .............................**40.00**
Friendly Village, mug, from $12 to .................................**15.00**
Friendly Village, plate, dinner; 10", from $12 to ...........**14.00**

**Rose Chintz, platter, 8", $40.00.**

Friendly Village, plate, luncheon; 9", from $9 to ................**12.00**

Friendly Village, plate, 7" sq, from $9 to ..............................**12.00**

Friendly Village, platter, 11½", from $30 to ....................**40.00**

Friendly Village, platter, 13½", from $35 to ....................**45.00**

Friendly Village, platter, 15", from $50 to ............................**60.00**

Friendly Village, salt & pepper shakers, pr ......................**40.00**

Friendly Village, sugar bowl, w/lid, from $35 to ..........**40.00**

Harvest Time, bowl, vegetable; 8", from $20 to ....................**25.00**

Harvest Time, plate, dinner; 10", from $12 to ....................**14.00**

Heritage Hall, bowl, vegetable; 8" ..................................**25.00**

Historical America, cup & saucer, jumbo ............................**30.00**

Indian Tree, bowl, soup; 7" .**10.00**

Indian Tree, creamer ..........**30.00**

Indian Tree, platter, 12" ......**35.00**

Indian Tree, sugar bowl, w/lid .**40.00**

Merry Christmas, bowl, cereal; 6", from $8 to ....................**12.00**

Merry Christmas, bowl, vegetable; with lid, from $80 to ...............**100.00**

Merry Christmas, plate, dinner; 10", from $12 to ............**18.00**

Old Britain Castles, bowl, cereal; 6", from $8 to ...............**12.00**

Old Britain Castles, bowl, vegetable; oval, from $30 to ...........................**35.00**

Old Britain Castles, coffeepot, from $80 to ....................**95.00**

Old Britain Castles, gravy boat, from $40 to ....................**48.00**

Old Britain Castles, plate, dinner; 10", from $12 to ...........**18.00**

Old Britain Castles, teapot, from $80 to ............................**90.00**

Old Mill, cup & saucer, from $12 to ....................................**15.00**

Old Mill, plate, dinner; 10", from $10 to ............................**14.00**

Rose Chintz, bowl, cereal; coupe, from $8 to ......................**12.00**

Rose Chintz, bowl, fruit; round or sq, from $7 to ..................**9.00**

Rose Chintz, bowl, vegetable; round or oval, from $20 to .............**30.00**

Rose Chintz, cup & saucer, from
$12 to ...............................**17.00**
Rose Chintz, gravy boat, from $35
to ......................................**45.00**
Rose Chintz, pitcher, 5½", from
$35 to .............................**45.00**
Rose Chintz, plate, dinner; 10",
from $10 to .....................**15.00**
Rose Chintz, platter, 11½", from
$30 to .............................**40.00**
Rose Chintz, platter, 15", from $60
to ......................................**70.00**
Rose Chintz, teapot, from $75
to ...............................**85.00**
Sheraton, bowl, cereal; 6" ....**10.00**
Sheraton, bowl, soup; 8" ......**14.00**
Sheraton, creamer ...............**30.00**
Sheraton, plate, dinner; 10" .**14.00**
Sheraton, plate, 6" .................**6.00**
Sheraton, platter, 11½" .......**35.00**
Sheraton, platter, 14", from $35
to ....................................**45.00**

# Kentucky Derby Glasses

Kentucky Derby glasses are
the official souvenir glasses sold
filled with mint juleps on Derby
Day. The first glass (1938), pic-
turing a black horse within a
black and white rose garland
and the Churchill Downs stadi-
um in the background, is said to
have either been given away as a
souvenir or used for drinks
among the elite at the Downs.
This glass, the 1939, and two
glasses said to have been used in
1940 are worth thousands and
are nearly impossible to find at
any price.

Our advisor for this category
is Betty Hornback; she is listed
in the Directory under Kentucky.

1941, aluminum .................**800.00**
1941, plastic Beetleware, from
$3,000 to ...................**4,000.00**
1945, short ......................**1,200.00**
1945, tall ...........................**425.00**
1946-47, ea .......................**100.00**
1948 ..................................**180.00**
1948, frosted bottom ..........**200.00**
1949 ..................................**180.00**
1950 ..................................**350.00**
1951 ..................................**450.00**
1952 ..................................**180.00**
1953 ..................................**135.00**
1954 ..................................**165.00**
1955 ..................................**135.00**
1956, 4 variations, from $175 to ...**400.00**
1957 ..................................**110.00**
1958, Gold Bar ..................**175.00**
1958, Iron Liege ................**175.00**
1959-1960, ea .......................**80.00**
1961 ..................................**100.00**
1962 ....................................**65.00**
1963 ....................................**47.00**
1964 ....................................**50.00**
1965 ....................................**55.00**
1966 ....................................**50.00**
1967-1968, ea ......................**47.00**
1969 ....................................**45.00**
1970 ....................................**55.00**
1971 ....................................**45.00**
1972-1973, ea ......................**37.50**
1974, Federal ....................**125.00**
1974, mistake ......................**18.00**
1974, regular ......................**16.00**
1975 ....................................**12.00**
1976 ....................................**14.00**
1976, plastic ........................**10.00**
1977 ....................................**10.00**
1978-1979, ea ......................**12.00**

**1980, 18.00.**

| | |
|---|---|
| 1981-1982, ea | **10.00** |
| 1983 | **9.00** |
| 1984 | **7.00** |
| 1984-1985, ea | **9.00** |
| 1986 | **8.00** |
| 1986 ('85 copy) | **18.00** |
| 1987-1988, ea | **8.00** |
| 1989-1991, ea | **6.00** |
| 1992-1994, ea | **4.50** |
| 1995-1996 | **3.00** |

## King's Crown

This is a pattern that's been around since the late 1800s, but what you're most apt to see on today's market is the later issues. Though Tiffin made it early, our values are for the glassware they produced from the '40s through the '60s and the line made by Indiana Glass in the '70s. It was primarily made in crystal with ruby or cranberry flashing, but some pieces (from Indiana Glass) were made with gold and platinum flashing as well. Tiffin's tumblers are flared while Indiana's are not, and because Indiana's are much later and more easily found, they're worth only about half as much as Tiffin's. Refer to *Collectible Glassware from the 40s, 50s, and 60s, Fourth Edition,* by Gene Florence (Collector Books) for more information.

| | |
|---|---|
| Bowl, flower floater, 12½" | **80.00** |
| Bowl, salad; 9¼" | **85.00** |
| Bowl, wedding/candy; footed, 6" | **30.00** |
| Cake salver, footed, 12½" | **75.00** |
| Candy box, flat, 6" | **60.00** |
| Compote, 7¼x9¾" | **45.00** |
| Creamer | **25.00** |
| Cup | **8.00** |
| Lazy susan, 8¾x24" | **225.00** |

**Pitcher, $175.**

| | |
|---|---|
| Plate, dinner; 10" | **37.50** |
| Plate, party; 24" | **155.00** |
| Plate, salad; 7⅜" | **12.00** |
| Plate, snack; w/indent, 9¾" | **15.00** |
| Punch cup | **15.00** |

Relish, 5-part, 14" ...............**95.00**
Stem, cocktail, 2¼-oz ...........**12.50**
Stem, oyster cocktail, 4-oz ...**14.00**
Stem, water goblet, 9-oz ......**12.00**
Tumbler, iced tea; footed, 12-oz ..**20.00**
Tumbler, juice; footed, 4-oz .**12.00**
Vase, bud; 9" ........................**75.00**

# Kitchen Collectibles

From the early patented apple peelers, cherry pitters, and food choppers to the gadgets of the '20s through the '40s, many collectors find special appeal in kitchen tools. Refer to *Kitchen Antiques, 1790 – 1940,* by Kathryn McNerney and *Kitchen Glassware of the Depression Years, Fifth Edition,* by Gene Florence for more information. Both are published by Collector Books.

See also Aluminum; Appliances; Clothes Sprinkler Bottles; Cookie Cutters and Molds; Egg Timers; Enesco; Fire-King; Glass Knives; Graniteware; Griswold; Clubs and Newsletters.

### Glass

Bowl, beater; green, Jeannette, from $25 to ....................**30.00**
Bowl, cobalt, 11⅝", from $70 to .**75.00**
Bowl, custard, flared sides, McKee, 8", from $15 to .**18.00**
Bowl, egg beater; Skokie Green, w/spout, McKee, from $22 to ..............................**25.00**
Bowl, green, Tufglass, tab handles, spout, from $35 to ..........**40.00**

Bowl, jade-ite w/decor, Hocking, 7½", from $15 to ..........**18.00**
Bowl, mixing; fired-on colors, set of 4, from $20 to ...............**28.00**
Bowl, mixing; green, 6½", from $12 to .............................**15.00**
Bowl, mixing; Hex Optic, pink, flat rim, Jeannette, 9", from $25 to ...........................**30.00**
Bowl, mixing; jade-ite, Hocking, 9", from $15 to ..............**18.00**
Bowl, Tom & Jerry, Skokie Green, McKee, from $75 to ......**85.00**
Butter dish, pink, rectangular, bow finial, from $50 to .**60.00**
Butter dish, rectangular with embossed ribs, Federal, 1-lb, from $30 to ....................**35.00**
Canister, caramel, matching lid, McKee, 40-oz, from $65 to **75.00**
Canister, Coffee (embossed), dark amber, sq w/tin lid ........**95.00**
Canister, Coffee in black letters on custard, sq w/tin lid, $35 to .....**40.00**
Canister, Coffee label on green, glass lid, 47-oz, from $50 to ......**55.00**
Canister, Dutch boy decal on clear, tin lid, from $15 to ........**20.00**
Canister, fired-on tulips, from $15 to .....................................**20.00**
Canister, Sugar in black letters on Delphite Blue, 40-oz ...**375.00**
Canning funnel, green, from $40 to .....................................**45.00**
Casserole, white clambroth, oval, Pyrex, w/lid, from $100 to .**125.00**
Cocktail shaker, dark amber, from $100 to ........................**110.00**
Coffee dripolator, crystal, sm, from $20 to .............................**25.00**
Crushed fruit/cookie jar, Party Line, green, Paden City, from $65 to .............................**70.00**

**Hocking Tulip pattern on white: Batter jug, $20.00; Syrup pitcher, $15.00; Pitcher, $20.00. (Photo courtesy Gene Florence)**

Cup, jade-ite, straight sides, Hocking, 6-oz, from $5 to ........**6.00**

Decanter, green, pinched teardrop, fluted stopper, Hocking, from $40 to ............................**45.00**

Egg cup, Chalaine Blue, from $15 to ....................................**18.00**

Grease jar, Red Tulips, Vitrock, from $20 to ....................**25.00**

Ice bucket, Party Line, amber, Paden City, from $27.50 to ..........**30.00**

Ice bucket, pink, Fry, w/lid, from $175 to ..........................**200.00**

Ice tub, Peacock Blue, from $35 to ...................................**40.00**

Knife rest, dark amber, from $17.50 to ........................**20.00**

Measure cup, green, 20-oz, from $125 to ..........................**150.00**

Measure pitcher, Delphite Blue, McKee, 2-cup, from $75 to ......................**85.00**

Mug, green clambroth, from $30 to ...................................**35.00**

Pitcher, Chesterfield, amber, from $90 to ............................**95.00**

Pitcher, custard, McKee, 2-cup, from $20 to ....................**22.00**

Reamer, Delphite Blue, sm, from $75 to ............................**95.00**

Reamer, grapefruit; milk glass, McKee, from $250 to ..**350.00**

Reamer, green clambroth, Hocking, from $150 to .............**175.00**

Reamer, Indiana Glass, dark amber, from $300 to ...**325.00**

Reamer, Skokie Green, McKee, lg, from $30 to ....................**35.00**

Reamer, Sunkist, black, from $700 to ...................................**750.00**

Refrigerater jar, Hex Optic, green, Jeannette, 4½x5", from $22 to ...................**25.00**

Refrigerator dish, Vitrock, Hocking, 4x4", from $15 to ............**18.00**

Shaker, fired-on blue, black lid, ea ...................................**6.00**

Shaker, green clambroth, Hocking, 8-oz, ea, from $17.50 to ..................**20.00**

Shakers, Chalaine Blue, ea, from $90 to ............................**95.00**

Spoon or fork, crystal w/cobalt handle, ea, from $27.50 to ...**35.00**

Syrup, amber, metal hinged lid, from $45 to ....................**50.00**

Syrup, fired-on green rings, from $15 to ..............................**18.00**

Tumbler, black, McKee, from $15 to ....................................**18.00**

Tumbler, green, footed, Paden City, from $10 to ............**12.00**

Tumbler, green clambroth, footed, from $12 to .....................**15.00**

Water bottle, green, canteen shape, Hocking, from $22 to ..............................**25.00**

## Gadgets and Miscellaneous

Apple corer, tin, round wood knob handle, ca 1877 .............**25.00**

Apple peeler, cast iron, 5-geared, marked Pat Pending .....**95.00**

Apple peeler, Goodell, ca 1880 ..**70.00**

Apple peeler, Hudson Pat 1882, cast iron ..........................**85.00**

Apple peeler, Lockey & Holland, cast iron, Pat 1856 ........**95.00**

Apple peeler, White Mountain #3, Goodell, ca 1898 ............**70.00**

Blueberry scoop, wood & wire w/handle, sm ..................**95.00**

Bowl scraper, plastic, American Beauty Cake Flour, 6x6" .**25.00**

Bread maker, Universal #8, metal, Pat December 25, 1906 .**65.00**

Butter curler, wooden w/sq grooved end ...................**75.00**

Can opener, cast-iron bull figural, head at blade, tail handle, 6½" ...............................**35.00**

Can opener, Dazey, electric .**28.00**

Canister, flour, sugar or utility; Porcelier, Country Life, ea ...........**35.00**

Casserole, Porcelier, Basketweave Cameo, w/lid, 8½" .........**55.00**

Cheese slicer, iron w/fine wire blade, 1920s, 6⅞" ..........**18.00**

Chopper, Tearless Onion and Vegetable Chopper, 1930s, M, $25.00; Funnel-strainer, aluminum, $10.00.

Cherry seeder, Champion, chrome, multiple action ..............**45.00**

Cherry seeder, Logan & Strobridge New Brighton, cast iron ................................**50.00**

Cherry seeder, New Standard Wobbly Wheel .............**110.00**

Cherry seeder, Rollman #8, cast iron & wood, clamps on, 12" ......................**65.00**

Chopper, flat steel blade, maple handle, 8¾", G ..............**45.00**

Chopper, wrought blade, cast tube iron handle, Pat Feb 1887 .**55.00**

Churn, Dazey #20 ..............**200.00**

Churn, Elgin, 2-qt ..............**200.00**

Churn, Lightning Butter machine, Pat Feb 6, 1917, 2-qt ..**120.00**

Churn, unmarked, glass, 1-gal .**95.00**

Coffeepot, Guardian Service, aluminum .........................**105.00**

Coffeepot, Porcelier, Serv-All Line, #576-D, platinum trim ..**65.00**

Cutter, biscuit; Kreamer, strap handle ............................**10.00**

Dough mixer, Landers, geared, crank .............................**85.00**

Doughnut cutter, Rumford, tin, 3¾x2½" dia ...................**20.00**

Egg poacher, wire, 5-compartment ............................**24.00**

Flour sifter, Bromwell, painted tin, ca 1940s-50s, EX ....**15.00**

Funnel, Dover, tin .................**12.00**

Grater, Acme Safety grater, box dated 1933, MIB ...........**20.00**

Grater, All in One Pat Pend, tin, ca 1940, 10⅝x4¼" .........**25.00**

Grater, nutmeg; Edgar, mechanical, 1896 ........................**75.00**

Grater, nutmeg; Little Rhody .**85.00**

Grater, nutmeg; tin & wood half-cylinder, 5¼x3", VG ......**85.00**

Grinder, food; Griswold #4, cast iron, w/3 blades .............**40.00**

Grinder/grater, cast iron/aluminum, Germany, clamps on, NM ................................**28.00**

Ice crusher, Dazey, chrome & black, standing style .....**22.00**

Juicer, Dazey, aluminum, wall mount ............................**17.00**

Knife sharpener, cast iron & wood, handle turns gears, 1900s ..**22.00**

Lemon squeezer, Griswold #2, cast iron ..............................**125.00**

Masher, heavy wire w/wooden handle, brass collar, 9¼" .....**25.00**

Masher, zigzag type w/fulcrum action, 11½" ..................**85.00**

Mayonnaise maker, Wessen Oil, glass w/embossed recipe .**45.00**

Pea sheller, Vaughan, hand-crank table model, EX ...........**55.00**

Percolator, Porcelier, Cattail, electric .................................**80.00**

Pie crimper, brass ................**35.00**

Pie tin, Mrs Wagner's Pies ..**20.00**

Pot scraper, American-Maid Bread ...........................**75.00**

Potato baker, Rumford ........**85.00**

Raisin seeder, Black Lightning, cast iron, clamps on ......**95.00**

Raisin seeder, Everette, wood & wire, hand held .............**95.00**

Rolling pin, Krispy Krust, MIB .........................**55.00**

Rolling pin, white stoneware, maple handles, 19x3" dia .........**200.00**

Sieve, Foley Food Mill, tin w/wood handles ...........................**12.00**

Sifter, Lee's Favorite Flour, tin, crank handle, 6x5", EX ...........................**28.00**

Slicer, vegetable; tin, straight cutter w/wire frame, 1900s, 12x4" ...............................**3.00**

Spatula, Wholesome Baking Powder, open handle, 11½" ...........**12.00**

Trivet, Wagner #8, aluminum .**35.00**

Urn, Porcelier, Barock-Colonial, #2007, electrical, gold trim .........................**125.00**

Waffle iron, Porcelier, Scalloped Wild Flowers, from $225 to ....................**300.00**

Whip, cream; Horlick Cream Whipper, black wire, 1930s, 9½" .................................**32.00**

Whisk, black tin & wire, coiled & straight, 1880s, 7½" ......**10.00**

# Knife Rests

Further research into the manufacture of knife rests by American companies has revealed that many different materials have been used in their production. Presently, several companies make them of pewter, and one in Massachusetts is using sterling silver. A company in New York state had been making pottery rests to match their table settings for several years, but they no longer do so.

The knife rest in our illustration was made by the Carvel-Hall company of Chrisfield, Maryland. (The trademark 'Carvel-Hall' was registered in 1905.) The company made these rests in both gold-tone and silver-colored metal.

Knife rests are still being made in Europe by companies in Germany, France, Austria, and Poland, to name but a few. These new rests are available in most fine jewelry or housewares shops in the United States. Knife rests have been used by European housewives for many years, and some are now finding their way to the United States via collectors and dealers. Some of the new rests carry these marks: Raynard (porcelain and metal), St. Louis (glass, several designs), Baccarat (glass), Sabino (opalescent glass), Riedel of Austria (glass), Atelier Bernard (pottery), and Lalique (frosted glass).

Our advisor for this category is Beverly L. Ales; she is listed in the Directory under California. It is important to note that prices vary from one area of the country to another. See also Clubs and Newsletters.

Atelier Bernard, terre mele, new ............................**20.00**
Baccarat, set of 12, MIB .**385.00**

**Unique Knife Caddy by Carvel-Hall: Gold set of six, MIB, $53.50; Silver set of six, MIB, $18.00. (Photo courtesy Beverly L. Ales)**

Cut glass, 4½-5", ea, from $98 to .............................**155.00**
Herend, Hungary, new ........**35.00**
Hutschenreuther, Germany .**17.00**
Lalique, Kyoto pattern, new, from $148 to .........................**190.00**
Raynard, metal, new, 6 for ...**115.00**
Raynard, porcelain, new ......**45.00**
Riedel, 2 designs, new, ea ...**34.50**
Rosenthal, Germany, Maria, from $20 to .............................**24.00**
Saping, 6 designs, new, ea ..**40.00**
St Louis, 3 designs, new, ea, from $36 to .........................**180.00**
Strawberry Diamond w/Fan cut glass, English, boxed pr .**120.00**
US Pewter, dog, new ...........**13.00**
US Sterling Silver, animals, new, from $40 to ....................**55.00**

# Kreiss

One of the newest areas of collecting interests are items marked Kreiss which were imported from Japan during the 1950s. It's so new, in fact, that we're not even sure if it's pronounced 'kriss' or 'kreese,' and dealers' asking prices also suggest an uncertainty. There are several lines. One is a totally off-the-wall group of caricatures called Psycho Ceramics. There's a Beatnick series, Bums, and Cave People (all of which are strange little creatures), as well as some that are very well done and tasteful. Others you find will be inset with colored 'jewels.' Many are marked either with an ink stamp or an in-mold trademark (some are dated).

Ashtray, man w/tomahawk, marked Psycho Ceramics ......................**35.00**
Ashtray, Wild Man head .....**25.00**
Bank, pink pig, sitting, 6¾", from $75 to .............................**80.00**
Bank, pink poodle .................**75.00**
Bank, Santa waving, unmarked, 6¼", from $25 to ...........**30.00**
Cookie jar, Beatnik .............**50.00**
Egg cup, Mrs Claus .............**35.00**
Figurine, bum in trash can, w/rhinestones ................**95.00**
Figurine, Cinderella ............**65.00**
Figurine, devil, 5" ................**32.00**
Figurine, elephant with drunk .................**125.00**
Figurine, farmer .................**25.00**
Figurine, Merrywolf ............**60.00**
Figurine, Siamese Dancer, 8" ........................**25.00**
Mug, man in garbage can ....**30.00**
Mug, 3-D caveman & cave-woman .........................**50.00**
Perfume bottle, skunk .........**80.00**
Salt & pepper shakers, bluebird, pr ....................................**35.00**
Salt & pepper shakers, puppy, lg, pr ....................................**25.00**

# Lefton China

Since 1940 the Lefton China Co. has been importing and producing ceramic giftware which may be found in shops throughout the world. Because of the quality of the workmanship and the beauty of these items, they are eagerly sought by collectors of today. Lefton pieces are usually marked with a fired-on trademark or a paper label.

Our advisor for this category is Loretta De Lozier, author of *Collector's Encyclopedia of Lefton China, Books I and II*; she is listed in the Directory under Iowa.

Angel, w/flowers, Happy Birthday, #5079, 6" ........................**45.00**
Ashtray, w/violets, sponge gold touches, #136, 3¾" ........**15.00**
Bank, bowling pin, #2644, 10" .**28.00**
Bank, kangaroo w/pink bow, #2778, 7¾" .....................**25.00**
Box, Garden Bouquet, footed, w/lid, #1894, 4" dia .......**40.00**
Box, Spring Bouquet, #8134, 4" ..**35.00**
Butter dish, Celery Line, #1301 ......................**25.00**
Coffeepot, Cuddles, #1448 ...**85.00**

**Creamer and sugar bowl, Miss Priss, #1508, pair from $45.00 to $55.00. (Photo courtesy Loretta De Lozier)**

Cookie jar, Scottish girl, #1173, 9¼" .................................**295.00**

Creamer & sugar bowl, Blue Paisley, #2374, pr .................**65.00**

Creamer & sugar bowl, Moss Rose, #3167 .............................**32.00**

Dish, Hollyberry, #10409, 7" .**20.00**

Figurine, camel, Bethlehem Collection, #06117, 6" ........**32.00**

Figurine, Colonial lady, Elizabeth, #343, 7½" ......................**75.00**

**Figurine, dog, #7328, 4½x5", $18.00.**

Figurine, pheasant w/open wings, #1547, 8½", pr .............**250.00**

Jam jar, Miss Priss, #1515 ..**75.00**

Mug, Roosevelt, #2379, 5½" .**45.00**

Planter, fish, #709, 10¼" .....**28.00**

Planter, rainbow trout, matt finish, #1465, 10½" ............**27.00**

Salt & pepper shakers, chickens, #3024, 4", pr ..................**18.00**

Salt & pepper shakers, Rustic Daisy, #4124, 6¾", pr ...**25.00**

Salt & pepper shakers, speckled roosters, #3136, 3", pr ...**28.00**

Teapot, Hollyberry, #10419, 7" .**85.00**

Teapot, Poinsettia, #4388, 6-cup, 8" .....................................**90.00**

Teapot, Rose Chintz, musical, #7543 .............................**95.00**

Vase, Christmas Rose, #07678 ..**22.00**

Wall plaque, Kitchen, Memories of Home, #00807, 6½" .......**22.00**

Wall plaque, mermaid in shell, #4489, 7", pr .................**80.00**

# Letter Openers

Here's a chance to get into a hobby that offers more than enough diversification to be both interesting and challenging, yet requires very little room for display. Whether you prefer the advertising letter openers or the more imaginative models with handles sculpted as a dimensional figure or incorporating a gadget such as a penknife or a cigarette lighter, you should be able to locate enough for a nice assortment. Materials are varied as well, ranging from silverplate to wood. Some are inlaid with semiprecious stones.

Our advisor for this category is Everett Grist, author of *Collector's Guide to Letter Openers* (Collector Books). Mr. Grist is listed in the Directory under Tennessee.

Advertising, AS&W Co, chrome steel, 3-dimensional nail-head handle ............................**12.00**

Advertising, Clarence A O'Brien/Hyman Berman, brass .......................**35.00**

Advertising, Fuller Brush man, black plastic ...................**6.00**

Advertising, Pfizer/Roerig/Unasyn, cast white metal, 3-D scalpel ..........**8.00**

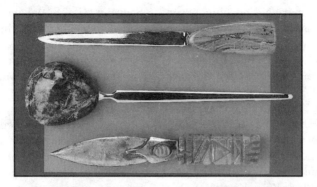

Top to bottom: Agate and steel, $12.00; Pyrite in jasper matrix and steel, $15.00; Green onyx and sterling, made in Mexico, $45.00. (Photo courtesy Everett Grist)

Advertising, Richmond Hosiery, TN, French ivory, leg & foot handle ............................**35.00**

Advertising, W&H Co... Sealtest..., genuine bronze, double sided ..............................**40.00**

Antler, genuine stag horn label, 3-dimensional, with leather sheath ............................**12.00**

Antler, stag, sterling collar & steel, machete point, Pat Nov 22, 1887 .........................**25.00**

Arts & Crafts, aluminum, Great Smoky Mountains, w/letter holder handle ................**12.00**

Arts & Crafts, copper, Vermont Hand Hammered..., w/monogram ..............................**12.00**

Brass, bell w/multicolor stars, marked ...from India by Sarna, 1952 ...................**15.00**

Brass, bird w/flowers, curved blade, marked China ....**10.00**

Brass, Capt John Smith, marked Jamestown-1607, ca 1957 ..**25.00**

Brass, elephant, smooth blade .**10.00**

Brass, feather top, chicken foot blade ............................**15.00**

Brass, horse leg & hoof, 3-dimensional, England .............**10.00**

Brass, nude 3-dimensional woman, Great Smoky Mountains ....................................**18.00**

Brass, Oriental dragon w/bottle opener handle, ornate blade ..............................**12.00**

Brass, trowel, circled floral design, round wooden handle .....**6.00**

Brass, unicorn, made in Taiwan .**10.00**

Combination, alpaca & abalone, coral eye, fish opener, smooth blade ..............................**20.00**

Desk set, brass, sword & stone letter opener & paperweight ......................**15.00**

Desk set, gold plate/wood/rhinestones, cat letter holder & pen/opener ......................**18.00**

Green onyx & sterling, Latin American motif, daggershaped blade .................**35.00**

Ivory, carved dragon motif, 2-sided, red butterflies, wavy blade ..............................**55.00**

Pewter, dancing frog, smooth blade, Metzke, 1979 ..**12.00**

Plastic, mermaid on blue, green
& gold sparkles, Made in
USA ...............................**6.00**

Plastic, red, Sacred Heart
Monastery, Hales Corners
WI ...................................**3.00**

Pot metal, figural lobster, gold-
colored w/red accents ....**8.00**

Pot metal, gold & black African
head w/red lips, smooth
blade .........................**25.00**

Resin, Black King, Kamehameha,
gold crown, made in
Hawaii .........................**6.00**

Silverplated, Mohawk trail,
Mohawk chief w/bow ....**75.00**

Souvenir, Elizabeth's coronation,
silverplate/enamel, England,
1953 ...............................**25.00**

Souvenir, George Washington sil-
houette/Mt Vernon, pot metal
& plastic .......................**12.00**

Souvenir, Gettysburg National
Museum, ruler ea side of
blade, blue plastic ........**4.00**

Souvenir, Grand Canyon AZ,
plastic & gold plate, black
blade ..............................**7.00**

Souvenir, Lincoln silhou-
ette/Lincoln Museum in
Washington DC, steel .....**6.00**

Souvenir, Lookout Mountain seal,
Lookout Mountain TN, cop-
per ...............................**10.00**

Souvenir, Mankato MN, wood
dagger shape, w/red on han-
dle tip ...........................**5.00**

Souvenir, Meka Denmark, silverplated w/enamel, Swiss
Cross ...........................**15.00**

Souvenir, Pensacola FL on blade,
white plastic, seashell han-
dle .................................**3.00**

Souvenir, U of S Alabama, plastic
or steel, made in USA,
w/sheath .........................**8.00**

Souvenir, wood, hand-painted
flowers, curved blade, knob
handle ...........................**20.00**

Sword, gold plate/steel, enamel
coat of arms, machete blade,
Drago ............................**18.00**

Sword, Viking; Norway, brass & silverplate, straight blade ..**25.00**

Sword, white metal, Fort
Conde on D handle, tex-
tured blade .................**5.00**

Sword, white metal, red enamel
coat of arms below handle,
Warwick .........................**8.00**

White metal, space shuttle handle,
marked Fort ..................**15.00**

Wood, African native head ..**12.00**

Wood, African nude native
woman, pointed head, silver
necklace .........................**15.00**

Wood, bust of English duke, ivory
eyes ...............................**25.00**

Wood, duck, hand-painted, green
head, Jasper, Canada ...**10.00**

Wood, duck, multicolor paint,
Dakin, China, 1987 .........**8.00**

Wood (light), Indian head ....**12.00**

Wood w/brass bell, painted, white
inlay ..............................**10.00**

# Liberty Blue

Take home a piece of American history!,' stated an ad from
the 1970s for this dinnerware
made in Staffordshire, England.
Blue and white depictions of
George Washington at Valley
Forge, Paul Revere, Independence

Hall — fourteen historic scenes in all — were offered on different place-setting pieces. The ad goes on to describe this 'unique...truly unusual..museum-quality...future family heirloom.'

For every five dollars spent on groceries you could purchase a basic piece (dinner plate, bread and butter plate, cup, saucer, or dessert dish) for fifty-nine cents on alternate weeks of the promotion. During the promotion, completer pieces could also be purchased. The soup tureen was the most expensive item, originally selling for $24.99. Nineteen completer pieces in all were offered along with a five-year open stock guarantee. For more information we recommend Jo Cunningham's book, *The Best of Collectible Dinnerware.*

Bowl, cereal; from $10 to .....**12.50**
Bowl, flat soup; 8¾", from $15 to ...............................**18.00**
Bowl, fruit; 5", from $4.50 to .**5.50**
Bowl, vegetable; oval ...........**40.00**
Bowl, vegetable; round ........**40.00**
Butter dish, with lid, ¼-lb ....................**55.00**
Casserole, with lid, from $65 to ......................................**75.00**
Coaster, from $8 to .............**10.00**
Creamer ...............................**18.00**
Creamer & sugar bowl, w/lid, original box .........................**80.00**
Cup & saucer, from $7 to ......**9.00**
Gravy boat, from $30 to ......**35.00**
Gravy boat liner ..................**15.00**
Mug, from $10 to .................**12.00**
Pitcher, milk ......................**115.00**

Plate, bread & butter; 6" .......**3.00**
Plate, dinner; 10", from $7 to .**9.00**
Plate, luncheon; scarce, 8¾" .**17.00**
Plate, scarce, 7" .....................**9.50**
Platter, 12", from $35 to ......**45.00**
Platter, 14" ...........................**80.00**
Salt & papper shakers, pr ...**38.00**
Soup ladle, plain white, no decal, from $30 to ....................**35.00**
Soup tureen, w/lid, from $250 to ...........................**350.00**
Sugar bowl, no lid ................**15.00**
Sugar bowl, w/lid .................**35.00**
Teapot, w/lid, from $95 to .**125.00**

# License Plates

Early porcelain license plates are treasured by collectors and often sell for more than $500.00 per pair when found in excellent condition. The best examples are first-year plates from each state, but some of the more modern plates with special graphics are collectible too. Prices given below are for plates in good or better condition.

Our advisor for this category is Richard Diehl, who is listed in the Directory under Colorado.

Alabama, 1971 ......................**5.00**
Alaska, 1966 .........................**19.50**
Arizona, 1974 ........................**5.50**
California, 1938 ..................**25.00**
Delaware, 1983 .....................**8.50**
Florida, 1952 ......................**25.00**
Georgia, 1996, Olympics ......**20.00**
Hawaii, 1975 ........................**10.50**
Illinois, 1948 .........................**16.50**
Indiana, 1976 ........................**3.50**
Kentucky, 1950 ...................**25.00**

Maine, 1940 .......................**10.50**
Maryland, 1919 ...................**30.00**

**Massachusetts, porcelain, blue and white, 1913, 5½x14", EX, $$75.00.**

Michigan, 1954 .....................**12.50**
Mississippi, 1968 ..................**6.50**
Montana, 1941 .....................**20.00**
New Jersy, 1916 ...................**40.00**
New Mexico, 1925 ...............**30.00**
New York, 1973 .....................**5.50**
North Carolina, 1981, First in
　　Flight ............................**10.50**
Ohio, 1959 .............................**7.50**
Oklahoma, 1919 ..................**35.00**
Pennsylvania, 1930 .............**12.50**
Rhode Island, 1934 .............**19.50**
South Carolina, 1961 ..........**12.50**
South Dakota, 1926 .............**18.50**
Tennessee, 1963 ...................**10.50**
Texas, 1958 ..........................**12.50**
Utah, 1949 ...........................**25.00**
Vermont, 1987 ......................**12.50**
Virgina, 1949, pr .................**35.00**
Washington DC, 1965 ..........**15.50**
Wisconsin, 1939 ...................**14.50**
Wyoming, 1968 ......................**5.50**

# Little Red Riding Hood

This line of novelties and kitchenwares has always commanded good prices on the collectibles market. In fact, it became valuable enough to make it attractive to counterfeiters, and now you'll see reproductions everywhere. They're easy to spot, though, watch for one-color eyes. Though there are other differences, you should be able to identify the imposters armed with this information alone.

Little Red Riding Hood was produced from 1943 to 1957. The Regal China Company was by far the major manufacturer of this line, though a rather insignificant number of items were made by the Hull Pottery of Crooksville, Ohio, who sent their whiteware to the Royal China and Novelty Company (a division of Regal China) of Chicago, Illinois, to be decorated. For further information we recommend *The Collector's Encyclopedia of Cookie Jars, Vol I*, by Joyce and Fred Roerig (Collector Books).

Bank, standing ...................**850.00**

**Spice canister, minimum value, $750.00. (Photo courtesy Pat and Ann Duncan)**

Butter dish .........................**550.00**
Canister, cereal ..............**1,475.00**
Cookie jar, closed basket, minimum value ..................**360.00**
Creamer, top pour, no tab handle ...........................**575.00**
Mustard jar, w/spoon .........**575.00**
Pitcher, batter ....................**575.00**
Salt & pepper shakers, 3¼", pr ...........................**195.00**
Spice jar, sq base, from $750 to ........................**1,000.00**
Sugar bowl, crawling .........**400.00**
Sugar bowl, w/lid, from $575 to ..........................**675.00**
Teapot ................................**365.00**
Wall pocket, from $450 to ..**550.00**

## Lu Ray Pastels

Introduced in 1938 by Taylor, Smith, and Taylor of East Liverpool, Ohio, Lu-Ray Pastels is today a very sought-after line of collectible American dinnerware. It was first made in these solid colors: Windsor Blue, Surf Green, Persian Cream, and Sharon Pink. Chatham Gray was introduced in 1948 and is today priced higher than the other colors. For more information, we recommend *Collector's Guide to Lu-Ray Pastels* by Kathy and Bill Meehan.

Bowl, coupe soup; flat ..........**15.00**
Bowl, fruit; Chatham Gray, 5 " .........................**12.50**
Bowl, lug soup; tab handle ..**19.00**
Bowl, mixing; 7" ..................**70.00**
Bowl, vegetable; oval, 9½" ...**16.00**
Bowl, 8¾" ............................**75.00**

Butter dish, Chatham Gray, rare color, w/lid .....................**90.00**
Casserole .............................**85.00**
Chocolate pot, AD; straight sides ........................**360.00**
Coaster/nut dish .................**65.00**
Coffee cup, AD .....................**20.00**
Creamer ................................**8.00**
Egg cup, double ...................**18.00**
Gravy boat ...........................**22.00**
Jug, water; footed ...............**85.00**
Muffin cover, w/underplate ..**105.00**
Nappy, vegetable; round, 8½" ......................**15.00**
Pitcher, any color other than yellow, bulbous w/flat bottom .....**75.00**
Pitcher, yellow, bulbous w/flat bottom ...............................**55.00**
Plate, 10" ............................**20.00**
Plate, 8" .............................**15.00**
Platter, oval, 13" .................**16.00**
Salt & pepper shakers, pr ...**13.00**
Sugar bowl, w/lid .................**11.00**
Teacup ..................................**8.00**
Teapot, curved spout, w/lid .**75.00**
Tumbler, juice ......................**45.00**

## Lunch Boxes

In the early years of this century, tobacco companies often packaged their products in tins that could later be used for lunch boxes. By the 1930s oval lunch boxes designed to appeal to school children were being produced. The rectangular shape that is now popular was preferred in the 1950s. Character lunch boxes decorated with the faces of TV personalities, super heroes, and Disney and cartoon characters are especially sought after by collectors today. Our values are for excellent condition lunch boxes only (without the thermos unless one is mentioned in the line).

Our advisor for this category is Terri Ivers; she is listed in the Directory under Oklahoma. Refer to *Pictorial Price Guide to Vinyl and Plastic Lunch Boxes and Thermoses* and *Pictorial Price Guide to Metal Lunch Boxes and Thermoses* by Larry Aikens (L-W Book Sales) for more information. For an expanded listing, see *Schroeder's Collectible Toys, Antique to Modern* (Collector Books).

A-Team, plastic, 1985, red, w/thermos, EX .........................**25.00**
Adam 12, metal, 1972, VG ..**45.00**
Annie, vinyl, 1981, w/thermos, VG ...............................**45.00**
Atom Ant, metal, 1966, G ...**60.00**
Basketweave, metal, 1968, M ......................**100.00**

**Charlie's Angels, NM, $75.00. (Photo courtesy June Moon)**

**The Munsters, 1965, with King Seeley Thermos, EX-, $85.00. (Photo courtesy June Moon)**

Bee Gees, metal, 1978, EX ..**40.00**
Care Bears, metal, 1983, w/thermos, M ..........................**40.00**
Dukes of Hazzard, metal, 1980, w/thermos, M ................**50.00**
Family Affair, metal, 1969, w/thermos, EX .......................**135.00**
Ghostbusters, plastic, 1986, purple, EX ..............................**20.00**
Ghostland, metal, 1977, EX .**65.00**
Gremlins, metal, 1984, w/thermos, EX ...................................**20.00**
Hansel & Gretel, metal, 1982, EX ...............................**85.00**
Happy Days, metal, 1976, VG **30.00**
Incredible Hulk, metal, 1978, EX ..............................**30.00**
Knight Rider, metal, 1981, w/thermos, M ..........................**85.00**
Luggage Plaid, metal, 1955, EX ...........................**65.00**
Magic Lassie, metal, 1978, w/thermos, EX .........................**85.00**
Miss Piggy, plastic, 1980, EX ......................**15.00**
Osmonds, metal, 1973, w/thermos, EX .................................**75.00**

Peanuts, vinyl, 1969, w/thermos, M ...................................**130.00**

Pete's Dragon, metal, 1978, EX .........................**45.00**

Planet of the Apes, metal, 1974, w/thermos, EX ..............**95.00**

Raggedy Ann & Andy, metal, 1973, VG .........................**35.00**

Rescuers Down Under, metal, 1977, VG ........................**35.00**

Scooby Doo, plastic, 1984, w/thermos, EX ..........................**50.00**

Space: 1999, metal, 1975, EX .**35.00**

Star Wars, metal, 1978, w/thermos, EX .........................**65.00**

Teenage Mutant Ninja Turtles, vinyl, 1988, blue softee, EX .........................**8.00**

### Thermoses

Archies, plastic, 1969, NM ..**40.00**

Battle of the Planets, plastic, 1979, M ..........................**18.00**

Care Bear Cousins, plastic, 1984, M .....................................**9.00**

Drag Strip, plastic, 1975, EX .**24.00**

Flintstones, metal, 1967, M ..**75.00**

GI Joe, metal, 1967, M ........**80.00**

Happy Days, plastic, 1977, EX .........................**15.00**

Heathcliff, plastic, 1982, EX ....**10.00**

Howdy Doody, plastic, 1977, EX ............................**25.00**

Kung Fu, metal, 1974 ..........**18.00**

Magic Lassie, plastic, 1978, EX ............................**20.00**

Osmonds, plastic, 1973, EX ..**20.00**

Rambo, plastic, 1985, M ......**10.00**

Sesame Street, plastic, 1985, EX ...............................**3.00**

Superman, plastic, 1978, M ..**15.00**

Waltons, plastic, 1973, EX ..**16.00**

# Magazines

Some of the most collectible magazines are *Life* (because of the celebrities and important events they feature on their covers, *Saturday Evening Post* and *Ladies' Home Journal* (especially those featuring the work of famous illustrators such as Parrish, Rockwell, and Wyeth), and *National Geographics* (pre-WWI issues in particular). As is true with any type of ephemera, condition and value are closely related. Unless they're in fine condition (clean, no missing or clipped pages, and very little other damage), they're worth very little; and cover interest and content are far more important than age.

See also National Geographics; TV Guide.

American Detective, 1936, January, Vol 4 #2, crime cases, VG ...**5.00**

American Weekly, 1950, November, Leyendecker cover, EX .................**20.00**

Argosy, 1965, Dr Sam Sheppard cover, EX .........................**7.00**

Art Photography, 1956, April, Sophia Loren cover, VG .**10.00**

Baseball Digest, 1951, DiMaggio cover, VG .......................**25.00**

Boy's Life, 1937, July, HC Christy cover, VG .......................**10.00**

Boy's Life, 1969, June, Mickey Mantle w/Mickey Jr cover, EX ................................**40.00**

Collier's, 1945, June, Truman cover, VG .........................**6.00**

Collier's, 1956, March 2, Grace Kelly & Prince Ranier cover .....**15.00**

Cosmopolitan, 1953, May, Marilyn Monroe cover, Oklahoma, EX ...................................**45.00**

Cosmopolitan, 1955, October, Audrey Hepburn cover, VG .............**9.00**

Country Song Roundup, 1957, August, Elvis Presley cover, VG ...................................**15.00**

Ebony, 1967, Star Trek cover, VG ...................................**5.00**

Esquire, 1941, November, Vargas & Petty art ....................**20.00**

Esquire, 1978, August 15, Robert Kennedy cover, VG .........**3.00**

Family Circle, 1944, March 24, Constance Dowling/Danny Kaye cover, VG ...............**3.00**

Family Circle, 1946, January 25, Bob Hope cover & article, VG ..................................**7.00**

Family Circle, 1949, June, girl w/puppy on cover, VG .....**3.00**

Fortune, 1932, August, VG .**10.00**

Fortune, 1949, Ben Shahn cover, EX ..................................**30.00**

Gentleman's Companion, 1980, May, VG .........................**10.00**

Ladies' Home Journal, 1941, July 1941, Bette Davis cover .**15.00**

Ladies' Home Journal, 1947, February, Ingrid Bergman article, EX ...................................**5.00**

Ladies' Home Journal, 1956, March, Grace Kelly article, EX ...................................**3.50**

Ladies' Home Journal, 1967, June, Twiggy cover, EX ............**2.00**

Liberty, 1946, December 21, Song of the South article, EX ..**5.00**

Life, 1941, January 6, Katherine Hepburn cover ..............**18.00**

Life, 1941, September 9, Ted Williams cover, EX .......**50.00**

Life, 1942, March 2, Ginger Rogers cover, EX ......................**15.00**

Life, 1949, October, Princess Margaret cover, EX .............**15.00**

Life, 1950, June 12, Hopalong Cassidy cover, NM ..............**45.00**

Life, 1951, July 30, Gary Crosby cover, VG .........................**4.00**

Life, 1956, April 23, Jayne Mansfield cover, EX ...............**28.00**

Life, 1958, July, Roy Campanella cover, EX .......................**20.00**

Life, 1962, June 22, Marilyn Monroe cover, NM, from $24 to ................................**30.00**

Life, 1966, April 15, Louis Armstrong cover, EX ...........**35.00**

Life, 1968, April 12, Dr Martin Luther King shooting ...**15.00**

Life, 1969, December 12, Apollo 12 article, VG ......................**10.00**

Life, 1971, March 12, Jackie Kennedy cover, VG .........**5.00**

Life, 1978, November, Mickey Mouse's 50th Birthday, EX .............**15.00**

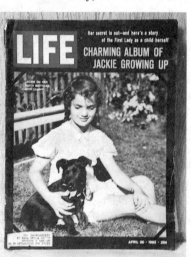

**Life, April 26, 1963, Jackie Kennedy cover, EX, $10.00.**

Look, 1927, December, Shirley Temple/Santa Claus cover, EX ..................................**35.00**

Look, 1963, December, Kennedy & family cover, Special Edition ..............................**15.00**

Look, 1966, December 13, John Lennon cover, VG+ .......**28.00**

McCall's, 1944, June, Irene Dunne & Dorothy Lamour photos, G ........................**4.00**

McCall's, 1951, June, Greta Garbo cover & article, VG+ .....**10.00**

McCall's, 1956, Helen Hayes article, VG ..............................**8.00**

McCall's, 1956, March, Duchess of Windsor cover, EX ..........**8.00**

McCall's, 1961, March, Jack Parr & Emily Post articles, VG ...**8.00**

Modern Romance, 1941, June, VG ..................................**11.00**

Newsweek, 1957, July 1, Stan Musial cover ..................**15.00**

Newsweek, 1972, January 10, Who Can Beat Nixon? ..**12.00**

Playboy, 1960, January, Stella Stevens cover, NM ........**40.00**

Playboy, 1960, May, Ginger Young cover, EX ........................**18.00**

Playboy, 1979, August, Dorothy Stratten, NM .................**15.00**

Popular Photography, 1937, August, swimsuit cover, VG ............................**15.00**

Redbook, 1949, July, Rudy Vallee article, EX ......................**5.50**

Redbook, 1956, Frank Sinatra cover, EX .........................**5.00**

Rolling Stone, 1971, #88, Morrison Memorial, EX ..............**100.00**

Saturday Evening Post, 1946, March 2, Norman Rockwell cover, EX .......................**10.00**

Saturday Evening Post, 1953, November 21, VG+ .........**4.00**

Saturday Evening Post, 1956, May 19, Rockwell cover, VG .**15.00**

Saturday Evening Post, 1957, June 29, Rockwell cover, EX ..............................**18.00**

Saturday Evening Post, 1961, June 14, Burt Lancaster article, VG ...........................**3.00**

Sports Illustrated, 1956, June 18, Mickey Mantle cover, EX .**150.00**

Sports Illustrated, 1957, Sugar Ray Robinson cover, EX ........**30.00**

Sports Illustrated, 1963, June 10, Cassius Clay cover, EX .**95.00**

Sports Illustrated, 1974, March 18, Babe Ruth cover, EX .....**45.00**

Sports Illustrated, 1984, April 23, Darrel Strawberry cover, VG ..................................**6.00**

Sports Illustrated, 1984, December 10, Michael Jordan cover, EX ..................................**40.00**

Time, 1948, May 17, Eddie Arcaro cover, VG+ .....................**25.00**

Time, 1954, May 31, Native Dancer (race horse) cover, EX ..............................**18.00**

Time, 1964, January 3, Martin Luther King cover, EX .**30.00**

Woman's Home Companion, 1950, March, VG+ .....................**2.50**

# Marbles

Because there are so many kinds of marbles that interest today's collectors, we suggest you study a book on that specific subject such as one by our advisor Everett Grist (see Directory, Tennessee), published by Collector Books. In addition to his earlier work, *Antique and Collectible Marbles*, he has written a book on *Machine-Made and Contemporary Marbles,* now in its second edition. His latest title is *Everett Grist's Big Book of Marbles*, which includes both antique and modern varieties. All are published by Collector Books.

Remember that condition is extremely important. Naturally, chips occurred; and though some may be ground down and polished, the values of badly chipped and repolished marbles are low. In our listings, values are for marbles in the standard small size and in excellent to near-mint condition unless noted otherwise. Watch for reproductions of the comic character marbles. Repros have the design printed on a large area of plain white glass with color swirled through the back and sides. While common sulfides may run as low as $100.00, those with a more unusual subject or made of colored glass are considerably higher, sometimes as much as $1,000.00 or more. See also Clubs and Newsletters.

Akro Agate, Flinty, red, ⅝" ......**15.00**
Akro Agate Imperials, in box .**900.00**
Akro Agate Popeye Corkscrew, dark blue & yellow, ⅝" .**35.00**
Akro Camelian Agate .....**1,000.00**
Banded Lutz, opaque black base ......................**250.00**
Banded Swirl, bright colors .**100.00**
Bennington, pink, 1" ...........**15.00**

Box, Akro Agate, metal, w/marbles, rules & bag ......**1,200.00**
Box, Christensen Agate & Co, Guineas, set of 24 ....**6,000.00**
China, glazed, single color, intersecting lines, 1" .............**10.00**
Comic, Cotes Bakery .........**800.00**
Comic, Tom Mix ..............**2,500.00**
Crockery, unglazed, lined ....**10.00**
Decorated china, glazed, rose, 1¾" ........................**1,200.00**
Decorated china, glazed, rose, ⅝" ...........................**350.00**

**Divided Core, red, white, and blue with yellow and green ribbon, ten outer lines of alternating yellow and white, ⅝", $40.00; 1¾", $180.00. (Photo courtesy Everett Grist)**

End of the day, Onionskin Lutz, pink & white core, NM .**175.00**
End of the day, pontil mark, 1¾" ......................**1,200.00**
Gooseberry, transparent amber, ⅝" ...................................**95.00**
Indian swirls, 1¾" ..........**2,700.00**
Indian swirls, ⅝" .................**95.00**
Marble King, Rainbow, wasp, 1" ...........................**10.00**
MF Christensen & Sons, slag, red ...............................**10.00**

298

Onionskin Lutz, 1¾" .......**1,700.00**
Peltier, Christmas Tree, ¾" .**800.00**
Peltier, Ketchup & Mustard, ¾" ........................**425.00**
Peltier, Peerless Patch, black aventurine, ¾" ..............**65.00**
Peltier, Rebel, ¾" ...............**725.00**
Peltier, Superman, ¾" .......**650.00**
Peppermint Swirl, mica in blue bands ...........................**450.00**

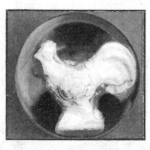

**Sulfide, rooster (EX detail), 1¾", polished, otherwise M, $110.00.**

Sulfide, American bison or buffalo, 1¾" ................................**350.00**
Sulfide, baby in a basket, 1¾" .....................**500.00**
Sulfide, child & dog, 1¾" ..**1,200.00**
Sulfide, child crawling, 1¾" ...**600.00**
Sulfide, common unpainted animals, clear glass, 1⅝", minimum value ...................**150.00**
Sulfide, lamb in light amber glass, 1¾" ...........................**2,000.00**
Sulfide, Little Boy Blue, 1¾" ...................**600.00**
Sulfide, numerals 2 & 1, 1¾" .**500.00**
Sulfide, papoose in cradle board, 1¾" ..............................**800.00**
Sulfide, Santa Claus, 1¾" .**700.00**
Transparent swirl, solid core, 1¾" ...........................**425.00**

# Match Safes

Match safes became popular around 1850. By the early 1900s they were commonplace. These small containers were designed to safely carry matches on one's person. They were made from numerous materials including tin, brass, sterling, gold, tortoise shell, and aluminum. Widely used at the turn of the century as a medium for advertising, most safes can be distinguished from other smalls by the presence of their rough striking surface. Match safes have been and are still being reproduced; there are many sterling reproductions currently on the market.

Our advisor for this category is George Sparacio, who is listed in the Directory under New Jersey.

Agate, cylindrical, brass trim, 2⅝x1", EX ...................**195.00**
Anheuser Busch, lg A & eagle, plated brass, 2⅞x1½", EX ....**95.00**
Arm & Hammer, thermoplastic, slip top, 3x1½", EX .......**95.00**
Book form, combo stamp/match, plated brass, 1⅞x1⅜", EX ........**50.00**
Cherubs motif, sterling, Unger Bros, 2x2", EX .............**275.00**
Cigars, banded, figural, plated brass, 2¾x1½", EX .....**175.00**
Climax Specialty ad, black & white, celluloid wrap, 2¾x1½", EX ...................**75.00**
Combo, stamps/pick/pencil/matches, silverplate, English, 2½x 1½" .............................**225.00**

Dog/Indian princess inserts, metal w/plated brass ends, 2¾x1½" .........................**45.00**

Fleur-de-lis motif w/3 garnets, sterling, 2⅜x1⅜", EX ........................**175.00**

Hidden photo, plain front, sterling, English, 2x1¾", EX .....**225.00**

Horse hoof form, plated brass w/celluloid trim, 2¼x1½", EX ..............................**175.00**

Jackknife form, 2 simulated blades, plated brass, 2⅞x1⅛", EX ................................**220.00**

Krupp Munitions, bull's-eye design, plated brass, 2⅝x1⅝", EX ................................**125.00**

Life preserver form, ship insert, plated brass, 1¾" dia, EX .................**295.00**

Mythical figure embossed 1 side, sterling, Carter, 2¼x1¼", EX ..............................**135.00**

Order of Masons, insert type, metal w/plated brass ends, 2¾x1½" ..........................**65.00**

Oriental motif w/working compass, brass, 2⅝x1¼", EX .......**225.00**

Oyster shell form, silver solder, Wallace, 3x1⅞", EX ....**175.00**

President Harrison figural portrait type, brass, 2¾x1¾", EX ..............................**300.00**

Sailboat motif, sterling, 2½x1⅝", EX ................................**125.00**

Serpent & rococo motif, sterling, Gilbert, 2½x1⅜", EX ...**115.00**

Shoe form, aluminum w/advertising on sole, 2⅞x1¼", EX ........................**135.00**

Shoe form, papier-mache, 1¼x3", EX ................................**125.00**

Shrew figural, plated brass, leather ears & tail, 2⅛x⅝", EX ..............................**265.00**

Standard Oil advertising, color graphics, celluloid wrap, 2¾x1½" ........................**150.00**

Tooth figural w/pig surmount, plated brass, 2⅝x1", EX .....**135.00**

Trick, coffin shape w/double lids, wood, 3x1¼", EX ...........**75.00**

Trousers w/suspenders form, pewter, 2⅞x1¼", EX ...**155.00**

United Brewery...Against Prohibition, celluloid wrap, 2¾x1½" ........................**125.00**

Wolf's head figural, plated brass w/glass eyes, 1x2", EX ........................**250.00**

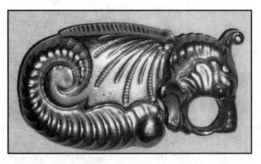

**Figural brass sea horse with glass eyes, 2x1⅛", EX, $350.00. (Photo courtesy George Sparacio)**

# McCoy

A popular collectible with flea market goers, McCoy pottery was made in Roseville, Ohio, from 1910 until the late 1980s. They are most famous for their extensive line of figural cookie jars, more than two hundred in all. They also made amusing figural planters, as well as dinnerware, and vases and pots for the florist trade. Though some pieces are unmarked, most bear one of several McCoy trademarks. Beware of reproductions made by a company in Tennessee who used a very close facsimile of the old McCoy mark. They made several cookie jars once produced by McCoy as well as other now-defunct potteries. Some of these (but by no means all) were dated with the number '93' below the mark.

For more information refer to *The Collector's Encyclopedia of McCoy Pottery* by Sharon and Bob Huxford and *McCoy Pottery, Collector's Reference & Value Guide,* by Margaret Hanson, Craig Nissen, and Bob Hanson (both available from Collector Books). See also Cookie Jars. See Clubs and Newsletters for information concerning the newsletter *The Nelson McCoy Express.*

Ashtray, bird at side of flower blossom, unmarked, 5¼", from $20 to ...................25.00

Cornucopia, Sunburst Gold, 4x3¼", from $20 to .......25.00

Creamer, Sunburst Gold, McCoy mark, 2¾x5½", from $25 to .........................30.00

Dog feeder, Man's Best Friend..., brown, 1930s, 7½", from $50 to ...................................60.00

**Fan vase, flower form, 1953, $55.00.**

Fernery, embossed antelope & leaves, pastel, NM mark, 1940s, 9½" ......................35.00

Fernery, Hobnail, pastel matt, NM mark, 1940s, 5½", from $20 to ............................30.00

Flower bowl ornament, fawn, white, NM mark, 4¼", from $40 to ............................60.00

Flower bowl ornament, peacock, white, unmarked, 4¾", from $40 to ............................60.00

Flower holder, angelfish figural, green, unmarked, 1940s, 6", from $100 to ................150.00

Flower holder, fish figural, yellow or rose, NM mark, 4¼", from $60 to ............................80.00

Flower holder, pigeon figural, yellow or rose, NM mark, 4", from $60 to ....................80.00

Flower holder, turtle figural, ivory or green, NM mark, 4¼", from $30 to .............................40.00

Flower holder, witch figural, brown or green, USA mark, 3", from $100 to .......... **150.00**

Flowerpot, Butterfly, color other than coral, NM mark, 3¾", from $25 to .................... **35.00**

Heart vase, pink, unmarked, 1940s, 6", from $45 to ... **60.00**

Ivy vase, Butterfly, blue, USA mark, 4½", from $30 to .. **40.00**

Jardiniere, Basketweave, white or green, unmarked, 7½", from $40 to ............................ **60.00**

Jardiniere, Blossomtime, McCoy mark, 6" sq, from $40 to ...................... **50.00**

Jardiniere, Hobnail, pastel matt, USA mark, 1940s, 3½", from $30 to ............................ **40.00**

Lamp base, horse figural, black, unmarked, 1950s, 8¼", from $65 to ............................ **95.00**

Matchbox holder, flower on white, McCoy mark, 1970s, 5¾", from $30 to .................... **40.00**

Pitcher, elephant figural, white, NM mark, 1940s, 7x5", from $250 to ........................ **300.00**

Pitcher, embossed stripes, glossy, McCoy mark, 1953, 9½", from $25 to ............................ **50.00**

Planter, banana form, yellow pastel, NM mark, 8½", from $30 to .................................... **40.00**

Planter, baseball glove form, unmarked, 6x6", from $125 to ................................ **150.00**

Planter, bird dog, hand decorated, McCoy mark, 8½x12½", from $150 to ........................ **175.00**

Planter, bird figural, white or green, USA mark, 4½", from $20 to ............................. **25.00**

Planter, bird of paradise, gold trim, McCoy mark, 12½", from $40 to .................... **50.00**

Planter, clown & pig figural, McCoy mark, 8½", from $60 to .................................... **75.00**

Planter, double cache; hummingbird, pink & green, marked, 11", from $60 to ............ **75.00**

Planter, duck w/egg, yellow w/decor, McCoy mark, 7x3¼", from $25 to .................... **30.00**

Planter, Fruit Line, grapes, 1953, 6½x5", from $75 to ..... **100.00**

Planter, lamb figural, painted details, McCoy mark, 1954, 5", from $60 to .................... **75.00**

Planter, Madonna, white, McCoy mark, 1950s, 6", from $250 to ................................ **300.00**

Planter, Mary Ann shoe, pastel, NM mark, 1940s, 5", from $20 to .................................... **35.00**

Planter, Old Mill, gold trim, McCoy mark, 6½x7½", from $50 to ............................ **60.00**

Planter, pomegranate, realistic, McCoy mark, from $75 to .. **100.00**

Planter, poodle figural, black w/red cold paint, McCoy mark, 7½" ...................................... **65.00**

Planter, puppy figural, brown spots, McCoy mark, 6¼x6", from $60 to .................... **75.00**

Planter, rabbit w/carrot, cold paint, McCoy mark, 7¼", from $75 to ........................... **100.00**

Planter, shell form, pastel matt, NM mark, 1940s, 7½x5½", from $25 to .................... **40.00**

Planter, stork at side of baby in basket, McCoy mark, 1956, 7", from $40 to .................... **50.00**

Planter, Wild Rose, McCoy mark, 1952, 3½x8", from $40 to ........................**50.00**

Planter vase, donkey figural, glossy, unmarked, 7", from $25 to ............................**30.00**

Porch jar, embossed decor, green, NM mark, 1940s, 11x9½", from $100 to ................**125.00**

Porch jar, embossed floral, cylindrical, McCoy mark, 11", from $100 to ..........................**150.00**

Stretch animal, lion, pastel, unmarked, 1940s, 7½x5½", from $175 to ................**225.00**

Teapot, Daisy, brown to green to white, McCoy mark, from $40 to ....................................**50.00**

Teapot, Ivy, hand decorated, McCoy mark, 6-cup, from $40 to ....................................**50.00**

Tray, hands figural, white, NM mark, 1940s, 8½", from $80 to ................................**100.00**

Vase, bud; Grecian, ivory w/green spray, McCoy mark, 7¼", from $25 to ............................**30.00**

Vase, Butterfly, standard glaze, handles, USA, 10", from $100 to ....................................**125.00**

Vase, Butterfly figural, colors other than coral, USA, 7½x5½", from $50 to ......................................**60.00**

Vase, cornucopia; matt colors, McCoy mark, 8x7½", from $60 to ....................................**75.00**

Vase, embossed tulip, sm handles, dark green, McCoy mark, 9", from $40 to ....................**50.00**

Vase, grape, gold trim, McCoy mark, 9", from $75 to ...**90.00**

Vase, hand w/glove figural, NM mark, 8¼", from $50 to ..**60.00**

Vase, hyacinth, McCoy mark, 8", from $60 to ....................**75.00**

Vase, peacock, green or white, McCoy mark, 1948, 8", from $35 to ............................**45.00**

Vase, poppy, pink w/green leaves, McCoy mark, 8½", from $200 to ..................................**300.00**

Vase, sailboat (embossed), sq foot, NM mark, 9", from $35 to ........**50.00**

Vase, swan figural, pastel, unmarked, 1940s, 6", from $20 to ............................**25.00**

Vase, triple lily, white or yellow, McCoy mark, 8½", from $40 to ..................................**60.00**

Vase, trumpet neck, upturned handles, green, McCoy mark, 1940s, 8¼" ....................**35.00**

Vase, Uncle Sam, yellow gloss, marked, 7½", from $50 to ....................**60.00**

Vase, yellow, waisted cylinder w/low handles, USA, 1940s, 10", from $45 to ............**65.00**

Wall pocket, Blossomtime, applied flower, label, 8", from $60 to ..................**85.00**

Wall pocket, clock, burgundy & blue w/gold trim, McCoy mark, 8", from $150 to ..........**200.00**

Wall pocket, clown, McCoy mark, 1940s, 8", from $100 to ..........................**125.00**

Wall pocket, Dutch shoe, McCoy mark, late 1940s, 7½", from $40 to ............................**50.00**

Wall pocket, fan, Sunburst Gold, McCoy mark, 1950s, 8½", from $60 to ..................**75.00**

Wall pocket, lady w/bonnet, McCoy mark, 1940s, 8", from $40 to ............................**75.00**

Wall pocket, leaf, yellow & green, McCoy mark, 7", from $35 to ..........................**50.00**

Wall pocket, lily bud, pink pastel, NM mark, 6", from $50 to ........**75.00**

Wall pocket, pear on leaves, natural, 1950s, 7x6", from $50 to ................................**60.00**

Wall pocket, umbrella, black matt, McCoy mark, 1950s, 8¾", from $60 to ....................**75.00**

## Melmac Dinnerware

Melmac was a product of the postwar era, a thermoplastic material formed by the interaction of melamine and formaldehyde. It was popular because of its attractive colors and patterns, and it was practically indestructible. But eventually it faded, became scratched or burned, and housewives tired of it. By the late '60s and early '70s, it fell from favor.

Collectors, however, are finding its mid-century colors and shapes appealing again, and they're beginning to reassemble melmac table services when pristine, well designed items can be found.

Our advisors for this category are Gregory R. Zimmer and Alvin Daigle Jr., authors of *Melmac Dinnerware*; they are listed in the Directory under Minnesota. See also Russel Wright.

**Aztec, Debonaire, Flite-Lane, Mar-Crest, Restraware, Rivieraware, Stetson, Westinghouse**

Bowl, cereal; from $2 to .........**3.00**
Bowl, soup; from $3 to ...........**4.00**
Butter dish, from $5 to ..........**7.00**
Cup & saucer, from $2 to ......**3.00**
Gravy boat, from $5 to ...........**6.00**
Plate, salad; from $2 to .........**3.00**
Tumbler, 10-oz, from $7 to ....**8.00**

**Boontoon, Branchell, Brookpark, Harmony House, Prolon, Watertown Lifetime Ware**

Bowl, cereal; from $4 to .........**5.00**
Bowl, serving; from $8 to ....**10.00**
Bread tray, from $8 to .........**10.00**
Plate, compartment; from $10 to ..............................**12.00**
Plate, dinner; from $4 to .......**5.00**
Platter, from $8 to ...............**10.00**
Tidbit tray, 2-tier, from $12 to ..**15.00**

**Fostoria, Lucent**

Bowl, cereal; from $7 to .........**9.00**
Butter dish, from $15 to ......**18.00**
Cup & saucer, from $8 to ....**12.00**
Plate, dinner; from $6 to .......**8.00**
Sugar bowl, w/lid, from $12 to .**15.00**

## Metlox

Since the 1940s, the Metlox company of California has been producing dinnerware lines, cookie jars, and decorative items which today have become popular collectibles. Some of their best-known patterns are California Provincial (the dark green and burgundy rooster), Red Rooster (in red, orange, and brown), Homestead Provincial (dark green and burgundy farm scenes), and Colonial Homestead (farm scenes done in red, orange, and brown). See also Cookie Jars.

Our advisor for this category is Carl Gibbs, Jr.; he is listed in the Directory under Texas. Mr. Gibbs is the author of *Collector's Encyclopedia of Metlox Potteries* (Collector Books).

**Modern Masterpice, Angelfish vase, #1814, Romanelli design, 8½", from $75.00 to $90.00.**

Blueberry Provincial, creamer, 6-oz ...................................**22.00**
Blueberry Provincial, salt & pepper shakers, pr ..............**24.00**
California Aztec, cup & saucer .**20.00**
California Geranium, bowl, salad ..........................**65.00**
California Geranium, plate, dinner ..................................**12.00**
California Ivy, bowl, salad; 11¼" ..........................**90.00**
California Ivy, cup & saucer .**15.00**
California Ivy, plate, salad; 8" .**12.00**
California Ivy, salt & pepper shakers, sm, pr .....................**28.00**
California Ivy, teapot, 6-cup ..**110.00**

California Provincial, butter dish ............................**95.00**
California Provincial, coaster, 3¾" ..............................**30.00**
California Provincial, cup & saucer ..........................**18.00**
California Provincial, egg cup .**35.00**
California Provincial, tumbler, 11-oz ....................................**40.00**
California Strawberry, plate, dinner; 10¼" ........................**13.00**
California Strawberry, salt & pepper shakers, pr ..............**24.00**
Homestead Provincial, bowl, soup; 8" ....................................**30.00**
Homestead Provincial, gravy boat, 1-pt ...............................**49.00**
Homestead Provincial, plate, bread & butter; 6⅜" ......**10.00**
Homestead Provincial, rooster pepper ...........................**38.00**
La Mancha, bowl, divided vegetable; 10¾" ..................**45.00**
La Mancha, mug, 10-oz .......**20.00**
Lotus, bowl, fruit; 5½" .........**16.00**
Lotus, sugar bowl, w/lid, 11-oz .**38.00**
Navajo, chop plate, 13" ........**65.00**
Navajo, plate, bread & butter; 6½" ...............................**40.00**
Provincial Fruit, bowl, salad; 11⅛" .............................**70.00**
Provincial Fruit, sugar bowl ...................**22.00**
Red Rooster Provincial, bowl, divided vegetable; 12" ...**65.00**
Red Rooster Provincial, butter dish ...............................**75.00**
Red Rooster Provincial, candle holder ...........................**50.00**
Red Rooster Provincial, mug, lg, 1-pt ....................................**38.00**
Red Rooster Provincial, pitcher, 1-qt ....................................**70.00**

**Poppet, Casey Policeman, #019, from $35.00 to $45.00. (Photo courtesy Carl Gibbs Jr.)**

Red Rooster Provincial, tumbler, 11-oz ..............................**34.00**

Sculptured Daisy, casserole, w/lid, 1½-qt ..............................**90.00**

Sculptured Daisy, compote, footed, 8½" .................................**80.00**

Sculptured Grape, creamer, 10-oz .................................**28.00**

Sculptured Grape, cup & saucer, 7-oz .................................**16.00**

Sculptured Grape, salt & pepper shakers, pr ....................**26.00**

Sculptured Zinnia, salad fork & spoon .............................**55.00**

**Sculptured Zinnia, Cup and saucer, $14.00; Dinner plate, $13.00; Coffeepot, from $80.00 to $90.00. (Photo courtesy Carl Gibbs Jr.)**

Vineyard, coffeepot, 8-cup ...**90.00**
Vineyard, plate, dinner; 10¾" .**13.00**
Woodland Gold, bowl, cereal; 5⅝" .............................**14.00**
Woodland Gold, butter dish, oval .........................**55.00**
Yorkshire, plate, salad ........**12.00**
Yorkshire, tumbler, lg .........**25.00**

# Miller Studio

Brightly painted chalkware plaques, bookends, thermometers, and hot pad holders modeled with subjects that range from Raggedy Ann and angels to bluebirds and sunfish were the rage during '50s and '60s, and even into the early 1970s you could buy them from the five-&-dime store to decorate your kitchen and bathroom walls with style and flair. Collectors who like this 'kitschy' ambience are snapping them up and using them in the vintage rooms they're re-creating with period appliances, furniture and accessories. They're especially fond of the items marked Miller Studio (an importing firm). Most but not all of their pieces are marked and carry a copyright date. If you find an unmarked item with small holes on the back where stapled-on cardboard packaging has been torn away, chances are very good it's Miller Studio as well.

Angels, cherub's face, orange, 1954, pr, from $18 to ....**20.00**
Animals, bear toothbrush holder, M17, tan & brown, 1954, from $16 to ...........................**18.00**

Animals, bunny toothbrush holder, yellow & black, from $30 to .....**32.00**

Animals, cat w/pencil holder, yellow & black, 1957, from $10 to ....................................**12.00**

Animals, horse head, brown, 1951, from $12 to .....................**14.00**

Animals, pig, blue & white, sm .**10.00**

Animals, poodle plaques, black & white, round, 1957, pr, from $20 to .............................**25.00**

Animals, Scottie dog head, yellow & black, pr, from $8 to .**10.00**

Birds, bluebird, blue to yellow, 1970, sm, pr, from $5 to .**7.00**

Birds, cardinal, red, 1972, pr, from $5 to .................................**7.00**

Birds, crested cockatoo, M30, light blue-gray, 1957, pr, from $18 to ....................................**20.00**

Birds, flying pheasant, M36, red, 3-pc set, from $25 to .....**30.00**

Birds, owl, white, 1978, 11", pr, from $8 to .......................**10.00**

Birds, swan, pink, oval, 1965, pr, from $8 to .......................**10.00**

Figures, Dutch boy & girl, yellow & red, 1953, pr, from $25 to ........................**28.00**

Figures, Raggedy Ann & Andy, blue & orange, pr, from $28 to ....................................**32.00**

Fish, family, blue, 9", 4-pc set, from $10 to ....................**12.00**

Fish, frolicking pr w/starfish, yellow, 3-pc set, from $10 to .........**12.00**

Fish, gaping pr w/bubbles, pink, 7", 4-pc set, from $8 to .**10.00**

Fish, male & female, black, 1954, pr, from $12 to .**14.00**

Fruit, cherry plaque, pink, yellow & black, sq, 1956, pr, from $18 to ....................................**20.00**

Fruit, grapes on wood, gold, 1964, from $10 to ....................**12.00**

Hot pad holder, peach w/funny face, yellow, 1972, pr, from $8 to ....................................**10.00**

Hot pad holder, sunflower, Let's Be Happy, yellow & green, 1973, pr .........................**14.00**

Note pad, bird, Make a Note, yellow & red, 1964, from $16 to ................................**18.00**

Note pad, fruit, Don't You Forget It, blue & red, 1968, from $10 to ....................................**12.00**

Note pad, owl w/pencil holder, red & yellow, 1970, from $10 to ................................**12.00**

Thermometer, fruit bunch, 1981, from $10 to ....................**12.00**

Thermometer, potbelly stove, Weather Watcher, gold, 1965, from $13 to ....................**15.00**

Thermometer, Sniffy Skunk, M55, black & yellow, 1954, from $28 to .............................**30.00**

# Model Kits

The best-known producer of model kits today is Aurora. Collectors often pay astronomical prices for some of the character kits from the 1960s. Made popular by all the monster movies of that decade, ghouls like Vampirella, Frankenstein, and the Wolfman were eagerly built up by kids everywhere. But the majority of all model kits were vehicles, ranging from 3" up to 24" long. Some of the larger model vehicle makers were AMT, MPC, and IMC. Condition is very important in assessing the value of a kit, with built-ups priced at about 50% lower than one still in the box. Other things factor into pricing as well — who is selling, who is buying and how badly they want it, locality, supply, and demand.

For information about Aurora models, we recommend *Aurora, History and Price Guide,* by Bill Bruegman (Cap'n Penny Productions, Inc); to learn more about models other than Aurora, refer to *Collectible Figure Kits of the '50s, '60s & '70s, Reference and Value Guide*, by Gordy Dutt (see Directory under Ohio for ordering information), and *Classic Plastic Model Kits* by Rick Polizzi (Collector Books). For additional listings we recommend *Schroeder's Collectible Toys, Antique to Modern* (Collector Books). See Clubs and Newsletters for International Figure Kit Club; *Model Toy Collector Magazine.*

Adams, Hawk Missle Battery #154, 1958, MIB ...........**70.00**
Airfix, Ankylosaurus #3801, 1981, MIB ...............................**30.00**
AMT, Flintstones, Family Sedan #496, 1974, MIB ...........**90.00**
ANT/Ertl, Airwolf Helicopter, 1984, M (EX sealed box) ..........**23.00**
Anubis, Star Trek: The Next Generation #9204, Borg Ship, 1992, MIB ......................**70.00**
Apex, Russian Carrier Rocket Vostak, 1990s, MIB ......**19.00**
Atlantic, Goldrake-Toei Animation, Actarus Figure Set #GK1, 1978, MIB ..........**14.00**

Aurora, Black Falcon Pirate Ship #210, MIB ......................**50.00**
Aurora, Comic Scenes, Lone Ranger #188, 1974, M (VG+ box) ................................**40.00**
Aurora, Creature From the Black Lagoon #426, 1963, assembled ..............................**65.00**
Aurora, Dr Jekell as Mr Hyde #482, 1972, MIB (sealed) ..............**210.00**
Aurora, Gladiator #406, 1964, MIB ..............................**155.00**
Aurora, Guys & Gals, Scotch Lad #419, 1957, MIB ...........**70.00**
Aurora, King Kong, 1972, glow-in-the-dark, assembled & painted, EX ............................**80.00**
Aurora, Lone Ranger #808, 1967, MIB ..............................**250.00**
Aurora, Monster Scenes, Frankenstein #633, 1971, assembled ..................................**100.00**
Aurora, Prehistoric Scenes, Cro-Magnon Woman, 1971, MIB ........................**100.00**
Aurora, Superboy #478, 1974, M (VG sealed box) ............**65.00**
Aurora, Superman, 1964, assembled ................................**35.00**
Aurora, Wolfman #450, 1972, MIB ..............................**120.00**
Bachmann, Dogs of the World, German Shepherd, 1960s, M (EX box) ........................**35.00**
Bandai, Godzilla #502526, 1984, MIB ................................**50.00**
Bandai, Thunderbird #536188, 1984, MIB ......................**40.00**
Billiken, Phantom of the Opera, 1982, NMIB .................**175.00**
Dark Horse, King Kong #K1092, 1992, MIB ......................**60.00**

**Monogram, Flip Out Beachcomber, 1965, NMIB, $375.00. (Photo courtesy June Moon)**

Eldon, Matador Missile & Launcher, 1960, MIB ...............**75.00**

Fundimensions, Six Million Dollar Man, MIB ......................**40.00**

Hawk, Explorer 18 Satellite #553, 1968, MIB ......................**70.00**

Hawk, Weird-Ohs Char-Icky-Tures, Francis the Foul #535, 1963, MIB ......................**50.00**

Horizon, Robocop #10, 1989, MIB ............................**60.00**

Imai, Capt Scarlet, Spectrum Helicopter #2015, 1992, MIB ............................**80.00**

ITC, Cocker Spaniel #3824, 1959, MIB ...............................**30.00**

Kaiyodo, Nelonga, 1990s, M (EX box) ...............................**50.00**

Lunar Models, Lost in Space, Chariot #SF009, MIB .**120.00**

Monogram, Battlestar Galactica #6028, 1979, MIB .......**200.00**

Monogram, Dracula #6008, 1983, MIB ...............................**45.00**

MPC, Batman #1702, 1984, MIB (sealed) .........................**50.00**

MPC, Superman #1701, 1984, MIB (sealed) ..................**60.00**

Revell, Bomarc Missile #1806, 1957, MIB .....................**80.00**

Revell, Douglas DC-7 United, 1974, MIB (sealed) ........**25.00**

Revell, John Travolta's 1979 Pontiac Firebird #1387, 1979, MIB ...............................**35.00**

Screamin', Star Wars, C-3PO #3500, 1993, MIB .........**45.00**

Testors, Davey the Cyclist #731, 1993, MIB (sealed) ........**15.00**

Toy Biz, Storm #48659, 1996, MIB (sealed) .........................**30.00**

Tsukuda, Ghostbusters, Sta Puft Man, 1984, sm, MIB .....**40.00**

## Moon and Star

A reissue of Palace, an early pattern glass line, Moon and Star was developed for the market in the 1960s by Joseph Weishar of Island Mould and Machine Company (Wheeling, West Virginia). It was made by several companies. One of the largest producers was L.E. Smith of Mt. Pleasant, Pennsylvania, and L.G. Wright (who had their glassware made by Fostoria and Fenton, perhaps others as well) carried a wide assortment in their catalogs for many years. It is still being made on a very limited basis, but the most collectible pieces are those in red, blue, amber, and green — colors that are no longer in production. The values listed here are for pieces in red or blue. Amber, green, and crystal prices should be 30% lower.

Ashtray, allover pattern, moons form scallops at rim, 4 rests, 8" dia ..............................**25.00**

Ashtray, moons at rim, star in base, 6-sided, 8½" .........**25.00**

Banana boat, allover pattern, moons form scallops at rim, 12" ...................................**45.00**

Basket, allover pattern, moons form scallops at rim, solid handle, 9" ......................**75.00**

Bell, pattern along sides, plain rim & handle, blue opalescent, 6" ..........................**45.00**

Bowl, allover pattern, footed, crimped rim, 7½" ..........**35.00**

Butter dish, allover pattern, scalloped base, ¼-lb, 8½" ....**45.00**

Butter/cheese dish, patterned lid, plain base, 7" dia ..........**65.00**

Cake plate, allover pattern, low collared base, 13" dia, minimum value .....................**65.00**

Cake stand, allover pattern, footed, 8", from $32 to ........**38.00**

Candle holders, allover pattern, flared & scalloped foot, 6", pr ..............................**50.00**

Candle holders, allover pattern, flared base, 4½", pr .......**25.00**

Candle lamp, patterned shade, clear base, 2-pc, 7½" .....**25.00**

Candy dish, allover pattern on base & lid, footed ball shape, 6" ....................................**25.00**

Canister, allover pattern, 1 or 2-lb, from $12 to ....................**15.00**

Chandelier, ruffled dome w/font, amber lg .....................**250.00**

Cheese dish, pattered base, clear plain lid, 9½", from $65 to ...........**70.00**

**Cigarette lighter, brass lighter unit, allover pattern, 3¾", from $50.00 to $60.00.**

Compote, allover pattern, footed flared crimped rim, 5" ..**22.00**

Compote, allover pattern, footed, patterned lid & finial, 7½x6" ..........................**40.00**

Compote, allover pattern, raised foot on stem, patterned lid, 12x8" ..............................**75.00**

Compote, allover pattern, scalloped rim, footed, 5x6½", from $18 to ..............................**20.00**

Compote, allover pattern, scalloped rim, footed, 7x10" ..........**45.00**

Console bowl, allover pattern, scalloped, flared foot, 8" ......**25.00**

Creamer, allover, raised foot w/scalloped edge, 5¾x3" .................**35.00**

Creamer & sugar bowl (open), disk
foot, sm, from $25 to .....**28.00**

Epergne, allover pattern, 1-lily, flared
bowl, scalloped foot .............**95.00**

Goblet, water; plain rim & foot,
4½" .................................**12.00**

Goblet, water; plain rim & foot,
5¾" .................................**15.00**

Jardiniere, allover pattern, patterned lid & finial, 9¾" ..**85.00**

Jardiniere/tobacco jar, allover
pattern, patterned lid &
finial, 6" ........................**50.00**

Jelly dish, allover pattern, patterned lid, stemmed foot,
10½" ............................**65.00**

Lamp, oil or electric; allover pattern, all original, 24", from
$200 to ......................**250.00**

Lamp, oil; allover pattern, 10",
from $100 to ....**120.00**

Nappy, allover pattern, crimped
rim, 2¾x6" ......................**18.00**

Plate, patterned body & center,
smooth rim, 8" ...............**35.00**

Relish dish, allover pattern, 1
plain handle, 2x8" dia ..**40.00**

Salt Celler, allover pattern, scalloped rim ........................**8.00**

Salt & pepper shakers, allover
pattern, metal tops, 4x2",
pr ............................**25.00**

Sherbet, pattern body & foot w/plain
rim & stem, 4¼x3¾" .......**25.00**

Sugar shaker, allover pattern,
metal top, 4½x3½" ........**50.00**

Syrup pitcher, allover pattern,
metal lid, 4½x3½" .........**75.00**

Toothpick holder, allover pattern, scalloped rim, sm flat foot .........**10.00**

Tumbler, iced tea; no pattern at
flat rim or disk foot, 11-oz,
5½" .................................**20.00**

# Mortens Studios

Animal models sold by
Mortens Studios of Arizona during
the 1940s are some of today's most
interesting collectibles, especially
among animal lovers. Hundreds of
breeds of dogs, cats, and horses
were produced from a plaster-type
composition material constructed
over a wire framework. They
range in size from 2" up to about
7", and most are marked. Crazing
and flaking are nearly always present to some degree. Our values
are for animals in excellent to
near-mint condition, allowing for
only minor crazing.

Beagle, recumbent ...............**48.00**
Bloodhound, #877 ..............**150.00**
Boxer, #556, mini .................**65.00**
Cocker Spaniel, brown, #786 .**75.00**
Collie pup, #818, mini .........**55.00**
Dalmatian, #854 .................**95.00**
Doberman, #785 ..................**95.00**
English Setter, #848 ............**65.00**
German Shepherd, #556, mini .**65.00**
Irish Setter, #856 ................**95.00**
Pekingese, #553, mini ..........**65.00**
Pointer pup, recumbent, #503 ...**75.00**
Pomeranian, #739 ...............**95.00**
Poodle, gray, 4" ...................**70.00**
Pug, #738 ..........................**125.00**
Springer Spaniel, #745 ........**95.00**

# Moss Rose

Though the Moss Rose pattern
has been produced by Staffordshire and American pottery companies alike since the mid-1800s,

**Pin tray, $5.00; Ashtray/cigarette box, from $15.00 to $18.00. (Photo courtesy April Tvorak)**

the line we're dealing with here was primarily made from the late 1950s into the 1970s by Japanese manufacturers. Even today you'll occasionally see a tea set or a small candy dish for sale in some of the chain stores. (The collectors who're already picking this line up refer to it as Moss Rose, but we've seen it advertised just lately under the name Victorian Rose, and some companies called their lines Chintz Rose or French Rose, so don't be surprised if we adopt one of those names later on.) The pattern consists of a briar rose with dark green mossy leaves on stark white glaze. Occasionally an item is trimmed in gold. In addition to dinnerware, many accessories and novelties were made as well.

Our advisor for this category is April Tvorak; she is listed in the Directory under Pennsylvania. For further information on items made by Lefton, see *The Collector's Encyclopedia of Lefton China* by Loretta DeLozier (Collector Books). Refer to *Schroeder's Antiques Price Guide* for information on the early Moss Rose pattern.

| | |
|---|---|
| Bowl, sauce | **4.00** |
| Bowl, soup | **8.00** |
| Butter dish | **18.00** |
| Cottage chese dish | **15.00** |
| Cup & saucer | **6.00** |
| Cup & saucer, demitasse | **8.00** |
| Egg cup, sm | **8.00** |
| Incense burner, gold trim, 3-footed, w/dome lid, 3¼" | **15.00** |
| Plate, dinner | **7.00** |
| Plate, salad | **5.00** |
| Platter | **15.00** |
| Teapot | **25.00** |
| Teapot, demitasse | **30.00** |
| Teapot, electric | **22.00** |

# National Geographics

The *National Geographic Magazine* was first introduced in October 1888. There was only one issue that year, and it together with the three published in 1889 make up Volume I, the most valuable group on the market. Volume I, No. 1, alone is worth about $12,000.00 in very good condition. A complete set of magazines from 1888 to the present is worth approximately $30,000.00 to

$60,000.00, depending on condition, as condition and price are closely related. As time goes by, values of individual issues increase. The most sought-after years are pre-World War: 1888 – 1914. Still, some postwar and recent issues command good prices. Prices are for single monthly issues, complete with all pages, covers, and ads. Note that there are a few special out-of-print issues that are worth more.

Our advisor for this category is Don Smith (listed in the Directory under Kentucky), who offers a value guide including special issues and maps.

| | |
|---|---|
| 1915 – 1916, ea | **11.00** |
| 1917 – 1924, ea | **9.00** |
| 1925 – 1929, ea | **8.00** |
| 1930 – 1945, ea | **7.00** |
| 1946 – 1955, ea | **6.00** |
| 1956 – 1967, ea | **5.50** |
| 1968 – 1989, ea | **4.50** |
| 1990 – present, ea | **2.00** |

# Niloak

Produced in Arkansas by Charles Dean Hyten from the early 1900s until the mid-1940s, Niloak (the backward spelling of kaolin, a type of clay) takes many forms — figural planters, vases in both matt and glossy glazes, and novelty items of various types. The company's most famous product and the most collectible is their Swirl or Mission Ware line. Clay in colors of brown, blue, cream, red, and buff are swirled within the mold, the finished product left unglazed on the outside to preserve the natural hues. Small vases are common; large pieces or unusual shapes and those with exceptional coloration are the most valuable. Refer to *The Collector's Encyclopedia of Niloak, A Reference and Value Guide,* by David Edwin Gifford (Collector Books) for more information.

Note: The terms '1st art mark' and '2nd art mark' used in the listings refer to specific die-stamped trademarks. The earlier mark was used from 1910 to 1924, followed by the second, very similar mark used from then until the end of Mission Ware production. Letters with curving raised outlines were characteristic of both; the most obvious difference between the two was that on the first, the final upright line of the 'N' was thin with a solid club-like terminal.

Ashtray, wooden shoe, 1 rest, N mark, 2½x5" ..................**20.00**
Bowl, 8 lg scallops, matt, block letters mark, 8" dia ...........**50.00**
Bowl/vase, Mission/Swirl, 3-color swirl, 1st art mark, 2½x5" .....................**100.00**
Box, Mission/Swirl, knobbed lid, 2nd art mark, 4½x3½" ..**265.00**
Cornucopia, graceful lines, glossy, block letters mark, 8½" .**45.00**
Figurine, donkey, stubborn, facial features, hand-tooled, marked, 3" .....................**70.00**
Figurine, retriever, sitting, matt, marked, 4½" ..................**45.00**

Flower frog, Mission/Swirl, unmarked, 1x3½" .........**75.00**

Flowerpot w/saucer, basketweave, gloss, 4½" ......................**35.00**

Jar, Mission/Swirl, bulbous, 2nd art mark, w/lid, 6½" ...**450.00**

Jug, glossy, mini, 3½" ..........**15.00**

Matchstick holder, Mission/ Swirl, cylindrical, 2nd art mark, 2" ......................**90.00**

Mug, Mission/Swirl, barrel shape, 1st art mark, 4½" .......**200.00**

Pin dish, open flower shape, matt, 3½" dia ..........................**20.00**

Pin tray, Mission/Swirl, 2nd art mark, 1¼x3¾" dia ........**80.00**

Pitcher, hand-thrown, detail on applied handle, glossy, 4" ..........................**30.00**

**Castware planter, deer figural, marked Niloak in low relief, 7", $40.00. (Photo courtesy David Gifford)**

Planter, cradle, matt, 4x6" ..**35.00**

Planter, polar bear w/attached sq basket, matt, 3½" ..........**75.00**

Planter, rooster, crowing, detailed feathers, marked, 9" .....**45.00**

Puff box, Mission/Swirl, flared base, 1st art mark, 4½x3¼" dia ...............................**350.00**

Salt & pepper shakers, various shapes, matt, from 2-3", from $20 to ...........................**35.00**

Stein, Mission/Swirl, flared base, 1st art mark, 4½" .......**250.00**

Tile, Mission/Swirl, unmarked, 4½x4½" .........................**85.00**

Tumbler, Mission/Swirl, 5½" ..**65.00**

Vase, hand-thrown, semigloss, Hywood by Niloak, 4" ...**40.00**

Vase, Mission/Swirl, bulbous, 2nd art mark, 10¼" ............**300.00**

Vase, Mission/Swirl, flat rim, early art mark, 4½" ...............**70.00**

Vase, Mission/Swirl, gourd shape, unmarked, 9⅛" ..........**180.00**

Vase, Mission/Swirl, hourglass shape, 2nd art mark, 3½" ..**95.00**

Vase, Mission/Swirl, ovoid, early art mark, 8½" ..............**250.00**

Vase, Mission/Swirl, pear shape, 1st art mark, 8" ..........**250.00**

Vase, Mission/Swirl, trumpet neck, 1st art mark, 10" ..........**250.00**

Vase, Mission/Swirl, 4-color swirl, 2nd art mark, 3¼" ........**80.00**

# Nippon

In complying with American importation regulations, from 1891 to 1921 Japanese manufacturers marked their wares 'Nippon,' meaning Japan, to indicate country of origin. The term is today used to refer to the highly decorated porcelain vases, bowls, chocolate pots, etc., that bear this term within their trademark.

Many variations were used. Refer to *The Collector's Encyclopedia of Nippon Porcelain* (there are five volumes in the series) by Joan Van Patten (Collector Books) for more information. See also Clubs and Newsletters.

Ashtray, autumn leaves in relief, 4-rest, M in Wreath mark, 2½" ..............................**325.00**
Basket vase, multicolored roses w/heavy gold beads, unmarked, 7½" ...........**450.00**
Bowl, fruit; fruit in relief, handled, M in Wreath mark, 7½" .....**225.00**

**Bowl, squirrel in relief, footed, 9",
from $450.00 to $550.00.**

Cheese dish, sampan scene, slant lid, Rising Sun mark, 7¾" ....**185.00**
Coffeepot, river scene, earth tones, stick handle, Maple Leaf mark, 7" .......................**150.00**
Condensed milk container, gold overlay on white, Maple Leaf mark ............................**175.00**
Humidor, florals w/moriage, squirrel finial, unmarked, 7½" ....**750.00**

Inkwell, Deco flowers on blue, M in Wreath mark, 4" .....**275.00**
Letter holder, flowers on cream, M in Wreath mark, 4½x6" ......**200.00**
Mug, 2 clown children w/rabbit on white, unmarked, 3¾" .**120.00**
Pitcher, Deco-style flowers at top, w/lid, M in Wreath mark, 5½" .............................**150.00**
Pitcher, Dutch lady at water's edge, M in Wreath mark, 4½" ..........................**350.00**
Plaque, cockatoo on perch, M in Wreath mark, 10" .......**325.00**
Plaque, windmill scene, M in Wreath mark, 10" .......**275.00**
Sugar bowl, floral band on cream, handled, w/lid, M in Wreath mark ..............................**80.00**
Sugar shaker, roses on cobalt w/gold, Maple Leaf mark, 4¼" ...........................**250.00**
Tea set, boy in sailor suit w/gun, child-size, 15-pc ..........**300.00**
Tray, Wedgewood type, canted corners, sq handles, M in Wreath mark, 10" ....................**350.00**
Urn, moriage dragon & trim, lg handles, unmarked, 11" ......**425.00**
Vase, kangaroo scene, sm gold handles, 12" ...............**275.00**
Vase, man on camel, ornate brown handles, M in Wreath mark, 9¼" ..............................**550.00**
Vase, moriage dragon, gourd form w/shaped rim, Maple Leaf mark, 8" ......................**350.00**
Vase, mums, pink on cobalt, classic form, Maple Leaf mark, 18" ..............................**900.00**
Vase, ocean & gull scene, gold handles, M in Wreath mark, 8½" ...........................**600.00**

Vase, sampan scene, angular handles, footed, M in Wreath mark, 6" ......................**150.00**

Vase, sunset scene, gold handles, bottle neck, M in Wreath mark, 11" .....................**375.00**

Vase, windmill scene, earth tones, handled, M in Wreath mark, 13" ...............................**400.00**

Vase, woodland scene w/brown sky, handled, M in Wreath mark, 10½" .................**625.00**

# Noritake

Since the early 1900s the Noritake China Company has been producing fine dinnerware, occasional pieces, and figural items decorated by hand in delicate florals, scenics, and wildlife studies. Azalea and Tree in the Meadow are two very popular collectible lines you will find listed here. Refer to *The Collector's Encyclopedia of Noritake, First and Second Series*, by Joan Van Patten; and *Early Noritake* by Aimee Neff Alden (all published by Collector Books) for more information.

## Azalea

Bonbon, #184, 6¼" ...............**50.00**

Bowl, oatmeal; #55, 5½" ......**28.00**

Bowl, vegetable; #101, oval, 10½" ..........................**60.00**

Cake plate, #10, 9¾" ............**40.00**

Casserole, #16, w/lid ..........**115.00**

Condiment set, #14, 5-pc .....**65.00**

Creamer & sugar bowl, #401, gold finial ...........................**155.00**

Berry creamer and sugar shaker, #122, $160.00 for the pair.

Cup & saucer, #2 .................**20.00**

Jam jar set, #125, 4-pc ......**155.00**

Mustard jar, #191, 3-pc .......**60.00**

Plate, bread & butter; #8, 6½" ........................**10.00**

Plate, grill; #38, 3-compartment, 10¼" .............................**165.00**

Plate, soup; #19, 7⅛" ..........**25.00**

Platter, #17, 14" ...................**60.00**

Relish, #119, 4-section, rare, 10" ...........................**150.00**

Relish, #18, oval, 8½" .........**20.00**

Spoon holder, #189, 8" .......**115.00**

Toothpick holder, #192 ......**135.00**

Vase, #187, fan form, footed .**185.00**

## Tree in the Meadow

Basket, Dolly Varden ........**125.00**

Bowl, soup ...........................**20.00**

Bowl, vegetable; 9" ..............**35.00**

Butter pat .............................**15.00**

Butter tub, open, w/drainer ..**35.00**

Cheese dish ..........................**45.00**

Compote ...............................**50.00**

Condiment set, 5-pc ............**45.00**

Cup & saucer, demitasse .....**35.00**
Gravy boat ...........................**50.00**
Lemon dish ..........................**15.00**
Relish, divided ....................**35.00**
Sugar bowl, #204 ................**25.00**
Tea set, 3-pc .......................**100.00**

## Miscellaneous

Cake plate, floral center with turquoise rim, pierced handles, red mark, 9½", from $45.00 to $55.00. (Photo courtesy Joan Van Patten)

Basket vase, lovebirds on yellow w/gold, M in Wreath mark, 5¾" ...............................**135.00**
Bowl, irises on white, gold handles, M in Wreath mark, 10½" ............................**75.00**
Bowl, roses on ivory, pink scalloped rim, M in Wreath mark, 5" ...................................**40.00**
Bowl, snow scene, 3 integral handles, M in Wreath mark, 6½" ............................**55.00**
Chip & dip set, river scene at sunset, M in Wreath mark, 9¾" ...........................**80.00**

Chocolate pot, gold design on white, M in Wreath mark, 9" .............................**110.00**
Egg cup, river scene w/windmill, M in Wreath mark, 3½" ...........................**30.00**
Jam jar, strawberries on tan, rose finial, M in Wreath mark, 5½" ...........................**100.00**
Lemon dish, lemon & leaves in relief, M in Wreath mark, 6", $45 to .............................**65.00**
Potpourri jar, floral wreath on blue, rose finial, M in Wreath mark ...........................**110.00**
Shaker, river scene w/tree & sailboat, M in Wreath mark, 2½" ...........................**60.00**
Tray, Deco fruit border, gold handles, M in Wreath mark, 11" .............................**95.00**
Vase, green fan form w/floral band on rim, M in Wreath mark, 6½" ..............................**150.00**
Wall pocket, swan scene, M in Wreath mark, 8" .........**110.00**

# Novelty Telephones

Novelty phones representing well-known advertising or cartoon characters are proving to be the focus of a lot of collector activity — the more recognizable the character the better. Telephones modeled after product containers are collectible too, and with the intense interest currently being shown in anything advertising related, competition is sometimes stiff and values are rising. For further information we recommend *Schroeder's*

*Collectible Toys, Antique to Modern* (Collector Books).

AC Spark Plug, figural, M ..**35.00**
Airpane, Northern Telecron, 1970s, NM .....................**85.00**
Alvin, M ................................**60.00**
Bugs Bunny, Warner Exclusive, MIB ..............................**100.00**
Cabbage Patch Girl, 1980s, EX, from $60 to ....................**75.00**
Charlie Tuna, 1987, MIB, from $50 to ............................**65.00**
Flintstones, green & red plastic, cardboard dial, 6", VG ...**100.00**
Ghostbusters, M .................**100.00**
Keebler Elf, NM .................**100.00**
Lazy Pig, MIB ......................**65.00**
Little Green Spout, EX ........**75.00**
Mario Brothers, 1980s, MIB .**50.00**
Mickey Mouse, Western Electric, 1976, EX ......................**175.00**
Oscar Mayer Weiner, EX ....**65.00**
Snoopy, Romper Room, 10", EX ...**25.00**

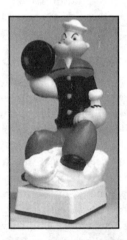

**Popeye, marked KFS Inc. 1982 COM VU I, Hong Kong, from $100.00 to $125.00. (Photo courtesy Joyce Roerig)**

Snoopy as Joe Cool, 1980s, MIB .........................**55.00**
Spider-Man, climbing down chimney, NM, from $165 to .......................**200.00**
Super Bowl XIX, full-size football w/handset, NM ..............**70.00**
Tang Lips, MIB, from $125 to .**150.00**
Tetly Tea Man, EX ............**100.00**
Winnie the Pooh, sq base, M, from $225 to .........................**250.00**
Ziggy, 1989, MIB .................**75.00**

# Occupied Japan

Items with the 'Occupied Japan' mark were made during the period from the end of World War II until April 1952. Porcelains, novelties, paper items, lamps, silverplate, lacquer ware, and dolls are some of the areas of exported goods that may bear this stamp. Because the Japanese were naturally resentful of the occupation, it is felt that only a small percentage of their wares were thus marked. Although you may find identical items marked simply 'Japan,' only those with the 'Occupied Japan' stamp command values such as we have suggested below. For more information we recommend the series of five books on Occupied Japan collectibles written by Gene Florence for Collector Books. Items in our listings are ceramic unless another material is noted, and figurines are of average, small size. See also Clubs and Newsletters.

Ashtray, Basilique Ste Anne de Beaupre, metal, 3", from $4 to ....................................**5.00**

Ashtray, Wedgwood type, white on blue, 4 rests, 2⅝", from $8 to ...................................**10.00**

Box, Scottie dog figural, metal, 2½x3½", from $12.50 to ...............**15.00**

Bud vase, angel blowing horn beside vase, MIOJ mark, 2½", from $10 to ....................**12.50**

Christmas ornaments, bells (12), M in MIOJ box, from $30 to ........................**35.00**

Cigarette box, embossed metal, 3½x4¼", from $18 to .....**20.00**

Creamer, Blue Willow, child size, 1½-2", from $15 to ........**17.50**

Crumb butler, souvenir of Washington DC, metal, from $5 to ............................**6.50**

Cup & saucer, floral band on white, Nasco Fine China, from $8 to ...............................**10.00**

Cup & saucer, floral chintz-like pattern on white, Merit, from $10 to .............................**12.50**

Cup & saucer, pink floral on white, swirled, ornate handle, Sanjo .....................**15.00**

Cup & saucer, tomato form, child size, from $7.50 to ........**10.00**

Cup & saucer, vining floral on white, Merit, from $10 to ..............**12.50**

Doll, celluloid, nude, 4¾", from $12.50 to ........................**15.00**

Fan, floral on paper, wooden sticks, from $12.50 to ...**15.00**

Figurine, ballerina, net dress, 4½", from $22.50 to ...............**25.00**

Figurine, Black fiddler, 5", from $40 to ...........................**42.50**

Figurine, boy boxer, red hair, black mark, 4½", from $12.50 to .**15.00**

Figurine, cat w/fiddle, 2", from $6 to ......................................**7.50**

Figurine, clown, marked EL in circle, 4½", from $20 to .....**25.00**

Figurine, Colonial couple seated, painted bisque, Andrea, 7", pr ...............................**150.00**

Figurine, couple at piano, 4", from $20 to .............................**22.50**

Figurine, Cupid beside flower, painted bisque, 4", from $25 to ...................................**30.00**

Figurine, Dutch water girl, 4", from $10 to ....................**12.50**

Figurine, flamingo, Miami souvenir, 5½", from $12.50 to ..........**15.00**

Figurine, geisha w/fan, Ardalt Lenwile China, 3¾", from $32.50 to ........................**35.00**

Figurine, girl w/accordion, red mark, 4½", from $8 to ..**10.00**

Figurine, Hummel-type boy & girl gardeners on base, Paulux, 5½" .....................................**55.00**

Figurine, Hummel-type boy w/flute, 4½", from $20 to .............**25.00**

Figurine, Japanese warrior, 8", from $35 to ...................**40.00**

Figurine, man w/violin, painted bisque, 9", from $55 to ..**60.00**

Figurine, Siamese dancer, 5" .**5.00**

Figurine, Spaniel, brown & white, 4½x5½", from $15 to .....**17.50**

Figurine, villain & lady, blue mark, 7½", from $50 to .............**55.00**

Lamp base, Colonial couple on base, painted porcelain, 11" .....**30.00**

Novelty, lady's slipper, Pico, 2¾", from $6 to ........................**7.50**

Planter, couple w/rabbits, Paulux, painted bisque, 5¼x7¼" .**175.00**

**Planters, bird perched on flowering branch at side of basket shape, from $35.00 to $50.00; Bird figural, from $8.00 to $10.00. (Photo courtesy Gene Florence)**

Planter, duck w/scarf, 3¼x4", from $8 to ...............................**10.00**

Planter, flamingo, 3", from $15 to ..................................**17.50**

Planter, Hummel-type girl w/basket, 4¾", from $10 to ....**12.50**

Planter, rabbit w/cart, blue, 2½x6", from $12.50 to ..**15.00**

Plaque, Colonial couple, painted bisque, Paulux, 6½x6x1¼" .**45.00**

Plate, Hybrid Cattelya (flower on white), Rosetti, 8¼" ......**22.50**

Powder jar, windmill scene on heart shape, 2¾", from $10 to ..................................**12.50**

Tea set, floral, 2-place, child size, from $30 to ....................**35.00**

Tray, divided; US Capitol/ Washington Monument embossed on metal, 6" ......................**7.50**

Umbrella, paper & wood, MIOJ on metal tip, 18" closed, from $25 to .....................................**27.50**

Wall plaque, mallard in flight, EX quality, 5-6½", ea, from $22.50 to .....................**25.00**

# Old MacDonald's Farm

Made by the Regal China Co., items from this line of novelty ware designed around characters and animals from Old MacDonald's farm can often be found at flea markets and dinnerware shows. Values of some pieces are two to three times higher than a few years ago. The milk pitcher is especially hard to find.

Our advisor for this category is Rick Spencer; he is listed in the Directory under Utah.

Butter dish, cow's head .....**220.00**

Canister, flour, cereal or coffee, med, ea ........................**220.00**

Canister, pretzels, peanuts, popcorn, chips or tidbits, lg, ea ....**300.00**

Canister, salt or sugar, med, ea ..........................**220.00**

Canister, soap or cookies, lg, ea ..........................**300.00**

Cookie jar, barn ................**275.00**

Creamer, rooster ...............**110.00**
Grease jar, pig ...................**175.00**
Pitcher, milk ......................**400.00**
Salt & pepper shakers, boy & girl,
  pr ....................................**75.00**
Salt & pepper shakers, churn, gold
  trim, pr ..........................**90.00**
Salt & pepper shakers, feed sacks
  w/sheep, pr .................**195.00**
Spice jar, assorted lids, sm, ea .**100.00**
Sugar bowl, hen .................**125.00**
Teapot, duck's head ...........**250.00**

# Paper Dolls

Though the history of paper dolls can be traced even farther back, by the late 1700s they were being mass produced. A century later, paper dolls were being used as an advertising medium by retail companies wishing to promote sales. But today the type most often encountered are in book form — the dolls on the cardboard covers, their wardrobe on the inside pages. These have been published since the 1920s. Celebrity and character-related dolls are the most popular with collectors, and condition is very important. If they have been cut out, even when they are still in fine condition and have all their original accessories, they're worth only about half as much as an uncut doll. In our listings, if no condition is given, values are for mint, uncut paper dolls. For more information, we recommend *Price Guide to Lowe and Whitman Paper Dolls* by Mary Young (see

the Directory under Ohio). For an expanded listings of values, see *Schroeder's Collectible Toys, Antique to Modern* (Collector Books). See also Clubs and Newsletters.

Annie Laurie, Lowe #1030, 1941, uncut, M ........................**75.00**
Baby Sparkle Plenty, Saalfield #2500, 1948, uncut, NM .**50.00**
Cowboys & Cowgirls, Lowe #1286, 1950, uncut, M ..............**25.00**
Dinah Shore & George Montgomery, Whitman #1970, 1959, cut, EX .................**35.00**
Dr Kildare & Nurse Susan, Lowe #2740, 1962, uncut, M ..**50.00**
Elly May (Clampett), Watkins/Strathmore #1819-A, 1963, uncut, NM ..........**50.00**
Faye Emerson, Saalfield #2722, 1952, uncut, M ............**125.00**
Goldilocks & the Three Bears, Lowe #2561, 1955, uncut, M ..............................**35.00**

**Happy Days Fonzie, Toy Factory, 1976, complete and uncut, M, from $20.00 to $25.00. (Photo courtesy Greg Davis and Bill Morgan)**

Here Comes the Bride, Lowe #2562, 1955, uncut, M ..**30.00**

In Our Backyard, Lowe #1027, 1941, uncut, M .............**60.00**

Joanne Woodward, Saalfield #4436, 1958, fold-out book, uncut, EX ......................**85.00**

Laugh-In, Saalfield #1325, 1969, complete & unused, NM .**50.00**

Malibu Skipper, Whitman #1952, 1973, uncut, M .............**10.00**

**Mrs. Beasley, Whitman, 1973, complete and uncut, from $20.00 to $25.00.**

My Fair Lady, Ottenheimer #2961-0, 1965, uncut, EX .........**35.00**

Ozzie & Harriet, Saalfield #4319, 1954, uncut, M ...........**100.00**

Partridge Family, Artcraft #5137, 1971, uncut, NM ..........**40.00**

Rosemary Clooney, Lowe, #2569, 1956, uncut, M .............**125.00**

Sally & Dick, Bob & Jean, Lowe #1023, 1940, uncut, M .........................**50.00**

Square Dance, Lowe #968, 1950, uncut, M ......................**25.00**

Twinkle Twins, Lowe #521, 1944, uncut, M ......................**25.00**

Wee Wee Baby, Lowe #1045, 1945, uncut, M ......................**50.00**

# Paperback Books

Though published to some extent before then, most paperback book collectors prefer those printed from around 1940 until the late 1950s, and most organize their collections around a particular author, genre, publisher, or illustrator. Remember (as is true with any type of ephemera) — condition is extremely important. Unless noted otherwise, our values are given for books in near-fine condition. (Book dealers use the term 'fine' to indicate 'mint' condition.)

Albert, MH; All the Young Men, Cardinal C-389, 1960, G ................................**5.00**

Allingham, M; Gyrth Chalice Mystery, Avon 70572, VG ........**40.00**

Armstrong, Charlotte; The Unsuspected, Pocket 444, 1947, VG ....................**13.00**

Arneson, DJ; Mork & Mindy Code Puzzles..., Cinnamon House, 1979, from $5 to ..............**8.00**

Aroeste, Jean Lissette; All Our Yesterdays, Bantam Fotonovel, 1978, VG .......**7.50**

Arrow, Wm; Planet of Apes #1, Visions From Nowhere, Ballantine, 1976 ..................**6.00**

Avallone, Michael; Cannonball Run, Leisure 993, 1981, VG ............................**4.00**

Avallone, Michael; Man From UNCLE, Ace G-553, 1965, VG ..............**10.00**

Bensen, DR; Swashbuckler, Bantam 10245, EX+ ...............**5.00**

Berman, C; Penny Marshall & Cindy Williams, Tempo Books, 1977, from $5 to ..**8.00**

Bixby, Jerome; Star Trek, Day of the Dove, Bantam Fotonovel, 1978, NM .......................**15.00**

Blake, Ken; Professionals #10, Cry Wolf, Sphere 1659, 1981, VG ...................................**5.00**

Blinn, William; Starski & Hutch, #1-#8, Ballantine, 1975-78, ea, from $3 to .........................**5.00**

Blish, James; Star Trek 3, Bantam F4371, 1969, VG .............**8.00**

Bloch, Robert; Psycho, Crest, 1961, 4th printing, VG ...........**13.00**

Boulle, P; Bridge Over River Kwai, Fontana, 1958, 7th printing, NM ...................................**7.00**

Bowdler, Roger; Magnum PI, Granada 13516, 2nd printing, 1981, VG .........................**8.00**

Braden, Tom; Eight Is Enough, Fawcett Crest, 1975, from $5 to ......................................**8.00**

Brandner, Gary; Cat People, Gold Medal 1-4470, 1982, VG .**4.00**

Brewster, Dennis; I Dream of Jeannie, Pocket Books, 1966, from $25 to ....................**30.00**

Bronte, Emily; Wuthering Heights, Pocket 7, 1941, 18th printing, NM .................**25.00**

Burke, John; Dr Terror's House of Horrors, Pan G692, 1965, G ..............................**10.00**

Burke, John; Magnificent Air Race, Pan X410, 1965, VG ........**8.00**

Burroughs, ER; Tarzan of the Apes, Ballantine, 1966, 3rd printing, VG ....................**6.00**

Cadin, Martin; Six Million Dollar Man, Cyborg #1, Warner, 1972, from $3 to .............**5.00**

Caillou, Alan; Khartoum, Signet P2941, 1966, VG .............**6.00**

Carter, John; New Avengers #2, Eagle's Nest, Futura 7471, 1976, VG .........................**8.00**

Chandler, Raymond; Marlow, Pocket 75434, 5th printing, 1969, VG .........................**5.00**

**Charteris, Leslie; The Saint, Let Her Kill Herself, Saint Mystery Library #128, 1960, VG, $10.00.**

Charteris, Leslie; Saint Steps in Mystery, Hodder 132, 1963, VG .**8.00**

Christie, Agatha; Death on the Nile, Bantam, 23rd printing, 1978, VG .........................**4.00**

Church, Ralph; Mork & Mindy, Pocket Books, 1979, from $3 to ....................................**5.00**

Clifford, Francis; Naked Runner, Signet P3112, 1967, VG .**6.00**

Cogan, Mike; Presidio, Pocket 66876, 1988, VG ..............**4.00**

Cogswell, Theodore; Spock, Messiah!, Bantam 10159, 1976, VG ...**5.00**

Cohen, Joel; Jimmie Walker the Dyn-O-Mite Kid, Scholastic, 1976, from $5 to ..............**8.00**

Cohen, Joel; Six Million Dollar Man & Bionic Woman, Scholastic, from $3 to .....**5.00**

Collins, Wilkie; Moonstone, Fontana 2820, 2nd printing, 1972, VG ..........................**6.00**

Costigan, Lee; Hard Sell, Tower 44-429, 1964, VG ............**8.00**

Daniels, Dorothy; Strange Paradise, Paperback Library, 1969, VG ........................**10.00**

Daniels, Norman; Smith Family #1, Meet the Smiths, Berkley, 1972, VG ..........................**6.00**

Davies, Fredric; Man From UNCLE, Cross of Gold Affair, Ace, 1968, VG .................**8.00**

Deck, Carol; David Cassidy Story, Curtis Books, 1972, from $5 to .....................**8.00**

Deming, Richard; Mod Squad #1-#5, Pyramid Books, 1968-70, ea, from $5 to ..................**8.00**

Dexter, Colin; Service of All the Dead, Bantam 27239, 1988, VG ....................................**4.00**

Dey, Susan; Cooking, Cleaning & Falling in..., Tiger Beat, '72, from $10 to ....................**15.00**

Dey, Susan; For Girls Only, Tiger Beat, 1971, from $10 to .**15.00**

Dicks, Terrance; Dr Who, Android Invasion, Pinnacle, 1983, VG ......................**4.00**

Doherty, Linda; Hardy Super...Word Finds, Tempo Books, 1977, from $5 to ..**8.00**

Drew, Wayland; Dragonslayer, Del Ray 29694, 1981, EX ...........................**5.00**

Du Maurier, Daphne; Rebecca, Garden City, 1940, VG .**20.00**

Edwards, Herb; Island of Love, Gold Medal, 1963, EX .....**5.00**

Einstein, Charles; No Time for More, Dell D224, 1958, VG ........**13.00**

Eklund, Gordon; Star Trek, Starless World, Bantam 12371, 1978, NM ......................**10.00**

Ellson, Hal; Games, Ace H-32, 1967, EX ..........................**9.00**

Exbrayat, Charles; Ravishing Idiot, Popular PC1051, 1965, VG .....................................**7.00**

Fairbairn, Douglas; Shoot; Dell 8077, 1976, VG ................**4.00**

Fairman, Paul W; World Grabbers, Monarch 471, 1964, NM ...........................**30.00**

Fleming, Ian; From Russia w/Love, Pan X236, 1964, VG ..............................**7.00**

Follett, Ken; Key to Rebecca, Signet AE3509, 17th printing, VG ....................................**4.00**

Forbes, Colin; Avalanche Express, Pan 25324, 1977, VG ......**5.00**

Foster, Alan Dean; Black Hole, New English Library, 1979, NM ....................................**6.00**

Franklin, Max; Dead, Award NA1301, 1974, VG ..........**5.00**

Friedman, Michael J; Star Trek, Call to Darkness, Pocket, 1989, VG ..........................**5.00**

Fuller, Roger; All the Silent, Pocket 50056, 1964, VG ............**10.00**

Gardner, John; Stone Killer, Award AQ1181, 1973, VG ..........**5.00**

Gipe, George; Back to the Future, Berkley 08025, 1985, VG ......................**4.00**

Golden All-Star Book, Donnie & Marie, Golden Press, 1977, from $5 to ........................**8.00**

Goldman, Wm; Marathon Man, Pan 24704, 1976, VG ......**6.00**

Graf, LA: Star Trek, Death Count, Pocket 73922, 1992, VG .**5.00**

Griffen, Elizabeth L; Shaggy Dog, Scholastic TX1111, 1975, VG ......................**5.00**

Grove, Martin A; Real Donnie & Marie, Zebra Books, 1977, from $3 to ........................**5.00**

Hammer, Earl Jr; The Homecoming, Avon, 1970, 1st printing, $3 to ...............................**5.00**

Hine, Al; Bewitched, Dell, 1965, from $10 to ....................**15.00**

Houston, David; Lindsay Wagner: Superstar of Bionic Woman, 1976, from $5 to .............**8.00**

Hudson, James A; Meet David Cassidy, Scholastic Books, 1972, from $5 to .............**8.00**

Johnston, William; Happy Days #1-#8, Tempo Books, 1974-77, ea, from $5 to .................**8.00**

Johnston, William; Nanny & Professor, #1-#2, Lancer Books, 1970, from $8 to ...........**10.00**

Johnston, William; Sweathog Grail, Ace, 1976, 1st printing, from $5 to ......................**8.00**

Koziakin, Vladmir; Hardy Boys Mystery Mazes, Tempo Books, 1977, from $5 to .............**8.00**

Lee, Howard; Kung Fu #1-#4, Warner, 1974, ea, from $3 to .............**5.00**

Leighton, Frances Spatz; Patty Goes to Washington, Ace, 1964, from $10 to .........**15.00**

Lewis, Mary; Mork & Mindy Puzzlers, Cinnamon House, 1979, from $5 to ........................**8.00**

Matcha, Jack; Brady Bunch NY Mystery, Tiger Beat, 1972, from $5 to ........................**8.00**

Paul, Rose; Bionic Woman's Brain Teasers, Tempo Books, 1976, from $5 to ......................**10.00**

Paul, Rose; Six Million Dollar Man's...Puzzles, Tempo Books, 1976, from $3 to ..**5.00**

Ross, Marilyn; Strangers at Collins House, Paperback Library, 1968, VG ..........**8.00**

Saint, HF; Memoirs of an Invisible Man, Dell 21122, 1988, VG ................................**5.00**

Saperstein, David; Cocoon, Jove 08400, 1985, VG .............**4.00**

Saunders, David; Mod Squad, Belmont 91-254, 1962, G ............................**6.00**

Saville, Andrew; Bergerac & Fatal Weakness, Penguin 10622, 1988, VG .........................**5.00**

Schumer, Arlen; Visions From Twilight Zone, Chronicle Books, 1990, M .............**27.00**

Sellers, Con; Too Late the Hero, Pyramid T2247, 1970, VG ...................**5.00**

Serling, Rod; More Stories From Twilight Zone, Bantam, 1965, NM ................................**15.00**

Seskin, Jane; Fantasy Island #1-#2, Ballantine, 1978-79, ea, from $5 to ......................**8.00**

Shapiro, Lionel; Sealed Verdict, Bantam 347, 1948, EX .**20.00**

Shatner, Lisabeth; Captain's Log: William Shatner's, Pocket, 1989, VG ........................**10.00**

Sheckley, Robert; 10th Victim, Ballantine U5050, 1965, NM ............................**13.00**

Shulman, Irving; Notorious Landlady, Gold Medal S1197, 1962, VG ..................................**12.00**

Sky, Kathleen; Death's Angel, Bantam 14703, 1981, VG ........**6.00**

Spillane, Mickey; Delta Factor, Signet Y6592, date unknown, VG ....................................**4.00**

Spillane, Mickey; Girl Hunters, Signet D2266, 1963, VG .**7.00**

Steffanson, Con; Laverne & Shirley #1-#3, Warner Books, 1976, ea, from $5 to ......**10.00**

Stone, Andrew L; Cry Terror, Signet 1508, 1958, EX ..**13.00**

Stratton, Chris; Bugaloos Rock City Rebels, Curtis Books, 1971, from $15 to ..........**20.00**

Stratton, T; Man From UNCLE, Invisibility Affair, Ace, 1967, VG ....................................**8.00**

Sucharatkul, Somtow; Alien Swordmaster, Pinnacle 42441, 1985, VG ..........................**5.00**

Thomas, Kenneth; Devil's Mistress, Gold Medal S802, 1958, VG ..................................**10.00**

Trevor, Leslie; Police Woman #2, Assassin, Award AQ1452, 1975, VG ..........................**6.00**

Tubb, EC; Breakaway, Pocket 80184, 1975, VG ..............**6.00**

Tynan, Kathleen; Agatha, Ballantine 27586, 1979, EX ..................**5.00**

Vardeman, Robert E; Klingon Gambit, Pocket 45358, 2nd printing, VG ....................**4.00**

Verne, Jules; Master of World, Ace D-504, 1961, VG ..............**8.00**

Wallant, Edward L; Pawnbroker, Pan X336, 1964, VG .......**7.00**

Wellard, James; Action of the Tiger, Avon T-188, 1957, VG ................................**8.00**

Willis, Maud; Bionic Woman, A Question of Life, Starr, 1977, from $8 to ......................**12.00**

# Pennsbury

From the 1950s through the 1970s, dinnerware and novelty ware produced by the Pennsbury company was sold through tourist gift shops along the Pennsylvania turnpike. Much of their ware was decorated in an Amish theme. A group of barbershop singers was another popular design, and they made a line of bird figures that were very similar to Stangl's, though today much harder to find.

Ashtray, Amish, round ........**25.00**
Ashtray, Eagle, 7½x5" .........**40.00**
Bowl, pretzel; Amish couple .**80.00**
Bowl, vegetable; Red Rooster, 2-part, 9½x6¼" .................**50.00**
Chip 'n dip, Red Rooster, 11" **85.00**
Coaster, Horowitz ................**30.00**
Coffeepot, Hex, 2-cup ..........**50.00**
Creamer & sugar bowl, Hex .**40.00**
Cruet, Amish, pr ................**100.00**
Figurine, blue jay, 10½" ....**600.00**
Mug, beer; Eagle ..................**42.00**
Mug, beer; Gay Ninety ........**45.00**
Mug, coffee; Amish couple, 3¼" .**27.50**
Mug, coffee; Black Rooster ..**35.00**

Pie plate, Amish couple by apple tree, 9" ..........................**65.00**
Pitcher, Amish man & heart, 4" .**35.00**
Pitcher, Black Rooster, 4" ...**35.00**
Plaque, Baltimore & Ohio RR, train, 5¾x7¾" ..............**65.00**
Plaque, Don't Stand Up While Room Is in Motion, 6" ...**30.00**
Plaque, Such Schmootzers, 4" .**22.50**
Plate, Christmas angel, 1970 ..**40.00**
Plate, Green Rooster, 8" ......**18.00**
Platter, dinner; Red Rooster, 10" ..............................**35.00**

**Pretzel bowl, Gay Ninety, 8x12", $85.00.**

Relish, Red Rooster, Christmas tree shape, 14½x11½" ..**85.00**
Salt & pepper shakers, Hex, 2½", pr ..................................**30.00**
Tray, Dutch Haven, octagonal, 4" ..............................**30.00**
Tray, Tulip & Heart, 4" .......**30.00**
Wall pocket, clown ..............**75.00**
Warming plate, Picking Apples, electric ..........................**95.00**

# Pez Dispensers

Originally a breath mint targeted for smokers, by the '50s Pez had been diverted toward the kid's candy market, and to make sure the kids found them appealing, the company designed dispensers they'd be sure to like — many of them characters the kids could easily recognize. On today's collectible market, some of those dispensers bring astonishing prices!

Though early on collectors preferred the dispensers with no feet, today they concentrate primarily on the character heads. Feet were added in 1987, so if you want your collection to be complete, you'll buy both styles. For further information and more listings, see *Schroeder's Collectible Toys, Antique to Modern* (Collector Books). Our values are for mint dispensers. Very few are worth collecting if they are damaged or have missing parts. See also Clubs and Newsletters.

Bambi, no feet ......................**75.00**
Batman, no feet ...................**15.00**
Bugs Bunny, no feet ............**20.00**
Captain America, no feet .....**85.00**
Charlie Brown, w/feet & tongue ..**10.00**
Clown w/Collar, no feet .......**65.00**
Daffy Duck, no feet .............**15.00**
Dalmatian Pup, w/feet ........**50.00**
Donkey, w/feet, whistle head .**10.00**
Elephant, no feet, orange & blue, flat hat ..........................**100.00**
Foghorn Leghorn, w/feet .....**95.00**
Fozzie Bear, w/feet, from $1 to ..**3.00**
Girl w/feet, blond hair .........**15.00**
Hulk, no feet, light green, remake ..........................**3.00**
Jerry Mouse, w/feet, plastic face ...**15.00**
Koala, w/feet & whistle head .**40.00**

Lamb, w/feet & whistle head .20.00
Li'l Bad Wolf, w/feet ............20.00
Merlin the Mouse .................20.00
Mr Ugly, no ft .......................45.00
Octopus, no feet, black ........75.00
Odie, w/feet ...........................5.00
Olive Oyl, no feet ...............200.00
Panda, no feet, diecut eyes ..30.00
Parrot, w/feet & whistle head ..10.00
Pinocchio, no feet ...............150.00
Pirate, no feet .......................45.00
Raven, no feet, yellow beak .60.00
Santa Claus (A), no feet, steel
    pin ............................125.00
Scrooge McDuck (A), no feet .35.00
Skull (A), no feet, from $5 to .10.00
Smurf, w/feet .........................5.00
Snowman (A), no feet ..........10.00
Spider-Man, no feet, from $10
    to ..............................15.00

**Zorro, no feet, with Zorro logo, $75.00, no logo, $45.00; King Louie, no feet, orange, $20.00.**

## Pfaltzgraff Pottery

Since early in the 17th century, pottery has been produced in York County, Pennsylvania. The Pfaltzgraff Company that operates there today is the outgrowth of several of these small potteries. A changeover made in 1940 redirected their efforts toward making the dinnerware lines for which they are now best known. Their earliest line, a glossy brown with a white frothy drip glaze around the rim, was called Gourmet Royale. Today collectors find an abundance of good examples and are working toward reassembling sets of their own. Village, another very successful line, is tan with a stencilled Pennsylvania Dutch-type floral design in brown. It was discontinued little more than a year ago, and already prices are starting upwards as shoppers turn to secondary market sources to replace and replenish their services. The line is so extensive and offers such an interesting array of items, it is sure to have collector appeal as well.

Giftware consisting of ashtrays, mugs, bottle stoppers, a cookie jar, etc., all with comic character faces were made in the 1940s. This line was called Muggsy, and it is also very collectible, with the mugs starting at about $35.00 each. For more information, refer to *The Collector's Encyclopedia of American Dinnerware* by Jo Cunningham (Collector Books) and *Pfaltzgraff, America's Potter*, by David A. Walsh and Polly Stetler, published in conjunction with the Historical Society of York County, York, Pennsylvania.

Christmas Heritage, cheese tray, #533, 10½x7½", from $5 to .**7.00**

Christmas Heritage, plate, dinner; #004, 10", from $4 to ......**5.50**

Gourmet Royale, ashtray, #AT32, skillet shape, 9", from $10 to ................**15.00**

Gourmet Royale, baker, #321, oval, 7½", from $18 to ..**20.00**

Gourmet Royale, bean pot, #11-2, 2-qt, from $28 to ..........**30.00**

Gourmet Royale, bean pot, #30, w/lip, lg, from $45 to .....**50.00**

Gourmet Royale, bowl, cereal; #934SR, 5½", from $6 to .**8.00**

Gourmet Royale, bowl, salad; tapered sides, 10", from $25 to ...................................**28.00**

Gourmet Royale, bowl, vegetable; #341, divided, from $20 to ........................**24.00**

Gourmet Royale, butter dish, #394, ¼-lb stick type, from $12 to .............................**14.00**

Gourmet Royale, casserole, hen on nest, 2-qt, from $75 to ..**95.00**

Gourmet Royale, casserole, stick handle, 3-qt ...................**30.00**

Gourmet Royale, chafing dish, w/handles, lid & stand, 8x9" ...........................**35.00**

Gourmet Royale, chip 'n dip, #311, molded in 1 pc, 12", from $15 to ....................................**20.00**

Gourmet Royale, creamer, #382, from $5 to ........................**7.00**

Gourmet Royale, flour scoop, sm, from $12 to ...................**15.00**

Gourmet Royale, jug, #384, 32-oz, from $32 to ...................**36.00**

Gourmet Royale, ladle, 3½" bowl w/11" handle, from $18 to .............................**20.00**

**Gourmet Royale, four-part serving tray, metal center handle, from $20.00 to $25.00.**

Gourmet Royale, mug, #391, 12-oz, from $6 to ........................**8.00**

Gourmet Royale, plate, dinner; #88R, from $3.50 to ........**4.50**

Gourmet Royale, plate, salad; 6¾", from $3 to ........................**4.00**

Gourmet Royale, platter, #337, 16", from $25 to ...........**30.00**

Gourmet Royale, relish dish, #265, 5x10", from $15 to ........**17.00**

Gourmet Royale, salt & pepper shakers, #317/318, 4½", pr, $12 to .............................**14.00**

Gourmet Royale, shirred egg dish, #360, 6", from $10 to ....**12.00**

Gourmet Royale, teapot, #381, 6-cup, from $20 to ............**25.00**

Heritage, butter dish, #002-028, from $6 to ........................**8.00**

Heritage, cup & saucer, #002-002, 9-oz .................................**3.00**

Muggsy, bottle stopper, head, ball shape ...........................**85.00**

Muggsy, cookie jar, character face, minimum value ..........**250.00**

Muggsy, mug, character face, ea, from $35 to ...................**38.00**

Muggsy, shot glass, character face, from $45 to ...................**50.00**

Village, baker, #236, rectangular, tab handles, 2-qt, from $12 to ........................**15.00**

**Village, loaf pan, $15.00.**

Village, baker, #24, oval, 10¼", from $9 to ...................**12.00**

Village, baker, #240, oval, 7¾" .........................**7.50**

Village, bowl, batter; w/spout & handle, 8", from $30 to .........................**35.00**

Village, bowl, mixing; #453, 1-qt, 2-qt, & 3-qt, 3-pc set, from $40 to ...................................**50.00**

Village, bowl, serving; #010, 7" ..**9.00**

Village, bowl, vegetable; #011, 8¾" ..................................**12.00**

Village, butter dish, #028 ......**8.00**

Village, casserole, w/lid, #315, 2-qt ...................................**28.00**

Village, coffeepot, lighthouse shape, 48-oz, from $35 to ...........**40.00**

Village, cookie jar, #540, 3-qt, from $20 to .............................**25.00**

Village, cup & saucer, #001 & #002, from $3.50 to .........**4.50**

Village, gravy boat, #443, with saucer, 16-oz, from $12 to ...................**15.00**

Village, pedestal mug, #90F, 10-oz ...................................**4.50**

Village, plate, dinner; #004, 10¼", from $3.50 to ...................**4.50**

Village, soup tureen, #160, w/lid & ladle, 3½-qt, from $40 to ......................**45.00**

# Pie Birds

What is a pie bird? It is a functional and decorative kitchen tool most commonly found in the shape of a bird, designed to vent steam through the top crust of a pie to prevent the juices from spilling over into the oven. Other popular designs were elephants and black-faced bakers. The original vents that were used in England and Wales in the 1800s were simply shaped like funnels.

From the 1980s to the present, many novelty pie vents have been added to the market for the baker and the collector. Some of these could be obtained from Far East Imports; others have been made in England and the US (by commercial and/or local enterprises). Examples can be found in the shapes of animals (dogs, frogs, elephants, cats, goats, and dragons), people (policemen, chefs with and without pies, pilgrims, and carolers), or whimsical figurals (clowns, leprechauns, and teddy bears). New for the 1990s is an array of holiday-related pie vents.

Consequently a collector must be on guard and aware that these new pie vents are being sold by dealers (knowingly in many instances) as old or rare, often at double or triple the original cost (which is usually under $10.00). Though most of the new ones can't really be called reproductions since they never existed before, there's a black bird that is a remake, and you'll see them everywhere. Here's how you can spot them: they'll have yellow beaks and protruding white-dotted eyes. If they're on a white base and have an orange beak, they are the older ones. Another basic tip that should help you distinguish old from new: older pie vents are air-brushed versus being hand painted. Please note that incense burners, one-hole pepper shakers, dated brass toy bird whistles, and ring holders (for instance, the elephant with a clover on his tummy) should not be mistaken for pie vents.

Our advisor for this category is Lillian M. Cole, who is listed in the Directory under New Jersey. See also Clubs and Newsletters.

Bird, all-black or all-white, imported, 4" .....................**4.00**

Bird, black or white, wide mouth, marked England ...........**35.00**
Bird, multicolor, Morton Pottery .............................**18.00**
Black-faced chef & cook, multicolor paint, Taiwan, pr .....**10.00**
Bluebird, speckled, black details, USA, 1940s-50s, 4½" ....**25.00**
Chef, white, pinhole vent, 1995 reproduction ...................**5.00**
Funnel, aluminum, England .**25.00**
Grimwade, funnel, England .**50.00**
Pyrex, funnel, sizes vary, ea .**15.00**
Rooster, multicolor, marked Cleminson or Cb ...........**28.00**
Rowland's Hygienic Patent, England ...............................**70.00**
SB signed, England, 1980s to present ...............................**30.00**

# Pin-Back Buttons

Because most of the pin-backs prior to the 1920s were made of celluloid, collectors refer to them as 'cellos.' Many were issued in sets on related topics. Some advertising buttons had paper inserts on the back that identified the company or the product they were advertising. After the 1920s lithographed metal buttons were produced; they're now called 'lithos.'

Our advisors for miscellaneous pin-back buttons are Michael and Polly McQuillen; they are listed in the Directory under Indiana. See also The Beatles; Elvis Presley; Political.

Bruce Lee Game of Death, 1979 ..**20.00**

Catwoman, DC Comics, multicolored, 2" ..............................**4.00**

Certified Hershey's Chocolate Lover ................................**5.00**

Chessie, shows mascot kitten, black & white, 1½" ........**2.00**

**Dumbo D-X, Walt Disney, red, gray on white, $28.00.**

Foist Family, Edith Bunker photo, 1972 ................................**18.00**

GE Safety Committee, red, gold & green, 1" ..........................**8.00**

Gene Autry, photo on blue, purple or red ground, 1950s, 1¼" ....**25.00**

Hard Rock Cafe, Save the Planet, multicolored ....................**5.00**

John Travolta for President, Midland Records, 1976, 1½" .............**20.00**

Lion King, features all characters, 1993, 3" ...........................**5.00**

Lion King, Simba, I'm Gonna Be King, 1993, 2¼" ..............**5.00**

Little Mermaid, purple lettering, 1980s, 3" ..........................**5.00**

Lone Ranger, Sunday Herald & Examiner, 1930s ...........**30.00**

Lost in Space 30th Anniversary, Dec 2-3, 1995, limited edition, 1½" .................................**15.00**

Mickey Mouse, Mod Mickey, Beny-Albee, late 1960s, 3½" ..**20.00**

Peanuts, Snoopy Come Home, 1972, yellow, 6" ............**15.00**

Peanuts, We Love You Charlie Brown, 1¼" .....................**5.00**

Pocahontas, Sing Along Songs video button, 1995, rectangular ....................................**8.00**

Reebock, Pump It Up!, blue & orange ............................**2.00**

Reno, Biggest Little City in the World ..............................**3.50**

Rin-Tin-Tin, Screen Gems, 1956, head shot ......................**20.00**

**Roy Rogers and Dale Evans, Charles Starret Famous Cowboy Series, black and white litho, 1¼", $15.00 each.**

Sal Mineo Fan Club, multicolored, 3" .......................................**5.00**

Sea World, Shamu & His Crew, multicolored, 2½" ............**4.00**

Talespin, image of Baloo, 1980s, 3" .......................................**3.00**

Woodstock 1969, purple, red & white ..............................**18.00**

Yogi Bear for President, 1964, red, white & blue, 3" ...........**50.00**

## Pep Pins

In the late '40s and into the '50s, some cereal companies packed a pin-back button in each box of their product. Quaker Puffed Oats offered a series of movie star pin-backs, but Kellogg's Pep Pins are probably the best known of all. There were eighty-six different Pep Pins, so theoretically if you wanted the whole series, as Kellogg hoped you would, you'd have to buy at the very minimum that many boxes of their cereal. Pep Pins came in five sets: the first in 1945, three more in 1946, and the last in 1947. They were printed with full-color lithographs of comic characters licensed by King Features and Famous Artists — Maggie and Jiggs, the Winkles, and Dogwood and Blondie, for instance. Superman, the only D.C. Comics character, was included in each set. Most Pep Pins range in value from $10.00 to $15.00 in NM/M condition; any not mentioned in our listings fall into this range. The exceptions are evaluated below.

Our advisor for Pep Pins is Doug Dezso; he is listed in the Directory under New Jersey.

| | |
|---|---|
| Bo Plenty | 30.00 |
| Corky | 16.00 |
| Dagwood | 30.00 |
| Dick Tracy | 30.00 |
| Felix the Cat | 85.00 |
| Flash Gordon | 30.00 |
| Flat Top | 30.00 |
| Jiggs | 25.00 |
| Kayo | 20.00 |
| Maggie | 25.00 |
| Mama De Stross | 30.00 |
| Mama Katzenjammer | 25.00 |
| Olive Oyl | 30.00 |
| Orphan Annie | 25.00 |
| Phantom | 80.00 |
| Popeye | 30.00 |
| Rip Winkle | 20.00 |
| Superman | 42.00 |
| Uncle Walt | 20.00 |
| Winkles Twins | 90.00 |

# Political Collectibles

Pennants, posters, badges, pamphlets — in general, anything related to a presidential campaign or politicians — are being sought by collectors who have an interest in the political history of our country. Most valued are items from a particularly eventful period or those things having to do with an especially colorful personality.

Our advisors for this category are Michael and Polly McQuillen; they are listed in the Directory under Indiana. See also Clubs and Newsletters.

| | |
|---|---|
| Badge, press; 1964 Republican Convention, w/white ribbon, EX | 85.00 |
| Badge, 1948 GOP Convention, Philadelphia PA, NM | 65.00 |
| Badge, 1956 Connecticut Constitutional Convention Staff Member, EX | 35.00 |
| Badge, 1956 GOP Convention, San Francisco CA, elephant w/flag, EX | 75.00 |
| Badge, 1960 GOP Convention, Sergeant at Arms, pink ribbon, EX | 55.00 |
| Ballpoint pen, John F Kennedy bust portrait, 1917-63 | 12.50 |

Bandana, Humphrey (blue) & Muskey (red) w/a donkey, EX .............................**45.00**

Brochure, Ronald Reagan as host of GE Theatre, 1954, 14x 10½", EX .......................**20.00**

Bumper sticker, Jimmy Carter for President in '76, 12" .......**2.00**

Bumper sticker, Re-Elect Hillary's Husband in 1996, M .......**1.25**

**Bust, John F. Kennedy, bronze-colored plastic, U.S. Steel/World's Fair Unisphere, 5", $25.00.**

Campaign stamp, A Vote for Goldwater Is a Vote for America, multicolor ........................**1.00**

Charm bracelet, John F Kennedy & family, nickel-plated, 7½", EX ................................**25.00**

Delegate key, 1960 Chicago Republican Convention, EX ...........................**28.00**

Handbill, Greet President Nixon, 1971, M ...........................**3.50**

Handkerchief, President Hoover portrait, 1932, 17x17" .**100.00**

Key, 1968 Democratic Convention, brass, lg, M ...................**20.00**

License plate, Herbert Hoover for President, 3x5", VG ......**35.00**

License plate, LBJ for the USA, red, white & blue, EX ...**30.00**

License plate, Reagan, red, white & blue, 1981, M ............**10.00**

License plate, Wallace for President, portrait & flag, 6x12" ..........................**9.00**

Money clip, John F Kennedy, 1917-63, MIB ...............**10.00**

Mug, Jimmy Carter caricature, brown ceramic ...............**20.00**

Pennant, Vote Dewey, Republican, green felt, 1958, 13", VG .**30.00**

Plate, President & Mamie Eisenhower, portraits, 12", NM ...........................**24.00**

Postcard, John & Jackie Kennedy, full-color photo, 9x6", M .**5.00**

Poster, Lyndon Johnson campaign, photo, red, white & blue, 1964, NM .............**20.00**

**Poster, Nixon Impeaches, by G. Duoos, green, yellow, and white, 1974, 23x35", $75.00.**

Poster, Robert Kennedy, Kennedy for President, 1968, 12x16", NM ................................**35.00**

Sheet music, Eisenhower inauguration, 1953 .....................**8.00**

Sunglasses, paper, Go Goldwater, San Francisco Convention, NM ................................**25.00**

Tab clip, McGovern ................**2.00**

Ticket, 1948 Republican Convention ...............................**10.00**

Wristwatch, Spiro Agnew, Dirty Time, running ...............**50.00**

## Pin-Back Buttons

Celluloid pin-back buttons ('cellos') were first widely used in the 1896 presidential campaign; before that time medals, ribbons, and badges of various kinds predominated. By the 1920s buttons with designs lithographed directly on metal ('lithos') became more common. The most attractive and interesting designs are found on 'classic' buttons made between 1900 and 1915, and they (along with the plainer but very scarce buttons for presidential candidates of the 1920s) are also the most expensive.

Prices for political pin-back buttons have increased considerably in the last few years, more due to speculative buying and selling rather than inherent scarcity or unusual demand. It is still possible, however, to find quality collectible items at reasonable prices. In flea markets, recent buttons tend to be overpriced; the goal, as always, is to look for less familiar items that may be priced more reasonably.

Most collectors look for presidential items, but buttons for 'causes' (such as civil rights and peace) as well as 'locals' (governors, senators, etc.) are becoming increasingly popular as well. Picture buttons are the most desirable, especially the 'jugates' which show both presidential and vice-presidential candidates. Recently, 'coattail' items, featuring presidential and local candidates on the same button, have attracted a lot of interest. Most buttons issued since the 1964 campaign, with a few notable exceptions, should be in the range of $2.00 to $10.00.

Condition is critical: cracks, scratches, spots, and brown stains ('foxing') seriously reduce the value of a button. Prices are for items in excellent condition. Reproductions are common; many are marked as such, but it takes some experience to tell the difference. The best reference book for political collectors is Edmund Sullivan's Collecting Political Americana, the second edition of which has been recently published.

Adlai Stevenson portrait, Best in View, 1952, 1½", EX .....**70.00**

Click w/Dick, red, white & blue, 1960, M ............................**2.50**

Clinton & Gore portraits, Hope Not Fear, black on gold ..**1.50**

Colonel North, American Hero .**5.00**

Dick Gephardt for President, red, white, blue & black ............**50**

For Peace McGovern, caricature w/dove, multicolor, 3½" ..**4.50**

Robert F. Kennedy pin-backs, red, white, and blue with black and white portraits, 3" – 4": Kennedy for U.S. Senator, $15.00; Robert F. Kennedy For U.S. Senate, $45.00.

Harry S Truman, 1884-1972, black & white portrait ..............**5.00**

Hubie Baby, stylized letters, red & white, M ..........................**4.00**

I Like Ike, 1952, ⅞", EX ........**3.00**

I'm for Nixon, flasher, M .....**10.00**

In Memory of LBJ, 1908-1973, 4" ................................**15.00**

John F Kennedy color portrait w/red rim, 3", M ..............**5.00**

Lesbians & Gay Men for Clinton/Gore, red, white blue, lg ..............................**1.25**

March on Washington November 15, red on yellow, ca 1969, 1¾" ..................................**3.00**

McGovern/Eagleton, NM .......**5.00**

Nixon & Agnew portraits, natural colors, lg, M .....................**4.00**

Nixon in '72, stylized letters, red, white & blue ....................**2.50**

Pat Brown for Me, red, white & blue, 1962, sm .................**1.50**

Presidente Nixon, Ahora mas que nunca!, blue on white, 1972 .............................**2.50**

Register for LBJ, Stetson hat, blue & white ...........................**4.00**

Robert F Kennedy full-color portrait, 1968, 3½" .............**10.00**

Strom Thurmond for President, 2-color, 1968 .......................**3.50**

Students for Kennedy, JFK portrait, red, white & blue, EX ..............................**5.00**

The Choice: Trust w/Muskie, Nothing w/Nixon, 1972 ...**2.00**

Vote Gore, Senator...Tennessee (father of Vice President), flasher ...........................**12.00**

Vote McGovern, dove, 1972, 1¼", EX ...................................**15.00**

Wallace for President, Stand Up for America, portrait, 3" .**3.00**

We Want Mamie, portrait, red, white & blue ..................**12.50**

Willkie portrait, red, white & blue border, 1940, 1¼", EX ..**25.00**

WIN (Whip Inflation Now), 1970s .............................**1.50**

## Poodle Collectibles

It is speculated that the return of servicemen following

World War II sparked an interest in all things French. Although debatable, it was widely accepted that poodles were of French origin. Thus the poodle trend of the late '40s through the mid-'60s was born. During this era, poodles were featured in a wide variety of items that included apparel, figurines, household items, and toys. The poodle trend lost popularity and eventually faded as the flower-power movement of the late '60s and '70s brought rejection of materialism. Fortunately for collectors, poodle memorabilia survived and can be found today.

Our advisor for this category is Elaine Butler, author of *Poodle Collectibles of the '50s and '60s*; she is listed in the Directory under Tennessee.

**Night light, poodle puppy figural, unmarked, from $20.00 to $25.00. (Photo courtesy Elaine Butler)**

Clothes hamper, painted scene on patterned vinyl, Lucite handle ................................**70.00**

Decanter, upright white poodle, Garnier, w/corkscrew, from $15 to ............................**20.00**

Dish towel, printed poodle on linen, from $4 to .............**6.00**

Figurine, ceramic w/much coleslaw, turquoise w/gold, 1950s, from $30 to ........**35.00**

Figurine, w/parasol, white ceramic, unmarked, from $20 to ................................**25.00**

Figurine, white ceramic w/black angora trim, from $8 to .**12.00**

Kleenex holder, black metal rectangle w/white painted poodle, Ransbury ...............**20.00**

Perfume holder, poodle figural, various sizes, ea, from $25 to ................................**40.00**

Pin, gold-tone figural, marked Sarah Coventry, from $15 to ................................**20.00**

Pin, gold-tone figural w/blue rhinestone eyes, unmarked, from $10 to ....................**15.00**

Pincushion/nodder, enameled figural, cushion on back, Florenza ................................**35.00**

Planter, poodle pulling cart, painted ceramic, unmarked, from $15 to ............................**20.00**

Planter, poodle puppy, paper label: Napcoware Japan, #136 in mold ..............................**10.00**

Purse, embroidered scene on cotton, plastic handle, from $8 to ................................**10.00**

Tablecloth, turquoise polka dots & border w/black poodles, from $20 to ..................**25.00**

Toy, hard plastic, marked Breyer, from $30 to ....................**40.00**

Toy, push puppet, unmarked, M, from $3 to ........................**5.00**

Toy, tan vinyl & black cashmere, marked Dream Pet, from $8 to ...................................**10.00**

Tumbler, juice; black silhouette, flared foot & rim, set of 4, from $10 to ....................**15.00**

## Precious Moments

Precious Moments, little figurines with inspirational captions, were created by Samuel J. Butcher and are produced by Enesco Inc. in the Orient. They're sold through almost every gift store in the country, and the earlier, discontinued models are becoming very collectible.

Our advisor for this category is Rosie Well; she is listed in the Directory under Illinois. Refer to *Precious Collectibles*, a magazine published by Rosie Wells Enterprises Inc. for more information. See also Clubs and Newsletters.

Bell, We Have Seen His Star, E-5620, Hourglass mark ..**40.00**

Bell, Wishing You a Merry Christmas, E-5393, Cross mark ............................**45.00**

Doll, Aaron, 12424, Olive Branch mark ............................**140.00**

Doll, Angie, Angel of Mercy, 12491, Cedar Tree mark .........**225.00**

Doll, Timmy, E-5397, Dove mark .....................**155.00**

Figurine, Blessed Are the Pure in Heart, E-3104, Triangle mark ............................**50.00**

Figurine, Brighten Someone's Day, 105953, Bow & Arrow mark ............................**25.00**

Figurine, Brotherly Love, 100544, Olive Branch mark .......**95.00**

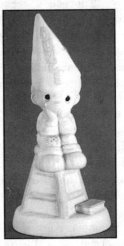

**Figurine, Nobody's Perfect, 'Dunce' boy, 1982, Hourglass mark, 7¼", $75.00.**

Figurine, Friends Never Drift Apart, 100250, Olive Branch mark ..............................**65.00**

Figurine, God Sent His Son, E-0507, Fish mark ............**95.00**

Figurine, Jesus Loves Me, E-1372B, Hourglass mark ..............**50.00**

Figurine, Let the Whole World Know, E-7165, Hourglass mark .**125.00**

Figurine, Lord Keep Me on the Ball, 12270, Olive Branch mark ..............................**70.00**

Figurine, Love Is Sharing, E-7162, Fish mark ....................**145.00**

Figurine, May Your Birthday Be Warm, 15938, Dove mark .........................**35.00**

Figurine, May Your Future Be Blessed, 525316, Trumpet mark .............................**40.00**

Figurine, Mother Sew Dear, E-2850, Cross mark ........**250.00**

Figurine, My Love Will Never Let You Go, 103497, Cedar Tree mark ...............................**45.00**

Figurine, No Tears Past the Gate, 101826, Olive Branch mark .........................**115.00**

Figurine, Sending You a Rainbow, E-9288, Dove mark .......**85.00**

Figurine, Sharing Our Joy Together, E-2834, Olive Branch mark ...............................**65.00**

Figurine, Sharing Our Season Together, E-0519, Cross mark ............................**150.00**

Figurine, This Land Is Our Land, 527386, Vessel mark, from $350 to .........................**425.00**

Figurine, To a Special Dad, E-5212, no mark ...............**70.00**

Figurine, To Tell the Tooth You're Special, 105813, Cedar Tree mark ............................**150.00**

Figurine, You Have Touched So Many Hearts, 527661, Butterfly mark .........................**38.00**

Frame, God's Precious Gift, 12041, Cross mark ....................**50.00**

Frame, The Lord Bless You & Keep You, E-7166, Olive Branch mark .................**50.00**

Musical, Come Let Us Adore Him, E-2810, Fish mark .................**145.00**

Musical, Peace on Earth, E-4726, Hourglass mark .........**120.00**

Musical, Silent Night, 15814, Dove mark ...........................**100.00**

Musical, Wishing You Were Here, 526916, Trumpet mark .........................**110.00**

Ornament, Baby's First Christmas, E-2362, Dove mark .......................**35.00**

Ornament, Bundles of Joy, E-2374, Hourglass mark ...........**120.00**

Ornament, But Love Goes on Forever, E-5627, Triangle mark .......................**130.00**

Ornament, Love Is Kind, E-5391, Dove mark ....................**35.00**

Plate, Jesus Loves Me, E-9275, Fish mark ......................**35.00**

Plate, The Hand That Rocks the Future, E-2596, Cross mark .........................**40.00**

Thimble, God Is Love, Dear Valentine, 100625, Dove mark .............................**20.00**

Thimble, The Lord Bless You & Keep You, 100633, Cedar Tree mark .............................**15.00**

## Purinton

Popular among collectors due to its 'country' look, Purinton Pottery's dinnerware and kitchen items are easy to learn to recognize due to their bold yet simple designs, many of them of fruit and flowers, created with basic hand-applied colors on a creamy white gloss. For more information we recommend *Purinton Pottery, An Identification and Value Guide,* by Susan Morris (Collector Books).

**Canister, Palm Tree, $200.00; Matching range shakers, $75.00. (Photo courtesy Pat Dole)**

Baker, Maywood, 7" .............**15.00**
Bank, Uncle Sam, 4½" .........**50.00**
Bowl, cereal; Pennsylvania Dutch, 5¼" ...................................**20.00**
Bowl, fruit; Apple, scalloped border, 12" ..........................**40.00**
Bowl, vegetable; Normandy Plaid ...........................**18.00**
Candle holder, Saraband, 6x2" .**50.00**
Coffee server, Seaform, 9" .**125.00**
Cookie jar, Fruit, oval, red trim, 9" ..................................**60.00**
Cup & saucer, Provincial Fruit, 2½", 5½" ........................**20.00**
Decanter, Mountain Rose, 5" ..**45.00**
Jar, grease; Apple, with lid, 5½" ......................**85.00**
Jug, honey; Apple, 6¼" ........**55.00**
Jug, Kent, Normandy Plaid, 1-pt, 4½" .................................**20.00**
Lamp, TV; Red Feather, 8½" .**75.00**
Planter, Ming Tree, 5" .........**40.00**
Planter, sprinkler shape, Red Tulip, 5½" ......................**65.00**
Plate, chop; Intaglio, 12" .....**25.00**
Plate, dinner; Apple, 9¾" ....**15.00**

Platter, meat; Intaglio, 12" .**30.00**
Salt & pepper shakers, Crescent Flower, round, 2¾", pr ...........................**65.00**
Teapot, Fruit, 2-cup, 4" .......**30.00**
Toothpick holder, rolling pin shape, 5" ......................**25.00**
Tumbler, Apple, 12-oz, 5" ....**20.00**
Wall pocket, Mountain Rose, 3½" ...........................**65.00**

**Range bowl, Mountain Rose, with lid, 5½", $65.00. (Photo courtesy Susan Morris)**

# Puzzles

Of most interest to collectors of vintage puzzles are those made of wood or plywood, especially the early hand-cut examples. Character-related examples and those representing a well-known personality or show from the early days of television are coming on strong right now, and values are steadily climbing in these areas. For an expanded listing, see *Schroeder's Collectible Toys, Antique to Modern* (Collector Books). See also Rock 'n Roll.

Adventures of Gulliver, frame-tray, Whitman, 1969, complete, 14x11", NM .........**35.00**

Andy Panda, frame-tray, Walter Lantz, 1963-63, 11x8", EX ...........................**10.00**

Aquaman, jigsaw, Whitman, 1968, 100 pcs, EX (EX box) ........................**35.00**

Batman, jigsaw, APC, 1973, NM (NM canister) ................**25.00**

Bee Gees, jigsaw, 1979, MIB .**20.00**

Broken Arrow, frame-tray, Built-Rite, boxed set of 4, MIB ........................**65.00**

Buffalo Bill, jigsaw, Built-Rite, 1956, 100 pcs, EX (EX box) ..................**25.00**

Bullwinkle, jigsaw, Whitman, 1960, complete, EX (EX box) ..........................**25.00**

Captain Kool & the Kongs, frame-tray, 1978, M (sealed) ...**15.00**

Chilly Willy, frame-tray, Walter Lantz, 1962-63, 11x8", EX ...........................**10.00**

Combat, jigsaw, Jaymar, 1960s, NMIB ...........................**20.00**

**Disney Movie Classics, Bambi and Friends, Jaymar, #105, 100 pieces, 18x13", MIB, $10.00.**

**CHiPs, Ponch and John, HG Toys #483-01, 150 pieces, 1977, from $8.00 to $10.00. (Photo courtesy Greg Davis and Bill Morgan)**

Davy Crockett Indian Attack, jigsaw, Jaymar, EX (EX box) ......................**35.00**

Deputy Dawg, jigsaw, Whitman, 1972, 100 pcs, NM (EX box) ..................**15.00**

Dondi, frame-tray, Jaymar, 1961, 14x11", NM ...................**15.00**

Dracula, jigsaw, 1974, EX (EX canister) .........................**20.00**

Fat Albert, jigsaw, Whitman, 1975, 100 pcs, NM (EX box) ..........................**20.00**

Gunsmoke, jigsaw, Whitman, 1969, 100 pcs, MIB .......**35.00**

Hardy Boys, jigsaw, 1978, EX (EX box) ..............................**25.00**

Howdy Doody, frame-tray, Whitman, 1953, 15x11", NM .........................**20.00**

Impossibles, frame-tray, Whitman, 1967, 14x11", EX .......................**25.00**

Lassie & Timmy, frame-tray, Whitman, EX ................**25.00**

Little Lulu, jigsaw, Whitman, 1973, set of 4, MIB .......**70.00**

Mary Poppins, frame-tray, Jaymar, 1964, NM ..............**20.00**

Mary Poppins, jigsaw, Jaymar, 1964, MIB ......................**40.00**

Milton the Monster, jigsaw, Whitman, 1967, NMIB .........**50.00**

Mr Magoo, frame-tray, Jaymar, 1967, complete, 10x13", EX .............................**15.00**

Peter Pan, frame-tray, Jaymar, 1950s, EX .....................**20.00**

Princess of Power, frame-tray, 1985, 14x11", EX ..........**10.00**

Road Runner, jigsaw, Whitman, 1980, EX (EX box) ..................**20.00**

Roger Ramjet, frame-tray, Whitman, 1966, EX ..............**20.00**

Shotgun Slade, jigsaw, Milton Bradley, 1960, 100 pcs, NMIB ..........................**30.00**

Sleeping Beauty, frame-tray, Whitman, 1958, various images, 11x14", ea .**20.00**

Snow White & the Seven Dwarfs, jigsaw, Jaymar, 1940s, 300 pcs, NMIB .....................**50.00**

Steve Canyon in China, jigsaw, Jaymar, 1950s, EX (EX box) ..........................**15.00**

Tammy, jigsaw, Whitman, 1964, MIB ..............................**40.00**

Tom & Jerry, frame-tray, 1954, EX ..................................**30.00**

Twinkles, frame-tray, Whitman, 1962, rare, 14x11", NM ..........................**55.00**

Underdog, frame-tray, Whitman, 1976, 11x8", EX ...........**15.00**

Wyatt Earp, frame-tray, Whitman, 1956, EX ..............**25.00**

Yogi Bear, jigsaw, Whitman, Jr, 1960s, 63 pcs, NMIB ....**25.00**

# Radios

Novelty radios are those that carry an advertising message or are shaped like a product bottle, can, or carton; others may be modeled after the likeness of a well-known cartoon character or disguised as anything but a radio — a shoe or a car, for instance. It's sometimes hard to recognize the fact that they're actually radios. To learn more, we recommend *Collector's Guide to Novelty Radios, Books I and II,* by Marty Bunis and Robert F. Breed (Collector Books).

Transistor radios are also popular. First introduced in 1954, many feature space-age names and futuristic designs. Prices here are for complete, undamaged examples in at least very good condition. All are battery operated and AM unless noted otherwise. For further information, we recommend *Collector's Guide to Transistor Radios, Second Edition,* by Marty and Sue Bunis (Collector Books). If you have vintage radios you need to evaluate, see *Collector's Guide to Antique Radios, Fourth Edition* (Bunis, Collector Books).

## Novelty Radios

Ajax Laundry Detergent, AM/FM, box style, Hong Kong, 4¾", from $50 to .....................**75.00**

Binoculars, AM only, braided strap, 3⅜x4¼", from $30 to ......**45.00**

Blinking Pig, bib overalls, 6½x3¼", from $15 to .....**25.00**

Borden Milk Shake Chocolate Flaver (English & French), from $40 to .....................**50.00**

Canada Dry, can form, French along bottom, from $20 to ..........**30.00**

Coors Light, can form, AM/FM, bright aluminum label, from $20 to .............................**35.00**

Drum, plastic w/paper label, Midland Electronics, Taiwan, from $35 to .....................**50.00**

Evel Knievel, tire shape, Hong Kong, 6" dia, from $35 to .............**50.00**

Fanta Orange (French & English), can form, from $20 to ...........................**35.00**

Ghostbusters, FM, Concept 2000, China, 1986/1989, 4" sq, from $20 to .............................**30.00**

Grand Old Dad Deluxe Scotch Whiskey, Hong Kong, bottle form, 5½" ......................**50.00**

Jewelry box, knight & castle motif, Japan, 10x6", from $40 to ....................................**50.00**

Kodak Instant Color Film, sq package, Hong Kong, from $50 to .............................**60.00**

Lawry's Seasoned Salt, AM only, beverage can case, from $35 to ....................................**50.00**

Marlboro Cigarettes, package form, Japan, 13¼", from $75 to ................................**100.00**

Miller High Life, glossy label on can form, from $25 to ...**30.00**

Mork (of Mork, & Mindy), Concept 2000, 1979, EX ..............**35.00**

MusiCooler, red & white cooler shape, Hong Kong, 10x12", from $30 to ....................**40.00**

Nabisco Nacho 'n Corn Things, box style, Hong Kong, 3½x5", from $35 to ............................**50.00**

Nature Valley Granola, box style, Hong Kong, 3½x5", from $50 to ....................................**75.00**

Old Milwaukee Beer, baseball cap, AM/FM, 2 ear plugs, from $25 to ....................................**40.00**

Orange 'C' Plus, 3-D orange w/sticker label, 3½" dia, from $35 to ............................**50.00**

Penguin, wings for tuning & volume, Hong Kong, 6½", from $60 to ............................**75.00**

Pool table (jewelry box), wooden, cue stick & 3 balls on top, Japan ............................**50.00**

Princess of Power, Power Tronic by Nasta, Mattel, 1985, 5", from $15 to ....................**25.00**

Quick Quaker Oats, old style label, size of standard beverage can ......................**100.00**

Radio (like Philco Model 70), cathedral style, AM/FM, China, 8" ......................**25.00**

Snapple, badge type, from $45 to ..**55.00**

Spam, can shape w/white top, 3¾x3⅜", from $40 to .....**50.00**

Starforce Robot, white plastic, movable arms, Hong Kong, 6", from $40 to ....................**60.00**

Television set, 'channel' selector is tuner, Dryco, Korea, from $35 to ....................................**50.00**

**Transistor Radios**

Admiral, Y2226 Golden Eagle, vertical, yellow plastic, AM, 1962, 3⅜" ..............................**30.00**

Admiral, Y2441 Power Eight, horizontal, leather, AM, 1963, 7¼" ................................**15.00**

Admiral, 7M12, horizontal, red & white plastic, AM, battery, 1958, 5⅞" ......................**60.00**

Admiral, 751, leather, 8 transistors, AM, battery, 1959, from $15 to ............................**20.00**

Airline, GEN-1254A, horizontal, M/W logo, AM, battery, 1965 ............................**35.00**

Aladdin, AL65, vertical, 6 transistors, AM, battery, 1962, 3½" ............................**125.00**

Angel, ATR-23 Boys Radio, vertical, plastic, 2 transistors, AM, 4⅜" ................................**60.00**

Arvin, 9562, horizontal, tan, 7 transistors, AM, battery, 1957, 11⅜" ......................**55.00**

Bulova, 660 Series, vertical, plastic, AM, battery, 1959, 5¾" ....**85.00**

Capehart, T6-203 Incomparable, vertical, AM, battery, 1961, from $35 to ....................**50.00**

Columbia, 400R, vertical, red, 4 transistor, AM, battery, 1960 ...**55.00**

Coronato, RA60-9917A, horizontal, watch radio, AM, battery, 1963 ............................**75.00**

Emerson, 842, horizontal, leather, AM, battery, 1956, 9½" .**45.00**

General Electric, P808A, horizontal, white plastic, AM, 1961, 7⅛" ................................**20.00**

General Electric, 677, horizontal, red plastic, AM, 1955, 5½" ....**125.00**

Golden Shield, #3608, vertical, plastic, AM, battery, 1961 ......**35.00**

Hitachi, KH-960H Hiphonic, horizontal, black, AM/FM, battery, 1965 ......................**25.00**

Kowa, KT-31, vertical, 3 transistors, AM, battery, 1960, from $75 to ............................**95.00**

Maco, AB-175, horizontal, 7 transistors, AM, battery, 6½" ....**30.00**

Melodic, GT-586, vertical, 6 transistors, AM, battery, 1961 ..**30.00**

Motorola, 76T1, horizontal, charcoal leatherette, AM, battery, 1957 .............................**55.00**

Norelco, L1W32T/02G, horizontal, 8 transistors, AM/FM, battery, 1965 ......................**25.00**

**Orion, Deluxe, plastic, six transistors, AM, battery, 4½x2½x1½", from $125.00 to $150.00. (Photo courtesy Marty and Sue Bunis)**

Panasonic, R-100, horizontal, leatherette, AM, battery, 7⅝" ............................**20.00**

Philco, T-4J-124, horizontal, plastic, 4 transistors, 1959, 5⅞" ..............................**55.00**

RCA, 1-T-4J Hawaii, vertical, gray plastic, 8 transistors, AM, 1959 .............................**35.00**

Realtone, TR-970, vertical, plastic, 9 transistors, 1963, 6" ..**65.00**

Sanyo, 7S-P6 Personal All Wave, horizontal plastic, AM, battery, 6" ..........................**25.00**

Silvertone, 211, vertical, plastic, 6 transistors, AM, 1959, 6¼" .........**40.00**

Sony, TR-810, horizontal, plastic, 8 transistors, AM, battery, 1959 .............................**55.00**

Sony, 2R-27, vertical, plastic, 8 transistors, AM, battery, 4" ...**30.00**

Tempest, HT-1251, vertical, plastic, 14 transistors, AM, 4¼" ...**30.00**

Toshiba, 7P-130S, horizontal, plastic, 7 transistors, AM, 1963, 5⅞" ......................**45.00**

Truetone, DC3270, horizontal, plastic, 9 transistors, AM, 5⅞" ..............................**40.00**

Valiant, HT-1200 High Fidelity, vertical, plastic, AM, battery, 4¼" ..............................**35.00**

Westinghouse, HP11P5, horizontal, blue plastic, 5 transistors, 1957 .............................**85.00**

Zenith, Royal 90, vertical, plastic, AM, battery, 4¼" .........**35.00**

# Ramp Walkers

Ramp walkers date back to at least 1873 when Ives produced a cast-iron elephant walker. Wood and composite ramp walkers were made in Czechoslovakia and the

**Wilson Walkers: Little Red Riding Hood, $40.00; Clown, $30.00; Nurse, $30.00. (Photo courtesy Randy and Adrienne Welch)**

USA from the 1920s through the 1940s. The most common were made by John Wilson of Watsontown, Pennsylvania. These sold worldwide and became known as 'Wilson Walkies.' Most are two-legged and stand approximately 4½" tall.

Plastic ramp walkers were manufactured primarily by the Louis Marx Co. from the 1950s through the early 1960s. The majority were produced in Hong Kong, but some were made in the USA and sold under the Marx logo or by the Charmore Co., a subsidiary of Marx.

The three common sizes are 1) small premiums about 1½" x 2"; 2) the more common medium size, 2¾" x 3"; and 3) large, approximately 4" x 5". Most of the smaller walkers were unpainted, while the medium and large sizes were hand or spray painted. Several of the walking types were sold with wooden or colorful tin lithographed ramps.

Randy Welch is our advisor for ramp walkers; he is listed in the Directory under Maryland. For more extensive listings and further information, see *Schroeder's Collectible Toys, Antique to Modern* (Collector Books).

Astro & George Jetson, Marx ..**90.00**
Bunny carrying carrot, plastic .**60.00**
Dachshund, plastic ..............**15.00**
Donald Duck pushing wheelbarrow, Marx ....................**25.00**
Duck, plastic ........................**15.00**
Elephant, plastic ................**20.00**
Fred & Wilma on Dino, Marx ..**60.00**
Goat, plastic ........................**20.00**
Indian Chief, Wilson ...........**45.00**

Little King & Guards, Marx .**70.00**

Mad Hatter w/March Hare, Marx ............................**50.00**

Mickey Mouse pushing lawn roller ............................**35.00**

Minnie Mouse pushing baby stroller ..........................**35.00**

Monkey, Czechoslovakian ...**30.00**

Policeman, Czechoslovakian .**60.00**

Reindeer, plastic ..................**40.00**

Santa Claus, Wilson ............**75.00**

Spark Plug, Marx ..............**200.00**

Top Cat & Benny, Marx ......**65.00**

# Records

Records that made it to the 'Top Ten' in their day are not always the records that are prized most highly by today's collectors, though they treasure those which best represent specific types of music: jazz, rhythm and blues, country and western, rock 'n roll, etc. Many search for those cut very early in the career of artists who later became superstars, records cut on rare or interesting labels, or those aimed at ethnic groups. A fast-growing area of related interest is picture sleeves for 45s. These are often worth more than the record itself, especially if they feature superstars from the '50s or early '60s.

Condition is very important. Record collectors tend to be very critical, so learn to watch for loss of gloss; holes, labels, or writing on the label; warping; and scratches. Unless otherwise noted, values are for records in like-new condition —

showing little sign of wear, with a playing surface that retains much of its original shine, and having only a minimal amount of surface noise. To be collectible, a sleeve should have no tape, stickers, tears, or obvious damage. In our listings, 45s are assumed to be with the original sleeve. Refer to *The American Premium Record Guide* by Les Docks for more information on extended play and 78 rpm records. See also Clubs and Newsletters.

### Children's Records

Alice in Wonderland, Golden, 45 rpm, 1950s, EX (EX sleeve) ......................**25.00**

Alice in Wonderland, Toy Toon Records, picture disks, 1952 ..........................**15.00**

Archies Jingle Jangle, Stereo, 33⅓ rpm, 1969, EX (EX sleeve) ......................**15.00**

Ballad of Davy Crockett, Golden, 45 rpm, 1950s, NM (EX sleeve) ..........................**14.00**

Batman's Pal Robin, 45 rpm, 1966, EX (NM figural sleeve) .**30.00**

Birthday Song for You, Voco 35215, picture disk, 1948, 5" sq ..................................**20.00**

Bozo's Christmas Album, 33⅓ rpm, 1973, EX (EX sleeve) ......**10.00**

Bunny Easter Party, Voco EB ½, picture disk, 1948, diecut, from $25 to ...................**35.00**

Cinderella, Toy Toon Records, picture disk, 1952 ..............**15.00**

Ferdinand the Bull, Golden, 45 rpm, 1950s, EX (EX sleeve) .....**25.00**

Frontierland, Golden, 45 rpm, 1950s, EX (EX sleeve) ..**25.00**

Jacob's Dream, Bible Story, picture disk, 1948 ..............**15.00**

Little Jack Horner, Pix 104, picture disk, 1941, 10", from $75 to ....................................**90.00**

Little Red Riding Hood, 33⅓ rpm, 1968, VG (VG sleeve) ...**10.00**

Loopy DeLoop, Golden, 45 rpm, 1960, NM (EX sleeve) ...**12.00**

Mary Poppins, Buena Vista, 33⅓ rpm, 1964, NM (EX sleeve) ........................**15.00**

Music From Disneyland, Decca, 33⅓ rpm, 1950s, NM (EX sleeve) ...........................**40.00**

Old McDonald Had a Farm, Voco, picture disk, 1948, 7", from $10 to ............................**15.00**

Peter Pan, You Can Fly, Golden, 45 rpm, 1950s, EX (EX sleeve) ..........................**25.00**

Popeye the Sailor Man, 33⅓ rpm, 1960s, VG (VG sleeve) ..**10.00**

Robin Hood, Toy Toon Records, picture disk, 1952, from $10 to ....................................**15.00**

Rover the Strong Man, Voco, picture disk, diecut, 7", from $25 to ....................................**30.00**

Shepherd Boy, Bible Storytime, picture disk, 1948, from $10 to ....................................**15.00**

Songs From Mother Goose, Toy Toon Records, picture disk, 1952, from $10 to ..........**15.00**

Ten Little Indians, Toy Toon Records, picture disk, 1952, from $10 to ....................**15.00**

Terry & the Pirates, Record Guild of America F501, picture disk, 1948 ..............................**40.00**

Thor, Golden Books, 33⅓ rpm, EX (EX sleeve) ....................**24.00**

Three Little Kittens, Disneyland, 45 rpm, 1962, EX (EX sleeve) ........................**10.00**

Three Stooges Songbook, Coral, 33⅓ rpm, EX (EX sleeve) .......**40.00**

Thumbelina, Golden, 78 rpm, 1951, VG (VG sleeve) ......**3.00**

Tom Cat the Tightrope Walker, Voco, picture disk, diecut, 1948, from $25 to .........**30.00**

Wagon Train, Golden, 45 rpm, 1950s, EX (EX sleeve) ..**25.00**

Westward Ho the Wagons, DBR #67, 78 rpm, 1950s, M (NM sleeve) ...........................**50.00**

When Jesus Was Born, Bible Storytime, picture disk, 1948, from $10 to ....................**15.00**

Wonder Woman, Shadybrook, 45 rpm, 1977, w/theme song, M (VG sleeve) ....................**75.00**

Woody Woodpecker, Golden, 33⅓ rpm, 1963, EX (NM sleeve) .........**30.00**

## LP Albums

Annette Narrates Tubby Tuba, M .................................**25.00**

Beasley, Jimmy; Fabulous Crown 5014 ..............................**30.00**

Beatles, Rock & Roll Music, Capitol SKBO-11537, double album ............................**35.00**

Berry, Chuck; St Louis to Liverpool ...............................**50.00**

Blues Brothers, Briefcase of Blues, Atlantic SD19217 .........**20.00**

Brigadoon, movie soundtrack, Gene Kelly photo sleeve .**6.00**

Burnette, Johnny; Hits & Other Favorites, Liberty .........**25.00**

Cash, Johnny; Hymns by..., Columbia 1284 ..............**30.00**

Darren, James; Love Among the Young, Colpix, 1959 ......**25.00**

Diamonds Are Forever, United Artists, 1971 ....................**8.00**

Doors, LA Woman, Electra, diecast cover ..............................**35.00**

Ed Sullivan Presents My Fair Lady, VG .........................**5.00**

Ford, Tennessee Ernie; Ol' Rockin' Ern, Capitol 888 ...........**20.00**

Garland, Judy; Judy in Love, Capitol 1961, M ..............**8.00**

Gore, Leslie; It's My Party, from $35 to ............................**45.00**

Grateful Dead, Blues for Allah .**25.00**

Grateful Dead, Skeletons From the Closet ........................**8.00**

Greene, Lorne; Welcome to the Ponderosa, 1964 ............**12.00**

Ice Station Zebra, MGM, 1968, NM ..................................**8.00**

Jan & Dean, Filet of Soul, Liberty LRP-3441 ......................**25.00**

Jones, George; Salutes Hank Williams, Mercury 20596 .................**30.00**

Jones, Jimmy; Good Timin', from $40 to ............................**50.00**

King, BB; Singing the Blues, Crown 5020 ..................**30.00**

Kingston Trio, Sold Out ........**5.00**

KISS, Crazy Nights, M ........**30.00**

Lennon, John; Imagine, w/all inserts, from $25 to ......**40.00**

Limelighters, Tonight in Person ..**3.00**

Man From UNCLE & Other TV Themes, Metro, 1965 ....**20.00**

Marley, Bob & Wailers; Rebel Music ............................**20.00**

McDaniels, Gene; Tower of Strength, Liberty 3215 .**40.00**

Moody Blues, Go Now, picture disc, AKP 5 ....................**30.00**

Nelson, Ricky; Songs by Ricky, Imperial 9082 ................**40.00**

Newton, Wayne; Golden Archive Series, VG ......................**3.00**

Orlons, Wah-Watusi, Cameo, 1960 ..............................**20.00**

Pink Floyd, The Wall, from $15 to ....**30.00**

Platters, Around the World, Mercury 1950s, NM .............**15.00**

Redding, Otis; Dictionary of Soul, from $40 to ....................**50.00**

Reeves, Jim; Girls I Have Known, RCA 1685 ......................**15.00**

Rolling Stones, Tattoo You, 1981, from $10 to ....................**15.00**

Sherman, Bobby; Here Comes Bobby, Metromedia, 1970, NM ..................................**12.00**

Snow, Hank; Country Guitar, Victor 3267 ..........................**25.00**

## 45 rpms

Adams, Jo Jo; Didn't I Tell You, Chance 1127 ..................**30.00**

Anderson, Bill; City Lights, TNT 9015 ..............................**30.00**

Avons, Baby, Hull 722 ........**20.00**

Ball, Earl; Party of One, Pathenon 101 ..............................**10.00**

Beach, Bill; Peg Pants, King 4940 ............................**35.00**

Belew, Carl; I'm Long Gone, Sowder 248 ..........................**12.00**

Big Five, Blue Eyes, Shad 5019 ..**12.00**

Blue Chips, Promise, Groove 0006 ..............................**8.00**

Bowles, Doug; Cadillac Baby, Tune 206 ......................**25.00**

Brown, Billy; Flip Out, Columbia 41297 ............................**12.00**

Brown, Jimmy; It's Over, Capitol 3255 ...............................**15.00**

Byron, Jimmie; Sidewalk Rock, Teen 113 .......................**12.00**

Carl, Steve; Curfew, Meteor 5046 ..........................**40.00**

Carter, Bob; Fortunate Few, Den 11229 ............................**10.00**

Cassell, Tommy; Go Ahead On, Cassell 58½ ...................**20.00**

Chaplin, Paul; Nicotine, Harper 100 ...............................**8.00**

Chavis Brothers, Humpty Dumpty, Ascot 2177 .................**8.00**

**CHiPs, California Hustle, Windsong Records, 1979, from $10.00 to $15.00. (Photo courtesy Greg Davis and Bill Morgan)**

Climbers, My Darlin' Dear, J&S 1652 ...............................**40.00**

Clingman, Loy; I'm Low, Low, Low; Dot 15567 .............**10.00**

Cooper, Dolly; Wild Love, Ebb 109 ..................................**8.00**

Craig, Pee Wee; Rambling Man, Choice 1000 ...................**15.00**

Cubans, Tell Me, Flash 133. **15.00**

Dalton, Big Lloyd; Jenny, Yucca 135 .................................**10.00**

Day, Margie; Ho Ho, Cat 118 ...................................**7.00**

De Vore, Jay; Doggone Mean, Bodark 004 ....................**12.00**

Dee, Ronnie; Action Packed, Back Beat 522 ........................**10.00**

Dixie Blues Boys, My Baby Left Town, Flair 1072 .........**20.00**

Douglas, Mel; Cadillac Boogie, San 1506 ..............................**30.00**

Draper, Rusty; Pink Cadillac, Mercury 70921 ......................**8.00**

**Fisher, Eddie; Green Years, Coca-Cola advertising, RCA Victor, M, $12.00.**

Edwins, Charles; I Got Loose, Duke 124 .......................**10.00**

Electras, You Lied, Infinity 012 .**15.00**

Execs, Walking in the Rain, Fargo 1055 ..............................**15.00**

Fisher, Brien; Fingertips, Spangle 2001 ..............................**12.00**

Five Crystals, Hey Landlord, Kane 25592 ............................**10.00**

Five J's, My Darling, Fulton 2454 ...........................**20.00**

Flames, So Alone, Aladdin 3349 ........................**30.00**

Ford, Jimmie; We Belong Together, Stylo 2105 ...............**12.00**

Four Tops, Where You Are, Riverside 4534 ......................**20.00**

Frazier, Calvin; Little Baby Child, Savoy 858 ......................**10.00**

Geno, Sonny; Rumble Rock, Rip 130 ...................................**12.00**

Gibson, Daddyo; Night Train, Checker 848 ....................**8.00**

Griffins, My Baby's Gone, Mercury 70913 .............................**20.00**

Guitar Dave, Zoro, Central 291 ..**8.00**

Harlan, Billy; I Wanna Bop, Brunswick 55066 ..........**20.00**

Heralds, Eternal Love, Herald 435 ...................................**40.00**

Hobkins, Ford; Ya Fine, Fine, Fine; Apex 7757 ............**20.00**

Hornets, Crying Over You, Flash 125 ...................................**20.00**

Jackson, Lee; Please Baby, Keyhole 115 ..........................**12.00**

Jerome, Ralph; Rockhouse, KP 1007 ...............................**18.00**

Jivers, Ray Pearl, Aladdin 3347 ...**40.00**

Kidd, Billy (The); Crazy Guitar, Jane 107 ........................**10.00**

King, Albert; COD, Coun-Tree 1006 .................................**8.00**

Lanier, Don; Pony Tail Girl, Roulette 4021 ................**10.00**

Law, Art; Kitty Kat Rock, Gulfstream 1051 ..................**30.00**

Lee, Jimmy; Chicago Jump, Bandera 2506 ......................**15.00**

Lightfoot, Papa; Jumpin' With Jarvis, Aladdin 3304 ....**30.00**

Lintons, Lost Love, Erica 005 ..**6.00**

Louis, Bobby; Call of Love, Capitol 4272 ...............................**15.00**

Louise, Paul; Cock-A-Doodle, Eko 502 ...................................**30.00**

Love, Billy; Drop Top, Chess 1508 .................................**30.00**

Marquees, Wyatt Earp, Okeh 7096 ...............................**15.00**

Martells, Forgotten Spring, Cessna 477 .............................**20.00**

McGuire, Lowell; Leave My Girl Alone, Nasco 6007 ........**12.00**

McVoy, Carl; Little John's Gone, Hi 2002 ..........................**10.00**

Mints, Night Air, Lin 5007 ..**12.00**

Mitchell, Billy; Bald Headed Woman, Atlantic 974 ....**20.00**

Murphy, Don; Mean Mamma Blues, Cosmopolitan 2264 .........**40.00**

O'Neal, Grady; Baby Oh Baby, Bella 2205 .....................**30.00**

Oliver, Bobby; Lucille, Lucky Four 1006 ...............................**8.00**

Pejoe, Morris; You Gonna Need Me, Vee Jay 148 ..........**30.00**

Possessions, No More Love, Britton 1003/1004 ................**15.00**

Prager, Billy; Crystal 106 ...**20.00**

Pretty Boy, Bip Bop Bip, Atlantic 1147 ...............................**20.00**

Prodigals, Marsha, Falcon 1011 ..**20.00**

Reed, Al; Top Notch Grade A, Winner 700 ..........................**10.00**

Renowns, Wild Ones, Everest 19396 .............................**15.00**

Robinson, Dick; Boppin' Martian, MCI 1006 ......................**25.00**

Rocketones, Mexico, Melba 113 .**20.00**

Sailor Boy, Country Home, Dig 116 ...................................**20.00**

Shaul, Lawrence; Tutti Frutti, Reed 1049 ......................**30.00**

Shepperd, Buddy; That Background Sound, Sabina 510 .................**12.00**

Smith, Shelby; Rockin' Mama, Rebel 728 ......................**20.00**

Sneed, Leslie; Oh, Baby Doll, Cascade 103 .........................**15.00**

Stevens, Ray; Cat Pants, Capitol 4030 ...............................**10.00**

Tads, You Reason, Dot 15518 ..**15.00**

Taylor, Bob; Don't Be Unfair, Yucca 110 .......................**20.00**

Thompson, Loretta; Hi De Ho Rock & Roll, United 214 ........**20.00**

Tiny Stokes, Blackfoot Boogie, Big T 235 .............................**15.00**

Turley, Richard; Makin' Love to My Baby, Fraternity 845 ......**15.00**

Turner, Big Joe; TV Mama, Atlantic 1016 ..................**10.00**

Vidaltones, Forever, Josie 900 .**10.00**

Visuals, My Juanita, Popular 117 ...............................**10.00**

Wayne, Billy; I Love My Baby, Hill Crest 778 .......................**40.00**

West, Sonny; Rave On, Atlantic 1174 ...............................**15.00**

Williams, Lester; Let's Do It, Duke 123 .................................**15.00**

Williams, Sonny Boy; Alice Mae Blues, Duplex 9005 .......**15.00**

Wray, Lucky; Teenage Cutie, Starday 608 ...........................**30.00**

Young, Donnie; Shakin' the Blues, Decca 31077 ..................**15.00**

## 78 rpms

Arkansas Charlie, Texas Trail, Vocalion 5292 ................**15.00**

Barlow, Jerry; Louisiana Baby, OT 103 ....................................**7.00**

Borton, Godfrey; Two Little Orphans, Bell 1187 .........**8.00**

Canada, Marmon; Born in Hard Luck, Gennett 6972 ......**20.00**

Carter, Floyd; Flemington Kidnap Trial, Oriole 8847 .........**10.00**

Clarke & Howell, Birmingham Jail, Supertone 9536 .....**15.00**

Crystal Spring Ramblers, Down in Arkansas, Vocalion 03856 .**10.00**

Dixie Crackers, The Old Bell Cow, Paramount 3151 ...........**30.00**

Four Virginians, Swing Your Partner, Okeh 45181 ...........**20.00**

Grey, Wallace; Little Mamie, Champion 15832 ...........**12.00**

Hawkins, Uncle Billy; Turkey In The Straw, Champion 15084 ............................**8.00**

Hughey, Dan; Red River Valley, Champion 15710 ...........**10.00**

Jones, Hiram; Sailor's Hornpipe, Homestead 16492 .........**20.00**

Lawson, Jimmie; Tennessee Blues, Victor 20477 ......**15.00**

Maddux Family, Stone Rag, Decca 5393 ................................**7.00**

Martin, Dan; Cross-Eyed Butcher, Superior 2824 ................**20.00**

Miller, John; Highway Hobo, Superior 2839 ...............**25.00**

New, Jim; Wreck of the Six Wheeler, Timely Tunes 1564 ..........**15.00**

Ozark Rambler, Wreck of the 1262, Paramount 3322 .**20.00**

Potter & James, Down on the Farm, Champion 9541 ..**12.00**

Reeves & Moody, Sweet Evelina, Victor 21188 ..................**15.00**

Rodeo Trio, Arkansas Traveler, Victor V40136 ................**8.00**

Shelor Family, Big Bend Gal, Victor 20865 .......................**15.00**

Stone, Jimmy; Midnight Boogie, Imperial 8137 ...............**10.00**

Tennessee Drifters, Mean Ole Boogie, Dot 1002 .................**10.00**

Vass Family, Deep Blue Sea, Decca 5432 ....................**10.00**

West Virginia Ridge Runners, Dill Pickle Rag, Superior 2794 .**40.00**

Wonder State Harmonists, Turnip Greens, Vocalion 5275 ..**12.00**

# Red Wing

Taking their name from the location in Minnesota where they located in the late 1870s, the Red Wing Company produced a variety of wares, all of which are today considered noteworthy by pottery and dinnerware collectors. Their early stoneware lines, Cherry Band and Sponge Band (Gray Line), are especially valuable and often fetch prices of several hundred dollars per piece on today's market. Production of dinnerware began in the '30s and continued until the pottery closed in 1967. Some of their more popular lines — all of which were hand painted — were Bob White, Lexington, Tampico, Normandie, Capistrano, and Random Harvest. Commercial artware was also produced. Perhaps the ware most easily associated with Red Wing is their Brushware line, unique in its appearance and decoration. Cattails, rushes, florals, and similar nature subjects are 'carved' in relief on a stoneware-type body with a matt green wash its only finish.

We have listed only their very collectible dinnerware lines here; for more information, we recommend *Red Wing Art Pottery, Books I and II*, by B.L. Dollen. To learn about their stoneware production, refer to *Red Wing Stoneware, An Identification and Value Guide,* and *Red Wing Collectibles,* both by Dan and Gail de Pasquale and Larry Peterson. All are published by Collector Books. See also Clubs and Newsletters.

### Dinnerware

Blossom Time, cup, from $4 to .**6.00**
Blossom Time, saucer, from $5 to ................................... **7.00**
Bob White, bowl, cereal .......**22.00**
Bob White, cocktail tray ......**75.00**
Bob White, plate, 8" ...............**8.00**
Bob White, relish, 3-part .....**30.00**
Capistrano, bowl, lug soup; 6" ..**8.00**
Capistrano, platter, 13" .......**35.00**
Chevron, bowl, custard ........**18.00**
Chevron, drip jar .................**37.50**
Greenwichstone, plate, bread & butter, from $4 to ...........**6.00**
Greenwichstone, plate, 10", from $5 to ................................**8.00**
Hearthstone, bowl, sauce; from $3 to ...................................**6.00**
Hearthstone, relish tray, center handle, from $15 to ......**22.00**
Lexington Rose, cream soup .**17.00**
Lexington Rose, plate, bread & butter ..............................**5.50**
Lotus, beverage server ........**45.00**
Lotus, butter dish ................**28.00**
Magnolia, bowl, salad; lg, from $10 to ...................................**15.00**
Magnolia, cup & saucer .........**7.00**
Morning Glory, bowl, cereal .**10.00**
Morning Glory, celery tray ..**18.00**
Morning Glory, plate, 10½" .**10.00**
Pepe, creamer ......................**10.00**
Pepe, platter, 15" ................**22.00**
Random Harvest, bowl, salad; 12" ..............................**45.00**
Random Harvest, teapot .....**85.00**
Reed, egg cup ......................**16.00**

Reed, jug, ball form, 32-oz ...**28.00**
Round-Up, casserole, 2-qt ...**95.00**
Round-Up, platter, 13" ........**90.00**
Round-Up, sugar bowl .........**40.00**
Smart Set, bowl, soup ..........**17.50**
Smart Set, creamer ..............**17.50**
Smart Set, plate, 6½" ............**7.50**
Tampico, butter dish, ¼-lb ..**32.50**
Tampico, cake stand ............**50.00**
Tampico, mug, coffee ...........**50.00**

**Tampico, gravy boat with attached underplate, $50.00.**

Town & Country, bowl, mixing; dusk blue .....................**125.00**
Town & Country, plate, rust, 6½" ............................**10.00**
Town & Country, shakers, Shmoo shape, mixed colors, pr .**75.00**
Village Green, sugar bowl, brown w/aqua lid, from $6 to ..**10.00**
Village Green, teapot, brown w/aqua lid, 5-cup, from $18 to ...............................**26.00**

## Miscellaneous

Ashtray, radiant orange gloss, contoured, #746, 6", from $24 to ....................................**30.00**
Ashtray, wing form, red, bottom mark, from $48 to .........**65.00**
Bowl, Belle, snow white w/orange interior, label, low, oval, #881, 8" ....................................**35.00**

Bowl, coral/blue leaf shape, #1251, 1950s, 12", from $42 to .**54.00**
Bowl, Deluxe, ivy embossed on green w/flecks, #B2504, 14½" ..........................**75.00**
Bowl, Gothic, green w/brown trim, #937, 1950s, 10", from $40 to ..........................**52.00**
Bowl, Textura, teardrop shape, gray w/coral interior, #B2108, 11¼" ..............................**40.00**
Bowl, yellow w/flecks, rectangular, footed, #M1603, 1960s, 10", from $32 to ...................**42.00**
Candle holder, leaf motif, turquoise gloss, #1286, 1940s, 8", from $30 to ..............**38.00**
Candle holder, salmon semimatt w/scalloped edge, #1619, 1950s, 4½" ....................**20.00**

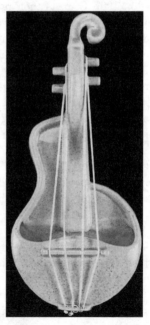

**Planter, mandolin with plastic strings, marked M/1484, USA, 13½", from $25.00 to $35.00.**

Candle holders, teardrop shape, cinammon gloss, #1409, 1960s, 5", pr .................**36.00**

Cornucopia, blue & Colonial Buff w/flecks, #442, 1950s, 15", from $68 to .....................**80.00**

Jardiniere, pink w/flecks, scalloped top, #M1610, 1960s, 6", from $18 to .....................**25.00**

Planter, lamb figural, blue matt, paper label, 1940s, 6½", from $110 to ..........................**145.00**

Planter, violet; black semimatt, #B1403, 1960s, 6", from $28 to ....................................**36.00**

Planter, yellow w/light green flecks, #1552, 1950s, 6", from $28 to .............................**36.00**

Vase, blue glossy swirl, #952, 1940s, 6", from $48 to ..........................**60.00**

Vase, brown leaves on yellow gloss, #1204, 1940s, 10", from $48 to .............................**65.00**

Vase, embossed leaves, white w/brown wash, #1096, 1940s, 9", from $72 to ..............**84.00**

Vase, fan form, metallic brown/Tahitian Gold, #892, 1960s, 7½" .....................**50.00**

Vase, Floraline, prism type, Cypress Green semimatt, #1633, 1960s, 7" ...........**45.00**

Vase, green semimatt, trophy shape w/low handles, #1053, 1940s, 8" .......................**50.00**

Vase, orange shell shape, white interior, #1295, 1950s, 7", from $36 to ...................**48.00**

Vase, Prismatique, celadon with orange interior, #798, 1960s, 8", from $60 to ..........................**74.00**

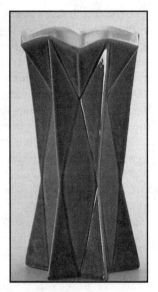

**Vase, Prismatique, #797, 11", from $68.00 to 82.00.**

Vase, stylized pitcher form, cinnamon gloss, #819, 1960s, 12", from $58 to ....................**72.00**

Vase, Tropicana, Shell Ginger, metallic brown, #B2007, 12", from $42 to ....................**54.00**

Vase, white bamboo motif w/green interior, #1400, 1960s, 8", from $30 to ....................**42.00**

Vase, white semimatt, embossed leaves, handles, #1115, 7¼", from $52 to ....................**68.00**

Vase, yellow gloss swirl, flared rim, #1590, 1950s, 10", from $48 to .............................**56.00**

# Rock 'n Roll

Concert posters, tour books, magazines, sheet music, and other items featuring rock 'n roll stars from the '50s up to the present are today being sought out by collectors who appreciate this type of music and like having these mementos of their favorite preformers around to enjoy.

Our advisor for this category is Bojo (Bob Guttuso); he is listed in the Directory under Pennsylvania. See also Beatles; Elvis Presley; Paperback Books; Records.

AC/DC, balloon, black w/white logo, promotional, MIP (sealed) ...........................**6.00**

Aerosmith, ticket, 1978, unused, M, from $15 to .............**20.00**

Alice Cooper, photo, on-stage scene, black & white, 8x10" .......................**5.00**

Boy George, poster, color, 24x36", M .....................................**12.00**

Carpenters, money cubes, Lucite cube w/shredded money, promotional ........................**28.00**

Cars, program, 1984, NM, from $12 to .............................**18.00**

Doors, bumper sticker, radio promo, vintage ................**7.00**

Duran Duran, puffy stickers, set of 6, MIP .............................**5.00**

Electric Light Orchestra, necklace, pewter UFO-shaped pendant on chain .........................**15.00**

Elton John, pennant, Capt Fantastic, paper photo on felt, 1970s, M .....................................**25.00**

Elton John, poster, Elton in mink jacket, 22x32", M .........**12.50**

Fleetwood Mac, belt buckle, Penguin cutout in circle, 1977, EX .............................**18.00**

Frank Zappa, tour program, 1980, M .....................................**12.00**

Grateful Dead, postcard, Without a Net, Rick Griffin art, NM ..............................**6.00**

Hall & Oats, sticker, radio promo, NY, 1985, NM ................**4.00**

Ike & Tina Turner, postcard, unused, NM, from $8 to .**10.00**

Jackson 5, game, Shindana, 1972, MIB (sealed) ................**175.00**

James Taylor, ticket, 1977, unused, NM ...................**10.00**

Janis Joplin, photo, hair blowing at microphone, black & white, 8x10" ...............................**5.00**

Jefferson Starship, sticker, Spitfire, girl & dragon, 1976, NM ....................**6.00**

Jimi Hendrix, postcard, 1980s reprint of 1968 concert, M .**4.00**

Kinks, booklet, TV Guise, resembles TV Guide, 1975, EX .........**10.00**

KISS, doll (Paul), M, $100.00; Buckle, brass, $30.00; Transistor radio, NM, $110.00. (Photo courtesy June Moon)

KISS, coin, Mardi Gras, logo & face portraits, 1979, M .**35.00**

KISS, Colorforms, complete, w/instruction sheet, EX (VG+ box) ................................**90.00**

KISS, game, On Tour, complete, VG+ ..............................**75.00**

KISS, pencils, set of 4, MIP (sealed) .........................**40.00**

Led Zepplin, patch, Zoso original promo, EX .....................**15.00**

Madonna, photo, beach portrait, black & white, 8x10", NM .**5.00**

Marshall Tucker Band, beer mug, plastic, color image, M .**18.00**

Metallica, program, 1988-89, EX, from $20 to ....................**25.00**

Michael Jackson, puppet, Moonwalker outfit, Puppet Kooler, 1988, MIB ......................**30.00**

Monkees, ballpoint pen .......**45.00**

Monkees, finger puppet, Davy, EX ................................**28.00**

Monkees, sunglasses, w/original hang tag ........................**45.00**

Monkees, writing tablet, photo cover, M .........................**30.00**

Motley Crue, puffy stickers, set of 5, MIP .............................**5.00**

Pink Floyd, ticket, California, 1977, unused, NM ........**22.00**

Pointer Sisters, sticker, color photo, 7x7" .....................**6.00**

REM, group photo, black & white, 8x10", NM ......................**5.00**

Rolling Stones, program, 1966, M .................................**15.00**

Rolling Stones, rub-off transfers, 1983, MIP (sealed) ........**12.00**

Stray Cats, decal tattoos, 9 on sheet, M .........................**6.00**

U2, ticket, Zoo TV Concert, unused, 1992, EX .........**18.00**

Van Halen, poster, David Lee Roth & group, 1982, 23x35", M ....**15.00**

Van Halen, puffy stickers, set of 5, MIP .................................**4.00**

# Rooster and Roses

Here's a line of dinnerware that seemed to appear out of the blue — suddenly there it was, by the tablefuls at the flea markets, by the *boothfuls* at the antique malls. It's Rooster and Roses, a quaint and provincial line of dinnerware made in Japan from the '40s and '50s. The rooster has a yellow breast with black crosshatching, a brown head, and a red crest and waddle. There are full-blown roses, and the borders are yellow with groups of brown diagonals. Several companies seem to have made the line, which is very extensive. In the short time we've been recording shapes, we've found more than seventy-five. Already it's becoming harder to find!

Our advisor for this category is Jacki Elliott; she is listed in the Directory under California.

Ashtray, rectangular, 3x2" ....**9.50**

Bell, from $25 to .................**35.00**

Bowl, cereal; from $10 to .....**14.00**

Bread plate, minimum value .**15.00**

Butter dish, ¼-lb, from $20 to .**25.00**

Carafe, w/handle & stopper lid, 8" ....................................**85.00**

Casserole dish, w/lid ............**65.00**

Cheese dish, slant lid, from $40 to ...................................**55.00**

Coffee grinder, rare, from $75 to ..............................**85.00**

Creamer & sugar bowl, w/lid, lg ..............................**25.00**

Cup & saucer, from $15 to ..**25.00**

Egg cup, from $20 to ............**25.00**

Egg plate ..............................**28.00**

Jam jar, attached underplate, from $25 to ....................**35.00**

Match holder, wall mount, from $40 to ............................**45.00**

Mug, rounded bottom, medium, from $12 to ....................**15.00**

Napkin holder, from $30 to .**40.00**

Pitcher, bulbous, 5", from $18 to ..............................**22.00**

Pitcher, 3½", from $12 to ....**14.00**

Plate, dinner; from $25 to ...**35.00**

Recipe box, from $25 to .......**35.00**

Rolling pin, minimum value....**50.00**

**Salt box, from $45.00 to $55.00.**

Toast holder, minimum value ..**75.00**

# Roselane Sparklers

A line of small figures with a soft shaded finish and luminous jewel eyes was produced during the late 1950s by the Roselane Pottery Company who operated in Pasadena, California, from the late 1930s until possibly the 1970s. The line was a huge success. Twenty-nine different models were made, including elephants, burros, raccoons, fawns, dogs, cats, and fish. Not all pieces are marked, but some carry an incised 'Roselane Pasadena, Calif.,' or 'Calif. U.S.A'; others may have a paper label.

Angelfish, 4½", from $20 to .**25.00**

Basset hound, sitting, 4" .....**15.00**

Basset hound puppy, 2" .......**12.00**

Bulldog, fierce expression, looking right, sm ........................**12.00**

Bulldog, sitting, slender body, looking right ..................**25.00**

Cat, Siamese, sitting, jeweled collar, 7" ..............................**25.00**

Cat, standing, tail arched over back, jeweled collar, 5½" ..........**25.00**

**Siamese cat, recumbent, head right, 7" long, from $20.00 to $25.00. (Photo courtesy Lee Garmon)**

Chihuahua, sitting, left paw raised, 6½" ....................**25.00**

Cocker spaniel, 4½" ............**20.00**

Deer, standing, head turned right & looking downward, 5½" ...........................**25.00**
Deer w/antlers, standing, jeweled collar, 4½" .....................**22.00**
Elephant, sitting, 6" ...........**25.00**
Fawn, 4½x1½" ....................**20.00**
Kangaroo w/babies ...............**35.00**
Kitten, sitting, 1¾" .............**12.00**
Owl, 5¼" ...............................**25.00**
Owl baby, 2¼" ......................**12.00**
Pig, lg .....................................**25.00**
Pouter pigeon, 3½" ..............**20.00**
Racoon, standing, 4½" .........**20.00**
Whippet, sitting, 7½" ...........**25.00**

# Royal China

Several lines of the dinnerware made by Royal China (Sebring, Ohio) are very collectible. Their Currier and Ives pattern (decorated with scenes of early American life in blue on a white background) and the Blue Willow line are well known, but many of their others are starting to take off as well. Since the same blanks were used for all patterns, shapes and sizes will all be the same from line to line. Both Currier and Ives and Willow were made in pink as well as the more familiar blue, but pink is hard to find and not especially collectible in either pattern.

Our advisor for this category is BA Wellman; he is listed in the Directory under Massachusetts. See Clubs and Newsletters for information on *Currier &*

*Ives China by Royal.*

### Blue Willow

Bowl, fruit nappy; 5½" ...........**4.50**
Bowl, soup; 8¼" ....................**10.00**
Cup & saucer .........................**6.00**
Gravy boat .............................**15.00**
Pie plate, 10", from $12 to ...**24.00**
Plate, salad; 7¼" ....................**7.00**
Sugar bowl, w/lid .................**12.00**
Tray, tidbit; 2-tier ................**35.00**

**Blue Willow, water pitcher, $65.00.**

### Colonial Homestead

Bowl, cereal; 6¼" .................**10.00**
Bowl, vegetable; 10" .............**20.00**
Casserole, angle handles, w/lid ......................**65.00**
Creamer .................................**5.00**
Pie plate ..............................**25.00**
Plate, dinner; 10" ...................**4.00**
Plate, salad; rare, 7¼" ..........**6.00**
Platter, oval, 13" .................**24.00**

### Currier and Ives

Bowl, cereal; tab handles, 6¼" .......................**35.00**

**Currier & Ives, butter dish, ¼-lb., $35.00; Salt and pepper shakers, $36.00 for the pair.**

Bowl, fruit nappy; 5½" ...........**4.00**
Bowl, soup; 8" .......................**12.00**
Casserole, angle handles, w/lid ....................**100.00**
Creamer, round handle, tall ..................**30.00**
Cup, round handle, tall, 9" ....**8.00**
Gravy boat, tab handle, from $25 to ....................................**35.00**
Gravy boat liner, restyled, Birthplace of Washington stamping ........................**30.00**
Mug, coffee ...........................**27.00**
Plate, calender; ca 1970s-85, ea, from $15 to .....................**20.00**
Plate, salad; 7¼" ..................**12.00**
Plate, snack; w/cup & well, 9" .........................**25.00**
Platter, tab handles, 10½" ..**28.00**
Salt & pepper shakers, pr ...**36.00**
Spoon rest, wall hanging .....**35.00**
Sugar bowl, no handles, w/lid ..................**28.00**
Tray, tidbit; 3-tier ................**75.00**
Tumbler, iced tea; glass, 12-oz, 5½" ................................**18.00**

Tumbler, old fashion; glass, 3¼" .......................**17.00**

## Memory Lane

Bowl, fruit nappy; 5½" ...........**3.00**
Bowl, soup; 8¼" .......................**7.50**
Bowl, vegetable; 10" .............**20.00**
Cake plate, w/handles, 10" ..**12.00**
Gravy boat liner, from $12 to ........................**15.00**
Plate, bread & butter; 6¼" ....**2.00**
Plate, salad; rare, 7¼" ...........**7.00**
Salt & pepper shakers, pr ...**12.00**
Sugar bowl, w/lid ..................**9.00**
Tumbler, iced tea; glass ......**12.00**

## Old Curiosity Shop

Bowl, cereal; 6½" .................**10.00**
Bowl, fruit nappy; 5½" ...........**4.00**
Bowl, vegetable; 10" .............**18.00**
Cake plate, w/handles, 10" ....................**15.00**
Cup & saucer ..........................**5.00**
Plate, bread & butter; 6¼" ....**2.50**

Salt & pepper shakers, pr ...**15.00**

# Royal Copley

Produced by the Spaulding China Company of Sebring, Ohio, Royal Copley is a line of novelty planters, vases, ashtrays, and wall pockets modeled after appealing puppy dogs, lovely birds, innocent-eyed children, etc. The decoration is airbrushed and underglazed; the line is of good quality and is well received by today's pottery collectors.

Our advisor for this catgory is Joe Devine, editor of *Royal Copley, Books I and II,* originally published by Leslie Wolfe; Mr. Devine is listed in the Directory under Iowa. See Clubs and Newsletters for *The Copley Currier.*

Ashtray, bow & ribbon, embossed mark, 5" .........................**25.00**
Ashtray, mallard figural, paper label only, 2" .................**15.00**
Figurine, cockatoos, embossed mark, 8¼" ......................**45.00**
Figurine, cocker spaniel, 6¼" .....................**25.00**
Figurine, kingfisher, paper label, 5" ....................................**30.00**
Lamp, dancing girl base, original shade ..........................**100.00**
Pitcher, Daffodil, pink, green stamp on bottom, 8" .....**45.00**
Pitcher, Pome Fruit, green stamp, 8" ..................................**45.00**

Planter, barefoot boy & girl, paper label only, 7½", ea ........**35.00**
Planter, coach, green stamp on bottom, 3x6" ..................**20.00**
Planter, deer & fawn, raised letters on bottom, 9" .........**30.00**

**Planter, deer beside stump, 8¼", from $18.00 to $25.00.**

Planter, dog in picnic basket, paper label, 7¾" ............**75.00**
Planter, duck at US Mail box, paper label only, 6¾" ....**50.00**
Planter, elephant w/ball, paper label, sm, 6" ..................**30.00**
Planter, Indian boy & drum, paper label only, 6½" ..............**24.00**
Planter, kitten in cradle, paper label, 7½" ......................**95.00**
Planter, rooster walking, white, embossed mark, 5½" .......................**45.00**
Planter, trailing vine & leaf, paper label, 4x7½" ..................**15.00**
Planter, white poodle w/black flowerpot, paper label only, 7" ..................................**48.00**

Razor blade receptacle, barber pole, paper label, 6¼" ...**60.00**
Vase, parrot on stump, 5" ...**18.00**
Wall pocket, bamboo, paper label, 7" .....................................**45.00**

# Royal Haeger, Haeger

Manufactured in Dundee, Illinois, Haeger pottery has recently become the focus of much collector interest, especially the artware line and animal figures designed by Royal Hickman. These were produced from 1938 through the 1950s and are recognized by their strong lines and distinctive glazes. For more information we recommend *Haeger Potteries Through the Years* by David Dilley (L-W Books).

Ashtray, #R-1095, Lincoln, 7" .**30.00**
Bowl, #R-510, dolphin, 15" ..**35.00**
Bowl, #R-967, starfish, 14" ..**65.00**
Bowl, #312-H, swan, 18" .....**40.00**

Candle holder, #R-203, fish, 5" .**45.00**
Candle holder, #R-433, triple, pink & blue mottled Mauve Agate, 11" ...................................**30.00**
Centerpiece, #514, mermaid on stomach w/bowl, white w/gold trim, 14" ........................**95.00**
Dish, #R-278, Spiral Plume, 9" ....**45.00**
Dish, #3169, sleek curved shape w/integral handles, 11" ..**25.00**
Figurine, #R-1440, poodle, 8" ..**55.00**
Figurine, #R-424, bucking bronco w/cowboy, 13" ..............**150.00**
Figurine, #R-648, leopard, 6" ..**45.00**
Flower block, #R-730 ..........**20.00**
Lamp, #5173, Cabbage Rose, 24" ..............................**30.00**
Pitcher, #R-G42, 10" ............**35.00**
Planter, #R-1747, jack rabbit, oyster color ........................**35.00**
Planter, #R-883, racing horses, 18" ..............................**125.00**
TV lamp, #6140, sailfish .....**65.00**
Vase, #R-1190, pine cone, 12" .**50.00**

**Little People jar with lid, Bennington Brown Foam glaze, from $15.00 to $18.00.**

**Vase, Earth Graphic Wraps, 11", $25.00.**

Vase, #R-659, alligator, 14½" ..**40.00**
Vase, #3306, horse head, 8¾" .**45.00**
Wall pocket, #R-287, birdhouse w/bird, mottled Mauve Agate glaze, 9" .........................**65.00**

## Royal Ruby

Among Anchor Hocking's Ruby Red assortment, you'll find dinnerware lines, various vases and novelties — even beer bottles. Ruby Red was simply a color. It was produced as early as 1938 and as late as 1977. Collectors appreciate the rich ruby hue of the glassware, its versatility, and (for now, at least) its reasonable prices. For a thorough study of the subject, we recommend *Collectible Glassware from the 40s, 50s, and 60s*, by Gene Florence (Collector Books).

Ashtray, leaf shape, 4½" .......**5.00**
Bowl, berry; 8½" .................**17.50**
Bowl, deep, 10" .....................**40.00**

Bowl, fruit; Bubble, 4½" ........**8.00**
Bowl, fruit; 4¼" .....................**5.50**
Bowl, salad; 11½" .................**33.00**
Bowl, soup; 7½" ....................**12.50**
Cigarette box/card holder, 6⅛x4" .........................**60.00**
Creamer, flat ..........................**8.00**
Cup .........................................**6.00**
Cup & saucer, Bubble ..........**12.00**
Goblet, ball stem .................**11.00**
Ice bucket .............................**35.00**
Ivy vase, ball shape, 4" ..........**6.00**
Pitcher, straight, 42-oz ........**30.00**
Pitcher, tilted, 3-qt .............**35.00**
Plate, dinner; 9⅛" ...............**11.00**
Plate, salad; 7" .......................**5.00**
Plate, sherbet; 6¼" .................**4.00**
Plate, 13¾" ...........................**25.00**
Punch cup, 5-oz .....................**3.00**
Saucer ...................................**2.50**
Stem, cocktail, 4½-oz ...........**10.00**
Stem, iced tea, 14-oz ...........**20.00**
Stem, juice, Bubble, 4-oz .....**10.00**
Stem, juice, 4-oz ..................**10.00**
Stem, sherbet, 6-oz ...............**8.00**
Sugar bowl, flat .....................**8.00**
Tidbit, Bubble, 2-tier ..........**37.50**

**Pitcher, $40.00; Tumblers, $7.00 each.**

Tumbler, iced tea; footed, 12-oz, 6" ..................................**15.00**

Tumbler, juice; footed or flat, 5-oz ....................................**7.50**

Tumbler, lemonade; Bubble, 16-oz, 5⅞" ...............................**16.00**

Tumbler, water; footed, 10-oz, 5" ...................................**6.50**

Tumbler, wine, footed, 2½-oz .**14.00**

Vase, either style, 6⅜" .........**17.50**

# Russel Wright Dinnerware

Dinnerware designed by Wright, at one time one of America's top industrial engineers, is today attracting the interest of many. Some of his more popular lines are American Modern, manufactured by the Steubenville Pottery Company (1939 – 59), and Casual by Iroquois, introduced in 1944. He also introduced several patterns of melmac dinnerware and an interesting assortment of spun aluminum serving and decorative items such as candleholders, ice buckets, vases, and bowls.

To calculate values for items in American Modern, use the high end for Cedar, Black, Chutney, and Seafoam; add 50% for Bean Brown, White, Glacier Blue, and Cantaloupe. For patterned lines, deduct 25%. In Casual, Brick Red, Cantaloupe, and Aqua items go for about 200% more than any other color, while those in Avocado Yellow are priced at the low end of our range of suggested values. Other colors are in between, with Oyster, White, and Charcoal at the higher end of the scale. Glassware prices are given for Flair in Crystal and Pink; other colors are higher. Add 100% for Imperial Pinch in Cantaloupe. Ruby is very rare, and market value has not yet been established. Coral and Seafoam are the more common colors in Flair glassware; other colors run about 10% to 15% higher. For more information refer to *The Collector's Encyclopedia of Russel Wright Designs, Second Edition,* by Ann Kerr (Collector Books). Mrs. Kerr is listed in the Directory under Ohio.

Bowl, bouillon; Sterling, 7-oz, from $14 to .............................**16.00**

Bowl, divided vegetable; Flair ....................**25.00**

**Melmac pieces in the Dogwood pattern: Cup & saucer, $11.00; Lug soup, $12.00; Dinner plate, $10.00.**

Bowl, fruit; Iroquois Casual, 9½-oz, 5½", from $10 to ......**12.00**

Bowl, salad; Ideal Adult Kitchen Ware, from $20 to .........**25.00**

Bowl, vegetable; Highlight, oval, from $65 to ....................**75.00**

Bowl, vegetable; White Clover, 8¼", from $27 to ...........**30.00**

Chop plate, Iroquois Casual, 13⅞", from $30 to ....................**50.00**

Chop plate, White Clover, decorated, 11", from $25 to ......**28.00**

Coffeepot, AD; Iroquois Casual, w/lid, from $75 to ........**100.00**

Creamer, American Modern, from $12 to .............................**15.00**

Creamer, Home Decorator or Residential ..........................**10.00**

Creamer, White Clover, decorated, from $18 to .............**20.00**

Cup, Meladur, from $7 to ....**10.00**

Cup, Sterling, 7-oz, from $10 to ..**15.00**

Cup, White Clover, from $12 to ..**15.00**

Cup & saucer, Home Decorator or Residential ......................**8.00**

Cup & saucer, redesigned; Iroquois Casual, from $18 to .......**20.00**

Gravy boat, American Modern, 10½" .............................**25.00**

Highball, Bartlett Collins Eclipse, 3", from $10 to .............**15.00**

Lug soup, American Modern, from $15 to .............................**20.00**

Lug soup, Home Decorator or Residential ..........................**3.00**

Mug, Iroquois Casual, 13-oz, from $60 to .............................**85.00**

Old fashioned, Imperial Twist, from $35 to ....................**50.00**

Pitcher, cream; Sterling, 9-oz, from $14 to ....................**16.00**

Plate, dessert; Meladur, 6¼", from $5 to .................................**6.00**

Plate, dinner; American Modern, 10", from $10 to ............**12.00**

Plate, dinner; Flair ..............**10.00**

Plate, dinner; Highlight, from $25 to .....................................**30.00**

Plate, dinner; Meladur, 9", from $8 to ...............................**10.00**

Plate, dinner; Sterling, 10¼", from $10 to .............................**15.00**

Platter, Flair ........................**25.00**

Salt shaker, American Modern, from $6 to ........................**8.00**

Sauce boat, American Modern .**50.00**

Sherbet/fruit dish, Highlight, from $20 to ............................**22.00**

Soup, Meladur, 12-oz, from $10 to ...................................**12.00**

Stem, cocktail; Old Morgantown/ Modern, 3-oz, from $25 to .......................**30.00**

Stem, iced tea; Imperial Pinch, 14-oz, from $30 to ..............**35.00**

Stem, iced tea; Old Morgantown/ Modern, 15-oz, from $25 to ...........**30.00**

Sugar bowl, Highlight, from $35 to ...................................**50.00**

Tumbler, Home Decorator or Residential ..........................**15.00**

# Salt Shakers

You'll probably see more salt and pepper shakers during your flea market forays than T-shirts and tube socks! Since the 1920s they've been popular souvenir items, and a considerable number has been issued by companies to advertise their products. These advertising shakers are always good, and along with miniature shakers (1½" or under) are some of the more valuable. Of course, those that have a crossover interest into other categories of collecting — Black Americana, Disney, Rosemeade, Shawnee, Ceramic Arts Studios, etc. — are often expensive as well. There are many good books on the market; among them are *Salt & Pepper Shakers, Identification & Values, Books I, II, III, and IV*, by Helene Guarnaccia; and *The Collector's Encyclopedia of Salt & Pepper Shakers* (there are two in the series) by Melva Davern. All are published by Collector Books. See also Advertising Characters; Ceramic Arts Studio; Character Collectibles; Disney; Gas Station Collectibles; Shawnee; Rosemeade; Clubs and Newsletters.

Airplanes, painted ceramic, blue w/black, sm, pr, from $15 to ......................**18.00**

Alligators, painted ceramic, realistic, tails up, pr ..............**12.00**
Bacon & egg, painted ceramic, pr, from $10 to ....................**12.00**
Ball canning jars, plastic, complete w/sealing rings & metal handles, pr ......................**7.00**
Banana & pineapple people, painted ceramic, w/boxing gloves, pr ................................**35.00**
Banana people reclining, painted ceramic, pr, from $12 to .....................**15.00**
Bear holding 2 fish (shakers), painted ceramic, set .....**15.00**
Black porter w/2 barrel shakers at sides, Japan, 7½", 3-pc set .**35.00**
Boxers, painted bone china, 1 begging, 1 standing, pr ......**12.00**
Boxing gloves & bag, painted ceramic, pr, from $10 to .**12.00**
Buffalo, painted ceramic, realistic, pr ..................................**15.00**

**Couple with baby, painted ceramic, unmarked, from $30.00 to $35.00.**

Cabbage heads, painted ceramic, realistic, lg or sm pr, from $10 to ...................................**12.00**

Cactus & Mexican man in sombrero sleeping, painted ceramic, pr ...............................**10.00**

Camel holds shakers on back, painted ceramic, 3", set, from $25 to .............................**40.00**

Cats in pajamas, painted ceramic, pr ....................................**18.00**

Champagne bottle & ice bucket, painted ceramic, w/original label, pr ..........................**18.00**

Child in top hat, painted cramic, stacking, Japan, 5", pr .....................**45.00**

Clam shells, painted ceramic, realistic, sm, pr, from $10 to ...**12.00**

Clowns, painted ceramic, marked Napco, marked 1957, pr .**24.00**

Colonial couple, painted ceramic, Japan, 5", pr ..................**35.00**

Cookies, painted ceramic, black w/white cream filling, pr .**22.00**

Corn people, painted ceramic, pr ...............................**15.00**

Cow & moon, painted ceramic, brown & yellow, pr .......**28.00**

Cupcakes, painted ceramic, pr .**16.00**

Drum & bugle, painted ceramic, Arcadia, miniature, 2", pr .........**45.00**

Ducks, painted clay pottery, Mexico, pr ..............................**10.00**

Eskimo couple, painted ceramic, he with fish, she with basket, pr .......................**15.00**

Fawns, painted ceramic, realistic, 1 standing, 1 sitting, pr ....**26.00**

Fireplace logs, painted ceramic, unglazed bottoms, 2½", pr ..**18.00**

Fishing creel & hat, painted ceramic, pr, from $6 to ...**8.00**

Fruit basket tray w/2 fruit shakers, painted ceramic, 3½", $25 to ....................................**40.00**

Golf ball & bag, painted ceramic, white & brown, pr, from $8 to ..................................**10.00**

Grasshoppers on watermelon slices, painted ceramic, pr, from $6 to .......................**8.00**

Hammer & bruised thumb, painted ceramic, pr, from $10 to .**12.00**

Hippos, painted bone china, brown & white, 1 w/mouth open, pr .........................**26.00**

Ice cream cones, yellow w/white ice cream, pr ..................**10.00**

Ice cream soda & straws in holder, painted ceramic, pr, from $12 to ....................................**15.00**

Indians on horseback w/headdresses & tomahawks, painted ceramic, pr ...............**22.00**

Japanese lady at well, 2 lotus shakers ea side, painted ceramic, set ...................**50.00**

Kitchen sink & stove, painted ceramic, yellow, pr, from $10 to ....................................**12.00**

Lady holds 2 hat boxes (shakers), painted ceramic, set, from $55 to ...............**65.00**

Lady w/poodle & man w/packages, painted ceramic, comic, Japan, 5", pr ..................**90.00**

Lion male & female, painted bone china, marked HP Relco, pr ....................**28.00**

Lion tamer & lion, man w/whip in hand, meek lion, painted ceramic, pr ....................**15.00**

Lobsters, painted ceramic, bright red, pr, from $10 to .............................**12.00**

Mary & lamb, painted ceramic, blue dress, lamb w/brown collar, pr ..............................**30.00**

Masks of Comedy & Tragedy, painted ceramic, white & black, pr ..........................**20.00**

Mermaids, painted bisque, Florida on tails, Kenmar, 3½", pr ......**49.00**

Mouse w/cheese wedge, painted ceramic, gray & yellow, pr .**8.00**

Native w/bone in hair, painted ceramic, bone is 2nd shaker, pr ....................................**95.00**

Nuns, pink plastic w/white bases, pr, from $4 to ..................**8.00**

Old lady & shoe, painted ceramic w/gold trim, pr ..............**32.00**

Onions, pearly white, painted ceramic, pr .....................**12.00**

Oriental boy w/shakers on his back, painted ceramic w/gold trim, pr ...........................**15.00**

Ostriches, painted ceramic, comic, pr, from $10 to ..............**12.00**

Owls, tan lustre w/multicolor details, comic, pr, from $8 to ...............................**10.00**

Oxen (shakers) pulling hay wagon, painted ceramic, set .....**15.00**

Parrots, painted bisque, green on brown stump, pr, from $8 to ...............................**10.00**

Pelicans, metal, white w/orange, on green base, marked Miami, pr ....................................**35.00**

Piano benches, painted ceramic, tan w/white & black, pr, from $8 to ...............................**10.00**

Pick & shovel, painted ceramic, silver-gray & yellow, pr, from $8 to ...............................**10.00**

Pigs, painted ceramic, sleeping, 1 cradles the other at side, pr ...**10.00**

Pineapple slices, painted ceramic, yellow, pr, from $10 to .**12.00**

Rabbits on motorcycles, painted ceramic, pr ....................**25.00**

Rabbits on tray, painted ceramic, 5¼" L, from $25 to ........**40.00**

Rabbits playing banjos, painted ceramic, blue & cream, German, pr ..........................**35.00**

Ring-neck pheasants, painted ceramic, holes in chest, pr, from $5 to ........................**7.00**

Sad-eyed pup & garbage can, painted ceramic, unmarked, 1960s, 5", pr .................**35.00**

Sailboat & lighthouse on tray, painted ceramic, 3-pc set, from $15 to ....................**18.00**

Scarecrow couple, painted ceramic, American pottery, 3", pr .**28.00**

Scotsman w/bagpipes & 2 egg shakers on tray, painted ceramic, Canada ...........**18.00**

Shaving brush & lather mug, painted ceramic, pr .......**35.00**

Shriner's hats, painted ceramic, marked Temple Treasures..., pr, from $20 to ..............**25.00**

Smiley faces, Have a..., painted ceramic, TreasureCraft USA, 4", pr ..............................**29.00**

Swordfish, leaping, painted ceramic, pr, from $12 to ...........**15.00**

Telephone & directory, painted ceramic, blue w/black & gold, pr, from $8 to ................**10.00**

Thimble & thread, painted ceramic, pr, from $10 to .........**12.00**

Tigers, painted ceramic, cartoonlike, yellow w/black, sitting, pr ....................................**12.00**

Toaster, plastic, yellow w/black & white toast shakers, set .**15.00**

**Snowmen on Christmas tree-shaped tray, red and white painted ceramic, unmarked, from $15.00 to $20.00. (Photo courtesy Helen Guarnaccia)**

Toucans, painted ceramic, bright colors, pr, from $20 to....**22.00**

Turkey & roaster, painted ceramic, brown & yellow, pr, from $10 to ............................**12.00**

Typewriter people, painted ceramic, pr, from $65 to .........**75.00**

Water faucets, painted ceramic, blue w/black, pr, from $8 to .........................**10.00**

Watermelon slices, painted ceramic, pr ..............................**12.00**

Wedding bells, painted ceramic, ivory w/satin bows on top, 1940s, pr .......................**15.00**

Whales on beach balls, painted ceramic, pr, from $10 to .**12.00**

## Scottie Dogs

An amazing array of Scottie dog collectibles can be found in a wide range of prices. Collectors might choose to specialize in a particular area, or they may enjoy looking for everything from bridge tallies to original portraits or paintings. Most of the items are from the 1930s and 1940s. Many were used for advertising purposes; others are simply novelties. For further information we recommend *A Treasury of Scottie Dog Collectibles* by Candace Sten Davis and Patricia Baugh (Collector Books).

Ashtray/match holder, black amethyst glass ..............**50.00**

Bank, sitting Scottie w/oversized head, ceramic, black & white, 5" ....................................**20.00**

**Barrette, green Bakelite, ca 1940s, from $30.00 to $50.00. (Photo courtesy Candace Sten Davis and Patricia Baugh)**

Bookends, ceramic, white lustre w/black trim, red bow tie, 6½", pr ....................................**35.00**

Cake pan, copper Scottie figure, 1990s, 12x16" ................**75.00**

Clock, Playful Scottie, Lux, 3¼x4¼" ........................**225.00**

Clothes brush, SyrocoWood head w/red bristles, 1940s, 7" .**45.00**

Cookie stamp, glazed stoneware, 1990s, 2" dia ..................8.00

Corkscrew, metal figural Scottie w/coiled tail, 1940s-50s, 4x2" ............................25.00

Cutting board, wood cutout, 1990s, 10x12" .............................25.00

Door knocker, Scottish Terrier, brass, 4x2" ......................15.00

Figurine, Begging His Share, Hummel, ca 1956 ........185.00

Inkwell, head, glass, hinged, 3" ..150.00

Lighter, standing Scottie w/pull-out mechanism, wooden base, 2½x3" .............................35.00

Paper plate, 2 Scotties at play on red fluted rim, 1950s, 8x8" .........................20.00

Pitcher, juice; fired on red & black Scotties 1940s ...............40.00

Powder jar, transparent pink glass w/Scottie on lid, rectangular ..............................40.00

Salt & pepper shakers, sitting dogs, silver-tone metal, 1940s, 3" ......................30.00

Soap dish, white ceramic w/black Scottie in center, oblong, 1980s .............................15.00

Wall tapestry, Scottie watching 2 dogs playing, 38x20", M ............................35.00

# Scouting Collectibles

Founded in England in 1907 by Major General Lord Baden-Powell, scouting remains an important institution in the life of young boys and girls everywhere. Recently scouting-related memorabilia has attracted a following, and values of many items have escalated dramatically in the last few years. Early first edition handbooks often bring prices of $100.00 and more. Vintage uniforms are scarce and highly valued, and one of the rarer medals, the Life Saving Honor Medal, is worth several hundred dollars to collectors.

Our advisor for this category is Rolland J. Sayers, author of *A Complete Guide to Scouting Collectibles*; he is listed in the Directory under North Carolina.

## Boy Scouts

Arm band, Nat'l Jamboree Service Corps, 1973 ...................20.00

Binoculars, plastic, 12 power, 1950, VG ........................12.00

Book, Boy Scout Book of Scout Stories, Crump, 1953 ...........4.00

Book, Boy Scout Firefighters, Crump, EX ......................4.00

Calendar, 1967 World Jamboree, complete, 42x22" ...........20.00

Coin, BSA, Get Out & Vote, 1952 .............................2.00

Drum, tin w/japanned band, Boy Scout Band, repairs, 12" dia .....................150.00

Field glasses, Official BSA, 1933-37 ...................................20.00

Flag, 1935 or 1937 Jamboree Troop Contingent, 36x60" ......100.00

Hat, broad-brimmed, felt, ca 1920-50 .....................................15.00

Lapel pin, Explorer Award, sterling silver, ca 1958-68 ..35.00

Map, Nat'l Jamboree Official, color, 1960-89, ea ............2.50

**Paperweight, Boy Scouts, emblem form, Be Prepared at base, brass and silver finish, 4", $18.00.**

Morse code set, early, complete in box ..................................**20.00**
Patch, Build-Serve-Achieve Round up, 1961 ..................................**3.00**
Patch, hat; Nat'l Jamboree Official, green, 1969 ..............**5.00**
Patch, Tenderfoot Air Scout Candidate, tan sq, 2-prop, 1948-58 ..................................**30.00**
Patch, 50th Jubilee ..............**15.00**
Plaque, award, 1960, 6x9" .....**8.00**
Postcard, Robert Baden-Powell, 1857-1941, death issue ........................**4.00**
Poster, 1935 Nat'l Jamboree, Rockwell art, 20x30" ..............**100.00**
Scarf, Nat'l Jamboree, Valley Forge, 1957 ..................**12.00**
Slide, Nat'l Jamboree Region 7, metal contingent type, 1957 ..........................**3.00**
Yearbook, Official BSA, 1st edition, 1915, EX ..............**17.50**

## Girl Scouts

Badge, First Class, khaki twill ........................**7.00**
Book, Girl Scout Collectibles, Degenhardt, 1989 .........**40.00**
Camera, Official GSA, Brownie, box-type, 1949 ...............**20.00**
Camera, Official GSA, Univex, 1937 ...............................**50.00**
Certificate, Brownie Law, embossed, 1920 .............**15.00**
Cookie cutters, GSA, green handle, 1950, complete set ........................**12.00**
Cup, aluminum, collapsible, 1950 ...............................**5.00**
Emblem, collar; GSA, brass, 1918 ...........................**10.00**
Medal, Merit, GSA, 1920, w/ribbon ...............................**75.00**
Pin, GSA Tenderfoot, 1923-34 .**4.00**

**Mess kit, Girl Scout, M in torn box, $27.60.**

Pin, Mariner, 1940 ...............**15.00**
Postcards, GSA, color, 1951-52, set of 4 ...............................**5.00**
Uniform, GSA-Brownie, middy & bloomers, 1918 ............**200.00**
Wings, Brownie, 1926 .........**15.00**

# Sewing Items

Sewing notions from the 1800s and early 1900s, such as whimsical figural tape measures, beaded satin pincushions, blown glass darning eggs, and silver and gold thimbles are pleasant reminders of a bygone era — ladies' sewing circles, quilting bees, and beautifully hand-stitched finery. With the emphasis collectors of today have put on figural ceramic items, the pincushions such as we've listed below are coming on strong. Most were made in Japan; some were modeled after the likenesses of Disney characters.

Our advisor for figural sewing items is Carole Bess White (see the Directory under Oregon); she is the author of *Collector's Guide to Made in Japan Ceramics, Identification and Values* (there are three in the series). If you're interested in sewing machines, we recommend *Toy and Miniature Sewing Machines, Books I and II,* by Glenda Thomas. All of these books are published by Collector Books.

## Figural Ceramic Pincushions

Bird on tree next to mushroom, 3¾" ...............................**22.00**
Black child w/lg head, lustre trim, cushion hat, 2¾", from $50 to ...........................**75.00**
Bust of boy, bow tie, multicolor matt, head is cushion, 3", from $28 to ...........................**38.00**

Calico dog, tongue out, paws hold lustre top-hat cushion, from $17 to ...........................**36.00**
Camel w/cushion basket on back, multicolor lustres, 4", from $30 to ...........................**40.00**
Carriage & pr of horses, lustre trim, 1¾" ......................**18.00**
Cat w/bass fiddle, card-suit cushion, multicolor lustres, from $18 to ...........................**28.00**
Chick w/open beak next to sq cushion, lustre trim, 2½" ........**20.00**
Clown girl in tub, lustre trim, 3" ...............................**35.00**
Cockatiel, lustre trim, black mark, 2¾" ...............................**20.00**
Colonial man w/violin sits by cushion basket, from $11 to .**20.00**
Dachshund holding top hat, lustre trim, 3¾" ......................**28.00**
Deco flat-sided pelican, cushion in back, lustre trim, from $13 to .......**24.00**
Deco rocking horse w/boy on back, lustre trim, 3½" ............**25.00**
Dog next to radio, lustre trim, black mark, 3" ...............**38.00**
Donkey pulling barrel cushion, lustre trim, 1¾", from $18 to ...............................**28.00**
Foo dog by open flower holding cushion, 3", from $16 to ..........................**24.00**
Girl w/big hat & suitcase, matt, black mark, 4¼" ............**38.00**
Hans & Gretchen boy & girl, multicolor lustre trim, 4", pr, from $75 to ...........................**125.00**
Horse & coach w/cushion top on tray, lustre trim, 2¾", from $17 to ...........................**23.00**
Kewpie-like figure w/basket cushion, 4", from $30 to .......**45.00**

**Three Little Pigs with musical instruments, multicolor lustre and shiny glazes, all Japan, from 3" to 3¼", from $30.00 to $40.00 each. (Photo courtesy Carole Bess White)**

Lady (tall) w/basket, black mark, 5¾" ...............................**38.00**

Lady w/shawl by flower cushion, cat at feet, 2¾", from $9 to ..........................**18.00**

Man in baseball cap, cushion on legs, lustre trim, 2¾", from $26 to .............................**36.00**

Man with accordion, cushion behind, lustre trim, 3¾", from $19 to ..................**23.00**

Man w/bird on head, lustre trim, 3" ....................................**36.00**

Monkey holding orange, matt, black mark, 2¼" ......**20.00**

Potbellied stove w/Canadian Mountie cushion, brown, 5", from $12 to ....................**18.00**

Sailor boy, painted bisque, hat is cushion, 3¼", from $23 to ............................**33.00**

Spaniel w/basket cushion on its back, lustre trim, 4", from $28 to ....................................**38.00**

Teacher w/book & cane before flat-sided cushion, lustre trim, from $23 to ...................**28.00**

## Thimbles

Advertising, aluminum, from $2 to ....................................**6.00**

Austria, aluminum w/stone top ...**4.00**

Brogan, sterling, fleur-de-lis ..**50.00**

Germany, sterling, leaf border ....**35.00**

Haviland, china ....................**15.00**

Italy, Murano glass ..............**10.00**

Ketchum & McDougal, sterling with gold-plated band .**40.00**

Muhr, gold, faceted rim .....**100.00**

Simons, sterling, Columbian Expo ..........................**300.00**

Simons, sterling, marked Priscilla ................................**40.00**

Simons, sterling, target band ..**25.00**

Simons, sterling, 10 panels .**30.00**

Simons, 14k gold ................**110.00**

Unmarked, base metal ..........**5.00**

Unmarked, English sterling, zipper pattern ....................**30.00**

Wedgwood, Jasperware .......**25.00**

## Toy Sewing Machines

Betsy Ross, 1949, 6¼x7¾x4¼" .**100.00**

Britain's Petite, pink plastic, 1980s, 8¾x10x8¾" ........**40.00**

Casige, metal w/yellow flowers, Germany, 7½x8", from $75 to ................................**95.00**

Decker, cast aluminum, Saarbruken Germany, 1950s, from $150 to .........................**175.00**

Holly Hobbie, manual or battery-operated, 1977-82, 9¼" L ...............................**25.00**

Jet Sew-O-Matic, metal, manual, Straco/West Germany, from $45 to .............................**65.00**

Little Betty, metal, manual, Straco/England, from $65 to ...............................**85.00**

Little Modiste, electric, wood base, 1950s, 7" L ....................**60.00**

Little Princess, plastic, manual, Frankonia/Hong Kong, from $25 to .............................**50.00**

Sew Mistress, various colors, battery-operated, Japan, from $45 to .............................**65.00**

Sew-n-Play, plastic, battery or hand-operated, 9½" L................................**25.00**

Singer Sewhandy #20, pressed steel & cast iron, 1940s, MIB, from $75 to .................**100.00**

Strawberry Shortcake, pink plastic, 1980s, 8¾" L ...........**45.00**

Universal, orange & white plastic, manual, Unitoys Ltd, from $20 to .............................**30.00**

## Miscellaneous

Chatelaine, Victorian brass, oval, 3 chains+measure, 2½x2" .........................**85.00**

Crochet hook, bone, style B ...**5.00**

Darner, pink glass, handled half sphere, Czechoslovakian, 4" .....................**85.00**

Darner, sterling, from chatelaine, egg ea end, hollow needle tube ..............................**75.00**

Display card, Blue Shield, 24 Singer 15¢ needle packets, from $10 to ....................**15.00**

Doll, Gofun (oyster shell paste), cushion body w/tool loops, Japan, from $14 ...........**17.00**

Dress pattern, Simplicity, 1920s flapper style ..................**27.00**

Embroidery scissors, figural bird, old German silver .........**55.00**

Embroidery skein, in Art Noveau 'Asiatic' Filo Selle 9 paper, 1890s ...............................**1.50**

Knitting counter, celluloid, labeled Knit-Count, early 1900s .**45.00**

Measure, celluloid winking pig, tape comes from mouth, 1½", from $40 to ....................**55.00**

Measure, china kitten, plaid, red cloth tongue pull, shiny, 3", from $12 to ....................**18.00**

Needle book, Army-Navy cover, ship, plane & American eagle, from $5 to ........................**8.00**

Needle book, Atomic cover, couple on rocket ship, from $3 to .**5.00**

Needle book, Broadway, shows 2 ladies sewing, Made in Occupied Japan ........................**2.50**

Needle book, Century of Progress views, 6½x4½" ................**2.00**

Needle book, Sewing Susan cover, 4 ladies in sewing circle, from $2 to ................................**4.00**

Needle book, Sweetheart cover with lady sewing, from $2 to ..............................**5.00**

Needle case, leatherette w/carnation & needles on cover, Patent 1914 ..................**25.00**

Needle case, sterling, embossed hare & Toby jug, 3⅜" ...**80.00**

Pincushion, footed pressed glass base w/sq cushion, 6½x5" ......................**42.00**

Pincushion, sterling base w/flower topper, velvet cushion, Tiffany ......................**150.00**

Pincushion, wood pedestal base w/round cushion, green & black paint ....................**9.50**

Pincushion/tape measure kit, corduroy kitten on ball, from $6 to ...................................**10.00**

Scissors, George & Martha Washington engraved silver, German ..............................**85.00**

Scissors sharpener, chromed metal, Kenberry, 2¼x1¼" oval .................................**2.50**

Sewing bird, all rosewood, mid-1800s ..........................**250.00**

Sewing box, child's; round w/girl & doll cover, Pressman, complete ..............................**42.00**

Sewing kit, salt shaker shape w/cushion top, needles inside ......................**20.00**

Sewing kit, WWI army green metal cylinder, thimble top ..........................**15.00**

Shuttle, for narrow loom, wood w/metal gears ................**15.00**

Shuttle, tatting; silver w/engraved swirls, German .............**48.00**

Shuttle, tatting; sterling w/engraved flowers, 2" .**65.00**

Tape measure, advertising, metal case w/Graybar Electric, 1½" dia ...................................**17.50**

**Measure, celluloid sailing ship, red and white, 2x2¼", from $100.00 to $125.00.**

Tape measure, figural walnut, bright metal case, Goldinger NY 1982 ........................**47.50**

Tape measure, red & white plastic case, early, from $1 to ........................**3.00**

Threader, Rawlinson's Cleaning, plastic cylinder w/metal loop, 2½" ...................................**7.50**

Tracing wheel, metal w/black wood handle, Eureka, 6" ..........**6.50**

Workbox, child's; cardboard w/paper Colonial lady, German, 6x3½" ...................**15.00**

# Shawnee

The novelty planters, vases, cookie jars, salt and pepper shakers, and 'Corn' dinnerware made by the Shawnee Pottery of Ohio are attractive, fun to collect, and still available at reasonable prices. The company operated from 1937 until 1961, marking their wares with 'Shawnee, U.S.A.,' and a number series, or 'Kenwood.' Note: Large shakers with decals and gold trim are very hard to find and have a minimum value of $225.00 for the pair.

Our advisor for this category is Richard Spencer; he is listed in the Directory under Utah. Refer to *The Collector's Guide to Shawnee Pottery* by Janice and Duane Vanderbilt, and *Shawnee Pottery, An Identification and Value Guide,* by Jim and Bev Mangus (both by Collector Books) for more information. See also Cookie Jars; Clubs and Newsletters.

Ashtray, magnolia blossom, marked USA, from $18 to ......................**20.00**
Bank, Howdy Doody, marked Bob Smith USA, 6½", from $450 to ..................................**550.00**
Bowl, fruit; Corn Line, #92, 6", from $40 to ...................**45.00**
Bowl, fruit; Valencia, 5", from $15 to ....................................**20.00**
Bowl, mixing; Lobster Line, #8, 8", from $30 to ...................**35.00**
Bowl, vegetable; Corn Line, #95, 9", from $45 to .............**50.00**
Bud vase, Valencia, from $15 to ...........................**17.00**
Creamer, Corn Line, #70, from $26 to ....................................**28.00**
Creamer, elephant, white w/red ears, marked USA, from $35 to ....................................**40.00**
Creamer, Lobster Line, #70, from $24 to .............................**26.00**
Egg cup, Valencia, from $14 to .**16.00**
Figurine, lamb, flowers around neck, bow in tail, unmarked, from $25 to ...................**30.00**

Flowerpot, Bow Knot, w/saucer, marked USA, 4¼", from $8 to ...................................**10.00**
Grease jar, Laurel Wreath, yellow, blue or green, USA, ea, from $28 to .............................**30.00**
Mug, Lobster Line, #69, 8-oz, from $45 to .............................**50.00**
Pitcher, ice; Valencia, marked USA, from $35 to ..........**40.00**
Pitcher, Pennsylvania Dutch, marked USA 10, from $55 to ...............................**60.00**
Pitcher, Tulip, marked USA, from $65 to .............................**75.00**
Planter, Basketweave, red, marked USA 150, 9½" L, from $6 to ..................................**8.00**
Planter, Dutch windmill, gold trim, Marked Shawnee 715, from $28 to ....................**32.00**
Planter, lovebirds perched on stump, marked USA, from $10 to ....................................**12.00**

**Planter, giraffe figural, #521, from $25.00 to $30.00. (Photo courtesy Jim and Beverly Mangus)**

**Platter, Corn, #96, 12", $45.00; Pitcher, Corn, #71, $65.00.**

Plate, Corn Line, #68, 10", from $35 to ..............................**40.00**

Plate, Valencia, 10¾", from $12 to ...................................**14.00**

Range set, Corn Line, 3-pc, from $110 to ..........................**115.00**

Range set, Lobster Line, 3-pc, from $110 to .........................**115.00**

Salt & pepper shakers, birds, heads down, sm, pr, from $20 to ....................................**25.00**

Salt & pepper shakers, Dutch boy & girl, gold & decals, lg, pr ......................**135.00**

Salt & pepper shakers, flowerpots, gold trim, sm, pr ...........**55.00**

Salt & pepper shakers, Muggsy, gold trim, lg, pr ...........**265.00**

Salt & pepper shakers, Puss 'n Boots, sm, pr .................**48.00**

Salt & pepper shakers, Swiss Kids, lg, pr, from $40 to ..........**45.00**

Salt & pepper shakers, Valencia, pr, from $25 to ..............**30.00**

Snack jar/bean pot, Lobster Line, lobster finial, #925 ......................**650.00**

Snack set, Corn Line, from $350 to .................................**365.00**

Sugar bowl, Wave, yellow, blue or green, marked USA, ea, from $22 to ............................**24.00**

Teapot, Corn Line, #75, 30-oz, from $75 to ....................**85.00**

Teapot, Dutch style, bright yellow, marked USA 10, 10-oz, from $35 to .............................**40.00**

Teapot, Pennsylvania Dutch, marked USA, 30-oz, from $200 to .........................**225.00**

Teapot, Swirl, blue, green or yellow, marked USA, 6-cup, from $30 to .............................**35.00**

Tray, utility; Valencia, from $15 to ...................................**18.00**

Utility jar, covered basket, gold trim, marked USA, from $100 to ...................................**110.00**

Vase, cornucopia; marked USA, 3½", from $12 to ...........**14.00**

Vase, gold philodendrons & handles, marked Shawnee 805, 6½", from $35 to ...........**40.00**

Vase, Valencia, from $14 to ..**16.00**

Wall pocket, Little Bo Peep, marked
USA 586, from $30 to .....**35.00**

# Sheet Music

The most valuable examples of sheet music are those related to early transportation, ethnic themes, Disney characters, a particularly popular actor, singer, or composer, or with a cover illustration done by a well-known artist. Production of sheet music peaked during the 'Tin Pan Alley Days,' from the 1880s until the 1930s. Covers were made as attractive as possible to lure potential buyers, and today's collectors sometimes frame and hang them as they would a print. Flea markets are a good source for sheet music, and prices are usually very reasonable. Most are available for under $5.00. Some of the better examples are listed here. Refer to *The Sheet Music Reference and Price Guide, Second Edition* (Collector Books), by Anna Marie Guiheen and Marie-Reine A. Pafik and *Collector's Guide to Sheet Music* by Debbie Dillon (L-W Book Sales) for more information.

All In, Down & Out, McPherson, Bowman & Smith, 1906 .**10.00**

And So Goodbye, Allie Wrubel, 1938 .................................**5.00**

Beautiful Chimes at Sunset, Arthur Lange, 1914 ........**5.00**

By the Old Mill Where the Water Lilies Grow, Morgan, 1912 ...........................**5.00**

**Paper Doll, Johnny S. Black, Mills Brothers black and white photo cover, $5.00. (Photo courtesy Anna Marie Guiheen and Marie-Reine A. Pafik)**

Carmen, Georges Bizet ..........**5.00**

Color My World, James Pankow, 1970 .................................**3.00**

Cynthia, Richard Kountz, 1950 ......................**2.00**

Day & Night, Johnson, 1933 .**5.00**

Down in the Depths, Cole Porter, Movie: Red, Hot & Blue, 1936 ..............................**5.00**

Estelle, Frankie Carle, 1930 .**5.00**

Fairy Tales, BC Hilliam, Musical: Buddies, 1919 ...............**10.00**

For the Good Times, Kris Kristofferson, 1968 .....................**5.00**

Garland of Roses, Streabbog, 1936 .................................**5.00**

Go Away Little Girl, Carole King, Photo: Donny Osmond, 1962 ..............................**5.00**

Goldfinger, Bricusse, Newley & Barry, Movie: Goldfinger, 1964 .................................**3.00**

Guy Is a Guy, Oscar Brand, Photo: Doris Day, 1952 ..............5.00

Heart's Heaven, Robert L Remmington & Bayley Jordan, 1922 ..................................5.00

Ho Ho Song, Red Buttons & Joe Darion, Photo: Red Buttons, 1953 ..................................5.00

I Beg of You, Elvis Presley, 1957 ...........................20.00

I'll Know, Swerling, Burrows & Loesser, Musical: Guys & Dolls, 1950 ......................5.00

I Love Them All, Sandy Linzer, Photo: Nancy Sinatra, 1970 ...3.00

I Love You So Much It Hurts, Floyd Tillman, Photo: Perry Como, 1948 ......................3.00

I'm Gonna Meet My Sweetie Now, Benny Davis, 1927 ..........3.00

I've Got the Sun in the Morning, Irving Berlin, Movie: Annie Get Your Guns, 1946 ....10.00

I Was Lucky, Jack Meskill & Jack Stern, 1935 ......................3.00

Ida Belle, Smith & Duke, 1952 .3.00

If I Loved You More, Charles Newman & Fred Coots, 1938 ..............................3.00

If I Ruled the World, Bricusse & Ornadel, Photo: Tony Bennett, 1963 ........................5.00

In My Arms, Loesser & Grouya, 1943 ..................................3.00

Irene, McCarthy & Tierney, Musical: Irene, 1919 ...............5.00

It's a Good Day, Peggy Lee & Dave Barbour, 1946 .................3.00

Just Ask Your Heart, Joe Ricci, Photo: Frankie Avalon, 1959 ......................................3.00

La Cucaracha, Carl Fields, Photo: Don Pedro, 1935 ..............5.00

Let Your Love Walk In, Joe Greene, Photo: De Castro Sisters, 1955 ..........................5.00

Little Small Town Girl, Jules Loman & Hugo Rubens, 1945 ............................3.00

Love Won't Let Me Wait, Bobby Eli & Vinnie Barrett, 1975 ............................3.00

Many Tears Ago, Jenny Lou Carson, 1945 ..........................3.00

Mid the Hush of the Corn, Gordan Temple ..............................5.00

Mother at Your Feet Is Kneeling by Sister, Sister SC, 1948 ............................3.00

My Heaven Is Home, Kerr & Collins, 1928 ...................5.00

My Wubba Darling, Kay & Sue Werner, 1939 ...................5.00

No Stone Unturned, Lester M Cox & Melvin Herman, 1953 ............................3.00

**Think It Over, Dan Coats, Cheryl Ladd color photo cover, Kengorus Music, 1978, from $8.00 to $10.00. (Photo courtesy Greg Davis and Bill Morgan)**

Old Folks, Dedette Lee Hill & William Robinson, 1938 ......................**3.00**

One Morning in May, Mitchell Parish & Hoagy Carmichael, 1933 ................................**5.00**

Sew the Buttons On, John Jennings, Musical: Riverwind, 1963 ................................**3.00**

Starlit Hour, Mitchell Parish & Peter DeRose, 1939 .........**5.00**

That Old Dream Peddler, Al Sterwart & Pepe Delgado, 1947 .............................**5.00**

There's a Tear in My Beer Tonight, Kuhn, Cornell & Asherman, 1946 ..............**5.00**

Thumper Song, Bliss, Sour & Manners, Movie: Bambi, 1942 .............................**10.00**

Tommy, Scott & Sachs, 1928 ..**5.00**

Two Weeks With Pay, Joan Whitney & Alex Kramer, 1947 .........................**3.00**

Unchained Melody, Hy Zaret & Alex North, 1955 .............**3.00**

Very Good Advice, Hilliard & Fain, Movie: Alice in Wonderland, 1951 ......................**10.00**

Watching, Bert Meyers & Joe Solman, 1920 ........................**5.00**

We'll Be Together Again, Laine & Fisher, 1945 ....................**3.00**

When April Comes, Paul Weston & Doris Schaefer, 1950 ..........................**5.00**

When Our Soldier Boys Come Home, Gus Kahn, 1944 ..**5.00**

When the Sun Comes Out, Koeler & Arlen, 1941 ...................**3.00**

When You're Gone Away, Goldsmith & Goldsmith, Movie: Babes, 1975 .....................**2.00**

# Shell Pink Milk Glass

Made by the Jeannette Glass Company from 1957 until 1959, this line is made up of a variety of their best-selling shapes and patterns. The glassware has a satiny

**Relish, six compartments with embossed decor, 16" long, $38.00.**

finish, and the color is the palest of peachbloom. Refer to *Collectible Glassware of the 40s, 50s, and 60s* by Gene Florence (Collector Books) for more information and an expanded listing.

Bowl, Florentine, footed, 10" .**27.50**
Bowl, Pheasant, footed, 8" ...**37.50**
Cake stand, Harp, 10" .........**45.00**
Candle holders, 2-light, pr ..**37.50**
Candy jar, grapes, 4-footed, w/lid,
    5½" ................................**20.00**
Compote, Windsor, 6" ..........**20.00**
Honey jar, beehive shape,
    knotched lid .................**40.00**
Pitcher, Thumbprint, footed, 24-
    oz ...................................**27.50**
Punch base, tall, 3½" ..........**35.00**
Punch cup, 5-oz ......................**6.00**
Relish, vineyard design, 4-part, 8-
    sided, 12" ......................**40.00**
Snack tray, w/cup indent,
    7¾x10" ..........................**9.00**
Stem, water goblet; Thumbprint,
    8-oz ..............................**12.50**
Tray, lazy susan; complete
    w/base ........................**190.00**
Tumbler, juice; footed,
    Thumbprint, 5-oz ............**8.00**
Vase, 7" ................................**35.00**

# Shot Glasses

Shot glasses, old and new, are whetting the interest of today's collectors, and they're relatively easy to find. Basic values are given for various categories of shot glasses in mint condition. These are general prices only. Glasses that are in less-than-mint condition will obviously be worth less than the prices given here. Very rare and unique items will be worth more. Sample glasses and other individual one-of-a-kind oddities are a bit harder to classify and really need to be evaluated on an individual basis.

Our advisor for this category is Mark Pickvet, author of *Shot Glasses: An American Tradition*. He is listed in the Directory under Michigan. See also Clubs and Newsletters.

Barrel shaped, from $5 to .....**7.50**
Carnival colors, plain or fluted,
    from $100 to ...............**150.00**
Depression, colors, from $10 to .**12.50**

**Left to right: Cobalt, $15.00; Depression glass, dark yellow, from $10.00 to $12.00; Souvenir, ruby stain, from $35.00 to $50.00. (Photo courtesy Mark Pickvet)**

Frosted w/gold designs, from $6
    to ...................................**8.00**
General, gold designs, from $6
    to ...................................**8.00**
General, porcelain, from $4
    to ...........................**6.00**
Nudes, from $25 to .............**35.00**
Pop or soda advertising, from
    $12.50 to ........................**15.00**
Porcelain tourist, from $3.50 to ....**5.00**
Sayings & toasts, 1940s-50s, from
    $5 to ................................**7.50**

Square, general, from $6 to ...**8.00**
Standard glass w/pewter, from
$7.50 to ..........................**10.00**
Taiwan tourist, from $2 to ....**3.00**
Whiskey or beer advertising, mod-
ern, from $5 to ...............**7.50**

# Silhouette Pictures

Silhouettes and reverse
paintings on glass were commercially produced in the US from
the 1920s through the '50s.
Some were hand painted, but
most were silkscreened. Artists
and companies used either flat
or convex glass. Common subjects include romantic couples,
children, horses, dogs, and cats.
Many different styles, sizes, colors, and materials were used for
frames. Backgrounds also vary
from textured paper to colorful
lithographs, wildflowers, or butterfly wings. Sometimes the
backgrounds were painted on
the back of the glass in gold or
cream color. These inexpensive
pictures were usually sold in
pairs, except for the advertising
kind, which were given by merchants as gifts.

Our advisor for this category
is Shirley Mace, author of *The
Encyclopedia of Silhouette Collectibles on Glass* (Shadow Enterprises); she is listed in the Directory under New Mexico.

Art Publishing, flat, lady & candles on gold foil, #AP810-20,
8x10" ..........................**25.00**

Benton, Colonial couple, BG 68-26,
$40.00. (Photo courtesy Shirley
Mace)

Benton, convex, birdbath/couple in
garden, wood frame, #BG68-
139, 6x8" ......................**20.00**
Benton, convex, couple on horses,
mountain at sunset, #BG45-
207, 4x5" ......................**27.00**
Benton, convex, girl w/water from
well on ivory, #BG45-182,
4x5" ..............................**30.00**
Benton, convex, lady on horse
w/dog, colorful ground,
#BG68-200, 6x8" ...........**38.00**
Benton, convex, Plas-Stone dog's
head on pink, #BG68-216,
6x8" ..............................**40.00**
Buckbee-Brehm, flat, lady's head
on gold, 4½x5½" ............**15.00**
Butterfly wing, convex, palms on island,
real wings, #BW3D-1, 3" ......**24.00**
Deltex, flat, lady w/parasol/man at
tree, silver foil, #DE810-1,
8x10" ..............................**35.00**
Fisher, flat, To My Mother verse,
white swans, flower ground,
4½x7" ..............................**24.00**

Flowercraft, flat, couple on bridge, flower ground, wood frame, 4x10" ............................**28.00**

Newton, flat, lady at spinning wheel, advertising on ground, 6x8" ..............................**20.00**

Peter Watson, convex, hand-painted, boy & girl, #PW5D-7, 5" dia ......................**25.00**

Reliance, flat, lady at vanity, butterfly wing ground, #RE912-20, 9x12" ........................**45.00**

Reliance, flat, Sprint in Park, boy, girl & mother, #RE44-87, 4" sq .....................**18.00**

# Soda Pop

A specialty area of the advertising field, soft drink memorabilia is a favorite of many collectors. Now that vintage Coca-Cola items have become rather expensive, interest is expanding to include some of the less widely known flavors — Dr. Pepper, Nehi, and Orange Crush, for instance.

If you want more pricing information, we recommend *Huxford's Collectible Advertising* by Sharon and Bob Huxford. Our advisors for this category are Donna and Craig Stifter; they are listed in the directory under Illinois.

### Coca-Cola

Since it was established in 1891, the Coca-Cola Company has issued a wide and varied scope of advertising memorabilia, creating what may well be the most popular field of specific product-related collectibles on today's market. Probably their best-known item is the rectangular Coke tray, issued since 1910. Many sell for several hundred dollars each. Before 1910 trays were round or oval. The 1903 tray featuring Hilda Clark is valued at $6,000.00 in excellent condition. Most Coca-Cola buffs prefer to limit their collections to items made before 1970.

For more information we recommend *Collectible Coca-Cola Toy Trucks* by Gael de Courtivron, *B. J. Summers' Guide to Coca-Cola,* and *Goldstein's Coca-Cola Collectibles.* *Huxford's Collectible Advertising* has a large Coca-Cola section. All are published by Collector Books.

Apron, cloth bib type, white w/phrase & tilted bottle graphic, EX ................**115.00**

**Calendar, girl with bottle, 1948, framed, 10½x26½", $130.00. (Photo courtesy Dunbar Gallery)**

Ashtray, glass, round, Have a Coke/Drink Coca-Cola on rim, M .....................................**30.00**

Blotter, Friendliest Drink on Earth, 1956, NM+ .........**15.00**

Blotter, Have a Coke, couple w/bottle, receding logo, 1947, NM ................................**20.00**

Bottle carrier, cardboard, 6 for 25¢, white on red, 1939, EX ...........................**50.00**

Bottle carrier, wood, cutout handle, wing logos, 1930s-40s, VG+ .............................**100.00**

Bottle opener, metal bottle shape, flat, 1950s, EX+ ............**22.00**

Bottle topper/bottle, cardboard diecut hot-air balloon, King Size, EX ..........................**32.00**

Calendar, 1925, complete, EX ..**1,200.00**

Calendar, 1933, complete, VG+ ..**350.00**

Calendar, 1943, complete, VG+ ..**250.00**

Calendar, 1950, complete, EX+ ..**240.00**

Carton display, cardboard, 2-tier, Shop Here..., 38x14x20", EX+ ...**200.00**

Carton display, wire rack, 3-tier, Take Home a Carton 25¢, 58x17", NM .................**275.00**

Change receiver, plastic, Try One..., Frozen Coca-Cola mascot, 1960s, NM+ ...**200.00**

Clock, maroon metal, Drink Coca-Cola on red center dot, 1950s, 18" dia, VG+ ................**150.00**

Clock, plastic, Things Go Better with Coke, 1960s, sq, EX ...............**100.00**

Clock, 1980 reproduction of Sessions regulator, oak, NM .........................**325.00**

Coupon, Free Drink, 1934 Chicago Century of Progress, NM ...............................**38.00**

Decal, Drink Coca-Cola in Bottles, 1950s, 9x15", NM+ .......**45.00**

Decal, script logo, 1950s, 10x28", EX ................................**20.00**

Dispenser, streamline, red, 1940s, EX ...............................**375.00**

Display bottle, green glass, w/cap, 1960s, 20", NM+ ...........**80.00**

Doll, Frozen mascot, stuffed striped cloth, 1960s, NM+ ........**150.00**

Fan, cardboard, wooden handle, Sprite boy & bottle on yellow dot, G+ ...........................**50.00**

Fly swatter, wire mesh, looped wire handle, NM ...........**50.00**

Game, Broadsides, Compliments of..., Milton Bradley, 1940s-50s, EX+ ......................**80.00**

Game, Down the Mississippi Race Game, saleman's incentive, 1956, EX+ ......................**50.00**

Game, NFL Football Game, ca 1964, NM ......................**15.00**

Game, Santa Ring Toss, 1980s, VG .............................**10.00**

Handkerchief, cloth, Kit Carson, white & black print on red, 21", EX ........................**120.00**

Lighter, flip top, 75th Anniversary, contour logo, M .............**40.00**

Menu board, plastic light-up, Good w/Food, fishtail logo, 19x49", NM ...............................**200.00**

Menu board, tin, Things Go Better w/Coke, green board, 28x20", EX ................................**85.00**

Miniature case w/bottles, plastic, EX ................................**25.00**

Patch, Drink...in Bottles, red, 1950s, 7" dia, VG+ ....**20.00**

Pillow, #16 race-car shape, stuffed print cloth, 1970s, 15", NM ....................**100.00**

Pin-back button, Member Hi-Fi Club, multicolored, 1950s, EX ...............................**20.00**

Playing cards, Be Really Refreshed, masquerade party, 1960, NMIB .................**165.00**

Playing cards, Zing! Refreshing New Feeling, 1963, EXIB .........**70.00**

Pocket mirror, 1911, VG+ .**150.00**

Pocket mirror, 1916, EX ....**200.00**

Push bar, tin, Coke Adds Life..., contour logo, black, 1970s, 32", EX+ ........................**35.00**

Puzzle, jigsaw, 2000 pieces, NMIB ...........................**25.00**

Radio, vending machine, Drink..., red & white, 1963, VG ......**65.00**

Record, 45 rpm, Let's Go Go Go for Three in a Row, 1966, EX+ ..............................**20.00**

Sign, bottle shape, tin, 16", 1947, VG ..................................**65.00**

Sign, button, tin, bottle on red, 1950s, 36", EX .............**275.00**

Sign, cardboard, Enjoy..., bongo couple, 1960s, 39x22", VG ............................**50.00**

Sign, cardboard, Here's Something Good!, party, 1951, 27x16", VG ..............................**350.00**

Sign, fishtail, tin, Drink..., white on red, 6x12", NM+ ....**160.00**

Sign, plastic light-up, Drink..., red & white, 1960s, horizontal, EX ...............................**150.00**

Sign, porcelain, ...Sold Here Ice Cold, 1955, 12x29", EX ......................**200.00**

Sign, tin, Drink..., couple w/bottle, red, 1942, 32x56", EX .........................**525.00**

Thermometer, bottle shape, tin, 1950s, 17", NM+ .........**160.00**

Thermometer, plastic, gauge atop cube base w/contour logo, 1980s, EX ......................**25.00**

Tip tray, 1909, EX+ ..........**875.00**

Tip tray, 1916, EX+ ..........**275.00**

Tip tray, 1920, EX+ ..........**260.00**

Toy airplane, Albatros, red & white w/black, 1973-74, EX+ .........................**100.00**

Toy truck, Matchbox #37, even load, 1950s-60s, 2¼", NMIB ......................**115.00**

Tray, 1935, 13x11", EX+ ...**330.00**

Tray, 1940, 11x13", NM ....**325.00**

Tray, 1942, NM+ ...............**350.00**

Tray, 1947, 13x11", VG .....**200.00**

Tray, 1957, M ...................**325.00**

Watch, 100th Anniversary, round gold-tone face, black leather strap, M ......................**125.00**

## Dr. Pepper

A young pharmacist, Charles C. Alderton, was hired by W.B. Morrison, owner of Morrison's Old Corner Drug Store in Waco, Texas, around 1884. Alderton, an observant sort, noticed that the drugstore's patrons could never quite make up their minds as to which flavor of extract to order. He concocted a formula that combined many flavors, and Dr. Pepper was born. The name was chosen by Morrison in honor of a beautiful young girl with whom he had once been in love. The girl's father, a Virginia doctor by the name of Pepper, had discouraged the relationship due to their youth, but Morrison had never forgotten her. On December 1, 1885, a U.S. patent was issued to the creators of Dr. Pepper.

Bottle opener, metal lion's head, etched lettering/design, 3", EX ..................85.00

Bottle topper, Madelon Mason, EX ..............................150.00

Bottle topper, Sandy Carleson, NM+ ............................250.00

Bottle topper, Virginia Kavanagh, NM ..............................220.00

Calendar, 1951, complete, EX+ .100.00

Clock, Drink a Bite To Eat, round w/glass front, metal frame, EX ..............................150.00

**Clock, lights up, 15" diameter, NM+, $400.00.**

Decal, hand pouring Dr Pepper over ice cream, 1950, 13x9", NM ..................................50.00

Fan, cardboard, wooden handle, girl w/bottle, Earl Morgan art, EX ..................................75.00

Fan pull, cardboard, beach girl w/umbrella, G ...............80.00

Match holder, tin, 1940s-50s, 6", NMIB ..........................200.00

Menu board, tin, ...When Hungry, Thirsty or Tired, 1940s, 27x19", VG+ .................250.00

Postcard, Free! 6 Bottles of Dr Pepper, arrow points to 6-pack, NM ......................15.00

Sign, cardbaord, Join Me!, girl in car, framed, 1940s, 32x40", NM ..............................575.00

Sign, cardboard, Madelon Mason on white, 1940s, 19x23", G+ ..............100.00

Sign, flange, Fountain..., yellow, red white stripes, 1961, 15x22", NM .................750.00

Sign, paper, Try Frosty Pepper...Ice Cream, 1950s, 17x22", EX+ ..................65.00

Sign, porcelain, Drink..., white on red, curved corners, 9x24", NM ..............................160.00

Sign, tin, Drink Dr Pepper, Good for Life, white on red, 1936, 7x20", VG+ ..................350.00

Thermometer, tin, Hot or Cold, Enjoy the Friendly..., 1950s, 16", EX .........................175.00

Tray, You'll Like It Too!, girl w/bottles, 1930s-40s, rectangular, VG+ ...................280.00

## Hires

Did you know that Hires Root Beer was first served to fairgoers at the Philadelphia Centennial in 1876? It was developed by Charles E. Hires, a druggist who experimented with roots and herbs to come up with the final recipe. The company originally chose the Hires boy as their logo, and if you'll study his attire, you can sometimes approximate a guess as to when an item he appears on was manufactured. Very early on he appeared in a dress, and from 1906 until 1914 it was a bathrobe. He sported a dinner jacket from 1915 until 1926.

Bottle carrier, wood w/dovetailed corners, Quarter Case, VG+ ..................**30.00**

Bottle topper, cardboard, 10¢ Off/Try a Real Black Cow, EX .............................**12.00**

Clock, light-up, glass face, Drink..., red, white & blue, 15" dia, EX .........................**385.00**

Clock, logo & frothy mug on woodgrain, black frame, sq, EX .**75.00**

Coupon, Free Drink, pictures Hires Boy, VG+ .............**38.00**

Display, cardboard, lady on phone, holds 6-pack in center, 34x14", NM ............................**120.00**

Menu board, tin, ...In Bottles, blue & white striped bottom, 28x20", NM ................**125.00**

**Sign, embossed tin, Enjoy Hires Root Beer, 1932, 28x11", NM, $350.00. (Photo courtesy Craig and Donna Stifter)**

Mugs, white ceramic hourglass shape, blue stamped Hires, 4-pc, 7", NM+ ..................**185.00**

Recipe book, EX ...................**65.00**

Recipe folder, boy leaning back w/glass looking at Hires sign, VG ..................................**20.00**

Sign, cardboard, diecut image of Hires Boy pointing, EX+ .**85.00**

Sign, paper, So Good w/Food..., hostess w/plate, 34x54", NM+ ........ **400.00**

Sign, tin, Ask for Hires in Bottles, white on blue, 10x29", VG+ .........**135.00**

Sign, tin, R-J logo on blue, 7x12", EX ..................................**70.00**

Thermometer, bottle shape, tin, Since 1876 label, 29", NM ........**250.00**

Trade card, bust image of girl in paper hat, M .................**18.00**

Tray, lady in center, Haskell Coffin art, HD Beach litho, 13x10", EX+ ...............**300.00**

### Nehi

Calendar, 1927, girl with bottle on beached boat, wood frame, 21x11", EX .**200.00**

Clock, Drink Nehi Orange & Other Flavors, round w/glass front, 15", NM ......................**325.00**

Menu board, tin, Drink...Special Today, 1930s-40s, 28x20", EX ............................**100.00**

Pocketknife, Remington, metal, boot-shaped handle, EX ........................**110.00**

Sign, flange, Drink Nehi Ice Cold/bottle on panel, 1940s, 13x18", NM .................**525.00**

Sign, paper diecut, Square Deal Service/No Fooling Here, 1930s, 8x10" .................**75.00**

Sign, tin, Curb Service/Nehi Sold Here Ice Cold, 1950s, 28x20", NM+ ..............................**160.00**

Sign, tin, Drink Nehi Beverages, bottle at right, 1932, 12x30", EX+ ..............................**250.00**

Sign, tin, Drink Nehi Beverages, bottle on oval, 1953, 17x44", EX ...............................**300.00**

Sign, tin, Gas Today/Drink Nehi Ice Cold Sold Here, 42x15", EX+ ..............................**475.00**

Sign, tin, Nehi Quality Beverages, bottle graphic, 1940s, 20x6", EX ...............................**100.00**

Trade card, girl in bathtub folds down to serving 2 men, VG+ .....................................**85.00**

## Nesbitt's

Cooler, picnic, aluminum, rectangular with embossed name, G ........................................**100.00**

Dispenser, screw-on base, glass top w/chrome lid, paper label, NM ..............................**225.00**

Dispenser, 1-gal glass bottle inverted on pink glass base, 18", EX .........................**325.00**

Distance chart, cardboard with steel frame, ca 1955, 31x7", EX+ ...............................**40.00**

Sign, cardboard, boy & girl with bottle smiling down at clown, 19x26", EX+ .**125.00**

Sign, cardboard, family barbecue scene with phrase, 1940s, 25x36", EX+ ..................**250.00**

Sign, cardboard, picnicking couple, distant mountain, 25x36", G+ ...................**75.00**

Sign, porcelain, Nesbitt's Orange, geometric ground, 1950s, 12x25", NM .................**375.00**

Sign, tin, A Soft Drink Made From Real Oranges, bottle, 27x27", NM ..............................**300.00**

Sign, tin, Enjoy... A Delicious Drink, bottle, 1940s, 33x33", NM ..............................**275.00**

Sign, tin/cardboard, Don't Say..., professor w/bottle, 9" dia, EX ...............................**125.00**

Thermometer, tin, black, 1938, 23", EX ........................**200.00**

Thermometer, tin, white, 16", EX+ ..............................**75.00**

Thermometer, tin, yellow, 27", VG+ ..............................**200.00**

## Orange-Crush

Calendar, 1946, complete, 31x16", VG ...............................**125.00**

Clock, bottle cap logo, glass front, metal frame, Pam, 15" dia, EX ...............................**275.00**

Dispenser, glass bowl w/beveled base, top spigot, 1930s-40s, NM ..............................**325.00**

Display w/bottle, Drink...Demand This Bottle, graphics, 1930s, EX+ ..............................**350.00**

Menu board, Drink Orange-Crush, blackboard bottom, 19x13", G+ ..................................**85.00**

Menu board, glass case w/menu slots on either side of logo, NM+ ..............................**500.00**

Pitcher & glass set, fluted pitcher w/flared-top glasses, NM .**100.00**

Sign, cardboard standup, sunbather w/bottles, 1930s-40s, 18", EX ........................**200.00**

**Sign, framed paper, ballerina image by Walt Otto, 1936, 31x15", NM, $425.00. (Photo courtesy Craig and Donna Stifter)**

Sign, reverse glass, Fresh!, Drink..., Crushy w/bottle, 10" dia, VG+ ......................**200.00**

Sign, tin, Ask For...Carbonated Beverage, bottle, 1940s, 32x56", EX ..................**475.00**

Sign, tin, Drink..., Crushy logo lower left, 9x27", EX ...**220.00**

Sign, tin flange, There's Only One..., curved corners, 12x18", NM .................**450.00**

Stamp holder, celluloid book shape, Whitehead & Hoag, 1x1", EX .........................**90.00**

Street marker, brass, Safety First..., 4" dia, EX .......**325.00**

Syrup can, 1-gal, 1950s, empty, EX+ ...............................**35.00**

Thermometer, dial type w/aluminum frame, 1950s, 12½" dia, NM .........................**35.00**

Thermometer, masonite, white, amber bottle, 1930s, 16", NM ............................**250.00**

Thermometer, porcelain, white, amber bottle, 1940s-50s, 15", EX ...............................**325.00**

Thermometer, tin, bottle shape, 1950s, 29", NM ..........**300.00**

Thermometer, tin, orange, Crushy logo, G .........................**115.00**

Thermometer, tin, turquoise, 1950s, 15", EX .............**130.00**

Toy truck, diecast windup, London Toy, Canada, scarce, 6", VG ..............................**100.00**

Tray, boy & girl at piano, 14" dia, EX+ ...............................**25.00**

## Pepsi-Cola

Pepsi-Cola has been around about as long as Coca-Cola, but since collectors are just now beginning to discover how fascinating this line of advertising memorabilia can be, it's generally much less expensive. You'll be able to determine the approximate date your items were made by the style of logo they carry. The familiar oval was used in the early 1940s, about the time the two 'dots' between the words were changed to one. But the double dots are used nowadays as well, especially on items designed to be reminiscent of the old ones — beware! The bottle cap logo was used from about 1943 until the early to mid-'60s with variations. For more information refer to *Pepsi-Cola Collectibles* by Bill Vehling and Michael Hunt and

*Introduction to Pepsi Collecting* by Bob Stoddard.

Ashtray, ceramic, round w/mini bottle & lamp shade, EX+ .**275.00**

Blotter, Pepsi & Pete The Pepsi Cops, 1939, EX+ ...........**80.00**

Bottle, miniature, painted label, 3½", VG (NM cap) .........**18.00**

Bottle, miniature, paper label, 4½", EX+ .......................**25.00**

Bottle carrier, cardboard, Bigger-Better, 1940, NM+ ........**75.00**

Bottle carrier, cardboard, 6-pack, horizontal stripes, 1950, VG .....................**28.00**

Bottle carrier, wood, dowel handle, 1940, EX ......................**100.00**

Bottle opener, multicolored tin litho bottle shape, 1930s, 4", EX ................................**40.00**

Calendar, 1941, complete, EX+ .**325.00**

Calendar, 1947, complete, NM .**85.00**

Charm, gold-tone, shamrock w/horseshoe on chain, NM .............**60.00**

Clock, light-up, bottle cap on yellow, Swihart, 1950s, 15" dia, EX+ .............................**400.00**

Clock, plastic light-up, Say Pepsi Please, 1970s, 22x16", EX+ ...........................**30.00**

Cooler, 4-legged wooden box w/cast-iron opener, tin sign, 32x35", VG .................**350.00**

Dispenser, metal streamline style, red, white & blue, 1950s, NM .................**550.00**

Dispenser, plastic box w/stainless steel parts, red, white & blue, VG+ .............................**250.00**

Display rack, wire, 3-tiered, bottle cap sign, 1940s, 42x22", VG .............................**175.00**

Fan, cardboard w/wooden handle, Pepsi cops, 1940, 12", NM+ .........**120.00**

Fountain pen, blue & white stripes, VG ....................**35.00**

Lighter, can shape, silver-blue w/white diagonal stripes, 1960s, EX+ ....................**50.00**

Menu board, tin, wood-look frame w/rope border, 1940s, 30x20", NM ..............................**250.00**

Menu board, tin blackboard, yellow raised rim, 30x20", EX+ ............................**35.00**

Menu board, wood w/double row of slots, ribbon logo, 1940s, 20x25", EX .................**750.00**

Paperweight, glass, rectangular w/rounded corners, VG .**50.00**

Pocket mirror, ...The Light Refreshment, rectangular, EX+ ..............................**100.00**

Push bar, porcelain, Enjoy Pepsi Iced, red on white, 32", EX ....................**150.00**

Push bar, porcelain, Have a Pepsi, cap logos, yellow, 1950s, 32", NM ..............................**220.00**

**Sign, tin diecut bottle cap, 1951, 18" diameter, $175.00. (Photo courtesy Craig and Dinner Stifter)**

Radio, fountain dispenser, red, white & blue, leather strap, 1950s, EX ....................**375.00**

Salt & pepper shakers, early bottles w/oval labels, EXIB, pr ............................**165.00**

Salt & pepper shakers, swirled bottles, 5½", NM, pr .....**20.00**

Sign, bottle cap shape, porcelain, P-C logo, 19", EX ........**325.00**

Sign, bottle cap shape, tin, P-C logo, 19", VG ...............**125.00**

Sign, cardboard, Be Sociable..., 2 couples, horse, dog, 26x38", EX+ ..............................**120.00**

Sign, cardboard, The Light Refreshment, birdcage, 1957, 11x25", EX ...................**100.00**

Sign, cardboard, Think Young..., black couple, 14x30", VG .**40.00**

Sign, plastic diecut, cowboy kid roping popcorn & Pepsi, 14x18", EX+ ..................**60.00**

Sign, porcelain, Enjoy..., cap on yellow & white, 12x29", VG+ ..........................**225.00**

Sign, tin, bottle bursting through yellow ground, 20x27", VG+ ............**335.00**

Sign, tin, P-C Bigger & Better 5¢, red, blue on yellow, 10x20", NM ..............................**100.00**

Thermometer, tin, blue w/white & gray border, 16", VG ...........................**275.00**

Thermometer, tin, red & white on blue, 1930s-40s, 27", VG+ ..........**300.00**

Thermometer, tin, white & yellow, 1956, 27", EX ..............**150.00**

Thermometer, tin, yellow, 1267, 28", EX ..........................**75.00**

Tray, Coast to Coast/Bigger & Better, 1930s, 11x14", EX+ ..........**350.00**

## Royal Crown Cola

Bottle topper & bottle, cardboard, Santa in wreath, EX ..........................**18.00**

Clock, blue numbers 12-3-6-9 & blue crowns on white, round, EX ...............................**130.00**

Cooler, picnic, metal box, red on yellow, 20x18x12", EX .**150.00**

Sign, bottle shape, tin, pyramid label, 12", NM+ ..........**230.00**

Sign, cardboard, RC Mad Mad Cola, girl w/bottle on white, 22x34", NM ...................**55.00**

Sign, cardboard, RC Tastes Best! Says Bing Crosby, w/horse, 22x34", EX .................**150.00**

Sign, cardboard, So Bubbly Fresh!, family boating scene, 27x49", VG ...............................**125.00**

Sign, reverse glass, We Serve...Smooth — Mellow, bottle, 19x12", EX+ ........**1,050.00**

**Thermometer, red and white painted tin, 26x10", NM, $60.00.**

Sign, tin, bottle on white, raised border, 36x16", NM ...**450.00**

Sign, tin, Drink...Best Taste Test, bottles, red, 18x58", EX ...........................**250.00**

Sign, tin, The Fresher Refresher, white & red, 28x8", NM+ ............**125.00**

Sign, tin, We Serve...Ice Cold, mountain graphics, 1936, 3x20", NM ...................**120.00**

Thermometer, tin, blue, bottle next to gauge, 1960s, 17", NM .............................**230.00**

Thermometer, tin, red, white & yellow, yellow arrow up, 26", VG ..................................**45.00**

Thermometer, tin, white, bottle next to gauge, 14", EX+ ........**100.00**

## 7-Up

Though it was originally touted to have medicinal qualities, by 1930 7-Up had been reformulated and was simply sold as a refreshing drink. The company who first made it was the Howdy Company, who by 1940 had changed its name to 7-Up to correspond with the name of the soft drink. Collectors search for the signs, thermometers, point-of-sale items, etc., that carry the 7-Up slogans.

Ashtray, glass, decorative border around logo in center, G .**15.00**

Bill hook, celluloid button, I'd Hang for a Chilled 7-Up, EX+ ...........................**35.00**

Bottle topper w/bottle, boy in beanie w/bottle, EX .......**32.00**

Bottle topper w/bottle, cardboard, various holidays, EX, ea .**22.00**

Calendar, 1943, General McArthur, complete, VG+ ................**35.00**

Clock, neon, Fresh Up With..., tilted bottle, 15x15", EX ..**340.00**

Clock, plastic light-up, Get Real Action..., sq, EX+ ..........**75.00**

Cuff links, enameled logo, M, pr ...............................**30.00**

Display, glass, bottle in iceberg, 1940s-50s, 9x7x8", NM .**375.00**

Doll, 7-Up Spot, plush & felt w/suction-cup hands, 1988, 6", MIB ...............................**10.00**

Menu board, tin, wood-tone, red oval logo, 1940s, 23x9", EX+ .........................**225.00**

Money clip, enameled dollar symbol w/logo, M .................**30.00**

Music box, can shape, Love Story theme, NM ....................**50.00**

Push bar, porcelain, Fresh Up w/Seven Up!, white, 32", NM+ ...........................**220.00**

Sign, cardboard, lady on ironing break, 1955, self-framed, 12x23", NM .................**100.00**

Sign, cardboard standup, family around TV, 16x12", EX+ .**40.00**

Sign, flange, 7-Up Likes You, green & white, scroll design, 10x13", NM .................**200.00**

Sign, porcelain, bubbles logo, white & black on red, 1951, 20x17", NM+ ...............**425.00**

Sign, tin, Fresh Up!.... white & black on red, octagonal, 14x14", VG .................**175.00**

Thermometer, dial type, 7-Up Likes You on red center dot, 12", NM ........................**200.00**

Thermometer, porcelain, white, The Fresh Up Family Drink, 15", EX .........................**130.00**

Toy truck, tin, friction, driver in clear plastic dome, 1950s, 9", EX+ .............................**335.00**

# Stangl

The Stangl Company of Trenton, New Jersey, produced many striking lines of dinnerware from the 1920s until they closed in the late 1970s. Though white clay was used earlier, the red-clay patterns made from 1942 on are most often encountered and are preferred by collectors. Decorated with both hand painting and sgraffito work (hand carving), Stangl's lines are very distinctive and easily recognized. Virtually all is marked, and most pieces carry the pattern name as well.

Ashtray/coaster, Garden Flower .**16.00**
Bowl, cereal; Thistle, 5½" ....**12.00**
Bowl, divided vegetable; Magnolia .......................**30.00**
Bowl, fruit; Country Garden, 5½", from $12 to ....................**15.00**
Bowl, Kiddieware, Little Bo Peep ...........................**100.00**
Bowl, lug soup; Chicory, 5½" .**12.00**
Bowl, lug soup; Lyric, 5½" ...**12.50**
Bowl, Orchard Song, 12" .....**24.00**
Bowl, salad; Fruit, 11" .........**45.00**
Bowl, salad; Wild Rose, 10" .**60.00**
Bowl, vegetable; Garden Flower, 10" .................................**38.00**
Bread tray, Fruit .................**35.00**
Butter dish, Thistle .............**40.00**
Cake stand, Rooster ............**32.00**
Casserole, Amber Glo, 6" .....**15.00**
Casserole, Fruit & Flowers, 8" .**70.00**

Creamer, Blueberry .............**12.50**
Creamer, Chicory, revised .....**7.50**
Creamer, Lyric .....................**12.50**
Creamer, Wild Rose .............**15.00**
Cup & saucer, Magnolia ......**12.50**
Cup & saucer, Rooster .........**20.00**
Egg cup, Amber Glo ...............**6.00**
Gravy boat, Golden Harvest .**15.00**
Mug, Sculpted Fruit ............**20.00**
Pitcher, Town & Country, 2½-qt .............................**80.00**
Plate, Amber Glo, 10" ............**7.50**
Plate, Blueberry, 11" ...........**20.00**
Plate, Chicory, 8" ...................**9.00**
Plate, chop; Blueberry, 12½" .**32.00**
Plate, Country Garden, 10" .**15.00**
Plate, Fruit, 6" .......................**4.00**
Plate, Lyric, 10" ...................**15.00**
Plate, Thistle, 6¼" ................**6.00**
Plate, Town & Country, 8" ..**20.00**
Relish, Chicory .....................**20.00**
Salt & pepper shakers, Chicory, pr ..................................**22.50**

**Golden Harvest, relish tray, 11¼" long, $25.00.**

Salt & pepper shakers, Magnolia, pr .....................................**20.00**

Sauce boat, Fruit .................**20.00**

Server, Rooster, center handle ...**12.50**

Sherbet, Garden Flower ......**20.00**

Spoon rest, Town & Country .**30.00**

Sugar bowl, Fruit & Flowers .**18.00**

Sugar bowl, Wild Rose, individual ................................**15.00**

Teapot, Amber Glo ..............**30.00**

# Star Trek Collectibles

Star Trek has influenced American culture like no other show in the history of television. Gene Roddenberry introduced the Star Trek concept in 1964, and it has been gaining fans ever since. The longevity of the television show in syndication, the release of six major motion pictures, and the success of Star Trek the Next Generation and Star Trek Voyager television shows have literally bridged two generations of loyal fans. This success has spawned thousands of clothing, ceramic, household, jewelry, and promotional items; calendars; plates; comics; coins; costumes; films; games; greeting and gum cards; party goods; magazines; models; posters; props; puzzles; records and tapes; school supplies; and a wide assortment of toys. Most of these still turn up at flea markets around the country, and all are very collectible. Double the value given for an excellent condition item when the original box or packaging is present. For further information and more listings, see *Schroeder's Collectible Toys, Antique to Modern* (Collector Books).

Accessory, Communicator set, Mego, 1974, complete, MIB .....**125.00**

Accessory, Telescreen Console, Mego, 1975, MIB ........**125.00**

Accessory, USS Enterprise Bridge, Mego, 1975, MIB ........**125.00**

Binoculars, Larami, MOC ...**80.00**

Book, Star Trek Quiz Book, Signet, 1977, softcover, VG ..........**5.00**

Book & record set, Passage to Moauv, Peter Pan, 1979, MIP .............................**10.00**

Bop Bag, Spock, 1975, M .....**50.00**

Communicators (Wrist), Motion Picture, 1974, MIB .....**100.00**

Figure, Admiral Kirk, Generations, Playmates, MOC ....................**25.00**

Figure, Data, Next Generation, Galoob, 2nd series, 3¾", MOC ...........................**40.00**

**Figure, Klingon, Mego, 1979, 12½",
MIB, $75.00.**

Figure, Ferengi, Next Generation, Galoob, 3¾", MOC ........**12.00**

Figure, Gorn, Mego, 2nd series, 1974-76, 8", MOC, to .........**350.00**

Figure, Ilia, Motion Picture, Mego, 1979, 3¾", MOC, from $15 to ...........................**20.00**

Figure, Kirk, Star Trek III, Ertl, 3¾", MOC .....................**25.00**

Figure, Klingon, Mego, 1st series, 1974-76, 8", MOC ..........**55.00**

Figure, Klingon, Motion Picture, Mego, 1979, 12", MIB, from $200 to ........................**250.00**

Figure, Picard, Next Generation, Galoob, 3¾", MOC ........**12.00**

Figure, Scotty, Star Trek III, Ertl, 3¾", MOC .....................**25.00**

Figure, Spock, Motion Picture, Mego, 1979, 12", MIB, from $100 to ........................**125.00**

Figure, Spock, Motion Picture, Mego, 1979, 3¾", MOC, from $40 to ...........................**50.00**

Figure, The Keeper, Mego, 2nd series, 1974-76, 8", MOC, from $250 to ........................**300.00**

Figure, Worf, Next Generation, Galoob, 3¾", MOC ........**12.00**

Iron-on transfers, 4 different, General Mills, 1979, M, ea ...............**5.00**

Ornament, Enterprise Ship, Hallmark, 1st series, MIB ..................**350.00**

Patch, Motion Picture, Kirk & Spock, M .......................**35.00**

Playing cards, Star Trek: The Wrath of Kahn, complete, MIB ..............................**15.00**

Rubber stamp, Motion Picture, M ..................................**8.00**

Sticker book, Next Generation, 1992, unused, EX ...........**5.00**

**Galileo talking store counter display with Galileo ornament, NM, $125.00. (Photo courtesy June Moon)**

Vehicle, Ferengi Fighter, Next Generation, Galoob, 1989, NRFB .............................**55.00**

Vehicle, Klingon Warship, Dinky, MIB, from $75 to ..........**85.00**

Vehicle, Shuttlecraft Galileo, Next Generation, Galoob, NRFB ........**50.00**

Wastebasket, Motion Picture, M .............................**35.00**

# Star Wars Collectibles

Capitalizing on the ever-popular space travel theme, the movie *Star Wars* with its fantastic special effects was a mega box office hit of the late 1970s. A sequel called *Empire Strikes Back* (1980) and a third adventure called *Return of the Jedi* (1983) did just as well, and as a result, licensed merchandise flooded the market, much of it produced by the Kenner Company.

Original packaging is very important in assessing a toy's worth. As each movie was released, packaging was updated, making approximate dating relatively simple. A figure on an original *Star Wars* card is worth more than the same character on an *Empire Strikes Back* card, etc.; and the same *Star Wars* figure valued at $50.00 in mint-on-card condition might be worth as little as $5.00 'loose.' Especially prized are the original 12-back *Star Wars* cards (meaning twelve figures were shown on the back). Second issue cards showed eight more, and so on. For more information we recommend *Modern Toys, American Toys, 1930 to 1980,* by Linda Baker. See *Schroeder's Collectible Toys, Antique to Modern,* for an expanded listing.

Accessory, Bespin Gantry, Star Wars, Micro Collection, EX .........**25.00**
Accessory, Ewok Village, Return of the Jedi, MIB ..............**100.00**
Accessory, Tripod Laser Cannon, Empire Strikes Back, MIB .**20.00**
Belt, Return of the Jedi, Lee, 1983, EX ....................................**8.00**
Case, Laser Rifle, NM (EX box) .**45.00**
Comb & Keeper, Return of the Jedi, MOC ....................**18.00**
Figure, Admiral Ackbar, Return of the Jedi, 3¾", MOC ........................**25.00**
Figure, Anakin Skywalker, Star Wars, 3¾", w/accessories, NM ..............................**30.00**

Figure, AT-AT Driver, Empire Strikes Back, 3¾", w/accessories, NM ......................**10.00**
Figure, AT-ST Driver, Return of the Jedi, 3¾", w/accessories, NM ..................................**8.00**
Figure, Barada, Power of the Force, 3¾", MOC ...........**60.00**
Figure, Ben Obi-Wan Kenobi, Star Wars, 3¾", w/accessories, NM ......................**20.00**
Figure, Bib Fortuna, Return of the Jedi, 3¾", MOC .............**20.00**
Figure, C-3PO, Star Wars, 3¾", w/accessories, NM .........**10.00**
Figure, Chewbacca, Power of the Force, 3¾", MOC, from $125 to ...................................**135.00**
Figure, Chief Chirpa, Return of the Jedi, 3¾", w/accessories, NM ...................................**8.00**
Figure, Death Squad Commander, Empire Strikes Back, 3¾", MOC ...........................**75.00**
Figure, Dengar, Empire Strikes Back, NMOC (41-back) .......................**55.00**
Figure, Emperor, Return of the Jedi, 3¾", MOC .............**35.00**
Figure, General Madine, Return of the Jedi, 3¾", MOC ......**18.00**
Figure, Greedo, Star Wars, 3¾", w/accessories, NM .........**10.00**
Figure, Han Solo, Return of the Jedi, 3¾", lg head, MOC ........................**85.00**
Figure, Imperial Commander, Empire Strikes Back, 3¾", MOC (41-back) ..............**55.00**
Figure, Imperial Stormtrooper, Empire Strikes Back, 3¾", MOC (41-back) ..............**30.00**
Figure, Jawa, 12", MIB .....**225.00**

Vehicle, B-Wing Fighter, Return of the Jedi, Kenner, 1983, MIB, $185.00. (Photo courtesy June Moon)

Figure, Lobot, Empire Strikes Back, 3¾", MOC .........**30.00**

Figure, Luke Skywalker, Return of the Jedi, X-Wing Pilot outfit, MOC .............................**50.00**

Figure, Luke Skywalker, 12", EX (VG box) ......................**285.00**

Figure, Princess Leia Organa, 12", NM ...............................**100.00**

Figure, Rebel Commando, Empire Strikes Back, 3¾", w/accessories, NM .......................**8.00**

Figure, R2-D2, Power of the Force, 3¾", MOC ......................**70.00**

Figure, Stormtrooper, Return of the Jedi, 3¾", MOC ......**35.00**

Figure, Walrus Man, Star Wars, 3¾", with accessories, NM ................**10.00**

Figure, Yoda, Empire Strikes Back, 3¾", orange snake, NM ............................**20.00**

Figure, 4-Lom, Return of the Jedi, 3¾", with accessories, NM .............................**10.00**

Fun poncho, Darth Vader or C-3PO, 1977, MIP, ea .......**30.00**

Mask, Boba Fett, Don Post, hard plastic, EX ...................**100.00**

Mask, Klaatu, Don Post, hard plastic, EX .....................**40.00**

Night light, Return of the Jedi, 6 different, MIP, ea .........**10.00**

Play-Doh, Empire Strikes Back, complete, MIB ...............**42.00**

Presto Magix Transfer Set, Wicket, set of 40, MIB ..........**18.00**

Speaker phone, Darth Vader, MIB ...........................**145.00**

Stickpin, R2-D2, 1977, diecast metal figure, NMOC ..................**25.00**

Vehicle, Boba Fett's Slave I, Star Wars, EX ......................**25.00**

Vehicle, Ewok Assault Catapult, NRFB ..........................**25.00**

Vehicle, Landspeeder, Star Wars, EX (VG box) .................**40.00**

Vehicle, Snowspeeder, Star Wars, diecast, VG ...................**25.00**

Vehicle, Twin-Pod Cloud Car, Star Wars, diecast, EX .........**25.00**

Vehicle, Y-Wing Fighter, Return of the Jedi, MIB .............**100.00**

Doll sets, Cafe Ole with Burrito, Mint Tulip with Marsh Mallard, Almond Tea with Marza Panda, 6", each scented set: $12.00. (Photo courtesy June Moon)

# Strawberry Shortcake Collectibles

Strawberry Shortcake came onto the market around 1980 with a bang. The line included everything to attract small girls — swimsuits, bed linens, blankets, anklets, underclothing, coats, shoes, sleeping bags, dolls and accessories, games, toys, and delightful items to decorate their rooms. It was short lived, though, lasting only until near the middle of the decade.

Our advisor for this category is Geneva Addy; she is listed in the Directory under Iowa.

Book, Cooking Fun, EX .......**10.00**
Candle, Apple Dumplin', MIP .**20.00**
Charm, Strawberry Shortcake, NM ................................**18.00**
Clothes rack, wood, MIB .....**75.00**
Comb & Keeper, MIP, from $15 to ...................................**20.00**
Doll, Almond Tea, MIB .......**24.00**
Doll, Angel Cake, 6", MIB ...**25.00**

Doll, Apple Dumpling, MIB ..**25.00**
Doll, Berry Baby Orange Blossom, 6", MIB ..........................**25.00**
Doll, Butter Cookie, 6", MIB ..**25.00**
Doll, Mint Julip, MIB ..........**25.00**
Doll, Strawberry Shortcake, 12", NRFB .............................**25.00**
Dollhouse ...........................**125.00**
Dollhouse furniture, living room, 6-pc basic, rare, M ........**85.00**
Figure, Merry Berry Worm, MIB ............................**20.00**
Figures, any, PVC, 1", MOC .**10.00**
Lamp, ceramic, VG ..............**50.00**
Radio, transistor, M ............**35.00**
Storybook play case, M ........**35.00**
Stove, VG ............................**30.00**
Stroller, Coleco, 1981, M .....**85.00**
Suitcase, Strawberry Shortcake, cloth, VG ......................**45.00**
Tablecloth, round, EX ..........**30.00**
Toy chest, M ........................**40.00**

# Swanky Swigs

Swanky Swigs are little decorated glass tumblers that once

contained Kraft Cheese Spread. The company has used them since the Depression years of the 1930s up to the present time, and all along, because of their small size, they've been happily recycled as drinking glasses for the kids and juice glasses for adults. Their designs range from brightly colored flowers to animals, sailboats, bands, dots, stars, checkers, etc. There is a combination of 223 verified colors and patterns. In 1933 the original Swanky Swigs came in the Band pattern, and at the present time they can still be found on the grocery shelf, now a clear plain glass with an indented waffle design around the bottom.

They vary in size and fall into one of three groups: the small size sold in Canada, ranging from 3¹⁄₁₆" to 3¼"; the regular size sold in the United States, ranging from 3⅜" to 3⅞"; and the large size also sold in Canada, ranging from 4³⁄₁₆" to 5⅝".

A few of the rare patterns to look for in the three different groups are small group, Band No. 5 (two red and two black bands with the red, first); Galleon (two ships on each glass in black, blue, green, red, or yellow); Checkers (in black and red, black and yellow, black and orange, or black and white, with black checkers on the top row); and Fleur-de-lis (black with a bright red filigree design).

In the regular group: Dots Forming Diamonds; Lattice and Vine (white lattice with colored flowers); Texas Centennial (cowboy and horse); Special Issues with dates (1936, 1938, and 1942); and Tulip No. 2 (black, blue, green, or red).

Rare glasses in the larger group are Circles and Dots (black, blue, green, or red); Star No. 1 (small stars scattered over the glass in black, blue, green, or red); Cornflower No. 2 (dark blue, light blue, red, or yellow); Provincial Cress (red and burgundy with maple leaves); and Antique No. 2 (assorted antiques in lime green, deep red, orange, blue, and black).

Our advisor for this category is Joyce Jackson, she is listed in the Directory under Texas.

Antique #1, any color, Canadian, 3¼", ea ............................**8.00**
Antique #1, any color, Canadian, 4¾", ea ..........................**20.00**
Antique #2, any color, Canadian, 1974, 4⅝", ea ................**25.00**
Bachelor Button, red, white & green, Canadian, 1955, 3¼" ..........**6.00**
Bachelor Button, red, white & green, Canadian, 1955, 4¾" ........**15.00**
Band #1, red & black, 1933, 3⅜" ..............................**3.00**
Band #2, red & black, Canadian, 1933, 4¾" ......................**20.00**
Band #3, white & blue, 1933, 3⅜" ..............................**3.00**
Band #4, blue, 1933, 3⅜" .......**3.00**
Bicentennial Tulips, any color, 1975, 3¾", ea .................**15.00**
Bustlin' Betty, any color, Canadian, 1953, 4¾", ea ..................**20.00**
Carnival, any color, 1939, 3½", ea ..................................**6.00**

Blue Tulip, 4½", from $12.00 to $15.00; Bustling Betty, 3¼", from $7.50 to $10.00; Sailboat, 3½", from $10.00 to $12.00.

Checkerboard, white w/blue, green or red, Canadian, 1936, 4¾", ea .....................................**20.00**

Circles & Dot, any color, Canadian, 1934, 4¾", ea .................**20.00**

Circles & Dot, any color, 1934, 3½", ea .............................**4.00**

Coin, Canadian, 1968, 3⅛" or 3¼", ea .....................................**2.00**

Colonial, clear w/indented waffle design, 1976, 4⅜" .............**1.00**

Cornflower #1, light blue & green, Canadian, 1941, 3¼" ......**8.00**

Cornflower #1, light blue & green, Canadian, 1941, 4⅝" ........................**20.00**

Cornflower #1, light blue & green, 1941, 3½" ..........................**3.00**

Cornflower #2, any color, Canadian, 1947, 3¼", ea ..............**8.00**

Cornflower #2, any color, Canadian, 1947, 4¼", ea ....................**20.00**

Cornflower #2, any color, 1947, 3¼", ea .............................**3.00**

Dots Forming Diamonds, red, 1935, 3½" ......................**25.00**

Ethnic Series, any color, Canadian, 1974, 4⅝", ea ..................**20.00**

Forget-Me-Not, any color, Canadian, 1948, 3¼", ea ..............**8.00**

Forget-Me-Not, any color, 1948, 3½", ea .............................**3.00**

Galleon, any color, Canadian, 1936, 3⅛", ea .................**30.00**

Hostess, clear & plain w/indented groove base, Canadian, 1960, 5⅝" .....................................**5.00**

Hostess, clear & plain w/indented groove base, 1960, 3¾" ....................**1.00**

Jonquil (Posy pattern), yellow & green, Canadian, 1941, 3¼" .............................**8.00**

Jonquil (Posy pattern), yellow & green, Canadian, 1941, 4⅝" ..........................**20.00**

Jonquil (Posy pattern), yellow & green, 1941, 3½" .............**3.00**

Kiddie Kup, any color, Canadian, 1956, 3¼", ea ...................**6.00**

Kiddie Kup, any color, Canadian, 1956, 4¾", ea .................**20.00**

Kiddie Kup, any color, 1956, 3¾", ea ......................................**3.00**

Lattice & Vine, white w/blue, green or red, 1936, 3½", ea .....**25.00**

Petal Star, clear, Kraft Cheese Spreads 50th Anniversary, 1983, 3¾" ........................**1.00**

Petal Star, clear w/indented star base, Canadian, 1978, 3¼" ....................................**2.00**

Provencial Crest, red & burgundy, Canadian, 1974, 4⅝" ....**25.00**

Sailboat #1, any color, 1936, 3½", ea ....................................**12.00**

Sailboat #2, any color, 1936, 3½", ea ....................................**12.00**

Special Issue, California Retail Grocers Merchants, red, 1938, 3½" ...................................**50.00**

Special Issue, Del Monte Violet, 1942, 3½" ......................**50.00**

Sportsmen Series, hockey/skiing/ football/baseball/soccer, 1976, ea ....................................**25.00**

Stars #1, any color, Canadian, 1934, 4¾", ea .................**20.00**

Stars #1, any color other than yellow, 1935, 3½", ea ..........**4.00**

Stars #1, yellow, 1935, 3½" .**25.00**

Stars #2, clear w/orange stars, Canadian, 1971, 4⅝" ........................**12.00**

Texas Centennial, any color, 1936, 3½", ea ..........................**30.00**

Tulip (Posy pattern), red & green, Canadian, 1941, 3¼" ......**8.00**

Tulip (Posy pattern), red & green, Canadian, 1941, 4⅝" ........................**20.00**

Tulip (Posy pattern), red & green, 1941, 3½" ........................**4.00**

Tulip #1, any color, Canadian, 1937, 3¼", ea ..................**8.00**

Tulip #1, any color, Canadian, 1937, 4⅝" ......................**20.00**

Tulip #1, any color, 1937, 3½", ea ..................................**4.00**

Tulip #2, any color, 1938, 3½", ea ..............................**20.00**

Tulip #3, any color, Canadian, 1950, 3¼", ea ...................**8.00**

Tulip #3, any color, Canadian, 1950, 4¾", ea .................**20.00**

Violet (Posy pattern), blue & green, Canadian, 1941, 3¼" ........**8.00**

Violet (Posy pattern), blue & green, Canadian, 1941, 4⅝" .....**20.00**

Wildlife Series, bear/goose/ moose/fox, Canadian, 1978, 4⅝", ea ..........................**20.00**

# Swizzle Sticks

Swizzle sticks, stirrers used for mixed drinks, first became popular in 1934 with the end of prohibition. They may be made of Bakelite, metal, wood, plastic, or glass. Collectors fall into two categories: those who prefer figural glass examples and those who like the advertising sticks. Advertising sticks in glass and plastic are the most popular today. Eagerly sought by collectors are Bakelite bats, railroad sticks, airline sticks, and World's Fairs-related sticks.

Our advisor for this category is Tom Maimone; he is listed in the Directory under New York. Mr. Maimone has written several articles on swizzle sticks and is a member of the International Swizzle Stick Collectors Association.

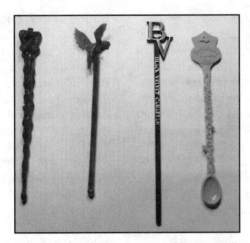

Advertising, plastic, common varieties, left to right: Seagram 7, Corby's, Black Velvet, Seagram's Gin, individual values from 10¢ to 25¢. (Photo courtesy Tom Maimone)

## Advertising

Airline, American Airlines logo .25
Airline, TWA, plastic giraffe ....25
Bakelite, bat, Essex House, NY ...........................**5.00**
Bakelite, bat, Jack Dempsey's .**10.00**
Glass rod, amber, Gilbey's Liquor ...........................**2.00**
Glass rod, cobalt blue, Lincoln Hotel ...............................**2.00**
Glass tube w/rolled paper inside, cobalt blue spoon end ...............................**4.00**
Glass tube w/rolled paper inside, Green River Whiskey .....**2.00**
Las Vegas clubs, plastic, 1970s-80s, ea ...............................**25**
Metal, golf club shape, Old Taylor Whiskey ...........................**2.00**
Plastic, common varieties (Seagrams, etc), ea, from 10¢ to ...........................**25**

Plastic, figural ballerina, Tropicana, Havana Cuba ...**2.00**
Plastic, figural skull, Ivanhoe, Chicago ...........................**1.00**
Railroad, plastic, NY Central, straight stick .....................**25**
Railroad, plastic figural domeliner train ...............................**5.00**
Wooden knocker, Concord Hotel, NY ...................................**2.00**
Wooden knocker, Lou Walter's, Latin Quarter .**2.00**
World's Fair, cobalt blue glass, Souvenir NY 1939 ...................**8.00**

## Figurals

Angel, clear glass, 1970s .......**2.00**
Bird, multicolored glass, Czechoslovakian, 1930s ...........**8.00**
Christmas tree, green glass, 1970s ...........................**2.00**

# Teapots

The continued popularity of teatime and tea-related items has created a tighter market for collectors on the lookout for teapots. Vintage and finer quality teapots have become harder to find, and those from the 1890s and 1920s will reflect age with three and four digit prices. Examples from the 1700s and 1800s are most often found in museums or large auction houses. Teapots listed here represent examples still available at the flea market level.

Most collectors begin with a general collection of varied teapots until they decide upon the specific category that appeals to them. Collecting categories include miniatures, doll or toy sets, those made by a certain manufacturer, figurals, or a particular style (such as Art Deco or English floral). Some of the latest trends in collecting are Chinese Yixing (yee-shing; teapots from an unglazed earthenware in forms taken from nature), 1950s pink or black teapots, Cottageware teapots, and figural teapots (those shaped like people, animals, or other objects). While teapots made in Japan have waned in collectibility, collectors have begun to realize many detailed or delicate examples are available. Of special interest are Dragonware teapots or sets where a dragon is molded in relief. Some of these sets have the highly desired lithophane cups — where a Geisha girl is molded in transparent relief in the bottom of the cup. When the cup is held up to the light, the image becomes visible.

*Teapots, The Collector's Guide,* by Tina M. Carter is available from the author for $16 postage paid; she is listed in the Directory under California. Two quarterly publications are also available; see Clubs and Newsletters for information on *Tea Talk* and *TeaTime Gazette.*

Aluminum, polished, black handle, marked USA, 2-cup .......**20.00**
Brass, allover embossed design, on stand, China ..................**85.00**
British Royal Navy or Army, brown, coralene, rope mark, NM ................................**35.00**
Brown Betty, Made in England, 8-cup ..................................**40.00**
Brown Betty, Ridgeway, paper label, 2-cup ....................**25.00**
China, dragon, marked China, 2-cup, in padded basket .**110.00**
Cobalt w/gold, souvenir china, Made in Germany .........**35.00**
Copper, stacking creamer & sugar, bell is lid, marked Mexico .........................**30.00**
Cube, floral design, England .**25.00**
Cube, red or cobalt, Hall .....**30.00**
Czechoslovakia, bright floral design, 1-cup .................**22.00**
Disney, characters in decal, marked Treasure Craft .**25.00**
Dragonware, dragon in relief, marked Made in Japan .**32.00**
Ellgreave, red & black, marked Div of Wood & Sons ......**42.00**
Frank Lloyd Wright, commemorative, Art Deco, Copco, 1993 ........**32.00**

House form, hand-painted, resin collectible, Japan, modern ..**15.00**

Majolica style, twin-tea, Made in Japan, on tray ...............**28.00**

Majolica-style basket & fruit, Wade, 1980s, 6-cup .......**30.00**

Majolica style w/fruit, Inarco paper label ....................**22.00**

Miniature souvenir, teapot, cup, saucer & stand, Made in Japan ............................**14.00**

Moss Rose, electric, marked Japan, 1960s, 4-cup ......**22.00**

Occupied Japan, brown, raised mark in porcelain, 2-cup .......................**12.00**

Pottery, gray w/ribbed section, common, unmarked US, 2-cup ...............................**12.00**

Princess Diana/Prince Charles, decal on white china, unmarked ......................**45.00**

Royal Gadroon pattern, dogwood flowers, pottery, Harker, NM ..............................**25.00**

Violets decal on fine china, Japan paper label, 1-cup .........**18.00**

White china, Oriental shape, wicker handle, unmarked ....**15.00**

**Ceramic Figurals**

Andy Capp, lid is cap, Wade, England ...............................**55.00**

Bluebird, hand-painted, cheery face, marked Japan ......**48.00**

Carousel horse, eagle mark, Heritage Mint Collectibles ...............**30.00**

Cat holding fish, white w/floral decor, marked China ....**22.00**

Conch shell shape, bail handle, marked Japan, sm ........**25.00**

Cottage Ware, marked hand-painted, Made in Japan .........**24.00**

Cottage Ware, Price Brothers, England, 6-cup ..............**65.00**

Deer, painted red nose, fawn forms handle, no mark, Japan .**18.00**

Elf, Germany, paper label, 6-cup, NM .................................**45.00**

Jim Beam, cartoon characters design, Wade limited edition, 1995 ..............................**55.00**

Orange w/comical face, embossed Florida, no mark ...........**15.00**

Owl, brown glaze w/hand-painted details, impressed Japan mark ..............................**22.00**

Peasant-style girl, marked Red Wing ..............................**70.00**

Precious Moments, Your Friendship Hits the Spot, 1993 .........................**65.00**

Sadler, English cottage, London Heritage or Minster series, current ..........................**35.00**

Snail, head is spout, bright glazes, impressed Japan mark .**20.00**

Tom the Piper's Son, detail variations, marked USA (Shawnee), from $65 to ..**150.00**

Tomato, red glaze, no mark, 6-cup ...............................**25.00**

Tony Wood, colonial man 1 side, lady on other, England .**45.00**

# Tiara Exclusives

Collectors are just beginning to take notice of the glassware sold through Tiara in-home parties, their Sandwich line in particular. Several companies were involved in producing the lovely items they've marketed over the years, among them Indiana Glass, Fenton, Dalzell Viking, and L.E.

**Bell, Sandwich, $15.00; Salt and pepper shakers, pr, 4¾", from 12.00 t0 $15.00.**

Smith. In the late 1960s Tiara contracted with Indiana to produce their famous line of Sandwich dinnerware (a staple at Indiana Glass since the late 1920s). Their catalogs continue to carry this pattern, and over the years, it has been offered in many colors: ruby, teal, crystal, amber, green, pink, blue, and others in limited amounts. We've listed a few pieces of Tiara's Sandwich below, and though the market is unstable, our values will serve to offer an indication of current values. Unless you're sure of what you're buying, though, don't make the mistake of paying 'old' Sandwich prices for Tiara. To learn more about the two lines, we recommend *Collectible Glassware from the 40s, 50s, and 60s, Fourth Edition,* by Gene Florence (Collector Books).

Ashtray, Sandwich, 4 rests, 7⅜", from $5 to ..........**7.00**

Basket, Sandwich, footed, 10", from $25.00 to .........................**32.00**
Bowl, salad; Sandwich, 5", from $2 to ......................................**3.50**
Bowl, vegetable; Sandwich, flared sides, 8" dia, from $10 to ...............................**12.00**
Butter dish, Sandwich, high domed lid, 6", from $18 to .........**25.00**
Candle holder, Sandwich, 8½", pr, from $15 to ...................**20.00**
Canister, Sandwich, 7½", from $8 to .....................................**10.00**
Canister, Sandwich, 8⅞", from $10 to .....................................**12.00**
Creamer, Sandwich, footed, 5", from $6 to .......................**8.00**
Cup, Sandwich, 9-oz, $2.50 to ..**3.50**
Dish, relish; Sandwich, 3-compartment, 12", from $10 to ..**12.00**
Egg tray, Sandwich, 12", from $10 to .....................................**14.00**
Goblet, wine; Sandwich .........**6.00**
Pitcher, Sandwich, 68-oz, to .**25.00**

Plate, dinner; Sandwich, 10", from $6 to ...................................**8.00**

Platter, Sandwich, footed, from $12 to ..............................**15.00**

Platter, Sandwich, 16" dia, from $10 to ..............................**15.00**

Saucer, Sandwich, 6", from $1 to ......................................**2.00**

Sugar bowl, Sandwich, footed, 2 handles, open, 5", from $4 to ....................................**5.00**

Tray, serving; Sandwich, high rim, 10", from $9 to ...............**12.00**

Tumbler, Sandwich, footed, 10-oz, 6½", from $6 to ...............**8.00**

Vase, Sandwich, footed, 3¾", from $6 to ...................................**8.00**

Betty Boop w/toothbrush & cup, KFS, plate #261, 4¾" .....................**85.00**

Boy in knickers, Japan, plate #223, 4¾", from $65 to ..................**80.00**

Boy w/dog, Japan, hanger, plate #26, from $70 to ...........**90.00**

Cat on pedestal, Japan (Diamond T), plate #225, 5⅞" .....**175.00**

Clown juggling, Japan, hanger, plate #60, 5", from $75 to ............................**90.00**

Clown w/mask, Japan (Goldcastle), plate #62, from $100 to .................**135.00**

Donald Duck, WDE, bisque, plate #83, 5¼", from $250 to .**275.00**

# Toothbrush Holders

Children's ceramic toothbrush holders represent one of today's popular collecting fields, with some of the character-related examples bringing $150.00 and up. Many were made in Japan before WWII.

Our advisor for this category is Marilyn Cooper, author of *A Pictorial Guide to Toothbrush Holders*; she is listed in the Directory under Texas. Plate numbers in the following listings correspond with her book.

Andy Gump & Min, Japan, bisque, plate #221, 4" ................**85.00**

Bear w/jacket, Japan (Goldcastle), plate #13, 5½" .**95.00**

Bear w/scarf & hat, Japan, hanger, plate #16, 5½", from $80 to ...................................**90.00**

**Dog, brown and multicolored semimatt, Japan, 6¼", from $50.00 to $75.00; Bonzo, blue lustre, Japan, 5¾", from $115.00 to $220.00. (Photo courtesy Marilyn Cooper)**

Ducky Dandy, Japan, hanger, plate #84, 4¼", from $150 to ............................**175.00**

Humpty Dumpty, Pat Pending, bisque, plate #114, 5½" ......................**175.00**

Lion, Japan, plate #118, from $75 to ......................................**85.00**

Mary Poppins, Japan, plate #119, 5¾" ...............................**150.00**

Mexican boy, Japan, hanger, plate #120, 5½", from $80 to ...............................**95.00**

Peter Pumpkin-Eater, Japan, plate #129, 4⅞" .............**90.00**

Pirate w/lg boots, Japan, hanger, plate #131, 5¼" .............**90.00**

Schnauzer, Germany, plate #283, 3⅛" .................................**115.00**

Soldier w/sash, Japan, plate #149, 6" .....................................**90.00**

Three Bears w/bowls, Japan (KIM USUI), plate #248, 4" .........................**100.00**

Traffic cop, Germany, plate #243, 5¼", from $325 to .....**375.00**

Uncle Willie, Japan/FAS, plate #157, 5⅛" .......................**85.00**

# Toys

Toy collecting is a very popular hobby, and if purchases are wisely made, there is good potential for investment. Most of the battery-operated toys made from the '40s through the '60s were made in Japan, even though some were distributed by American companies such as Linemar and Cragstan, who often sold them under their own names. Because of their complex mechanisms, few survive. Condition is very important in evaluating a battery-op, and the more complex their movements, the more they're worth.

Japanese wind-up toys are another fun and exciting field of toy collecting. The fascination with Japanese toys stems from their simplistic but exciting actions and strong colors. Many of the boxes these toys came in are almost as attractive as the toys themselves!

Toys from the 1800s are rarely if ever found in mint condition but should at least be working and have all their original parts. Toys manufactured in the 20th century are evaluated more critically. Compared to one in mint condition, original box intact, even a slightly worn toy with no box may be worth only about half price. Character-related toys, space toys, toy trains, and toys from the '60s are among the most desirable. Several good books are available, if you want more information: *The Golden Age of Automotive Toys, 1925 – 41,* by Ken Hutchison and Greg Johnson; *Modern Toys, 1930 – 1980,* by Linda Baker; *Collector's Guide to Tootsietoys,* by David E. Richter; *Toys, Antique and Collectible, Antique and Collectible Toys,* and *Character Toys and Collectibles,* all by David Longest; *Motorcycle Toys, Antique and Contemporary,* by Sally Gibson-Downs and Christine Gentry; *Matchbox Toys, 1947 – 1996, Second Edition,* by Dana Johnson; and *Schroeder's Collectible Toys, Antique to Modern.* All are published by Collector Books.

See also Action Figures; Breyer Horses; Hartland; Character Collectibles; Star Trek; Star

Wars; Western Heroes; Club and Newsletters.

## Battery-Operated

ABC Toyland Express, MT, 1950s, litho tin, 14½", EX ......**160.00**

Acrobat Cycle, Aoshin, 1970s, plastic, 9", NM (EX box) .....**150.00**

Acrobat Robot, SH, 1970s, mostly plastic, 4½", EX ..........**100.00**

Antique Gooney Car, Alps, 1960s, litho tin, 9", MIB ........**350.00**

Apollo-X Moon Challenger, TN, plastic, 16", EX ...........**185.00**

B-Z Rabbit, MT, 1950s, litho tin, 7", EX ...........................**125.00**

Ball Playing Dog, Linemar, 1950s, tin & plush, 9", M .......**175.00**

Barnyard Rooster, Marx, 1950s, litho tin, 10", EX .........**200.00**

Batmobile, AHI, 1977, plastic, radio control, 8", NM (NM box) ...............................**275.00**

Bear the Cashier, MT, 1950s, litho tin & plush, 7½", MIB .....................**425.00**

Beep Beep Greyhound Bus, Cragstan, 1950s, litho tin, 20", EX ...............................**225.00**

Billy Blastoff Space Scout, Eldon, 1968, 4½", EX .............**200.00**

Bimbo the Drumming Clown, Cragstan, 1950s, litho tin & cloth, MIB ...................**675.00**

Bubble Kangaroo, MT, 1950s, litho tin, rare, 9", EX ..........**400.00**

Buttons the Puppy w/a Brain, Marx, 1960s, tin & plush, 12", EX ...............................**400.00**

Calypso Joe, Linemar, remote control, tin w/cloth clothes, 10", EX ...............................**600.00**

Chiefy the Fire Dog, Alps, 1969, litho tin, 9", EX ..........**100.00**

Clang-Clang Locomotive, Marx, 1950s, litho tin, 10½", EX .**65.00**

Clown's Popcorn Truck, TPS, 1960s, mostly plastic, 6", EX ...**275.00**

Cock-A-Doodle-Doo Rooster, Mikuni, 1950s, litho tin, 8", EX .............................**165.00**

Cycling Daddy, Bandai, 1960s, tin & plastic w/cloth clothes, 10", MIB ............................**225.00**

Docking Robot, Daiya, 1960s, litho tin, 16", EX .................**200.00**

Dolly Seamstress, TN, 1950s, litho tin, 7", M (NM box) .....**385.00**

Fido the Xylophone Player, Alps, 1950s, tin & plush, rare, 9", MIB ............................**475.00**

FiFi Poodle, Alps, MIB, $45.00.

Fishing Polar Bear, Alps, tin & plush, 10", MIB ...........**325.00**

Funland Cup Ride, Sonsco, 1960s, litho tin, MIB .............**375.00**

Godzilla, Mattel, 1977, plastic, 19", NM (NM box) .......**255.00**

Hamburger Chef, K, 1960s, litho tin, 9", EX ...................**225.00**

Happy Clown Car, Y, 1960s, litho tin, 6½", EX ................**200.00**

Hoop Zing Girl, Linemar, 1950s, celluloid & tin, rare, 12", MIB ............................**575.00**

Hot Rod Racer #7, Cragstan, 1950s, litho tin, 8", MIB ..........**325.00**

Hungry Sheep, MT, 1950s, litho tin, 9", EX ....................**200.00**

Jolly Penguin, TN, 1950s, tin & plush, remote control, 7", EX ............................**200.00**

Josie the Walking Cow, Daiya, 1950s, plush & tin, EX .**200.00**

Laughing Clown, SH, 1960s, litho tin, 15", EX .................**400.00**

Major Tooty, Alps, 1960s, litho tin, 14", MIB .....................**275.00**

Mickey Mouse Krazy Kar, Marx, plastic, EX (EX box) .....**75.00**

Mighty Kong, Marx, 1950s, plush & tin, remote control, 11", EX ......**500.00**

Mighty Mike the Barbell Lifter, K, 1950s, tin & plush, 12", M .**300.00**

Monorail Rocket Ship, Linemar, 1950s, litho tin, 10", EX .**275.00**

Moon Express, TPS, 1950s, litho tin, 12", EX ..................**250.00**

Mother Goose, Yonezawa, litho tin, MIB ........................**250.00**

Mr Magoo Car, Hubley, 1961, tin w/cloth top, 9", M ........**300.00**

Nutty Mad Indian, Marx, 1960s, tin & vinyl, 12", MIB ..**175.00**

Nutty Mads Car, Linemar, 1960s, litho tin, MIB ..............**275.00**

Pee Pee Puppy, TN, 1960s, tin & plush, 9", NM ..............**150.00**

Pete the Spaceman, Bandai, 1960s, litho tin, 5", MIB ........**200.00**

Pretty Peggy Parrot, Rosko, litho tin & plush, 10", EX (EX box) ............................**425.00**

Radar Scope Space Scout, SH, 1960s, litho tin, 9", EX .**275.00**

Roaring Tiger, Rosko, tin & plush, 11", NMIB ...................**200.00**

**Santa on Go-cart, TM, 10¼", NM, $165.00.**

Shooting Gallery Gorilla, MT, 1950s, litho tin, rare, 10", MIB ............................**350.00**

Space Capsule #5, MT, 1960s, litho tin & plastic, 10½", EX ..........................**300.00**

Tom Tom Indian, Y, 1960s, tin w/cloth clothes, 10½", EX .............**165.00**

Vanguard Satellite Launcher, Remco, 1960s, MIB .....**275.00**

Whirlybird Helicopter, Remco, 1960s, litho tin, NMIB .**250.00**

Zintar Robot, Ideal, 1971, 6", NM (VG box) ......................**285.00**

Zoom Boat F-570, K, 1950s, litho tin, remote control, 10", NMIB .........................**225.00**

### Friction

Auto Transporter, SSS, litho tin, w/4 cars, 12", NM (EX box) ........................**200.00**

Circus Jeep, Y, litho tin, 6", EX (VG box) ......................**200.00**

Cocker Spaniel, Marx, litho tin, rare, 12", NM ..............**175.00**

Daredevil-Acrobat Stunt Motorcycle, Alps, litho tin, 5", NMIB ...........................**250.00**

Disneyland Jeep, Marx, litho tin, 10", EX .........................**200.00**

Dream Car, Cragstan/Ashitoy, tin & plastic, 7½", EX (EX box) ...........................**275.00**

Electric Locomotive, TN, marked Union Pacific, litho tin, 13", NMIB ...........................**125.00**

Flintstone Log Car, Marx, 1977, plastic, 5", MIB ...........**175.00**

Goofy's Stock Car, Marx, litho tin, 6", NM .........................**250.00**

Greyhound Escorter, Lowell Toy, litho tin, 6", EX (EX box) ..........**175.00**

Huckleberry Hound Car, Marx, 1962, tin w/vinyl figure, 4", NMIB ...........................**300.00**

Jupiter Rocket, Japan, litho tin, 8", NM (EX box) ..........**235.00**

Magic Fire Car, MT, litho tin & vinyl, 7", NMIB ..............**75.00**

Matador Rocket Launcher, K, litho tin, EX (VG box) .........**235.00**

Mickey Mouse Motorcycle, Linemar, litho tin, 4", NM ............**275.00**

Moon Rocket #3, MT, 1950s, litho tin, 7", NM (EX box) ...**400.00**

Planet of the Apes Prison Wagon, AHI, plastic, NM (EX box) ........**100.00**

Roaring Roadster, Nosco, plastic w/visible engine, 8", NM (NM box) ..............................**200.00**

Rocket XB-115, SH, litho tin & plastic, 12", MIB .........**175.00**

Space Explorer, Hong Kong, 1960, plastic, rare, 7½", MIB .**250.00**

Space Tank X-4, TN, litho tin, 7¼", MIB ..............................**175.00**

Sparkling Hot Rod Racer, Marx, plastic, 7", NM (VG box) ........**200.00**

Super Sonic Race Car No 36, MT, litho tin, 9", NM (NM box) ........**200.00**

Tom & Jerry Scooter, Marx, 1972, plastic, 4½", MIB ........**100.00**

X-3 Racer, Bandai, litho tin, 7", EX (EX box) ........................**200.00**

Yogi Bear Car, Marx, litho tin & vinyl, 4", NM (EX box) .**275.00**

Z-26 Space Patrol, KO, tin & plastic, 6" dia, EX ..............**135.00**

## Wind-Ups

Alpine Express, Ohio Art, litho tin, 33" base, EX (EX box) .**125.00**

Archie Jalopy, Marx/Mexico, litho tin, 7", EX ....................**300.00**

Babes in Toyland, Linemar, litho tin, 6", NM (EX box) ....................**350.00**

Bedrock Express Train, Marx, 1962, litho tin, 12", EX ............**250.00**

Bill the Ball Blowing Whale, KO, litho tin, NM (NM box) .**150.00**

Bimbo Clown Car, Joustra, litho tin, 4½", NM ...............**175.00**

BO Plenty & Baby Sparkles, Marx, litho tin, 9", MIB ........**475.00**

Candy Loving Canine, TPS, litho tin, 6", NM (NM box) ..**225.00**

Capitol Hill Racer, Unique Art, litho tin, 17", NM (NM box) ...**325.00**

Circus Monkey, GNK, litho tin w/paper umbrella, rare, 7½", NMIB ...........................**300.00**

Climbing Fireman, Marx, plastic & tin, EX (EX box) ......**250.00**

Climbing Tom Tom Monkey, MT, litho tin, 13", EX .........**125.00**

Clown Riding Cart, GK, litho tin, 5½", EX ......................**385.00**

Dancing Cinderella & Prince, Irwin, 1950, plastic, 5½", NMIB ............................**175.00**

Dopey Walker, Marx, 1938, litho tin, 8", EX ....................**350.00**

Dump Truck, Wells, litho tin w/balloon tires, 10", VG .......**175.00**

Express Parcels Truck, Distler, litho tin w/spoke wheels, EX ............................**285.00**

Fire Chief Car, Hoge, pressed steel, w/decal, 15", VG ...........**225.00**

Flipo the Dog, Marx, 1940, litho tin, 4", NM (EX box) ...**250.00**

Fliver Bug, Buffalo Toy, 1937, red-painted tin, 6½", NMIB .**250.00**

**GI Joe and his Jouncing Jeep, Unique Art, 1941, marked CR 5-4065, forward and reverse action, 8", EX, $250.00. (Photo courtesy Scott Smiles)**

Groolies Car, Yone, litho tin, 4¾", NM (EX box) ...............**250.00**

Hand-Standing Clown, Chein, litho tin, 5", EX, from $125 to ...............................**150.00**

Hercules Ferris Wheel, Chein, litho tin, 17", NM ........**385.00**

Hopping George Jetson, Marx, litho tin, 4", NM ..........**275.00**

Ice Cream Cart, Occupied Japan, litho tin & celluloid, 3", NM ......................**175.00**

Looping Plane, Marx, 1930s, litho tin, 7½" wingspan, EX ..........................**150.00**

Merry-Go-Round, Wyandotte, w/boats & airplanes, litho tin, 5½", EX ........................**400.00**

Milton Berle Car, Marx, litho tin & plastic, 6", NMIB, from $425 to ..................................**525.00**

Monkey Golfer, TPS, litho tin, 4½", NM (G box) ........**250.00**

Monkey on Motorcycle, Gama, litho tin, 7", VG ...........**350.00**

Moon Astronaut, Daiya, litho tin, 9", VG ..........................**375.00**

Moon Orbiter, Yonezawa, plastic, 4", NMIB ......................**150.00**

Native on Alligator, Chein, litho tin, 15", EX ..................**250.00**

Pango-Pango African Dancer, TPS, litho tin, 6", MIB .........**300.00**

Pig, Chein, 1938, litho tin, 5", EX, from $125 to ...............**150.00**

Pinocchio the Acrobat, Marx, 1939, litho tin, 11", VG .........**350.00**

Popeye w/Spinach Can, vinyl w/cloth clothes, 10", NM .............**175.00**

Pussy Cat Chasing Butterfly, TPS, plush & tin, 5", MIB ...................**200.00**

Reading Santa Claus, Alps, tin & vinyl w/cloth clothes, 7", NMIB ...........................**200.00**

Santa Claus on Sled, Occupied Japan, celluloid, 8", EX (EX box) ............................**175.00**

Sheriff Sam Whoopee Car, Marx, 1960s, litho tin & plastic, 5½", EX ................................**250.00**

Skeeter Duck, Lindstrom, litho tin, 9", EX (G box) .........**75.00**

Skippy the Tricky Cyclist Clown, TPS, litho tin, 6", EX (EX box) ............................**250.00**

Spacecraft Jupiter, K, litho tin & plastic, 5" dia, NM (EX box) ...........................**155.00**

Telephone Bear, Alps, tin & plush w/cloth clothes, 6½", NMIB .........................**150.00**

Tricky Taxi, Marx, green-painted tin, 4½", NM (G box) ..**200.00**

Trolly Bus, Joustra, tin w/balloon tires, 12", NM (EX box) .**400.00**

Twikki Robot (Buck Rogers), plastic, 7", NM ....................**125.00**

Waltzing Royal Couple, Irwin, plastic, 5", NM (VG box) ....**150.00**

Whoopee Cowboy, Marx, 1932, litho tin, 8", EX ...........**350.00**

# Trolls

The first trolls to come to the United States were molded after a 1952 design by Marti and Helena Kuuskoski of Tampere, Finland. The first to be mass produced in America were molded from wood carvings made by Thomas Dam of Denmark. As the demand for these trolls increased, several US manufacturers became licensed to produce them. The most noteworthy of these were Uneeda doll company's Wishnik line and Inga Dykin's Scandia House True Trolls. Thomas Dam continued to import his Dam Things line.

The troll craze from the '60s spawned many items other than dolls such as wall plaques, salt and pepper shakers, pins, squirt guns, rings, clay trolls, lamps, Halloween costumes, animals, lawn ornaments, coat racks, notebooks, folders, and even a car.

In the '70s, '80s, and '90s, more new trolls were produced. While these trolls are collectible to some, the avid troll collector still prefers those produced in the '60s. Remember, trolls that receive top dollar must be in mint condition.

For more information we recommend *Collector's Guide to Trolls* by Pat Peterson (Collector Books). See also Clubs and Newsletters.

Astronaut, Dam, 1964, 11", EX ...........................**125.00**

Ballerina, Dam, red hair, green eyes, original outfit, MIP ..........**55.00**

Carrying case, Ideal, w/molded waterfall, M ...................**25.00**

Cave girl, Dam, white hair, flannel leopard skin outfit, 3", EX ..............................**25.00**

Clown, Dam, 1965, painted-on clothes, 5½", NM .........**250.00**

Cook-Nik, Uneeda Wishnik, 1970s, bendable, 5", MOC ........**40.00**

Cow, Dam, white hair, 3½", EX ...........................**45.00**

Eskimo, Dam, 1965, brown hair, painted-on clothes, 5½", EX .....................**75.00**

Girl, bank, Dam, 1960s, green or yellow felt dress, 8", EX, ea ..**25.00**

**Wishnik Troll dolls in cases with accessories, Ideal, $45.00 each. (Photo courtesy June Moon)**

Girl w/pigtails, unmarked, blond hair, yellow felt dress & hat, 3", EX ............................**20.00**

Good Luck-Nik, Uneeda Wishnik, 1970s, M in original tube .**30.00**

Grandpa Claus, Dam, 1977, white hair, 14", EX, from $100 to ........**125.00**

Judge, Uneeda Wishnik, gray hair, 5½", EX ..........................**30.00**

Moonitik, Uneeda Wishnik, mohair body w/rubber feet, rare, 18", EX ...............**100.00**

Nursenik, Uneeda Wishnik, 1970s, 6", MOC .............**50.00**

Outfit, any style, MIP, ea ....**15.00**

Pirate, bank, Dam, 1960s, red hair, felt clothes, 8", EX .........**30.00**

Playboy bunny, unmarked, blond hair, clip hands, 3½", EX ............................**15.00**

Playhouse, Wishnik Mini Trolls, Ideal, 1960s, EX ............**20.00**

Poppa-He-Nik, Wishnik, gold hair, green felt outfit, 5", EX .**25.00**

Santa, bank, Dam, 1960s, felt clothes, rare, 8", EX ......**45.00**

Vending Machine Trolls, 1960s, several variations, ea from $5 to ...................................**10.00**

# TV Guide

For most people, their *TV Guide* spends a week on top of their TV set or by the remote and then is discarded. But to collectors, this weekly chronicle of TV history is highly revered. For many people, vintage *TV Guides* evoke happy feelings of the simpler days of their youth. They also search for information on television shows not to be found in reference books. As with any type of ephemera, condition is very important. Some collectors prefer issues without address labels on the cover. Values are given for guides in fine to mint condition.

Our advisor is Jeffrey M. Kadet, of *TV Guide* Specialists; he is listed in the Directory under Illinois.

1953, June 19, Ed Sullivan .**42.00**

1953, May 15, David & Ricky Nelson ................................**87.00**

1954, March 26, Jackie Gleason ..........................**56.00**

1954, September 4, Eddie Fisher ............................**25.00**

1955, August 27, Groucho Marx ........................**56.00**

1955, January 15, I've Got a Secret cast ..............................**24.00**

1956, April 14, Grace Kelly Coronation issue ...................**22.00**

1956, June 16, Father Knows Best cast ...............................**64.00**

1957, February 9, Hugh O'Brian of Wyatt Earp ..................**22.00**

1957, May 11, James Arness as Matt Dillon ....................**42.00**

1958, February 22, Rosemary Clooney ..........................**15.00**

1958, June 7, Pat Boone ......**11.00**

1959, February 14, Alfred Hitchcock ...............................**11.00**

1959, May 30, Steve McQueen .............**90.00**

1960, February 27, Robert Stack of the Untouchables ....................**15.00**

1960, October 1, Dinah Shore ......................**15.00**

1961, February 4, Clint Eastwood ...........................**95.00**

1961, January 6, Vince Edwards ...................**15.00**

1961, July 1, Flintstones .....**75.00**

1962, August 4, Dennis the Menace cast ..........................**27.00**

1963, January 12, Arnold Palmer .......................**17.00**

1963, September 21, Richard Chamberlin ...................**20.00**

1964, August 15, Wagon Train cast ...............................**16.00**

1964, March 14, Beverly Hillbillies cast ...............................**25.00**

1965, January 2, Munsters cast ...............................**75.00**

1965, July 24, Raymond Burr .**10.00**

**1965, May 8 – 14, Bob Denver and Tina Louise on cover, from $20.00 to $30.00. (Photo courtesy Greg Davis and Bill Morgan)**

1966, April, 2, Dean Martin .**25.00**

1966, October 1, Vietnam War ......................**18.00**

1967, July 22, Bonanza cast .**72.00**

1967, May 27, F Troop cast .**15.00**

1968, April 20, Barbara Feldon of Get Smart ......................**18.00**

1968, July 20, Big Valley cast ..**60.00**

1969, June 14, Glen Campbell .......................**8.00**

1970, August 15, Johnny Carson by Norman Rockwell ....**10.00**

1970, December 12, Ed Sullivan & the Muppets ...................**9.00**

1971, January 9, Andy Griffith .......................**30.00**

1971, September 4, Jack Lord of Hawaii Five-O ..............**15.00**

1972, January 29, David Janssen ......................**23.00**
1972, July 1, Carol Burnett ..**10.00**
1973, January 20, Bob Newhart cast ..................................**7.00**
1973, November 17, Frank Sinatra ..................................**13.00**
1974, August 3, Emergency cast ...**9.00**
1974, January 26, David Carradine of Kung Fu .............**12.00**
1975, February 15, Rookies cast .............................**7.00**
1975, September 6, Fall Preview ...........................**28.00**
1976, March 6, Rockford Files cast ................................**7.00**
1977, March 19, Last Mary Tyler Moore Show ...................**27.00**
1977, October 15, Ed Asner of Lou Grant ..............................**8.00**
1978, April 8, Alice cast .........**8.00**
1978, July 1, Fantasy Island cast ..............................**7.00**
1979, February 3, CHiPs cast .**13.00**
1980, May 3, Mork & Mindy cast .............................**12.00**
1981, February 14, WKRP in Cincinnati cast ................**9.00**
1982, March 13, Three's Company cast ..................................**7.00**
1983, December 10, Tom Selleck ...............................**7.00**
1984, June 9, Remington Steele cast ...............................**15.00**
1985, February 2, Cagney & Lacey by Amsel .........................**7.00**
1986, April 5, Family Ties cast ...**8.00**
1987, October 17, Dolly Parton of Dolly .............................**12.00**
1988, June 11, Thirtysomething cast ..................................**7.00**
1989, May 6, TV Is 50 .........**13.00**
1990, March 17, Simpsons ..**15.00**

1991, May 18, Murphy Brown cast ..................................**6.00**
1992, March 21, Magic Johnson ..**5.00**
1993, April, Heather Locklear .**6.00**
1994, July 2, Reba McIntire ..**9.00**
1995, July 22, Dean Cain as Superman .......................**8.00**
1996, June 1, Jerry Seinfeld .**6.00**

# Universal

Located in Cambridge, Ohio, Universal Potteries Incorporated produced various lines of dinnerware from 1934 to the late 1950s, several of which are very attractive, readily available, and therefore quite collectible. Refer to *The Collector's Encyclopedia of American Dinnerware* by Jo Cunningham (Collector Books) for more information.

See also Cattail.

Ballerina, bowl, cereal ...........**5.00**
Ballerina, creamer & sugar bowl ...........................**20.00**
Ballerina, gravy boat ...........**12.00**
Ballerina, shakers, pr ..........**12.00**
Bittersweet, pitcher, w/lid, low .......................**40.00**
Calico Fruit, bowl, serving; tab handles ..........................**12.00**
Calico Fruit, custard cup, 5-oz .**6.00**
Calico Fruit, utility shaker .**12.00**
Largo, creamer .......................**6.00**
Refrigerator Ware, canteen jug, blue & white, various decals, ea ...................................**20.00**
Woodvine, bowl, mixing; 4" .**19.00**
Woodvine, gravy boat ..........**12.00**
Woodvine, sugar bowl, w/lid .**18.00**

Zinnias, casserole ................**13.00**

# Valentines

Valentine collecting has become more and more prevalent over the last several years, due in part to public awareness of their diverse subject matter. Whatever the interest of the collector, there is probably a type of Valentine that will appeal to his or her interest, whether it be advertising, smoking, transportation, comic characters, movie personalities, etc.

Please keep these factors in mind when assessing the value of your valentines: age, condition, size, category, and whether or not an artist's signature is present. All of these factors were taken into consideration when the following valentines were evaluated. It is also important to remember that prices tend to be higher on the East Coast than the West, primarily due to higher demand.

Our advisor for this category is Katherine Kreider; she is listed in the Directory under Pennsylvania.

In the listings that follow, HCPP stands for honeycomb paper puff, and MIG indicates valentines marked Made in Germany.

Dimensional, Dove Cote w/child, 6¾x4x3", EX ....................**5.00**
Dimensional, floral w/children, Germany, 4½x3x2½", EX ................................**3.00**
Dimensional, rowboat w/child & cat, Germany, 5x6x1½", NM ............................**35.00**
Dimensional, Viking ship, Germany, 9¾x9x5", EX .......**50.00**
Dimensional, 3-wheeled carriage, Germany/1900s, 9½x9½x2½", EX ..................................**50.00**
Flat, big-eared golfer, Germany, early 1900s, 8½x4¾", EX ..........**10.00**
Flat, Dutch maiden, Tuck, Germany, 1900s, 8x5", VG ...................**5.00**
Flat, Minnie Mouse, 1960, 4x3", EX .....................................**3.00**
Flat, monkey & monkey grinder, USA, 1940s, 3½x3", VG ..**1.00**
Flat, sailor & Boston bull, USA, 1940s, 5½x4", EX ............**5.00**
Flat, scuba diver w/original rubber hose, USA, 1940s, 8½x5½", EX ..................................**5.00**
Flat, Shirley Temple caricature, mid-1900s, 4x2¾", EX ....**3.00**
Greeting card, Hallmark, 1950s, 7½x6½", EX .....................**1.00**
Greeting card, steam engine, Hallmark, 1950s, 7x8x5", EX ..............................**10.00**
Greeting card, Whitney, ca 1940s, 4x6", EX ...........................**1.00**
Greeting card, Whitney, early 1900s, 7½x6½", NM ......**15.00**
HCPP, basket (sm version), 1920s, 6x5x3", EX .......................**3.00**
HCPP, mushroom w/children, early 1900s, Germany, 11x9x5", EX ...................**10.00**
HCPP, pedestal w/cherub & flowers, 1920s, 10x8½x4¼", EX ..............................**10.00**
Mechanical-flat, ace of hearts, Germany, 7x5¼", EX .........................**5.00**

Mechanical-flat, airplane w/child, Germany, 6¾x8¼", EX ...**5.00**

Mechanical-flat, Black children rooster, Germany/Katz, 1925, 12x8", EX ......................**10.00**

Mechanical-flat, circus elephant w/dog, 1950s, 9½x7½", EX .**1.00**

Mechanical-flat, cowboy, 1920s, 6x4", VG ..........................**1.00**

Mechanical-flat, donkey w/extended neck, Germany, 7¼x2½", EX ...................................**5.00**

**Mechanical-flat, girl in band, 1940s, USA, 6x5½", $3.00. (Photo courtesy Katherine Kreider)**

Mechanical-flat, Little Bo Peep, Germany, early 1900s, 9x8½", NM ................................**15.00**

Mechanical-flat, polo pony, Germany, 1940s, 9x7½", EX .................**3.00**

Mechanical-flat, Uncle Tom, USA, 1930s, 4¾x4", EX ...........**5.00**

Novelty, Ballyhoo magazine, ca 1920s, 4¾x4", EX ...........**5.00**

Novelty, clockwork musical card, Hallmark, 1950s, 9½x7½x1", NM ................................**5.00**

Novelty, finger puppet, 1950s, 6½x3¼", NM ...................**3.00**

Novelty, hanging heart made of HCPP, 1920s, 8x6½", VG .**5.00**

Novelty, heart-shaped candy box, 1900s, 3x2½x1", VG ........**3.00**

Novelty, kaleidoscope, Germany, 1927, 7x4", EX ................**3.00**

Novelty, Mousketeers, USA, 1950s, 4x2", NM ..............**2.00**

Novelty, peach bathing beauty, USA, 1940s, 4¾x3¾", EX .**2.00**

Novelty, Peter, Peter, Pumpkin Eater, USA, 4x3¼", EX ..**3.00**

Novelty, Three Blind Mice, USA, 1940s, 5x4", EX ..............**3.00**

Novelty, Winnie the Pooh, USA, 1960s, 5½x2¾" ................**2.00**

## Vernon Kilns

From 1931 until 1958, Vernon Kilns produced hundreds of patterns of fine dinnerware that today's collectors enjoy reassembling. They retained the services of famous artists and designers such as Rockwell Kent and Walt Disney, who designed both dinnerware lines and novelty items. Examples of their work are at a premium. See also Clubs and Newsletters.

Anytime, plate, 10" ...............**7.00**

Arcadia, bowl, serving; oval, 10" ..........................**25.00**

Brown-Eyed Susan, bowl, cereal; 6" ...................................**15.00**

Brown-Eyed Susan, cup & saucer .......................**10.00**

Brown-Eyed Susan, tidbit, 2-tier ...........................**30.00**

Calico, plate, dinner; 10½" ..**18.00**
Chintz, bowl, fruit; 5½" .........**8.00**
Chintz, cup ............................**8.00**
Chintz, platter, 12" ..............**25.00**
Early California, bowl, lug chowder;
 tab handles, w/lid, 6" ......**39.00**
Early California, coaster, 4½" .**25.00**
Early California, plate, salad;
 7½" ...............................**12.00**
Early Days, bowl, lug chowder;
 6" ..................................**15.00**
Early Days, salt & pepper shakers,
 pr ...................................**24.00**
Early Days, teapot, 6-cup ....**65.00**
Fantasia, bowl, goldfish, #121 .**375.00**
Fantasia, bowl, sprite, hand paint-
 ed, #125 .......................**325.00**
Fantasia, figurine, satyr, 4½" .**250.00**

**Fantasia, Centaur figurine, #11, 10½", from $1,200.00 to $1,400.00.**

Gingham, bowl, rim soup; 8½" ..**15.00**
Gingham, spoon rest ............**40.00**
Homespun, bowl, fruit; 5½" ...**8.00**
Homespun, plate, bread & butter;
 6" ...................................**5.00**

Lei Lani, cup & saucer, demi-
 tasse ............................**35.00**
Linda, cup & saucer .............**12.00**
May Flower, butter tray & lid ..**45.00**
May Flower, platter, 13½" ..**20.00**
Melinda, coffeepot, 8-cup .....**65.00**
Modern California, pitcher, 1-pt .**25.00**
Mojave, sugar bowl, w/lid ....**14.00**
Native California, pitcher, 2-qt .**40.00**
Organdie, bowl, fruit; 5½" .....**5.00**
Organdie, casserole, w/lid, individ-
 ual ..................................**25.00**
Organdie, cup & saucer, demi-
 tasse ..............................**25.00**
Organdie, plate, luncheon; 9½" .**9.00**
Plate, Edvard Grieg, Composer,
 8½" ................................**25.00**
Tam O'Shanter, carafe, w/stop-
 per ..............................**45.00**
Tickled Pink, bowl, chowder .**12.00**
Tickled Pink, plate, dinner; 10" ..**9.00**
Tweed, plate, chop; 12" ........**55.00**
Vernon 1860, salt & pepper shak-
 ers, pr ...........................**20.00**
Wheat, creamer ...................**15.00**
Wheat, relish, leaf shape, 12" .**25.00**
Winchester 73, plate, 6" ......**40.00**
Winchester 73, tumbler .......**45.00**

# View-Master Reels and Packets

   View-Master, the invention of William Gruber, was first introduced to the public at the 1939 – 1940 New York World's Fair and at the same time at the Golden Gate Exposition in California. Since then, thousands of reels and packets have been produced on subjects as diverse as life itself. Sawyers' View-Master even made two different stereo cameras for the general public, enabling people to make their own personal reels, and then offered a stereo projector to project the pictures they took on a silver screen in full-color 3-D.

View-Master has been owned by five different companies: the original Sawyers Company, G.A.F. (in October 1966), View-Master International (in 1981), Ideal Toy Company, and Tyco Toy Company (the present owners).

Unfortunately, after G.A.F. sold View-Master in 1981, neither View-Master International, Ideal, nor Tyco Toy Company have had any intention of making the products anything but toy items, selling mostly cartoons. This, of course, has made the early non-cartoon single reels and the three-reel packets desirable items.

The earliest single reels from 1939 to 1945 were not white but dark blue with a gold sticker in the center. They came in attractive gold-colored envelopes. Then they were made in a blue and tan combination. These early reels are preferred, as the print runs were low.

Most white single reels are very common, since they were produced by the millions from 1946 through 1957. There are exceptions, however, such as commercial reels promoting a product and reels of obscure scenic attractions, as these would have had smaller print runs. In 1952 a European division of View-Master was established in Belgium. Most reels and items made there are more valuable to a collector, since they are hard to find in this country.

In 1955 View-Master came up with the novel idea of selling packets of three reels in one colorful envelope with a picture or photo on the front. Many times a story booklet was included. These became very popular, and sales of single reels were slowly discontinued. Most three-reel packets are desirable, whether Sawyers or G.A.F., as long as they are in nice condition. Nearly all viewers are common and have little value except the very early ones, such as the Model A and Model B. These viewers had to be opened to insert the reels. The blue and brown versions of the Model B are rare. Another desirable viewer is the Model D, which is the only focusing viewer that View-Master made. Condition is very important to the value of all View-Master items, as it is with most collectibles.

Our advisor for this category is Mr. Walter Sigg, who is listed in the Directory under New Jersey.

Camera, Mark II, w/case ...**100.00**
Camera, Personal Stereo, w/ case ..........................**100.00**
Close-up lens, for Personal Camera ...............................**100.00**
Film cutter, for cameras ....**100.00**
Packet, Addams Family or Munsters, 3-reel set .............**50.00**
Packet, Belgium made, 3-reel set, from $4 to ......................**35.00**

Packet, miscellaneous subject, 3-reel set, from $3 to ........**50.00**

Packet, scenic, 3-reel set, from $1 to ....................................**25.00**

Packet, TV or movie, 3-reel set, from $2 to ......................**50.00**

Projector, Stereo-Matic 500 .**200.00**

Reel, Belgium made, from $1 to .**10.00**

Reel, blue, from $2.50 to .....**10.00**

Reel, commercial, brand-name product (Coca-Cola, etc), from $5 to ..............................**50.00**

Reel, gold center, gold-colored package ..........................**10.00**

Reel, Sawyers, white, early from 25¢ to ..............................**5.00**

Reel, 3-D movie preview (House of Wax, Kiss Me Kate, etc) ................**50.00**

Viewer, Model B, blue or brown, ea .................................**100.00**

Viewer, Model D, focusing type .**30.00**

## Tru-View

Tru-Vue, a subsidiary of the Rock Island Bridge and Iron Works in Rock Island, Illinois, first introduced their product to the public at the 1933 Century of Progress Exposition in Chicago. With their popular black and white 3-D filmstrips and viewers, Tru-Vue quickly became the successor to the stereoscope and stereocards of the 1800s and early 1900s. They made many stereo views of cities, national parks, scenic attractions, and even some foreign countries. They produced children's stories, some that featured personalities and night-clubs, and many commercial and instructional filmstrips.

By the late 1940s, Sawyers' View-Master had become a very strong competitor. Their full-color seven-scene stereo reels were very popular with the public and had cut into Tru-Vue's sales considerably. So it was a tempting offer when Sawyers made a bid to buy out the company in 1951. Sawyers needed Tru-Vue, not only to eliminate competition but because Tru-Vue owned the rights to photograph Disney characters and the Disneyland theme park in California.

After the take-over, Sawyers' View-Master continued to carry Tru-Vue products but stopped production of the 3-D filmstrips and viewers. Instead they adopted a new format with seven-scene 3-D cards and a new 3-D viewer. These were sold mainly in toy stores and today have little value. All of the pictures were on a cheaper 'Eastmancolor' slide film, and most of them have today faded into a magenta color. Many cards came apart, as the glue that was used tends to separate quite easily. The value of these, therefore, is low. (Many cards were later remade as View-Master reels using the superior 'Kodachrome' film.) On the other hand, advertising literature, dealer displays, and items that were not meant to be sold to the public often have considerable collector value.

When G.A.F. bought View-Master in 1966, they gradually phased out the Tru-Vue format. See also Clubs and Newsletters.

Card, from $1 to .....................**3.00**

**Eight Is Enough, View-Master #K76, GAF, 1980, from $15.00 to $20.00. (Photo courtesy Greg Davis and Bill Morgan)**

Filmstrip, children's story, from $1 to ................................**3.00**

Filmstrip, commercial (promoting products), from $20 to ..**50.00**

Filmstrip, instructional, from $5 to ...................................**15.00**

Filmstrip, ocean liner ..........**15.00**

Filmstrip, personality (Sally Rand, Gypsy Rose Lee, etc), from $15 to ....................**20.00**

Filmstrip, scenic, from $1 to **.5.00**

Filmstrip, World's Fair ..........**7.50**

## Wall Pockets

If you've been interested enough to notice, wall pockets are everywhere — easily found, relatively inexpensive, and very diversified. They were made in Japan, Czechoslovakia, and by many, many companies in the United States. Those made by companies best known for their art pottery (Weller, Roseville, etc.) are in a class of their own, but the novelty, just-for-fun wall pockets stand on their own merits. Examples with large, colorful birds or those with unusual modeling are usually the more desirable. There are several books we recommend for more information: *Collector's Guide to Wall Pockets, Affordable and Others*, by Marvin and Joy Gibson (L-W Books); *Collector's Encyclopedia of Wall Pockets* by Betty and Bill Newbound; *Wall Pockets of the Past* by Fredda Perkins; and *Collector's Guide to Made in Japan Ceramics* (three in series) by our advisor, Carole Bess White, who is listed in the Directory under Oregon. (The last three are all published by Collector Books.) See also Cleminson; McCoy; Shawnee; other specific manufacturers.

Bird & berry, brown & yellow tones, Czechoslovakia, 8" ..........**45.00**

Cornucopia w/applied bird, various colors, marked Patented 149244, 7" ......................**20.00**

Deco flower on cone form w/lustre trim, Japan, 7¼" ..........**35.00**

Dustpan w/decor, American Art Potteries, #81, 8" ..........**25.00**

Dutch boy w/goose beside stone wall, made in Japan, 6" **.18.00**

Oriental lady w/basket on back, bright colors, Japan, 8" **.25.00**

Rooster, white w/red & green details, Engle Studio, 12" ..............**65.00**

Sailboat, white w/gold lustre, Brown China Co, Sebring OH, 5¾" .................................**20.00**

Squirrel eating nut, brown tones, unmarked Japan, 4⅜" ..**12.00**

Telephone, crank model, white w/multicolor floral decor, L&F Ceramics ........................**20.00**

Umbrella, painted berries & leaves on white, Orion sticker, 6⅜" ................................**12.00**

**Yellow basketweave with handles, Japan, 6½", from $20.00 to $25.00. (Photo courtesy Fredda Perkins)**

# Western Heroes

Interest is very strong right now in western memorabilia — not only that, but the kids that listened so intently to those after-school radio episodes featuring one of the many cowboy stars that sparked the air-waves in the '50s are now some of today's more affluent collectors, able and wanting to search out and buy toys they had in their youth. Put those two factors together, and it's easy to see why these items are so popular. For more information, we recommend *Character Toys and Collectibles, First and Second Series,* by David Longest; *The Lone Ranger* by Lee Felbinger; and *The W.F. Cody Buffalo Bill Collector's Guide* by James W. Wojtowicz. All are published by Collector Books. See also Banks; Character Watches; Coloring Books; Comic Books; Games; Puzzles.

### Davy Crockett

Davy Crockett had long been a favorite in fact and folklore. Then with the opening of Disney's Frontierland and his continuing adventures on 1950s television came a surge of interest in all sorts of items featuring the likeness of Fess Parker in a coonskin cap. Millions were drawn to the mystic and excitement surrounding the settlement of our great country. Due to demand, there were many types of items produced for eager fans ready to role play their favorite adventures.

Bank, dime register, metal w/canted corners, 2½" sq, EX .**300.00**

Bank, plaster figure, VG ...**130.00**

Birthday card, Happy Birthday Grandson, 1950s, EX ....**10.00**

Doll, Reliable/Canada, rubber w/cloth outfit & coonskin cap, 10", EX ......................**175.00**

Figure, France, 1950s, hand-painted lead, 4", EX ............**125.00**

Flashlight, 1950s, lithographed tin w/red plastic top, 3", NM .**65.00**

Hat, England/Walt Disney, lithographed cardboard, NMIB .**75.00**

Indian Craft set, Pressmen, complete, NM (NM box) ....**125.00**

Paper plate, Walt Disney, 1950s, M ....................................**15.00**

Pistol & knife, Multiple, plastic, NM (NM card) ...............**75.00**

Planter, Napco, marked S90Em 4x4½", EX .......................**75.00**

Push-button puppet, 1950s, rare, NM ...............................**200.00**

Ring from gumball machine, 1960s, EX ......................**15.00**

Stamp/storybook, Simon & Schuster, 1950s, EX ...............**25.00**

T-shirt, Norwick, 1950s, multicolored image on white, EX .**25.00**

T-shirt transfer, NM ............**15.00**

Wastebasket, lithographed tin, oval, 10x9", EX .............**155.00**

## Gene Autry

First breaking into show business as a recording star with Columbia Records, Gene went on to become one of Hollywood's most famous singing cowboys. From the late 1930s until the mid-'50s, he rode his wonder horse 'Champion' through almost ninety feature films. He did radio and TV as well, and naturally his fame spawned a wealth of memorabilia originally aimed at his young audiences, now grabbed up just as quickly by collectors.

Cowboy Paint Book, 1940, NM .**50.00**

Flip book, Pocket Television Theatre, 1st in series, EX, from $50 to ............................**75.00**

Lariat flashlight, 1950, MIB ..**65.00**

Outfit, Leslie-Henry, 1940s, w/vest & chaps, NMIB, from $200 to ........................**300.00**

Postcard, advertising Gene Autry shirts, black & white, M ..**16.00**

Song book, 1946, 46-page, EX .**20.00**

Spurs, Leslie-Henry, 1950s, EX, pr, from $50 to ..............**60.00**

## Hopalong Cassidy

One of the most popular western heroes of all time, Hoppy was the epitome of the highly moral, role-model cowboys of radio and the silver screen that many of us grew up with in the '40s and '50s. He was portrayed by Bill Boyd who personally endorsed more than 2,200 items targeting Hoppy's loyal followers. If you just happen to be a modern-day Hoppy aficionado, you'll want to read *Collector's Guide to Hopalong Cassidy Memorabilia* by Joseph Caro (L-W Book Sales). See Clubs and Newsletters for information on *Cowboy Collector Newsletter*.

Bank, 1950s, bronze plastic bust, marked Springfield..., 4", EX ........................**65.00**

Binoculars, marked Sports Glass Chicago, metal & plastic w/decals, EX ...............**165.00**

Chaps, 1950s, black suede w/image of Hoppy, VG, pr .......................**85.00**

Display, Langendorf Bread loaf, 1951, 5x512", EX ..........**25.00**

Drum, Rubbertone/Wm Boyd, 1950, 5" dia, EX .........**300.00**

**Fun with Hoppy Field Glasses, 5¼", EXIB, $295.00.**

Film, Danger Trail, Castle Films, 1950s, 16mm, NM ...................**30.00**

Folder, Whitman, complete w/paper & envelopes, NM ...................**100.00**

Hand puppet, 1950s, cloth & vinyl, scarce ..........................**200.00**

Iron-on transfer, 1950s, black steer head w/Deputy, 2x7", EX ..................................**25.00**

Magazine, International Photographer, 1937, EX .............**165.00**

Magazine ad, Grape Nuts Cereal, full page, EX .................**35.00**

Money clip, silver w/photo insert ..........................**50.00**

Pencil, 1950s, name etched in silver, EX ..........................**15.00**

Photo album, black & white, NM .........................**275.00**

Picture Gun & Theater, Stephens, w/metal gun, theater & 2 slides, NMIB ...............**300.00**

Pocketknife, 1950s, black & white, 3½", VG ........................**50.00**

Rug, 1950, embroidered image of Hoppy & Topper in front of fence, NM .....................**225.00**

Sheet music, Wide Open Spaces, w/photo of Hoppy & Topper, VG ...................................**45.00**

Spurs, metal w/name screened on leather, EX ..................**225.00**

Tie clip, Anson, 1950, bust image, MIB .............................**250.00**

Wallet, 1950, plastic & metal w/image of Hoppy & Topper, VG (box) ......................**250.00**

## The Lone Ranger

Recalling 'those thrilling days of yesteryear,' we can't help but remember the adventures of our hero, The Lone Ranger. He's been admired since that first radio show in 1933, and today's collectors seek a wide variety of his memorabilia; premiums, cereal boxes, and even carnival chalkware prizes are a few examples. See Clubs and

Newsletters for information on *The Silver Bullet.*

Bank, 1938, metal book shape, image & name on leather cover, 3", VG ...............**200.00**
Binoculars, Harrison/TLR, 1949, NM (EX box) ...............**225.00**
Crayon tin, Milton Bradley, 1950, marked Lone Ranger Crayons, 6x5", EX .........**65.00**
First Aid kit, Victory Corp, 1942, from $75 to ....................**95.00**
Hairbrush & comb set, TLR, 1939, wood w/decal, NM (G box) .**125.00**
Horseshoe set, Gardner Games, 1950s, rubber w/wood posts, EX (EX box) ...............**200.00**
Magic slate, Whitman, 1978, EX, from $45 to ....................**75.00**
Matchbook, 1938, advertising Lone Ranger Ice Cream, EX .........................**30.00**
Newspaper ad, Frontier Town, 1948, EX, from $35 to ...**55.00**
Outfit, TLR, complete with hat, mask & bandana, EX .....................**200.00**

**Lone Range Wallet, Hidecraft, 1948, NM, $125.00.**

Paint box, Milton Bradley, 1938, M ....................................**80.00**
Party horn, lithographed tin, 5", NM ................................**30.00**
Spoon, figural handle, 1938, EX, from $75 to ....................**95.00**
Stamp set, Larami, 1981, MIP, from $12 to ....................**25.00**
Token, Good Luck, 1938-40, EX, from $85 to .................**125.00**

## Roy Rogers

Growing up during the Great Depression, Leonard Frank Sly was determined to make his mark in the entertainment industry. In 1938 after landing small roles in films featuring Gene Autry and others, Republic Studios (recognizing his talents) renamed their singing cowboy Roy Rogers and placed him in his first leading role in *Under Western Stars.* By 1943 he had become America's 'King of the Cowboys.' And his beloved wife Dale Evans and his horse Trigger were at the top with him. Fans mourn his recent passing.

Our advisor for this category is Robert W. Phillips; he is listed in the Directory under Oklahoma. Mr. Phillips is the author of *Silver Screen Cowboys, Hollywood Cowboy Heroes, Roy Rogers, Singing Cowboy Stars,* and *Western Comics;* all are highly recommended. See Clubs and Newsletters for information on the Roy Rogers—Dale Evans Collectors Association.

Ad sheet, Dream of Santa, 1950s, shows toys, 4 pages, EX .**35.00**

Book bag, 1950s, brown vinyl w/shoulder strap, image on front, VG ......................**65.00**

Camera, Herbert George Co, EX, from $75 to ..................**100.00**

Cowboy & Indian Kit, Colorforms, complete, NM (VG box) .**150.00**

Flashlight, Bantam, 1974, red & white plastic, 3¼", NM ..**165.00**

Horseshoe set, Ohio Art, 1950s, NM ..............................**200.00**

Membership card, Roy Rogers Fan Club, 1947, EX, from $40 to ..........................**60.00**

Modeling clay, Standard Toycraft, complete, NM (NM box) .**125.00**

Mug, Dayton, 1950, plastic head figure, 4½", NM ............**70.00**

Nodder, black script signature on sq gold base, MIB .......**250.00**

Outfit, Merit Playsuits, 1950s, complete, NMIB ..........**350.00**

Paint-By-Number set, Avalon, 1950s, unused, EX (EX box) ........................**165.00**

Photo, multicolored w/printed signature, 8x10" ................**15.00**

Pull toy, NN Hill, 1955, Roy on Trigger, wood & tin, 9½", NMIB ..........................**525.00**

Raincoat & hat, yellow vinyl w/black fringe & trim, EX ..........**350.00**

Salt & pepper shakers, boot shape, EX, pr ............................**95.00**

Scarf, 1950s, silk w/facsimile signature, EX .....................**40.00**

Slippers, 1950s, leather cowboy-boot style w/image & lettering, EX ..........................**175.00**

Tent, Hettrick, 1950s, yellow canvas teepee syle, 54", EX ......**250.00**

Toothbrush, Owens Brush Co, from $40 to ....................**60.00**

Wall plaque, signed Many Happy Trails..., chalkware, 8x7", EX ..............................**275.00**

Window card, Man From Oklahoma, 14x22", EX .........**175.00**

Yo-yo, photo image of Roy & Trigger, EX ..........................**25.00**

## Miscellaneous

Annie Oakley, sewing kit, Pressman, 1950s, MIB, from $40 to ................................**50.00**

Bonanza, cup, 1960s, features Adam & the Ponderosa, tin, EX ..................................**30.00**

Bonanza, sweatshirt, Norwich, 1960s, cotton w/portraits, child size, VG ..............**150.00**

Bonanza, woodburning set, ATF Toys, 1960s, MIB, from $225 to ..................................**250.00**

Cheyenne, cowboy gloves, fringed w/name & horse head image, M ..................................**40.00**

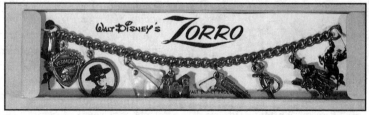

**Zorro bracelet, Walt Disney, 1957, MOC, $150.00. (Photo courtesy June Moon)**

Texas Ranger, Spurs with Jangles, Toy Town, 1950s, MIB, $35.00; Gloves, 1950s, M, $35.00. (Photo courtesy Dunbar Gallery)

Dale Evans, Colorforms Dress-Up Kit, EX (EX box) ...........**75.00**

Daniel Boone, canoe, Multiple, 1965, rubber, inflatable, 18", EX ................................**85.00**

Daniel Boone, film view, Acme, 1964, w/2 films, MIB, from $15 to .............................**20.00**

Gabby Hayes, sheriff's set, 1950s, NMOC ...........................**80.00**

Gunsmoke, pencil case, Hasbro, 1961, blue cardboard w/decal, 4x9", EX .........................**30.00**

Pecos Bill, figure, metal, 6", NM ...**35.00**

Range Rider, chair, 1956, wood w/image on black fabric back, 24", EX ..........................**85.00**

Rifleman, hat, Tex-Felt, 1958, red w/photo image on label, NMIB ...........................**75.00**

Rin-Tin-Tin, magic pictures, Trans-O-Graph, 1956, NMIB .........................**50.00**

Rin-Tin-Tin, outfit, Pla-Master, 1955, Corp Rusty 101st Cavalry, NMIB .....................**135.00**

Straight Arrow, manuscript, 1952, Stage Rider, EX ..............**5.00**

Tales of Wells Fargo, coloring set, Transogram, 1959, EX (EX box) ...............................**65.00**

Tom Mix, flashlight, 1930s, bullet shape, 3", EX, from $60 to .**75.00**

Wild Bill Hickok, outfit, Yankeeboy, 1948, complete, NMIB ......................**200.00**

Wyatt Earp, guitar, 24", EX .**125.00**

Wyatt Earp, spurs, Selcol, plastic, NMOC ...........................**50.00**

Zorro, cape, Carnival Creations, NMOC ...........................**65.00**

Zorro, charm bracelet, gold-tone w/black highlights, 5 charms, NMIB .............................**65.00**

Zorro, cup, Melmac, white w/image of Zorro, EX ...................**25.00**

Zorro, key chain/flashlight, 1950s, plastic, EX .....................**60.00**

Zorro, pocketknife, Riders of the Silver Screen series, NMIB .........**50.00**

Zorro, rug, 1950s, full-color cotton pile, EX ........................**185.00**

# Westmoreland

Originally an Ohio company, Westmoreland relocated in Grapesville, Pennsylvania, where by the 1920s they had became known as one of the country's largest manufacturers of carnival glass. They are best known today for the high quality milk glass which accounted for 90% of their production. For further information we recommend contacting the Westmoreland Glass Society, Inc., listed in Clubs and Newsletters. See also Glass Animals and Birds.

Ashtray, Colonial, purple slag .**30.00**
Basket, Paneled Grape, #1881, Brandywine Blue, split handle, oval .........................**45.00**
Bell, Cameo, #754, Beaded Bouquet trim, Dark Blue Mist .........................**35.00**
Bell, Paneled Grape, #1881, milk glass, shaped base ........**35.00**
Bonbon, Daisy, #205, Brown Mist ............................**30.00**
Boudoir lamp, English Hobnail, #555, milk glass, stick-type ........**45.00**
Bowl, console; Paneled Grape, #1881, milk glass, round, 12" ..............................**55.00**
Bowl, Lotus, #1921, milk glass, oval ...............................**30.00**
Bowl, Paneled Grape, #1881, milk glass, cupped, 8" ...........**45.00**
Bowl, Paneled Grape, #1881, milk glass, lipped, 9" .............**50.00**
Bowl, Paneled Grape, #1881, milk glass w/gold trim, cupped, 8" ...................**50.00**
Bowl, Paneled Grape, #1881, milk glass, belled, 9½" ..........**55.00**
Bowl, Rose Trellis, #1969, milk glass w/hand-painted decor, 10" .....................................**75.00**
Butter dish, Paneled Grape, #1881, milk glass, ¼-lb .**30.00**
Cake plate, Lattice, milk glass, footed ............................**35.00**

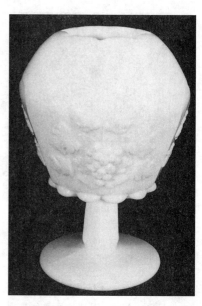

**Paneled Grape, ivy ball, milk glass, #1881, $45.00. (Photo courtesy Frank J. Grizel)**

Cake plate, Paneled Grape, #1881, milk glass, low foot, 2½" dia .........................**75.00**
Candelabra, Lotus, #1921, milk glass, 3-light, pr ............**68.00**
Candle holders, Beaded Grape, #1884, milk glass, pr, from $25 to .........................**30.00**
Candle holders, Spiral, #1933, black, pr..........................**40.00**
Candlesticks, Paneled Grape, #1881, Bermuda Blue, pr ...............**35.00**
Candy dish, Beaded Bouquet, #1700, Colonial pattern, milk glass ..............................**35.00**
Candy dish, Paneled Grape, #1881, Dark Blue Mist, crimped, footed, 8" ........**35.00**
Compote, Blue Mist, #1902, w/lid ..........................**35.00**

428

Compote, Paneled Grape, #1881, milk glass, ruffled edge, footed, 6" ..............................**45.00**

Creamer, Paneled Grape, #1881, milk glass, 8-oz, 5" ........**25.00**

Egg cup, American Hobnail, #77, milk glass ......................**10.00**

Egg plate, Paneled Grape, #1881, milk glass, center handle, 10" ..............................**45.00**

Fairy lamp, Irish Waterford, #1932, ruby on crystal, footed ...**65.00**

Goblet, English Hobnail, #555, milk glass, barrel form, footed ...................................**12.00**

Goblet, water; American Hobnail, #77, milk glass ..............**10.00**

Goblet, water; Paneled Grape, #1881, milk glass ..........**16.00**

Jardiniere, Paneled Grape, #1881, milk glass, round, footed, lg ......................**35.00**

Pin tray, Heart, #1820, Blue Mist ............................**30.00**

Plate, dinner; Paneled Grape, #1881, milk glass, 10½" .**35.00**

Plate, Forget-Me-Not, boy fishing, black ..............................**65.00**

Plate, Paneled Grape, #1881, Bicentennial decoration, limited edition ..................**225.00**

Plate, Princess Feather, #201, Golden Sunset, 8" .........**45.00**

Plate, Zodiac, #25, crystal w/blue, ruby or yellow stain, 15", ea ........................**95.00**

Punch set, Fan & File, Ice Blue, miniature ......................**45.00**

Rose bowl, English Hobnail, #555, milk glass, 4½" ..............**15.00**

Sugar bowl, Paneled Grape, #1881, Brandywine Blue, 2½x3" ..............................**15.00**

Tidbit tray, Paneled Grape, #1881, Light Blue Mist, 1-tier, 8" .**35.00**

Trinket box, #1902, Purple Mist, heart shape ..................**25.00**

Tumbler, juice; Della Robbia, #1058 ............................**35.00**

Tumbler, water; Paneled Grape, #1881, milk glass ..........**16.00**

Vase, Old Quilt, #500, milk glass, flared top, footed, 9" .....**65.00**

Vase, Paneled Grape, #1881, milk glass, footed, 11½" ........**65.00**

Water set, Old Quilt, #500, Ice Blue, 7-pc ...................**150.00**

## Wexford

Made since 1967 by Anchor Hocking, this line was at one time very extensive; a few pieces remain in production yet today. You'll see it at flea markets everywhere. Its appearance is both elegant and serviceable, and so far, anyway, it isn't at all expensive. In

**Della Robbia, plate, #1058, 14", $95.00. (Photo courtesy Frank J. Grizel)**

**Creamer, 8-oz., $2.50.**

his new book *Anchor Hocking's Fire King and More*, Gene Florence lists seventy-six different pieces and says we can assume there will be even others turn up as collectors become more familiar with the market. The vast majority is crystal, but Mr. Florence lists Pewter Mist and green as well, along with an assortment of fired-on colors.

Bowl, serving; scalloped top, 14" .............................**10.00**

Cake stand ...........................**10.00**
Decanter, 32-oz ....................**12.00**
Goblet, footed, 10-oz .............**3.50**
Mug, 15-oz ............................**6.00**
Plate, scalloped, 9½" .............**3.00**
Salt & pepper shakers, 8-oz, pr .**3.00**
Tumbler, iced tea; 15 or 16 oz, ea .................................**3.50**
Tumbler, wine/juice; 6-oz ......**2.00**
Vase, footed, 10½" ...............**12.50**

# DIRECTORY

The editors and staff take this opportunity to express our sincere gratitude and appreciation to each person who has in any way contributed to the preparation of this guide. We believe the credibility of our book is greatly enhanced through their participation. Check these listings for information concerning their specific areas of expertise.

You will notice that at the conclusion of some of the narratives, the advisor's name is given. This is optional and up to the discretion of each individual. We hope to add more advisors with each new edition to provide further resources to you, our readers. If you care to correspond with anyone listed here in our Directory, you must send a SASE with your letter.

## Alabama
Cataldo, Gene
Gene's Cameras
2614 Artie St., SW Ste. 37-327
Huntsville, 35804
205-536-6893

## California
Ales, Beverly L.
4046 Graham St.
Pleasanton, 94566-5619
510-846-5297
Specializing in knife rests; editor of *Knife Rests of Yesterday and Today*

Andrews, Dan
27105 Shorewood Rd.
Rancho Palos Verdes, 90275
310-541-5149
Specializing in breweriana and beer cans

Carter, Tina
882 S. Mollison
El Cajon, 92020
619-440-5043
Specializing in teapots, tea-related items, tea tins, children's and toy tea sets, plastic cookie cutters, etc. Book on teapots available. Send $16 (includes postage) or $17 for California residents, Canada: add $5 to above address.

Cox, Susan
Main Street Antique Mall
237 E Main St.
El Cajon, 92020
619-447-0800 or fax 619-447-0185
Author of *Frankoma Pottery, Value Guide and More;* also specializing in American pottery (California pottery in particular), Horlick's advertising, matchbooks, and advertising pencils

Elliott, Jackie
9790 Twin Cities Rd.
Galt, 95632
209-745-3860
Specializing in Rooster and Roses

Harrison, Gwynne
P.O. Box 1
Mira Loma, 91752-0001
909-685-5434
Buys and appraises Autumn Leaf; edits newsletter

Lewis, Kathy and Don
Whirlwind Unlimited
187 N Marcello Ave.
Thousand Oaks, 91360
chatty@ix.netcom.com
Authors of *Chatty Cathy Dolls, An Identification and Value Guide,* and *Talking Toys of the 20th Century*

Rosewitz, Michele A.
3165 McKinley
San Bernardino, 92404
909-862-8534
rosetree@sprintmail.com
Specializing in glass knives made in USA circa 1920s through 1950s

Synchef, Richard M.
22 Jefferson Ave.
San Raphael, 94903-4104
Fax 415-507-9944
Specializing in Beatnik and Hippie collectibles

Utley, Bill; Editor
*Flashlight Collectors of America*
P.O. Box 4095
Tustin, 92781
714-730-1252 or fax 714-505-4067
Specializing in flashlights

Van Ausdall, Marci
P.O. Box 946
Quincy, 95971-0946
916-283-2770
Specializing in Betsy McCall dolls and accessories; edits newsletter

## Connecticut
Sabulis, Cindy
P.O. Box 642
Shelton, 06484
203-926-0176

Specializing in dolls from the '60s – '70s (Liddle Kiddles, Barbie, Tammy, Tressy, etc.); co-author of *The Collector's Guide to Tammy, the Ideal Teen*

## Colorado
Diehl, Richard
5965 W Colgate Pl.
Denver, 80227
303-985-7481
Specializing in license plates

## District of Columbia
McMichael, Nancy
P.O. Box 53310
Washington, 20009
Author of *Snowdomes* (Abbeville Press); editor of *Snow Biz,* a quarterly newsletter

## Florida
Kuritzky, Lewis
4510 NW 17th Pl.
Gainesville, 32605
352-376-3884
Author of *Collector's Guide to Bookends*

Poe, Bill and Pat
220 Dominica Cir. E
Niceville, 32578-4068
850-897-4163 or fax 850-897-2606
Buy, sell, trade, fast-food collectibles, cartoon chararter glasses, PEZ, Smurfs, Califorinia Raisins; send $3 for a 70-page catalog published 2 times, January and July

## Idaho
McVey, Jeff
1810 W State St. #427
Boise, 83702
Author of *Tire Ashtray Collector's Guide* available for $12.95 postpaid; send SASE for my 300+ sale item catalog

## Illinois
Garmon, Lee
1529 Whittier St.
Springfield, 62704
217-789-9574
Specializing in Borden's Elsie, Reddy Kilowatt, Elvis Presley, and Marilyn Monroe

June Moon
245 N Northwest Hwy.
Park Ridge, 60068
847-825-1441 or fax 847-825-6090
Specializing in character collectibles

Jungnickel, Eric
P.O. Box 4674
Naperville, 60567-4674
630-983-8339
Specializing in Indy 500 memorabilia

Kadet, Jeff
TV Guide Specialists
P.O. Box 20
Macomb, 61455
309-833-1809
Buying and selling of *TV Guide* from 1948 through the 1990s

Klompus, Eugene R.
The National Cuff Link Society
P.O. Box 346
Prospect Hts., 60070
847-816-0035
Specializing in cuff links and men's accessories

Stifter, Craig and Donna
P.O. Box 6514
Naperville, 60540
630-789-5780
Specializing in soda memorabilia such as Coca-Cola, Hires, Pepsi, 7-Up, etc.

Wells, Rosie
Rosie Wells Enterprises, Inc.
R.R. #1
Canton, 61520
Editor of secondary market price guides on Boyds Bears, Hallmark, Precious Moments, Cherished Teddies, and others

## Indiana
Hoover, Dave
1023 Skyview Dr.
New Albany, 47150
Specializing in fishing collectibles

McQuillen, Michael and Polly
P.O. Box 50022
Indianapolis, 46250
317-845-1721
Specializing in Political memorabilia

## Iowa
Geneva D.
P.O. Box 124
Winterset, 50273
515-462-3027
Specializing in Imperial Porcelain, Pink Pigs, and Strawberry Shortcake collectibles

The Baggage Car
3100 Justin Dr., Ste. B
Des Moines, 50322
515-270-9080
Specializing in Hallmark

De Lozier, Loretta
1101 Polk St.
Bedford, 50833
712-523-2289
Author of *Collector's Encyclopedia of Lefton China, Identification and Values* (Collector Books)

Devine, Joe
D&D Antique Mall
1411 3rd St.
Council Bluffs, 51503
712-232-5233 or 712-328-7305
Specializing in Royal Copley

## Kansas

Anthony, Dorothy J.
World of Bells Publications
2401 S Horton
Ft. Scott, 66701-2790
Author of *World of Bells*, #5 ($8.95); *Bell Tidings* ($9.95); *Lure of Bells* ($9.95); *Collectible Bells* ($10.95); and *More Bell Lore* ($11.95); autographed copies available from the author; please enclose $2.00 for postage

## Kentucky

Hornback, Betty
707 Sunrise Ln.
Elizabethtown, 42701
502-765-2441
Specializing in Kentucky Derby and horse racing memorabilia

Smith, Don

Don Smith's National Geographic Magazine
3930 Rankin St.
Louisville, 40214
502-366-7504
Specializing in *National Geographic* magazines and related material; guide available

## Louisiana

Langford, Paris
415 Dodge Ave.
Jefferson, 70121
504-733-0676
Author of *Liddle Kiddles*; specializing in dolls of the 1960s – 70s

## Maryland

Losonsky, Joyce and Terry
7506 Summer Leave Ln.
Columbia, 21046-2455
Authors of *The Illustrated Collector's Guide to McDonald's® Happy Meal® Boxes, Premiums, and Promotions©*, ($11 postpaid); *McDonald's Happy Meal Toys in the USA* in full color ($27.95 postpaid); *McDonald's® Happy Meal® Toys Around the World*, full color, ($27.95 postpaid); and *Illustrated Collector's Guide to McDonald's® McCAPS®*, ($6 postpaid); autographed copies available from the authors

Welch, Randy
27965 Peach Orchard Rd.
Easton, 21601-8203
410-822-5441
Specializing in walking figures, and tin wind-up toys

Yalom, Libby
The Shoe Lady
P.O. Box 7146
Adelphi, 20783
301-422-2026
Specializing in glass and china shoes and boots. Author of *Shoes of Glass* (with updated values) available from the author by sending $15.95 plus $2 to above address

## Massachusetts

Bruce, Scott
P.O. Box 481
Cambridge, 02140
617-492-5004
Publisher of *Flake* magazine; author of books; specializing in buying, selling, trading cereal boxes, cereal displays, and cereal premiums; free appraisals given

Wellman, BA
P.O. Box 673
Westminster, 01473-1435
Specializing in all areas of American ceramics; identification and price guides available on Ceramic Arts Studio; researcher on Royal China

White, Larry
108 Central St.
Rowley, 01969-1317
978-948-8187; larrydw@erols.com
Specializing in Cracker Jack; author of books; has newsletter

## Michigan

Dipboye, Marilyn
33161 Wendy Dr.
Sterling Hts., 48310
Editor of *Cat Talk* newsletter (subscription $20 per year US or $27 Canada)

Gilbert, Carol Karbowiak
2193 14 Mile Rd. 206
Sterling Hts., MI 48310
Specializing in Breyer

Pickvet, Mark
P.O. Box 90404
Flint, 48509
Author of *Shot Glasses: An American Tradition*, available for $12.95 plus $2.50 postage and handling from Antique Publications, P.O. Box 553, Marietta, OH 45750

## Minnesota

Zimmer, Gregg
4017 16th Ave. S
Minneapolis, 55407
612-721-7543
Co-author of book; specializing in Melmac

## Missouri

Allen, Col. Bob
P.O. Box 85

St. James, 65559
Author of *A Guide to Collecting Cookbooks;*
specializing in cookbooks, leaflets, and
Jell-O memorabilia

Bowman, Kevin R.
P.O. Box 471
Neosho, 64850-0471
417-781-6418 (6pm-9pm CST)
Specializing in sporting goods; lists available

Duncan, Pat and Ann
Box 175
Cape Fair, 65624
417-538-2311
Specializing in Holt Howard, Lefton,
Roseville

McCale, Helen L.
1006 Ruby Ave.
Butler, 64730-2500
816-679-3690
Specializing in Holly Hobbie

# Nevada
Hunter, Tim
4301 W Hidden Valley Dr.
Reno, NV 89502
Fax 702-856-4354
Author of *The Bobbing Head Collector and
Price Guide*

# New Hampshire
Apkarian-Russel, Pamela
Chris Russell
and The Halloween Queen
4 Lawrence St. & Rt. 10
Winchester, 03470
Specializing in Halloween collectibles, post-
cards of all kinds, and Joe Camel

Holt, Jane
P.O. Box 115
Derry, 03038
Specializing in Annalee dolls

# New Jersey
Cole, Lillian M.
14 Harmony School Rd.
Flemington, 08822
908-782-3198
Specializing in collecting pie birds, pie vents,
and pie funnels; also pie bird research

Dezso, Doug
864 Paterson Ave.
Maywood, 07607
Author of *Candy Containers* (Collector
Books); specializing in candy containers,
nodders, Kellogg's Pep pin-back buttons,
Shafford cats, and Tonka toys

Litts, Elyce
P.O. Box 394
Morris Plains, 07950
Specializing in Geisha Girl (author of
book); also ladies' compacts

Palmieri, Jo Ann
27 Pepper Rd.
Towaco, 07082
201-334-5829
Specializing in Skookum Indian dolls

Sigg, Walter
3-D Entertainment
P.O. Box 208
Swartswood, 07877
Specializing in View-Master and Tru-View
reels and packets

Sparacio, George
P.O. Box 791
Malaga, 08328
609-694-4167
Specializing in match safes

Visakay, Stephen
P.O. Box 1517
W Caldwell, 07007-1517
cocktailshakers@webtv.net
Specializing in vintage cocktail shakers (by
mail and appointment only); author of *Vintage Bar Ware*

Yunes, Henri
971 Main St., Apt. 2
Hackensack, 07601
201-488-2236
Specializing in celebrity and character dolls

# New Mexico
Mace, Shirley
Shadow Enterprises
P.O. Box 1602
Mesilla Park, 88047
505-524-6717 or 505-523-0940
shadow-ent@zianet.com
Author of *Encyclopedia of Silhouette Col-
lectibles on Glass* (available from the author)

# New York
Dinner, Craig
Box 4399
Sunnyside, 11104
718-729-3850
Specializing in figural cast-iron items (door
knockers, lawn sprinklers, doorstops, wind-
mill weights, etc.)

Eisenstadt, Robert
P.O. Box 020767
Brooklyn, 11202-0017
718-625-3553 or fax 718-522-1087
Specializing in gambling chips and other
gambling-related items

Gerson, Roselyn
P.O. Box 40
Lynbrook, 11563
516-593-8746
Collector specializing in unusual, gadgetry,
figural compacts, and vanity bags and purses; author of *Ladies' Compacts, of the 19th*

*and 20th Centuries* ($36.95 plus $2 post-paid), *Vintage Vanity Bags and Purses,* and *Vintage and Contemporary Purse Accessories* (Collector Books); edits newsletter

Iranpour, Sharon
24 San Rafel Dr.
Rochester, 14618-3702
716-381-9467 or fax 716-383-9248
SIranpour@aol.com
Specializing in advertising and promotional wrist watches; editor of *The Premium Watch Watch*

Lederman, Arlene
Lederman Antiques
79 S Broadway
Nyack, 10977
914-358-8616
Specializing in vintage cocktail shakers, 18th through 20th-century antiques, American, European, furniture, glass, decorative accessories, and collectibles

Luchsinger, Paul P.
1126 Wishart St.
Hermitage, 16148
412-346-2331
Specializing in antique and unusual corkscrews

Maimone, Tom
53 W Court St.
Warsaw, 14569
716-786-5674
Specializing in advertising and figural swizzle sticks

Weitman, Stan and Arlene
101 Cypress St.
Massapequa Park, 11758
516-799-2619 or fax 516-797-3039
Authors of *Crackle Glass, Identification and Value Guide, Volumes I and II* (Collector Books)

## North Carolina

Brooks, Ken and Barbara
4121 Gladstone Ln.
Charlotte, 28205
704-568-5716
Specializing in Cattail Dinnerware

Marfine Antiques
Finegan, Mary
P. O. Box 3618
Boone, 28607
828-226-23441 @14.00
Author of Johnson Brother Dinnerware, order from the author plus shipping and handling

Retskin, Bill
P.O. Box 18481
Asheville, 28814

704-254-4487 or fax 704-254-1066
matchclub@circle.net
Author of *The Matchcover Collector's Price Guide,* and editor of *The Front Striker Bulletin,* the official publication of the American Matchcover Collecting Club (AMCC)

Sayers, Rolland J.
Southwestern Antiques and Appraisals
P.O. Box 629
Brevard, 28712
Author of *Guide to Scouting Collectibles,* available from the author for $19.95 plus $3.50 postage

## North Dakota

Farnsworth, Bryce L.
1334 14 1/2 St.
S Fargo, 58103
Specializing in Rosemeade

## Ohio

Bruegman, Bill
137 Casterton Ave.
Akron, 44303
330-836-0668 or fax 330-869-8668
Author of *Toys of the Sixties; Aurora History and Price Guide;* and *Cartoon Friends of the Baby Boom Era.* Write for information about his magazine and mail-order catalog.

Budin, Nicki
679 High St.
Worthington, OH 43085
614-885-1986
Specializing in Beatrix Potter and Royal Doulton

Cassity, Brad
1350 Stanwix
Toledo, 43614
419-385-9910
Specializing in Fisher-Price pull toys and playsets up to 1986 (author of book)

Cimini, Joan
63680 Centerville-Warnock Rd.
Belmont, 43718
Specializing in Imperial; also has Candlewick matching service

Dutt, Gordy
*Gordy's / KitBuilders Magazine*
Box 201
Sharon Center, 44274-0201
330-239-1657 or fax 330-239-2991
Author of *Collectible Figure Kits of the '50s, '60s, and '70s* ($24 US postpaid or $25 Canadian); specializing in models other than Aurora, Weirdos, and Rat Finks

Grubaugh, Joan
GB Publications
2342 Hoaglin Rd.

Van Wert, 45891
419-622-4411 or fax 419-622-3026
Author of *Gerber Baby Dolls and Advertising Collectibles* ($39.95 plus $4 postage)

Kerr, Ann
P.O. Box 437
Sidney, 45365
513 492-6369
Author of *Collector's Encyclopedia of Russel Wright Designs* (Collector Books) also interests in 20th-century decorative arts

Lerner, Michael
32862 Springside Ln.
Solon, 44139
Phone or fax 216-349-3776
Specializing in MAD Collectibles

Marsh, Thomas
914 Franklin Ave.
Youngstown, 44502
216-743-8600 or 800-845-7930
Publisher and author of *The Official Guide to Collecting Applied Color Label Soda Bottles* Volumes I and II ($28.95 each postpaid)

McGrady, Donna S.
154 Peters Ave.
Lancaster, OH 43130
614-653-0376
Specializing in Gay Fad

Young, Mary
P.O. Box 9244
Wright Bros. Branch
Dayton, 45409
Author of books; specializing in paper dolls

## Oklahoma
Ivers, Terri
Terri's Toys and Nostalgia
206 E Grand
Ponca City, 74601
580-762-8697 or 580-762-5174
Fax 580-765-2657
toylady@poncacity.net
Specializing in character collectibles, lunch boxes, advertising items, Breyer and Hartland figures, etc.

Phillips, Robert W.
Phillips Archives of Western Memorabilia
1703 N Aster Pl.
Broken Arrow, 74012
918-254-8205 or fax 918-252-9362
rawhidebob@aol.com
One of the most widely published writers in the field of cowboy memorabila, biographer of the Golden Boots Awards, and author of *Roy Rogers, Singing Cowboy Stars, Silver Screen Cowboys, Hollywood Cowboy Heroes,* and *Western Comics: A Comprehensive Ref-*

*erence*; research consultant for TV documentary *Roy Rogers, King of the Cowboys* (AMC-TV/Republic Pictures/Galen Films)

## Oregon
Coe, Debbie and Randy
Coes Mercantile
Lafayette School House Mall #2
748 3rd (Hwy. 99W)
Lafayette, 97137
Specializing in Elegant and Depression glass, art pottery, Cape Cod by Avon, Golden Foliage by Libbey Glass Company, Gurley candles, and Liberty Blue dinnerware

Morris, Tom
Prize Publishers
P.O. Box 8307
Medford, 97504
503-779-3164
Author of *The Carnival Chalk Prize*

White, Carole Bess
PO Box 819
Portland, 97207
Specializing in Japan ceramics; author of books

## Pennsylvania
BOJO/Bob Gottuso
P.O. Box 1403
Cranberry Twp., 16066-0403
Phone or fax 724-776-0621
Specializing in the Beatles and rock 'n roll memorabilia

Greenfield, Jeannie
310 Parker Rd.
Stoneboro, 16153-2810
724-376-2584
Specializing in cake toppers and egg timers

Kreider, Katherine
Kingsbury Antiques
P.O. Box 7957
Lancaster, 17604-7957
717-892-3001
Specializing in valentines from the 1800s to 1960s; author of *Valentines With Values* ($22.90 includes shipping and handling; PA residents please include 6% sales tax) and *One Hundred Years of Valentines* (book available from author)

Posner, Judy
R.R. 1, Box 273
Effort, 18330
http://www.tias.com/stores/jpc
judyandjef@aol.com
Specializing in figural pottery, cookie jars, salt and pepper shakers, Black memorabilia, and Disneyana; sale lists available; fee charged for appraisal

Turner, Art and Judy
Homestead Collectibles

P.O. Box 173
Mill Hall, 17751
717-726-3597
Specializing in Jim Beam decanters and Ertl
diecast metal banks

Tvorak, April and Larry
P.O. Box 94
Warren Center, 18851
717-395-3775; april@epix.net
Specializing in Kitchen Independence,
Kitchen Prayer Ladies, Pyrex, Fire-King
(guides available), and Holt Howard

## Tennessee
Butler, Elaine
233 S Kingston Ave.
Rockwood, 37854
Author of *Poodle Collectibles of the '50s and
'60s* ($21.95 postpaid)

Daigle, Alvin Jr.
Boomerang Antiques
Gray, 37615
423-915-0666
Co-author of book; specializing in Melmac
Dinnerware

Grist, Everett
P.O. Box 91375
Chattanooga, 37412-3955
417-451-1910
Author of books on animal dishes, aluminum, advertising playing cards, letter
openers, and marbles

## Texas
Cooper, Marilyn M.
P.O. Box 55174
Houston, 77255
Author of *The Pictorial Guide to Toothbrush
Holders* ($22.95 postpaid)

Jackson, Joyce
900 Jenkins Rd.
Aledo, 76008
817-441-8864
Specializing in Swanky Swigs

Nossaman, Darlene
5419 Lake Charles
Waco, 76710
817-772-3969
Specializing in Homer Laughlin China information and Horton Ceramics

Pringle, Joyce
Chip and Dale Collectibles
3708 W Pioneer Pky.
Arlington, 76013
Specializing in Boyd art glass, Summit, and Moser

Woodard, Dannie
P.O. Box 1346
Weatherford, 76086
817-594-4680

Author of *Hammered Aluminum, Hand
Wrought Collectibles*

## Utah
Spencer, Rick
Salt Lake City
801-973-0805
Specializing in Shawnee, Roseville, Weller,
Van Telligen, Regal, Bendel, Coors, Rook-
wood, Watt; also salt and pepper shakers,
cookie jars, etc., cut glass, radios, and silver
flatware

## Virginia
Cranor, Rosalind
P.O. Box 859
Blacksburg, 24063
Author of *Elvis Collectibles* and *Best of Elvis
Collectibles* (each at $19.95 with $2.50
postage), available from the author

Henry, Rosemary
9610 Greenview Ln.
Manassas, 20109-3520
703-361-5898
checker@erols.com
Specializing in cookie cutters, stamps, and
molds

Reynolds, Charlie
Reynolds Toys
2836 Monroe St.
Falls Church, 22042-2007
703-533-1322
Specializing in banks, figural bottle openers,
toys, etc.

Windsor, Grant
P.O. Box 3613
Richmond, 23235-7613
Specializing in Griswold

## Washington
Palmer, Donna
Our Favorite Things
3020 Issaquah
Pine Lake Rd. #557
Issaquah, 98027
206-392-7636
General line but specializing in Scottie dog
collectibles

Thompson, Walt
Box 2541
Yakima, 98907-2451
Specializing in charge cards and credit-relat-
ed items

## Wisconsin
Helley, Phil
Old Kilbourn Antiques
629 Indiana Ave.
Wisconsin Dells, 53965

608-254-8659
Specializing in Cracker Jack items, radio premiums, dexterity games, toys (especially Japanese wind-up toys), banks, and old Dells souvenir items marked Kilbourn

Wanvig, Nancy
Nancy's Collectibles

P.O. Box 12
Thiensville, WI 53092
Author of book; specializing in ashtrays

# CLUBS AND NEWSLETTERS

Akro Agate Collectors Club
*Clarksburg Crow*
Roger Hardy
10 Bailey St.
Clarksburg, WV 26301-2524
304-624-4523
Annual membership fee: $20

American Bell Assn.
International, Inc.
P.O. Box 19443
Indianapolis, IN 46219

The American Matchcover Collecting Club (AMCC)
P.O. Box 18481
Asheville, NC 28814
704-254-4487 or fax 704-254-1066; match-club@circle.net;
Dues: $23 per year; includes quarterly issues of *The Front Striker Bulletin*, a membership roster and card, free matchcovers, and full membership privileges; offers appraisal service for estate and insurance purposes if SASE is enclosed

*Antique and Collector Reproduction News*
Mark Chervenka, Circulation Dept.
P.O. Box 71174
Des Moines, IA 50325
800-227-5531
Monthly newsletter showing differences between old originals and new reproductions; subscription: $32 per year

*The Antique Trader Weekly*
P.O. Box 1050
Dubuque, IA 52004-1050
Subscription: $32 (52 issues) per year; sample: $1

Autographs of America
Tim Anderson
P.O. Box 461
Provo, UT 84603
801-226-1787 (afternoons, please)
Free sample catalog of hundreds of autographs for sale

*Autumn Leaf*
Bill Swanson, Editor
807 Roaring Springs Dr.
Allen, TX 75002-2112
972-727-5527

*Avon Times*
c/o Dwight or Vera Young
P.O. Box 9868, Dept. P.
Kansas City, MO 64134
Send SASE for information

*The Baggage Car*
3100 Justin Dr., Ste. B
Des Moines, IA 50322
515-270-9080 or fax 515-223-1398
Includes show and company information along with current Hallmark listings

*Betsy McCall's Fan Club*
Marci Van Ausdell, Editor
P.O. Box 946
Quincy, CA 95971
DREAMS707@aol.com
Subscription: $12.50 per year or send $3 for sample copy

*The Bobbing Head Doll Newsletter*
Tim Hunter
4301 W Hidden Valley Dr.
Reno, NV 89502
702-856-4357 or fax 702-856-4354;
thunter885@aol.com

Bookend Collector Club
Louis Kuritzky, M.D.
4510 NW 17th Place
Gainsville, FL 32650
352-377-3193; lkuritzky@aol.com

Boyd's Crystal Art Glass
*Jody & Darrell's Glass Collectibles Newsletter*
P.O. Box 180833
Arlington, TX 76096-0833
Published 6 times a year; subscription includes an exclusive glass collectible produced by Boyd's Crystal Art Glass; LSASE for current subscription rates or send $3 for sample copy

*The Candy Gram* Newsletter
Joyce L. Doyle
P.O. Box 426
North Reading, MA 01864-0426

CAS Collectors Association (Ceramic Arts Studio) *CAS Collector Newsletter*
P.O. Box 46
Madison, WI 53701
608-241-9138
Subscription: $18.50 for 6 issues per year

Cat Collectors Club
*Cat Talk* Newsletter
Marilyn Dipboye
33161 Wendy Dr.
Sterling Hts., MI 48310
810-264-0285
Subscription: $20 per year

*Collectible Flea Market Finds* Magazine
Goodman Media Group, Inc.
1700 Broadway
New York, NY 10019
800-955-3870
Subscription: $18.97 for 4 issues per year

*Collector Glass News*
P.O. Box 308
Slippery Rock, PA 16057
Subscription: $15 per year for 6 issues

Compact Collector Chronicles
*Powder Puff* Newsletter
P.O. Box 40
Lynbrook, NY 11563
Contains information covering all aspects of compact collecting, restoration, vintage ads, patents, history, and articles by members and prominent guest writers. A 'Seekers and Sellers' column and dealer listing is offered free to members.

*The Cookie Jar Collectors Express*
Paradise Publications
Box 221
Mayview, MO 64071
816-584-6309

*Cookie Jarrin' With Joyce: The Cookie Jar Newsletter*
R.R. 2, Box 504
Walterboro, SC 29488

*Cookies*
Rosemary Henry
9610 Greenview Ln.
Manassas, VA 22110
Subscription: $12 per year

*The Copley Courier*
1639 N Catalina St.
Burbank, CA 91505

*Currier & Ives China by Royal*
c/o Jack and Treva Hamlin
R.R. 4, Box 150
Kaiser St.
Proctorville, OH 45669
614-886-7644

*Czechoslovakian Collectors Guild International*
P.O. Box 901395
Kansas City, MO 64190

*Depression Glass Daze*
Teri Steel, Editor/Publisher
Box 57
Otisville, MI 48463
810-631-4593
The nation's marketplace for glass, china, and pottery

*Doll Castle News* Magazine
P.O. Box 247
Washington, NJ 07882
908-689-7042 or fax 908-689-6320

Doorstop Collectors of America
Jeanie Bertoia
2413 Madison Ave.
Vineland, NJ 08630
609-692-4092
Membership: $20 per year, includes 2 newsletters and convention; send 2-stamp SASE for sample

*The Ertl Replica*
Mike Myer, Editor
Hwys. 136 & 20
Dyersville, IA 52040
319-875-2000

FBOC (Figural Bottle Opener Collectors)
Linda Fitzsimmons
9697 Gwynn Park Dr.
Ellicott City, MD 21043
301-465-9296
Please send SASE for information.

*Fiesta Club of America*
P.O. Box 15383
Loves Park, IL 61132-5383
Subscription: $20 for 1 year and includes newsletter

*Fiesta Collector's Quarterly*
China Specialties Inc.
P.O. Box 471
Valley City, OH 44280
Subscription: $12 per year

Fisher-Price Collector's Club
Jeanne Kennedy
1442 N Ogden
Mesa, AZ 85205
Monthly newsletter with information and ads; send SASE for more information

*FLAKE, The Breakfast Nostalgia Magazine*
P.O. Box 481
Cambridge, MA 02140
617-492-5004
Subscription: $20 per year; free 25-word ad with new subscription

*Flashlight Collectors of America Newsletter*
Bill Utley

P.O. Box 4095
Tustin, CA 92681
714-730-1252 or fax 714-505-4067
Subscription: $12 per year; single copies and
back issues are $3 each

*Florence Collector's Club Newsletter*
c/o Florence Collector's Club Membership
Chairman
P.O. Box 122
Richland, WA 99353
Subscription: $20 per year

Frankoma Family Collectors Association
c/o Nancy Littrell
P.O. Box 32571
Oklahoma City, OK 73123-0771
Membership dues: $20 (includes quarterly
newsletter and annual convention)

*The Front Striker Bulletin*
Bill Retskin
P.O. Box 18481
Asheville, NC 28814
704-254-4487 or fax 704-254-1066
http://www.matchcovers.com
Quarterly newsletter for matchcover collec-
tors $17.50 per year for 1st class mailing +
$2 for new member registration

*Grandma's Trunk*
The Millards
P.O. Box 404
Northport, MI 49670
616-386-5351
Auction and set price lists in newspaper format for all types of paper ephemera; subscription: $5 yearly bulk rate or $8 for 1st
class

Griswold & Cast Iron Cookware Association
Grant Windsor
P.O. Box 3613
Richmond, VA 23235
804-320-0386
Membership: $15 per individual or $20 per
family (2 members per address) payable to
club

*Hall China Collectors' Club Newsletter*
P.O. Box 360488
Cleveland, OH 44136

Head Hunters Newsletter
c/o Maddy Gordon
P.O. Box 83 H
Scarsdale, NY 10583
For collectors of head vases; subscription:
$20 yearly for 4 quarterly issues. Ads free to
subscribers

*International Figure Kit Club*
Gordy's
P.O. Box 201
Sharon Center, OH 44274-0201
330-239-1657 or fax 330-239-2991

International Nippon Collectors Club
(INCC)
c/o Phil Fernkes
112 Oak Ave N
Owatonna, MN 55060
Publishes newsletter 6 times per year

International Perfume and Scent Bottle
Collectors Association
Randall B. Monsen, President
P.O. Box 529
Vienna, VA 22183
Fax 703-242-1357

*Just for Openers*
John Stanley
3712 Sunningdale Way
Durham, NC 27707-5684
919-419-1546
For collectors of bottle openers

*Knife Rests of Yesterday and Today*
Beverly L. Ales
495 Linden Way
Pleasanton, CA 94566-6879
Subscription: $20 per year for 6 issues

*The Laughlin Eagle*
c/o Richard Racheter
1270 63rd Terrace South
St. Petersburg, FL 33705

The Lovin' Connection (for Pillsbury
Collectors)
2343 10000 Rd.
Oswego, KS 67356
316-795-2842

Marble Collectors' Society of America
P.O. Box 222
Trumbull, CT 06611

*McDonald's®*
*Collector Club*
1153 S Lee St., Ste. 200
Des Plaines, IL 60016
http://www.concentric.net/~Gabrielc/McD-
club2.htm

*Model & Toy Collector Magazine*
Toy Scouts, Inc.
Bill Bruegman
137 Casterton Ave.
Akron, OH 44303-1552
330-836-0668 or fax 330-869-8668

National Association of Avon Collectors
c/o Connie Clark
6100 Walnut, Dept. P
Kansas City, MO 64113
Send large SASE for information

*National Blue Ridge Newsletter*
Norma Lilly
144 Highland Dr.
Bloutville, TN 37617
Subscription: $15 per year

The National Cuff Link Society
Eugene R. Klompus, President
P.O. Box 346
Prospect Hts., IL 60070
847-816-0035
Membership: $25 per year

National Depression Glass Association
Anita Woods
P.O. Box 69843
Odessa, TX 79769
915-337-1297

National Graniteware Society
P.O. Box 10013
Cedar Rapids, IA 52410

National Imperial Glass Collectors'
Society, Inc.
P.O. Box 534
Bellaire, OH 43906
Dues: $15 per year (+$1 for each additional
member of household), quarterly newsletter:
*Glasszette*

National Reamer Association
c/o Debbie Gilham
47 Midline Ct.
Gaithersburg, MD 20878

National Society of Lefton
Collectors
*The Lefton Collector* Newsletter
Loretta DeLozier
11101 Polk St.
Bedford, IA 50833
712-523-2289

National Valentine Collectors Association
Evalene Pulati
P.O. Box 1404
Santa Ana, CA 92702
714-547-1355

*The Nelson-McCoy Express*
Carol Seman, Editor
7670 Chippewa Rd., Ste. 406
Brecksville, OH 44141-2310
McCjs@aol.com

The Occupied Japan Club
c/o Florence Archambault
29 Freeborn St.
Newport, RI 02840-1821
Publishes *The Upside Down World of an O.J.
Collector,* a bimonthly newsletter. Information requires SASE.

*On the Lighter Side*
International Lighter Collectors
Judith Sanders, Editor
136 Cir. Dr.

Quitman, TX 75783
903-763-2795 or fax 703-763-4953
Annual convention held in different cities in
the US; send SASE when requesting information

*Paper Collectors' Marketplace*
Doug Watson, Publisher/Editor
470 Main St.
Scandinavia, WI 54977-0128
715-467-2379 or fax 715-467-2243 (8 am to 8 pm)
Subscription: $19.95 for 12 issues per year

*Paper Doll News*
Emma Terry
P.O. Box 807
Vivian, LA 71082

*Paper Pile Quarterly*
Ada Fitzsimmons,
Publisher/Editor
P.O. Box 337
San Anselmo, CA 94979-0337
Subscription: $17 per year

Peanut Pals
Robert Walthall, President
P.O. Box 4465
Huntsville, AL 35815
205-881-9198
Associated collectors of Planters Peanuts
memorabilia, bimonthly newsletter *Peanut
Papers;* annual directory sent to members;
annual convention and regional conventions;
dues: $20 per year (+$3 for each additional
household member); membership information: P.O. Box 652, St. Clairsville, OH,
43950. Sample newsletter: $2

*Pez Collector News*
Richard & Marianne Belyski, Editors
P.O. Box 124
Sea Cliff, NY 11579
Phone or fax 516-676-1183

*Pie Birds Unlimited Newsletter*
Lillian M. Cole
14 Harmony School Rd.
Flemington, NJ 08822
908-782-3198

*Pottery Collectors Express*
P.O. Box 221
Mayview, MO 64071-0221

*The Premium Watch Watch*
Sharon Iranpour, Editor
24 San Rafael Dr.
Rochester, NY 14618-3702
716-381-9467 or f a x  716-383-9248; SIran
pour@aol.com

*The Prize Insider Newsletter for Cracker
Jack Collectors*
Larry White

108 Central St.
Rowley, MA 01969
978-948-8187
larrydw@erols.com

Political Collectors of Indiana
Michael McQuillen
P.O. Box 50022
Indianapolis, IN 46250
317-845-1721
Official APIC (American Political Items Collectors) Chapter comprised of over 100 collectors of presidential and local political items

*Quint News*
Dionne Quint Collectors
P.O. Box 2527
Woburn, MA 01888
617-933-2219

*Record Collectors Monthly*
P.O. Box 75
Mendham, NJ 07845
201-543-9520 or fax 201-543-6033

*Red Wing Collectors Newsletter*
Red Wing Collectors Society, Inc.
c/o Doug Podpeskar
624 Jones St.
Eveleth, MN 55734-1631
218-744-4845
Please include SASE when requesting information.

*Rosevilles of the Past* Newsletter
Jack Bomm, Editor
P.O. Box 656
Clarcona, FL 32710-0656
407-294-3980
Send $19.95 per year for 6 to 12 newsletters

*Roy Rogers – Dale Evans Collectors Association*
Nancy Horsley, Exec. Secretary
P.O. Box 1166
Portsmouth, OH 45662-1166

Salt and Pepper Novelty Shakers Club
Irene Thornburg
581 Joy Rd.
Battlecreek, MI 49017
616-963-7953

Shawnee Pottery Collectors' Club
c/o Pamela Curran
P.O. Box 713
New Smyrna Beach, FL 32170-0713
Send $3 for sample copy

The Shot Glass Club of America
Mark Pickvet, Editor
P.O. Box 90404
Flint, MI 48509

*The Silver Bullet*
Terry and Kay Klepey

P.O. Box 553
Forks, WA 98331
For Lone Ranger enthusiasts and collectors; send SASE for current subscription information

*Snow Biz*
c/o Nancy McMichael
P.O. Box 53262
Washington, D.C. 20009
Quarterly newsletter (subscription: $10 per year) and collector's club, annual meeting/swap meet

The Soup Collector Club
David and Micki Young, Editors and Founders
414 Country Lane Ct.
Wauconda, IL 60084
847-487-4917; soup club@aol.com
Membership: 6 issues per year for $22 donation per address

Tea Talk
P.O. Box 860
Sausalito, CA, 94966
415-331-1557; teatalk@aol.com
4 quarterly issues: $17.95

*The TeaTime Gazette*
P.O. Box 40276
St. Paul, MN 55104
612-227-7415
1leamer@aol.com
4 quarterly issues: $18.95

*Toy Shop*
700 E State St.
Iola, WI 54990
715-445-2214
Subscription (3rd class) $23.95 for 26 issues

*Toy Trader*
100 Bryant St.
Dubuque, Iowa 52003
Subscription in US $24 for 12 issues

*The Trick or Treat Trader*
C.J. Russell
and The Halloween Queen
P.O. Box 499
4 Lawrence St. & Rt. 10
Winchester, NH 03470
halloweenqueen@cheshire.net; subcription: $15 per year for 4 issues or $4 for sample copy

*Troll Monthly*
5858 Washington St.
Whitman, MA 02382
800-858-7655 or 800-858-Troll

*Vernon Views* Newsletter for Vernon Kilns collectors
P.O. Box 945
Scottsdale, AZ 85252

Quarterly issue available by sending $10 for a year's subscription

View-Master Reel Collector
Roger Nazeley
4921 Castor Ave.
Philadelphia, PA 19124
215-743-8999

*Vintage Fashion & Costume Jewelry*
Newsletter/Club
P.O. Box 265
Glen Oaks, NY 11004
718-969-2320 or 718-939-3095
Yearly subscription: $15 (US) for 4 issues; sample copy available by sending $5

*The Wade Watch, Ltd.*
8199 Pierson Ct.
Arvada, CO 80005
303-421-9655 or 303-424-4401
Fax 303-421-0317
Subscription: $8 per year (4 issues)

Westmoreland Glass Society
Steve Jensen, President
4809 420 St. SE
Iowa City, IA 52240
319-337-9647

*The Willow Word*
Mary Lina Berndt, Publisher
P.O. Box 13382
Arlington, TX 76094
Subscription: $23 (US) for 6 20-page issues per year; includes free ads to readers and lots of photos

World's Fair Collectors' Society, Inc.
Michael R. Pender, Editor
P.O. Box 20806
Sarasota, FL 34238
813-923-2590
Dues: $17 per year in US, $18 in Canada

# Index

**445**